MW01014396

PARENT–CHILD RELATIONS

PARENT-CHILD RELATIONS

A GUIDE TO RAISING CHILDREN

Hisham Altalib
AbdulHamid AbuSulayman
Omar Altalib

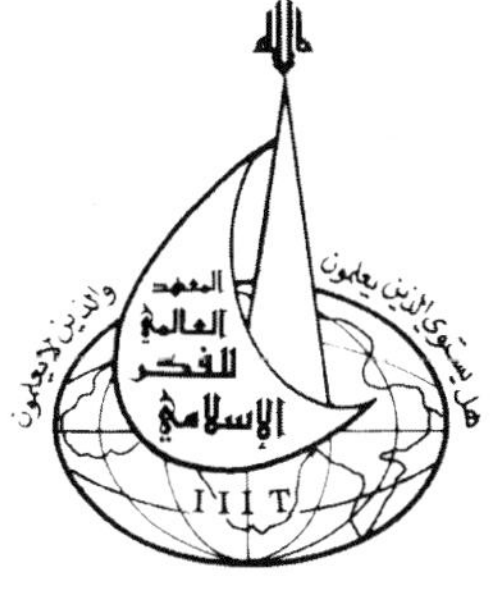

THE INTERNATIONAL INSTITUTE OF ISLAMIC THOUGHT
LONDON • WASHINGTON

The International Institute of Islamic Thought
P.O. Box 669, Herndon, VA 20172, USA
www.iiit.org

London Office
P.O. Box 126, Richmond, Surrey, TW9 2UD, UK
www.iiituk.com

ISBN 978-1-56564-582-0 hardback

Typesetting and cover design by Ian Abdallateef Whiteman
Illustrations and picture research by Hanna Whiteman

Images © iStockphoto
Image p.62 © Timstirling | Stock Free Images & Dreamstime Stock Photo
Image p.144, www.morguefile.com/creative/hogg
Image p.226 http://blog.timesunion.com/parenting/11891/mamas-boys-get-second-chance-at-home/
Image p.250 http://www.stockfreeimages.com © Akhilesh | Stock Free Images & Dreamstime Stock Photos
Image p.250 http://www.stockfreeimages.com © Spepple22 | Stock Free Images & Dreamstime Stock Photos
Image p.333 © Mnj7th | Stock Free Images & Dreamstime Stock Photos
Image p.425 © Derocz | Stock Free Images & Dreamstime Stock Photo

Printed by Gutenberg Press Ltd, Malta

The Authors

Hisham Yahya Altalib

Dr. Hisham Yahya Altalib was born in Mosul, Nineva, Iraq in 1940. He holds a B.Sc. in electrical engineering from Liverpool University (1962) and a Ph.D. in electrical engineering from Purdue University in Lafayette, Indiana, USA (1974).

During his employment as an electrical engineer, Dr. Altalib soon became active in Islamic work in North America, which continues to this day. He has held several positions in various Islamic organizations, including first full-time director of the Leadership Training Department of the Muslim Students Association of the United States and Canada (MSA) (1975–1977) and secretary general of the International Islamic Federation of Student Organizations (IIFSO) in 1976. He has conducted many training camps and seminars in America and abroad.

A founding member and Director of the SAAR Foundation (1983–1995), as well as founding member of the International Institute of Islamic Thought (IIIT) in 1981, he is also the author of *Mithāq al-Sharaf al-Da'awy* (Arabic) and the well-known book *A Training Guide for Islamic Workers*, which to date has been translated into over 20 languages. He is currently the director of finance of the IIIT.

He is a father and a grandfather.

AbdulHamid Ahmad AbuSulayman

Dr. AbdulHamid Ahmad AbuSulayman was born in Makkah in 1936, where he completed his high school education. He holds a B.A. in commerce from the University of Cairo (1959), an M.A. in Political Science from the University of Cairo (1963), and a Ph.D. in International Relations from the University of Pennsylvania (1973).

He has held various positions throughout his career, including secretary for the State Planning Committee, Saudi Arabia (1963–1964); founding member of the Association of Muslim Social Scientists (AMSS) (1972); secretary general of the World Assembly of Muslim Youth (WAMY) (1973–1980); chairman, Department of Political Science at King Saud University, Riyadh, Saudi Arabia (1982–1984); and Rector of the International Islamic University (IIU), Malaysia (1988–1998).

Instrumental in organizing many international academic conferences and seminars, Dr. AbuSulayman is currently the president of the International Institute of Islamic Thought (IIIT) and author of many articles and books on reforming Muslim societies, including *The Islamic Theory of International Relations: New Directions for Islamic Methodology and Thought*; *Crisis in the Muslim Mind*; *Marital Discord: Recapturing the Full Islamic Spirit of Human Dignity*; *Revitalizing Higher Education in the Muslim World* and *The Qur'anic Worldview: A Springboard for Cultural Reform*.

He is a father and a grandfather.

Omar Hisham Altalib

Dr. Omar Hisham Altalib was born in Kirkuk, Iraq in 1967 and left to the USA with his parents in 1968. He graduated from George Mason University in 1989 with a B.A. in Economics and a B.A. in Sociology and holds an M.A. (1993) and a Ph.D. (2004) in Sociology from the University of Chicago. He was granted a Graduate Student Fellowship from the National Science Foundation (1989–1992) and became an Adjunct Professor of Sociology at Daley College, Chicago (1998) and at Indiana University Northwest, Gary, Indiana (1999).

He was an Assistant Professor of Sociology and Criminology at Ashland University, Ohio (2000–2003) and served as Senior Knowledge Engineer at Science Applications International Corporation at Alexandria, Virginia (2005–2006). He was Assistant Professor of Sociology at the International Islamic University, Malaysia (2009–2011). Dr. Altalib has authored several articles on the family, education, endowments, charitable organizations and social work. He frequently attends academic conferences and travels worldwide.

Acknowledgements

What a blessing it was when the Board of Trustees of the International Institute of Islamic Thought (IIIT), decided to entrust the authors with the great responsibility of writing this work.

To Dr. Ahmad Totonji, Dr. Fathi Malkawi, Dr. Jamal Barzinji, and Dr. Yaqub Mirza, we offer our heartfelt thanks for keeping the wheels of IIIT in motion while we worked on the completion of this book.

We offer our gratitude to the reviewers who offered valuable suggestions for improving the text, particularly Batoul Tu'mah, Zainab Alawi, Michèle Messaoudi, Wanda Krause, Maida Malik, Sara Mirza and Gasser Auda. To Dr. Iqbal Unus who reviewed the first table of contents. To Lina Malkawi and Zeena Altalib who prepared and formatted the initial artwork and made valuable contributions to the manuscript.

Our thanks also go to:

Akbar Ali Mir, Ashraf Sabrin, Saif Altalib, Zaid Altalib, Noha Altalib and Mahmoud Sherif who typed and copied several drafts of the book.

Dr. Tanveer Mirza and Salma Ashmawi, who provided real life examples through the parenting workshops held at ADAMS (All Dulles Area Muslim Society) in Herndon, Virginia, USA.

Junaina Abdullah, who helped in reviewing a set of videos on parenting, and to Layla Sein for her insightful comments.

Hasan Altalib, for providing the many enriching references and useful comments on the presentation, contents, and format of the text.

We have been fortunate to have Salwa Medani in our office who worked diligently on the manuscript and improved it on a daily basis. A great blessing descended on us in the person of Shiraz Khan in our London office. She is a very special and remarkable editor who is a goldmine of creativity and critical feedback and a wonderful source of encouragement.

We are deeply indebted to Dr. Imad-ad-Dean Ahmad, president of the Minaret of Freedom Foundation, for his meticulous editing, invaluable additions, and enriching suggestions.

We are extremely grateful to Sylvia Hunt for her rigorous copy-editing, to Salma Mirza for her extensive proofreading, and to Abdallateef Whiteman for his admirable design and layout. Special thanks also go to Hanna, Abdallateef's daughter, for her exquisite hand drawn illustrations. Our profound appreciation is extended to the staff of the IIIT London Office for the quality of their work and supervision of the production of the final version.

The invaluable suggestions and professional insight of the education and psychology experts, Dr. Ishaq Farhan, Dr. Abdul Latif Arabiyyat, Dr. Mahmoud Rashdan, Dr. Fathi Malkawi, and Dr. Abdul Rahman al Naqeeb who contributed significantly to the quality of the book.

We thank our families for providing a comforting and supportive environment to ease the pressures around us while we worked on the manuscript. Special appreciation goes to Dr. Ilham Altalib, Dr. Hisham's life partner for 46 years, without whose unlimited encouragement and sacrifice this work would not have seen the light of day. Her insights and invaluable comments on parenting were a continual source of inspiration in bringing the work to fruition. The bulk of time spent on this work was "borrowed" from family time together and in particular our grandchildren Yusif and Ameen, seven and five years old.

All praise goes to the All-Knowledgeable and All-Powerful, Who gave us the strength to accomplish the task.

Dedication

TO OUR BELOVED mothers and fathers, who flooded us with love, sacrifice, and compassion throughout our lives, cherishing our development and raising and nurturing us to the best of their ability. Although lacking in training and formal education, they emulated the practice of their parents before them, using wisdom, commonsense, and the verified experiences of past generations and civilizations, to teach us righteousness, faith, and self-reliance. May God shower His blessings upon their souls.

To all the parents on our planet today, struggling hard to raise successful children, who, though they mean well, yet need the necessary knowledge and skills to communicate wisely with their children, and create the happy loving family relationships and home environment we all so dearly desire.

To all the families who wish to raise their children to become men and women of caliber, possessing values and qualities of righteousness, honesty, courage, compassion, creativity, and faith, as well as strength of mind and a sense of responsible independence.

To our wives and children, who have endured much hardship and strain over the years, exuding endless patience and unfailing encouragement while we worked on the research and writing of this book.

To all of the above we dedicate this humble effort.

May the Compassionate Almighty, the One and Only, accept our sincere endeavors in trying to bring harmony, peace, and improvement to humankind.

Contents

History of this Book

THIS BOOK HAS been written for all parents, whoever they are and wherever they may be. However, its concept is part of the long-term vision of the International Institute of Islamic Thought (IIIT) to arouse the Muslim world from the intellectual stagnation and decay into which it has fallen and to recapture the intellectual dynamism that once symbolized its great civilization. To promote its vision on parenting, the book focuses on the intellectual and moral regeneration of the Muslim mind and psyche through the medium of education. Although an examination of the methodology behind the intellectual demise of the Muslim world is not addressed here, Islamic Thought reform is the main theme promoted in IIIT publications and conferences to help revive Muslim intellectualism.

Practically, it is imperative that parents know how to raise good children since the psychological foundations of values and personality are largely developed at home in early childhood. We will therefore focus primarily on how cultural, educational, and social skills training in the home is the basis for the proper intellectual, psychological and emotional development of a child. Although the home is the source of the behavioral patterns influencing the child's thought processes in determining right from wrong, it is not enough simply to know what is right and to mechanically do it. Human will and emotion have to accept and desire what the mind considers to be right and to act accordingly; this is where the role of parents is pivotal. Schools and educational institutions teach historical data, facts, physical and technical skills, and provide information, which are to be complemented by the child's home and family life, for it is the latter that develops character, social skills and emotional strength.

This work is meant to contribute to child development and upbringing and different forms of human leadership development. IIIT has organized many conferences and published key works to serve this purpose including: *A Training Guide for Islamic Workers* (translated into more than 20 languages), *Dalīl Maktabat al-Usrah al-Muslimah* (Guide to a Muslim Family Library), and *Azmat al-Irādah wa al-Wujdān al-Muslim* (Crisis in the Muslim Will and Psyche).

The idea to write a book on parent–child relations was suggested during a meeting of IIIT's Board of Trustees in August 1994 on Tioman Island, Malaysia. It was to be the third in a series of books to be published on human development and interpersonal communication by the Institute. Far earlier, and in response to a request by the IIIT, Dr. Isma'īl al Fārūqī authored in 1982 *Tawḥīd: Its Implications for Thought and Life* (a Muslim training manual on the issues of belief and *'aqīdah*). Later in 1991, the IIIT and the International Islamic Federation of Student Organizations (IIFSO) jointly published the widely successful *A Training Guide for Islamic Workers*, the second book in the series, which sought to educate Muslims in effective personal, group and leadership skills. This book is to be considered the third book in the series.

Recognizing the importance of the family unit, Dr. AbdulHamid AbuSulayman, Rector of the International Islamic University, Malaysia

(1988–1998), established a new mandatory course (culminating in a Diploma) on Family and Parenting with a view to disseminating the rationale and moral value of good parenting to students as well as to produce enough teachers to teach the course.

In addition, IIIT founders had initiated a series of leadership training seminars organized in three phases. The idea of producing a book on parenting was given precedence during phase 3:

Phase 1 (1975–1990) consisted of definition, preparation, propagation, and mobilization. It dealt with the skills and tools of activism needed to improve the efficiency and performance of work. This phase culminated in the publication of *A Training Guide for Islamic Workers* (1991), the second book in the series noted above.

Phase 2 (1991–2000) institutionalized training with the efforts of competent trainers including Dr. Omar Kasule in Kuala Lumpur, Dr. Iqbal Unus in Washington, Dr. Anas al-Shaikh-Ali in London and Dr. Manzoor Alam in New Delhi. They conducted numerous training programs worldwide.

Phase 3 was to focus on parenting in the twenty-first century. While Phases 1 and 2 targeted youth activists, it became increasingly clear that character building was an equally essential component that began at birth. As such, IIIT decided to emphasize the significant role that parents can play using good parenting skills to raise righteous citizens and future leaders imbued with principled leadership traits within a healthy and conducive home environment for children to grow. Hence, the publication of this work.

Parenting is not a job to be underestimated or taken lightly. It has a huge impact on the type of children we raise, the type of society in which we live, and ultimately the type of civilization we leave for future generations. As such, it should be given the utmost consideration and be made top priority. We cherish this belief deeply and strongly encourage and invite other authors to further develop each of the topics covered in this book with additional research and instructional materials. IIIT has already established several academic teams to develop further materials on these topics and has translated them into major world languages. This book is only the first step in promoting the case for proper parenting at the practical level.

According to many experts, "the largest trade in the world, the most important task, the greatest task, and the best investment of human beings is cherishing and raising children."

Aims and Objectives

THIS EASY-TO-READ book addresses the one billion parents of our world today, both Muslims and those of other faiths, as well as non-parents, grandparents and relatives who wish to benefit from its advice. It is not aimed at scholars and specialists in particular. Its specific focus is on the goals of parenting, highlighting problems and offering solutions, as well as outlining methods to develop and raise people of righteousness, moral caliber and who will demonstrate leadership qualities.

The main objectives of the work are to:

• Emphasize the importance of good parenting in raising children and families, by making parental responsibility a duty and a top priority, not just theoretically but practically.

• Show parents "how" to acquire the necessary education and skills to implement proper parenting techniques in order to raise righteous citizens of firm character and sound morals, who have the qualities needed to become the building blocks of society and future human civilization.

• Finally, to help parents to create a happy, harmonious and functional family home environment, with supportive relationships amongst all the family members.

In Part One, we deal with the rationale behind good parenting, defining what it is and how it can be implemented to form a very real solution for the regeneration of the Muslim world as well as society as a whole. We also outline the status of parenting as practiced today, including reviewing sources of information available to the Muslim world and the world's industrialized countries, on parenting. We sought to examine how to raise children of sound moral character who possess qualities for active social change. The methods and tools needed to promote physical and emotional strength are highlighted in Part Two of the book. Part Three focuses on character-building and discusses the impact of too much television as well as computer and video games on children and family life while providing practical alternatives to their excessive use.

At the end of each chapter, we have included user-friendly exercises to be performed by both parents and children. The main purpose is to promote ongoing dialog and communication among family members so they can come to know each other well, enjoy time together, participate in decision making, and exchange skills. This will help establish good dynamic family relationships and a happy home environment. Very few activities require outside resources like the use of a library, consulting other parents, or seeking professional advice. We strongly recommend that families do these activities at home or around dinner tables outside the home. It is hoped that these participatory and interactive discussions/activities will fill an important yet missing gap in daily parenting, facilitating discussions pertaining to internal family issues that are rarely tackled and usually marginalized. These discussions and family reflections are a worthwhile aim in themselves.

Finally, this book and the issues it tackles will be followed by the publication of additional works on the subject, categorized under two major themes:

1: (a) Understanding the Role of Parents in Education, Faith, and Skills Training; (b) Happy Families: Necessary Incubators for Developing Future Potential Leaders.

In terms of 1(a) the idea is to help parents understand and accept their role in developing their children's concept of faith and leadership skills. In terms of 1(b) the focus will be on establishing a pleasant and comfortable family home environment to act as an "incubator" to nurture pious people who are potential leaders with a sense of civic responsibility. Issues of communication, praise, criticism, anger, and family time spent together represent the practical steps needed to build and provide the correct environment. In addition, the idea that "children are good observers, but poor analysts" will be illustrated. Practical tests will be provided for parents to see how children deal in real life with others, including with each other, grandparents and other relatives, guests, neighbors, the poor, the community, animals, plants, the environment and the world in general.

2: Role Models for Good Parenting are a Must: The Parents – the Prophets.

Parents will be made aware of the importance of their own behavior in relation to child development. Since children are imitators, parents must be the best role models they can be so that by emulating them children can be the best they can be.

The life of Prophet Muhammad ﷺ furnishes the best example of how to emulate being a father, a grandfather, a great friend of children and a great leader. Indeed, in studying the behavior of the Prophet ﷺ and using his conduct as a blueprint we will set the standard by which to apply the advice given in this entire work.

Finally, if parents do their best and succeed in implementing our suggestions, we hope to set in motion a positive cycle: the raising of healthy and happy children who are active participants in society and who themselves will eventually make exemplary parents.

If at some stage in life, mothers and fathers are ever asked: "What did you do to make your life worthwhile?" they can respond with confidence: "I was a great parent." Maybe a happy grandparent too!

Introduction

HUMAN BEINGS ARE created in the best of forms and are capable of being highly sophisticated. As such, raising a child demands theoretical and practical knowledge concerning the development of infants and children. Since new parents generally have little experience of parenting, they need to learn how to deal with children even before they are conceived.

Unfortunately, although we strive hard to accumulate wealth to have nice homes, cars, and furniture, we neglect to put the same effort into child rearing, hoping or assuming that things will turn out for the best without proper preparation. Parenting should not be left to chance, for the gamble is great and the stakes are high.

Parents usually acquire knowledge by trial and error and may become more effective with their later children than their firstborn, having learned from their initial experience. However, the problem is that by the time these priceless lessons are learned, it will often be too late. The early children will have been raised and will have become mature adults, making it almost impossible to put this learning into effect.

Good parenting really matters and cannot be left to sort itself out. It is a challenging job which needs constant attention. An overview of the task ahead, therefore, has to be appreciated and an honest commitment given to ourselves, our spouses, and our families.

An important aspect of child rearing, which we stress throughout this work, is communication. Effective communication with children will help them develop into happy and responsible adults. It is crucial to know how and when to talk to children, and more importantly, how to listen to them with patience and understanding. Parents, while they love their children unconditionally, need to start improving their communication and listening skills with them. Communication is a two-way act, and should not be brought to a standstill. Parents are to help their children develop their utmost potential without using force. Exposing themselves to the real-life situations of other mothers and fathers will help parents apply new skills and techniques in coping with difficult situations.

Parents also need to reconsider some of the older practices, for old is not always gold. As times change, new circumstances emerge requiring new and creative treatments and responses. Naturally, all parents hope that their children will turn out to be the best. We will highlight some of the common mistakes that are innocently made by parents as well as the many problems commonly faced.

Another area we explore in this work is developing "leadership" traits in children. This may seem an odd feature to give attention to. In this regard, however, we would like to point out that when referring to leadership, we do not mean the ambitious hunt for power, but rather developing people of strength, moral fiber, caliber, ethics, and other qualities necessary to become active members of society with a sense of civic responsibility.

To many teenagers today, home has degenerated to the level of being merely a hotel and a restaurant. Creating a happier and more peaceful home environment for both parents and children is a necessity. Home is not just a place, it is an incubator, a platform and a stage where family members are actors and communication is the script. Everyone must learn 'to play' their part. It is sad to see that many parents and children today are unable to get along with one another, thus creating a dysfunctional home. Some parents and children are afraid or suspicious of one another, and many of them do not know how to improve their relationship. They may even give up trying to understand one another and, frustrated and angry, may just withdraw emotionally, and ultimately abandon their relationship completely.

Although parenting is an enormous responsibility, it should not be given up in despair. It is never too late to overcome challenges and we can still improve our relationships if we avoid blaming ourselves for our past blunders. It is no use saying: "If we only did this or did not do that." Regrets, and constant dwelling on the "if only" scenario, is destructive and serves no purpose but to hurt us further. Although we might have made wrong choices that hurt our families, we must keep in mind that our intentions were for the best. We need to spend less time looking back, and far more time looking ahead. Rather than filling our minds with what we could have or should have done, we need to focus on what we can do right now for a brighter tomorrow. We can also make a pledge to our children to improve ourselves by becoming better parents, considering the past as a life lesson and the future as a chance for change. It may help to visualize the past as sculpted marble or hardened concrete, and the future as pliant clay, still to be molded.

Many parents today (ourselves included) wish that they had known the art and science of good parenting before having had children. Had they done so, there may have been a drastic improvement in the raising of their children. Most parents will feel that much more time could have been spent nurturing relationships. Looking back on our own particular lives, it is painfully apparent that there existed a wealth of experience that we missed, and priceless enriching moments that could have been shared. We hope that our children will forgive us for our mistakes and hope that new parents in turn will avoid these mistakes. We also pray that God Almighty shields every parent from learning his/her lesson the hard way, by first-hand experience!

Our approach in this work is to give guidance by focusing on prevention, not treatment. We do not assert that we can treat problems like drug addiction, alcoholism, depression, crime, and sexually transmitted diseases. However, we can provide a "preventive" measure, a family guide to minimize the chances of experiencing these pitfalls through awareness.

Proper parenting requires skills and preparation so that children can be successful and make their parents proud of them. Fortunately, much more information and techniques are available about parenting than ever before. While there are no short cuts to parenting, just as there are no short cuts to anything worthwhile, it is never too late to start being a better parent, for you are a parent now and forever, whether your children are 4 or 40.

Raising a child to be a happy and well-balanced adult is the hope of all parents. This book will multiply your chances of accomplishing this and realizing your dream of a successful, wholesome relationship with your children. A wise person once said, "It is not where your dreams take you but where you take your dreams." Although the best time to raise your teenager was a decade ago, the second best time is today, so use it. God Almighty will bless your sincere intentions and effort.

We have included statistical data from many sources to give the reader a sense of direction and hope. Statistics change frequently, they are only meant to be taken as a guide and not as a fixed reality.

Many experts have commented on the format and production of this series. Some reviewers recommended publishing the work in many booklets, others suggested separating theory from practical application, while yet others thought it better to produce a "DIY" (Do It Yourself) guide where theory and application should go together. We see the merits of all these options. However, for now, we are offering this first edition in the current format. We are hoping to receive valuable feedback and comments from our readers to incorporate them in future editions of the work, to be published in different sizes and formats.

It is not humanly possible to successfully address many ethnic cultures in one book; however, it is hoped that the translated editions in various languages will be adapted toward those specific readerships by local teachers and leaders.

The English translation of verses from the Holy Qur'an have been taken from Yūsuf 'Alī and Muhammad Asad's interpretations with a few modifications where necessary by the authors.

This work is the culmination of the authors' experiences in the Muslim world and the West. It attempts to synthesize and to capture the wisdom of divine revelation, prophetic guidance, and human achievements from both the Muslim heritage and Western culture. It is an effort to show how these great wisdoms complement each other when properly analyzed and evaluated. Thus, it offers a unique and humble contribution to the realm of the Parent–Child Relationship.

THE AUTHORS

January 2013, Washington, D.C., USA

She Came Crying in 1969

WITH TEARS IN her eyes the mother said: "Brother Altalib, please help me. It is my daughter. I raised her and gave her everything she asked for. She is now nineteen and she ran away with her boyfriend last night. I don't know where she is."

I said: "Sister, what do you mean you gave her everything?"

She said: "Food, clothes, toys, money – everything she needed!"

I asked: "Did you teach her about the religion, the Qur'an, the lives of the prophets, and Muslim history?"

She said: "No, but I gave her everything!"

I said to myself: "Alas! We raise our children oblivious of God and deprived of strong moral training, yet expect them to become like the righteous, Abū Bakr, 'Umar, and 'Alī! Oranges and apples do not grow on oak trees! We are nineteen years too late! We do not live by bread alone."

It took a year of patience, love, and wisdom to restore the girl and her husband (former boyfriend) to the blessings of God and the enjoyment of a righteous life with four children in the subsequent years of the marriage.

If you really want to respond to your children, you need to have a PERSONAL relationship with them. They need to know that you are dependable and that you will be there whenever they need you. Investing time, money, and effort in your children is the best "investment" you can make!! Your child is appealing to you, saying loudly Mom, Dad, please:

> "Don't walk in front of me, I may not follow you,
> Don't walk behind me, I may not lead you,
> Walk beside me and just be my friend." (Albert Camus)

Do you hear the cry?

PART ONE

Parenting: Setting the Foundation

CHAPTER 1

Good Parenting: What is it and How do We Begin?

Introduction

WHEN ONE SEES a happy family living in harmony, with a peaceful and relaxed home environment, and (above all) well-adjusted, pious children, this is not the result of chance. It is the result of hard work and effort to develop good parent–child relationships. Good parenting is a long-term investment and is the key to great success in the emotional, psychological, and physical development of children.

In essence, good parenting provides a warm, loving environment in which children can flourish. Such an environment is essential for forging relationships that improve communication and bring children and parents closer together. Successful communication requires positive attitudes, not harsh or judgmental ones, that encourage children to strive for excellence.

Muslim parenting today is quite problematic. Most parents do not take courses in parenting and they lack knowledge, experience, and parenting skills. They rely solely on instinct and common sense, which is usually outdated and inherited from ancestors who are either uninformed or for whom parenting has a different cultural meaning. There are others who are educated but imitate Western cultures blindly. Parents may also follow other ill-informed parents and neighbors. Some parents try to fulfill their unfulfilled wishes through their children. There are some who neglect or postpone parental duties. Owing to a lack of understanding or lack of time they delegate parenting to babysitters, schoolteachers, relatives, television, and computer games. This is particularly a feature of some oil-rich countries where the "malpractice" of importing babysitters has impacted negatively on children's characters.

We aim to help parents rectify all of the above, and to eliminate or reduce their innocent mistakes. In a sense, we offer a good "insurance policy" against most of the common pitfalls parents are likely to encounter.

Unfortunately, parenting today is largely taken for granted with little thought given to what this tremendous role entails. In fact, how many of us parents have ever thought seriously about the task we are entrusted with? It will help if we do so, for we will come to realize that parenting requires its own set of skills, strategies, and planning.

CONSIDER THE FOLLOWING QUESTIONS:
Question 1: Which task requires knowledge of management, psychology, sociology, anthropology, nursing, culinary art, and communication?
Question 2: Which task does not require a degree, a certificate or a license to practice?
Question 3: Which task is one of the most misunderstood and neglected?
Question 4: Which task has endured the most abuse and violence?
Question 5: Which task is so crucial that it affects people's lives even as adults?
Question 6: Which task is the most important teacher for a child?

Answer: **Parenting**.

Think about it: we do not hire mechanics, plumbers, electricians, or doctors unless they are qualified for the job, yet the majority of us become parents without any training. We study for

16 years to earn a college degree, yet can easily become parents as teenagers, without even preparing for the great responsibility that lies ahead. Again, although we know that we must have a license to drive a car, to hunt for deer, or to fly a plane, we do not feel that it is necessary for people to be trained for parenthood.

So what is it that the majority of us, of course meaning well, do when raising children? Although numerous parenting theories and good advice are available to parents, they are generally ignored and parents blithely carry on hoping that everything will turn out for the best. They may exert some effort, attend Parent–Teacher Association (PTA) meetings at school, keep a general "eye on things," worry about grades, attend family outings for the sake of being there, and make other superficial efforts. But aside from this, parents tend to do little else.

Although there is no all-encompassing fast-track model we can use, there are procedures that can be implemented to help us achieve our goal. Along the way, we come to realize that the road to good parenting is always under construction, and that although we may make improvements, we cannot expedite the process. Do not look for "short cuts," to successful parenting because they do not exist.

SIX THEORIES, NO CHILDREN; SIX CHILDREN, NO THEORIES

"Before I got married, I had six theories about bringing up children; now, I have six children and no theories."

JOHN WILMONT, EARL OF ROCHESTER
(Brown 1994)

Phases of Child Development

Let us begin by first understanding that children go through different phases of development. It is beneficial for parents to familiarize themselves with these stages, for in each stage the requirements and demands of parenthood change. The phases of child development can be divided as follows: Infants, toddlers, and preschoolers (ages 0–7); pre-teens (ages 8–11); young teens (ages 12–14); and young adults (ages 15–22). In each of these stages, children require different physical, emotional, social, and psychological resources from parents.

Ultimately, the child grows from a state of total dependence to one of nearly total independence. It is important for parents and offspring to negotiate these transitions successfully. Conflict theorists note how parents and young adults compete for power and resources. Each wants to control the other, and they often have different ideas about how resources (money, space, and time) should be allocated. As children become adolescents and adults, parents need to redirect their energy away from their children toward their own lives. Then the equation reverses when the parents become old and possibly dependent on their children. Independence translates into interdependence, where there will always be mutual advice, consultation, and sharing and caring between children and parents.

The Way We Raise Our Children: Different Parenting Styles

Let us also recognize that there are four broad parenting styles that many parents adopt (of course parenting styles do not always fit into these categories).

1) **Authoritarian / dictatorial**: Parents demand obedience, and severely punish disobedience.
2) **Authoritative**: Parents expect their children to be responsive to their demands, yet they are also responsive to the demands of their children. These parents explain their rules clearly and provide different well-considered reasons for rules and regulations, so the children realize that the parent's demands are not haphazard, arbitrary, or meaningless.
3) **Permissive**: Parents allow their children to do as they please. There is little conflict, because permissive parents defer to their children's wishes.
4) **Democratic**: Parents try to negotiate with their children, and include their children in decision-making.

In general sociologists prefer authoritative parenting. Examine your own parenting style and decide under which of the four broad categories you could be placed. Ask yourself why you have chosen to adopt a particular style or why you have fallen into a "a particular style". Self-analysis of this type will allow you to rethink your methods by focusing on the positive areas, and improving those that are wanting.

A Note on Authoritarian / Dominant Parenting: A Culture of Coercion and Fear

There is a prevalent belief, particularly amongst Muslim parents and some minorities, that the Authoritarian style of parenting is an effective way in which to prevent deviant behavior in their children. Interestingly it is based on a mindset which seems to focus on prevention of bad conduct rather than the encouragement of positive mental attitudes and good behavior. Control and fear take precedence over harmonious family relationships and the result can be maladjusted children with widespread repercussions for society at large. For this reason, and because of the popularity of this style, we have decided to focus a little more deeply on this issue.

The prevalent behavior of Muslim parents is that of rigid rule enforcement and domination, and lack of dialog, participation, and consultation. The seeds of authoritarian practices are planted within the family from infancy, and then permeate outside the home to invade schools, social institutions, and eventually the government and political systems.

Within the family, the father has forceful authority over the children, the older brothers over the younger ones, and the boys over the girls. The males are generally the dominant "bosses" and the whole atmosphere is devoid of the concepts of partnership and responsibility. In contrast, the Prophet ﷺ encouraged the concept of pastorship (derived from the Latin for shepherd) and stated:

> You are all shepherds [pastors] and you are all responsible for what you are assigned to [your parish]. (AL-BUKHĀRĪ)

The general practice is that parents issue unexplained orders and instructions to children with an arbitrary list of do's and don'ts. When the children ask for explanations, the routine answer is "do as you are told," "that's the way it is," "do as I say, not as I do," or "do not argue too much." Sometimes inquisitive children may be reprimanded and accused of being disrespectful, impolite, or disobedient. To silence inquisitive children, some parents may give inaccurate responses to questions, instead of saying they do not know the answer.

This is not to say that these parents do not care for their children; on the contrary, they love and care greatly for their families. Nevertheless, in trying to be strict and in control what they are in effect becoming is domineering. Furthermore, domineering is not the same as training, which is what it is sometimes confused with. This domineering practice does not help to raise children who are emotionally, psychologically, and mentally sound. To raise strong children, parents need to engage children in participative consultation. The Qur'an states:

> *Who [conduct] their affairs by mutual consultation.* (Qur'an 42:38)

> *And it was by God's grace that you [O Prophet] did deal gently with your followers: for if you had been harsh and hard of heart, they would indeed have broken away from you. Pardon them, then, and pray that they be forgiven. And take counsel with them in all matters of public concern; then, when you have decided upon a course of action, place your trust in God: for, verily, God loves those who place their trust in Him.* (Qur'an 3:159)

Although the coercive approach may result in children giving apparent respect to their parents, it will be a hollow respect founded on fear, rather than conviction and love. Fear, both learned and instinctual, is discussed in more detail in Chapter 15. This authoritarian approach is extended into the educational system, where children's respect for teachers is not built on love of learning, but rather on fear of a teacher's displeasure and/or punishment. The result is that children may not do well academically. The coercive approach is reinforced by the educational system in some countries, where most teaching is based on learning by memorization, rather than comprehension and participation. Based on this system, parents and schools have little to congratulate themselves for. All they have done is help contribute to the "manufacture" of individuals whose social behavior is aligned with dictatorial and authoritarian institutions. This is the slave-like attitude that we find in government administrations, political parties, social movements, police departments, national armies, corporations, and factories. Those few individuals who escape this educational system and do not succumb to the tyranny of society, have little recourse. They behave hypocritically and follow the crowd, or become misfits and thorns in the side of a deeply flawed system, with consequent suffering and frustration.

There exists a crisis in the Muslim mind and in the psychological and emotional upbringing of Muslim children. The lack of a coherent methodological approach and the fragmentation and compartmentalization of knowledge are responsible for the distortion of Muslim culture and thought. The lack of attention given to skilled parenting is equally responsible for the serious emotional and psychological deprivation of young children. The current approach of many Muslims toward parenting does not incorporate the Qur'anic vision of *'imrān* (creating and developing a civilization), *itqān* (perfection), and *tafakkur* (exploration); rather, it is literal, slavish, and imitative. Instead of being scientific, objective, and methodical, Muslims are superstitious. They are overwhelmed with the idea of jinn and magic, and miss out on the fruits of a scientific mentality.

It is widely perceived that the responsibility for solving the intellectual stagnation, and crisis of mind that has almost paralyzed the Ummah, falls squarely on the shoulders of thinkers and educators. However, although they have an important role to play, ultimately, it is to parents that we should look for a solution. Once convinced, parents will certainly do their best to raise healthy, free, and well-adjusted children capable of shouldering the mantle of leadership, and bringing about a positive change in society, ultimately reversing the paralysis of the Ummah.

Today's sad state of parenting can be characterized as follows:

- Overwhelming illiteracy among parents, which is an obstacle to seeking knowledge and learning skills;
- A culture of fear which breeds a "slave mentality" devoid of creativity and initiative;
- Blind imitation of and obedience to others ("herd mentality") without critical analysis; and
- A domineering and coercive approach at home and in the public domain.

Parenting can make or break a family, a society, and a civilization. Civilization building is never ending and is not a one-time job; rather, it is a way of life and a dynamic continuous process. It has a beginning but no end. Civilization continues to grow, improve, and develop. It is a matter of continuous exploration, discovery, and improvement (*ihsān*). We encourage parents to think of the big picture, and to think of the repercussions of their parenting practices on society at large.

When children are raised in a state of fear and oppression, they become afraid to take risks and afraid to make decisions. Eventually they end up lacking a sense of responsibility and are unable to make decisions. Fearful children also adopt self-indulgent attitudes that lead to a lack of participation in public affairs, and that inhibit them from questioning a leader's authority, resulting in authoritarian and dictatorial regimes. Children brought up like this will end up tolerating corruption and shying away from performing their duties toward society. Team spirit is lost in the process, preventing the establishment of those institutions necessary for building societies. The backward-looking and rigid culture of superstition and irrationality inculcated in the fresh young minds of children ensures the absence of development in science and technology.

The golden age of Islamic civilization flourished because all these factors were kept in mind while children were being raised. For example, the practice of breastfeeding was seen as an integral aspect of child rearing, where attention was given to the child's necessary emotional and psychological development. Indeed, the answer to the question "why did such a great civilization decline to become the lowest of the low?" lies in one important aspect: the way we raise our children, starting from birth. Lack of focus on good parenting is the key missing dimension in the great and numerous reform efforts in Muslim history.

What Can Predict Parenting Style?

Is there a link between our interactions with our parents and the way we interact with our children? Parents who abuse their own children often say they were themselves mistreated as children. Can a person's positive childhood experiences with his/her own parents forecast the eventual development of a warm, sensitive, and stimulating style of parenting? Is there an intergenerational transmission of parenting style?

A parent's own child-rearing history makes a cumulative contribution to his/her eventual parenting style. In general, parents who experienced more supportive child rearing in any period of their childhood became warm, sensitive, stimulating parents to their own children. Supportive parenting is associated with improved cognitive development by the age of three. (Baumrind 2008)

Fathers tend to interact differently than mothers with their babies and toddlers. While most fathers and mothers are similar in their responsiveness, stimulation, affection, and teaching, fathers tend to engage in more physical play than mothers. Both parents, however, play more physically with sons than with daughters. Mothers' and fathers' level of education is also associated with children's eventual performance in school and other areas. Interestingly, the more years of education a father has, the more supportive a mother tends to be with their children. (Ricks 1985)

Aside from mirroring our parents' style of raising children, we sometimes oppose our parents' style of raising children. There may be some differences in child-rearing practices from generation to generation. Nearly half of grandparents think their grandchildren are being raised differently than the way they raised their own children. Half of that group state their offspring are more lenient with their grandchildren than they were as parents. Fewer than half say their children give their grandchildren fewer household responsibilities than their children were given and their grandchildren have more opportunities than they provided to their own children (Zogby International 2006).

Regardless of the parents' own childhood, "family of origin," education, or income, healthy parents discover that having their own children is an opportunity to rethink the way(s) in which they were raised. They may repeat or improve on their parents' method with their own children as they grow.

Ultimately, however, no matter how much parents do, their children are independent individuals and they are personally accountable and responsible for their actions. All that parents can offer is support and guidance. One day they will be very happy and proud to declare: "We were good parents."

Beginning Good Parenting: An Overview of the Task Ahead

Good parenting starts before a child is conceived. Before marriage, one needs to choose a good spouse. After marriage, the pregnant mother has to look to her health, and her nutrition, and avoid harmful substances entering her body. The father has to take care of her to the best of his ability, alleviate as many of her duties and work as possible, and allow her enough rest, sleep, and relaxation. Here we offer parents an overview of the task ahead and the knowledge and skills necessary to achieve good parenting. It is helpful to know the real scope of the challenges facing parents so that they do not overestimate or underestimate the difficulties facing them. If they think parenting is too easy, they will not feel the need to prepare themselves for it. If they think it is too difficult, they may despair and give up.

Although parenting may be the most rewarding, stimulating, and ultimately pleasurable experience one ever goes through, it can also be the most demanding. One's whole life is a series of tests, and raising children is one of the most challenging. Romantic notions, therefore, will need to be put aside and certain realities grasped. Good parenting is not simple, and is never without mistakes. Children will try their parents' patience and test their endurance, and even when they are not near, will preoccupy their hearts and minds. One's life changes dramatically with the arrival of children.

All children have talent and potential, as do all parents. Parenting is not something that has to be faced alone. Many parents have a support network to help care for their children, including teachers, nannies, relatives, religious leaders, and friends.

Once children are conceived, we can begin by applying the following guidelines. It helps to keep a broader picture in mind to avoid being swamped with the confusion of many do's and don'ts. Begin by trying to understanding the following eight principles to help you view your family life and home in a balanced way.

Keep parenting lighthearted. Tell yourself that although we may commit "stupid" mistakes innocently, you cannot spell "STUPID" without **U** and **I**.

1. UNDERSTAND THAT CHILD DEVELOPMENT IS A LONG AND SOPHISTICATED PROCESS

Raising righteous children, active citizens, and potential good leaders is a daily task that takes years, not months. Although romance may fail us and friendships may end, the parent–child bond is more powerful and indestructible, weathering the worst of storms to remain one of the strongest and most enduring relationships on earth.

2. SET THE RIGHT GOALS AND STRIVE CONSTANTLY TO IMPROVE

Goals help us avoid confusion and define action. They make clear where we want to go and how to travel there (we have devised a parenting goals chart discussed in subsequent chapters). Without goals or a road map, parents may make mistakes unknowingly because they have no defined objectives against which to measure their actions. This does not mean that mistakes will not happen; they will! The point is to recognize mistakes and learn from them by becoming more responsible. The same applies to children: have we given our children clear instructions? Have we guided them on how to live in harmony with us? Have we given them the necessary skills so that they can live up to our expectations?

3. PUT INTO PRACTICE THE PRINCIPLES LEARNED AND SHARE PRACTICAL EXPERIENCES WITH OTHER PARENTS

If we examine the literature on parenting, or seek counseling, we will find much guidance to help us. Although parents may agree on general principles, they often fail to put them into practice (due to lack of skills, experience, or just the day-to-day chores). However, when they share their practical experiences with other parents, it can help both parties achieve

better parenting skills. Whether we are single, married, at home, or employed outside the home, parenting is a job too important to do in isolation.

4. BE GOOD ROLE MODELS AND TEACH CHILDREN SELF-RELIANCE

One of the most important things that parents can teach their children is how to manage without them. It is in the home that children learn dignity, courage, self-discipline, love, compassion, interdependence, and responsibility. Lecturing is not enough to provide children with the necessary tools to become men and women of admirable character. A parent's good example is better than many sermons.

5. TEACH CHILDREN TO DISCERN RIGHT FROM WRONG

When parents hear stories about the poor behavior of other children, they often remark: "My child cannot do that. My child is different." It is wrong to assume that our child is immune from bad behavior and will naturally turn out to be successful. In reality, a child may behave contrary to our wishes. This should come as no surprise for our children are basically no different from the thousands of other children who socialize and live around us. Since we are all the descendants of Adam and Eve (harboring their genes), we are all capable of discerning right from wrong and acting upon this internal knowledge. Facing similar challenges and living in a close environment, everyone is bound to make mistakes, the only difference being that some of us will make more mistakes than others, and some of us will repent and rectify, whereas others will not. Although everyone is unique, we face many similar experiences. There is hardly an issue in our lives that has not been experienced, in some way or another, by someone else.

6. WORK HARD TO DEVELOP AND INCULCATE KEY CHARACTER TRAITS

In terms of the bigger picture, the re-emergence of a truly humane civilization can only be achieved with the establishment of sound institutions. These institutions must be comprised of individuals who possess strong and impeccable character, devoid of selfishness, lust, and corruption. These personalities must furthermore possess the qualities of honesty, humbleness, and love of others. Good character traits are rarely the product of chance; they are the result of happy homes, stable environments, and committed parents.

7. DEVELOP THE ART OF CONVERSATION

Talk! Have discussions with your children on anything and everything, on what you did during the day, on how you feel about issues, and on what your child thinks about x, y, and z. It is important for children to learn how you articulate your thoughts. Make communication a priority and come to know and understand your child. Aside from developing relationships, talking is also critical for language development and articulation. Do not seek refuge in television, the Internet, and/or computer games to keep the child out of your way. Lack of talking results in dead intellect and passivity. We have devoted a chapter to the negative influence of watching too much television. Communication includes serious discussions and humorous interchange. Parents should joke and play with their children, because humor strengthens relationships and banishes boredom. Parents spend so much time bringing up children that they forget to ***enjoy*** them and this is a huge loss. Children are in a complete world of their own, and have great capacity for happiness and play. It is sad to see morose, boring parents, who prefer to watch television programs rather than go out and about with their children, make them laugh, and have fun with them. Since life is full of pressure and anxiety, children can provide the best medicine to alleviate stress by helping parents escape into their childish world, albeit only for a while. Some parents feel that playing with children shows a weakness or lack of seriousness about life. The reality is that when you laugh with children, you allow them to feel confident and unafraid of you, tension levels go down, an invisible bond of love is shared, and children feel free to express themselves. To joke and laugh is an essential part of communication.

8. ENJOY GOOD PARENTING!

This follows on from the previous point. The principles outlined above are meant to be applied with compassion and fun. Sometimes, success-obsessed parents are so focused on goals that they let the simple pleasures of family life slip by. Be aware of this. Good parenting is a holistic concept and a compassionate task since the experience of parenting is as important as the realization of the objectives.

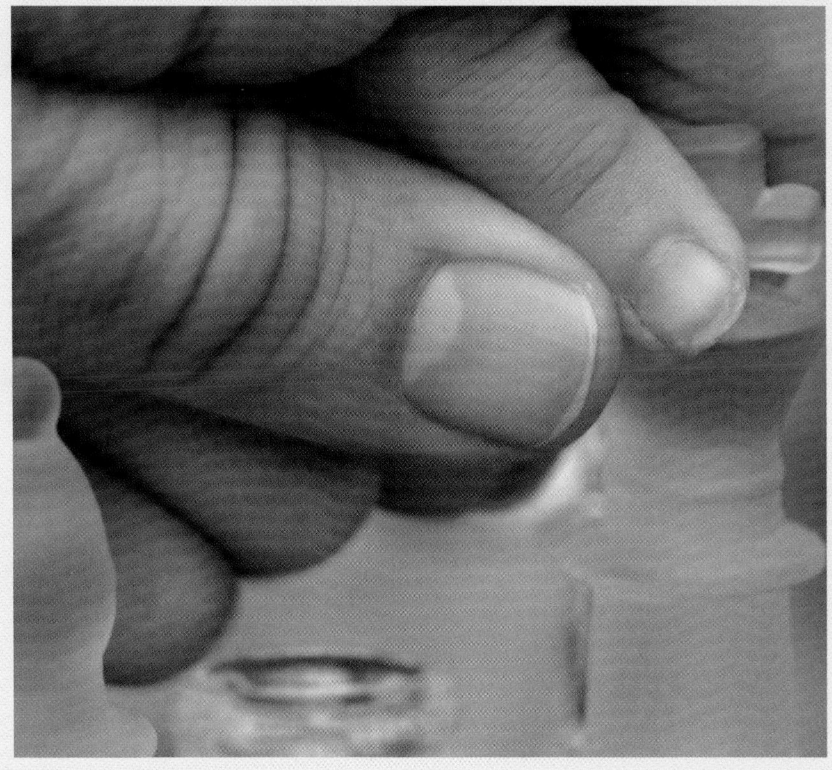

Quality Time and ACTIVE ENGAGEMENT with Children

Parents may often claim that they spend a lot of time WITH their children. Actually, what they mean is not WITH but in proximity of their children. That is, they may be in the same room as their child but watching TV, reading, on the phone, reviewing emails, or conversing with other guests. What is needed is ACTIVE ENGAGEMENT with children. This implies reading together, playing sports and games together, solving puzzles together, cooking and eating together, discussing things together, joking together, shopping together, building blocks together, and washing dishes together. In other words, not simply being in a child's company whilst simultaneously leaving the child alone but being an active participant and partner in activities with the child.

This is good quality time with enough quantity time spent through ACTIVE ENGAGEMENT.
No babysitting, nor delegation can replace interaction with parents, both of them!

HASAN ALTALIB

Utilizing Sources of Information on Parenting

One of the ways in which to begin good parenting would be to consult sources of expert advice and tips.

Muslim Sources vs. Western Sources
Parenting literature is widely available in North America (Table 1.1). For Western parents much information is available on good parenting; and there are many books, libraries, and websites providing resources and information to help make parenting more rewarding and effective.

Table1.1 Availability of Literature on Parenting

Library	No. of titles
Library of Congress	2,464
Consortium of 6 Universities, USA	3,215
Fairfax County Public Library, Virginia	432
National Library of Canada	362

Sources: United States Library of Congress (www.loc.gov)
Fairfax County Public Library (www.fairfaxcounty.gov/library)
Library and Archives Canada (www.collectionscanada.gc.ca)

In contrast, when would-be Muslim parents seek advice on parenting from Muslim sources, what is available to them? Al-Tall and al-Qaysi (in Arabic 1990) emphasize the scarcity of high-quality Muslim literature on parenthood. Few books provide practical details on how to instill acceptable values and character in children. Parents face difficulties in utilizing the classical books on parenting. The old ones deal with different times and challenges, and they lack clear classification, indexing, and referencing. Parenting information for Muslims is scattered over a vast variety of writings including: literature on jurisprudence, Qur'anic commentaries (*tafsīr*), historical works, Sufi poetry, and books of exhortation.

Dr. al-Za'balawi (in his book in Arabic on teen upbringing) states that there is little Islamic literature on child rearing, and very few specialized writings on adolescence. The Muslim Students Association of the United States and Canada (MSA) published the first Islamic coloring book for children in 1973. Such books were not available then, and parents who settled in the West felt the scarcity of literature for children.

Dr. Manazir Ahsan, Director of the Islamic Foundation in Leicester, England, mentions that although Muslim communities in the West have been able to establish a good number of institutions, mosques, and schools, they have not been able "to produce adequate literature in English to cater to the teaching requirements of their younger generation, both at home and at school" (D'Oyen 1996).

The literature produced is far too small and much more is needed. The Islamic library today is deficient in books on child rearing and parenting. Most of the literature addresses adult education, and little is written about child development and adolescent psychology. Vast amounts of literature have been written by jurists on formal aspects of marriage contracts; the rights and duties of husbands, wives, and children; the technicalities of divorce, and the calculation of inheritance. There is a need for more Islamic books that focus on the family and the relationships among siblings, particularly the social, psychological, and developmental aspects. When parents look for advice on family issues, most of the books they encounter concentrate on formalistic and legalistic (*fiqhī*) issues.

Furthermore, Muslim history books taught in high schools in the Arab world tend to ignore human interaction and personal development, and focus mostly on political issues and regulating peace and war among nations.

Little space is devoted to the human love, affection, and respect shown by the Prophet Muhammad ﷺ toward children, his kindness in dealing with them, his respect for them, and his willingness to join in their games. The Prophet did not have the opportunity to raise his own sons because they died in infancy, yet he raised his daughters (Fāṭimah, Zaynab, Ruqayyah, and Umm Kulthūm) and contributed to the raising of his grandchildren, and the children of his relatives and the community. He also raised his young cousin 'Alī ibn Abī Ṭālib and his adopted son Zayd ibn Ḥārithah. It is amazing how the Prophet ﷺ paid so much attention to children and showed them care, kindness, and respect while at the same time being totally occupied with establishing a new society and a new state, which was under constant threat of being annihilated by its enemies.

Little attention has been paid by men to child rearing because, for the most part, it has been done by women. Exploration and elaboration of the actions of Muslim women, known in Islamic literature as the Mothers of the Believers, is not undertaken enough. Indeed, much of it has been lost or devalued. We need to encourage scholars to investigate and develop literature on how the Prophet's wives and the female Companions raised children. This will help introduce an important dimension to the role of women in social development and expand the Islamic library in women's studies. Furthermore, this literature should include a study of the actions of women who have successfully raised potential leaders, both male and female, in recent times. Unless we do this, the guidance that "Paradise lies at the feet of the mother" will be nothing more than a pious platitude.

The emphasis to date has been on abstract values and objectives, rather than on practical ways and means to develop character and values in children. Not enough attention is paid to the understanding and analysis of development and growth, making it hard for parents to apply parenting principles in their daily lives. Practical techniques, relevant skills, and real-life examples are needed. One distraction has been the centuries' long colonization of Muslim countries, during which time the top priority was given to the liberation of the land, while *tarbiyah* (education and training) was ignored. Social change, good management, and development were at the bottom of the agenda. Writing about parenthood was not a priority and no serious research was undertaken into the subject for a long time.

Muslim reformers like Ibn Saḥnūn, Ibn al-Jazzār, and 'Alī al-Qabsy, all in Qayrawan, Tunis, placed more emphasis on breastfeeding, and how to control, discipline and punish children in the classroom as well as compensation for teachers. Not enough attention was devoted to child psychology, child development, education, and parenthood. This may partly explain why the great reformist movements could not revive Muslim civilization in spite of the genius and sincere efforts of their leaders. To be able to establish a thriving society, we need to have an excellent knowledge of child rearing and character building. We also need sound education, strong faith, and proper skills. It is interesting to note how the Qur'an describes the prophets as role models to emulate. Leadership qualities can be developed early if we have a deeper understanding of the art and science of parenting.

In 2002, Professor Mumtaz Anwar of Kuwait University was commissioned by IIIT to research available literature on parenting for Muslims. He found a lack of good parenting books for Muslims, and also that there are very low literacy rates in many parts of the

Muslim world, especially among women. Most Muslim parents depend on personal observation and experience in raising children, which is not enought for successful child rearing. Even for educated Muslim parents, there is a lack of high-quality literature on good parenting and no real formal training available. Although it is difficult to gauge how much literature on parenting is available in all the languages of the Muslim world, we assert that it is not enough. Clearly, an urgent need exists to produce high-quality literature on parenting, based on character building, values, and righteousness, which also deals with the relevant problems of communities today including problems at a local level.

Qualities of the Prophets (Found in the Qur'an)

Qur'anic Terms	تعابير قرآنية
Honest	صدّيقاً
Compassionate and Merciful	رؤوف رحيم
Knowledge and Wisdom	حُكماً وعلماً
Increase (referring to *Ṭālūt*) in Physical Strength and Knowledge	زاده بسطة في العلم والجسم
Strong and Trustworthy	القوي الأمين
Professional and Trustworthy	حفيظ عليم

Should Parenting be Taught in High Schools?

> **If parenting is a responsible task, why then do we not teach formal courses in schools? Seven out of ten people think that parenting is something we have to learn or be taught.**
>
> LONGFIELD AND FITZPATRICK 1999

The world has changed since the end of the Second World War. Earlier generations of the same family used to live in the same village or town. Grandmothers and grandfathers, aunts, uncles, and older siblings were available to offer advice and help with childcare. Family life now is becoming more challenging. Many single-parent families exist and there are more marital breakdowns and working mothers than before. As the art of transmitting good parenting has fragmented we need to fill the role of "parenting teacher" left vacant by the shrinking extended family network. Should we look towards schools to do this? Furthermore, bringing up the second child may be easier than the first because we learn so much more. If we can pass on this experience, formally and/or informally, should we not do so?

Although providing courses on parenting sounds logical and appealing, in reality it is far from it. We need to be clear as to what we require such courses to teach. The role of "parenting teacher" is also a problem. Family life is not a pure science: it is also about feelings, relationships, and intimacy. Those who argue against teaching about parenting in high schools claim that parenting should not be taught as rigid formulas in classes run by government agencies. Educational institutions that like to interfere in private family life and meddling politicians should not be allowed to lay their hands on the intricacies of family relations. Professional help in parenting is useful, yet parents must not abdicate their role to teachers and professionals. Since every family is unique, parents are advised to resort to their wisdom, intuition and personal judgment. Learning from one's own mistakes is quite helpful and family autonomy should be preserved. Parenthood, unlike mathematics, is not a theoretical subject. Teachers who are able to teach theory may not be so able to teach a practical course on parenting.

According to psychotherapist Donald Winnicott,

"All my professional life I have avoided giving advice. With the best of intentions, doctors were especially liable to get in the way between mothers and infants, parents and children."

WINNICOTT 1992

Furthermore, in giving guidance on parenthood, we need to be careful to avoid improper external intervention in family life as well as becoming authoritarian. This may undermine the confidence and accountability of parents. Untrained teachers should not act as a conciliation or arbitration service for addressing family conflicts.

Having said this, however, there are beneficial elements of a well structured course that cannot be overlooked. Instead of throwing the baby out with the bath water, we must teach the value of responsibility that results from starting a family, as well as the time and cost involved. The example of parenting courses discussed below is taken from the United Kingdom but the Muslim world itself is also starting to teach parenting. For instance, it is encouraging to know that in 1998, the International Islamic University in Malaysia introduced a course on marriage and parenthood for students and a Diploma in Parenting Education to train teachers.

BRITISH GUIDELINES FOR HIGH SCHOOL COURSES

As discussed, there has to be a delicate equilibrium between parents and schools, which is not to be upset by the introduction of compulsory classes. Further, although health agencies and charities offer help to new parents on pregnancy, birth, and caring for infants, the teaching of social aspects and values may be controversial.

The British government started teaching a formal parenting class to school children in 2000. Family breakdown and single parenthood present a serious problem for Britain, and have reached alarming levels in Europe (Woolf 1999). Based on the advice given by educationists, civil servants, and psychologists, the British government introduced guidelines for teaching pupils the following topics: (Burgess 2009)

- Dealing with conflicts in marriage
- Punishing children appropriately
- Practical tips on how to cope with a child's tantrum in a supermarket
- Expected roles of mothers and fathers
- Costs and practicalities of bringing up children
- Nurturing of self-esteem in children and parents with praise
- Relative value of material things against love and security
- Responsibilities alongside rights and independence
- Value of marriage
- Time management skills
- Dealing with stresses in family life

The British government felt that this curriculum would help reduce the number of teenage pregnancies and criminal behavior in children. Learning to live with family rules is the first step toward learning to live within society's laws and to avoid incarceration.

> Although parenting is challenging, it is the most enjoyable, rewarding, stimulating and ultimately pleasurable experience most of us are ever likely to have.
>
> (BATOOL AL-TOMA, AUTHOR AND MOTHER, PERSONAL LETTER)

A science requires methodologies, structures, strategies, and assumptions.
An art requires wisdom, tact, intuition, love, and common sense.
Child rearing is a science, an art, and a spiritual endeavor.

Are Our Children Abnormal?

Owing to the complexities of child rearing, some parents think that their offspring are abnormal. A mother said: "Several years before we had children, my husband and I surprised our neighbors by cleaning their house while they were away. They had three small children, who had many toys scattered throughout their house. Six hours after we started, we collapsed, exhausted on their couch, shaking our heads in disbelief. This can't be normal. If it is, we're never having children. Two years and two children later, I know just how normal our neighbor's house was. Our own living room has the same children-live-here look now."

FABER AND MAZLISH 1982

Children are the Future of Humanity –
Through Children We Can Change the World

- Children are likely to live up to what you believe of them: If you tell your children "You can do it", they will do it. If you tell them "You cannot do it," they will not do it.
- A nation is the sum of its families and the sum of its men and women.
- If we want to change a nation, we have to change the home.
- For every child at risk, there is also a family at risk.
- Smart is not something you simply are; but something you can become.
- To change the family we have to change ourselves.
- As your children grow, your role as a parent should evolve from a manager to a consultant, from an onsite supervisor to a mentor.

Verily, God does not change people's condition unless they change their inner selves; and when God wills people to suffer evil [in consequence of their own evil deeds], there is none who could avert it: for they have none who could protect them from Him. (Qur'an 13:11)

Conclusion

Whether courses are formally taught or not, one thing is certain: Good parenting and its repercussions on society at large are coming to be widely recognized. Confronting the realities of marriage, parenthood, child development and child care before they actually happen can be an effective measure to prevent many of the dilemmas future parents may otherwise face. However, while it would be a logical step to go beyond teaching sex education to teaching the outcome of sexual relations, in the form of babies and how to raise them, this should not be viewed as replacing the role of parents themselves. If parents realize the potential of their role and the success it brings to themselves and to society, they will be willing to comprehend the art and science of good parenting and happily sacrifice all they can for the sake of their offspring. Relying on governments, schools, or the media to produce model citizens is, at best, a gamble, and at worst, a lazy evasion of the parents' duties. Who can put more wholehearted effort into the welfare of children than their parents? No other entity can compete!

Activities

ACTIVITY 1: DID YOU EVER WONDER WHY?

Discuss the following with your children and cite personal experiences from relatives and friends. Consider why:

Someone can be a great scholar, but a social failure
A parent can be loving and warm, but not spend time with the family
A person can be religious, but irrational
A person can have great self-confidence, but mistrust others
A person can be a great thinker, but highly disorganized
A person can spend generously on himself, but be stingy toward others
A person can be rich, but a miser

Proper parenting could have played a significant part in correcting these issues!

ACTIVITY 2: YOUR PARENTING STYLE

Which child-rearing approach appeals to you most? Identify one weakness in your parenting style and take the necessary steps to improve it. Discuss this with your children.

ACTIVITY 3: A LIST OF CHILDREN'S COMMON MISBEHAVIOR

Is My Child Unique?

Some parents think that their children are either much better than others or much worse, as if they are a special breed. Actually, children share the majority of traits with their contemporaries. Hence, sharing experiences among parents is rewarding. Prepare a list of problem behaviors that apply to your children, and discuss how to improve each one. To motivate the child, begin with items that are easier to correct.

MAKE A LIST: "WHAT IS WRONG WITH MY CHILD?"

Listed below are some problem behaviors shown by some children:

Failing in school
Being lazy
Under-eating or overeating

Having a hair style you disapprove of
Answering back
Being with friends you do not like

Refusing to pray
Refusing to help in the house
Sulking in long silence

Refusing to tidy up
Taking silly risks
Disrespecting elders

Staying out late at night
Disliking being at home
Never wanting to go out

Stealing
Lying
Smoking

Swearing and cursing
Watching too much TV
Hitting other people

Arguing back
Watching horror videos
Eating junk food

Being rude to neighbors/grandparents
Wearing clothes you disapprove of
Playing loud music/TV/radio

Not washing properly
Staying too long in the bathroom
Leaving things all over the house

Note to Parents: *Do your circumstances allow you to reverse the exercise and let your children make a list of "what is wrong with my parents?!" Do you have the courage and the wisdom to engage them in this exercise?!*

ACTIVITY 4: REFLECTIONS ON A POEM

Ask your family to sit together and have one child recite this poem aloud. Request from all your family members to reflect on their personal behavior toward each other and offer some concrete suggestions for improvement.

I ran into a stranger as he passed by
"Oh, excuse me, please" was my reply

He said, "Please excuse me too;
I wasn't watching for you"

We were polite, this stranger and I,
We went on our way saying goodbye.

But at home a different story is told,
How we treat our loved ones, young and old.

Later that day, cooking the evening meal
My son stood beside me very still.

When I turned, I nearly knocked him down.
"Move out of the way," I said with a frown.

He walked away, his little heart broken.
I didn't realize how harshly I'd spoken.

While I lay awake in bed,
A small voice came to me and said,
"While dealing with a stranger,
Common courtesy you use,
But the family you love, you seem to abuse.

Go and look on the kitchen floor,
You'll find some flowers there by the door.

Those are the flowers your son brought for you
He picked them himself: pink, yellow and blue

He stood very quietly not to spoil the surprise
You never saw the tears that filled his little eyes.

By this time, I felt very small,
And now my tears began to fall.

I quietly went and knelt by his bed;
"Wake up little one, wake up," I said.

"Are these the flowers you picked for me?"
He smiled, "I found them, out by the tree.

I picked them because they're pretty
like you.
I knew you'd like them, especially the
blue."

I said, "Son, I'm very sorry for the way
I acted today;
I shouldn't have yelled at you that way."

He said, "Oh, Mom, that's okay.
I love you anyway."

I said, "Son, I love you too,
And I do like the flowers, especially the
blue."

ANONYMOUS

ACTIVITY 5: TODAY'S PARENTS VS. YESTERDAY'S

Consider these questions and discuss them with your children:
Are you closer to your children than you were with your parents at that age? (76% of American parents said Yes.)

Do you talk with your children more than your parents spoke to you while you were in college? (71% of American parents said Yes)
(Kantrowitz and Peg 2006)

Ask the whole family to think of ways to increase their interactions and contact, citing stories of grandparents and relatives as much as possible. These stories can help ground the family identity and parentage of children. It can also teach national history that is not centered on a colonial view of events often found in the history books of industrialized countries.

ACTIVITY 6: AS A PARENT, YOU CAN MAKE A DIFFERENCE!!!

Discuss the following with your children.

A friend told me: "It doesn't matter what I do with my child. I am only one person!"

If every individual in the world stopped trying to make a difference because s/he was "only one person," who would be left to make that difference? This is a fallacy. We know that the prophets of God were individuals, as were the great Companions, scholars, and many wise men and women in history. They changed the world. Think of Steve Jobs and Bill Gates.
Then ask yourself: who has made a difference in your life? Is it a relative, friend, teacher, coach, or religious leader? Tell your story to the children and ask them to share about who has made a difference in their life.

ACTIVITY 7: CHILDREN: WHAT DO YOU EXPECT FROM YOUR PARENTS?

Ask one of your children to read the story "The Giving Tree" by Shel Silverstein aloud. Then ask the children what they expect from you. What, when, and how? Afterward state what you expect from your children!

"The Giving Tree" by Shel Silverstein is a tale about a relationship between a young boy and a tree in a forest. The tree always provides the boy with what he wants. In the boy's youth the tree provides its branches for the boy to swing on. Later the tree provides shade in which to sit, apples to eat, and branches with which to build a home. As the boy grows older he requires more and more of the tree but gives nothing back to the sad tree that yearns for the boy's company. In the ultimate act of self-sacrifice, the tree lets the boy, who is now a man, cut her down so the boy can build a boat in which he can sail. The boy leaves the tree, now a stump. Many years later, the boy, now an old man, returns to the tree seeking a quiet place to sit and rest. The tree offers its stump and is glad to finally have the boy's company.

CHAPTER 2

The Family Unit: Why is it Important? What are its Functions?

Introduction

WHAT IS A FAMILY and what purpose does it serve? How does it function? What are its goals? What makes it strong? What destabilizes it? What contributions should each member make to its success? How is success to be measured? The answers to all these questions have a direct effect on good parenting and how children are raised. In this chapter, we attempt to examine these and other issues. We will also make parents and readers aware of the great capacity of the family unit to effect positive social change. The family not only transforms its members but ultimately society as a whole. We will also examine how parenting is practiced in the Muslim world and in the West.

In Chapter One we introduced parents to the question of why good parenting matters, how parenting is learned, and how the parenting style we choose to adopt affects the kind of people our children become. Becoming good parents goes beyond the nuts and bolts of applying key principles. Parenting requires an awareness of the nature of the family unit and its interconnectedness, the major focus of this chapter. This chapter will also make constant reference to love, care and security. A loving family environment responds to both the needs of children and the needs of parents. Good parenting prepares children to become responsible adults with a sense of civic responsibility.

We also touch on the issues of single-parent families, divorce, changes in family size and current family conditions in the Muslim world. The instability facing many Muslim families may seem to have little bearing on child rearing, but the reality is that stable family units are essential to forging stable and dynamic societies. Progressive societies cannot exist without healthy family units, and this is particularly true for the Muslim world which has yet to reverse its decline.

Some define the "family" as a group of people related to one another, others as a social unit, and yet others as a group consisting of parents and children living together in a household. Although there are many views of the family, definitions of the traditional family are often closely related to marriage and children. It is also through marriage that the family unit often evolves, since marriage is not merely a partnership of two individuals, but a merger of two extended families. The modern family unit (particularly in the West) has transformed considerably over the years,

changing from an extended to a nuclear structure. In addition, family size has changed (people are having less children).

However, a family ought to be much more than the sum total of its parts. A family is part of the larger culture, and ideally, a whole culture in itself. It is important for us to understand the greatness of the roles we play within family. A family is a little house of worship, a little government, and a little school of goodness.

Transition to Parenthood

When we think of a family, we normally think of parents and children. First time parents undergo a transition from a dyad (two people) to a triad (three people) upon the arrival of the first child. With the arrival of children parents enter a new phase of life. Parents go through a period of adjustment due to the changes in lifestyle that children bring (including hardships and tensions as well as joy and happiness). When a baby is born to a Muslim family certain traditional rites take place to welcome the newborn (Zaydan, Abdul Kareem, in Arabic, 1993):

- Make the call to prayer in the newborn's ears. Al-Ḥākim reported from Abū Rāfi' that he saw the Prophet ﷺ recite the *Adhān* (primary call for prayers) in the ear of al-Ḥasan, the son of 'Alī, when his mother Fāṭimah delivered him.
  Calling the *Adhān* in the right ear and the *iqāmah (immediate call for prayers)* in the left ear upon birth declares the oneness of God, affirms the message of Prophet Muhammad ﷺ and reminds believers to perform prayers for the baby in the future.
- Name the baby upon his/her arrival without delay. It is crucial to give the baby a good meaningful name (since you are setting a role model for the child to aspire to). This does not have to be an Arabic name or a historic name, and could be the name of a non-Muslim who is a great model for the child to emulate. The meaning of the name should be good, and it is worth considering giving a name which is easy to write and pronounce in more than one language.
- Organize an *'aqīqah (celebration of birth)* for the baby. *'Aqīqah* (in Arabic) refers to the animal slaughtered as a sacrifice for a newborn child. The Prophet ﷺ slaughtered one ram for his grandsons al-Ḥasan and al-Ḥusayn. This is to take place on the seventh day after birth or later. The meat can be cooked and people can be invited to eat it at a community feast (*walīmah).* The meat should be used to feed the family and the people of the community, both poor and rich. The animal has to be a wholesome and healthy one without defects. Upon slaughtering the animal the following prayer is to be said, "In the name of Allah, for Your sake and from You Oh Almighty God, this is the *'Aqīqah* of the baby [name]."
- Ahmad and al-Tirmidhī reported that the Prophet ﷺ said: "Every child is mortgaged by its *'aqīqah*, which should be slaughtered seven days after childbirth, the child's hair should be shaved, and the child should be named." This is recommended and is not obligatory. In addition the Prophet ﷺ told his daughter Fatimah to weigh the shaved hair of the baby with silver and donate the silver to the poor. Jews have similar observances but for Christians baptism often meets their requirements.

Effects of Children on Marital Stability

The family unit is immediately put under pressure with the arrival of children. Parenthood, although a great gift, is not always the exciting event that it is sometimes assumed to be. Upon becoming parents, couples should realize that life will never be the same again, and prepare themselves accordingly for the challenges that lie ahead. Parents will need to sacrifice some of their interests for those of the baby; and the capability of being a mother or father will come into question. It will not be easy, especially for mothers, to cope with the fatigue of being constantly on call for the baby. Fathers may not come home to a cheerful wife, a happy child, and a spotless house, and many fathers, may

Mothers: You Cannot be All Things All the Time! There is No Such Thing as a Mother who has no work.

Do not try to be a perfect spouse, parent, homemaker, and full-time career person at the same time. You can do different things at different times. Children change your life significantly, so embrace the changes, be family-friendly, and be flexible.

see their wives overworked, unhappy, and unable to take care of them as before.

Motherhood involves mental, physical, and emotional exhaustion. Little sleep and constant care of the baby will take a toll on even the strongest of relationships, and ultimately may cause the marriage to suffer.

Financial issues become more significant as couples struggle with house and job responsibilities while caring for a child. This can also have an adverse effect on married life. Life can be particularly stressful for parents who work full-time. Some parents avoid putting their children with childcare agencies and work alternate shifts to enable one parent to always be at home with the child. Although this is good for the child, it is not optimal for the husband and wife, who become like two ships passing in the night. In such cases the relationship can deteriorate rapidly. Parents may have petty disagreements or destructive struggles over whose turn it is to clean the house or wash the dishes. Parents who feel guilty about the lack of time spent with children may exacerbate matters further by cutting back on "couple time" in favor of "child time." Other parents spoil their children with gifts, money, and junk food (rather than spending time with them), putting even more financial and social pressure on themselves.

Such pressures will put the marriage under strain, especially if the couple's limited time together is turned into complaint sessions instead of intimate chats. Marital conflict between parents impacts negatively on children. Many parents suffer from lack of communication which leads to misunderstanding and unresolved conflict. Children should not be treated as "small adults" who are expected to always behave like grown-ups. It is also wrong to treat children as annoying, it is their habit to be persistent and to ask questions. Their physical, emotional, and developmental needs must be fulfilled.

The following are a few suggestions to help parents manage the transition to parenthood. The change in family dynamics from being husband and wife to being mothers and fathers will hopefully be less stressful.

> Let families take care of families, and society will take care of itself.
>
> CONFUCIUS

1. Schedule some daily or weekly time to spend alone together as a couple. This could include going for a walk, doing some exercise, or having dinner together. Talking on the phone during the day or getting up a few minutes early to focus on each other is helpful. Sharing babysitting time with other trusted parents is also a good practice.
2. Share expectations with your spouse. Discuss any anxieties which you may have concerning your new role as parents. Talk about the impact of parenthood on your health, your relationship, and your jobs.
3. Spend time on eating meals together, worshipping together, having sex, and exercise. Since the baby's demands will take up all your time, make time for communication even if the dirty clothes and unwashed dishes have to wait.
4. Express your disagreements and do not be afraid of conflict. Regard a fight as an indication that something is wrong in the relationship, and seek counseling together.
5. Talk with a trusted friend or a wise co-worker who has experienced the transition from spouse to parent. This helps to alleviate feelings of isolation. Make sure you speak with a person of the same gender, and do not reveal anything about your spouse that is private.

Parenting is based on an inseparable partnership between father and mother – each having a different assignment but a complementary role. Even when playing with their child, parents provide different needs. The mother embraces the child, comforts him on her chest, and floods him with love and affection. The father holds him away from his chest, throws him in the air (only after two years of age) and catches him, lets him ride on his back, and wrestles with him on the floor. All these exercises teach thc child self-reliance and expose the child to a controlled level of roughness, aggressiveness, and risk-taking. Both parents need to fulfill their roles to develop the child's personality. As a father, parenting is a partnership with your wife; your job as the protecting father is irreplaceable. You have to know when to "parent" and when to "befriend"– that is, when to step in to protect and when to let your child "learn a lesson."

Regardless of how children affect the parents' feelings about marriage, children bring more commitment to the marital relationship. Figure 2.1 illustrates that the more children a couple has, the more likely it is that they will stay married. Parents of dependent children keep their marriage together to maintain continued access to a higher standard of living for their children. Parents (especially mothers) with small children feel more pressure to stay married, even if they are unhappy. Although children may reduce or increase happiness, they certainly increase stability, since more pressure exists to avoid divorce.

Effect of Children on Marital Stability

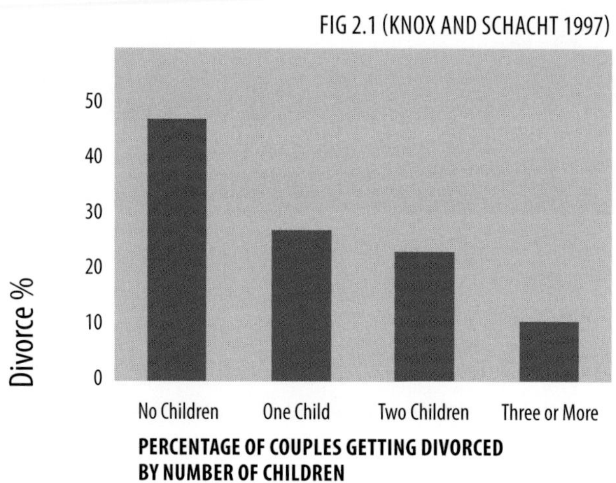

In his book *Gross National Happiness*, Arthur Brooks explains that in the United States parents are much more likely to be happy than non-parents. One reason is that children lend meaning to life. Married religious people (who are twice as likely to attend church every week) are more likely than singles to be happy not because they may be richer, but because their life is more enriched. (Brooks 2008)

WHO SHOULD DO WHAT

Parents: Create a happy home.
Children: Learn from your parents, and support them.
Grandparents: Bring the family together across generations.
Friends: Help the parents.
Teachers: Educate the children.
Reformers: Show parents how to practice good parenting.

Living with Children is Only a Passing Stage

And, behold, with every hardship comes ease.
Verily, with every hardship comes ease! (Qur'an 94:5–6)

Although parents of infants sometimes feel that the sleepless nights will never end, before they know it, their children are grown and gone. Unlike the marital relationship, the parent–child relationship inevitably moves toward separation. Just as the marital partners were alone before their children came, they will be alone again after their children leave. Parenthood is only one important phase in marriage and in life. For parents, the time spent living with children constitutes about one third of their lifetime and more than half of their married life. However, once a parent, always a parent. The relationship continues indefinitely even after children get married and leave home. Also, the relationship should continue whether the kids are nearby or thousands of miles away. Parents then grow into the phase of being grandparents.

Family Size Now and Then in the United States

Shrinking family sizes have affected relations within the family unit. With fewer siblings, children can get more attention from parents. The family ties become stronger and more intense. At the same time children may not acquire the skills that result from taking care of younger siblings. The Baby Boomer generation (the 77 million Americans born between 1946 and 1964) has, as boomer parents, raised between them an estimated 80 million children only. While their income and education is high,their family size is small. Birth control devices and abortion are more available, making it easier to have less children. In the old days, parents thought of children like cooking sweets: the first few might not turn out right, but you could always make more!! Now many families have one or two children only, so they focus on them and give them a great deal of attention. Family size has also become smaller due to the rise of two-career couples, the high mobility rate of families, and the long distance between parents and their relatives.

In 1960, 77 percent of American women had left home, married, and had children by age 30. In 2000, only 46 percent of American women had left home, married, and had children by age 30! The median age of marriage in the United States in the year 2000 was 27 for men and 25 for women. In 1950 the median age of marriage in the U.S. was 22 for men and 20 for women (KANTROWITZ AND TYRE 2006).

The Single-parent Family Unit

One in four children lives in a single-parent home in the United States (12 million children). About two million American parents are single mothers and one million parents are single fathers. The number of single fathers has almost doubled in ten years (Leland 1996). Single-parent families are increasing and there are two main reasons for this: divorce and children being born out of wedlock (born out of wedlock is the term used to describe children born to parents who are not married to each other).

Marriage (and all its commitments) is undesirable to some couples who prefer to live together without being married (cohabit). Almost 3 million children in the United States live in households with unmarried parents (about 4 percent of children, according to the U.S. Census Bureau): 1.8 million children lived with their mom and her partner, whereas 1.1 million lived with their dad and his partner. (U.S. CENSUS BUREAU, 2002)

Cohabiting in Perspective: The 2000 Census of the United States counted 4.9 million households in which the head of the household had an unmarried partner of the opposite sex. This was an increase from 3 million households in which the head of the household had an unmarried partner of the opposite sex in 1990.

Out of 105.5 Million Households in the USA in 2000:

- 54.5 million were married couples.
- 4.9 million were unmarried couples with opposite sex partners.
- 0.6 million were unmarried couples with same-sex partners.

The Case of "No-Fault Divorce"

No-fault divorce is a form of divorce where both partners agree to end the marriage and the judge does not require any reason to be given. Some people want to end this kind of divorce. In response to rising divorce rates, Ronald Reagan, then Governor of California, and himself divorced, signed the first law in 1969 that allows couples to have a no-fault divorce. Up until then, spouses had to prove that the other had done wrong in order for the judge to end their marriage (the most common reasons given for divorce were adultery, abuse or abandonment). Couples desperate to get away from each other lied in court or hired private detectives to spy on one another. The no-fault bill was designed to reduce the acrimony and shenanigans between couples who wanted a divorce. It allowed partners who both wanted to end the marriage to be able to do it amicably; even if one contested the divorce, the other could get it without accusing their spouse of wrongdoing. Every state, except New York, followed California and allowed no-fault divorce. In the three years after no-fault divorce was allowed, divorce rates jumped.

LELAND 1996

Single parents miss the great comfort and the advantages of the sincere loyal consultant: the other parent.

We stress that just because a child is born out of wedlock, this does not make either parent less of a parent. Raising children as a single parent requires a lot of stamina and self-reliance as well as a strong mental attitude. Juggling the demands of work and home is not easy. Single parenting is hard and exhausting, both mentally and emotionally. Single parenting is more demanding than dual parenting. Single parents have to fulfill two roles (that of the mother and the father): they single-handedly make all the financial decisions, enforce all the household rules, and handle all the children's conflict and misbehavior, and even when this has been achieved they must cope with loneliness. This does not mean to say that things are always better in two-parent families (far from it), but the work is harder for single parents, and their emotional needs are harder to fulfill. All parents need to have a positive mental attitude, especially single parents.

For children, growing up with a single parent means that they will lack the care and protection of a second parent (father or mother). Of course the missing parent does not have to be an absent parent. Though divorced, both parents can still play an active part in their children's lives. Children with one parent will also lack the same support system that children with two parents have. Single parents love and care for their children, and the more education, skills, and awareness they have, the less pain the children experience.

Below are some facts concerning the negative impact of single-parent homes on children (HARPER AND MCLANAHAN 2004):

- Single parent homes are less able to protect the well-being of women and adolescent children compared to the traditional married couple.
- Girls who grow up without both biological parents are more likely to become sexually active as teenagers.
- Children and teenagers living without their biological fathers are at greater risk of suffering physical, emotional, or sexual abuse.
- High school students from broken homes cause more problems in school.
- In some communities, children of single parents commit more crime.
- Children of single parents are more likely to be abused or neglected, and are more likely to end up in jail.

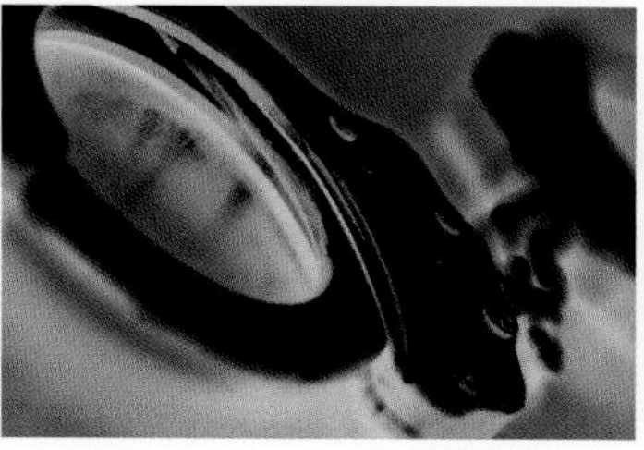

The principles of good parenting outlined in this book apply just as much to single parents as they do for two-parent families. All parents face similar problems but single-parent families will need to give extra attention to the following issues:

1. Exhibiting personal strength. If the parent falls apart, the child's world becomes unstable as there is no second parent to turn to. Therefore, single parents need to assess the situation and stay calm and confident. Their mental state and their emotional state must be strong.

2. Fulfilling two roles. The role of the missing parent needs to be fulfilled. Fathers, for instance, need to become more emotionally and spiritually close with their children. There are many self-help books which can guide parents in this.

3. Boosting self-esteem. The children should not be ashamed that they have only one parent, and they should know that they are just as good as someone from a two-parent home. Single parents need to provide their children with a good home and a happy family life. Teach children that Prophet Muhammad ﷺ lost both his parents at a young age. Be careful of overindulging the children in order to "make up" in some way for the lack of the second parent, and do not allow them to manipulate you by making you feel guilty.

4. Good communication. Constant communication between the parent and the child is necessary. The lives of both parent and child will be made easier by creating a loving, affectionate relationship and a supportive home environment.

Having said this, being a single parent does not mean that we have to raise our children without any support. It can be as joyful and as successful an experience as that of two-parent families (or maybe better, given that many two-parent families have high levels of marital conflict and tensions).

PRINCIPLES TO APPLY TO BE SUCCESSFUL SINGLE PARENTS

Listed below are a series of actions that single parents can do to raise successful children and to minimize parent-child struggles.

- Cultivate a network of friends and relationships. Make good friends and invite them and their children to social gatherings and meals with your children. Get to know other single-parent families (remember that even though you are a single parent, you are not alone). Close friends can provide you with emotional support, companionship, help in emergencies, childcare, and a sympathetic ear. Be discerning about those whose friendship you seek; choose caring, reliable, trustworthy and faithful people who will be there for you in times of need. If you have an extended family, then maintain these ties and visit one another regularly. Do not feel embarrassed to share your parenting load with family members and request their help when you need it.
- Organize numerous outings and joyful days with your children. Keep mementos of the occasions to remind you and your children of happy times and events.
- Share some of the decision-making and problem-solving with your children. This will raise their self-esteem and they will feel that they are valued members of the family. In single-parent families, each child's help and cooperation is needed every day. Working as a team and sharing the workload will reduce the pressures you face.
- Do not allow your anger or personal anxieties to affect your children. If you can see the world from their point of view, you will realize that children feel vulnerable. Children fear that if something happens to the parent, they will be alone in the world. Remember to turn to God for all your needs, and after having done all you can, leave your problems and fears in His caring hands.
- If you get divorced do not force the children into taking sides. Do not ask your children to choose between "good parent and bad parent". Children have immense loyalty to both parents, and feel guilty if having to reject one in favor of the other.
- Above all, be positive and God-centered. Remember that single parents with good parenting skills can raise children just as successfully without a partner. Do this by building a good support system – a circle of friends, relatives and neighbors. Raising good children is not about the number of parents, but the quality of parenting and the quality of the parent's worldview.

THE IMPACT OF SINGLE MOTHERHOOD ON THE PROPHETS: ISHMAEL, MOSES, JESUS, AND MUHAMMAD ﷺ

Some of the greatest prophets sent to humanity were raised in single-parent homes. Below we briefly recount the stories of the mothers of these four prophets. The strength and wisdom of these great women is truly inspirational for all parents.

Prophet Ishmael ‹ﷺ›

The Qur'an narrates the story of Ishmael:

Then, when [the son] reached [the age of] [serious] work with him, he said: "O my son! I see in a vision that I must offer you as a sacrifice: Now see, what is your view!" [The son] said: "O my father! Do as you are commanded: you will find me, if Allah so wills, one practicing patience and constancy!" (Qur'an 37:102)

We know that Prophet Abraham ‹ﷺ› did not stay long with his oldest son Ishmael, because he was conveying the message to the people of Iraq, Palestine, and Egypt. It was Ishmael's mother, Hajar, who raised him in the arid valleys of Makkah. Hajar taught Ishmael to be wise, trustworthy and self-confident.

Prophet Moses ‹ﷺ›

And so, [when he was born,] We inspired [thus] the mother of Moses: "Suckle him [for a time], and then, when thou hast cause to fear for him, cast him into the river, and have no fear and do not grieve – for We shall restore him to thee, and shall make him one of Our message-bearers!" (Qur'an 28:7)

It was the mother of Moses, trusting in God for the care of her baby, who cast Moses into the river. She then raised him herself after he refused to be breastfed from wet-nurses in the home of the Pharaoh. What a tremendous sacrifice she made! She entrusted God with the life of her child, and molded the leadership qualities of such a great prophet!

Prophet Jesus ‹ﷺ›

Behold! The angels said: "O Mary! Allah has chosen you and purified you – chosen you above the women of all nations..." (Qur'an 3:42)

Jesus was a fatherless baby brought up by the Virgin Mary. Mary was a single mother who embodied the highest possible standards of love, sacrifice, and integrity. She was described by Allah in an entire chapter in the Qur'an to be the purest chosen woman and the highest in faith.

Prophet Muhammad ﷺ

Muhammad was born an orphan and his mother, Amīnah bint Wahab, was a single parent. She raised him for six years, during which his exemplary character and personality were formed. Courage, love, honesty, creativity and self-confidence were instilled in him by his mother.

The impact of motherhood is immeasurable!

How much credit can we allot to mothers for their priceless contributions to parenting?

- Children come to this world knowing who their mother is, the mother tells the child who their father is!
- Imam Ahmad narrates that a man came to the Prophet ﷺ and said, "I have come to pledge allegiance to you for hijrah (migration) and I have left both my parents behind crying." The Prophet ﷺ said, "Go back, and the same way that you made them cry, make them laugh."
- It is said that during the funeral of his mother, a Muslim once wept and said, "Why should I not cry when one of my doors to Paradise has now closed?"

Can One Parent Substitute for the Other?

A mother cannot fully substitute for a father, and a father cannot fully substitute for a mother. Infants who develop a secure attachment to both parents thrive best. Mothers offer unlimited love, tenderness, breastfeeding, tolerance, and patience. Fathers offer strength, responsibility, louder voices, different smells, and scratchy cheeks: all useful stimuli to the infant. Generally, the loss of a mother is more severe for children than the loss of a father. A mother can provide protection and love, and her hopes tend to be more focused on the children. Full time homemakers show more concern for the children, and the children are in many ways more attached to her. The children fill her daily agenda. She has the dedication and ability to overwhelm the children with love and peace to make them succeed in life. (George Tremblay and Allen Israel, 1998)

There exists a misconception that a boy needs a father more than a mother, and a girl needs a mother more than a father. A father is as important to a daughter as to a son, though in somewhat different ways. Similarly, a mother is crucial in the upbringing of her sons. Fathers give girls feelings of strength, support, and security. A girl needs a father so that she can successfully relate to males. Otherwise, males may seem to her as being too mysterious or frightening or glamorous.

Can mothers play the role of fathers to their fatherless boys? The answer is that they cannot and that it is not necessary. Children's personalities are so constituted that even if they cannot remember ever seeing their father or mother, they can vividly imagine what their parents were like and describe them down to the smallest details. Children can patch together an ideal parent out of bits and pieces of other people's personalities. What a mother can do for a fatherless boy is to help him construct an image of his father by providing him opportunities to be with grandfathers, uncles and cousins in her presence. Also, she can expose her son to a friendly and trusted male schoolteacher, minister or Imam, in a safe and supervised environment. Under her guidance these men can provide good male role models for her son.

What Really Matters?

Forty years from now, it will not matter how much your bank account contained, what sort of house you lived in, or what kind of car you drove...What will really matter is how important you were in the life of a child and a grandchild.

A NOTE ON ISLAM AND DIVORCE

One of the main reasons for the rise in single-parent families is the rise in divorce rates. Divorce is prohibited in some cultures and religions (divorce was illegal in Brazil until 1977, Hindu law used to prohibit divorce, and divorce for Catholics is prohibited in the Phillippines). Islam discourages divorce but still allows it (according to certain strict procedures). Before divorce Muslims must go through family mediation and arbitration between the spouses. Islam requires wise and trusted relatives to try very hard to save the marriage, particularly if it affects children. The Prophet ﷺ said: "The most hated lawful act in the eyes of God is divorce." (Ibn Mājah). That said, Islam and other faiths recognize that marriages fail. It is regrettable but it does happen.

Parents must do everything possible to preserve their marriage. When divorce takes place and children are affected, parents must be honest with the children:

- Upon divorcing and remarrying, the children have to be carefully told the facts of what is really happening, without covering up or inventing stories. Parents need to make it clear why they are separating, and emphasize that it is not the children's fault and that they still love their children. A parent should never just vanish without giving an explanation. It can make the children bitter. The parent may believe that he is helping the children to avoid pain, but children reason that the parent did not even love them enough to explain to them what happened and at least say goodbye.
- Do not coerce children to accept the point of view of either parent or to take sides.

When stepparents and stepfamilies are involved, it serves no good purpose to try to push children to accept people who are not their biological relatives as if they were. There may be much tension, jealousy, and rivalry to deal with as relationships progress. It is far better for a child to accept a stepparent as "my mother's new husband" (or "father's new wife") than try to pretend he/she is their new parent.

Impact of Divorce on Children

Immediately after divorce, the income of households with children declines 21%. Thirty-eight percent of divorced or separated women with children live in poverty; the figure is 17% for men who get custody. Children of divorcees are more likely to drop out of school, have children out of wedlock and have poor mental health. SELTZER 1989

Parents and ex-spouses should deal with all family members in a kind, respectful, and tolerant way. The Qur'an advises us to behave properly in case of divorce:

> *A divorce may be [revoked] twice, whereupon the marriage must either be resumed in fairness or dissolved in a goodly manner. It is not lawful for you to take back anything of what you have ever given to your wives unless both [partners] have cause to fear that they may not be able to keep within the bounds set by God: hence, if you have cause to fear that the two may not be able to keep within the bounds set by God, there shall be no sin upon either of them for what the wife may give up [to her husband] in order to free herself. These are the bounds set by God; do not, then, transgress them: for they who transgress the bounds set by God – it is they, they who are wrongdoers!* (Qur'an 2:229)

Considerable tolerance is needed in case of divorce. Some children may never accept their stepparents; in these cases, all that can be done is to be kind and gentle and play for time. Later on, children will leave the home to set up their own homes. When a marriage ends after a long time of trouble, it is often a relief to the children. Children may experience feelings of mixed loyalty. Although it may be better without their father, they cannot admit this when they still love him and wish he was there. Children hope that things had worked out better. A caring stepparent can develop a beautiful bond of friendship that lasts a lifetime. A wise step-parent says to the step-child: "I am not your parent but the husband or wife of your parent and I do care for you".

A single parent with a teenager faces some different problems. The parent must be careful not to make the teenager excessively dependent, or try to put the teenager into the role of the absent partner. Teenage sons are NOT husbands, and teenage daughters are NOT wives. There is also the great danger of sexual abuse, physical abuse and mental abuse. The teenagers have too much to cope with at a time when they should be coping with their schoolwork. Single parents need to be prepared to let them pursue and develop their own lawful interests outside the home. No matter how lonely the parents happen to be, they should not be selfish.

Illegitimate children are not the same as children of a widowed or divorced parent living in a single-parent home. The main difference comes from the sense of belonging to a father. A deceased father still provides a needed sense of comfort for his children, who feel that they can identify and relate to him. This helps the mother to impart to the children the feeling of security and love. She can guide them and provide the friendly environment in which they can excel and surpass their peers who may have both parents and a seemingly better lifestyle. Along with her continual support, she can raise achievers if she provides the children with challenges to overcome difficulties. These mothers provide opportunities for their children to prove themselves and build self-confidence.

Advise for Divorced Parents

- Do not blemish the children's perception of the other parent.
- Try to keep a healthy communication between the children and the other parent and his/her relatives.
- Make the children feel that they are loved by both parents.
- Explain to the children that the separation of their parents does not harm their relationship with them.

Importance of the Family Unit in Islam

Islam has placed so much importance on preserving the family. First of all, the Qur'an asserts that human beings are the most honored and dignified of God's creatures, entrusted by their Creator to be His trustees on earth. Hence, they need to be trained and prepared for the task of trusteeship (*istikhlāf*). It is no coincidence that infancy is of the longest duration compared to all animals. The starting point in this "family school of education" is a healthy relationship between husband and wife. This should not be built on "businesslike deals", or legalistic rights and duties (although "family laws" are necessary as minimum protection). The husband–wife relationship should be built on *mawaddah* (compassion) and *raḥmah* (mercy). Without this foundation, the two wishes of the parents (articulated in verse 25:74 of the Qur'an) for a happy home and successful, pious children will not be realized. Single-parent families must also be compassionate and merciful with their children.

> *And those who pray "Our Lord! Grant unto us spouses and offspring who will be the comfort of our eyes and give us [the grace] to lead the righteous."* (Qur'an 25:74)

The family is necessary for human beings to realize their full psychological development. The Creator has fashioned us in the best way, including our physical and non-physical aspects. Our shape, height, color, movement, and appearance, and our psychological, spiritual, and mental aspects, have all been created in a coherent manner. God has also blessed us with tribes, communities, and nations.

> *Verily, We create human beings in the best [optimum] conformation.* (Qur'an 95:4)

During our life journey, we develop in stages in great and remarkable ways: from the fragility and weakness of infancy, through the stages of growth and learning, up to the peak of strength, and returning finally to the feebleness of old age (entailing loss of strength, knowledge, and memory). During this process, parents continue to grow psychologically, contributing much to their children, grandchildren, and the larger extended family. The need for healthy intimacy will remain unfulfilled if the individual does not become a spouse. It is only within the sanctity of marriage that men and women are able to experience optimum psychological intimacy. As the Qur'an puts it,

> *They [your wives] are your garment and you [husbands] are a garment for them.* (Qur'an 2:187)

Following marriage, another factor of growth comes into play: the desire to have children and start a family. At this stage, four different possibilities can occur, each with its own psychological outcomes. Either the couple will be barren, or have daughters only, or have sons only, or have both daughters and sons. Every one of these outcomes has an effect on parents and on children.

> *He bestows the gift of female offspring on whomever He wills, and the gift of male offspring on whomever He wills; or He gives both male and female [to whomever He wills], and causes to be barren whomever He wills: for, verily, He is All-Knowing, infinite in His power.* (Qur'an 42: 49–50)

The psychological rewards continue with the parents experiencing the pleasure of seeing their children become married, and then seeing them have children of their own (their grandchildren), allowing them to feel the continuation of their existence into the future.

We realize how different it is when we have only one child (a boy or a girl) in the family. It is not the same feeling when the child has brothers and sisters. Neither is it the same when the child has no aunts, uncles, grandfathers or grandmothers. Children are enriched when there is an extended family, and even more so with a larger extended family (from the two sides of the father and the mother). Opportunities for psychological enrichment occur when the children have a healthy set of relationships. This occurs in the context of various roles; for the female: as a daughter, a sister, a wife, a mother, an aunt, and a grandmother, and for the male: as a son, a brother, a husband, a father, an uncle, and a grandfather.

Once a Family, Always a Family!

If we die tomorrow, the company or the organization for which we are working can replace us in a matter of days. However, the family we leave behind will feel the loss for the rest of their lives. We pour ourselves more into work than into our own family, an unwise action indeed!

(Anonymous internet post)

F A M I L Y

F Father
A And
M Mother
I I
L Love
Y You

FAMILY OBJECTIVES ACCORDING TO THE QUR'AN

Good family traditions promote values that children may not learn at school.

Family life depends on setting the right family objectives, which are over and above the goal of simply having children. The family does not only produce children to preserve humanity from extinction. Maintaining the family for the sake of the family does not make sense, and thus family objectives must encompass far more than just self-preservation. The Qur'an states:

> *O human beings! Be conscious of your Sustainer, who has created you out of one living entity, and out of it created its mate, and out of the two spread abroad a multitude of men and women. And remain conscious of God, in whose name you demand [your rights] from one another, and of these ties of kinship. Verily, God is ever watchful over you!* (Qur'an 4:1)

Humans are created from a single soul (*nafs*), from that soul was then created a spouse, and from that soul and its spouse were created many men and women. Although the verse is in the singular form, the same process is emphasized in the plural form:

> *Allah has made for you mates from your selves, and made for you from your mates sons and daughters and grandchildren, and provided for you the best sustenance. Will they then believe in vain things and in God's bounties disbelieve?* (Qur'an 16:72)

The idea of putting human beings on earth to play a certain role is described in the following verse:

> *Behold, your Lord said to the angels: "I will create a vicegerent on earth." They said: "Will You place in it one who will spread corruption and shed blood? While we celebrate Your praises and glorify Your Holy [Name]?" He said: "I know what you know not."* (Qur'an 2:30)

The verse defines the role of every Human Being on earth: Trustee & Vicegerent (*khalīfah*). The role of the human being as a vicegerent is to develop the earth (*'imrān*) and spread justice (*'adl*). The Qur'an also states that life is a test, and that we are here to worship and serve God alone:

> *I have created jinns and human beings only so that they may worship Me.* (Qur'an 51:56)

Thus the objectives of the family include: Service to God, vicegerence, respecting God's sustenance and bounties, maintaining ties of kinship, and preserving each other's rights.

God also then specifies the relationship between spouses in the following verse, which focuses on tranquility, love, and mercy among family members:

> *And among His Signs is this: that He created for you mates from among yourselves that you may dwell in tranquility with them, and He has put love and mercy between your [hearts]; verily, in that are Signs for those who reflect.* (Qur'an 30:21)

Although love within the family is given a very high place, it is not the highest love in life. Among the attributes of Allah are Compassion, Justice, and Peace. The love for the Almighty and His Messenger is put at the highest level:

> *Say: "If it be that your fathers, your sons, your brothers, your spouses, or your kindred; the wealth that you have gained; the commerce in which you fear a decline; or the dwellings in which you delight are dearer to you than Allah or His Messenger or the striving in His cause; then wait until Allah brings about His decision: and Allah guides not the rebellious."* (Qur'an 9:24)

The foundation of love is love for our Creator. Loving the Creator is the highest order of love. Hence, you love your parents, children, and relatives even when they wrong you, because your love for them is derived from and depends upon your love for Almighty God. His bounties to you continue even when you misbehave. Love within the family is explained in the Qur'an:

> *... And remain conscious of God, in Whose name you demand [your rights] from one another, and of these ties of kinship. Verily, God is ever watchful over you!* (Qur'an 4:1)

> *for your Sustainer has ordained that you shall worship none but Him. And do good unto [your] parents.* (Qur'an 17:23)

In this network of love and care, the mother comes before the father, and she is the one who is to be taken care of first. When a man asked the Prophet ﷺ, "Who is worthy of my care and appreciation (*birr*) first?" he replied, "Your mother, your mother, your mother, then your father" (AL-BUKHĀRĪ).

Servants of the Merciful (*'ibād al-Raḥmān*) hope for two wishes to be granted: a happy family environment and the development of righteous leaders:

> *And those who pray "Our Lord! Grant unto us spouses and offspring who will be the comfort of our eyes and give us [the grace] to lead the righteous."* (Qur'an 25:74)

Joy and comfort is the objective of everyone in the family (including parents, grandparents, children, and grandchildren). Producing righteous leaders is a second objective. This can be achieved by teaching one's children trusteeship, worship of the Creator, development of the earth (*'imrān*), and love of God and His Messengers. Ignoring these essential principles will deprive the family of its happiness. The joy of parenting comes from seeing children behave correctly and in accord with their mission of life on earth.

Absorb these concepts, live up to them, and explain them to your children as they mature. This is the way to implant the seed of virtue and goodness in the heart and mind of the child. Even if the child grows up forgetting about God, one day the seed of faith will grow and bear fruit. Purity of faith should ideally be fed with "the purity of the mother's milk to the baby." Instill the foundation for good character. Set the child's priorities straight right from the beginning.

Such a foundation of righteousness strengthens the child's immunity against the rampant temptations around us. We cannot rely solely on external "policing" to protect society. The child's internal value system, sense of self-respect and power of self-control are the most effective mechanisms for the protection of society. Parents need to help children benefit from the wisdom of divine revelation by emphasizing faith, honesty, and compassion early on in their lives.

WHAT WENT WRONG WITH THE MUSLIM FAMILY?

Family values have suffered a decline over the decades. The rise in divorce rates, single-parent families, cohabiting couples, illegitimacy, poverty and insecurity has affected both children and parents. The Muslim family unit has unfortunately been no less immune to these developments, suffering its own particular problems and weaknesses. The Muslim family is supposed to hold the blueprint to success and stability. The answer to why it has declined is complex but lies partly in the decline of the Ummah itself. Deteriorating economic conditions, a deficient education system and a marginalization of sincere faith – all these factors have adversely affected the Muslim family unit.

Although the Ummah's heritage is a rich one, it has not been immune to contamination and the prevalence of wrong practices. These have to be identified and carefully removed to restore the pristine qualities that once gave the Ummah such success. We must sift out the inappropriate influences on our children or else we will be left with imbalanced adults harboring major character flaws.

The Qur'an requires Muslims to read (*iqra'*), reason (*ya'qilūn*), think (*yatafakkarūn*), contemplate (*yatadabbarūn*), and comprehend (*yafqahūn)*. Why do Muslims have some of the highest levels of illiteracy and yet why are they steeped in superstition? Muslims have been defeated, massacred, and humiliated during the last few centuries. Furthermore, robbed of their land, wealth, and hopes, they have developed a distorted worldview, a polluted culture, and a weak sense of self-confidence. They have lost much of their character and chosen money and power over morals and the common good. Laziness and greed have taken priority over common security and public interest. The Ummah faces corruption, disease, poverty, and famine.

Muslims are divided into 56 countries, several of which quarrel and fight with one another. They consume much and produce little, and live just to survive and eat rather than build and develop. Centuries of decay have warped their characters, distorted their universal outlook, polluted their culture, and caused the spread of a superstitious mentality. In addition to this, an imported European system of education spread throughout Muslim societies. The new generations lost confidence in themselves, their culture, their faith, and their ancestors. Children began to have doubts about their identity, which further weakened their self-esteem, dignity, and consciousness. They became more subservient, lacking the moral and spiritual stamina necessary for responsible and constructive behavior. Unity and harmony were shattered at home, in the neighborhood, and in society at large.

Muslim women and men began to blindly imitate the inappropriate practices of other cultures, which included nudity, showing off (*tabarruj*), improper sexual pursuits, and neglect of religious duties. This resulted in conflictual behavior, cultural disasters, and a family that was neither Islamic nor modern.

The unthinking pursuit of material gain and physical pleasure, de-spiritualized and demoralized both parents and children. The building block of society – the family – began to fail. Instead of nurturing worthy citizens (who are brave, creative, self-confident, and responsible), Muslim families began to produce spoiled and egocentric children instead. These children were takers rather than givers, self-centered rather than caring community members and servants, and more wasteful and harmful than helpful.

Many Muslim parents suffer from illiteracy, ignorance and apathy. Many Muslim children are stifled in their efforts to acquire knowledge and skills. Some Muslim societies suffer from oppressive tyrannical governments. Many Muslims face the following problems:

- Limited freedom to think, due to oppression and indoctrination;
- Limited freedom to question, inquire, and speak;
- Limited freedom to do business and prosper, due to corruption and mismanagement;
- Limited freedom of women, due to ignorance and male oppression; and
- Limited freedom of citizens to choose their leaders, due to suppression and tyranny.

Muslims cannot tackle all these factors overnight. Nevertheless, they can start with something that is within their control, and that is good parenting. To raise righteous, successful children and ultimately good citizens, Muslims need to change the authoritarian and oppressive styles of parenting currently in vogue in their countries and seriously reform their parenting practices.

CHILD DEVELOPMENT AND SOUND EDUCATION SYSTEM

There has been a serious attempt at reform to curb the slide into which the Muslim world began to drift. Many plans were put into effect. However, child education, an extremely important dimension, was missing in the reformers' agenda. Great scholars covered many disciplines (including theology, philosophy, politics, sociology, and economics), making a considerable and devoted contribution to reverse the decline of the Ummah and improve its situation. However, the diseases hindering the emergence of a righteous nation were not cured. The tremendous potential and capabilities of Muslim individuals and societies have

THE INADEQUACY OF MUSLIM EDUCATORS!

not been utilized effectively. The gap between Muslims and non-Muslims in creativity, performance, and achievements (in science and technology) has been widening for decades. The responsibility on scholars and educators is to explore the missing dimension and develop a solution. They would do well to examine the issues of child rearing, child development, and child education. They must start with parenting in the home. Unless the child's psyche and mentality become the focus of attention from parents and reformers, the Muslim world will continue to deteriorate and suffer from decadence and backwardness.

Historically, many traditional reformers focused mainly on religious rituals and their

legal and political aspects. Many modern Muslim secular reforms went in the other direction and focused on imitation of their former Western conquerors. The masses were left with hollow promises and hopes that never materialized. Many religious reformers were full of emotion and sentiment and proposed incomprehensible solutions that were based on an imitation of the golden age of Islam. There existed no real focus on the role and responsibility of women (wives and mothers) in raising children. Comprehensive scholarship and literature dealing with child development, child education, and parenting was lacking. There was a muted and inert response of the masses to the sincere calls of reformers, whether traditional religious or modern secular in their approach. Most Muslims were reactive rather than proactive. There were no planned actions utilizing careful methodologies derived from a deep analysis and understanding of the problem. The reformers did not properly address both the divine laws (*al-sunan al-Ilāhiyyah*) and the natural, social, and human sciences.

Muslims must realize the importance of raising good children and its long-term effects. The leading Companions of the Prophet ﷺ were adults when they were addressed by the Prophet ﷺ. Their basic characters had already been formed from infancy. They were raised as free, courageous people and were never oppressed by tyrants. The Prophet ﷺ pointed to the importance of a child's character building: "The best of them before Islam is the best of them after Islam if they understand (Islam)." The basic qualities of a person are already set in childhood. Whether during the pre-Islamic period or the post-Islamic period. Faith and skills can be taught later to the child, while good character cannot.

When the Prophet ﷺ began his mission, he was 40, Abū Bakr was 37, 'Uthmān was 36, 'Umar was 19, 'Alī was 12, while the Prophet's wife, Khadījah, was 55. Fundamental goals and values are set by the Qur'an, while the first steps toward achieving them are the responsibility of parents. Parents must initiate early character building, using the tools of psychology, sociology, communication, and education. Although basic human values and needs do not change, the techniques of parenthood need to be well researched, developed, and updated.

Realizing the importance of good parenting and that the position of nations is mostly determined by how we raise children, several courses have been developed worldwide to implement parenting skills, and bring the subject more widely into the public arena. Ignoring this window of opportunity is very costly, and no nation can afford such a big loss. Much benefit can be achieved by providing courses on parenting for parents and parents-to-be. Establishing community activities to promote the awareness of raising children is highly beneficial. Creating a special government ministry and/or establishing specialized institutions for constructive parenting in various countries would be a great service to humanity.

In a survey conducted jointly by the Washington Post and Harvard University the priorities of many men and women were found to be: "confronting psychological and economic pressures; strengthening family bonds; communicating with children effectively; and preferring that mothers spend most of their time at home with children." Good parenting is obviously the top priority.

AL-USRA MAGAZINE 2005

A CLOSER LOOK AT THE NEED FOR A SOUND EDUCATION SYSTEM

If we want to reform our children's education, we need to take a hard look at the education system in the Muslim world. Some Muslim schools today are criticized for their lack of understanding with regards to the nature of the child, for example, the way they may consider children's games a vice. The curriculum is not based on the stages of the child's development, for it is mostly coercive, dry, and inflexible. It ignores the inquisitiveness of children and their natural tendency to practice sport and play games. Instead, it relies on rote learning and memorization.

Historically, two distinct types of schooling could be identified in the Muslim world. First, there was the private, sound, and well-designed style of education for the children of the elite, such as the rulers and the rich. Their children were taught by highly qualified and compassionate teachers, who were called (*mu'addib*) in the private palaces. These teachers/tutors were instructed to prepare children for leadership and excellence. Rulers such as Mu'āwiyah ibn Abū Sufyān, 'Abd al-Malik ibn Marwān, al-Ḥajjāj al-Thaqafī, Hārūn al-Rashīd, and others had great teachers. These teachers were given the facilities needed to educate children in the disciplines of religion, culture, and literature, as well as certain skills and practices. One disadvantage of the system of one-on-one teaching is that children are deprived of the advantages of learning within a group of students. This is in marked contrast to the second system of the *kuttāb*, schools for the masses, where only some portions of the Qur'an and basic arithmetic were taught. Neither teachers nor facilities were adequate. Teachers used physical punishment as a means of disciplining the students, banned children from playing, and used memorization as the basic method of learning. This historical duality in the system of education exists to a large degree even today in some Muslim countries. Rich parents send their children to private schools either locally or abroad and the poor send theirs to ill-equipped public schools. The private schools have the financial resources to employ qualified teachers and follow both foreign and special curricula, as well as provide excellent facilities including laboratories, visual aids, libraries, computers, and playgrounds not available in the public schools. Unfortunately, these expensive private schools in Muslim countries usually produce students with a negative view of their native culture, legacy, and religion.

The real victim of inadequate schooling is the child. This loss of the "window of opportunity" to raise and educate the majority of the nation is difficult to rectify after the minds and hearts of individuals have been shaped. If we want to revive the Ummah, we have to change our way of child raising (parenting), as well as our system of education (schooling). Hence, there is a dire need to focus on the early years of childhood. To be successful, we should start by addressing the first teachers: parents. They are no doubt the teachers of the soul and the developers of character.

It is fair to say that a good, balanced model of parenting does not exist today in either the Muslim world or the West. Any society that is looking for social change should know that parenting is the key factor for achieving happiness – morally, spiritually, and materially. First of all, we should reform our concepts and practices of parenting. The approach to parenting should include both the heart and mind. The mind requires reasoning, logic, and strategies. The heart requires feelings, love, tact, and intuition. Constructive parenting should not lack either scientific knowledge or the artistic touch.

Civilization building (*'imrān*) needs many institutions, which can be successful only if they are managed by individuals who are honest, creative, effective, reliable and working within a consultative environment. Raising individuals strong in mind, body, spirit, and character is best entrusted to the family institution – the parents. This task cannot be left to schools, media, and governments, although they can help greatly. No entity is more able to deliver or is naturally eager to promote the best interests of children than the parents. There is a great selflessness and compassion which marks parenthood such that, where every person may wish him/herself to be the best in the world, it is only parents who will wish their children to be even better than they are.

If convinced, parents will sincerely sacrifice and do whatever it takes to raise children in the best possible way. When one talks to parents about the best interests of their children, they listen. They only need to understand how to realize them. Making parents aware of their responsibility is the starting point. Parenting is a lifelong task, not just the first five years, although this may be the most important period. At this early stage, parents are the major players, although later on they have the power to continue playing an effective role in shaping the character and lifestyle of their children if they know how to guide them correctly.

The Family Unit in America

In her book, *It Takes A Village to Raise a Child,* Hillary Clinton (1996) US Secretary of State, states that 40 percent of teenage girls become pregnant before the age of 20, and that one and a half million abortions are performed annually. Many Americans plan their weekend entertainment better than they plan their families. Clinton continues, the number of illegitimate births jumped from five percent in 1960 to 25 percent in 1996. Twenty percent of children live in poverty. Homicide and suicide kill almost 7,000 children every year; and 135,000 children bring guns to school each day. Children, rich and poor, suffer from abuse, neglect, and preventable emotional problems. One in three American adults is overweight, up from one in four during the 1970s.

Secretary Clinton writes that the average 17 year old has already seen 18,000 murders on TV. The average American student has spent between 15,000 and 20,000 hours watching television, compared with 11,000 hours in school. The average American child watches annually more than a thousand stylized and explicit rapes, murders, armed robberies, and assaults on television.

Why would a child watching the Nixon Watergate crisis in 1972, think it wrong for anyone to break into Democratic Party offices, when s/he will have watched many similar break-ins on TV every night and considered them to be heroic actions? Children become desensitized when they see many crimes daily and it becomes a normal part of their lives.

Parents need to be aware of the wrong messages their children are exposed to, protect them against it, and actively lobby for a reduction of these negativities. The vast quantities of American literature available on parenting have not made the required impact. Hence, we need to examine why, with so much advice and decades of research, parenting seems to be taking a turn for the worse.

The general emphasis in Hollywood is on physical appearance, the outer body rather than intellectual achievement and the beauty of morals and ethics. There are naked statues of men and women in public squares. Beauty contests focussed on women's bodies are common and are devoid of morality and spirituality. This has been commercialized to such an extent that there even exist beauty contests for dogs and cats! The Islamic doctrine is that God is beautiful and He loves beauty in everything; but the greatest focus is on the beauty of character, values, and morality.

When it comes to family problems such as drugs and issues of sexuality, the way we define the problem dictates the nature of the solution. If we define the issues as economic, the solution will be economic. If they are projected as social ills, the remedy will be basically social; if seen as physical the answer will be of a physical nature. For instance, it is often said that the drug problem is one of supply and not demand. This has led to a huge government investment in equipment, including boats and airplanes, to stop the supply. The focus is on the economics of the issue. In reality however, this has not solved the problem and drug lords continue to profit immensely by their sordid trade. It is time society also referred to these issues as moral, spiritual, and social and treated them accordingly.

COMMON MYTHS OF PARENTING IN AMERICA

The conflict between aims and means in American society creates a great deal of confusion in the minds of children. In his book *Why Johnny Can't Tell Right from Wrong*, William Kilpatrick (1993) explains that parents want their children to be honest, reliable, fair, self-controlled, and respectful. What prevents parents from developing these traits in their children? Part of the answer lies in the influence of powerful myths about child raising. We will look at these myths in more detail in a subsequent chapter, however a few common myths specific to the family unit in America are listed here. William Kilpatrick criticizes the following:

a) **Because the United States was built mainly on the idea of rugged individualism, when the U.S. was established, children should be brought up with no authority.** The man went out into the forest, built his house, grew his food, and established his own business, all the while protecting himself and his family from wild animals, thieves, and foreign governments. He ran away from authority. The early Christian pilgrims from different denominations came to what was then the Thirteen Colonies, a vast land where there was little or no government, to escape the harassment of dictatorial governments in England, France, and Germany, which suppressed their human rights and took away their freedom. Many Americans, who have benefited from the idea of limited government authority, think that it is better to bring up children with little or no authority at all. However, children need skillful parental care and authority to bring them up as loving people, whereas adults do not.

b) **The myth of the "Good Bad Boy."** "Bad" boys are portrayed as lovable and happy. Tom Sawyer and Buster Brown, two popular characters from American storybooks, are examples from the past, Dennis the Menace, Bart Simpson, The Little Rascals, and other "lovable" brats featured in films and on television are examples from the present. This tradition has a powerful hold on the imagination, so that the word "obedience" becomes a dirty word in the child's vocabulary.

c) **The myth that love by itself preserves a child's "natural goodness."** This is the idea conceived by Rousseau, that virtue will take care of itself if children are just allowed to grow in their own way. All that parents need to do is "love" their children; love, according to Rousseau, meaning non-interference and complete freedom.

The Seven Deadly Sins in Christianity
Gluttony, greed, sloth, envy, wrath, pride, and lust.

d) **The myth of "expert knowledge" that is always right and never wrong.** Parents have abdicated their responsibility and deferred to the "experts" in raising their children. The majority of child-rearing experts subscribe to the above myth of "natural goodness," so we have a situation where one myth supports another. Experts tend to place too much emphasis on the unique, creative, and spontaneous nature of children. Some experts only want parents to adjust themselves to their children, rather than parents teaching children to follow rules and obey authority.

e) **The myth that "moral problems are psychological problems."** Behavioral problems are seen as problems in self-esteem or the result of unmet psychological needs. Many child experts disagree with the idea that most behavioral problems are the result of desires and sheer "willfulness" on the part of children. Many books are devoted to "self-esteem," and the word "character" is not likely to be found anywhere. It is worth noting that a study of child-rearing articles in *The Ladies' Home Journal, Women's Home Companion,* and *Good Housekeeping* magazines for the years 1900, 1910, and 1980, found that one-third of them were about character development.

f) **The myth that "parents do not have the right to instill their values in their children."** Some people argue that children must create their own values. In reality, children have little chance to do that, since other people in society want to impose their own values as well. Does it make sense for parents to remain neutral bystanders when everyone else (from scriptwriters, to entertainers, to advertisers, to sex educators), insists on selling their own values to children? One way of defining values is to think of sins.

g) **The myth of "the Single-Parent Family being just as good as the Two-Parent Family."** Character formation is a difficult task, even when we know how to do it. Divorce makes character formation much more difficult. The rate of divorce is very high, affecting over half of American families. Children from single-parent homes are more at risk of falling victim to drug use, delinquency, emotional problems, and unwanted pregnancies. Having said this, we do not deny that children from all families are capable of healthy psychological adjustment. The British psychiatrist D. W. Winnicott once coined the phrase "good-enough mother," meaning that for a child to develop a healthy self, the mother must be a "good-enough mother" who relates to the child with "primary maternal preoccupation." This applies to fathers and mothers too in both single- and two-parent families. A caring parent in a single-parent family can indeed do a better job of raising children than uncaring parents in a two-parent family. Furthermore, if a single parent has extended family members helping out and a very family-friendly workplace (should s/he work), s/he may do a better job of parenting than an ignorant parent of a two-parent family. (We discussed single parents earlier in this chapter).

h) **The myth of the "pure secular family" as the best example to follow.**

In the Hebrew, Roman, and Greek civilizations of the past, and even in America during the eighteenth and nineteenth centuries, the idea of the sanctity of the home was the rule, not the exception. Many rituals or scripture readings took place in the home. Home life was linked to something larger than itself, to a larger vision and purpose. This twin vision of the family as being sacred in itself, and as set within a larger sacred framework, gave added authority to parents, and added strength to family bonds.

Families that have the loyalty of their children manage to convey a sense that they are engaged in important work: in continuing a faith, a tradition, a craft, philosophy, or a vision of the way things ought to be. Unfortunately, many families today do not stand for anything. Neither "little churches" nor "little governments," they are more like "little hotels and restaurants": places where one stays temporarily with no particular sense of commitment. In essence, the values and ethics have been trivialized and marginalized to the extent that "everything goes" and nothing matters!

What changed the family from a community to a collection of individuals, each pursuing his or her own fulfillment? Many modern American psychologists can be blamed. Their emphasis has not been on family or marriage, but rather on separation and individualism. Alfred Adler, considered the father of the optimistic American strand of psychology, called his theory "individual psychology" (the humanistic study of drives, feelings, emotions, and memory in the context of the individual's overall life plan). Dr. Sardar Tanveer (professor of education at the University of Cincinnati) states that the concepts of "I" and "myself" are strongly advocated in classrooms, where teachers tell students: "you decide, not your parents," "you do what you like." For example, a girl told her grandmother, "You can't give me orders, you are not even my mother." The grandmother responded, "But I am the mother of your mother." (Seminar at ADAMS Center, 1997)

In a spiritual environment, children do not "take orders" from parents, rather, all the family members draw from God as they understand God's commands in the sacred books. The presence of positive and clear religious rules showing right and wrong behavior makes religious parenting more authoritative than parenting by non-religious parents.

Religious patterns are more common in Eastern cultures, which have a strong sense of family and family ritual. Not much of tradition is left in American families, where the only daily ritual practiced regularly is the ritual of watching television. This is satirized by the opening credits of the television program called The Simpsons, which is, ironically, a television program. However, it would be a mistake to generalize and assert that Eastern cultures are better than Western cultures.

Family bonds in the United States have been weakened by the emergence of a "social contract" model of the family, where rational self-interest replaces absolute obligation. Our view is that these families do not work if their members regard them as a joint stock company, formed for their utility rather than being based on ties of duty and love. Raising children or making a marriage work over a lifetime requires personal sacrifices that may look irrational, if regarded from a cost–benefit basis.

> When a man came to 'Umar ibn al-Khaṭṭāb ﵁ and told him that he wanted to divorce his wife because he did not love her, 'Umar ibn al-Khaṭṭāb ﵁ said, "Woe to you! Are families only built on love? Where is your pastoralship and care?" (AL HASHMI, 1999)

The American Christian family with a firm religious commitment says grace before meals, and performs nightly devotions and regular family liturgies, which follow the Church's liturgical calendar. These actions give a sense of purpose and mission. The center of religious life is the home, which becomes a sacred place, and the priority is the children's moral and spiritual development. Great emphasis is placed on respect for parents and older relatives, such as grandparents, uncles, and aunts. Close contact is maintained with relatives, and major religious holidays are occasions for happy reunions. Therefore, it should come as no surprise that although practicing Orthodox Jewish groups live in densely populated urban areas, their children are remarkably free of drugs, violence, and irresponsible sex, evils from which other urban children suffer. Similar observations apply to American Muslim families.

LESSONS FROM THE COLUMBINE HIGH SCHOOL MASSACRE

The Columbine High School massacre of April 20, 1999, in Littleton, Colorado, resulted in 15 people dead, 26 injured, and hundreds traumatized. Several other violent incidents took place at schools in Georgia, Kentucky, Arkansas, and Virginia afterwards. The late Professor Dilnawaz Siddiqui focused on the problem of bad character. Some analysts blamed the shattered family system, others spoke of too much violence in the media, while others faulted the easy accessibility of guns and anti-personnel weapons similar to cluster bombs. Yet something significant was missing from the analysis, namely, *personal responsibility* and *accountability for one's actions*. Beliefs, intentions, and attitudes, as well as our words have consequences. We may

summarize Siddiqui's advice to parents as follows:

- Human communication, education, and interactions must promote proper values.
- Children must learn beliefs and standards of right and wrong.
- Relativistic interpretations of what is truth result in chaos in society. A relativist claims that what is right and wrong depends on the circumstances (not on eternal principles).
- A healthy child must learn core universal values (such as truth, honesty, justice, and peace).
- Good and evil ought not to have an equal chance to prosper anywhere. We must teach children positive beliefs and help eradicate negative ones as much as we can.

Instead of defending criminals as victims of society, we ought to hold everyone accountable for their actions. We should evaluate our actions in comparison with our principles. We should not assert that anybody else in our situation would behave in the same way or probably worse. Unless and until proper parenting occurs, we can expect these violent crimes to continue, if not rise.

TEACHING CHILDREN VALUES: THE CONSERVATIVE–LIBERAL DEBATE

In an article 'Only Way to Teach Values: Help Kids Discover Them' (*Chicago Tribune* 1998) Eric Zorn asserts that: "the only way to teach values is to help children discover them. The social conservatives emphasize the development of virtue, ethical thinking, and moral behavior. Children do not magically acquire these qualities any more than they magically learn math. Placing all hopes in character education outside the school has turned out to be naive in an era of fractured, busy families and value-light popular culture."

Eric Zorn supports character education in schools. He notes that the left has resisted the reintroduction of character education in schools because it might suggest unthinking conformity, narrow-mindedness, and intolerance. However, children who grow up without a good moral education are disadvantaged just as much as children who grow up poor, sick, homeless, or abused.

Children, Calculus, and Ethics

Children are not expected to discover the principles of calculus on their own. Similarly, when it comes to ethics, morality and values, parents have to teach their children.

Zorn quotes Larry Nucci: "The emerging compromise position recognizes that children cannot be spoon-fed the truth. They have to be engaged to think hard and discover it. But at the same time, however, they are not adults, and there is a definite role for educators to play in guiding them. Society must have shared values as a starting point – it is not just a free-for-all." How to do this without turning character education into simply "a collection of exhortations and extrinsic inducements designed to make children work harder and do what they are told" remains a problem according to Alfie Kohn. Kohn argued that the carrot-and-stick approach to moral education (now the dominant form), leaves children with a primitive understanding of virtue as "uncritical acceptance of readymade truths." This type of understanding does not really take root in a person's character, and does not lead to empathy, skepticism, and other morally sophisticated qualities. Introducing character education in schools is a good and necessary idea, it is certainly better than no character education at all! The middle ground seems to be: Do not force values on children, but do not leave them alone either, for they are young and need guidance. Parents have the responsibility to guide and help children to discover values themselves whenever possible.

> Children who grow up without a good moral education are disadvantaged just as much as children who grow up poor, sick, homeless, or abused.

Families in Muslim Countries vs. the United States

Our human knowledge is limited, it is not absolute. There are many challenges that families face no matter where they live. Yet some families face more serious problems than others. Urbanization, industrialization, and secularization have a great impact on families living in the city. Some of the problems in big cities in the United States are listed below:

- Non-marital sex is made inviting, attractive, and available, resulting in greater sexual promiscuity.
- Mixed dancing, mixed swimming, and arousing sex-oriented music are widespread.
- Dating, which entails physical contact (kissing, necking, pecking), is the approved system for men and women to get to know one another, and it is taught by parents to children as the acceptable norm.
- Nakedness in public locker rooms and bathrooms is common. Toilets may not have doors in some schools; privacy is lost in the bathroom.
- Abstinence before marriage is not emphasized enough. Condoms are distributed by some schools and even churches to unmarried young people.
- Some teachers tell children to "do as you like and feel" without moral restrictions, and that lust and desire should be let out and not suppressed. They also learn that the individual, not God, is the ultimate authority.
- Drinking alcohol is common and tolerated, and it is encouraged.
- Drug abuse is rampant. Guns and violence are common in schools and among children in public places. Television shows promote violence.
- Abortion is practiced widely. The family size is getting smaller, tending toward the nuclear family in contrast with the extended family.
- Many men wear tight clothing, and women wear make-up and perfume to become sexually attractive. Many people cover less of their bodies to be more tempting. Early marriage is not encouraged, resulting in irresponsible sexual practices.
- The divorce rate is high and single-parent-families are increasing rapidly.
- Children having children is becoming more common, and since teen marriages are discouraged, the result is more unwed mothers. Professor Olasky states that 85 percent of teenage mothers in the 1950s were married by the time their babies were born (Olasky 1994).
- Homosexuality is becoming an accepted, normal – and legal – practice. More states are legalizing same-sex marriage.
- More senior citizens are kept in nursing homes, rather than staying with their children and grandchildren.
- Virginity before marriage is rare. A virgin lady in her 20's may be considered unattractive and unwanted. The majority practice sex before marriage;

celibacy is in the minority.

- The family is disintegrating gradually, and family bonds (*ṣilat al-raḥm*) and values are becoming weaker.
- Sexual satisfaction with any consenting adult is considered a purely personal matter.
- Sexually transmitted diseases (STDs) are common, including AIDS.
- Families move their jobs and places of residence more frequently; they are highly mobile.
- Many women have to rely on themselves and no relative is obligated to assume his responsibility towards her as her guardian and protector, morally and financially.
- Women and men are more independent and more willing to take risks. More families have two working spouses.
- There is a weaker distinction between the roles of males and females.

On the plus side, urban families in the United States have many benefits:

- There is more civic participation and respect for the rights of others.
- They enjoy higher standards of living.
- There is a much higher level of literacy.
- There is more participation in social services and public works. Although family ties are weak, more reliance on social institutions is common in the United States.
- There is more freedom and more alternatives for achieving personal goals.

By comparison the family in the Muslim world has some of these characteristics:

- Marriage among relatives is much more common.
- Families in general are more authoritarian and protective. Compared with the United States, children lack self-confidence, courage, and innovation. They fear confrontation with their leaders and superiors.
- Stronger family ties act as the final guarantee of security in a society where social work and team spirit are weak.
- The family is a one-man management system, where little consultation takes place. Gender inequality among family members is more common.
- Many religious Muslim families are uninviting and dysfunctional. Religious events are experienced more as rituals and orders rather than joyous spiritual occasions.

Since more and more Muslim families now live in cities, it is important to recognize the difficulties that city people encounter. Parenting is harder in the city.

Stories of Muslims Living in Britain

Mr. Bakry, from Mosul, Iraq attended a top Military College in England. In the college's shower room, everyone bathed naked except Mr. Bakry, for he kept his underwear on. His officer wondered: "Why don't you take off your underpants?" Mr. Bakry carefully explained that Muslims do not expose their private parts (*'awrah*), for personal privacy is of major importance.

Mr. Muhammad, studying at the University of Birmingham, England was asked by his landlady: "Why don't you have a girlfriend? Are you a homosexual?" He explained that sex in Islam is only allowed between spouses!

The above generalizations are not meant to show which family system is better. They only raise relevant issues to think about and study in order to implement corrective tools of parenting in both systems. In reality, there has been a strong influence from Western culture on families and parenting in the Muslim world. These influences have had mixed results: some are positive, others are negative.

In secular educational systems, humans have replaced God as the ultimate authority, and materialism has been made the dominant ideology. The scientific understanding of the universe depends only on cause and effect. Although this scientific discourse provides us with many fascinating details about the material aspects of the universe, it does not offer a balanced comprehensive worldview of what we see and what is behind what we see. The Muslim worldview recognizes the Oneness of God (*tawḥīd*), the human trust (*amānah*), and responsibility for developing the earth (*'imrān – istikhlāf*), with full accountability in the Hereafter.

WESTERN INFLUENCE ON MUSLIM PARENTING

With the influx of Western media and the educational dominance of the West, secular family practices have had a considerable impact on Muslim families. In his book (in Arabic) *Towards Free Islamic Education* [*tarbiyah*] *in Muslim Governments and Countries*, Abu al-Hasan al-Nadwi calls for comprehensive reform of the education system. He cites the negative influence of Western curricula, which destabilize the personality and weaken the faith. A generation of graduates has been raised that is valueless, with schools producing rulers and administrators who fight religion, oppress the believers, and force their countries into economic ruin. Modern education that is imposed on Muslim societies produces young people who are confused, unable to struggle for a moral cause, or develop a balanced worldview encompassing the material and the spiritual.

What may be good for other cultures may not be suitable for Muslim children. When American scholars comment about the great success of Japanese schools, they emphasize that most of what is good for Japan is not suitable for the United States because they are two different cultural systems. Blind copying across cultures causes many problems. Parenting is a delicate task and should be tackled with knowledge and wisdom.

Nations respond to Westernization and modernity differently. Professor Ali Mazrui (State University of New York) explains that when the question "can we economically modernize without culturally having to Westernize?" was put to Japan, Turkey, and Africa, three different scenarios emerged. The Japanese responded: "Yes. We can have Western techniques and maintain the Japanese spirit." The Turks, who carry the legacy of Mustapha Kemal Atatürk, answered: "No, cultural

Westernization is the only route toward modernization." Kemalist Turkey throughout the twentieth century did all it could to impose Westernization onto its people, including abolishing the Arabic alphabet and adopting the Latin one; outlawing the fez (headdress for men); forcing women to adopt Western dress codes; and establishing a fanatically secular state. Colonial and post-colonial Africa answered: "Cultural Westernization implementation without economic modernization," which in fact was the worst of both worlds (The Association of Muslim Social Scientists Bulletin 2002).

Parenting in Britain and the United States

A UNICEF Survey, which ranked 21 wealthy countries in six categories (material well-being, health and safety, education, peer and family relationships, behaviors and risks, and young people's own subjective sense of well-being) found that both the United States and Britain were in the bottom two-thirds of five of the six categories (UNICEF Report 2007). Children fared worse, despite high overall levels of national wealth, because of greater economic inequality and poor levels of public support for families in the U.S. and the U.K., with poorly developed services to meet the needs of families with children. It appears that America and Britain do not invest as much in children as continental European countries do. The following subcategories were included in the survey:

SUB CATEGORIES OF THE UNICEF SURVEY

Percentage Who Ate The Main Meal of The Day with their Families Several Times Per Week	Proportion of Children Who had "Kind" or "Helpful" Relationships with other Children
Health Coverage	Day-Care Services
Preventive Care for Children	Health And Safety
Incidences of Single-Parent Families	Infant Mortality
Risky Behaviors Among Children	Vaccinations for Childhood Diseases
Drinking Alcohol	Deaths from Injuries and Accidents Before Age 19
Risky Sexual Activity	Fighting In The Past Year
Percentage of Children who Lived in Single-Parent Homes or with StepParents	Children Being Bullied in the Previous Two Months.

Freedom or Truth?

One major issue in raising children is that of personal freedom. In modern industrialized nations, freedom becomes an objective in itself. Many parents grant almost limitless freedom to their children, which ultimately backfires for it serves to encourage the selfish desires of the child. Uncontrolled desires are dangerous because they can overtake God's ethical and compassionate guidance, enslaving people to the pleasures of material life. Entertainment and fun become addictive as the ultimate "meaning of life" to the child. In Islam, emphasis is placed on personal accountability and responsibility, which should not be replaced with a

flippant "live for the moment for tomorrow we die" attitude. The Qur'an describes this human phenomenon as follows:

> *Then do you see the one who takes as his god his own vain desire? Allah has, knowing [him as such], left him [to go] astray and sealed his hearing and his heart [and understanding] and put a cover on his sight. Who then will guide him after Allah [has withdrawn Guidance]? Will you not then receive admonition?*
>
> *And they say: "What is there but our life in this world? We shall die and we live and nothing but Time can destroy us." But of that they have no knowledge: they merely conjecture.*
>
> (Qur'an 45:23–24)

Freedom from desire leads to inward peace.

LAU-TZU, THE FOUNDER OF TAOISM – 6TH CENTURY BC

The first and best victory is to conquer self. PLATO, GREEK PHILOSOPHER

Freedom is a precious gift that is not to be irresponsibly used for pleasurable ends only, regardless of right and wrong. Freedom is a great ideal, for with it we can search for the TRUTH, find it, and then grasp it. The ultimate human quest is about finding the truth, which is a high and worthy aim. When freedom is used wisely for useful aims, it becomes a precious gift from the Creator so that humans choose to do what is right and correct and willingly shun what is evil and destructive. Children need to be guided to develop good habits, to make appropriate choices, and to hold truth as the highest value in their conscience – it comes before freedom. Every system in the universe has its limits and human freedom has to be orderly and constructive, with limits set according to a moral guidance, not chaotic and destructive. Parents are responsible for helping to develop within children appropriate attitudes and beliefs based on a value-laden system whose sources are authentic Divine Scriptures and the traditions of all the prophets, peace be upon them all.

To use our freedom to please God, we must acquire not only true divine knowledge but also knowledge of human nature. Combining both types of knowledge will save us from acting blindly and destroying the environment and ourselves. The Creator knows best and He alone is in the best position to guide us to the right path. With research, scientific experimentation, and knowledge, we will come closer to the true guidance of the Divine and discover the right answers to our questions in time.

Consider the family as an example. Many modern psychologists and sociologists tell us that the family unit is necessary and society will collapse without it. If humanity had not understood the need for family structure from the dawn of time, there might not have existed viable societies today. Various basic values like honesty, trust, respect for life and property, sexual restraint, equality, and freedom from oppression are fundamental requirements for human existence. Without these values society cannot flourish, and it is in the family unit that these values are best nurtured. So important are these values for humankind that instead of waiting for humanity to discover them (if at all), they have been ingrained into our very inner selves, our innate nature or *fiṭrah*, as well as being revealed to humanity as essential values from the beginning of human existence, in order for human life and society to thrive on this planet.

Hence, it is not a coincidence that Prophet Adam, who was to father humanity on earth, and Eve, the mother of humanity, were taught these basic eternal values so that they could teach them to their children immediately, and in turn all the future human race. God illustrates the sanctity of life in the story of Cain (Qābīl) and Abel (Hābīl). Just imagine, if Adam, Eve, and their children had been alcoholics, drug addicts or sexually permissive, what would have been the result?! Revelation is akin to a knowledgeable guide who shows us the way across a desert; without it, humanity would be lost and perish. Rightly-guided freedom produces civilized children and civil societies, who can survive because they have self-control, good habits, and proper environmental practices.

The universe is a perfect system: cells, atoms, and galaxies project a system of the highest order, and all these organized systems operate within set rules and limits. Ignoring these limits leads systems to disintegration. The Creator founded this universe on a precise and balanced measure with great emphasis on complementarity and integration. This concept of balance is mentioned three times in the following verses:

> *[At His behest] the sun and the moon run [exactly] their appointed courses; [before Him] prostrate themselves the stars and the trees. And the skies has He raised high, and has devised [for all things] a balance, so that you [too, O men,] might never transgress the balance [of what is right]: Weigh, therefore, [your deeds] with justice, and cut not the balance short!*
>
> (Qur'an 55:5–9)

Key values, therefore, must be preserved at all costs. People must not abuse life and commit suicide, even if suicide is what they desire when things go very wrong for them. People should not commit incest, even if this is what they desire. People should not become alcoholics or drug addicts, destroying themselves, their families, and their society. Guidance was given to humans through divine revelation since ancient times. Human knowledge is limited and it may take a long time before most people can fully appreciate the value of the family, and realize the problems caused by racism, suicide, alcohol consumption, drug abuse, and adultery. Divine guidance from the

In their zeal to get religion out of the classroom, they threw morality out of the window

very start of human life on earth sought to warn against these evil practices to allow humanity to realize its highest virtues.

Reverend and author Dr. Jerald F. Dirks, former ordained minister (deacon) in the United Methodist Church, who embraced Islam in 1993, when asked at a IIIT seminar what would be the single most important reform that he would like introduced into the religious church curriculum, responded: "To do away with the disease of relativism in values and morality which keeps changing dangerously without bounds." The basic message stays constant and preserved and does not change according to the wishes of a young generation. After all, the essential needs of human beings remain the same. The family system must be preserved and protected to avoid the disintegration of urbanized and modern industrialized families. Muslims can learn much from the positive aspects of Western freedom to liberate the oppressive and authoritarian ways of thinking and governing that have enslaved them and caused them to lag behind the West in development and progress. Muslims have lost their worldview as civilization builders. The *'adl* and *shūrā* system (system of justice and consultation), which is supposed to govern all affairs of Muslim politics and economics, and of social solidarity – including the family and parenting – has been replaced with tyrannical attitudes.

The West needs a vision to discipline its system of unguided freedom, whereas Muslim societies need liberation from strict and oppressive discipline. In other words, guide freedom in the West and free Muslims from the shackles of their misguided practices. Both societies need to learn from each other and balance their concepts and actions in line with true authentic Divine revelation.

THE STORY OF RONALD KELLER

We need a stable spiritual and value system to live happily with certain firm standards.

"Born in 1954 in the farm country of the northwestern United States, I was raised in a religious family as a Roman Catholic. The Church provided a spiritual world that was unquestionable in my childhood, if anything more real than the physical world around me; but as I grew older, and especially after I entered a Catholic university and read more, my relation to the religion became increasingly called into question, in belief and practice.

One reason was the frequent changes in Catholic liturgy and ritual that occurred in the wake of the Second Vatican Council of 1963, suggesting to laymen that the Church had no firm standards. To one another, the clergy spoke about flexibility and liturgical relevance, but to ordinary Catholics, they seemed to be groping in the dark. God does not change, nor the needs of the human soul, and there was no new revelation from heaven. Yet we rang in the changes, week after week, year after year; adding, subtracting, changing the language from Latin to English, and finally bringing in guitars and folk music. Priests explained and explained as laymen shook their heads. The search for relevance left large numbers convinced that there had not been much in the first place."

NUH HA MIM KELLER 2001

Where to Raise Children

A Case Study of the Culture Shock of Moving Between East and West

When families move from East to West or *vice versa*, they experience a culture shock either way. Here for instance is the true story of one unfortunate family returning to their Muslim country after graduating from College in the United States with two new children. Although they had the option of working in America, the family decided to return to the Middle East so that their children could learn Arabic and the Qur'an. Upon landing, the children started experiencing the civilizational shock of a new country and commented: "Yuck, this is a dirty place." Entering their apartment, anything that they touched dirtied

their hands. Although the parents had been assured that the apartment had been thoroughly cleaned, the carpets, the walls, the stairs, and the balcony were not really clean. Their real problem now was how to unpack in the midst of all the dust. The only solution was to clean the apartment themselves.

The second shock was that while the construction materials were expensive, the workmanship was mediocre. The bathroom doors could not be fully closed. The tiles were beautiful but uneven and slippery. The plumbing was shiny but leaking. In spite of the scarcity of water and the daily interruptions to the water supply, the taps leaked. In the third floor, the water pressure was low and one had to fill buckets with water and store it overnight.

Another shock was schooling. The private schools were expensive and the public schools were an educational disaster. The teachers needed training and the children in many ways lacked manners and discipline. Parents could only weigh the advantages and disadvantages of sending their children to school at all!!

Transportation was too slow owing to congestion and lack of road maintenance. Packed school buses could cause children to spend hours traveling to and from school. For many, it was quicker to walk than to drive. To visit a relative or a friend, one had to plan the journey like a major trip from city to city. Driving a car demanded the best of skills and all one's nerves (akin to entering a war zone and facing the vicious maneuvers of enemies).

In addition to the air pollution there was noise pollution. The children lost their privacy and peace of mind owing to the continual loud noises surrounding them, even within the home. Noises in the schools, the streets, and from the neighbors were even invading their bedroom. The only way to have a quiet moment was to travel to neighboring villages, a whole project in itself.

This is just one example of a possible culture shock that can occur to illustrate the issues that families who choose to move (whether from West to East or vice versa) can face. It cannot be generalized of course for not everybody will face the same difficulties or issues, nor does this imply that families should live in the East or the West. More to the point, each country has its own attractions and problems and each family is unique in its circumstances. There is no general directive of where it is best for children to live. Families who choose to move should realize that they have bought a package deal which will include negative and positive outcomes (and a wise decision for the family needs to be made). Life is a test indeed!

Two Missing Concepts in Western Thought

In several discussions held with the authors, Dr. Taha Alalwani, a trustee of IIIT, Virginia, explained how the West lacked two essential concepts: 1) God is the Greatest (*Allāhu Akbar*); and 2) God knows best (*Allāhu A'lam*). In terms of the first concept, when humans neglect the wisdom and authority of Almighty God in their affairs, they have in effect declared themselves "gods" in place of the Creator, the One and Only. If people become arrogant, misguided, and assume that they are free from error and the ultimate source of knowledge, then they can justify doing whatever they please to themselves, their families, their society, their world, and their environment. They may knowingly or unknowingly destroy the animal kingdom and the plant kingdom, and pollute the land, the sea, the air. Arrogance leads to the destruction of the order and balance of nature, and the skies and space around them (the ozone layer). Because humans have devalued the creation of God, they have tampered with the ecosystem and nature (such that clean air, pure water, and chemical-free meat and vegetables have become a rarity). Global warming is a real threat to human existence. No matter how much we progress in science and technology, we are still an insignificant proportion of the infinitely vast universe of the Creator.

Humbleness is to say that God Knows Best (*Allāhu A'lam*). The incredible scientific and technological discoveries of humankind up to the twenty-first century have caused many people to boast of human knowledge with arrogance. However, the irony is that the more we know, the more we discover how much more we do not know. Humbleness toward others and humility before God are essential ingredients of respectable scholarship. The truly great thinkers understand this. Humans should continually explore and discover new frontiers of knowledge. Remember that our desire to learn is due to the blessing of the Creator, the Supreme Being, who has endowed us with intelligence and provided us with the earth and the universe.

> It takes a great person to be truly *humble*, and a *humble* person to be truly great.

The Qur'an sheds light on the topic of knowledge:

> *...Of knowledge it is only a little that is granted to you [O humans!]*
> (Qur'an 17:85)

> *Nor shall they compass aught of His knowledge except as He wills.*
> (Qur'an 2:255)

> *Say: "If all the oceans were ink [wherewith to write] the words of my Lord, sooner would the ocean be exhausted than would the words of my Lord, even if we added another ocean like it for its aid."*
> (Qur'an 18:109)

Creed Values vs. Functional Values

It is the family which nurtures morality and values (such as truth, justice, love, courage, honesty, and responsibility). All these are based upon the concept of creed (*'aqīdah*), where fundamental values are put before functional values. The two are not always compatible. In some societies, the pleasure of life in this world is the ultimate objective. For Muslims, however, achieving eternal life in the Hereafter by living a good life in this world is the balanced ultimate objective. This means that achieving success in the afterlife does not contradict having a good life in this world; success in the Hereafter can and should be done without neglecting this world. Staying alive in this world is only a means to achieving eternal life. The Prophet advised a Bedouin how he should put his trust in God but, at the same time, follow the laws of the natural sciences as well as the laws of the social sciences. "Tether your camel [so that it does not go astray], and put your trust in God [asking for His Mercy while you are away]." A balance is needed between this worldly life and the Hereafter as follows:

> **"Work for your life in this world as if you are going to live forever, and work for the Hereafter as if you are going to die tomorrow."**
> (ABU-TALIB, 1996)

Talmudic scholars say: Live everyday as though it is your last day, for who knows whether or not that is the case.

A good case in point is to compare the condition of people who lived in former communist countries. Communism is supposed to care for workers more than capitalism, but in reality workers in communist countries experienced worse conditions. Though the functional values in communist countries were asserted to care for people, the deep-rooted values were those of conflict, oppression, and destruction for other classes of the society.

The capitalist profit-driven countries of the West did better than communist regimes because of the prevalence of deep-rooted Christian values of love, charity, and mercy. That is why these countries developed more care provisions for the poor and the needy, whereas the masses under communism suffered more.

Communism's eventual collapse was largely due to its tyrannical values and worldview. The ideology is based on conflict, confrontation, and the destruction of property rights. Although these regimes purported to establish the authority of the working class, in reality, the proletariat remained the oppressed majority, contrary to the declared aims of Marxist ideology.

The communist philosophy was skin deep,

dysfunctional and utopian, whereas the situation in the West was much better. Capitalism does not deliver a form of utopia on earth. Based on the concept of unguided freedom in personal ownership and a self-interest profit-driven philosophy, it has brought some unjust socio-economic conditions to the working people. However, deep-rooted religious values and Christian charity in the West have helped to alleviate some of the damaging effects on the poor working class, thus reducing some of the harm done by industrialization. This is in contrast to the communist party elites working for their own interests by means of the huge bureaucratic machine which they created. It was the working classes under communism who were the major victims of these regimes. Deeply-rooted charitable and religious values are crucial for the benefit of societies and individuals.

Although a vast body of literature and research on parenting exists in the West, our human knowledge is very limited indeed. People are not just a product "made in the USA" or "made in China," about which we have good knowledge. We are made by "The Creator of the Universe." Only our Maker and Fashioner knows everything about us. In her book *Parenting Experts: Their Advice, the Research and Getting it Right*, Jane Rankin, a psychologist, asserts that a considerable gap exists between what the gurus of parenting preach and what the continuing scientific research of the last 30 years shows. Popular Western parenting experts of the twentieth century like Benjamin Spock, T. Berry Brazelton, James Dobson, Penelope Leach, John Rosemond, and others differ on many important issues of parenting like spanking, setting limits, working mothers, daycare, potty training, television, etc.

Although we should encourage continual research on parenting, using all the available tools of the social, natural, and spiritual sciences, yet we must humble ourselves about the outcome of human research. We need to seek guidance and wisdom from Divine Knowledge.

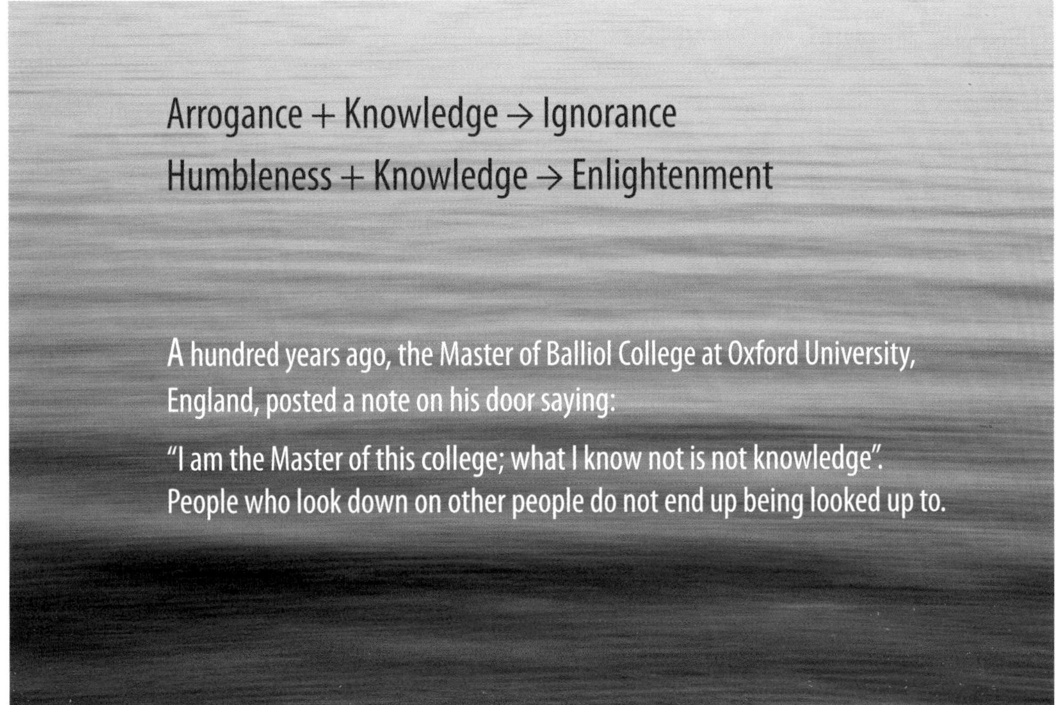

The Agricultural Model of the Family

Children are Like Plants, Parents are Like Gardeners

"Culture" comes from the word "cultivation". Children and human beings are similar to plants in so many ways. Both need care and tending and will grow best in a good environment that has been specially prepared for them. For the youngest plants, in areas with high pollution, the best environment is a greenhouse as plants need to be hardened off before being transplanted outside. It gives them a head start, for upon being transplanted, these plants grow larger, stronger, and more resilient to disease than other plants. Children need protection and nurturing for healthy moral development. "Then, our sons in their youth will be like well-nurtured plants" (Psalms 144:12). A child raised in a good home environment will be stronger, healthier, and more resistant to the moral diseases circulating in the larger culture. This analogy, so plain to agricultural societies, is less obvious in industrial societies, where most people have little experience of growing plants. However, children of course, are more than just plants. Plants are passive, whereas children are active bundles of energy, full of intellect and will. They need to play an active role in their own development and also need to learn to set limits to their own behavior. Children still need much assistance, and the best way for a parent to provide this is to encourage and enhance the development of good habits that will someday turn into sound character and high virtues.

Activities

ACTIVITY 8: THE THREE MAJOR WORRIES OF THE TWENTY-FIRST CENTURY

Discuss with the family: What are the causes of these three major worries and how can they be prevented?

In 1997, the late William Buckley (the Conservative columnist) and Senator George McGovern (the Liberal Democrat), during a graduation ceremony at South East State University, Cape Girardeau, identified three major worries:

The first is the deconstruction and dysfunction of the American family, resulting in a high percentage of illegitimate children. The second is the destruction of the environment, where a great deal of pollution is being poured onto the land, air, oceans, waterways, and forests. The third is alcoholism, which is destroying people's health and families.

ACTIVITY 9: APPLICATION OF ATTRIBUTES TO CHILDREN (ALPHABETICALLY)

Parents are to sit with their children and discuss each of the following traits and suggest one practical way to inculcate it in each child.

Children are...

Amazing, acknowledge them
Believable, trust them
Energetic, direct them
Innocent, delight with them
Joyful, appreciate them
Kindhearted, learn from them
Lovable, cherish them
Noble, esteem them
Open Minded, teach them
Precious, value them
Questioners, encourage them
Resourceful, support them
Spontaneous, enjoy them
Talented, develop them
Unique, affirm them
Yearning, notice them
Zany, laugh with them

(MEIJI 1999)

ACTIVITY 10: DISCUSSING THE REAL CAUSES OF VIOLENCE IN CHILDREN

Discuss with your children some horrible events from their experiences. In the United States, the Columbine High School Massacre was shocking. Two boys, aged 18 and 17, killed 15 people and injured 26, using guns and bombs. Shooting and laughing just as on TV, movies and video games, they then shot themselves dead. They had made 19 bombs at their homes. Such incidents were not rare: about 22 similar incidents in the United States took place in the following months. Why did they do it? Who is responsible? How could it have been prevented? What should be done to prevent similar incidents in the future? What lessons can be learnt? How do we cure the real causes of violence?

ACTIVITY 11: DEALING WITH SOCIAL PROBLEMS

Discuss with your family the causes and effects of smoking, taking drugs, illegitimate pregnancies, alcoholism, suicide, and divorce. Suggest practical ways of improving society with your family.

ACTIVITY 12: DR. SPOCK'S (1903–1998) PARENTING MODEL IN AMERICA: SOME LESSONS "DO AS I SAY, NOT AS I DO!"

Sit together to discuss your own experiences on parenting in the light of Dr. Spock's life story (Maier, *Newsweek*, 1998) paraphrased below:

Understanding the status of child raising in the United States will be incomplete if we do not consider Dr. Benjamin Spock's – the leading pediatric psychologist of the twentieth century – influence on modern parenting. His mother smothered him with love, rules, and high expectations. He divorced his alcoholic wife after 51 years of marriage. Dr. Spock established a pediatric practice and realized that *most children's problems were behavioral rather than medical*: temper tantrums, thumb sucking, refusal to eat, unwillingness to sleep, and an inability to be potty trained on schedule. He grew interested in Freud and underwent psychoanalysis twice.

He advised parents not to rush children but to cherish them. "Trust yourself. You know more than you think you do." He taught that love is what infants needed most from their mothers and fathers. He listened carefully to his patients, but not always to his own children. When a mother asked: "Should a young child see his parents *naked*?" he answered: "That is a hard one to give a simple answer to."

Dr. Spock's family was dysfunctional. "It is always harder to do the right job with your children than to write about it." His wife became an alcoholic, developed a mental illness and was later hospitalized. He was cold as a father and his two sons felt emotionally abandoned by him.

He admitted that he had been too career-driven and the family started practically hugging one another intensely to compensate for the past. He acknowledged, "I never kissed my two sons when they were young."

He instructed his sons to call their parents by their first names – a radical and seemingly enlightened move for the time. The father felt their upbringing should reflect his philosophy. To pretend that they are equals is really unreal; it was a gesture to the rest of the world, "This is my son, who calls me by my first name." When Dr. Spock talked to his sons, it often felt like an oral examination. The calm voice that characterized his books bore little resemblance to the blunt and condemning tones he used at home; he had no idea of his caustic effect as a father.

He insisted that his sons never embarrass themselves or disgrace the family's name in public. Outsiders' approval or disapproval was very important to him as a parent. The opinions of strangers and the Press mattered greatly to him. His boys dressed neatly and were told to be polite and neighborly. If John's smile waned or he seemed moody, Ben quickly prompted him out of it. "Don't be so grouchy, try and look a little more pleasant in public," he demanded.

Dr. Spock seemed in denial about his problems at home. His two sons had learned to keep a respectful distance from one another. Whatever conflicts Mike and John had with their father remained private. They played along with reporters and photographers when the news magazines and television reporters asked them to pose with him, and gave vague and short responses about their father's behavior at home.

He did not express love and true emotions to his children, who confessed publicly: "We never kissed our father." Dr. Spock has been more a symbol than a man, more an authority than a human father; he was a cold and strict father who ignored his children's emotional needs.

Spock blamed his own upbringing. "I never saw physical affection (clear-cut affection between father and son). My father loved me, and he did some kind things, but as far as physical affection is concerned, I'm trying to think if my father kissed me or the rest of the children on any particular occasion, I don't remember if my father kissed me or my siblings."

Lesson: Do not follow the experts' theories blindly. Such knowledge keeps evolving and changing, and unless we complement human findings with the guidance of revelation, we will go astray and cause more harm than good.

ACTIVITY 13: DISCUSSION OF CULTURE SHOCK

Parents to discuss with children their own experiences of cultural shocks. Then invite each child to explain his/her own visits to other countries or the cultures of their schoolmates from other races, religions, and ethnicities.

If the children have never visited their relatives abroad, it is highly recommended, finances permitting, to research and plan ahead for the family vacation to meet their relatives as often as conveniently possible.

ACTIVITY 14: MENTALITY OF TRUE LEADERS

Discuss the following quotations with your family:

"I have observed that the most effective leaders are rarely public office heroes. These men and women aren't high-profile champions of causes. They move patiently, carefully, and incrementally. They do what is right." (Badaracco 2002)

"Leaders may want to develop a herd mentality among their followers, but they should not succumb to such thinking themselves." (Steven B. Sample in *The Contrarian's Guide to Leadership*)

Conclusion: Doing the right thing is what matters, not what is most popular and fashionable! Discuss who can define what is right and how! Is it you, I, he, she, or the Almighty Creator?!

ACTIVITY 15: SHARING FAMILY HISTORY

Sit down with your children and share what you know of their ancestors.

Most families today do not share their family history with their children. Children need to know about the life, achievements, failures, jobs, experiences, activities, and strengths of their great-grandfathers and great grandmothers. Nina Abdullah, a parenting expert, teaches her clients how to draw family trees and genograms. A genogram is a diagram showing marriages, divorces, illnesses, and relationships between family members such as aunts, uncles, cousins, and grandparents on both the mother and father's side of the family. The Prophet ﷺ encouraged the Arab tribal tradition of telling stories about one's ancestors and memorizing one's family line as far back as possible (Campo, 2009). Some Somalis know 20 generations of their ancestors and meet often in a big tribal gathering to share what they know about their ancestors.

CHAPTER 3

Good Parenting: Setting the Right Goals

We aim to build good and strong children,
Who build good and strong families,
Who build good and strong communities,
Who build good and strong nations,
Who build a peaceful world

Setting the Right Goals: The First Step in Implementing Good Parenting

PARENTS SHOULD PRACTICE intelligent parenting. Although many parents plan their careers and annual holidays down to the finest detail, they fail to sit down and develop a plan together for themselves as a family unit. In fact, most will not even agree on any real intent, purpose, aspiration, or strategy for their family. With no goals, it is highly likely there will be little achievement. Lurching from work, to home, to shops, to schools, to holidays, and from crisis to crisis, hoping things will turn out for the best, is nothing short of playing Russian roulette with our children's future, allowing valuable time to slip by unnoticed. We need long-term goals and a strategy to realize them.

The proper approach to parenting considers the individual and the society as one integrated system. We cannot build a strong society without having strong and righteous individuals. Such individuals are not produced in a vacuum, for they need a social environment of solidity and cooperation. The objective of parents is to produce human beings who are vicegerents of God, who are strong and trustworthy, and civilized citizens, and whose mission in life is development and reform throughout the land. Without this message, human existence is purposeless and meaningless. The interests of individuals have to encompass this life and the Hereafter, the temporal as well as the spiritual, and the personal as well as the societal. This should be the overriding theme and world view of parents in the raising of children.

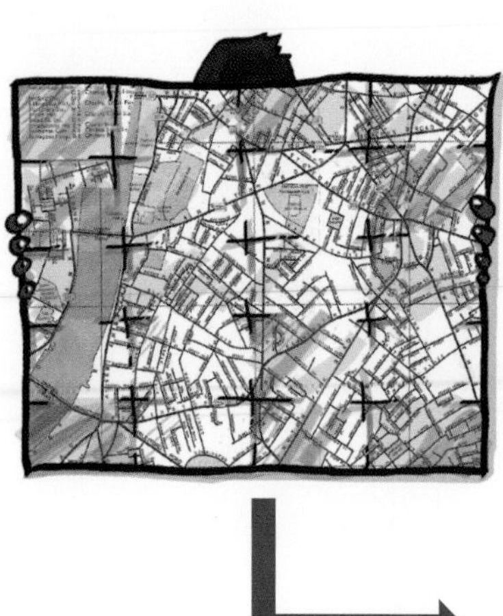

Good Parenting Goals Chart: Goals, Values, Means

The First Wish: Happy Family	The Second Wish: Raising Leaders of the Pious (Righteous)			
Communication Praise/Criticism Attitudes Feelings Calmness/Anger Touch, Kiss, Hug Joy, Jokes Mutual Understanding Family Time Together Alternatives to TV Family Meetings Family Meals Stress Management Games, Sports Active Engagement with Children	Physical Strength Health & Fitness	Personality Characters	Knowledge, Wisdom & Faith	Skills: Professionalism
	Choosing a Spouse Child Development Breastfeeding The Brain Miracle Health Nutrition Exercise Sleep Healthy Sex Avoiding Intoxicants	Courage Love Honesty Freedom Responsibility Independence Creativity Self-esteem Trust Respect Patience Humility & Humbleness	Education/Schooling Homework Enhancement, Encouragement, and Empowerment of Children Discipline vs. Punishment Faith Identity Extended Family	Reading Writing Computer skills Driving skills Chores Money & Time Management Giving Supplication (*du'aa*) Decision Making

Let us begin with focusing on the chart above. We call this the Good Parenting Goals Chart. This summarizes the goals we should try to set and outlines a road map of how to achieve them through instilling principles and values from childhood through to adulthood.

The overall goals themselves have been taken from a) the deep aspirations of parents beautifully summed up in verse 25:74 of the Qur'an, and b) a revealing hadith of the Prophet Muhammad ﷺ:

> *And those who say: "Our Lord, grant us from our spouses and our offspring joy and comfort, and make us leaders of the pious."* (Qur'an 25:74)
>
> People are like minerals [or metals, having their own character]; the best of people in the [pre-Islamic] age of ignorance (*jāhiliyyah*) are the best of them in [the age of] Islam, if they understand [and comprehend]. (AL-BUKHĀRĪ AND MUSLIM)

As specified in the chart, the goals have been divided into two broad categories with the second category further divided into four sub-categories. Parents need to revisit the chart continually to habituate themselves with its goals and values, to study them, to mentally keep track of them, and to benchmark action and development against them. This will insure that they do not slip into complacency or allow the daily duties of life to take over parental priorities.

A Closer Look at the Goals

1. GOALS TAKEN FROM THE QUR'ANIC VERSE: THE PRAYER OF BELIEVERS

THE SUPPLICATION that the believers request is for Almighty God to first grant them from their spouses and offspring *qurrata a'yun, (*a joy for their eyes). This phrase is repeated six times in the Qur'an and its literal meaning is: "comfort of our eyes, joy to our eyes, eyes that are gladdened by blissful delights". So in

essence the first wish concerns having a happy home and family life.

This does not refer to only the nuclear family but also a truly extended one, including the spouse, offspring, grandparents, uncles, aunts, and cousins. Some necessary conditions for a happy home include communication between parents and children; showing love and affection, and using praise and measured criticism appropriately in a constructive way. Additional conditions for a happy family include building positive attitudes, dealing with feelings in a considerate and sensitive way; smiling, kissing, hugging, touching and shaking hands with children; enjoying meals and doing chores together, and cracking jokes and welcoming each other.

The second request the believers make to their Lord is for their spouses and offspring to become the "imam of the pious". The word imam and its plural *a'immah* is repeated ten times in the Qur'an. Various commentaries explain this phrase "make us imam of the pious" as follows: Make us exemplars for others, a model for others, callers for righteousness, a guide for others, leaders of human beings, the foremost among those who are conscious of God, the archetypes of others, forerunners of others, and an object of imitation by our followers. Therefore, the second objective of the family is focused on raising pious and effective leaders and guides for humanity.

In this regard, we would like to point out that when referring to leadership, we do not mean the ambitious hunt for power, but rather developing people of strength, moral fiber, high caliber, ethics, and other character qualities necessary for good leadership. Furthermore, the word "leader" can have a negative connotation in the sense that it is not healthy for every member to compete for this single position. The fact that there can only be one formal "leader" of any group can create unnecessary competition, and develop feelings of thwarted ambition. If everyone hungered for this position, who would then be the "workers" or followers? Our aim is to inspire our children to embody the type of qualities that mark people of principled leadership. Any member of a society who participates and improves the status quo is a true leader; and this is how real progress is achieved.

Where are the Leaders? You are the Leaders

- We are the leaders we are waiting for.
- Leadership is not about being important, it is about serving something important.
- It is not whether you hold the position, but how well you lead.
- Leadership is doing what is right when only God is watching.
- Everyone is a leader to someone. Whether that someone be an employee, a spouse, a child, or oneself; you are a leader!

To reiterate, leadership qualities do not mean the ambitious hunt for power, prestige, position or money. Neither do they imply the teaching of dominance and control. Quite the opposite! What is proposed is that children are raised with a sense of generosity, humility, and a wider purpose, able to perceive of themselves as active and valuable members of society. Persons who can live with ease in a world of diverse opinions and who have the tremendous advantage of confidently setting the highest goals for themselves, and are not hampered by low self-expectations. Children who are afraid of society's disapproval of their faith or race are not children who can serve society. Given the nature of the society in which we live, these qualities should be given importance. If one does not teach one's children to be confident and lead rightly, they may be easily led, wrongly.

IN MUSLIM LEGACY, THE WORD "LEADER," (*QĀ'ID*) WAS NOT IN FACT USED BUT RATHER DEFINED BY THE FOLLOWING TERMINOLOGY INSTEAD:

Shepherd, pastor, custodian ***Rā'ī***
Trainer and educator ***Murabbī***
Foremost person, Exemplar ***Imam***
Discipliner, Character Builder ***Mu'addib***
Teacher ***Mu'allim***
Mentor, Guide ***Murshid***
Coach ***Mudarrib***

A leader is a person who guides other people and their work to achieve certain goals, while the *Murabbī* (trainer–educator) is the one who prepares and qualifies individuals to accomplish the goals. The Prophet ﷺ, for instance, chose ʿAmru ibn al-ʿĀṣ and ʿUbaydah ibn al-Jarrāḥ to lead armies, whereas he sent Muṣʿab ibn ʿUmayr to Madinah and Muʿādh ibn Jabal to Yemen as "shepherds, trainer–educators, and mentors" to raise and nurture righteous and enlightened individuals.

It is not a coincidence that many prophets were sheep herders, including Shu'ayb, Moses, Jesus, and Muhammad, peace be upon them all. The occupation of shepherd itself implies kindness, care, and compassion for followers. It also implies humbleness. These are the basic and essential qualities needed to raise children; how beautiful an analogy to see parents as shepherds tending their flock. Therefore, a leader is a shepherd, mentor, coach, and teacher.

A Leader or a Shepherd?!

The word "leader" (*qā'id*) is used in various cultures, but it is not used in the Qur'an or in the Hadith. Instead, the word "shepherd" is used in the following hadith:

All of you are shepherds and responsible for your wards under your care. The Imam [that is, ruler] is the shepherd of his subjects and is responsible for them, and a man is the shepherd of his family and is responsible for them. A woman is the shepherd of her husband's house and is responsible for it. A servant is the shepherd of his master's belongings and is responsible for them. A man is the shepherd of his father's property and is responsible for it. All of you are shepherds and responsible for your wards and the things under your care. (AL-BUKHĀRĪ)

2. GOALS TAKEN FROM THE HADITH OF THE PROPHET ﷺ

Prophet Muhammad ﷺ states:

People are like minerals [or metals, having their own character]; the best of people in the [pre-Islamic] age of ignorance (*jāhiliyyah*) are the best of them in [the age of] Islam, if they understand [and comprehend]. (AL-BUKHĀRĪ AND MUSLIM)

Many things can be learned from this hadith. One lesson is that character building must occur during early childhood. This is common for all human beings, Muslim and non-Muslim (as implied by the hadith). Courage, creativity, honesty, love and trustworthiness existed in many adults prior to the coming of Islam. The best of people are those who possess these character traits. Islam adds faith, wisdom, knowledge and divine guidance. The Prophet is telling us that the 'highest character' pagans can become the highest character Muslims, provided they understand Islam.

Best Polytheist—understands and comprehends Islam → Best Muslim

Some Muslims think that the courage, honesty, and trustworthiness of great Muslims (like 'Umar ibn al-Khaṭṭāb and Khālid ibn al-Waleed) came after they embraced Islam. The truth is, they were courageous, honest, and trustworthy before entering Islam. Islam complemented their pre-existing good character with wisdom, knowledge, and divine guidance.

This hadith focuses on character traits. There are some necessary conditions that need to be present in believers, such as physical fitness and good health (especially during pregnancy and breastfeeding). Alcohol, drugs, smoking, and extramarital sex are evils which harm the pregnant mother as well as the unborn child. Expectant mothers should avoid taking medicines, except as advised by a physician, and, moreover, they need good nutrition and enough sleep. Extra care and protection from viral and bacterial infections should be taken.

The kind of character traits we are seeking to develop are courage, honesty, creativity, trust, worthiness, love, and responsibility. These have a limited window of opportunity to develop. The first five years are therefore crucial. In addition, parents need to enable children to acquire the skills of reading, writing, speaking, driving, swimming, and using computers. They need to teach children patience, respect, and decision making. The earlier these skills are mastered, the more benefits they bring and the more doors of opportunity they open for the children.

Prophet Muhammad ﷺ was described by his friends and foes as being honest and trustworthy. This was his essential character prior to receiving the divine revelation. The Qur'an stresses the same theme of the afore-mentioned hadith (good character) when it describes the prophets, such as Noah (Nūḥ), Jonah (Yūnus), Abraham (Ibrāhīm), Ishmael (Ismā'īl), Moses (Mūsā), Saul (Ṭālūt), Jesus ('Īsā), Joseph (Yūsuf), Job (Ayyūb), and Jacob (Ya'qūb) (peace be upon them all). Moses is described as being "strong and trustworthy." Prophet Joseph describes himself as "qualified, professional and trustworthy." These descriptions include important qualifications for leadership: Strength (of body and character), professionalism (requiring knowledge and skills), and trustworthiness. In sum, the 25 prophets mentioned in the Qur'an are described as honest, wise, knowledgeable, merciful, compassionate, strong, trustworthy, patient, and fulfillers of promises. It is these key traits that we need to emphasize in parenting to raise and develop our children. Note the following verses of the Qur'an:

> *Also mention in the Book [the story of] Ishmael: He was [strictly] true to what he promised and he was a messenger [and] a prophet.* (Qur'an 19:54)

> *[Joseph] said: "Set me over the storehouses of the land: I am indeed trustworthy and knowledgeable."* (Qur'an 12:55)

> *When he [Moses] reached full age and was firmly established [in life], We bestowed on him wisdom and knowledge: for thus do We reward those who do good.* (Qur'an 28:14)

> *Said one of the [damsels]: "O my [dear] father! Engage him [Moses] on wages: truly the best of men for you to employ is the [one] who is strong and trustworthy..."* (Qur'an 28:26)

> *He [Saul] said: "Allah has chosen him above you and has gifted him abundantly with knowledge and bodily prowess; Allah grants His authority to whom He pleases. Allah cares for all and He knows all things."* (Qur'an 2:247)

> *Now there has come unto you a messenger [Muhammad] from amongst yourselves: it grieves him that you should perish: most anxious is he for you: to the believers is he most kind and merciful.* (Qur'an 9:128)

Coffee and Family Priorities

A parent picked up a large empty jar and filled it with golf balls. He asked his children if the jar was full. They agreed that it was. He then picked up a box of pebbles and poured them into the jar, shaking it lightly. The pebbles rolled into the open areas among the golf balls. He asked again if the jar was full. They agreed that it was. The parent next picked up a box of sand and poured it into the jar. The sand filled the remaining space. He asked if the jar was full. The children responded with "yes." The parent then produced two cups of coffee from under the table and poured the contents into the jar, filling the empty space between the sand. The children laughed.

"Now," said the parent, "I want you to imagine that this jar represents your life. The golf balls are the important things – worship, your future spouse and your children, your health, your friends, and your favorite passions – things that if everything else was lost and only they remained, your life would still be full. The pebbles are the other things that matter like your job, your house, and your car. The sand is everything else, like fun and the small stuff.

If you put the sand into the jar first, there is no room for the pebbles or the golf balls. The same goes for life. If you spend all your time and energy on the small stuff, you will never have room for the important things. Pay attention to the things that are critical to your success in the Hereafter and your happiness in this world. Pray more; give more in charity. Spend time and play with your children. Take care of your health. Go out to dinner with your spouse. Take time to study. There will always be time to clean the house and fix the disposal in the sink.

Take care of the golf balls first, the things that really matter. Set your priorities. The rest is just sand."

One child inquired what the coffee represented. The parent smiled. "I'm glad you asked. It just goes to show you that no matter how full your life may seem, there's always room for a couple of cups of coffee with a friend."

Conclusion

Fix Your Eyes on the Prize

Although this chapter has discussed the issue of goals and objectives in some detail, when all is said and done, goal-setting is simply a means to an end, and the end product, the raising of righteous children, has always to be kept in mind. It will have a direct impact on how one deals with children and how one develops in them the qualities required to play the roles that parents wish them to play when they become adults.

To achieve the goals we set for our children, we need to look at our own character and behavior. We need to:

1) Apply an appropriate balance of discipline with that of encouragement and empowerment.
2) Practice what we preach as much as possible and make our worldview a holistic concept in life, with a sense of identity and belonging. Admit your mistakes and apologize for them without making excuses.
3) Complement the above with faith and prayers. The Almighty responds to sincere people and helps them in His own way and at His own time.

The Bible states:

> "Train a child in the way that he should go, and when he is old, he will not depart from it."
>
> (Proverbs 22:6)

The future of this world and its security depend largely on its future generations. Parenting plays a pivotal role in the reform and regeneration of society and its effects should not be underestimated. Humanity itself faces great dangers and challenges and we need to be serious about our duty to acquire good parenting skills, and put them into practice. Our children will be the parents of the future, who will then teach the same values to their own children, thus starting a cycle that can only bring peace, justice and stability to the world. Life is not measured by how many breaths we take, but by the moments that take our breath away!

Activities

ACTIVITY 16: DISCUSSION OF THE HOME ENVIRONMENT

Ask each member of the family to answer these questions:

Do you feel happy when you enter the home?
Do you feel happy when you leave the home?
What can you do to make your home environment happier?

Identify one specific thing you require from each member to enhance happiness in the home.

ACTIVITY 17: PARENTS: TEACH YOUR CHILDREN

Review the following items and discuss how to teach them to your children. Address the issues that are lacking in your children's training.

- How to plant a flower they love; (your children love to play with dirt, digging, and water hoses).
- Not to litter.
- How to call you at work.
- How to dial 911 (999 or national emergency number) and when and why.
- To return what they borrow.
- To compliment others.
- Not to hurt others.
- Not to be afraid of animals but to respect and appreciate them.
- To make their word their bond.
- To clean their own mess.
- To share and care. Shared joy is double joy and shared sorrow is half sorrow.
- To respect authority, but not be in awe of it.
- To make friends with children of all races and colors, even those who do not speak a word of English.
- Not to be afraid to try new things, within safety limits.
- How to behave if they lose.
- How to win.
- Even if they are not the best at something, they can still enjoy it.
- When they are afflicted with a serious problem, to do their best and seek God's help.
- To wait for lower prices before buying.

- How to wash and fold their laundry.
- How to respect books.
- To be on time and to call if they are going to be late, always.
- To give things away.
- How to be tidy and nice in appearance.

Parents:

- Do not tell your child, "don't cry"; ask him why he is crying.
- Do not buy your child everything s/he wants, even if you can.
- Do not criticize your child's mistakes, but discuss their lack of effort.
- Believe in your child.
- Do not criticize your spouse in front of your child.
- Do not put a television or computer in your child's room.
- Do not use television as a babysitter.

ACTIVITY 18: SOME MISTAKEN PROVERBS IN ARAB CULTURE

Parents need to explain and refute some of the proverbs that are prevalent in Arab culture. These tend to emphasize the themes of self-absorption, lack of consideration, and hypocrisy.

> If you were not a wolf, you would be eaten by wolves. [This encourages dominance and aggressive behavior]
> The hand that cannot be bitten should be kissed. [Denotes hypocrisy]
> Why do I care! [Self-absorption, selfish outlook]
> If I die of thirst, let there be no rain. [Lack of consideration]
> Beware of the evil of those whom you favored. [Negative attitude]

ACTIVITY 19: A WORLDVIEW BASED ON TRUE FRIENDSHIP

Explain the following hadith, then narrate stories about your friendships that were incorrect, insincere, and not for the sake of the Almighty alone. The Prophet ﷺ said:

> "There is a group of the servants of God that even the prophets and martyrs will envy." They said, "Oh, Messenger of Allah, who are these people?" He said, "They are a people who love each other for the light of Allah, not for wealth or family ties. Their faces are filled with light and they are on pulpits of light; neither do they fear when the people fear, nor do they grieve when the people grieve." Then the Prophet ﷺ recited the verse, "Oh, verily, they who are close to God – no fear need they have, and neither shall they grieve." (Abū Dāwūd)

ACTIVITY 20: CALM DISCUSSION AMONG FAMILY MEMBERS: REGULARLY!

- Have a family meeting once a month to discuss the political, social, and economic situation of everyone in the family.
- Make sure that no undue tension and stress result from this possibly heated discussion.

CHAPTER 4

The Most Important Goal: Raising Children Who Love God

Introduction

ALTHOUGH IN THE previous chapter we examined some of the major goals and values that parents have to set in raising children, there is one particular overall objective that requires special emphasis, and that is faith in God. Raising children who *know of* God is very different than raising children who *love* God and are *conscious* of Him. Consciousness of God is the basis from which all other values will blossom and from which real success will result.

Our time with our children is limited, so we need to organize ourselves, begin a schedule and not leave it to some future date and person to do the job for us, hoping that spirituality and morality will somehow filter in.

The society in which we live continually promotes unbalanced rationalism, a way of thinking that excludes God from our lives. Be aware of schools that push God into the background.

The Current Approach to Inculcating Faith in Our Children

Before examining what we ought to do, let us examine what is happening in our family circles.

The misguided religious approach which Muslims often apply to life today may be described as formalistic and legalistic, and this in turn spills over into how Muslim children are raised. The dominant religious culture as it is practiced today tends to divide life into two main activities: religious rituals (*'ibādāt*) and business interactions (*mu'āmalāt*). In terms of religious rituals, this impacts on Muslim parenting by confining religious education to a simple enactment of rituals, which include ablution and praying five times a day (salah), fasting during Ramadan (*ṣawm*), and paying the poor-due (zakah). It also strictly governs social interactions, including the marriage contract (*zawāj*), business contracts (*'uqūd*), formal personal morals (*ādāb*), and memorization of basic beliefs (*kalimah* or *shahādah*). This is a legalistic way of practicing faith.

In addition, Muslim parents and families often neglect the importance of public-Ummatic duties and accountability, in favor of isolated personal advancement, giving little thought to moral responsibilities toward other members of society. As a result, children are not encouraged to participate in civic affairs, and as long as they have been taught the basics of prayers and reading the Qur'an, parents congratulate themselves on a duty well done. Children therefore grow up thinking that performing personal rituals is the central element of a moral life, and that if they perform these rituals, then they have performed all their religious and moral obligations in life. What this can amount to is an individualistic egotistical life style, one of mere survival and a negative public attitude. Unfortunately, this apathy has wider repercussions for ultimately it destroys public life and society, the result of which is that everybody is a loser.

In reality, worship (*'ibādāt*) really does not merely mean the performance of rituals alone, but also includes all the duties and actions required in a Muslim's life according to Islamic Law (Shari'ah), as well as values, like the promotion of what is good, avoiding evil, engaging in public struggle, and caring for others. If these qualities are not deeply rooted in the

emotional fabric (*wujdān*) of Muslim children, then they will pass this apathy on to their own children, and perpetuate a cycle of disastrous indifference. There is, therefore, a major imbalance and flaw in the sequence of religious education that overemphasizes the performance of rituals as a goal in itself and underemphasizes inner development and public concerns. The word *'ibādāt* really denotes *dhikr*, which means remembrance and communication with the Almighty to establish righteousness, morality, and good behavior.

A Culture of Self-Absorption: Lack of Participation in Public Affairs

Unfortunately there was a historical confrontation, polarization, and separation between Muslim scholars and thinkers on the one hand and oppressive and corrupt political leaders on the other. Muslim jurists have been isolated from public life and have focused mainly on the personal and individual aspects of people's lives, ignoring the public and societal concerns. Thus, the practices of public affairs, good governance, political participation, consultation (*shūrā*), civic duties, seeking social justice and establishing brotherhood have not been given their due importance. This has distorted the Islamic universal vision. A passive attitude toward public issues has affected the Ummatic team spirit and weakened group bonds necessary to generate public concern. A civilization cannot be sustained by a narrow-minded emphasis on personal salvation alone; it has to be complemented by a strong emphasis on social and public concerns. In other words the implementation of the concept of *istikhlāf* (the trusteeship of humankind) requires us to perform and develop, generation after generation, the mission of *'imrān* (the creation of a civilization based on the common good). Although concern for personal and family laws in Islamic jurisprudence (*fiqh*) is a necessary requirement, it is not, on its own, enough to produce builders of civilization.

Such a discourse helps to produce good but ultimately passive and submissive individuals and communities. People raised in a traditional, formalistic, and legalistic culture may perform their ablution, prayers, fasting, and pilgrimage rituals correctly, but they unfortunately do not incline toward good citizenship, public participation, and promoting service to society. Becoming dependent on governments to provide them with ready-made services, rather than shouldering their personal and public responsibilities, they become unable to think for themselves, or make decisions about their future, or increase their knowledge, or take care of themselves. In other words, apathy wins over active participation. Children raised in this way do not become free, ethical, innovative thinkers, team workers, or pioneers of social progress; instead, they ultimately grow up as timid and selfish egoists.

Individuals who live under oppressive political and religious authorities suffer from a bad situation; where social change is needed they generate sick societies and destructive behavior, clearly evident in the social misery of their environment and economy. While they avoid interest-bearing bank accounts, they are happy to cheat on their Income Tax returns and the payment of zakah, even though lying and cheating contravene the Shari'ah. They feel victorious when they have managed to escape being caught for smuggling and for deceiving custom officials.

Some parents emphasize self-centered behavior from the time their child is born to the time s/he reaches adulthood. More effort is put into what the children will wear than in teaching them to care for others and be kind to others, or to inculcate a sense of responsibility for people, the poor and needy in particular, and the environment in general. Many of us may buy expensive toys that break easily for our children, yet turn away from the suffering of a poor child on the road begging for food and clothes.

This way of looking at life has hurt our societies and public life. How can we explain, for instance, that the National Day in Bangladesh refers to the separation of Bangladesh from Pakistan? Why should the celebration of a division be lauded when we see European nations uniting and cooperating to enhance their common interests, when once they were enemies of one another? Brazil has unity despite the presence of many ethnic, religious, and linguistic groups, each with its own economic and social problems. Meanwhile, Muslim and Arab countries, despite their common language, culture, and common interests, continue to disintegrate. "Quarreling" Arab states and "poor" Muslim countries do little to help their citizens. Muslim numbers are on the increase, but not their status on the world scene.

Can religion be the reason for the Muslim world's fragmentation, disunity, pettiness and isolation? Do such poor qualities serve its interests? Do Muslims misunderstand their religion? There exists a split in the Ummah's mentality. Everyone has learnt to think only of himself or herself, and tries to preserve his/her immediate personal and family interests, while ignoring the Ummah's wider interests and those of other members of society, including relatives and neighbors. Muslim culture is becoming narrow-minded and distorted, void of neighborly feelings and the teamwork spirit that should be its hallmark. Muslims need to lift their heads out of the sand.

Compare this situation with the attitude of Abū Bakr, when he was willing to donate all his wealth to the community. The Prophet ﷺ asked him: "What did you leave for your family?" He answered: "I left them Allah and Allah's Messenger." Abū Bakr's action was a sign not only of his strong faith, but also of his conviction that the Prophet ﷺ and society would be able to take care of him and his family should they ever be in need. If Abū Bakr had felt that his family would have been forced to suffer and beg in the streets, he would have kept most of his wealth and donated a small part of it.

The current unhappy state of the Muslim world cannot be blamed on the fact that it consists of vast territories with many ethnic groups speaking many different languages, or that they are ruled by oppressive regimes or have suffered a history of colonialism etc. Islam promotes peaceful coexistence and social harmony. Muslims today comprise one-quarter of the world's population. Their disunity cannot be attributed to Islam because Islam teaches unity, brotherhood, solidarity, and compassion. Nor can it be attributed to political and economic factors since economic and political decline is a symptom, not a cause. The question then remains: What is responsible?

We believe that the answer lies in the Qur'anic verse:

> *Verily, never will Allah change the condition of a people until they themselves bring about change in their own souls.* (Qur'an 13:11)

We cannot stress this point enough: the poor condition of a people lies within themselves. Therefore, only by comprehending the Qur'anic vision and changing our inner characters can we change the condition of our own lives. This can only happen through proper parenting.

Education is a lifelong process and can be acquired from the cradle to the grave. Good parenting, however, is essential for establishing public concerns like a sense of responsibility, self-sacrifice, and caring for others. These values must be instilled during early childhood by parents nurturing the right emotional, social, and spiritual aspects of the personality. These have to be captured very early on when it is far simpler and more effective to do than during adulthood. Books of fiqh (legal rules) represent the basic religious and cultural reference manuals for Muslim personal development, and as such have great influence in building personality.

Therefore, it is necessary to revise the fiqh books by adding the missing dimensions of public concern for society and the whole of humanity. This dimension is explained clearly in the Qur'an and Hadith:

> *But those who, before them, had homes [in Madinah] and had adopted the Faith, show their affection to such as came to them for refuge, and entertain no desire in their hearts for things given to the [latter], but give them preference over themselves, even though poverty was their [own lot]. And those saved from the covetousness of their own souls; they are the ones that achieve prosperity.*
>
> (Qur'an 59:9)

The Prophet ﷺ said:
He who does not concern himself with the affairs of Muslims is not one of them.
(IBN MAS'ŪD)

Unless we care for others in society, such as the poor, the orphans, the neighbors, and those in need, we will not be able to become the best we can be. As we see from *Sūrah al-Mā'ūn* in the Qur'an:

> *Do you see the one who denies the Judgment [to come]? Then such is the person who repulses the orphan [with harshness], And does not encourage the feeding of the indigent. So woe to the worshippers, who are neglectful of their prayers, those who [want only] to be seen [by other people], but refuse [to supply even] neighborly needs.* (Qur'an 107:1–7)

There is a direct and strong linkage between personal worship and the well-being of society. Religious rituals must be linked to caring for orphans, feeding the poor, and helping neighbors. The real objective of worship is to prepare the worshiper for serving his/her fellow human beings. The existence of beggars in the streets of the Muslim world proves the existence of a lack of real sense of responsibility, which has taken root amongst people today.

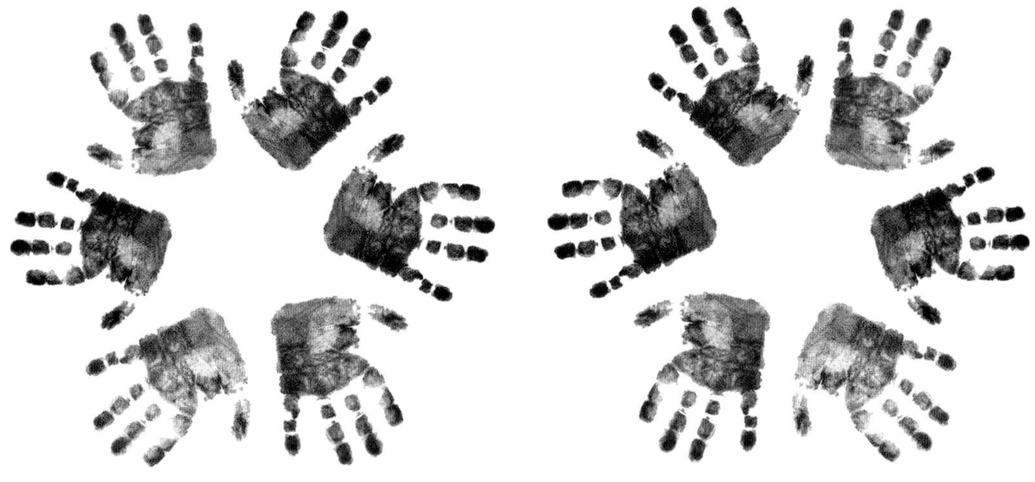

Lack of Personal Responsibility

Many people feel little or no responsibility for themselves, for others or for their future. In a society where hard work and honesty yield little or no benefit to the individual, the individual avoids both, and begs from others for support, demanding that they perform their duties toward him, while denying that he owes anything to himself or his family. The concept of responsibility for self is missing from contemporary Muslim societies. It is also a direct consequence of the prevalence of collectivism in the Muslim world. One should not confuse caring for others with collectivism, for collectivism is to give priority to the group over the individual. Tribalism and clannishness were the most primitive forms of collectivism in the Muslim world. Nowadays, these have been replaced with being a slave of the government. In intellectual terms, collectivism leads to "group think," or a herd mentality, which is the enemy of original individual thought (ijtihad), the mainspring of human progress. In economic terms, it removes any incentive for productivity from individuals, turning them into unproductive consumers. Psychologically, it removes the individuals' vision of themselves as the *khulafā'*. Collectivism promotes a culture of dependency, where one has no self-esteem. Ethically, it leads to moral cowardice. Politically, it leads to either rival factions attempting to impose their will upon one another or to the "strong man" imposing his will on the society.

In contrast with the above, the Qur'an appeals directly to individuals to choose to accept their role as *khulafā'* and to submit to Allah's Will, encouraging them to struggle to achieve good for themselves, for their community, and for society. If we truly want for others what we want for ourselves, then we will want others also to be rational, responsible, and free.

In many Muslim countries, children are taught to be passive and uncritical. They learn some outdated legal injunctions. Zakah is taught as a tax based on the number of camels you own. Students are taught to give bushels of barley and dates to the poor. Books on jurisprudence still contain chapters on how to deal with slaves and the correct method of buying and selling them! Young Muslims are being taught outdated and unnecessary information. A valuable opportunity is also being lost: that of developing compassion and concern for the needs of other people. This lack of compassion is a serious flaw in the character of the future generations of the Ummah.

The underlying reason for teaching a child about zakah is not how to calculate percentages for camels, dates, and barley, but to instill an understanding of the great concepts of social solidarity, kindness, sacrifice, generosity, as well as the importance of sharing with the desperate and needy. Far more important than the material aspects of the issue are the inculcation of deep feelings of compassion and empathy, as well as an appreciation of the suffering of the helpless and of the have-nots of society. It is the practice of brotherhood and the joy of giving by means of zakah and other charities that needs emphasis at this tender age, not the boring mathematical calculations.

A Distorted Culture: Backwardness and Superstition

Many Muslims today are backward-looking rather than forward-looking, and they are reactive rather than proactive. They wait until a problem occurs and then rush to try to do something about it (but rarely succeed), rather than planning ahead and thinking forward to prevent the occurrence of the problem in the first place. They are like the car driver who only looks at the rear mirror instead of the front windshield.

Another problem hampering Muslim progress is superstition, witchcraft, and obsession with the world of jinns. Islamic civilization was built on foundations of knowledge, science, objectivity, and reason. It is comforting to know that Muslim scholars, while they believed in the supernatural miracles of all the prophets, at the same time believed that the real miracle that Prophet Muhammad ﷺ left to humanity was the Qur'an. Qur'anic Revelation addresses the human intellect and is based on reason. The Qur'an calls for research, contemplation, exploration, and thinking. These are dominant and recurring themes in the Qur'an. It is this type of mentality which parents have to nurture in the minds of their children, so that they grow up believing in the community of reason while maintaining their firm faith in God and the Hereafter. Civilization is not built on superstition and witchcraft. One hears appalling stories of people resorting to the healing "powers" of spirits, jinns, stars, and magic in dealing with family affairs, rather than resorting to sound medical or psychological treatment. These practices are alien to the principles and spirit of Islam and harmful to children's intellect. Our role as parents is to inculcate the enlightened scientific mentality which the Qur'an emphasizes. The Qur'an affirms *al-sunan al-Ilahiyyah,* the laws of nature that govern human life and the physical universe. These divinely inspired natural laws applied fully to the Prophet ﷺ as explained in the verses:

> Say: "*I have no power over any good or harm to myself except as Allah wills. If I had knowledge of the unseen, I should have multiplied all good, and no evil should have touched me: I am but a warner, and a bringer of glad tidings to those who have faith.*"
>
> (Qur'an 7:188)

Say: "I am but a man like yourselves, [but] the Revelation has come to me, that your God is One God: whoever expects to meet his Lord, let him work righteousness, and, in the worship of his Lord, admit no one as partner."
(Qur'an 18:110)

This objective and scientific mentality produced one of the greatest civilizations the world has ever known. During its golden age, it was the Muslims who helped Europe out of the Dark Ages (into which it had sunk for centuries) and into the Enlightenment. (Al-Hassani 2011)

The French philosopher Roger Garaudy described the dimensions of Western civilization as follows:

Modern Western civilization owes its esthetic and legal system to the Roman and Greek civilizations, its morality to Christianity, and its scientific thinking to Muslims in Spain.

(AL HEWAR MAGAZINE 2002)

It is the duty of parents first and school teachers second to raise children of great intelligence, calibre and character, deeply entrenched with an understanding of divine and natural laws, the universe, and the human and social sciences.

The Wrong Worldview: Weakness and Fear

Prophet Muhammad ﷺ said:

"There will come a time when other nations will attack you, like the hungry people who devour a plate of food." A Companion responded: "Is it because of our smaller numbers, O Prophet of Allah?" The Prophet said: "No, you will be many then, but you will be like the foam on the ocean waves. Allah will take away the fear and respect of you from the hearts of your enemy, and He will instill in your hearts weakness (*wahn*)." Someone said: "What is *wahn*, O Prophet of Allah?" The Prophet answered: "'*Wahn*' is the love of this worldly life and hatred of death." (Abū Dāwūd)

The Balanced Way: The Wise Approach

We ask parents to take an honest look at their religious beliefs. A wise understanding of the practices and inner requirements of your religion will have a beneficial impact on how you raise your children. It is important to parent in a way that does not lead to a culture of fear, self-absorption, backwardness, and coercion.

The early scholars (*'alims, fuqahā'* and mullahs) emphasized both rituals and worship (*'ibādāt*). The Qur'an mentions *dhikr,* meaning remembrance of the Almighty. Both elements are essential for teaching children. Parents need to be aware of the Islamic worldview and to teach it to children at the age of discernment. Children should also be told that our duty is to develop life on earth according to the correct values and rules that God has revealed to humankind, and that worship is a means to achieve those ends. This will then lead them to understand the whole purpose of life as being to strive to do the right thing.

As parents, our behavior will be the model to which children will turn. Therefore, we should continually seek *dhikr* to remind us of our duty to do that which would improve our lives and please Him. In particular, we are required to do our best in maintaining a righteous life on earth, in taking care of our environment, seeking knowledge, and helping the oppressed to be liberated. Children will have a better understanding of the real meaning and aim of *'ibādāt* if they see parents practicing this, and if they are taught that life is meant to be a test of people's qualities and their struggle to do their best in both the private and public aspects of society.

The following verses establish the foundations of a worldview in the mind of the child:

> *Say: "Indeed, my prayer, my*
> *emotional devotion, my livelihood,*
> *and my demise are for Allah, the*
> *Lord of the worlds.*
> *There is no partner with Allah, and*
> *that is what I have been ordered,*
> *and I am at the forefront of those*
> *who submit."*
>
> (Qur'an 6:162–163)

> *Prayer restrains [one] from shameful*
> *and unjust deeds and aggression.*
> (Qur'an 29:45)

> *... and who give food – however*
> *great be their own want of it – unto*
> *the needy, and the orphan, and the*
> *captive [saying, in their hearts,] "We*
> *feed you for the sake of God alone:*
> *we desire no recompense from you,*
> *nor thanks."*
>
> (Qur'an 76:8–9)

Allah has promised, to those among you who believe and perform righteous deeds, that He will, of a surety, grant them in the land, inheritance [of power], as He granted it to those before them; that He will establish in authority their religion – the one which He has chosen for them; and that He will change [their state], after the fear in which they [lived], to one of security and peace: They will worship Me [alone] and not associate aught with Me; and whoever disbelieves after that, they are the rebellious ones.

(Qur'an 24:55)

Teach Children Love of the Qur'an

To raise children who love God, parents need to introduce the Qur'an to them so that it becomes more than just a sacred Book which is to be read on a few religious events and then shelved for the rest of the year. Should the emphasis be on giving information or should it be on the more important emotional and psychological development of the heart and soul of the child? Gaining knowledge and information continues throughout one's entire life, whereas healthy emotional and psychological development must occur early in childhood, mostly before the teen years.

What is happening today is that Muslims repeatedly frighten children from their early years with accounts of Hellfire (*jahannam*), rarely mentioning Allah's Love, Mercy, and Compassion, or the beauty of Heaven. We emphasize how they will burn in Hell if they disobey God or their parents or make mistakes. Meanwhile, we neglect to mention how they will be rewarded and served in Paradise if they act righteously, obey Allah, obey their parents, help others, and do what is right. We continually threaten children and remind them about punishments as if they are evil criminals, yet seldom encourage them or mention the love of God and the rewards they get for good behavior. In this environment, children grow into terrified and fearful adults. They harbor a negative attitude and lack self-confidence and, at worst, are discouraged from their faith altogether.

Teachers usually start teaching the Qur'an to children from the last Part (*juzu' 'ammah* or Part 30). This Part contains short chapters (surahs), which were revealed in Makkah at the beginning of the Revelation. These short chapters were aimed at the deviant and arrogant oppressors from the tribe of Quraysh and their cruel pagan leaders (like Abū Jahal and Abū Lahab). In these early chapters the Qur'an is addressing those who tortured Muslims, killed some of them, plotted to kill the Prophet ﷺ, and waged war to annihilate the believers. These surahs were meant to bring these tyrants to their senses, and the strong verses fell on their ears like thunder, because they contained dire warnings. Look at the following examples:

Destruction upon the hands of Abū Lahab, and destruction upon him.

(Qur'an 111:1)

Horror to every liar and gossiper.

(Qur'an 104:1)

Has there come unto thee the tiding of the Overshadowing Event? Some faces will on that Day be downcast, toiling [under burdens of sin], worn out [by fear], about to enter a glowing fire, given to drink from a boiling spring. No food for them save the bitterness of dry thorns. (Qur'an 88:1–6)

Horror to the cheaters. (Qur'an 83:1)

Say: "O you who reject Faith!"
(Qur'an 109:1)

When the Earth is shaken to its [utmost] convulsion. (Qur'an 99:1)

It is unfortunate that although this harsh form of address was not meant for innocent children, these are the very verses that are first taught to them nowadays. The reason for teaching these surahs is that they are very short and are considered easy to memorize. Instead of frightening children at this young age with an emphasis on Hell and punishment, we need to emphasize the love of God, the mercy of parents, and the beauty of Heaven. This fits into their psychology instilling feelings of security, love, warmth, generosity and tenderness during early childhood. It is better to begin with God's Love, His Mercy, Kindness, Compassion, Forgiveness, and Generosity, in addition to His many other beautiful attributes. **Children should also be told that they are good and that God loves them before teaching them that they should love God**. The sequence should be God's love (first) and then (second) their obligation to love God.

Once children begin to understand, parents can gently bring in the subject of Hell as punishment for evil doing. Surahs containing warnings and threats for committing major sins are supposed to be introduced when children can draw lessons from them instead of succumbing to fear. This is usually during the late childhood and teen years, when they are older and can better comprehend abstract ideas and the consequences of their actions.

Care needs to be taken over how we develop our children's mentality and psychology, especially when teaching the Qur'an. It is imperative that parents select the most suitable verses on which to focus during the different stages of their children's growing up. Most of the Companions (*Saḥābah*) of the Prophet ﷺ were introduced to the Qur'an when they were adults. At that age, the Qur'an had a profound effect on them. Their already courageous and strong character was strengthened and the Qur'an directed them to high moral standards. Specialists in Qur'anic sciences, together with education experts and social scientists, can advise parents on how to teach children, including the sequence of verses relative to their age. Certainly, all the verses of the Qur'an are to be taught during the life of the individual. However, the question is: In what sequence should they be taught? Which verses need to be emphasized and at what age? It is clearly not suitable to start with the whole of the 30th part just because it contains 37 short surahs. What is considered easier to remember should not be the only consideration.

Non-Arabic-speaking parents have to explain to their children the meaning of the verses in their own languages. Currently, emphasis is placed on simply being able to read the Arabic and memorize the verses without knowing the meaning. Parents are strongly recommended to acquire a good translation of the Qur'an and supplement their reading lessons with interpretation (*tafsīr*) lessons, so that they start to develop a relationship with the world view and message of the Qur'an. If parents are unable to do this, they can find a teacher and monitor what and how their children are taught. Recordings of the Qur'an can be played regularly at home so that children become familiar with its sound. It is important to establish a pattern of reading that is consistent and organized so that children become used to reading the Qur'an every day. Learning Arabic as a second language also helps children learn the Qur'an and interact with it first hand. Many good children's books have been

published containing stories of the prophets taken from scriptures, and the lessons to draw from these stories. Parents have to purchase or borrow these stories to supplement the Qur'anic readings so that children become familiar and comfortable with the Qur'an.

Teach Children Prayers: Continual Remembrance of God

There are many short prayers that bring to mind the idea of a watchful, caring God, Who is ever present with us. These are easy to introduce and help children acquire the habit of thanking Him, and seeking His guidance and protection. They also combat any attempt to push God into the background. Parents, for instance, should thank God out loud before they eat, and when finishing eating, and ask children to repeat the *du'ā'* (supplication) after them. Again, when entering the house, when leaving the house, when going to sleep, and when waking up, a point should be made of saying a *du'ā'*. This instills an attitude of gratitude. Simply saying *Bismillāh* (in the Name of God) when beginning an activity will be observed by children and copied. Although it may seem trivial and dull for children at first, it is worth persevering. Eventually this habit will promote in children the practice of *dhikr* and make this communication with the Almighty a natural aspect of their life. They will also come to realize God's merciful hand in everything.

When it comes to salah (ritual prayers), again, this should be made an important and natural element of the parents' daily life. Parents set the best example for their children. Make the call for prayers (*adhān*) in front of your children and treat the time for prayer seriously. The television should be switched off and everyone should be prepared so that the prayer starts in the right atmosphere. Parents should pray in front of their children with consciousness and calmness. Too often there is an impatience for the prayer to end, and this rush will be noticed by children and no doubt imitated without concentration on prayers. A *du'ā'* has to be made before and after the prayer so that the children learn to do the same; it can be a request for anything you feel you need from the Almighty.

Teach Children *Tawbah* (Repentance)

Children need to understand that actions have consequences, that misbehavior is shameful and is known to God, and that they need to repent when they have committed bad deeds. It is not enough for children to say sorry and move on. Children need to understand that one's regret of misbehavior needs to be addressed to God. This also opens the door to further God consciousness, and allows the parents to teach their children God's love and mercy. Children can then establish a deeper relationship with Him.

Parents will not be thanked for their teaching efforts by children; on the contrary, they are likely to encounter tantrums and all manner of resistance. Nevertheless, persistently explaining the situation in a firm voice and giving plenty of affection when *tawbah* has been made will reinforce in the children the practice of repenting and refraining from wrong actions. Later on when the children are older, if they hurt or do something wrong to others, they will know what to do to make amends with God.

Teach Children About Prophet Muhammad ﷺ and Other Prophets

Parents are advised to invest in a small library of books and acquire the habit of reading regularly with their children. They can read or narrate stories of the Prophet ﷺ (including his life, his childhood, his character and his message), stories of his grandchildren, and stories of his Companions. Prophetic stories enable children to enter the world of the prophets, form a strong association with them and emulate them as role models. These stories need to be tailored and addressed to the children's age group and center on aspects to which children can relate. Parents can also read to children stories of strong men and women and moral leaders throughout history.

Teach children about the achievements of Islamic civilization. Take children to museums and allow them to experience Islamic art, history, and architecture. Museums are a wonderful place for children to be inspired by history, and they often have activities for children, which parents can take advantage of. There are also excellent Internet sources devoted to this subject, for example, "1001 inventions," showcasing Muslim achievements of the past thousand years: http://www. 1001 inventions.com. It is recommended that parents also invest in a copy of the book, *1001 Inventions: Muslim Heritage in Our World.* This is an easy-to-read, beautifully illustrated guidebook taking readers through a thousand years of science and technology and into the lives of medieval pioneers whose ingenious inventions have helped create our world today. Websites and books/DVDs containing audio-visual material showing the great beauty of the world in which we live are also another great source of guidance. Children should be shown visually appealing films, especially those describing the wonders of creation (such as the miracle of the bee).

In addition, as children become older, the effects of a secular world view will encroach more deeply into their growing conscience. Be prepared to answer questions about topics such as the theory of evolution. Children will be vulnerable the minute they enter the wider world, and parents are extremely naive if they leave belief to filter in through a sort of Islamic osmosis. Once the knowledge of God and His creation are deeply ingrained in children, the sophistries of some secularist discourse will be easy to deal with. Children need a confident and firm foundation from which to deflect and/or ignore any attempts to distort their world view.

Teach Children *Ādāb* (Manners)

Islam's concept of behavior includes the concept of morals (*ādāb*). Children should be taught to say please and thank you, as well as *al-hamdulillah* (all praise be to God), *insha'Allāh* (if God wills), and *al-salām 'alaykum* (peace be upon you). Too often, this beautiful greeting is allowed to slip into a "hi", "hello", or "bye". Children need to be taught the *ādāb* of proper eating and drinking, wearing decent clothes, and how to act respectfully in a social setting.

It is important to keep children and the home environment clean, tidy, and organized so that they absorb these habits themselves. Do not spoil children; sometimes, it is better to cook a plain dish other than a fancy dinner so that they learn to value food when they are given a particularly delicious meal. Frequent exaggerated praise and admiration of children may instill vanity or arrogance. It is not necessary to buy them every toy they demand; if they really want something, then occasionally they can be allowed to work for it by doing little chores. They should be reminded that the Almighty God may give them something better. Working out alternative solutions, for instance, when they cannot have what they want, prepares children for the reality waiting for them in the real world, and all the values and discipline they learn will serve them well throughout their lives.

What Should You Tell Your Children First: They Love God or God Loves Them?

If children are taught to say "I love God, He created me and created the earth, the sun and the moon" what kind of message are they being given? First of all, children have no concept of God, for it is an abstract idea that they do not comprehend yet. What does it matter to them to love or not to love something that they do not know? Furthermore, for children, their existence as well as the universe around

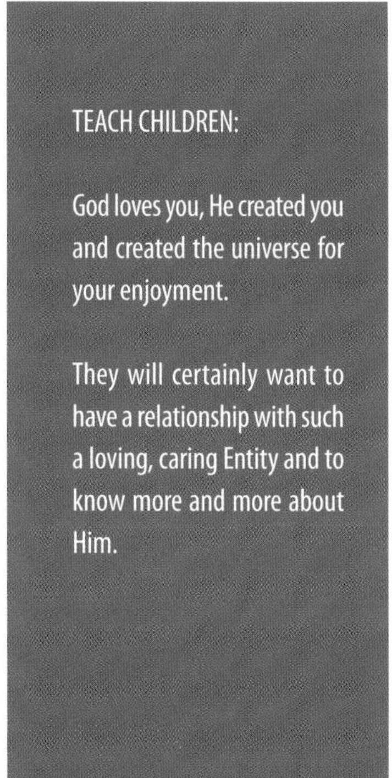

them is a matter of fact and it is nothing special. However, if the issue is reversed and the children are taught "God loves you, He created you and created the universe for your enjoyment," they will then want to know eagerly who this Being is who loves them, and cares for them and their pleasure. They will certainly want to have a relationship with such a loving, caring Entity and to know more and more about Him.

There is a strong relationship between worship, life, and voluntary submission to the Will of the Creator. Our good behavior has to be based on a desire to please Him, the Ultimate source of Goodness and Truth. The way to please God is to follow His directives and guidance to improve the quality of our lives as well as those of the people around us. We strengthen our spirituality by being good, hardworking, honest, useful, and helpful to others, thus moving closer to the Creator. We help ourselves by helping others, by respecting the rights of life, property, and honor; and by promoting justice, compassion, and freedom, avoiding tyranny, and resisting oppression. All of these struggles require a continual awareness and remembrance of God and His beautiful attributes. Observing the religious rituals strengthens this awareness and our love for the Almighty. In this way, we will be blessed and the sincere worshiper can gain the strength to succeed in doing what is good and right.

Know Thy Self: The Problem with Arab Education

There is a loud cry for learning, freedom, and ijtihad (research): The United Nations Arab Human Development Report (2009) shows a worrying trend across the modern Arab world in terms of scientific advancement and research. Today's Arabs lag behind other nations even in sustaining their own rich cultural tradition. A 1991 UN study showed that Arab countries have one of the lowest publication figures in the world. Europe is in the lead, producing over five times the number of publications in comparison with the Arab countries.

The report highlights an increasing disparity between Arabic countries and the rest of the world. In their obsession to control, authoritarian Arab states have stifled creativity and all argument. "Freedoms that are hostage to false matters of security, to censorship, and to self-appointed watchdogs of public morality are freedoms denied. The first victims of this denial are creativity, initiative, innovation and knowledge." (*The Economist* 2003).

Parents should not shun their responsibility towards children by relegating their role to governments. Parents, as role models and primary teachers to their children, must stand up to the challenge and become a major factor in effort to change society. Parents are the "ignition key" for the process of effective reforms; the drivers are the intellectual reformers and educators who teach parents what to do and how to do it. If the parents are convinced, they will eagerly do what is required. They possess a far-reaching moral influence on their children and can reshape the character of future generations.

Activities

ACTIVITY 21: PROGRESS OF JAPAN AND GERMANY VS. THE BACKWARDNESS OF MUSLIM COUNTRIES

In an informal meeting with a group of 3 couples, discuss these questions:

Why is it that many Muslim countries have not progressed, whereas Japan and Germany, which were decimated during World War II, are now among the leading nations of the world?

Why do some Muslim countries still throw garbage into rivers, have a poor education system, and export raw materials cheaply only to buy them back as highly expensive manufactured goods? For example, a ton of iron ore is exported for $2000 and then bought back as computers and electronic gadgets for millions of dollars.

Why does the Muslim world have some of the highest levels of illiteracy despite the Qur'anic injunction to read (*iqra'*)?

ACTIVITY 22: MAKING THE CONNECTION BETWEEN CHILDREN AND THEIR CREATOR – EARLY ON!

Although the five daily prayers remind us of God in a systematic way, there are many other activities which we need to connect with the Creator as we perform them.

Children need to be taught to do continual *dhikr* (remembrance) of the Creator. One effective way is to teach them to memorize the following supplications practiced by the Prophet ﷺ from the time of waking up to bedtime. These do not take long and they improve our state of mind and they orient our action in the right direction (especially on these two occasions, when we begin eating and when we finish eating). Parents may choose one or two items each week and ensure correct practice before going to the next one. Teach children the meaning of these supplications.

(If the Arabic is difficult to recite, it is acceptable to say them in the native language or in English).

Waking Up: Praise be to God, Who revived us after death and to Him is our resurrection

إذا أفاق من نومه قال: الحمد لله الذي أحيانا بعد أن أماتنا وإليه النشور

Seeing the Dawn Light: We woke up in the morning and the whole kingdom of the Universe belongs to God. All praise be to Allah.

إذا رأي نور الفجر قال: أصبحنا وأصبح الملك لله والحمد لله

Standing Before the Mirror: Praise be to the One Who perfected my creation. O Lord, perfect my manners as You perfected my creation.

إذا نظر إلى المرآة قال: الحمد لله الذي خلقني فسواني، اللهم حسن خُلُقي كما أحسنت خَلْقي

Getting Dressed: Praise be to Allah Who clothed me to cover my *'awrah* [private parts] and beautify my life.

إذا لبس ثوباً قال: الحمد لله الذي كساني ما أواري به عوراتي وأتجمل به في حياتي

Entering the *Masjid*: O Allah, open for me Your doors of mercy, and grant me the treasures of Your knowledge.

إذا دخل المسجد قال: اللهم أفتح لي أبواب رحمتك وانشر علي خزائن علمك

Upon Eating: Praise be to Him who fed us and satisfied our thirst and made us Muslims.

إذا أكل طعاماً قال: الحمد لله الذي أطعمنا فأشبعنا وسقانا فأروانا وجعلنا مسلمين

Drinking Water: Praise be to Allah who made the water sweet by His Mercy and not bitter and salty because of our sins.

إذا شرب الماء قال: الحمد لله الذي جعل الماء فراتاً برحمته ولم يجعله ملحاً أَجاجاً بذنوبنا

Entering the Bathroom: I seek refuge in Allah from the cursed Satan. O Allah, I seek refuge in you from dirt and filth.

إذا دخل الخلاء قال: أعوذ بالله من الشيطان الرجيم اللهم إني أعوذ بك من الخبث والخبائث

Exiting the Bathroom: O Allah, Grant me forgiveness. Praise be to Allah who saved me from harm and granted me good health.

إذا خرج من الخلاء قال: غُفرانك الحمد لله الذي أذهب عني الأذى وعافاني

Leaving the House: In the name of Allah, I rely on Him. I seek refuge in Him from leading or being led astray.

إذا خرج من البيت قال: بسم الله توكلت على الله اللهم إني أعوذ بك أن أضل أو أُضل

Entering the House: In the name of Allah, we enter, in His Name we exit, and upon Him we rely.

إذا دخل البيت قال: بسم الله دخلنا وبسم الله خرجنا وعلى الله توكلنا

ACTIVITY 23: APPRECIATING THE FAVORS AND BLESSINGS OF GOD

In the spirit of these formal supplications (above), children are requested to make their own personal requests to the Almighty in their own language and to discuss them with their parents.

ACTIVITY 24: PUTTING PROBLEMS INTO PERSPECTIVE

Let one child read aloud this true story and discuss it, adding your own experiences. Gratitude for the smallest things from God leads to contentment, which stops us from feeling jealous, bitter and sad. This is the secret of happiness and the cure for anxiety.

> I knew a young woman who was dealing with serious problems. Her parents were divorced, she was looking after a sick mother whilst holding down a full-time job and had financial problems. However, her attitude to life was cheerful: "If I can wake up in the morning and walk on my feet, I am perfectly all right!"

In other words focus on what you have and look (and strive) for the best possible outcome in life. The following hadith sums up this great attitude:

> The Prophet ﷺ said:
> "Whoever wakes up secure amongst his people, physically healthy, and has enough food for the day, it is as if the whole world had been gathered for him."
>
> (AL TIRMIDHĪ AND IBN MĀJAH)

ACTIVITY 25: SEVEN CONCEPTS TO TEACH CHILDREN

Let a child read the following hadith, then reflect on each principle and relate it to real experiences.

> "There are seven whom Allah will cover with His shade on the day when there is no shade except His shade: a just ruler, a youth who grows up worshiping Allah, a man whose heart is attached to the mosque when he leaves it until he returns to it, two persons who love each other for the sake of God and meet for that and part for that, a man who remembers God when he is alone and his eyes overflow with tears, a man who refuses the approaches of a highly positioned and beautiful woman, saying, 'I fear Allah', and a man who gives charity and conceals it so that his left hand does not know what his right hand gives." (AL-BUKHĀRĪ AND MUSLIM)

CHAPTER 5

Addressing Common Challenges and Pitfalls

Introduction

IN THE LAST few chapters we have tried to convey the ethos of a good, comprehensive parenting plan and outlined some key measures of putting this into effect. We have also stressed the importance of using one's natural parenting instincts, in conjunction with the plan, as a guide to raising good children. The approach we have used is flexible enough to allow parents to create their own foundation and make their own choices in raising their families, with the overall objective being to raise children who are pious, responsible, and socially skilled. We have also stressed that raising a good child has wider repercussions than simply our own peace of mind and a happy home life; it is a major building block of society and civilization itself. However, a good plan, although it makes the difficult enough task of parenting that much easier, is not complete unless it can guide one through some of the potential challenges and pitfalls of parenting. In this chapter we will be focusing on some of the difficulties of parenting, and providing some common-sense solutions. First we will look at some of the major challenges and then, in the following chapter, at some of the major pitfalls. Although we have touched on aspects of these in earlier chapters, it is hoped that seeing them as a coherent whole will allow parents to become more aware of the world that both they and their child live in and some of the hard issues they will face.

Major Challenges Facing Parents

Children say: Our parents are driving us CRAZY!

Parents say: Our children are driving us CRAZY!

STOP YELLING AT EACH OTHER!

Understand the Problems

Analyze the Issues and Solve them Together: **Patiently!!**

Our life is a series of difficult tests, and raising children is one of the most challenging. Nevertheless, the reward for passing the test of parenting is priceless. It is helpful for parents to know the real scale of the challenges facing them so that they do not overestimate or underestimate the task ahead. If they think parenting is too easy, they will not feel the need to prepare themselves for it. If they think it is too difficult, they may despair and give up. We will try to identify the difficulties, and hope that parents will experience some relief and satisfaction to discover that they are not alone in the struggle. It is enriching to discuss these difficulties with other parents, and many parents will be surprised at how much they have in common.

Here are some examples of the many challenges facing parents:

LACK OF EXPERIENCE

This is a major challenge when the first child arrives. Neither parent knows what to do in many situations. Although they may have learned some theories, they lack practical experience. Asking other parents can help greatly; it is on-the-job training without supervisors.

Parenting by the Ear, Literally!

Child guidance formerly was a simple matter, when your mother pulled you along by the ear.

DAY-TO-DAY PRESSURES

Parents often come under pressure resulting from a gender-based division of labor. Many mothers spend the day at home while fathers work outside the home. In the evening, mothers like to go out, whereas fathers prefer to stay at home. This can lead to friction if parents do not empathize with each other.

Fatherhood is Not Only Providing Material Needs

As we grow older, we must realize that being a great father is not just providing food and a roof over our children's heads.

THE DAILY GRIND: ACCEPTING THAT THE PARENTING TASK IS 24/7

There are no office hours for parenting and we might as well accept and embrace the fact that the parenting task is twenty-four hours a day, seven days a week, and fifty-two weeks a year, with no vacation. There is no such thing as "divorce" from one's children. Once a parent, commitment is made for the rest of one's life, and nothing should stand in the way of this commitment.

Which is Harder: Being a Father or the President of the United States?

"I can do one of two things, I can be president of the United States, or I can control my daughter Alice. I cannot possibly do both."

Theodore Roosevelt
(1858–1919), US President
(Porter and Cervantes 2007)

"One word of command from me is obeyed by millions… but I cannot get my three daughters to come down to breakfast on time."

British Officer Wavell
(1883–1950)
(Shaw 1998)

PARENTING IS AN INFLEXIBLE TASK

Once the child is born, parenthood cannot be postponed, rescheduled or neglected. Children have their own biological clocks, and parents should understand their development. Parents cannot slow down a child's growth, nor can they accelerate it. If they try to interfere, they will have a disaster on their hands. The world is in a hurry, but children are not. It is wise to adopt the pace of nature: its secret is patience.

PARENTING IS A LONG-TERM "INVESTMENT" OF TIME, EFFORT, AND MONEY

Parenting is a slow and involved process. It may take years before parents know whether their child is a righteous person or immoral.

PARENTS ARE ONLY ONE OF MANY INFLUENCES ON THEIR CHILDREN

Parents need to be aware of the world in which their children are growing up (which is constantly changing). Developments in technology for instance have thrown up ever greater challenges (in the form of television, internet, cell-phones, online chat rooms, digital music, DVDs, and computer games). Movie and pop star adulation has only mushroomed. If not plugged in to some device or other, children are surrounded by distractions galore. Parents are not fully free in raising their children and face competition from television actors, the Internet, and peers. There are many positive and negative influences on children. Although parents often take the credit – and the blame – for the way their children turn out, they are only one among many influences on child development. From a macro (societal) perspective, well-intentioned and committed parents still cannot make the Internet less filthy, the street gangs less violent, and the media less vulgar.

Although parents are the first significant influence; peer influence becomes increasingly important for children as they grow older, and remains so into the college years. During this time, children are likely to mirror the values and behavior of their friends. Teenagers often become attached to their peer groups, and may distance themselves from their parents. Siblings also have an important and sometimes lasting effect on one another's development; they are social mirrors and models (depending on the age) for one another. They may also be sources of competition and jealousy. Environmental variables also influence children, like geographic location, family size, the family's social class, the dominant religion, and race relations.

BABIES ARE UNABLE TO SPEAK

Just imagine how difficult it is to communicate with animals, and then think of babies. They are not fully able to speak, so it is hard to know their needs, feelings, and thoughts. We have to guess correctly. A child is not a small adult, and an adult is not a big child. Our advice is to read to babies and recite Qur'an to them, because babies remember words before they are able to speak.

Unimaginable Perception!
When I was a boy of fourteen, my father was so ignorant I could hardly stand to have the old man around. But when I got to be twenty-one, I was astonished at how much he had learned in seven years.

MARK TWAIN

Aha, Aha! Now I Know....
The children despise their parents until the age of 40, when they suddenly become just like them – thus preserving the system.

QUENTIN CREWE, AMERICAN WRITER

Children's Perceptions Change
Oh, to be only half as wonderful as my child thought I was when he was small, and only half as stupid as my own teenager now thinks I am.

REBECCA RICHARDS
(BROWN 1994)

Parenthood is a Timely Duty
"We are guilty of many errors and many faults, but our worst crime is of abandoning the children, neglecting the fountain of life. Many of the things we need can wait. The child cannot. Right now is the time his bones are being formed; his blood is being made; and his mind is being developed. To him we cannot say tomorrow. He is today."

G.MISTRAL,
NOBEL LAUREATE, CHILE, 1986

PARENTING IS INTERDISCIPLINARY

Parenting requires a complex set of skills (many of which we are unconscious of). Parenting involves several specialties, such as psychology, sociology, economics, medicine, biology, management, and art. Parenting is both an art and a science. As the world around us changes and throws ever more complex challenges in our direction good parenting skills become more needed. Having the highest degrees (whether in the sciences or the arts) does not necessarily produce a happy and contented family. Communication remains an essential component of good and effective parenting.

FATHER AND MOTHER SHOULD ACT AS A TEAM

Teamwork is not easy and is a major challenge for parents. Spouses have to be compatible to work well together. The spouse you choose is not only a wife or a husband, but also a future mother or father. How many of us think this way before getting married? Working as a team requires more than love and sincerity: it requires knowledge, skills, and the right attitude. It is important that parents do not play the blame game when things go wrong, each accusing the other of having caused the problem or not done enough. Their son or daughter is constantly changing, and a successful transition from childhood into adulthood requires a great deal of cooperation between the parents.

PARENTING IS A SKILL THAT REQUIRES GOOD MANAGEMENT OF RESOURCES

It may be possible to hire an accountant to take care of the family finances, a tutor to take care of education, and a nurse to take care of health issues. However, the task of family management cannot be delegated; if the parents cannot manage the family, no one else can. Family management requires parents to allocate love, affection, time, and attention. This is an inseparable part of parenthood, which has to be done by the parents themselves. One need only look at Marxist experiments in Soviet Russia, in which people other than the natural parents or family members took over the parenting task. The same was tried earlier by the Spartans in Greece. The result was a colossal failure for the children concerned. Good management of time and resources becomes even more important for single-parent families, who have to juggle a more intense schedule than those with two parents.

THE CHILDREN'S PERCEPTION OF THEIR PARENTS MAY BE THE OPPOSITE OF WHAT THEIR PARENTS INTEND

Children may interpret their parents' help as interference, their concern and love as babying, and their advice to them as bossiness. Although reality is important, for children, perception is reality. That is why it is important to ask children about their thoughts, feelings, and reactions. Ask you children: Did you like what I did for you?

KNOW WHAT TO TELL CHILDREN AND WHEN

The lessons adults may draw from stories may not necessarily be the same lessons children may draw. In addition, it is extremely tempting for parents to take advantage of children's innocence and ignorance to effect an outcome which makes the parent's life easier. When children are eating pomegranates, for instance, some parents tell them to eat all the seeds without leaving a single one on their clothes or furniture (to avoid stains difficult to remove later on). Instead of sticking to the facts, however, and to ensure the children's full cooperation, some parents resort to embellishment. They tell children that each pomegranate contains a special seed from Paradise (so that the children will then keenly eat every single seed so as not to miss the special gift of the blessed one). Similarly, in many homes, rice grains were cleaned and washed. To ensure that no rice was wasted in the process, mothers would tell their daughters to be very careful not to lose any grains because among them was one special one from Paradise.

These are useful and clever tricks employed

Telling Your Child: What and When?

At what age is this story appropriate? A lion, a wolf, and a fox hunted a cow, a goat, and a rabbit. The lion told the wolf: "Divide the prey." The wolf said: "The cow for you, the goat for me, and the rabbit for the fox." The lion pounced on the wolf and killed him. Then the lion turned to the fox: "How do you divide the prey?" The fox answered: "The rabbit for your breakfast, the goat for your lunch, and the cow for your dinner." The lion asked the fox: "Where did you learn such wisdom?" The fox said: "From the crushed head of the wolf." When such a story is told to children, they will learn fear, cowardice, and hypocrisy. However, if it is told to adults, they will learn how to be cautious and careful. Timing is critical when it comes to telling stories and teaching lessons to a child.

by parents to save time and money for themselves, as well as to teach children discipline, cleanliness, and responsibility. However, parents must be careful to explain to children once the age of discernment is reached, that these were nothing more than myths, thus clearing their minds of any superstition. A more pervasive myth fed to children is that of Santa Claus, who appears at Christmas time and showers children with gifts. It is detrimental if children believe Santa Claus is more important than God.

INADVERTENTLY INSTILLING WRONG CONCEPTS IN CHILDREN

Some well-intentioned parents have described the following incidents:

Incident 1: When Saleem refused to enter the bathroom at kindergarten, the teacher asked him why. He said, "My parents have told me that toilets are inhabited by jinns and Satans. I am scared to be alone with them."

Incident 2: A young boy, Hamid, was puzzled. He had been told that angels did not enter bathrooms, yet he had also been told that two angels were always looking over his shoulders to record all his deeds. Would the two angels then go into the bathroom with him?! He could not figure it out!

Some parents give the wrong explanation to children regarding the prohibition of eating pork. Children extrapolate that pigs are bad animals to be hated and treated with cruelty. Parents fail to explain to children that all animals are the beautiful creations of God, but some are not good to eat. All are created for a good purpose, and we have to be kind to animals and plants.

Some over-zealous and well-intentioned parents convey the wrong message of hating people who commit mistakes. They do not differentiate between the bad action and the actor. Hence, they hate smokers as well as smoking. This causes children to hate people instead of loving them and trying to correct their mistakes. The result is that children may come to think that they are superior to others and become arrogant.

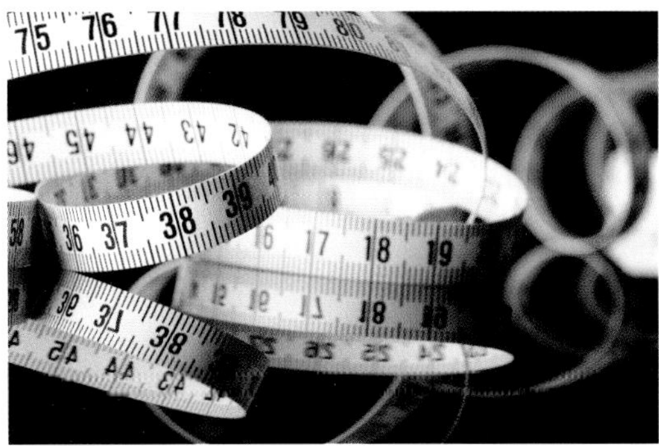

THE CHALLENGE OF CREATING A POSITIVE SELF-IMAGE

Surrounded by myths of the beautiful body, promoted by fashion magazines, Hollywood and glamorous pop stars, children (particularly teenage girls) can easily fall into the trap of eating disorders or an overly vain desire for makeup and clothes. This inflated concern with appearance is fuelled by a commercial media whose message is that 'thin' is beautiful.

For children, the transition from innocent childhood to mimicking adult life is coming at a younger age with all the attendant insecurities of not realizing the ideal of perfection demanded. This puts a great strain on parents who want their children to enjoy their childhood. The importance of instilling sound moral values, confidence, and good character therefore becomes ever more vital. Parents need to be aware of the corruption and premature sexualization of children by consumerism. (Williams 2002)

Children's sense of fulfillment has to come from community attachments, communication and family bonds and not the false sources of fulfillment championed by the media (i.e. money, power and fame).

Parenting Lessons from Moses in the Bible: What Moses Has to Say

Hear, O Israel: The Lord our God, the Lord is one. (Deuteronomy, 6:4)

Lesson 1: Set the right priorities! How do parents teach their children to set priorities? It does not matter what we know, if we do not know what matters. If we forget the ultimate (God), we become slaves to the immediate.

You shall love the Lord your God with all your heart, with all your soul, and with all your strength. (Deuteronomy, 6:5)

Lesson 2: The relationship is more important than the rules. The rule of rules is: Highlight a Few, Important, Relevant, Simple, and Transforming rules. Rules are not bad, yet they change behavior from the outside in, rather than the inside out. However, love changes the heart and motives of a person.

And these words which I command you today shall be in your heart. (Deuteronomy, 6:6)

Lesson 3: Internalize scripture. It is important that parents internalize these words from God themselves before instilling them into their children. These words have to be part of the parents before they can be part of the children. Parents cannot give away what they do not have, so they should practice what they preach. If it does not work at home, they should not try to export it.

You shall teach them diligently to your children. (Deuteronomy, 6:7)

Lesson 4: It is not the quantity of time that matters, but the quantity of quality time. Parents should welcome "teachable moments" and plan for them when they do not come naturally. Parents are prone to give their children everything except the one thing they need most: Time. Our society is work-oriented, not family-oriented. The issue is not prioritizing our schedule but scheduling our priorities.

Talk of them when you sit in your house, when you walk by the way, when you lie down, and when you rise up. (Deuteronomy, 6:7)

Lesson 5: What is worth remembering is worth repeating. Parents should verbalize, emphasize, repeat, and articulate values. It is important to be precise, concise, and simple. Show and Tell: Parents can introduce their children to relatives, leaders, members of Congress, pastors, imams, and guests, who embody the values that parents are teaching.

Conclusion

In spite of all the challenges, however, parenting is enjoyable, doable and full of its own rewards for both parents. The challenges are many (bad peer influences, sex in the media, miscommunication, and mismanagement). The misconceptions, pitfalls and myths are numerous (as we shall see in the next chapter).

Activity

ACTIVITY 26: COMMUNICATING IMPORTANT CONCEPTS

Explain to your children (citing examples of your own) the following:

It does not matter what you know if you do not know what matters (priorities).
The issue is not prioritizing our schedule but scheduling our priorities.
Fill your heart with the love of the Lord so that you can give love to others. You cannot give away what you do not have.

For Parents: Practice what you preach. A picture is worth a 1000 words. A practical example is a 1000 times better than a picture.

CHAPTER 6

Common Misconceptions, Pitfalls, and Myths to Avoid

Introduction

IN THE PREVIOUS CHAPTER WE HAVE STRESSED that the raising of a good child has wider repercussions than simply the parents' own peace of mind and a happy home life; it is a major building block of society and civilization. We have outlined the importance of goals and detailed some of the major challenges that parents should be aware of when raising children. In this chapter we focus on debunking some commonly held assumptions which masquerade as good advice for effective parenting, highlighting some of the pitfalls which parents fall into, and showing how to avoid them. We also debunk some commonly held myths. Another reason for looking at these pitfalls and myths is that a good parenting plan, although it makes the difficult task of parenting easier, is not complete unless it can guide parents over some of the potential stumbling blocks of parenting.

Debunking Commonly Held Misconceptions and Pitfalls

USING INHERITED METHODS BLINDLY

Most of us learn certain habits from our parents. These habits are not always useful, and some may be outdated or even harmful. One mother said: "The moment I was pregnant, I became my mother." Some parents, out of humility and gratitude, assert that their parents did the best job in rearing them. The experience for many of us will have been to receive much love and care from our well-wishing parents, may God bless their souls. However, not all of them would have possessed the means, knowledge, or skills, needed for constructive parenting.

BLIND IMITATION OF OTHERS

Blind imitation is the wrong way of parenting. Every child is special in some regard and what may be good for one child may not be good for another. Parents need to try to find out what is the best way to deal with their children. When consulting with other parents, they have to be aware of the various styles of parenting being practiced, for they differ considerably in the usefulness of their application to their own specific case. Some parents are permissive or democratic, whereas others are strict and dictatorial.

A NEW SURPRISE EVERY STEP OF THE WAY

"New fathers quickly learn that raising children is a kind of desperate improvisation."

(BILL COSBY, ACTOR)

"Parenting was not something you learned how to do; it was something you just did when the children arrived."

(ELKIND 1995)

FULFILLING UNFULFILLED WISHES THROUGH OUR CHILDREN

This is a common source of wrong parental behavior. There are parents who seek to fulfill through their children goals that they failed to achieve themselves, pushing their children to realize them. For instance, a parent who dreamt of being a doctor or engineer and did not become one, may dictate to his/her child to go into medicine or engineering, even though the child may not have the desire to do so. Children are not just an extension of their parents. They have their own independent wishes and ambitions.

It is tempting for parents to see their children as extensions of themselves. They try to correct their own flaws through their children,

even to right the wrongs done to their own parents in the past. If the parents were never good golf players they want their children to be champion golfers. If the parents are poor at mathematics, they want their children to be like Einstein. If the parents failed to become politicians, they want their children to win every political race. Parenthood is not a second childhood, and children are not miniature versions of their parents. From the beginning, they are individuals who must be respected for who they are and not what they are meant to become.

DELEGATING PARENTHOOD

It is often assumed that parenting can be carried out by the mother or the father. In fact, the father cannot replace the mother, nor can the mother replace the father, just as the right hand cannot replace the left hand nor the left replace the right. Each parent has a specific and crucial role. Nor can grandparents, other relatives, or babysitters take over the role of parenthood. These are all inadequate substitutes for the parents.

ASSUMING LOGIC IS ENOUGH WITH CHILDREN

Relationships between parents and children are not based on rational thinking alone, for habits and emotions enter the equation. Parents cannot convince children to eat fruit and vegetables by saying: "Eat it; it is good for you, it provides essential vitamins and minerals to stay healthy and strong." Although reasoning may be necessary, it is not enough.

ASSUMING ONE CAN WIN A WAR AGAINST ONE'S CHILDREN

Although parents may win some battles here and there, eventually the children will retaliate with revenge and hatred toward them. Parents may prevent by force their 10-year-old daughter from exercising her wild wishes, yet when she reaches the age of 13, she may run away from home and become pregnant, thus winning the war that her parents started against her. Their son may steal a car and cause a major accident. Parents only have one alternative: to win their children to their side. How is this done? By listening, discussing, loving, reasoning and understanding. It is a delicate task that requires patience and effective communication.

PARENTS RELYING ON THE FACT THAT THEY ARE BIGGER AND IN CONTROL

Children know that they will also eventually be strong. If parents use their strength to intimidate and bully their children, making them afraid of them, then children may use the same behavioral tactics when they reach adulthood. If the parents make their children feel that they are all on the same side, then the children will have a healthy relationship with others. They will realize that the parents' strength adds to their own strength. Parents who force their children do not realize that if they had used love and persuasion instead of coercion, they could have achieved the same results, perhaps even better. If love or force can achieve the same results, then why insist on force?

Just Treat them as Sons and Daughters
"You don't raise heroes, you raise sons. And if you treat them like sons, they will turn out to be heroes, even if it is just in your own eyes."
(SCHIRRA 2001)

PARENTS ASSUMING THEY CAN TREAT ALL THEIR CHILDREN IN THE SAME WAY

Parents may assume that all of their children are similar. This is not the case. Children in a family are like flowers in a bouquet; there is always one determined to face in the opposite direction to the way the arranger desires. Children differ in their tolerance of stress, in their capacity to learn, in their level of confidence in social situations, and in their hobbies. Parents soon become aware of the specialness of each child – of her or his difference from every other child that they know and from children about whom they have read. It is amazing how siblings can be very different. Some differences may be due to differences in sex and gender role socialization.

TREATING THE CHILD AS A SMALL ADULT

Parents may wrongly think that a child should be treated like a small adult. Al-Jarajrah (1988, in Arabic) explains that a child is not the same thing as a small man, as the Greeks and Romans believed. He asserts that the most crucial phase of our life is childhood. Humanity misunderstood the intricacies of the child's world until the mid-twentieth century, when Jean Piaget spoke of the cognitive development of children. The prevalent trend before then had been to follow the Graeco-Roman pagan belief of considering the child to be a miniature adult, and as a result, to apply the same ideas which applied to adults, to children. They are in fact entirely unequal ($\neq$): Child $\neq$ Small Adult, Adult $\neq$ Big Child.

In reality parents need to understand the child's psychology, which is not easy. It is easier to understand the biological needs of the baby (i.e. if a baby is hungry you feed it, if it is tired you rest it, or if it has filled its diaper you clean it). The psychological needs of the baby are harder to understand. It is difficult enough for adults to understand their own adult psychology, even though they may know themselves better than others.

Children are Training their Parents
"The value of marriage is not that adults produce children but that children produce adults."
(PETER DE VRIES IN COLOROSO 2002)

BUYING CHILDREN WHATEVER THEY WANT

Parents should not rush to buy their children whatever they want; they should not indulge their child's every whim. Parents are not there to wait on their children hand and foot but to teach them, to give them chores, and to help them understand that life is about giving and taking. This pitfall happens almost imperceptibly as parents become accustomed to buying things for the baby and, before they realize what is happening, are inundated by demands for clothes, CDs, DVDs, and toys by the child who is now older.

Some Myths of Parenthood Debunked

Raising children needs to be sufficiently romanticized so as to attract a sufficient number of spouses into the full-time role of parents, because society cannot continue without new members. Some parents may believe that child rearing is all fun, that good parents will produce good children, that love and intuition are enough for successful parenting, that children will appreciate the sacrifices parents make for them, that parenting comes naturally, and that family values are easy to instill. These beliefs do not reflect the realities of parenthood. Below we have summarized and paraphrased some of the widely held beliefs of parenthood (myths) that are not supported by facts. (Knox and Schacht 1997)

Myth 1: Rearing children is always fun. Future parents see television commercials of young parents playing with their children in the park, and they think that this is what child rearing is all about: endless fun. The truth is somewhat different.

The idea of fun implies that one can take it or leave it, whereas parents must stay with the children and continue to look after them, whether they are enjoying the experience or not. Once they have begun, they cannot quit when they feel like it.

Myth 2: Good parents inevitably produce good children. Many people assume that children who turn out "wrong" (drug users, thieves, prostitutes, or scam artists) have parents who did not do a good job. We tend to put all the blame on parents when children fail. However, many good parents who have done their best may have children who do not turn out well (for instance, think of Prophet Noah's son). Conversely, it is also often the case that parents may be bad whilst the children turn out to be good (for instance think of the prophetic cases of Moses, who was brought up in the house of the Pharaoh, and Abraham, whose father turned against him).

PARENTING IS REALLY FRUSTRATING, SOMETIMES

There are times when parenthood seems nothing but feeding the mouth that bites you.

Myth 3: Children are appreciative. Most parents think that if they give the children all they need, the children will recognize the sacrifices of the parents. This is not always true. Parents who give their children love, care, and nurturing may not be appreciated by their children. Some parents assume that their children will appreciate them if they give them material things (like clothes, games, computers, and cars). That assumption is frequently wrong. Some children think that they are entitled to everything that their parents are giving them, and feel no responsibility to appreciate what their parents have done for them.

Myth 4: Parenting comes naturally. Some people believe that there is no need for formal training in parenting. In many countries there are more driver education courses than parenting courses.

There are clear differences between novice and expert mothers. Novice mothers are less able to understand their children's goals and needs, and do not know what behavior to expect of the children as they grow older. Expert mothers, on the other hand, understand better the way children think and behave. Without training, people tend to duplicate the mistakes of their own parents.

Man Proposes, But God Disposes

You may plan very well for your first baby, but when it arrives, everything unplanned happens.

Myth 5: Family values are easy to instill. To many, family values mean the following:

- Respect for elders and other people.
- An appreciation of differences between people.
- The ability to calmly discuss differences and find cooperative ways to resolve them.
- Sticking with something good, even when it is difficult to do so.
- Making and keeping commitments.
- Maintaining personal integrity at all times.
- Helping others and serving the community.

Obviously, all the above and many more values cannot be easily taught.

Myth 6: Intuition, common sense, and love are enough. Parents need education and skills as well. Parenthood is an endless series of small events, periodic conflicts, and sudden crises, which call for timely responses. Responses bring consequences, since each response affects the child's personality, for better or for worse. Correctly responding to a child's needs is a skill that must be learned.

A child's character is shaped by experiences with different people and situations. Character traits cannot be taught arbitrarily. No one can teach loyalty by lectures, courage by correspondence, and manhood or womanhood by osmosis. Character building requires knowledge of child psychology and the phases of child development. Parents want their teenagers to have compassion, commitment, and courage. To do this, parents need to learn the right methods to translate desired ideals into successful outcomes.

Insanity and Wisdom!

"Insanity is hereditary; you get it from your children."

Sam Levenson (Brown 1994)

"The art of being wise is the art of knowing what to overlook."

William James (Lazear 1993)

FIRST HAND EXPERIENCE

PARENTING CAN BE LEARNT BY FIRST-HAND EXPERIENCE, BUT EXPERIENCE IS A HARD TEACHER: SHE GIVES THE TEST FIRST, AND THE LESSONS AFTERWARDS. TRY TO RECITE THE FOLLOWING SUPPLICATION: "OH GOD, MAY I NOT HAVE TO LEARN EVERY LESSON IN LIFE FROM FIRST-HAND EXPERIENCE."

Myth 7: The Misconception of Self-Martyrdom. Some parents believe (out of their good feelings) that they should burn themselves out for the sake of their children. Furthermore, they think that religion requires them to do just that. The fact is that wealth and children are to be considered a joy and ornament for parents, not a form of torture and suffering.

> *Wealth and children are an adornment of this world's life: but good deeds, the fruit of which endures forever, are of far greater merit in your Sustainer's sight, and a far better source of hope.* (Qur'an 18:46)

Parents, particularly mothers, are not supposed to enact unlimited sacrifice for their children, acting like servants for their needs. Mothers should be helped and served as well. They have to take care of themselves first, then the children.

Myth 8: The Top Responsibility for the Parent Is His/Her Relationship with the Children. On the contrary, the first responsibility is to one's own self, not one's relations with others.

> *On a Day when everyone will [want to] flee from his brother, and from his mother and father, and from his spouse and his children: on that Day, everyone will have their [own] concerns.* (Qur'an 80: 34–37)

Strike a balance between yourself, your children, and your Creator. The Prophet ﷺ said:

> Your spouse has a right over you, your body has a right over you, your Creator has a right over you, so give each their right. (AL-BUKHĀRĪ)

This includes parents taking care of their health, enjoyment, lawful desires, friendships and vacations.

Activities

ACTIVITY 27: DIFFICULT PERSONAL EXPERIENCES

From your own experience as a parent, can you relate why parenthood is difficult and how? Do this in a family meeting with your children. It may open their eyes to the hard realities of life.

ACTIVITY 28: DISCUSSION OF THOUGHTS ON PARENTING

Explain these verses in a family setting, with all the members present, then discuss your thoughts, detailing both the sufferings and the joys of raising children. Cite some actual stories of people you know!

> One father said: "Children are created to punish their parents," while the Qur'an says:
>
> *Wealth and children are an adornment of this world's life: but good deeds, the fruit of which endures forever, are of far greater merit in your Sustainer's sight, and a far better source of hope.* (Qur'an 18:46)
>
> *O you who believe! Truly, among your spouses and your children are [some that are] enemies to yourselves: so beware of them! But if you forgive and overlook, and cover up [their faults], verily Allah is Oft-Forgiving, Most Merciful.* (Qur'an 64:14)
>
> *Your riches and your children may be but a trial: but with Allah is the highest Reward.* (Qur'an 64:15)

CHAPTER 7

When Things Go Wrong

Introduction

THERE IS NO ultimate guarantee of success for any relationship and this includes the parent-child one. Things can and do go wrong. When you looked with pride on your beautiful new born baby, no doubt you were filled with hope and optimism. You prayed for the wonderful times you would be having with your child, and you expected love, obedience, and respect. You thought to yourself: "What a rewarding relationship this is going to be!"

Fifteen years later, you may think to yourself: "What on earth has gone wrong?" You did everything you had to do, you did your best, and you tried your utmost to raise your child with love, discipline, and faith. But how is it that your offspring has turned out to be a teenage Monster, with a capital M?

One parent was shocked to notice that his brilliant son who was a straight A student with excellent health actually had an emotional deficiency. He was immature psychologically. Some parents may not notice that their child has an emotional problem, particularly if the child is doing well in school and is normal physically and mentally. In fact, s/he may be top of the class, but lacking in emotional ability. A clue or a casual comment to the parents could come from teachers, friends, or relatives, and it should be considered seriously by the parents, who have to take remedial action.

One mother says: "We live in a fine suburb, our children went to the best schools, and we spent a lot of time with them as a family: camping, skiing, and swimming. Our son is now in prison. He held up a local grocery store one night, and got shot in the leg. We have stopped asking ourselves what we did wrong. He is twenty-three years old, and drifted into friendships with a group of guys who just decided they would steal one night."

This chapter examines what can be done when things go wrong. It is better to focus on how to handle the difficulties than to dwell inordinately on the past or question where we as parents failed. It examines issues of anger, tantrums, bullying, and teenage misbehavior. It also examines open communication as a vital tool to overcome the issues faced. There is no problem, no matter how big, which cannot be resolved.

When things do go wrong, which odds are they will, this should not automatically be equated with failure on the part of parents. It is not necessarily your fault or a deliberate error on your part. Your son or daughter is constantly changing, and the transition from childhood into adulthood causes friction. You should not blame yourself or your spouse. Parents need not be daunted by all the hardships that parenting entails. Obstacles can be overcome with good parenting, and it can and will be a rewarding experience. One's hopes and prayers, as well as the acquisition of knowledge, skills, and guidance from other parents, are requisite guarantees for success.

Anger, Rebelliousness, Tantrums, and Tears

Children are learning and growing all the time, and one of the things they will test is parental control and power. This can become a battle of wills. No amount of lecturing by the parents will stop headstrong children, who will scream and disrupt the whole household if they can to have their own way; or they may cry and cry endlessly until they are given attention. Parents can be brought to the verge of tears, and the easiest thing is to just give in. This is the wrong thing to do, for, in the long term, it reinforces the idea that this demand for attention will always work. Shouting, beating, and forcing children will not solve the problem either.

The solution is an intelligent method of discipline that will teach the children to respect your rules and leave control in your hands.

A FEW WAYS TO DISCIPLINE AN UNRULY CHILD

Discipline upgrades behavior, punishment suppresses behavior.

- Speak in a normal voice, emphasizing the consequences of bad behavior. The focus of the child should be on the consequences of non-obedience. If this does not work, then concentrate on voice and eye contact. This is the first step before any action is taken. Use a firm, calm voice, and do not shout.
- Let the child know you are serious and look directly into his eyes. Remind him a few times clearly and slowly. If he does not listen, approach closer to him, maintaining the voice and eye contact. Repeat calmly again.
- If this does not work, then apply the rule of consequences: give the child a list of things that will happen (consequences) if they do not listen. Consequences must be followed through to enforce respect, otherwise children will not take you seriously if you warn them. If they are screaming, whining, expressing anger, do not respond the same way. Inform the child calmly of the consequences and make sure he understands how long he has to obey. Give him time to comply, and do not try to demand immediate results. Once this is done, walk away.
- There are several "consequences" parents can apply. Observe your children, find out what they treasure, and what means a lot to them, and confiscate this for a time. It may be a favorite toy, or a trip somewhere. Once the child regrets and/or calms down, reward him with great affection for being good. You may have to follow up one consequence with another to reinforce the point if the child continues misbehaving.
- Designate a "naughty area" where s/he is to stay whilst you calmly continue unruffled with your work, until the child apologizes. Forgive him instantly and then forget about the incident quickly to change the mood. The idea of this "area," whatever name you choose to give it, is that it takes attention off the child and s/he feels the loss of privilege of being with others. This time is not for conversation, the child needs to be left alone. The spot you choose should also be a boring one or somewhere quiet, but not the child's bedroom. If he is sent to this area, set the length of time he must stay there. If he tries to talk in defense or in anger, ignore this.
- Reward children when they behave well. Do not bribe them to behave well or when they are throwing a tantrum. This is an inappropriate practice from which children learn nothing useful.

Bullying: Your Child and You

Bullying can affect anyone's child and spotting the signs early on can save much heartache and stress. Bullying occurs when your child is taunted, harassed or attacked. Parents need to be alert because many children are afraid to tell their parents when they are bullied. Look out for unusual behavior from your child and respond calmly when something is wrong. Bullying Online (http://www.bullying.co.uk), is a website dedicated to tackling bullying. It states, "Around 16 children in the UK kill themselves every year due to distress over bullying. Their schools often say they had no idea what was going on. But the bullies know exactly what they've been doing – and so do their friends. It's too late to have regrets when someone has died, or been made so ill they need medical treatment".

THE 'BULLYING ONLINE' WEBSITE LISTS SOME SIGNS THAT YOUR CHILD IS BEING BULLIED.

- Torn clothes
- 'Losing' money
- Falling out with previously good friends
- Being moody and bad tempered
- Being quiet and withdrawn
- Wanting to always stay at home
- Being aggressive with brothers and sisters
- Doing less well at schoolwork
- Having trouble sleeping
- Being anxious
- Coming home with cuts and bruises
- Asking for stolen possessions to be replaced

If Your Child is Being Bullied, What Next?

Most children will not want to talk about being bullied. The way parents handle this issue can be crucial, so not overreacting or demanding answers from your child is the key. Asking questions like "how was school today?" can be helpful in extracting vital information. However, many children may not want to talk about their school day and view questioning as intrusive. Noting unusual behavior is important.

Children need to feel comfortable and open enough to talk with their parents about things such as bullying, or general unhappiness in their lives. Open communication is important to establish in early childhood. Having such an open relationship with your children enables them to be open about their fears and to feel they can approach you about their problems, saving much time and effort. Demanding your child to tell you "what's wrong" will achieve nothing if your child feels uncomfortable discussing such matters with you.

SEVERAL STEPS WHICH CAN BE IMPLEMENTED REGARDING BULLYING

- Most schools have anti-bullying policies. Approaching your child's school should be the first step. Arranging to meet with your child's teacher to discuss this issue is the next step.
- Do not teach the child to retaliate, because ultimately, this is not the solution and may cause more trouble. Hitting another student is not likely to end the problem, and it could cause your child to be suspended or expelled.
- Keep calm as a parent, and do not panic, or rush to contact the parents of the child bullying your child. Although this is usually a parent's first response, sometimes it makes matters worse. It is better for school officials to contact the parents of the child who did the bullying.
- Speak regularly with your child and the school to see whether the bullying has stopped. If not, then contact the school authorities again.
- Help your child become more resilient to bullying by building up his/her confidence. Martial arts and self defense classes may facilitate this.
- Teach your child safety strategies. Teach him/her how to seek help from an adult when feeling threatened by a bully. Talk about whom s/he should ask for help and role-play what s/he should say. Assure your child that reporting bullying is not something to feel guilty about.
- Ask teachers to find things for the child to do during break and lunch time in a safe place.
- Consult websites such as (http://www.stopbullyingnow.hrsa.gov) and learn how other parents have coped and the strategies they have used.

Teenagers: Critique of the Notion of Adolescence

The adolescent years will perhaps be the most challenging stage of bringing up children. Dr. Imad al-Dean Ahmed argues that in an environment of freedom, adolescents can be leaders. Adolescence is defined as "the period between puberty and adulthood." Yet in early societies, puberty was considered the beginning of adulthood. The revealed religions have enshrined this fact in their rituals and laws. In Judaism, the youth at a bar mitzvah proclaims, "Today, I am a man." In Islam, a girl becomes a woman with the onset of menstruation and ritual prayer is obligatory on puberty. The adolescent years are a time in which young adults need to be given the responsibilities of adults to help them achieve maturity.

In the modern era, formal schooling for all has replaced the apprenticeship models of earlier societies. In order to force the general population into the formal educational system, it has been necessary to deny them the possibility of acting as adults. Even apprentice positions are not allowed in many places until the end of formal schooling, namely, high school (17–18 years old) or college (19–22 years old). Forcing children into a school system that acts *in loco parentis* (in place of parents) has required pretending that adolescents are children rather than immature adults. Further enshrined in law, not coincidentally, is the pretense that all children mature at the age of 18 or 21. In fact, children mature physically at about age 19, although they usually mature mentally earlier, while emotionally, people can mature at a wide range of ages (and some never seem to do so).

In the past, treating adolescents as adults encouraged their mental and leadership abilities and enhanced their emotional maturity. The modern model, treating adolescents as children, fosters dependency and insults their sense of self-worth. In traditional societies, 15 year olds participated in teaching, in business, in civil society, in warfare, and got married. In modern society, they are treated as younger children. For serious scholarship they must wait until college, if not graduate school.

This delay in giving adolescents adult responsibilities has extracted a heavy price. It is the cause of many of the problems society confronts with regard to its young people. In the first place, not all adolescents are suited to study. There is an intense resentment among most adolescents towards the school system into which they are confined. Those who are suited to scholarship resent being treated like children. Those denied from commerce by law until age 16 may engage in illegal commerce (such as drug dealing). Those who might otherwise have sought a place in civil society may take positions in gangs. Those who might have done well at less formal or more advanced studies may sit frustrated in their school classes. Many are diagnosed with "attention deficit disorder" because their minds are roaming elsewhere (not focused on the assignments which they find too boring to hold their attention). Additionally, young men and women, who would have in another era indulged their raging hormones within the sanctity of marriage, do not abstain from sex owing to the delay of marriage, but instead have children out of wedlock – or avoid children by a visit to the abortion clinic.

The legal remedies to these problems fall outside the scope of this book. However, it is important for parents not to make the mistakes that modern society has made. Do not treat young adults like children. Treat them as you would treat young colleagues at your place of employment. Be aware that they are in need of guidance and experience, but be equally aware that they need respect, responsibility, and mentorship. Encourage them to take on as much responsibility as possible. Give them some financial responsibility too: a Saturday job, perhaps, where they become accustomed to the world of work and earning an income.

Anger in Our Teenagers and in Ourselves

ANGER IS ONE LETTER AWAY FROM DANGER

Anger in teenagers is perhaps the most difficult emotion for parents to cope with. Linda Lebelle (Focus Adolescent Services) explains and analyzes the issue, using the following two examples to illustrate the case:

Example 1: Karen is a 9th-grader and has been feeling that nothing is worth it anymore. As hard as she tries, she just doesn't seem to fit in. The day before she had tried out for the school play, but when she got on stage, she froze up and just stopped in the middle of her audition. Now, everyone in the school must know about it and Karen is sure they're laughing at her. She'll never let them know how bad she feels. She knows what they're thinking and they're right – she isn't good enough and she'll never fit in. Karen hates them all.

Example 2: Chris punched his fist into the bedroom wall. But it wasn't enough. He picked up his soda can and threw it into the hall. The brown sugary liquid dripped down the walls and onto the carpeting. "You can't make me…!" he screamed. "I'm not going anywhere with you! I'll do what I want!" Chris ran down the stairs and out the front door. His father ran after him, yelling at him to get back in the house, but he had already gotten into his car and sped away. Chris was so mad at his father. He had better things to do than go visit family. He and his friends had plans, and his father wasn't going to run his life. He knew he'd feel better when he smoked some weed.

What do these young people have in common?

They're battling with anger. They are not getting what they want and things are not the way they think they should be. They are feeling intense displeasure or antagonism toward someone or something that comes with the realization that things are not always in their control.

Anger is a feeling, not a behavior.

Anger takes many forms – from indignation and resentment to rage and fury – and it is the expressions of the forms of anger – the behavior – that we see. Karen represses her anger and withdraws. Chris is defiant and destroys property. They will continue their behavior, or it may escalate, until they decide to look within themselves to the roots of their anger.

Anger can be harmful or healthy.

Anger is a frightening emotion. Its negative expressions can include physical and verbal violence, prejudice, malicious gossip, antisocial behavior, sarcasm, addictions, withdrawal, and psychosomatic disorders. This can devastate lives, destroy relationships, harm others, disrupt work, cloud effective thinking, affect physical health, and ruin futures.

But there is a positive aspect; it can show us that a problem exists, as anger is usually a secondary emotion brought on by fear. It can motivate us to resolve those things that are not working in our lives and help us face our issues and deal with the underlying reasons for the anger, specifically:

REASONS FOR ANGER

Abuse	**Anxiety**	**Substance Abuse**	**Grief**
Depression	**Alcohol Abuse**	**Trauma**	

Being the Parent of an Angry Teenager Brings up the Anger in Ourselves

Teenagers face a lot of emotional issues. They're faced with questions of identity, separation, relationships, and purpose. The relationship between teens and their parents is also changing as teens become more and more independent.

This can bring about frustration and confusion that leads to anger and a pattern of reactive behavior for both parents and teens. Unless we work to change our own behavior, we cannot help teens change theirs. We need to *respond rather than react* to each other and to situations. The intention is not to deny the anger, but to control that emotion and express it in a proactive way.

What Can We Do for Our Teenager and for Ourselves?

Listen to your teen and focus on feelings. Try to understand the situation from your child's perspective; be empathetic. Blaming and accusing only builds up more walls and ends all communication. Tell them how you feel, stick to facts, and deal with the present moment. Show that you care and show your love. Work towards a solution where everyone wins. Remember that feeling angry should not result in violent behavior.

Seek professional help for your teen, yourself, and your family when there is violence, chronic hostility, depression, or a risk of suicide.

A Few Principles of Good Communication

In an ideal world everything runs smoothly and according to plan: in the real world things go wrong. The goals parents will have set, the principles they will have applied, and the efforts they will have put into the family unit, will fail unless there is proper communication. When things go wrong do not allow levels of anger, frustration or disappointment to rise. Think calmly through the issues and practice good communication.

There are a few principles of good communication that can be applied. These will resolve many of the temper tantrums and power struggles which will begin to surface as children move into the pre-schooler, school age, and later, teenage years.

Allow your children to talk and listen to them without being condescending or impatient. Encourage them to talk about their day, to tell a story, or to discuss a problem. Try not to interrupt. The oral traditions of the past (in which storytelling and discussion were integral aspects of community and family life) have now been replaced with the visual traditions of today (TV, movies, and video games). Talking has many advantages; it gives children the confidence to express themselves, makes them more articulate, and inculcates a natural ability to discuss trivial or serious issues with parents. Although you as the parent are often tired and may find it difficult to talk, nevertheless, talking is well worth it. The child you talk with will grow and relate to you as a human being rather than the person who

We accuse others of "talking too much," but do we ever accuse them of "listening too much?" Listening is caring. The louder we talk, the quicker our children switch off.

simply feeds and clothes them. It will allow children to feel connected to parents and the home. Good communication will teach children the behavior and respect required when interacting with others, particularly respect for the parent. Do not put the children down, or make them feel stupid. Be aware of your own behavior: it should be polite, attentive, and controlled. The idea is to make children confident and secure, (two aspects of personality which they will carry into their adult lives).

Initiate intellectual discussions with your children. Debate issues and compare opinions. This will teach children critical thinking and develop their intellectual stamina. Do not underestimate the children's intelligence or negate their views on subjects.

A good time to talk is during dinner. If parents initiate a habit of keeping the television switched off, and eating food together on a table or on the floor, they will make life much easier when the children are older. TV takes attention away and blocks the development of deeper relationships, especially at meal times, which are a good opportunity to generate and experience family bonding.

Do not lose control of a situation by losing your temper, or resort to fear tactics to control your children. It is better to avoid communication until you have calmed down.

It still happens, even in the twenty-first century, that some mothers frighten their children with imaginary monsters (to prevent them from doing certain things such as going out at night). Mothers have invented monsters (or misrepresented the jinn) under different names (such as *dujjerah*, *su'luwwah* or *dāmiyyah*, an imaginary jinn-type creature completely wrapped in a black gown and having the feet of a donkey) to use fear as a form of control. Although these scare tactics keep children at home at night and away from possible physical harm, these tactics also backfire by building irrational fear in the minds of children. They may grow up fearful of the dark, being alone, small rooms, animals, thunder, lightning, and strangers. Although later on as adults they will come to discover that these fairytale monsters do not really exist, the emotional and psychological damage will have already been done. One possible reason why these practices are resorted to is the inability of parents to engage in deep analysis, and then lack of patience to develop viable alternatives.

Talk to children at their level, rather than towering above them like a giant. Be affectionate with them, place your hand lightly in theirs as you talk, or touch them with love, so they constantly feel a bond with you, and become used to expressing their feelings.

Activities

ACTIVITY 29: QUESTIONS AND RESPONSES FOR PARENTS AND TEENAGERS

The first step to identifying and managing anger is to look within ourselves. Parents and teens should sit together and ask these questions of themselves to bring about self-awareness. The point here is to initiate discussion rather than giving the right answers:

Where does anger come from?
What situations bring out this feeling of anger?
Do my thoughts begin with absolutes such as "must," "should," "always", "never?"
Are my expectations unreasonable?
What unresolved conflict am I facing?
Am I reacting to hurt, loss, or fear?
Am I aware of anger's physical signals (e.g., clenching fists, shortness of breath, sweating)?
How do I choose to express my anger?
To whom or what is my anger directed?
Am I using anger as a way to isolate myself, or to intimidate others?
Am I communicating effectively?
Am I focusing on what has been done to me rather than what I can do?
How am I accountable for what I'm feeling?
How am I accountable for how my anger shows up?
Do my emotions control me, or do I control my emotions?

ACTIVITY 30: A PROBLEM-SOLVING ACTIVITY

Gather two or three couples to discuss how you would tackle the issues of the young man in the example below. Then, compare your thoughts with the Prophet's ﷺ approach.

A young man came asking the Prophet ﷺ to permit him to practice fornication. The Companions present were shocked and started to scold him. The Prophet ﷺ said, "Bring him closer to me." After he had sat down, he asked him five consecutive questions: "Would you like it [adultery or fornication] for your mother, daughter, sister, paternal aunt, or maternal aunt?!" To each of the five questions, the young man answered: "I swear, by God, No! Oh, Messenger of Allah, may Allah make me a shield for you!" The Prophet ﷺ answered every response, "Neither do people like it for their mothers, daughters, sisters or aunts!" Then the Prophet ﷺ laid his hand on him and prayed, "Oh, Allah, forgive his sins, purify his heart, and protect his sex organ." (Aḥmad). The young man never contemplated the idea of fornication after that!

The Prophet ﷺ communicated with the young man, appealing to his dignity and self-respect, and helped him to develop effective self-control. Scolding, shouting or threatening him with punishment and Hell fire would not have helped the situation.

We can see that this method of treatment shows the difference that exists between theoretical knowledge and a deep psychological understanding of human emotions. The young man was seeking a solution while exploring his sexuality. The Prophet ﷺ did not preach to him about the sins that lead to punishment and Hell; instead, he appealed to his pure innate dignity and conscience. He used the psychological approach to achieve moral and religious objectives. This is not an isolated case study, but a school of thought rooted in a sound methodology focusing on the problem-solving approach to child development.

PART TWO

Child Development

CHAPTER 8

Character Building Cannot Wait

Introduction

Once parents decide to focus on good parenting, they need to begin character education immediately, for it is the foundation on which all else is built. The reward will be priceless.

CHARACTER BUILDING STARTS in infancy during the formative years of child development. It is precisely during these valuable stages of childhood that many fundamental aspects of one's personality traits are formed. Unfortunately, however, most of the leadership-training programs which exist are directed toward adults, not children. Human development literature in Muslim countries is primarily addressed to adults in high school or to those at college level and beyond.

What is meant by "character building?" Basic traits (like courage, love, freedom, honesty, responsibility, and creativity) constitute the essential components of the human personality and start developing from early infancy. Once set, they are difficult to undo, replace, or build later on in life. It is these characteristics which form the basis of one's future personality, and therefore, parents need to spend time and effort in nurturing them to the best of their ability. Although knowledge, experience, and skills are all important qualities for success, they come later and can be developed as children grow into adulthood. They serve an important function, contributing to the further refinement of the basic traits, to guide and enrich people to become better and wiser human beings. If the basic characteristics form the "hardware" of a person's personality, we may term education and faith the "software".

Someone who is a coward will not suddenly become brave later on in adulthood by simply taking a course on courage. Similarly, someone who is full of hate and cruelty will not suddenly become truly loving and caring by reading books on love and compassion. A liar does not automatically become honest and trustworthy by listening to advice on honesty. For most people, once their basic personality traits are formed (defining who they are and how they behave) it would be difficult to change them or to reshape their "hardware". The easiest and best way to instill the finest qualities is during the formative years of childhood.

The examples of Abū Bakr al-Ṣiddīq, 'Umar ibn al-Khaṭṭāb, Khālid ibn al-Walīd, and other Companions are notable. They teach us that the qualities of courage, trust, honesty, and leadership were already present in the character of these men, having been nurtured during their childhood. Islam complemented this good character by affirming the notable elements of their personality and adding faith, wisdom, and knowledge. Islam was able to inspire them with the sense of a civilized mission and imbue them with a new meaning, world view, and purpose to their lives. The firmness of their character did not diminish after they had embraced the new religion but continued to grow in strength. The Qur'an explains this phenomenon, applicable to the prophets as well as other human beings, when it mentions that once man has grown up and attained middle age God grants him knowledge and wisdom.

When he [Moses] reached full age, and was firmly established [in life], We bestowed on him wisdom and knowledge: For thus do We reward those who do good.
(Qur'an 28:14)

The Prophet ﷺ said:
People are like minerals [or metals, having their own character]; the best of people in the [pre-Islamic] age of ignorance (*jāhiliyyah*) are the best of them in [the age of] Islam, if they understand [and comprehend]. (AL-BUKHĀRĪ AND MUSLIM)

A good police officer and a bad criminal both need to possess courage and loyalty to be effective in their performance and useful to their groups. However, the police officer uses these characteristics to serve society, whereas the criminal uses them for harmful ends. Although courage and loyalty are necessary, they need to be value-oriented to be beneficial, otherwise they can be harmful and destructive.

Islam normally gives general guidance on most issues, yet it offers a more detailed road map when it comes to the family. Islam outlines a comprehensive family system and gives guidance on choosing a spouse, getting engaged, and writing the marriage contract (including the role of guardians and witnesses). Islam also gives guidance on sexual conduct, pregnancy, abortion, delivery, naming the baby, lineage, breastfeeding, baby care, wills and guardianship, education and training, gender differences and similarities, inheritance, child rights and duties, delinquency, care of orphans, adoption, widowhood, parenting and child raising, divorce, alimony, waiting period for marriage (after divorce or the demise of the husband), cessation period, menstruation, sibling relations, extended family, family bonds, grandparents, grandchildren, neighbors, and the dress code.

Parenting has to be regarded as a futuristic endeavor because it is responsible for preparing the high quality cadres of society, including its creative thinkers, wise scholars, hard workers, brave soldiers, strong athletes, and the great world leaders of human civilizations.

The following sections help parents focus on character building and educational development programs.

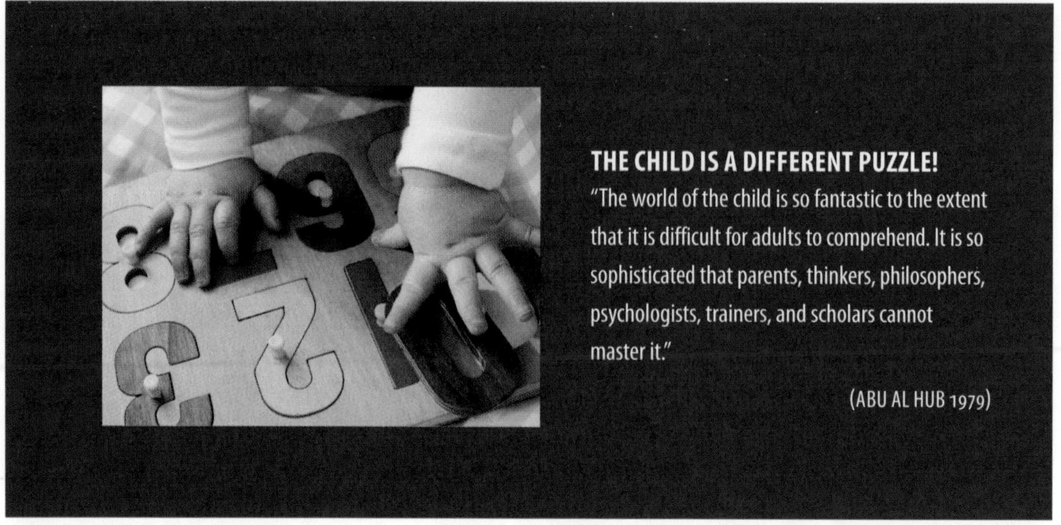

THE CHILD IS A DIFFERENT PUZZLE!
"The world of the child is so fantastic to the extent that it is difficult for adults to comprehend. It is so sophisticated that parents, thinkers, philosophers, psychologists, trainers, and scholars cannot master it."

(ABU AL HUB 1979)

Phases of Development

This section will deal with phases of human development necessary to allow parents to visualize the gradual development of their child from one stage to the next and to thereby understand better the peculiar needs of each stage. Whilst outlining the development status of the human body and mind during the years of growth, parents will also be shown how to capitalize on several aspects relative to each stage to optimize the outcome of parenting.

For example, some parents force their children to eat more, but they resist defiantly. Later on, their appetite suddenly increases and they begin to eat more, voluntarily. This is not due to the parents' insistence, but to natural growing up. Similarly, teenagers may suddenly revolt against parents and the environment, yet, as they grow up, this attitude subsides owing to the natural phases of development. Doctors advise parents to be fully aware when development milestones are reached. Not reaching these milestones at a certain age should sound an alarm that there might be a serious health problem.

A parent's best protection is to be well informed. They should not be afraid to ask their family physician for explanations. Nor should they be worried if their child does not reach each stage on time. Babies insist upon developing at their own pace. Although the development of a child follows a general human genetic pattern, it is also unique for each individual. To be successful, parents should set aside their dreams for their children and help them attain their own dreams. Children are not like their parents, for they possess an independent personality. Parents are advised to let reality be reality and adopt the pace of nature whose secret is patience.

How Far Can Pop Psychology be Trusted?

Although Muslims appreciate the various theories of psychology that prevail in societies today, they need to be particularly careful about theories on human development and behavior. For one thing, they are continually changing and psychologists are not in agreement on many issues. Muslims are not lost altogether, however, because they do have constant guidance from divine revelations, which allows them to keep on the right track and prevents them from vacillating between contradicting opinions.

An example is the endless debate on nature vs. nurture, genetics vs. the environment, which plagues psychologists. Wright (1998) states:

> "Psychologists can call off their century-long search for the key to rearing a good child – not because they've found it, but because it doesn't exist. Parents do not have any important long-term effects on the development of their child's personality."

Judith Harris (1998) asserts that around half of the difference in personality among children is unaccounted for by genetics. The crucial environmental influence is outside the home, where children absorb the values of their peers and find a niche in the local ecology. They become known as tough or nice or wacky or wicked, and personality traits start to harden. Granted, parents can shape behavior within the home. Nevertheless, in the wider world, the child is a different person, and there lie the roots of the budding adult.

Certainly, pop-psychological notions about how one can create a good child by a simple magical parenting style are not necessarily true. In fact, behavioral geneticists have learned that identical twins reared together are scarcely more alike than identical twins reared apart. Birth order can be a factor as well. Maybe younger siblings are treated differently by parents, or face some other "micro-environmental" effect, such as being bullied by other siblings.

A boy in Arkansas shoots schoolmates, whereas his younger brother does not. Why? Did alienation at school reach critical mass because he felt less loved at home than his brother? Did schoolyard rejection make him morose, hence impervious to a parenting style that worked well with his brother? Is that the key – parenting style should be calibrated to the child's different needs? No one seems to know.

Harris' core convincing message is that parents may wildly overestimate their influence and may usefully calm some nerves in this age of high-anxiety parenting. However, it may also do the opposite. These days, much parental fretting is already going into the shaping of peer groups and their context.

Parents can relax – science has not answered many of these questions. How long are parents going to wait for science to tell them how to deal with their children? Human beings need to put their trust in the stable Divine guidance of God and His Messengers. This is not a call for the rejection of psychological theories at all, yet serious research is needed that takes the guidelines of Revelation into account to help families in parenting. Godless theories will inflict more harm than good on human society. The answer to proper parenting lies in the wise combination of the Revelation of the Creator and the accumulation of human knowledge. And this is a continuing process.

Phases of Human Development in the Qur'an

Listed below are verses from the Qur'an dealing with the various phases of development of the human body.

> *Now let man but think from what he is created!*
> *He is created from a drop emitted,*
> *Proceeding from between the backbone and the ribs.* (Qur'an 86:5–7)

> *O mankind! If you have a doubt about the Resurrection, [consider] that We created you out of dust, then out of a [fertilized egg], then out of a leech-like stage, then out of a [chewed like] flesh, partly formed and partly unformed, in order that We might manifest [Our Power] to you; and We cause whom We will to rest in the wombs for an appointed term, then do We bring you out as babies, then [foster you] that you may reach your age of full strength; and some of you are called to die, and some are sent back to the feeblest old age, so that they know nothing after having known [much], and [further], you see the earth barren and lifeless, but when We pour rain on it, it is stirred [to life], it swells, and it puts forth every kind of beautiful growth [in pairs].* (Qur'an 22:5)

> *It is He Who brought you forth from the wombs of your mothers when you knew nothing; and He gave you hearing and sight and intelligence and affection: that you may give thanks [to Allah].* (Qur'an 16:78)

> *It is Allah Who created you in a state of [helpless] weakness, then gave [you] strength after weakness, then, after strength, gave you weakness and a hoary head: He creates as He wills, and it is He Who has all knowledge and power.* (Qur'an 30:54)

> *Man We did create from a quintessence [of clay];*
> *Then We placed him as a [fertilized egg] in a place of rest, firmly fixed;*
> *Then We made the fertilized egg into a leach-like stage; then of that leach-like stage We made a chewed-like flesh; then We made out of that chewed-like flesh bones and clothed the bones with flesh; then We developed from it another creature. So Blessed be Allah, the Best to create! After that, at length you will die. Again, on the Day of Judgment, will you be raised up.* (Qur'an 23:12–16)

There are several phases in the creation and growth mentioned above. They can be identified as follows:

- Dust – quintessence of clay. This is the material from which humans are created, as proven by scientific evidence: from earth they are created, to it they return, and from it they are resurrected.
- *Nafs wāḥidah* – a single soul is what the first couple, Adam and Eve, was created from. It is noteworthy to observe that the word *zawj* is consistently used in the Qur'an for a spouse, a pair, and a couple.
- Reproduction – from the first couple, the reproduction system is as follows: *nuṭfah*: fertilized egg (sperm + ovum) → *'alaqah*: leech-like (hook) → *muḍghah*: embryo (chewed-like substance) → *`iẓāman*: (bones) → *laḥman*: (flesh) covering the bones.
- Another creature (fetus) – (possibly after 4 months into pregnancy) may now be the embryo that develops into a new phase of life, into the human form. The fetus now is not a material thing only, but a partner with a soul who has a share of the parents' inheritance. S/he is a special partner, in that s/he has rights only, and no duties at all at this stage.
- Baby (*ṭiflan*) – born as a baby, a human being, with zero knowledge and a sense of total helplessness.
- Weaning (*fiṣāluhu*) for 2 years maximum – the infant suckles breast milk for no more than two years. Breastfeeding is strongly encouraged in five verses.
- Puberty – attaining the age (*al-ḥulum*) of nocturnal emission or menstruation with emphasis on growth and development of sexual hormones. Now they are able to reproduce and become parents.
- Youth (*ashudd*) – maturity of man or woman. According to Yūsuf 'Alī, the age of full strength is between 18 and 32, although the Prophet ﷺ allowed males as young as 15 to engage in battle. Maturity may come later for some than others. For those who do mature, the age of wisdom may be at about 40 and throughout middle age.
- Old age (*shaykh*, *shaybah*, *ardhal al-'Umur* and then *ḍa'f*) – feeblest old age, with fading memory and knowledge and increasing weakness. It is marked also by decrease in knowledge, until one knows nothing after having known much. By now, the human being has passed through the stages of weakness, then strength, then full strength, then weakness, and finally, feeblest old age.
- Death – upon attaining an appointed term by the Creator, the physical body, which developed from dust into a human, now returns to dust, waiting for the Day of Resurrection.
- Resurrection (*ba'th*) – thus completing the cycle of creation.

> *From the [earth] did We create you, and to it shall We return you, and from it shall We bring you out once again.* (Qur'an 20:55)

- Immortality – living in Heaven or Hell for part or all of eternity, subject to our deeds and the mercy of the Lord. This completes the cycle of the creation of the human being, from mortal to eternal.

The Qur'an puts these distinctive phases into the correct global perspective. Human beings did not exist, God then created a single entity, one soul (self). From that single soul the Creator created a spouse (it is not known how, for the Qur'an does not explain this). Then, these two spouses were married, and a new system of production came into being by mating, following a dignified system of formal marriage to preserve and protect the most important unit of society: the family of father, mother, and children.

The Miracle of Conception, Pregnancy and Delivery

D'Oyen (1996) explains that when the sperm of the father fertilizes the egg of the mother, the newly fertilized egg is hardly bigger than the dot on the lower-case letter "i" and for a few weeks it looks like a little piece of a chewed substance. When it is four weeks old, it has more human features and already has a tiny heart which has begun to beat until death – when it is still less than one inch long! By the fourth month of pregnancy, it is about six inches long and has become a perfectly formed human being complete with fingers, toes, and eyebrows. Although it does not breathe on its own yet, and its eyes remain closed, it can hear its mother's heartbeat, her voice, and other loud noises in the same way that one can hear sounds while one's head is under water. The fetus kicks and stretches and turns in every direction while sucking its thumb! Sometimes, it even swallows a bit of amniotic fluid and gets the hiccups. The mother can feel these movements. When thc baby grows bigger, the father can put his hand on the mother's stomach and feel the kicks and hiccups.

Sometimes, the mother cannot sleep at night because the baby wants to move about just when she wants to go to bed. She has to eat generous helpings of nutritious food so that the baby can grow. However, as the baby grows, it is harder for her to eat a big meal, for there is just not enough room! By the seventh month of pregnancy, the baby starts becoming heavy to carry around. Pregnant mothers need to be given special care and attention as well as help around the house. After about nine months, the baby weighs between 6 and 10 pounds and is between 18 and 21 inches

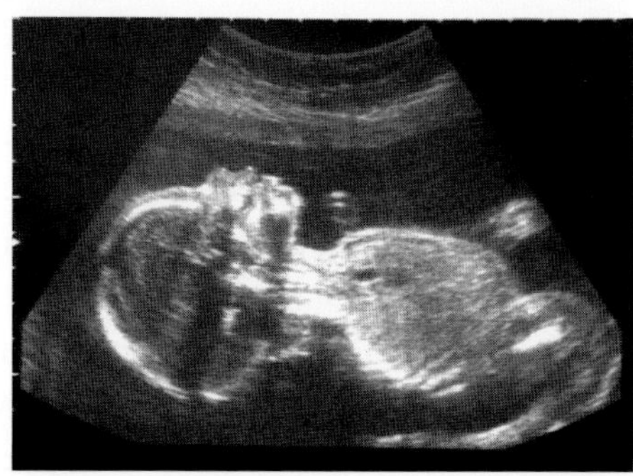

long. It can hardly move around inside the womb any more: it is time to begin its life in the outside world.

When the baby is ready to be born, the uterus, which God made the strongest muscle in the body, starts contracting to push out the baby. Like other animals, a woman's body is made to deliver without any help from a doctor. The birth is usually a safe and happy event, unlike the sometimes exaggerated dramatic scenarios on TV. In spite of the intense labor pain owing to strong contractions, most mothers are strong and brave for the sake of their child. They forget about the pain when they have their new, beautiful baby in their arms.

God describes the psychological status of pregnancy as *wahnan 'alā wahn*, travail upon travail or weakness upon weakness. Indeed, sometimes the mother feels itchy, restless, easily annoyed, oscillating quickly between feelings of depression and happiness, and worrying much. Allah granted her permission to refrain from fasting in Ramadan, for she can make up for this later when she is able to do so. During and after delivery for about 40 days she is excused from the regular five daily prayers. This is a strong hint to the husband and relatives to help her psychologically and physically with house chores. They are to ensure her good health with nutritious food, sound sleep, and peace of mind during breastfeeding.

Various Stages of Human Growth: From Birth to Old Age

Stages of growth take place on the physical as well as psychological levels and both areas have to be dealt with appropriately. The ages mentioned for each stage of growth are approximate.

Stages of Growth According to 'Umar ibn al-Khaṭṭāb

He identified the following stages:

The child is nurtured [raised] for seven years; becomes helpful for seven years; his physical development [height] stops at 23 years; his brain stops growing at 35 years and beyond that is only experience. (Tuffahah, 1979, in Arabic)

Two important questions are: When is character formed? Can anything be done about it later? Although no one knows the exact answers, fairly good generalizations, however, are useful. The general stages of growth are listed below:

BIRTH – 4 MONTHS

At birth, verse (16:78) asserts that human beings are born with no knowledge, although the Almighty has gifted them with hearing, sight, and cognition as the tools of acquiring knowledge, for which they should be thankful to their Creator.

From 0 to 4 months, the baby's glance wanders about vaguely, then babies seem to be more focused on scrutinizing people. They gaze at their mothers more than at other people. They startle at sudden noises and blink at bright lights, stretch their arms and bring them back, turn their heads from side to side. They will soon recognize the voices and faces of their parents, and they begin smiling, cooing, and babbling. By 4 months, the average baby can roll over. Boys' heads tend to be slightly larger than the girls' (Spock 1974).

The immunization schedules have to be followed. The baby should never be shaken, for the brain may not be completely settled yet. If the baby is crying and will not stop, and her temperature is normal, is it time to change the diaper? Time to eat? Sleep? Or just be held? The baby is crying owing to real needs. Crying, though difficult for parents, is normal. Parents need to consult their doctor or psychologist if the crying seems excessive and the baby cannot be soothed.

5–18 MONTHS

This stage of growth is perhaps the most significant in setting people's fundamental attitudes toward life. Babies begin to feel as separate individuals and insist on a bit of independence like wanting to hold their own bottles and not be cuddled too long. They form their first real attachment to the parents. If the parent is a warm person, they expect other people to be the same. Lovingness in the parent will foster love in them. If, on the other hand, their parent is cold and suspicious, they will develop in this direction. They will expect the rest of the world to be cold and, therefore, will find mainly its cold aspects. Regarding the concept of themselves, babies are led at this stage to an assumption that they are basically appealing or unattractive, good or unworthy. This is when they tend to become optimists or pessimists. If babies have had very little relationship with their parents, they will not relate well to things and ideas. Breastfeeding has a great impact on the baby's development, both physically and emotionally.

Parents should consult their doctor if the baby is not yet crawling, is unable to stand while supported or does not make sounds or point to objects. By six months, the baby ought to be able to sit without support, reach for an object with one hand and transfer it to the other, babble, and recognize his/her own name. Most babies – though not all – will be sleeping through the night. The first tooth often arrives around the age of six months. The baby should be holding his/her head up, have a coordinated gaze, and appear to hear and see normally. Parents have to recognize the difference between the "I'm hungry" cry and the "I need you" cry. In general, girls tend to reach developmental mile- stones, such as shaking rattles, a little faster than boys, though boys tend to grow faster.

By nine months they can crawl around and get into mischief. The baby recognizes different sounds and tries to imitate. The pincer grasp enables the baby to pick up small objects, and it may bang two objects together. Their world expands as crawling begins. Some babies will be pulling up to stand and begin walking while holding onto furniture. Nearly everything that babies touch goes in their mouths, because babies are used to sensing things through their mouth. The baby's hands will find ways into places that the parents never dreamed of.

By the time babies are one year old, they can walk and say a few words as well as feed themselves. They may learn to say Mommy or Daddy. Although there is still no real understanding of punishment, the baby does understand the meaning of "no." It is important to redirect the baby from an unwanted activity while being consistent. Before one year of age, babies do not know that they are misbehaving. They just know that there is a big wide world out there ready to be experienced.

Between 1 and 2 years, walking has been mastered. The baby – now a toddler – is becoming more independent and enjoys exploring. Toddlers can kick a ball, run, climb stairs using handrails, and scribble with crayons or markers. Toddlers operate on impulse, for they do not know polite behavior from rudeness or comprehend the difference between good and bad. Time-outs (removing a child from a situation and isolating him in a specific place) are preferred modes of discipline, about one minute per year of age. This age group does not understand reasoning or compromise. Parents need to try offering choices, not punishment, and give leeway for independence. There should be as few rules as possible, though consistency is important.

IT IS VERY BENEFICIAL FOR THE ADVANCEMENT OF LANGUAGE AND THE LOGICAL PARTS OF THE BRAIN TO EXPOSE THE BABY TO SOFT QUR'ANIC RECITATION, SOFT MUSIC, SOFT RECORDINGS OF SOUNDS OF NATURE, AND SUITABLE SONGS, *NASHĪD* (RELIGIOUS SONGS), AND RHYTHMS. THIS WILL HELP TO DEVELOP THE BABY'S VARIOUS BRAIN CENTERS.

Parents have to watch for a longer attention span, and parents should provide more activities like drawing and building with blocks. They need to consult their family physician if the baby's focus still seems short. Temper tantrums are frustrating, though generally not a cause for alarm. Hearing develops faster than sight; the baby responds to loud noises. It does not see clearly before six months. Cognition follows hearing and seeing.

18–36 MONTHS

Children during this stage acquire a definite sense of themselves as separate people with wishes of their own. However, they become more conscious of their dependence on their parents. The baby feels a number of conflicting pulls: independence versus dependence, cleanliness versus soiling, cooperation versus stubbornness, and affection versus antagonism. The personality of the children at the end of the third year will depend on their level of compliance or assertiveness, their inborn temperament and the warmth of the relationship that has developed with parents during this somewhat strained period.

Potty Wars Between Experts and Scientific Research

Brazelton tells parents to praise a child's toileting success, but "not too much" in order to maintain a relaxed environment. He says to toilet-train when children can follow instructions and imitate others – usually around the age of two.

Leach says: Don't bother to train before 15 months and don't expect children to be reliable, even in daytime, before the age of three. Don't nag. It can delay the process.

Rosemond believes that if the mother's ability to become an authority figure from caretaker is delayed much beyond the age of two then the child won't mature properly and will probably develop behavior problems later in life.

Research proves that different children learn at different times. Training for girls takes about nine months (more for boys) and that frequent prompting works.

(LEMONICK 1999)

For example, if parents are intensely dominating and the child is compliant by temperament, s/he may be made too submissive. If they are hostile and tactless, yet leave their child loopholes for fighting back, the child may become extremely hostile. If parents are grim-natured and make cleanliness a very serious matter, their child, if naturally docile, may become overly clean and scrupulous. If anxious parents hover over children, constantly watching them, and if children are impressionable, they may become overly dependent. Breastfeeding should be stopped at two years, thus giving children the encouragement to depend on themselves more and more. Various psychologists assert that a child's character is formed by three years of age. However, certain personality tendencies may be greatly modified in later childhood and adulthood if the environment or the pressures change.

Also, many other characteristics will not be formed until the later stages of childhood. The child's attitudes toward people of their own sex and the opposite sex will largely determine what kinds of friendships they will consider and what sort of marriages they will make.

In the first two years, a baby grows very quickly and changes greatly. Every month, something new is learned. After two years, children begin to slow down in their growth. Children run easily and start jumping, climbing, poking things, and may even ride a tricycle. They copy actions and words. They can draw semi-recognizable circles and squares, and can work simple puzzles. They should be interested in toilet training. At this stage, toddlers want to speak short sentences and know about 50 words.

Parents need to be patient with the constant flurry of "why" questions; it is important to encourage curiosity without being impatient. Positive reinforcements and time-outs are the best techniques of discipline. It is now a good time to start working on social skills like sharing and taking turns with others.

Speaking unintelligibly, showing little interest in other children, and falling frequently are all actions that parents should report to their family physician and psychiatrist.

Differences begin to even out: girls have a growth spurt, and boys begin to reach developmental milestones faster. Both should have a minimum 250-word vocabulary by age three.

4–7 YEARS

By four years old children may eat less than they did when they were two because they are not growing as fast and are less active. Children continue to grow steadily each year, learning new things every day until they reach the teenage years, when they go through another big change! A youngster's energy level between four and five is at an all-time high (they want to walk, run, skip, and jump), making parents long for the crawling stage! The child can throw a ball and ride a tricycle.

During this stage parents can explain why a behavior is wrong and discuss consequences (as long as the explanation is short). Encourage and reward good behavior while penalizing the bad. Keep an eye out for extreme unwillingness to leave the parent. The child should be toilet trained before the age of five and should want to be active, either alone or with others.

Children notice the difference between boys and girls and want to know the names of body parts. This is the phase of "Question" because children ask many questions (including those about sex). Parents should respond to these questions, otherwise the children will seek out answers from their friends, who will likely give false information. (Jaber 1977, in Arabic).

Gradually, children become more and more moody and emotional and tend to move rapidly from one extreme to the other: from too much love to hate and anger, from happiness to sadness. Children begin to feel afraid and become scared of the dark, animals, death, and God. They are frightened of being separated from their parents and losing them. Children acquire fear from their parents and other people around them. They imitate them in being frightened of spiders, strange places and loud sounds. (Jaber 1977, in Arabic).

Children may become jealous of others and this may lead them to aggression. Hence, it is crucial that parents treat all their children equally and fairly. The story of the jealousy of Prophet Joseph's brothers, leading to aggression against him, is a good example.

As the children grow, identification with the parent of the same sex may make the influence of that parent more important. The boys watch their father more closely doing gardening work and girls observe their mother carefully doing household work. Parents can inject love and respect into children by their example of mutual love and respect for each other and for the children. Doing things together, including playing, reading, and feeding animals, will help establish the foundations of trust, self-confidence, and open communication. Children learn religion from observing parents and doing the rituals together. If good manners are implanted into children before they are introduced to the outside world, it is more likely that they will be doing the right things when they are older.

7–14 YEARS

This is the age of elementary education and the onset of puberty. As boys and girls grow up, they begin to look and behave more and more like men and women. These changes usually begin somewhere between the ages of 9 and 13 for girls, and between 11 and 15 for boys. This time is called adolescence, the age when children mature into adults and become capable of having children themselves.

Many physical, mental, emotional, and spiritual changes take place during adolescence. Children discover that they begin to look different, feel different, and think differently than just a year earlier.

A girl who is nearing adolescence may suddenly gain weight in preparation for a growth spurt, and then grow several inches in a few months. Her hips begin to widen and her breasts begin to enlarge. Hair grows under her arms and around her private parts. A boy goes through a similar growth spurt, and he may eat a lot. His shoulders begin to widen. Hair grows under his arms, around his private parts and on his face and chest. His voice may start to sound deeper and more like a man's voice. Both boys and girls may discover that they outgrow their shoes every few months. This is the time when parents are to emphasize prayers more than before.

THE FOLLOWING DEVELOPMENTS ARE NOTICED (7–14 YEARS):

- Children become sensitive to criticism; feel angry easily, and are more moody and emotional.

- Children interact more with friends, from whom they gain their values and ethical standards. Hence, it is beneficial for parents to accompany/supervise them during social visits.
- Children feel shy and need encouragement to voice their opinions, which should be respected.
- Body muscles grow quickly and they become inclined to practice sports (such as running, climbing, swimming, and playing football, soccer and basket ball).
- They depend more on themselves for eating, clothing, and personal hygiene. It is time to teach them the etiquettes of eating, drinking, and socializing. Start to teach them the *du'ā'* (supplication) for each occasion. This is a period of "sexual inactivity" or inert sex. They prefer the company of their own gender. They should not be exposed to erotic imagery on TV, in magazines or in books. After 10 years of age, they should not sleep in the same bed with their siblings.

11–13 Years: Menstruation for Girls

Most girls begin to menstruate between the ages of 11 and 13 (the monthly period starts). For about 3-7 days each month, a small amount of blood is released from the vagina. This is a sign that they are becoming physically ready to have children. The bleeding is fine and does not hurt (it is nature taking its course, since human beings are created this way). This blood is the thin inner lining of the uterus. The two ovaries start to ripen one egg each month and a blood-rich lining forms in the uterus, a kind of nest in which the fetus can grow. Without the male sperm, the egg cannot grow and the lining becomes old, so the uterus disposes of it by menstruation. About every 27–30 days (lunar month), this natural process will take place all over again.

The Pain of Periods

Millions of women complain of discomfort during menstruation. Problems can last for days and range from mild to severe.

Symptoms include: bloating, cramps, breast tenderness, menstrual migraines, heavy or prolonged bleeding, mood swings and fatigue. (KALB 2003)

The first time a girl menstruates is an important event in her life. It means that she has reached puberty and is officially a young woman. From that moment on, she is responsible for all of her religious obligations (just like any adult Muslim woman) such as fasting, praying, and covering herself properly in front of male strangers. About half of all females experience some discomfort during menstruation. They may have cramps, feel tired or become irritable. Allah has excused women from fasting during Ramadan on the menstruating days, although they must make up the missed days after Ramadan. Also, women are prohibited from performing prayers (salah), sitting in a mosque or touching the Qur'an during the monthly period. The prayers do not need to be made up later. Feminine pads are used to catch the blood from menstruation to keep clothing clean. When a woman has finished menstruating, she takes *ghusl* (a shower or bath) in order to clean herself for prayers.

13–15 Years: When Boys Become Men

Boys release sperm when they have reached puberty and become young men. Sometimes, while they are dreaming at night, their penis becomes stiff and some sperm (*haywan manawi)* is released. This is called a nocturnal emission, because the sperm live in a liquid called semen (*many*), and when it comes out it dampens the underwear. This is a pure liquid and not urine, and is nothing to be ashamed of. It means that the boy is a man and physically able to become a father. From this point on, he is considered to be responsible for his religious obligations (like any adult Muslim man). Some boys do not experience nocturnal emissions, yet they are considered to be young men by the age of 15 according to the Shari'ah (Islamic Law), or when they have several other physical signs of puberty (such as the deepening of their voice). In any case, boys and girls should regularly pray and fast from the age of 12, even if they are slow to develop the signs of puberty.

"You have a wonderful child. Then, when he's thirteen, gremlins carry him away and leave in his place a stranger who gives you not a moment's peace."

JILL EIKENBERRY (BROWN 1994)

Some boys and men touch their private parts on purpose to have an erection and let some semen out by massaging, because they enjoy ejaculation. This is called masturbation. This behavior is encouraged in some liberal societies, and is not unlawful (*ḥarām*). Female masturbation and male masturbation is discouraged in Islam. Anyone who stimulates his private parts intentionally must make a new ablution (*wuḍū'*) before performing prayers. Anyone who has masturbated must cleanse himself by taking a shower (*ghusl*) to be ready for prayers.

14–21 Years

In this stage the voice becomes louder, rougher, and more masculine for boys, and softer and more feminine for girls. The muscles of boys grow stronger, and the breasts of girls grow larger and their body fat builds up. For boys, the legs and arms grow longer, the shoulders wider, and the feet bigger. Hair shows on the face and grows in the armpits and around the private parts. Temporary inconsistencies in the growth of the legs and arms cause noticeable clumsiness in walking and handling objects. They need some time for the adjustment and fine-tuning of their bodies.

Understanding Teenagers

In making decisions, teenagers may follow their emotions rather than rationality. Their hearts may conquer their minds and feelings and emotions may dominate over reason and thought. Teenagers are self-conscious: they spend a lot of time worrying about themselves and how they look. They may wear braces on their teeth to straighten them, get acne (pimples or spots) on their face, and be worried that they are too tall, too short, too fat or too thin. All the changes in their body can make them nervous and unsure of themselves. They may be worried about their future career and what kind of education to follow or which school to go to, and whom they will marry. All of these decisions can make teenagers irritable and anxious.

The hormones that cause the body to grow rapidly can also cause mood changes: boys may feel restless or angry for no apparent reason, and girls may cry or become irritable at the slightest thing. Sometimes, young people want to be treated as adults, but they want to act like children. Although these feelings can be confusing, they are normal as long as they do not become uncontrollable. Healthy people learn to control their feelings and think twice before speaking and acting on them.

According to Avicenna, we should start teaching the Qur'an as soon as the child is ready to receive it physically and mentally. Teach him the alphabet and the basis of religion. Then teach him select poems on the subjects of manners, praising knowledge and condemning ignorance, kindness to parents, doing good to others, and honoring and helping the weak and the poor. When the child has finished learning the Qur'an and the language, then he should be directed toward certain hobbies and activities compatible with his abilities and interests. (Al-Ibrashi 1976, in Arabic)

On the positive side, the mind and intellect begin to work better at around the age of 13 or 14, and teenagers can learn complicated things that they would not have been able to understand earlier. It is a good time to learn many skills which will be needed in life, such as cooking, taking care of children, and fixing things around the house. Teenagers learn many social skills, such as how to speak and socialize with others and participate in various organizations. They learn how to take on more responsibility for themselves and others, and may take a part-time job while they continue their education, or even begin to work full-time or volunteer.

Islam offers several preventive measures for teenagers at this stage, such as:

- lowering the gaze at the opposite sex
- playing sports to consume energy
- fasting on Mondays and Thursdays and breaking fast with others
- asking permission before entering someone's house
- avoiding *khalwah* (being alone with the opposite sex behind closed doors)
- brothers and sisters should sleep in separate beds (but could be in the same bedroom) after the age of 10. It is interesting to note that in Britain, housing regulations require children over the age of 10 of the opposite sex to have separate bedrooms (Housing Act 1985). This may be too much to ask, for if this rule were applied universally, the planet would be covered with mansions!

On the non-physical side, several issues are important to note:

- Teenagers develop a self-identity: Teenagers need some privacy and time alone. As they grow older, they may think about such things as: Who am I? Why am I here? What is life all about? Why are there so many problems in the world? It is a time when young people question many things they have learned, and look for answers and new ideas. Sometimes, this is a reason for tension and arguments with parents. Teenagers usually become more stable between the ages of 16 and 19. The period in which a child becomes an adult (11–19) is a long and difficult one that requires much patience and understanding from everyone in the family.
- Teenagers develop the ability for abstraction: They start to conceptualize and imagine. They can anticipate problems and devise solutions for the future. Unlike their earlier years, during which they could think only of the immediate present, they can now attach the proper meaning to time: past, present, and future. They realize the meanings of days, weeks, months, years, and centuries. They begin to feel a sense of history. Hence, their questions can transcend material things and go into the origins of life, the nature of the afterlife, aims and means, values and ethics, the beginning and end of the universe, and this life and the Hereafter.

- Teenagers develop a sense of religiosity: Adolescence is called the era of Religious Awakening, when teenagers argue their strong views about Heaven and Hell, sin and repentance, resurrection and eternity, fate and destiny, and freedom and determinism. During their twenties, they become more stable and objective in their outlook on life.
- Teenagers engage in daydreaming and fantasizing: Daydreaming takes place at this stage. It is an important way in which adolescents express their wishes to themselves. It is one of the characteristics of mental growth, which is a normal phenomenon provided that it is not overdone (it should not become an excessive part of their private or public life).

Did you ever wonder why the huge public demonstrations carried out in many countries are normally done by students? Whether these take place in Turkey, Egypt, Malaysia, Indonesia, Iran, or the USA.... It is because teenagers are highly energetic, emotional, passionate, and believe strongly in their opinions of reform or radicalism. It has much to do with their phase of development.

- Teenagers engage in criticizing others, starting with their parents: They may criticize their parents for their clothes, food, tastes, the way they raise their siblings, and compare them with their peers' parents. They may also criticize the schools, the society, and the government, and advocate radical methods of reforms and social change.
- Teenagers become idealists: Idealism is common among teenagers owing to their lack of experience in life.

Abstract Thinking + Lack of Experience → Idealism

Idealistic teens might reject the authority of their parents or society especially when the adolescents' ideas and solutions are continually rejected without a satisfactory explanation. Teens may become frustrated and restless and eventually isolated and alienated. Idealistic teenagers become helpless and hopeless, and may lose confidence in themselves and lose trust in others.

POSSIBLE CHAIN OF EVENTS
One thing may lead to another, as follows:

Teenage idealism and lack of experience → rejection by parents and society → conflict → isolation → alienation → desperation → mistrust → helplessness → hopelessness → apathy → passivity → inertia

- Teenagers feel lost: Teenagers face several options in life. However, because they make decisions by themselves without consulting parents or experienced individuals, they fail to make the right decisions. What is needed at this age is to create an atmosphere of indirect help, which is not binding on them, to make the correct decisions.
- Teens develop a sense of achievement: A sense of achievement is needed to prove themselves with some accomplishment. Well-defined responsibilities enable them to be successful. The absence of responsibilities makes them feel neglected and insignificant. Giving them too much or too hard a task makes them feel incapable and a failure. A balance must be sought.
- Teens have an ability to memorize: There are two common types of memorization: rote (mechanical) memorization and comprehension memorization (or the direct and the indirect). Direct learning by rote memorization is to retrieve passages with little or no understanding of the contents. Indirect comprehension includes understanding the contents and relating the meanings to other subjects as well as deducing new relationships among the elements of the contents. Development of direct mechanical memorization begins in childhood and peaks at about 15 years of age (al-Sayyid 1975). It then starts to decrease in sharpness, speed, and extent. However, indirect comprehension starts later yet continues to develop and grow during teenage years and up to middle age. What is learnt during early childhood is like carving on stone (retained for a long time) whereas that learnt during old age is analogous to writing on the surface of water (fading quickly).

21–35 Years: Young Adulthood

This is the age of maturity, strength, and reproduction for most people. Yusuf 'Ali in the twentieth century and 'Umar ibn al-Khaṭṭāb in the seventh century believed that the mind is fully developed by the age of 35; thereafter, development is based only on experience.

35–50 (maybe 60) Years: Middle Age

The middle years are when development is due not to physical growth but to education, training, and experience. Physical weakness (*ḍa'f*) gradually sets in.

60 Years and Older: *Shaykhūkhah* (Aging)

Old age sets in and ends in the feeblest age (*ardhal al-'umur*), where knowledge and memory start to dwindle. If people live long enough, their knowledge diminishes. It is like a computer's memory which is being gradually deleted. Alzheimer's disease affects old people by destroying their memory. Another name for this phase is *shaykhūkhah* (aging), *ḍa'fan* (weakness) *wa shaybah* (old age).

The life cycle begins with the birth of the baby (that knows nothing, but is equipped with hearing, sight, and *fū'ād*, the seat of affection). God invites human beings to be thankful to Him: *la'allakum tashkurūn*. Then babies go from weakness to strength and back to weakness during old age (*shaybah*). Between birth and old age humans become knowledgeable and God encourages them to attain comprehension and wisdom: *la'allakum ta'quilūn*. In the final stage of life – at the end of this journey – people must be righteous and avoid major sins. At 60, people have no excuse to commit vices, as explained by the Prophet ﷺ:

"By the age of 60, the All Forgiving God has given man all the excuses." (AL-BUKHĀRĪ)

The older we become, the more our memory fades away, but our reasoning power remains strong. A real blessing!

Lucky and blessed are those who start praising the Lord early in life and mature to the stage of wisdom to recognize and comprehend the essence and mission of creation and human beings on this earth.

A child does not develop according to a clock. Each child develops at its own pace and within its own pattern. A child's unique inner clock is the one that parents must focus on.

Capitalizing on the Phases of Development

The Baby is Our Window of Opportunity

The heart of the baby is pure and empty. It has a natural inclination for retention of everything and it is attracted by everything. (Imam al-Ghazālī)

The baby is ready to accept all the information and accepts all the instructions directed toward him. (Ibn Miskawayh)

This is the parents' golden chance to interact and teach their children to the maximum level possible!

BREASTFEEDING DURING THE FIRST TWO YEARS: This is the stage when important elements of the personality are being built. The outcome is a healthy child, both physically and emotionally. During infancy, the baby's brain centers, brain interconnections, and brain networks (in the form of trillions upon trillions of neurons) are being formed. Courage, creativity, love, honesty, attitudes, language, and logic, start being constructed during this stage. In addition to the countless medical advantages of breast milk, mothers transmit to their babies huge emotional advantages. Love, compassion, and self-esteem are transmitted with nursing in the first two years. Nursing mothers also benefit greatly from the intimate psychological relationship with the baby.

LOVE AND FEAR OF GOD: Children need to be introduced early to love, hope, and rewards from the Merciful, the Compassionate. The concepts of fear, punishment, and Hell must wait till the teenage years, when children comprehend abstract concepts and images. Owing to their highly impressionable minds in the early years, children's potential for freedom, creativity, and imagination is stifled when they are constantly threatened with Hell. Scaring children and intimidating them robs them of their courage, ability to take risks, make decisions, and have confidence in themselves.

MEMORIZATION: Shaykh Muhammad al-Ghazaly in *Kayfa Nataʿāmal Maʿa al-Qurʾān* (1992) raises the question of when to emphasize memorization of the Qur'an and when to focus on comprehension. He was looking for the right answer. It now seems that memorization should be stressed more than comprehension up to the teenage years, and then there should be more stress on comprehension and *tafsīr* (interpretation) from the early teens onwards. This way the best potential of the brain is utilized for the eventual harvest of early direct memorization and later comprehension.

ASPECTS OF *DAʿWAH*: This should be intensified during the teenage years, when children are most receptive to abstract concepts like Heaven, Hell, and the Hereafter. Their energy and emotions at this stage are highest and their passion can be directed to righteousness, spirituality, and sacrifice for the common good. Teenagers' emotions need to be balanced with rationality. They need to strengthen their worship rituals with knowledge to control their emotions during crises and to bolster themselves with reliance on the Almighty (*tawakkul*).

SENSITIVITY TOWARD CRITICISM DURING ADOLESCENCE: Teenagers must be coached tactfully so as not to hurt their feelings and injure their self-respect. The aim is to guide their development, not to cause them to lose their self-confidence. Encouragement and enhancement should be the approach in this phase. Jealousy and comparisons are on their minds as teenagers, hence the need to treat all their siblings fairly and equitably.

IDENTITY BUILDING SHOULD BE INTENSIFIED during adolescence, for this is when teenagers begin examining themselves, society, the universe, and metaphysics, *al-ghayb*, the unseen. This is the time to discuss the true concepts of *tawḥīd* (Oneness of God), *istikhlāf* (vicegerency of humankind), *'imrān* (civilization building), the world view, the objectives of life, and the relationship with oneself, with others, the environment, and the Creator.

LEARNING A SECOND LANGUAGE: This must not be left until the teenage years. It has to be started before the age of 10. This is when the language sounds are established through the brain neurons and interconnections. The earlier the better to be able to pronounce all the sounds of the alphabet like a native. Children possess a tremendous ability to learn several languages without much difficulty during their early childhood. "The youngest brains have the greatest aptitude for absorbing language, and someone who is bilingual at a young age will have an easier time learning a third or fourth language later on. Compared with adults or even high school students, young children are better able to learn German with near-native pronunciation or mimic the subtle tones of Mandarin" (Glod 2006). The same applies to learning Arabic and other languages.

The 6 Year Old Persian Ḥāfiẓ

(*Ḥāfiẓ* is one who can recite the whole Qur'an from memory; s/he may not even understand Arabic).

Sayyid Mohammad Husayn Tabatabai, whose mother tongue is Persian, memorized the whole Qur'an at the age of 6. His father says, "He was just 2 years old when I first realized his talent." The boy learned by listening to his mother who is also a *Ḥāfiẓah*. He memorized the verses by listening once or twice. He reads the Qur'an daily to retain what he memorizes. His favorite parts are the stories of the prophets, Joseph in particular. (MUSLIM NEWS 1998)

It is a miracle of the Qur'an that a person who does not understand Arabic can memorize it from cover to cover! Today, thousands of children who are less than 10 years of age of various races memorize the Qur'an in its original Arabic text.

The 4½ Year Old Syrian Ḥāfiẓ

The youngest child on record (4½ years) who memorized the whole Qur'an is Abdullah Ahmad Shghalah from Aleppo, Syria, born in 1996. He started memorizing the Qur'an at the age of three and completed it by four and a half. At the age of five he also memorized 1000 traditions of the Prophet ﷺ and more than 1000 lines of poetry.

The story started at his father's shop, when he noticed his son at the age of two singing Umm Kalthum's song "Ẓalamūnī al-Nās" upon hearing it once from the loud neighbor's radio. The parents decided to channel his potential toward the Qur'an. They started reading a few chapters to Abdullah who would memorize them upon second recital. In a few months, Abdullah also perfected pronunciation according to proper *tajwīd* rules.

At the age of five, Abdullah got First Prize in the Qur'anic National Competition in Syria, where the competitors' ages were between 14 to 30 years. He was the youngest to be first in Qur'anic competitions. (AL USRAH MAGAZINE 2005)

Memorization Between East and West

The practice in Muslim countries to enroll preschoolers in Qur'anic memorization schools is paying good dividends. Although the majority of Muslims (four-fifths) do not understand Arabic, they can memorize the whole Qur'an without comprehending owing to the peak of memorization brainpower in early childhood. Interpretation can come later during the teenage years. Nowadays, memorization as a system is not emphasized enough in the West, whether to memorize the Bible, poetry, or plays. However, earlier Christians used to memorize the Bible. Some Christian Arab children memorize the Qur'an, it gives them a tremendous communication edge in vocabulary, language, and brain power storage, retention, and retrieval.

Early Memorization of the Qur'an Helps Adults in High School

Dr. Yusuf Khaleefa (former Minister of Education, Sudan) reported:
Our experience with the *Ḥāfiẓ* from various *khalawī* (village madrasas) and schools in Sudan proved that those who memorize the Qur'an have a good memory for storing, retrieving, and comprehending complicated concepts and problems. These students, who had never attended regular secular schools, were given a 2-year preparatory course in the sciences to qualify them to enter the universities. Ninety percent of them passed the general entrance exam of the Republic. They were on par with other students who had attended secular schools for 12 years.
(Abdullah 1994) found that memorization in the early years can assist with strengthening memorization in later years of life.

Activity

ACTIVITY 31: ADVICE FOR PARENTS

Father and mother: Discuss the following items then decide on how to apply them to your children.

- Give your children a bit more than they expect and do it cheerfully.
- Don't believe all you hear or spend all you have.
- When you say, 'I love you,' mean it.
- When you say, 'I'm sorry,' look the person in the eye.
- Never laugh at your children's dreams. People who do not have dreams do not have much.
- In disagreements, fight fairly. No name calling.
- Do not judge people by their relatives.
- Talk slowly but think quickly.
- When someone asks you a question you do not want to answer, smile and ask, 'Why do you want to know?'
- Great love and great achievements involve great risk.
- Say 'bless you' when you hear someone sneeze.
- When you lose, do not lose the lesson.
- Respect yourself; respect others; and take responsibility for all your actions.
- Do not let a little dispute injure a great family bond.
- When you realize you have made a mistake, take immediate steps to correct it.
- Smile when picking up the phone. The caller will hear it in your voice.
- Spend some time alone.

Parents: Understand Some Phases of Your Children's Development

- **The age of Regulation: 1–7 years**
- **The age of Imitation: 8–12 years**
- **The age of Inspiration: 13–upward**

CHAPTER 9

The Road to a Healthy Child: Hygiene, Nutrition, Physical Exercise, and Sleep

Introduction: Health Comes First

A patient kept complaining of persistent pain to doctors. Finally one doctor told him "You spend too much time and money protecting your business assets of machinery and buildings, but you neglect your most important asset – your own body!"

THE OLD ADAGE "prevention is better than cure" will always hold true and is something on which parents need to focus. They should not just wait for disaster and then react. Any major mistake that parents commit concerning their baby's health may destroy his/her future. Parents have a double responsibility toward their own health and that of their children. Unfortunately, most people, instead of spending an ounce on prevention, spend a ton in the intensive care unit. Doing the right thing on time is inexpensive and easy, and the results are highly rewarding. Inaction makes us sorry and miserable. More dangerously, however, the damage to children's health may be permanent. It is not difficult to imagine the level of guilt felt over neglecting the health of one's children, when sickness happens that could have been prevented easily. It may then be too late to do anything, no matter how hard one tries and how much one spends.

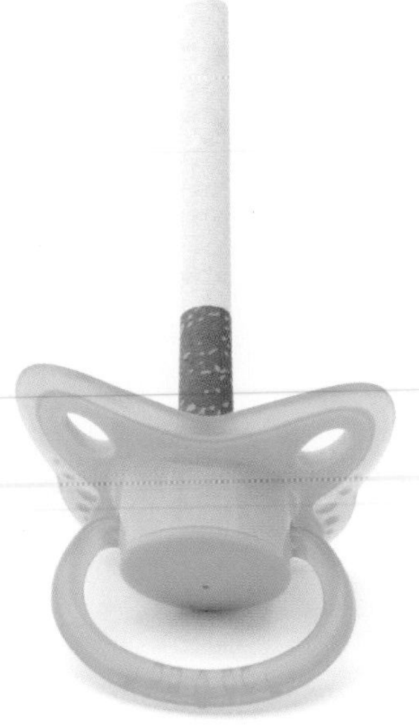

Health, therefore, is a top priority. It is not possible to have a good family, a good career, a good education, or a good time if one does not have good health. Furthermore, healthy minds come in healthy bodies and the necessary mental and psychological development of the baby will occur if the body is healthy.

Parents need to guarantee for their children clean water, good sanitation, nutritious food, timely vaccinations, regular exercise, and access to a doctor. Raising healthy babies starts before a child is conceived; one should choose a healthy spouse.

Pregnancy Time

The pregnant mother has a great responsibility for her fetus. Nutritious food, enough sleep, visiting the doctor regularly, and exercise are essential for a healthy delivery. She is to avoid risks of bacterial infections, as well as the intake of harmful substances (like drugs, unhealthy food, and alcohol). Smoking is one of the more harmful activities that a mother should not do during her pregnancy. A fetus absorbs everything from its mother, (nutrients and oxygen come via the placenta and umbilical cord), so smoking not only exposes the fetus to toxins in tobacco smoke, but it also damages placental function. Read the following warning put on cigarette packs sold in the United States:

SURGEON GENERAL'S WARNING

Smoking Causes Lung Cancer, Heart Disease, Emphysema, And May Complicate Pregnancy.

Smoke-Less Environment: If There is a Will, There is a Way!
Nations can reduce smoking considerably if they make the commitment to do so. It happened in the US.

No Smoking Allowed – In 1985 the number of municipalities with clean-indoor air ordinances was 202, by 2003 this had increased to 1631.

However, regardless of the law, parents should keep their children out of smoky environments, inside and outside the home.

If the mother contracts a viral infection, she is to consult the doctor immediately to avoid harming the fetus. This also applies during breastfeeding. Infections may cause the baby to be blind, deaf, mentally retarded, schizophrenic, or autistic. Mothers must have their blood tested during pregnancy to avoid hemolytic disease (which can lead to brain damage or the death of the baby).

After Delivery: The Controversy About Vaccination

The arguments for and against vaccination are presented here so that parents can make an informed choice.

After delivery, the doctor should examine the baby, particularly the eyes, ears, and reflexes. Boys should be circumcised to avoid infection. Many parents realize the necessity of immunization and follow the immunization schedule. However, 80% of them are unaware that most vaccinations are given before the age of two. It is amazing how we vaccinate chicks inside the egg three days before hatching, and calves are given their shots before they come home, while some of our children are not given their shots before they are two.

Vaccinations Can Do So Much!

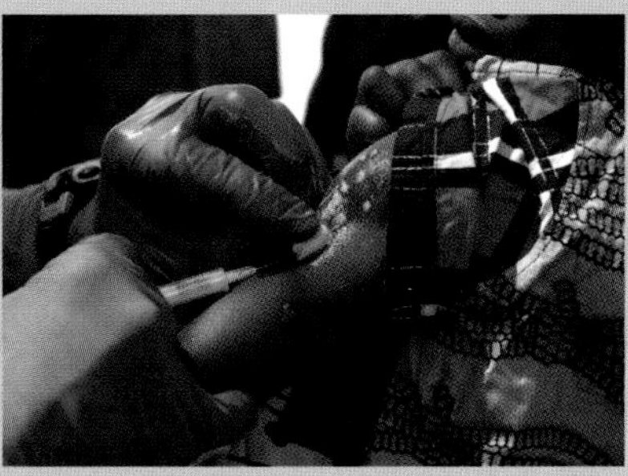

Six deadly "childhood" diseases – measles, polio, tuberculosis, tetanus, whooping cough, and diphtheria – kill millions of children each year. The vast majority are malnourished youngsters with little resistance to disease. The vaccines to prevent these diseases have been known for decades, and have eliminated the threat of these diseases from developed nations. Almost every child in America is immunized against major childhood diseases, but millions of children in developing nations remain at risk simply because they do not have access to vaccines. Twenty percent of children in developing countries still do not have access to immunizations, and each year nearly three million children worldwide die needlessly from vaccine-preventable illnesses.

("For the Children: The Gift of Health, Education, and Hope," Donation Pamphlet, UNICEF 2003)

Tell your children the story of vaccination: "It was Dr. Edward Jenner who produced the innovative idea of vaccination in 1796, a real story of creativity. In medicine there are three kinds of good ideas: the obvious ones, the not-so-obvious ones and the sort that Dr. Edward Jenner came up with. He had heard from his neighbors in rural Gloucestershire, England, that people who caught cowpox didn't get the more-lethal smallpox very often, and he suspected the first disease was triggering the body's defenses against the second. The notion must have sounded preposterous to his colleagues. At the time they didn't have words for the "immune system" and "germs" because they hadn't figured out either concept" (Carmichael 2007).

Nonetheless, Jenner believed in his idea. So did a mother who let him test it on her 8-year-old son, James Phipps, when cowpox broke out on her farm in the spring of that year. The doctor collected pus from an infected milkmaid, shot it into the boy, and waited. After six weeks he injected the boy with smallpox. He waited some more until he was sure James would not fall sick. Then he announced the dawn of an era. He had invented the vaccine. No doubt, Jenner sounded crazy when he proposed his idea; revolutionaries often do.

Vaccines have transformed the entire world by eradicating smallpox, and they have largely rid the developed world of polio and measles. Vaccination is one of the most important medical innovations of the past two centuries, and it is also one of the most cost-effective. Vaccines do not cure disease; they prevent it, which is better. If 100 people are immunized, they are not only kept healthy but also prevented from infecting thousands more.

Each year, vaccines save countless lives. However, millions of people still cannot have them. In vast areas of Africa, Asia, and Latin America, children do not receive any of the basic vaccines available in developed countries and, as a result, they die. Nor is anyone, anywhere, routinely and effectively immunized against the big global killers – HIV, tuberculosis, and malaria, which together take six million lives each year – because, even with all the power of modern medicine, good vaccines for those diseases do not exist yet.

THE CASE AGAINST VACCINATIONS

Most people are unaware of the possible side-effects of childhood vaccinations. The argument against vaccination explains that much of the success attributed to vaccination programs may have been due to improvements in public health (especially with regard to clean water and sanitation, less crowded living conditions, better nutrition, and higher standards of living).

> "All vaccines contain toxic chemicals, DNA from animal tissue & aborted fetuses, and foreign proteins in the form of either live or dead viruses and bacteria. Current vaccine technology is based on science that is over two hundred years old and which says that vaccines 'safely stimulate an immune response' ... Toxic chemicals added to vaccines create immunologic as well as nervous system problems because they are not easily eliminated from the body, they accumulate in brain and organ tissues, and they damage nerves. Foreign proteins and DNA, when not adequately neutralized and eliminated by the immune system, can penetrate through cellular membranes".
>
> (http://www.know-vaccines.org/parent.html)

The immune system takes years to fully develop, and does so by being exposed to bacteria and viruses (which the body learns to throw off with fevers, mucus, sweating, and rashes). Vaccinations deny children the chance to acquire natural life-long immunity from relatively harmless diseases (such as measles, mumps, rubella, chicken pox, and whooping cough). After vaccination, the body is left in a state of alert for something that may never happen. Thus, the immune system is more likely to become hypersensitive and subject to allergies.

Those against vaccination argue that good health is the best way to provide IMMUNITY from disease.

The bugs are not "out there" trying to get us. If we are healthy on the inside, the body can resist colds, flu, measles, or whatever might be around us. The key is SUSCEPTIBILITY.

(Sinclair 1995), (Head 1999)

To reiterate we leave parents to make an informed choice with their physicians whether to vaccinate or not.

Pediatricians recommend that children are given a regular check-up at ages six, eight, and ten, and annually from eleven onward. The beauty of these check-ups is that problems are discovered early enough and can be treated effectively, rather than being left unnoticed and allowed to develop into incurable diseases. Some countries give medical check-ups to elementary students at the beginning of the school year, which is highly commendable. Disorders in children (like the impairment of hearing, sight, or speech) are identified during these health exams. Parents must focus on the prevention of diseases. Beyond vaccinations, the minimum requirements for good health are hygiene, nutrition, sleep, and exercise.

Immunization is the World's Greatest Health Bargain

$15 to protect a child. While we have made tremendous gains during the last two decades in immunizing over 80 percent of the world's children, over two million children still die each year from the lack of this basic inexpensive public health service.

Cleanliness and Hygiene

Cleanliness is the most effective line of defense that human beings have against bacterial and viral infections. Normally, hands are the instruments with which infections are transmitted to the body (when people touch their eyes, mouth, nose, and ears). Hence, washing hands several times a day sends the germs down the drain.

American author Rose Wilder Lane (1886–1968) interestingly observed in her work, *The Discovery of Freedom* that, "People accuse the Prophet Muhammad of being a fanatic, but I found that he was only fanatical about one thing – cleanliness and hygiene".

The Prophet ﷺ praised the five daily ablutions before prayer: "The similitude of five prayers is like the streaming river passing by the gate of one of you in which he takes a bath five times daily."

(MUSLIM)

Men, Women and Hygiene

When it comes to hand hygiene habits, American women are cleaner than American men. 91% of people polled said they always washed their hands after using a public restroom. But an observational study in six public bathrooms in four major U.S. cities found that 75% of men stopped to clean their hands, compared with 90% of women.

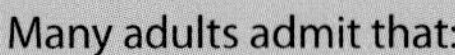

Many adults admit that:

42% of adults said they always washed their hands after petting a dog or cat

21% said they washed after handling money

32% said they washed their hands after sneezing or coughing

The single best defense against the spread of illness is to wash hands for 15 to 20 seconds with soap and water.

It is estimated that the U.S. spends more than nine billion dollars a year for diseases caused by not washing hands! (HYDE AND SANSONI, ASM, 2005)

QUESTION: How did the Spanish authorities during the "Inquisition" against Muslims and Jews detect those who were still Muslims at heart but pretending to be Christians after their forced conversions?

ANSWER: If the person remained very clean, then [it was considered that] he must still be a Muslim but pretending to be Christian. (AHMAD 1997)

Health: Some Islamic Practices

The Prophetic guidance in hygiene goes beyond washing of the hands, face, and arms five times a day. It mandates washing our hands before and after every meal and after using the bathroom.

Maintaining good health and hygiene may have been the most important contributions of Islam in the field of medicine. Arguably, clean water and good personal hygiene have saved more lives than all the antibiotics put together. They were inspired by the practice and sayings of the Prophet ﷺ, for example, "cleanliness is the other half of faith" (Tahoor and Iman/Muslim) and "a person's body has a right over him" (al-Dahaby 2004).

The Prophet ﷺ took traditional medicine when he fell ill and occasionally prescribed treatments. He was a vigorous and healthy individual who participated in many arduous physical activities (including numerous battles and the digging of the Trench when Madinah was about to be attacked). He could climb up to the Cave of Hira annually, which requires great physical effort.

Parents must make personal hygiene a priority for boys and girls before the age of puberty, and the earlier the better. Attention has to be devoted to personal cleanliness in children. Children will be responsible for praying, fasting, and other religious obligations just like adults, so they have to be well groomed and keep their bodies, clothing, and surroundings clean at all times.

CLEANLINESS IN THE TOILET

Muslims are obligated to keep their underwear and private parts as clean as possible. It is recommended that underpants, panties, and socks be changed daily to avoid unpleasant odors. If urine happens to splatter on clothing, it should be washed off until no color or smell remains. The Prophet ﷺ advised us to clean ourselves thoroughly after using the toilet (*istinjā'*), by first removing all traces of urine or feces with water or something clean and dry, such as toilet paper, using the left hand. Wash the private parts gently until no trace of impurities can be seen on the toilet paper. The private parts must be washed with water and then dried. Muslim homes may have either a special spray hose installed next to the toilet, or provide watering cans for this purpose. The left hand is used for cleaning and the right hand for eating to avoid contaminating food with impurities (even though hands are washed after using the toilet).

After cleaning with water, it is best to dry (especially for girls) to prevent infections, which can occur in damp underwear. Girls are to wipe from front to back rather than back to front. It is also recommended to wear loose cotton underwear, which "breathes" and dries more quickly than panties made from synthetic nylon or polyester. The hands are to be washed with soap after using the toilet to ensure hygiene and that no unpleasant odor remains under or around the fingernails. Short fingernails are strongly recommended by the Prophet ﷺ.

> Did you know that 98 percent of infections of babies come from putting their hands in their mouths? Prevent it by using clean pacifiers…
> (GOOKIN 1996)

HAIR AND NAILS

Hair that grows under the arms and around the private parts can be a source of bad odors. Combined with darkness and moisture, hair provides an ideal environment for bacteria to grow. If removed, the body odor is reduced and there is less chance of catching troublesome irritants, such as "jock itch" or body lice. The Prophet ﷺ said:

> Five practices are characteristics of the *fiṭrah* (the pure natural state, or the tradition of the prophets): circumcision, shaving the pubic hair, removing the hair of the armpits, clip ping the nails, and cutting the moustache short. (AL-BUKHĀRĪ)

Armpit hair and pubic hair may be removed by any relatively simple and fast method (including plucking, shaving, trimming, waxing) with any number of special depilatory creams and ointments, or using the new laser technology. Once every forty days is adequate for removal, or whenever it grows long. Underarm deodorant is recommended, especially before engaging in sports or going to school or visiting the mosque, to avoid offending others. All natural deodorants are highly recommended. Anti-perspirants, however, are dangerous, and should be avoided.

The habit some men and women have of changing their hair color is discouraged in Islam, as is the custom of growing their fingernails very long, or painting the finger and toenails with polish. Long fingernails collect dirt and can transmit disease (especially while preparing food). They are impractical, and one cannot make *wuḍū'* (ablution) properly when wearing nail polish since the water cannot reach the nails. It is permissible, however, to dye the fingernails with henna because it does not seal the nail surface. It is recommended that men use natural scents and perfumes, especially before going to the mosque. Women may use perfume within their homes, as long as there are no non-*maḥram* (legally marriageable) men present.

Do You Clean to Live or Live to Clean? Avoid Extremes!

- A lady earned the name Mrs. Clean, because she was too clean. She lived to clean. Her house was a sterile spotless environment. She gave hell to her children and deprived them of the joy of playing and socializing with others to avoid making any mess. The house was too clean for living. Happiness could not enter the house; it was too clean for it. She was divorced eventually, because the marriage environment was not clean enough for her. She sacrificed peace of mind for the sake of excessive cleanliness. Children are to be allowed some tolerable mess to be cleaned later. An obsession with anything is abnormal, even in cleanliness.
- A doctor once told of a neurotic patient in a mental hospital who washed his hands with soap every time he shook hands with others, including the medical professional staff.
- Children should be taught as early as possible to wash their hands before and after eating until it becomes a habit.

Islam's Healthy Habits for Body and Soul:

- Breastfeeding for infants (no more than two years).
- Circumcision for boys.
- Temporary abstinence from sex during the lady's monthly period.
- Regular bathing, and ablution five times a day.
- Washing hands before and after eating, and after going to the toilet.
- Dental care using *miswāk* (the equivalent of toothbrush and toothpaste today).
- Sleeping at night and working during the day.
- Abstinence from marital sex for forty days after childbirth.

Cleanliness is considered "half of the faith." The Qur'an prohibits eating pork meat or pork products, carrion, blood, and all intoxicants. Fasting from dawn to sunset daily for one month a year (*sawm*, Ramadan) brings rest to the body and has many medical values. Meditation and prayers bring psychological tranquility.

Circumcision in men causes 50 percent less chance of contracting HPV (Human Pappilloma Virus) from cervix infection in women, which in rare cases can lead to cervical cancer by the time they are 24 years old. HPV is by far the most common sexually transmitted disease in the United States.

The following are important Islamic medical instructions:

- Preserving life is required.
- Blood transfusions are allowed (after proper screening of the blood).
- Assisted suicide and euthanasia are not permitted.

- Autopsy is not permitted (unless required by law or the social good).
- Maintaining a terminal patient on artificial life support for a prolonged period in a vegetative state is discouraged.
- Abortion is not allowed (except to save the mother's life).
- Transplantation is allowed (with some restrictions).
- Artificial reproductive technology is permitted between husband and wife (only during the span of their marriage).
- Homosexuality is prohibited.
- A living will and medical power of attorney is encouraged.
- Genetic engineering to cure a disease is acceptable, but cloning requires further research to determine its acceptability.
- Organ donation is encouraged.

Nutrition

> The most important period in anyone's nutritional life is the first 1000 days. (THE ECONOMIST, MARCH 26, 2011)

Good nutrition is necessary for a healthy child. Not all food is nutritious; food is what we like to eat, but nutrition is what we need to eat. During the first two years, mothers, whenever possible, should breastfeed their babies for physical, emotional, social, mental, and psychological benefits. Before and after weaning the baby, a balanced nutritious diet is needed.

The daily intake has to include all food groups, like dairy, grain, fruits, vegetables, and meats, which provide essential vitamins and minerals for a growing child. Fruits and vegetables need to be washed because they may contain bacteria, chemicals, and dirt.

The Qur'an mentions all the necessary food sources known at the time as nice wholesome food (*azkā ṭa'āman*). They include the various kinds of meats (beef, camel, mutton/lamb, goat, fowl, and seafood), grains (wheat), pulses (beans and lentils), nuts, fruits and vegetables (grapes, figs, olives, pomegranates, dates, onions, garlic, and cucumbers), and milk and honey. Honey is particularly described as a cure and a healing substance for people. Children can be encouraged to eat honey regularly after the age of one.

OVERREATING

While the child has to eat from all nutritious types of food, overeating must be avoided. The Qur'an says:

> *O Children of Adam! Wear your beautiful apparel at every time and place of prayer: eat and drink: but waste not by excess, for Allah does not love the wasters.* (Qur'an 7:31)

Watch what you put into that "magnificent" body of yours. Remember, *what you eat affects you.* Learn how to "eat to live" and not "live to eat."

Parents are to provide pure, chemical-free water for children. There exists a misconception that a fat baby is healthy; this is not true. However, unlike adults, a certain proportion of fat in a child's diet is good.

Overweight Problems in America

We are a nation that eats with our eyes, not with our stomachs. The more we see food in our proximity, the more we eat.

(DR. SANJAY GUPTA, CNN, 2008)

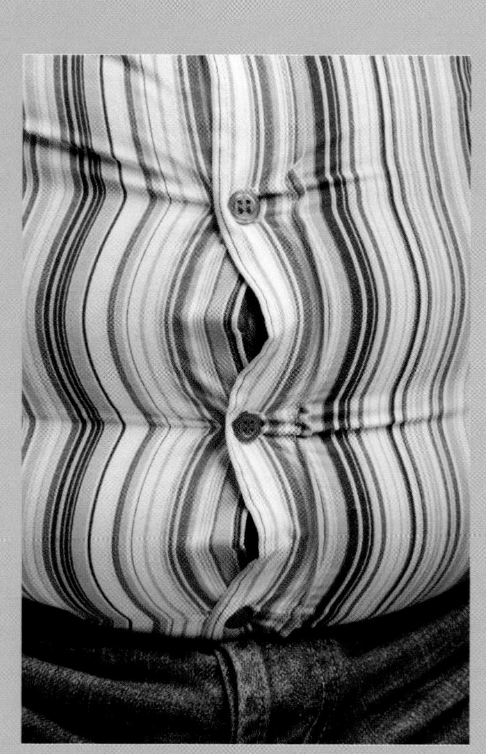

Parents: It is your chance to place healthy food around your children in appropriate places of the home!

36 percent of American women and 31 percent of men over age 20 are overweight. The average adult weighs eight pounds more than a decade ago. "Overweight" is defined as being 20 percent or more above your desirable weight. If you are 25 pounds above your desirable weight for an average 5'4" woman, and 30 pounds above your desirable weight for an average 5'10" man, then you are overweight.

Obesity among children is increasing at a faster rate than adults. A sedentary lifestyle with abundance of food are the root causes of obesity. The American food supply produces 3,700 calories a day for every man, woman, and child, a lot more than required.

(KUCZMARSKI ET AL, 1994)

The quality and balance of food intake is crucial; a child may be obese, yet s/he may be suffering from malnutrition. Parents can do much to train their children to form healthy eating habits.

The Child Who Refused to Say "*Alḥamdu Lillāh*" (Praise be to God)

A guest at our house told his seven-year-old son, after he ate 4 eggs, 4 slices of bread and a grilled cheese sandwich for breakfast, "My son, say Alḥamdu Lillāh (praise be to Allah)," signifying the end of eating. The son responded, "But father, I am still hungry! I am not finished! I do not want to say *Alḥamdu Lillāh* yet!" The host realized why he could not lift the child off the ground. The child was obese!!

Parents should Beware of Overeating, *Tukhmah* (Gluttony)

> The Prophet ﷺ said:
> The worst container that a Son of Adam can fill is his stomach. A few bites should be enough to sustain his body, but if he insists on eating, he should have a third of his stomach for food, a third for drink, and a third for his breath.
>
> (AḤMAD, AL-TIRMIDHĪ, AND OTHERS)

A Danish study found that teenagers in the United States are the most obese out of 15 developed nations. Nearly a third of children in the United States eat fast food every day. Worldwide bad nutrition is a leading factor in the death of millions of children, and leaves millions of others crippled, vulnerable to illness, and intellectually disabled. Nutrition for children plays its most vital role from conception to the age of three (UNICEF, 2003). Providing an environment for children in which junk food is absent, is a much more effective means of developing good dietary habits than forcing children to eat what is good for them. When boys overeat, it normally shows on their bellies; when girls overeat it shows on their hips, breasts and buttocks.

Man digs his own grave with his teeth!

IMAM AL-GHAZĀLĪ'S VIEWS ON EATING HABITS

Imam al-Ghazālī (1058–1111), one of the greatest reformers in Muslim history, said:

1. "The Muslim should not be the first to go to the dining room, nor to gaze at different dishes or at others eating. He must chew his food well and avoid wiping off food with his hands and clothes."
2. "Aversion to gluttony should be established in the child's mind by identifying gluttons, and rebuking gluttonous children in his presence, as well as praising those content with smaller quantities of food."
3. "A child should be trained to like giving others preference over himself in food and to be content with whatever is available for himself. He should be reprimanded for any inordinate desire for tasty food, drink, and splendid clothes."
4. "Overfeeding in infancy and childhood may be a factor in contributing to obesity later in adulthood, and obesity may cause the 'disease of the affluent.'"

Facts About Children and Nutrition

PREGNANCY TIME: To give your baby the best start, eat with the baby in mind even before you become pregnant. The first 4–6 weeks of pregnancy, when you may not know you are pregnant, are a critical time in a baby's development. Wives and expectant mothers are to take 400 micrograms of folic acid daily, which is necessary for the fetus' brain and spinal cord development. In this way, 50 to 70 percent of common nervous system defects can be prevented. A weight gain of 20–30 pounds during pregnancy is considered healthy. (Sutherland and Stoever 1997)

BETWEEN BIRTH AND PRE-TEENS: The dramatic growth of the first year lessens in the second year, along with appetite. Children normally gain only 6–8 pounds during their second year and may seem to lose interest in food. Children eat what they need when they are offered a healthy variety of food at each meal. Many toddlers in the United States have been fed low-fat diets by well-meaning parents and have become malnourished. There must be no "fat control" for children under the age of two. Fats provide energy as well as fatty acids for healthy skin. Fats also carry and help the body absorb vitamins A, D, E, and K. When the child is ready for cow's milk, use regular whole milk, not two percent or skim – at least until the age of two.

Only one-quarter of 2 to 5 year olds in the United States have a healthy well-balanced diet, compared with only 6 percent of teenagers.

PRE-TEENS AND TEENS: Although many children know the basic rules about health, they do not always follow them. Providing healthy food that pre-teenagers and teenagers will eat can be a challenge. An eight year old may eat whatever is put on the table, but a 14 year old may refuse foods s/he ate a month ago. Some solutions are to encourage children to help plan and prepare meals, and to avoid making food an issue. Mealtimes should focus more on sharing the day's events than on the food. Adolescents are growing more quickly than at any time since the first year of life. Girls need 2,000–2,500 calories a day to fuel their growth, and boys need

3,000–4,000 calories, with more active children needing the most calories. The increased nutritional needs of puberty often peak at 15 in girls and 19 in boys. Girls need extra calcium until they are about 25. Calcium increases the density of their growing bones and will help spare them from osteoporosis (weak bones) later. It is important that children do not miss a meal. Missing meals means losing important nutrients and eating small meals throughout the day is better than skipping meals and eating a big meal at night.

SAMPLE DIET FOR AGES 2 TO 10

According to the American Dietetic Association, children's daily diet should include:

- 6–11 servings of grain;
- 2–4 servings of fruits;
- 3 servings of vegetables;
- 2–3 servings of meat, poultry, fish and dried beans;
- 2–3 servings of dairy products; and
- Very small amounts of fats, oils, and sweets. Nuts and seeds are good sources of oil.
- For ages 1–5, a serving is about one tablespoon per year age.
- For any age, too much food on a plate is bad.

How can parents help their children eat enough of the main food groups each day? The answer is to make small amounts of healthy foods always available.

COMMONLY ASKED QUESTIONS

Most children do quite well nutritionally despite their erratic eating habits. They obtain what they need from food that is a quarter to a third of the size of an adult's food – about one tablespoon per year of age. Children will eat only foods that taste good to them. Here are some helpful hints to eating good food (Underwood and Kuchment 2008):

1. WHAT CHOICES SHOULD PARENTS GIVE THEM?

At mealtime, parents need to offer a range of nutritious items: protein, milk, fruit or vegetables, bread, and a second carbohydrate (like rice, noodles or potatoes). Then they have to let their children pick and choose from what is available. Parents should not feel that they have to limit themselves to foods they know their children like. Include at least one food they usually eat – even if it is bread or fruit. Vitamin deficiencies in children are rare, so in most cases a supplement is not needed.

2. IS IT ADVISABLE TO BE A VEGETARIAN?

The rule is to have a balanced diet of meat and vegetables. God created all these nice, wholesome foods for human beings for a good purpose. Therefore, they should eat from all allowable food, moderately. The more food that is cut out of children's diet, the greater their risk of nutritional deficiencies. Cutting out meat, poultry, and fish makes it harder for children to obtain enough iron. Human beings absorb only about 3–8 percent of the iron from vegetables and grains, compared with about 20 percent of the iron from meat. Eating a good source of vitamin C (an orange or a tomato) will help absorb more iron from the foods that are eaten. Vegetarian diets may be low in fat and calories, thus making it harder for children to meet caloric requirements.

3. BABIES ARE NOT SUPPOSED TO HAVE LOW-FAT DIETS. AT WHAT AGE IS IT SAFE TO CUT BACK ON THE FAT?

Fat intake should not be restricted for children under the age of two. Children of this age grow very rapidly and need fat for brain development. Fats also provide energy to maintain bodily functions, help the body absorb the essential vitamins A, D, E, and K, and carry the flavor in food, making it moist and easier to chew. Also, fat makes hormones. For children over the age of two, 30 percent of calories come from fat. When children are ready for cow's milk, they are to be given whole milk at least until they are two. After that, whole milk is still acceptable. So is two percent fat milk, one percent fat milk or skim milk – if the children have other good sources of fat in the diet. On a low-fat diet, children have to eat much more food to obtain the necessary calories. During a growth spurt, children need extra fat to obtain enough calories.

4. MY CHILD HATES MILK. HOW CAN HE OBTAIN ENOUGH CALCIUM?

It is particularly important for pre-teenagers and teenagers to obtain enough calcium, because they gain half their adult bone mass during adolescence. Milk is the best source of calcium, so if children will not drink it, it is possible to add it to the dishes that are prepared like soup, custard, pudding, and sauces. Other calcium-rich options include yogurt, cheese, and ice cream. Chocolate milk has more sugar than plain milk, but is still a good source of calcium.

5. IS IT CORRECT TO LET MY CHILD EAT BETWEEN MEALS?

Yes, absolutely, children need snacks. Children cannot eat much at one time because of their small stomachs, yet they have high energy requirements. They need something nutritious to eat every two to three hours. Snacks also help children obtain the nutrients that they missed at other meals. It is important, however, that snack times be structured. If the children eat breakfast at 7 o'clock, then a snack should not be offered until 9 or 10 – even if they are hungry before then. Sticking to a schedule can be difficult, especially if a child eats very little – after all, parents are so happy to have them eat something. Children who are allowed to nibble whenever they want wind up eating half as much as those who have set meals and snack times. When preparing snacks, think of them as little meals: fruits and vegetables, some protein, some starch, and some fat. A good snack might be organic cookies and milk, apples and peanut butter, or crackers, cheese, and fresh squeezed fruit juice.

6. BECAUSE EATING FRUITS AND VEGETABLES IS IMPORTANT, I WORRY BECAUSE MY CHILDREN DO NOT EAT THEM AT ALL. WHAT CAN I DO?

On average, American children are eating about 1½ servings of fruits and 2½ servings of vegetables a day. Many fruits and vegetables do not taste good to children. Nevertheless, it is important that they are continually offered, for eventually the children will eat some. To make these foods more child-friendly, one could try:

- Blending milk and fruit to make a smoothie.
- Offering dried fruit – raisins, bananas, apricots, and cherries – plain or baked into cookies or muffins.
- Adding vegetables to soups and casseroles.
- It is important to avoid bribery. Of course, children may eat their greens if dessert is the reward; however, they will not learn to like them in the long run. Children reason that if parents need to resort to tricks to make them eat a food, it cannot possibly taste good.
- Parents need not make eating everything on their plate a serious issue with children. If a child resists the broccoli and the brussel sprouts, then s/he could be offered milk and organic cookies (for calcium).

One Mother's Practice

When I was a child, we were expected to eat what was put on our plates without fuss. If I refused fatty meat and some fish, for example, my mother would:

- give me a lecture on wartime and post-war rationing;
- remind me of the starving millions in other parts of the world;
- serve the rejected food at the next meal.
- If we were hungry between meals, we could have brown bread and margarine. And that was it! Not everyone has money to throw around.

SYLVIA HUNT, UK

7. WHICH HIGH-FIBER FOODS DO YOU RECOMMEND FOR CHILDREN, AND WHY?

Parents need to feed children fruits, vegetables, bread grains, rice, and pasta. Some fiber-packed examples are: apples, figs, oranges, pears, strawberries, potatoes, beans, lentils, whole-wheat or pumpernickel bread, bagels, brown rice, bran cereal, and granola. Fiber helps prevent cancer and discourages overeating. Fiber reduces the absorption of fat and calories in the intestine, retains water and gives the feeling of fullness that satisfies hunger.

8. OUR FAMILY'S MOST FRANTIC TIME IS THE MORNING. DO WE REALLY NEED BREAKFAST?

Yes. It is important to do whatever it takes to make sure the family eats breakfast, even if that means getting up 15 minutes earlier. Children who miss breakfast have trouble concentrating at school and play. Breakfast fuels the brain as well as the body. An empty stomach leads to a weaker and less capable student.

9. MY DAUGHTER IS DETERMINED TO BE THIN. HOW CAN I TEACH HER TO EAT HEALTHILY INSTEAD OF CHOOSING NOT TO EAT?

Studies show that 78 percent of American adolescent girls wish to weigh less. Some avoid meat and so need high-protein alternatives (such as dried beans, lentils, peas, milk, cheese, eggs, and nuts). If one's daughter is going through puberty, it is important to explain to her that she needs the new layer of fat under her skin as an energy reserve for her growth spurt. If she still pulls back from the dinner table, then she needs be taken to the family physician and the nutritionist to discuss her eating habits.

10. SOME NIGHTS, FAST FOOD IS OUR ONLY FOOD. WHAT DO YOU SUGGEST?

Parents have to avoid consuming soda, fries, and burgers. Instead choose grilled chicken, salad, low-fat milk and yogurt. Top a pizza with grilled chicken, or tuna, and healthy vegetables.

11. IS YOUR CHILD A PICKY EATER?

Caregivers may inappropriately classify children aged two to five as "picky eaters," when in fact this is normal behavior. A child may be introduced to a new food at least 10 times before s/he will try it. Family meals together are important. Young children imitate their parents' eating behavior, and learn significantly from conversations about food. Yet, 51 percent of American children report that they do not eat with their families every day. By the age of three, familiarity is the single most important factor in determining which food a child will eat. While 75 percent of all children in the U.S. eat at least one vegetable each day, it is usually in the form of french fries. Tomato products, including salsa and spaghetti sauce, are also popular with children. Older children's food preferences change to emulate those of their peers. Milk consumption has decreased in the U.S. by 16 percent per child for children less than five years of age, while consumption of soft drinks has risen by 23 percent. Fifty-one percent of children miss the most important meal of the day – breakfast (US Department of Agriculture).

Which one comes first? Work or Breakfast? Never work before breakfast. If you have to work before breakfast, have your breakfast first!!

12. ARE SPICES GOOD OR BAD FOR HEALTH?

A study conducted by two scientists at Cornell University found that spices possess the ability to kill about thirty different bacteria that spoil food. Include onions, garlic, pepper, lemon and many herbs and spices (like parsley, oregano, thyme, cumin, cloves, mint and ginger) in the food. (Sherman and Billing, 1998)

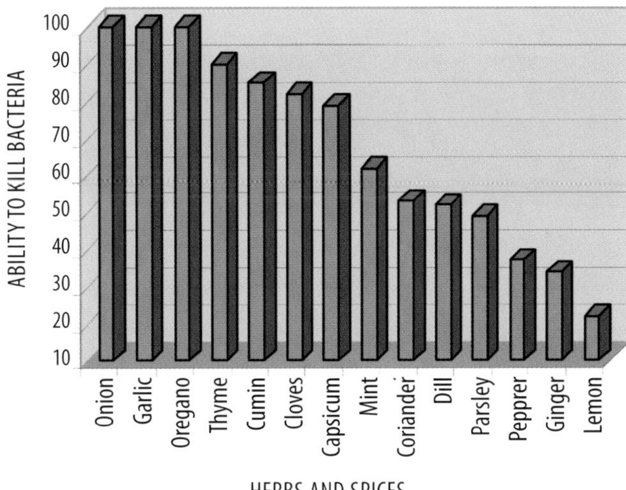

13. SCIENTISTS KEEP CHANGING THEIR MINDS, SO WHAT DO WE DO?

Scientists tell us to "forget what you know about eggs, margarine, and salt. The conventional wisdom has been overturned repeatedly by surprising new research; they seem to have gone mad. Hardly a week goes by without some expert somewhere issuing a new report declaring that a particular new food or vitamin or activity or condition will either restore your cardiovascular health or ruin it – and as often as not, the new advice seems to contradict the old" (Lemonick 1999).

What is the answer? Follow the basic directives of the Qur'an and the Prophet ﷺ about food and nutrition. Good nutrition is a matter of choosing healthy lifelong eating habits, which become set with age. Eat a moderate quantity from many varieties.

Qur'anic Directives on Food

> *O you who believe! Do not make unlawful the good things that Allah has made lawful for you, but commit no excess; for Allah does not love those given to excess. Eat of the things that Allah has provided for you, lawful and good; but fear Allah, in Whom you believe.* (Qur'an 5:87–88)

> *O Children of Adam! Wear your beautiful apparel at every time and place of prayer: eat and drink: but do not waste with excess, for Allah does not love the wasters.*
>
> (Qur'an 7:31)

Say: "Who has forbidden the beautiful [gifts] of Allah, which He has produced for His servants, and the things, clean and pure, [which He has provided] for sustenance?" Say: "They are, in the life of this world, for those who believe, [and] purely for them on the Day of Judgment." Thus do We explain the Signs in detail for those who understand. (Qur'an 7:32)

[To the honeybee] "*... and then eat of all manner of fruit, and follow humbly the paths ordained for thee by thy Sustainer." [And lo!] there issues from within their bellies a drink of many hues, wherein there is health for human beings. In all this, behold, there is a message indeed for people who think!* (Qur'an 16:69)

"*... Now send then one of you with this money of yours to the town: let him find out which is the best food [to be had] and bring some to you, that [you may] satisfy your hunger therewith: and let him behave with care and courtesy, and let him not inform any one about you...*" (Qur'an 18:19)

In sum:

- Eat all types of food, moderately. Eat a little bit of everything and not a lot of one thing.
- Being a vegetarian requires knowledge and expertise. Include moderate amounts of meat.
- Avoid pork, blood, carrion, alcohol, drugs, and smoking. These are not wholesome food but impure and harmful.
- Do not fill your stomach. Stop eating while you still like to eat more.
- Include honey in your daily diet. There is a cure and healing in honey.
- Use olive oil moderately (it provides you with HDL, the healthy cholesterol, and reduces LDL, the bad cholesterol).
- Avoid anything that has been given chemicals, pesticides and artificial additives.

The Pediatrician's Strange Prescription

When the father opened the sealed prescription envelope for his child, he found a $10 bill with a note from the pediatrician saying: "Buy a good wholesome meal for your child; she is undernourished."

This shows how parents neglect the essentials for their children to grow up healthy. The rat race society and the hurried lifestyle of parents cause them to neglect giving nutritious food to children. Parents need to provide the essential needs of their children during the early years of growth before it is too late. Both physical and emotional needs are crucial for children.

Children and Physical Exercise

> *"Let him [Joseph] go out with us tomorrow, that he may enjoy himself and play: and, verily, we shall guard him well."* (Qur'an 12:12)

"Come back here!" "Stop running around the house!" "I told you not to play ball in the house!" These are things that parents frequently say to their children. THEY ARE WRONG. They should be saying the opposite. "Go play basketball." "Go play soccer with your friends." "Go running and hiking."

Why is Physical Exercise Important for My Child?

Increased physical activity has been associated with an increased life expectancy and decreased risk of cardiovascular disease. Physical activity produces overall physical, psychological, and social benefits. Inactive children are likely to become inactive adults. Physical activity helps with:

- Controlling weight
- Reducing blood pressure
- Increasing HDL (good) cholesterol
- Reducing the risk of diabetes and some types of cancer
- Improved psychological well-being (including higher self-confidence and higher self-esteem)
- Teaching team spirit

AMERICAN HEART ASSOCIATION

About 21 percent of children aged 6–17 in the United States are obese. Overweight children are more likely to become overweight adults. Obesity in adulthood increases the risk of diabetes, heart disease, stroke, cancer, and other chronic disorders. The best way to combat obesity and other diseases is with exercise, beginning from childhood. Exercise promotes strength, flexibility, and endurance; it is particularly important for children aged two and up. For children, exercise means playing and being constantly active. An active child is more likely to have stronger muscles and bones, a leaner body, and a better outlook on life. Inactive children are more likely to develop diseases, strokes, obesity, and low HDL (good) cholesterol. Exercise helps children sleep better, and *makes* them more capable of handling daily physical and emotional challenges (like running to catch the bus in the morning, bending down to tie shoes, or studying for a test). Physical inactivity in childhood usually leads to physical inactivity in adulthood. (U.S. Center for Disease Control and Prevention)

CHILDREN AND SHOES

In an interesting article published in the *Guardian* newspaper, fitness expert Sam Murphy points out that going barefoot is best for children and warns that children's shoes can have a detrimental effect on a child's cerebral development. Tracy Byrne (a podiatrist specialising in

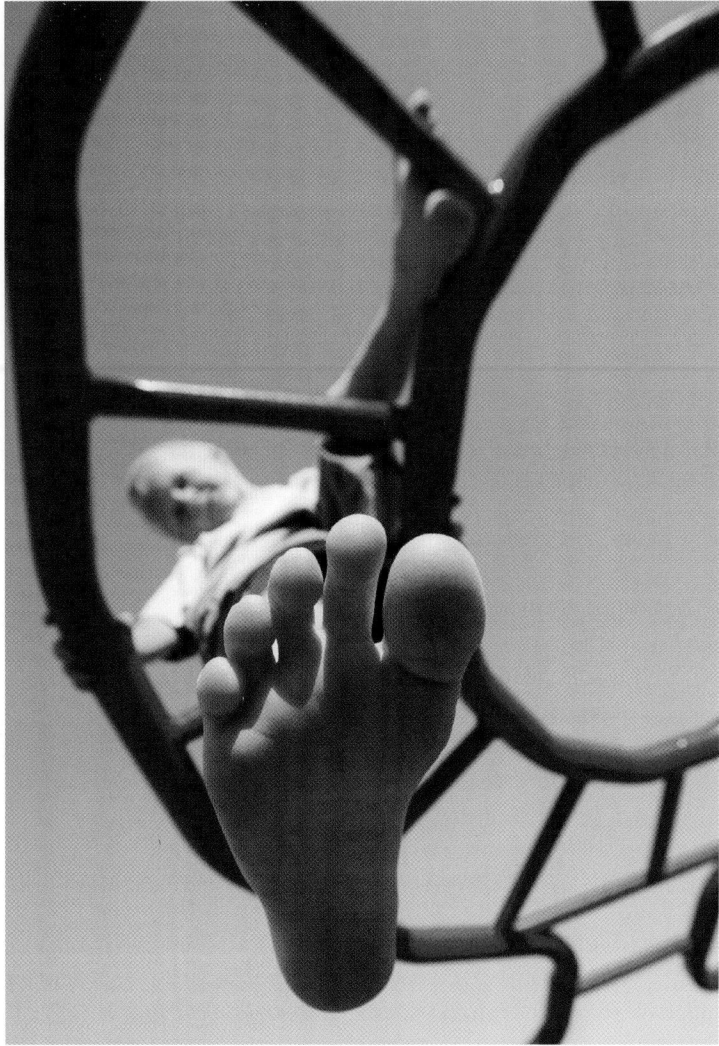

podopaediatrics) states that walking barefoot develops the muscles and ligaments of the foot, increases the strength of the foot's arch, contributes to good posture, and improves a child's awareness of where they are in relation to the space around them.

Shoes should not be a fashion statement. Shoes can be damaging for young feet. Research from the 2007 edition of the podiatry journal, *The Foot*, has shown some children's shoes to be completely rigid, without the necessary flexibility in the sole to allow for physical activities (leading to restriction in movement). Feet are at greater risk of damage from ill fitted or constricted shoes. It is harmful when feet have to conform to the shape and constriction of the shoe itself, rather than being allowed to develop naturally.

Parents need to put ergonomics ahead of fashion or attractiveness when buying children's shoes, and parents have to encourage children to go barefoot more often, (especially around the house, and wherever possible). (Murphy 2010)

WAYS TO PROMOTE ACTIVITY IN CHILDREN

Parents can do much to help children acquire the habit of exercising. Listed below are some suggestions:

- Reduce the time a child spends watching television, and playing video games. Owing to safety concerns, many children are left to watch television and do their homework until their parents come home. Ideally, children need to be active after school and study later in the day.
- Encourage the child to take part in activities that suit his/her age. Children under the age of two years should not watch television at all. (American Academy of Pediatrics)

- Teach children that physical activity is fun and that exercise comes in a wide variety of forms (playing tag, hop-scotch, sports). If the child has fun exercising, then s/he is bound to continue doing it.
- Do not use physical fitness as a punishment. It is a bad practice if a teacher orders a student to run five laps for getting in trouble.
- Parents are role models for their children and should exercise regularly. Take the stairs instead of the elevator, walk instead of driving, and jog instead of walking.
- Include the whole family in exercising. Parents should not sit on the couch and tell their children to go out and play.
- Combining regular physical activity with a healthy diet is the key to a healthy lifestyle. Children have to eat fruits, vegetables, and whole grains regularly.
- Encourage fun activities that promote strength, flexibility, and endurance. Strength can be built with an activity as simple as crossing the monkey bars, doing a hand-stand, or wrestling. Encourage competition in sit-ups, pull-ups, and push-ups.
- Teach children aerobic exercises. The heart beats faster, causing a person to breathe harder, which strengthens the heart and delivers oxygen to more body cells. Aerobic exercises include: basketball, volleyball, cycling, ice-skating, in-line skating, soccer, football, swimming, tennis, walking, jogging, and running.

Recommended Exercise Schedule

A children's exercise schedule is essential for their growth, and the minimum amount of exercise depends on their age. The National Association for Sport and Physical Education (NASPE) recommends:

Age	Minimum Daily Activity	Comments
Infant	No specific requirements	Physical activity encourages motor development
Toddler	1 1/2 hours	30 minutes planned physical activity AND 60 minutes unstructured (free play)
Preschooler	2 hours	60 minutes planned physical activity AND 60 minutes unstructured (free play)
School age	1 hour or more	Break up into separate exercise sessions of 15 minutes or more

The American Heart Association recommends that:

- All children age two and older should participate in at least 30 minutes of enjoyable, moderate-intensity activities every day.
- Children should perform 30 minutes of vigorous physical activities 3–4 days each week to achieve and maintain a good level of heart and lung fitness.
- If one's child does not have a full 30-minute break each day, then try two 15-minute or three 10-minute periods of vigorous activities.

Prophet Muhammad ﷺ said:

> "The strong believer is better and more lovable to God than the weak believer and there is goodness in all." (MUSLIM). (The word '*qawy*' in the Hadith refers to strength of faith and body).

The rule "use it or lose it" applies to body ligaments, heart muscles, and brain cells: Physical exercise is a must (not an option) for personal development. Although achieving a healthy physical condition is good, staying that way is a big challenge. Physical fitness has a positive impact on our energy level, mental attitude, and spiritual aspirations. If you run on Monday, then not again until Friday, do not try to double the miles on Friday to make up for it. Do not overwork yourself. Keep running, and work out at the gym or outside whenever possible.

Even babies need some exercise in between their daily feeding and sleeping. For babies from birth to one year, you can put them on their back, rotate their legs gently as if they are pedaling, place them on their stomach to encourage them to lift their head, and lay them on a blanket on the floor to move their body and reach for toys or other safe objects.

Sleep

It is essential for children to have enough sleep for good health and daily functioning. Normally, sleeping habits during infancy continue later in life. The Better Sleep Council in the U.S. reports nearly two-thirds of people say their job performance has been affected by lack of sleep; (26 percent of men and 13 percent of women admit to dozing off at their workplace). Sleep is meant to be taken at night. Our bodies are designed to wake during the day and sleep at night. Our bodies are designed to rest between evening and dawn (sunset and sunrise). There has to be some adjustment in extreme cases. For example, in northern Europe, the nights are very short in summer and very long in winter. At midsummer in northern Scotland, sunset is around 10.30 p.m. and sunrise around 3 a.m. (with only a twilight in between). In winter, sunset is around 3.30 pm and sunrise around 9 a.m.

> *And [have We not] created you in pairs,*
> *And made your sleep for rest,*
> *And made the night as a covering,*
> *And made the day as a means of subsistence?*
> (Qur'an 78: 8–11)

Day sleep will not fully substitute for the lost night sleep. Enough sleep at night helps one to become healthy and reduces the risk of disease.

Some Muslims are in the habit of staying awake all night in the fasting month of Ramadan and sleeping during the day! Switching night to day and day to night is not what fasting is meant to be. This upsets the natural pattern of our body rhythms.

With the setting of the sun, a sensitive mechanism lying at the base of our brain starts emitting chemical signals to our body parts to induce them to relax, preparing for sleep. With the approach of nightfall we start to yawn; our eyelids become heavy; and our movements slow down. As we fall asleep, the reception entry of our brain is blocked from the world around us. The action of sleep is controlled by the hormone melatonin and its precursor serotonin. Both chemicals manage the efficiency of sleep with the help of the darkness of night. The unnatural reversal of day and night upsets our built-in "biological clock" that induces us to rise feeling refreshed, energetic, and alert in the morning. By interfering with this innate clock, our sleep becomes disturbed and is insufficient to fulfill the needs of our body and mind.

With inadequate sleep, mental responses and abilities decline and physical reflexes and reactions slow down. This is particularly dangerous while working and driving, which demand alertness. The weakened responses contribute to inefficiency, miscalculations or mistakes, and accidents. Because sleep loss is cumulative, our brain keeps an accurate record of this debt that should be replaced with enough hours of quality sleep. Most scientists recommend seven to nine hours of night sleep for satisfactory mental and physical performance. The less we sleep, the less productive and energetic we become. Lack of sleep also results in irritability and grogginess, and it undermines our cognitive skills.

MEDICAL EFFECTS OF LOSING SLEEP

Diminished quality of sleep also interferes with immune cell repair and the stimulation of the immune fighter cells, impairing our defense mechanism and increasing the risk of infection and disease. Good sleep patterns improve our health, memory, alertness, mental responses and physical reflexes. Proper sleep enables us to work effectively and responsibly. Adequate sleep averts mistakes, erroneous decisions, wasted money, and possible disasters that may claim our lives. Our bodies and minds are interconnected. The brain, the nervous system, and the immune system are connected through neurotransmitters (brain chemicals) released by the sympathetic nervous system. Restful sleep enhances energy, mood, memory, thinking ability, and focus.

Beyond leaving people bleary eyed and dozing off at afternoon meetings, failing to obtain enough sleep or sleeping at odd hours heightens the risk of contracting a variety of illnesses, including cancer of the colon and breast, diabetes, heart disease, and obesity.

People in the West are shifting toward a 24-hours-a-day, seven-days-a-week society, and not sleeping enough like they used to do. The obesity epidemic is being driven in part by a corresponding decrease in the average number of hours of sleeping, possibly by disrupting the protein and hormones that regulate appetite.

Physiological studies suggest that a sleep deficit may put the body into a state of high alert, increasing the production of stress hormones and driving up blood pressure, a major risk factor for heart attacks and strokes. People who are sleep-deprived have a heightened state of inflammation in the body, which is a major risk factor for heart disease, stroke, cancer, and diabetes. Naps can help counter the harmful effects of sleep loss. Sleep influences

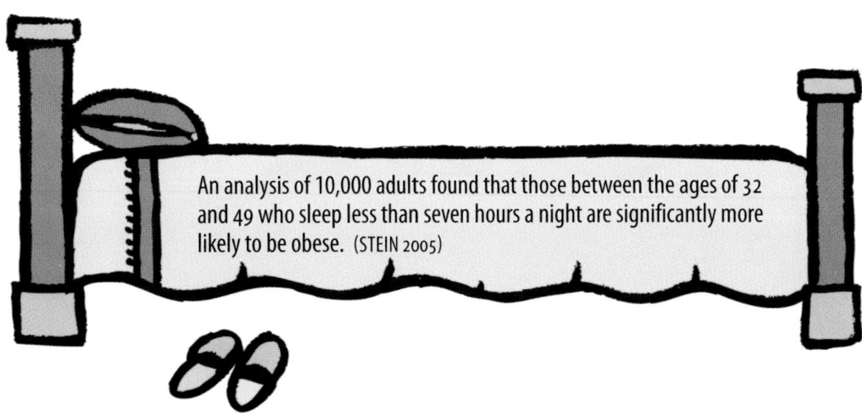

the functioning of the lining inside our blood vessels, which could explain why people are most prone to heart attacks and strokes during early morning hours. "Melatonin can prevent tumor cells from growing – it is cancer protective," says Eva Schernhammer of Harvard Medical School. If you are exposed to light at night you will produce less melatonin, increasing your cancer risk. (Stein 2005)

Other malignancies, including prostate cancer, may also be linked to sleep loss. People with disrupted sleep or people who are up late at night or get up more frequently in the night have the same problems. Even mild sleep deprivation disrupts the hormones ghrelin and leptin, which regulate appetite.

Early to bed, early to rise
Makes a man healthy, wealthy and wise.

Benjamin Franklin

Intoxicants: Drinking & Drug Prevention

Continuing our theme of focusing on physical well-being, parents and children must avoid using intoxicants. Intoxicants, including cigarettes, are hazardous to pregnant mothers, babies, and the father's sperm.

An ounce of prevention is worth a pound of cure.

A cigarette is a pinch of tobacco rolled in a paper with fire at one end and a fool on the other.

Alcoholism or drug addiction requires professional medical and psychological treatment. It is hoped that the following advice will prevent alcoholism and drug addiction. Major problems are not necessarily caused by a colossal mistake; they may be due to the accumulation of several minor factors. If parents are successful in creating a happy and loving family environment, their children will be less likely to seek satisfaction outside the home.

Alcoholism and the use of drugs (such as marijuana, cocaine, heroin, LSD) can cause massive damage to the brain's cells, as well as to the reproductive, circulatory, and the respiratory systems. These drugs cause brain damage, resulting in physical aggression, a distorted perception of reality, and lack of motivation. The abuse of even a mild drug like marijuana may be linked to schizophrenia.

CHILDREN AND TEMPTATION

Children may be invited by their friends or acquaintances to try illegal drugs. They need to be firm in their resolve to remain sober and drug-free. The adolescent years (14–20) are the most challenging time of life. Seeking knowledge and understanding of drugs is vital. Try role playing situations with children, so that they know how to act immediately if

temptation or peer pressure occurs.

One out of two people in America drinks alcohol or has tried some kind of illegal drug. Just talking about the dangers does not stop people from drinking or smoking – ironically, watching a terrible film about the effects of cigarette smoke in the lungs may send a smoker rushing straight out to have a cigarette. The pressures have to be discussed as well as how to resist them.

Parents need to explain to children the reasons behind the temptation to use drugs, which is largely due to the nice effects of "feeling high". This "artificial high" period of feeling good is temporary, and is accompanied by terrible "lows". Unless they are told this, children will, on meeting people who are seemingly enjoying drugs, think their parents have lied to them. They need to understand that this enjoyment comes at a heavy price, with very little short-term gain and very high long-term pain. The Qur'an describes accurately both sides of the issue when referring to wine and gambling. It states:

> *They ask you concerning wine and gambling. Say: "In them is great sin and some benefit for people; but the sin is greater than the benefit..."* (Qur'an 2:219)

Hence, the benefits of moderate social drinking and the possible good it may do for the heart or brain may be partly true. Nevertheless, the overall harm outweighs the little benefit by far.

EARLY DRUG USE SIGNS TO LOOK FOR: WHAT CAN PARENTS DO?

There are many signs of drug use, the most common are: Scorched tinfoil, spoons with bent handles, charred tin lids or bowls, mirrors and razor blades, screws of paper, discarded tins or bottles of solvent, cigarette papers, eye droppers, pill bottles, spatters of blood in the bathroom or on the teenagers' clothes, refusal to roll up their sleeves, change in appetite, sudden craving for sweet things, not going to bed, becoming impossible to wake up in the morning, odd phone calls, as well as furtive and secretive behavior. Children can become addicted to drugs without becoming scruffy or wild-eyed, and can do so in absolute secrecy. If parents are suspicious about their children, it is worth observing whether they have sore mouths, lips or noses, and whether they sometimes appear drunk or "blurred." If they are keeping company with known "sniffers," then parents should be alarmed.

Things parents can do to prevent the use of intoxicants:

- Strengthen the faith of the family by all possible means. Faith is the best defense. Drugs, alcohol, and gambling are strictly forbidden to a Muslim. The word *khamr* (used in verse 2:219 of the Qur'an) means a fermented and intoxicating substance, and applies to any substance that impairs the mind and makes the user lose self-control.
- Educate your family on the ills of smoking, drinking, and drugs and make them aware of the harmful effects. It helps if they can actually see someone suffered from drug abuse. Children could be assigned to write about the dangers of drugs and alcohol, socially, medically, and economically. Children should also be asked to give a presentation on the subject to the family. If they need money for their research, it is well worth it.
- Adult supervision is an excellent deterrent. Youngsters cannot do themselves harm if an adult is keeping an eye on them. They are not to be allowed to roam about late at night, nor should they be left alone in the house while parents go out to enjoy themselves. Parents have to make it a habit to socialize with the whole family together, whenever possible, and plan to maximize the time together inside and outside the home. Moreover, too much money at the teenagers' disposal will spoil them and enable them to purchase illicit drugs.
- Parents need to search their children's rooms, occasionally. Parents can explain firmly that they are aware of their child's need for privacy. Parents do not have to say "I'm doing this for your own good," but rather, "I have a duty toward your safety and well-being." This is not just a random invasion of privacy, but a search for a genuine reason, which teenagers are able to comprehend. Also children's pockets, bags, and wallets are to be searched from time to time without their knowledge.
- Too much privacy for children can be counter-productive. They should not be allowed to have a television set, a telephone, or a computer with Internet use in their bedrooms. Alcohol Concern (2009) highlights figures that suggest a large increase in the amount of alcohol being drunk by 11 to 13-year-olds in the U.K.
- Choose the right peers. Parents should select friends for their children among the community, relatives, and neighbors. Parents have to find the right kind of friends for their children; it is worth the effort.

Sometimes, in spite of all these preventive measures, one's son or daughter falls into trouble. Do not panic. The heartache, anger, and suffering that results can be overwhelming. Professional advice, together with counseling, will allow parents to solve the problem. It is important that parents control their feelings and put the situation into perspective. In many cases, much can be done with professional help to produce a total or partial cure and issues of treatment and intervention will be the logical steps to consider. What parents must not do is to hide away or fail to seek help, because of the stigma of having an addict in the family or the fear of the legal consequences. To help avoid extreme anger, parents can imagine that it is not their child, but a friend's child who has come to them, asking for advice. This is a useful tool to be able to think calmly and look for the appropriate solution without emotional outbursts. No one is alone in this predicament, for there are millions of families suffering in a similar way.

Parents need to share with their children the following:

1. Alcohol is the mother of all evils

A story about the dangers of intoxicating substances is related by 'Uthmān ibn 'Affān: A man was once forced to choose one of five evils: to tear up a copy of the Qur'an, kill a baby, worship an idol, drink alcohol, or sleep with a woman. He thought that the least evil would be to drink the alcohol. He drank, and then he slept with the woman, killed the child, tore up the Qur'an, and bowed in worship to an idol. The lesson: Alcohol can be the mother of all evils.

2. Cocaine Hurts the Fetus

In the mid 1980s in the U.S., there was an epidemic of cocaine. Paediatricians observed that babies born to pregnant women who had used cocaine were not like other infants. They were underweight, they trembled, they cried inconsolably, they recoiled from hugs or touches and they were startled at the slightest sound. As they approached school age, many of them could not sit still or focus, even on activities they enjoyed. Such cocaine babies would be a lost generation. (Begley 1998)

3. Not Every Child is Innocent

In 1987 the President of MYNA (Muslim Youth of North America) invited the Chief of Police of Herndon, Virginia, to conduct a seminar on Intoxicant Prevention at the IIIT (International Institute of Islamic Thought) auditorium in Herndon. The Chief narrated this story:

> I received many complaints about missing valuables in the area. I suspected one 14-year-old boy and went to his parents with a warrant to check the boy's room. His parents said emphatically, "It can never be our boy; he is a very good boy." I asked, "Did you ever check his room?" They said, "Never, he claims it is his private room and we're not allowed in, he always keeps it locked." When I broke into the room I found the missing valuables: TVs, cameras, stereos, watches and jewellery. I advised the parents: "Although you assigned him a private room, you own the house, you have a right to go in, and it is your duty to check it from time to time!"

Can this happen to your child? Not if you follow the Chief's recommendations!

ADVICE FROM AN ALCOHOLIC TO TEENAGERS

A pint of beer is too much, but a barrel is not enough!

Never start drinking alcohol; even with a single pint. Once you start you go down the road till one whole barrel will not satisfy you! Then you will go for the stronger stuff, the dangerous drugs.

ADDICTION VS. HEALTHY HOME CONNECTION

Parents should ask themselves a basic question: "Do we have a healthy relationship with our children? Or, do we feel disconnected from them?" A healthy relationship can be defined as feeling enthusiastic and excited to see one's children and your children are enthusiastic and excited to see you. When people feel connected to others, they want to be close to them. They enjoy sharing thoughts and talking with them.

People become addicted to alcohol and drugs when they feel disconnected. In the United States, over sixty million people are affected by alcohol. They are not inclined to play, talk, or think with their children. When parents are disconnected, alcohol, drugs, and smoking give children the substitute satisfaction that they crave. They connect with something that will give them pleasure and satisfaction.

People need to learn how to connect and to be close to their relatives. By going through shared experiences and going through a struggle together, family members become closer and more strongly bonded to one another. The parents' responsibility is continual observation of their kids and intervention with wise timing. There is no rest from this, for it is just like pushing a cart uphill gently, once one stops pushing, the cart will go downhill.

If their children attend parties, parents should find out what really happens at those parties. Parents will be alarmed to know that children have reported drinking alcohol and using drugs with religious youth groups, music groups, teachers, school counselors, doctors and policemen, both in school and outside school! Parents cannot abandon their responsibility by thinking that their children are in safe hands. Trust is not enough – they need to verify.

Parents should find out about their babysitters. They may search your medicine cabinets, looking for sleeping tablets to put the children to sleep in order to enjoy themselves freely! Normally, the best "babysitters" are grandparents, who possess the love and experience required.

Can a Child be Saved if Both Parents Smoke? Or Use Drugs? A Personal Story!

Although both my parents used to smoke, I never did. Why? Because my father used to tell me, "O my son, I am a victim of this bad habit, I wish I could leave it, but I don't have the strong will to do it. It is a mistake and it is ruining my health."

When I cleaned the hubble-bubble (shīshah/nargīlah) hose, which was full of tar and black paste, he told me "My son, all this filthy stuff is filling my chest now!"

If parents are committing a mistake, they have to admit this and explain to their children the consequences. Hopefully, the children will understand the lesson and avoid these ill practices. This principle can be applied to any bad habit: smoking, drinking, staying up too late, sleeping till noon, overeating, biting your nails, talking too loud or too much, being a bad listener, and sleeping too much. However, parents must be careful to choose the appropriate age and environment to explain their bad habits to prevent their children from losing trust and confidence in them and respect for them.

Establish a healthy connection with your children by being a role model. What should parents tell their children if the parents engage in smoking, drinking, or drug use? There is no substitute for being a good role model for one's children. Nevertheless, if parents are addicted to these ills and unable to purify themselves, the minimum is to admit their shortcomings. Explain the harms to your children, and advise them to avoid these mistakes. Show them how alcoholism and drug abuse is a tragedy. Being a liar or a hypocrite will make the situation worse, because children will assume that it is acceptable to be a liar or to be a hypocrite.

AFTERCARE PROGRAMS: RELIGION AS PREVENTION

If a son or daughter falls victim to intoxicants, therapy in a treatment center is only one phase of the cure; aftercare is the next vital phase. Without adequate aftercare, the gallant efforts that the parents, their child, and the treatment center have made can fade away. Aftercare means continuing the progress that was achieved in the treatment center and thus continuing the cure.

Parents have a difficult time with aftercare. The treatment program was intense and the child is so much better that the parents cannot imagine how the child could ever "backslide". Nevertheless, it is vital that they continue the treatment! Their son or daughter is just one disagreement away from misbehaving, one telephone call away from making contact with the wrong crowd, and one sip, snort, puncture, or swallow away from reverting to chemical abuse! The final battle is won or lost in aftercare!

Scott (1989), states that treatment centers for substance abuse almost always include a spiritual "higher power" concept. They do this even though God is ignored in the field of psychology.

Professional counselors know that religious programs are effective. Nothing else works as well.

The parents' immediate attention is required in the following cases: If their child is suicidal, out of control, endangering others, in need of chemical detoxification from chemical abuse, is going to be sent to a rehabilitation unit or sentenced to a reform school, and/or is in the wrong crowd.

If parents are forced to go to the government, they should arrange weekly visits with a wise religious person to keep their child in touch with God.

Breaking the Law

Using intoxicants may eventually lead the user to break the law and become a delinquent. A delinquent is a person under seventeen whose behavior is punishable by law. Most parents do not believe that their children will be jailed one day, yet it happens to many. It can be prevented if parents build up respect for the law in their children. If parents break speed limits, cut red lights, cheat on their tax returns, tell lies to customs officers, steal from the office or factory, and willingly concoct false excuse notes for children who are missing school, then their children will feel that the law really does not matter. If parents regard the police as the enemy, their children will not respect the police.

Some immigrants have the misconception that because they are living as a minority in a country governed by secular laws, they are free to violate these laws. To refute this misconception Shaykh Taha Jabir Alalwani, a trustee of the IIIT, states:

> Once a person enters a foreign country, s/he is in essence signing a "contract" with that state to obey their constitution

and laws. Having done that, a Muslim must honor all her/his agreements and contracts as the Qur'an and the Prophet ﷺ command us explicitly. If s/he does not intend to follow the laws of a country, s/he should either abstain from entering it or declare her/his unwillingness to obey their laws, in which case the courts will expel her/him.

If citizens within their country do not like a particular law, they can change it legally according to the democratic procedure as detailed by the constitution. Islam prohibits individuals from taking the law into their own hands and applying it as they like. This would undoubtedly lead to chaos, lawlessness, and injustice. At the same time, a Muslim may not commit injustice on the grounds that the civil law has commanded it. A Muslim is not allowed to obey a law requiring the performance of a *ḥarām* act. When a law is unjust, peaceful civil disobedience is the way to change it, as has been demonstrated by Thoreau, Gandhi and Martin Luther King. Long before any of them, the Prophet Muhammad ﷺ defied the pagan Quraysh rulers and led his people peacefully and non-violently on the pilgrimage to Makkah that resulted in the Treaty of al-Ḥudaybiyyah in 630 CE.

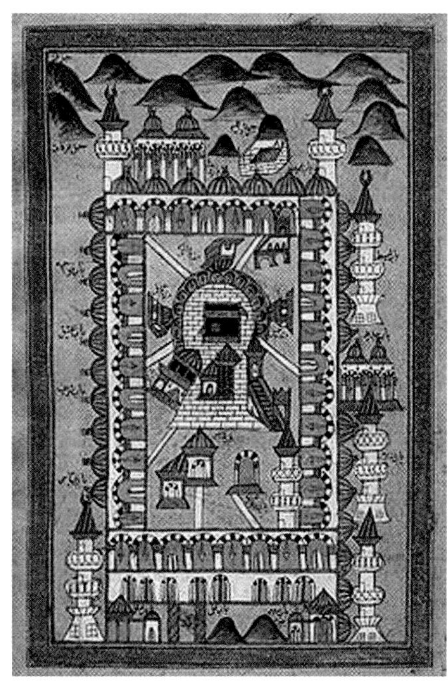

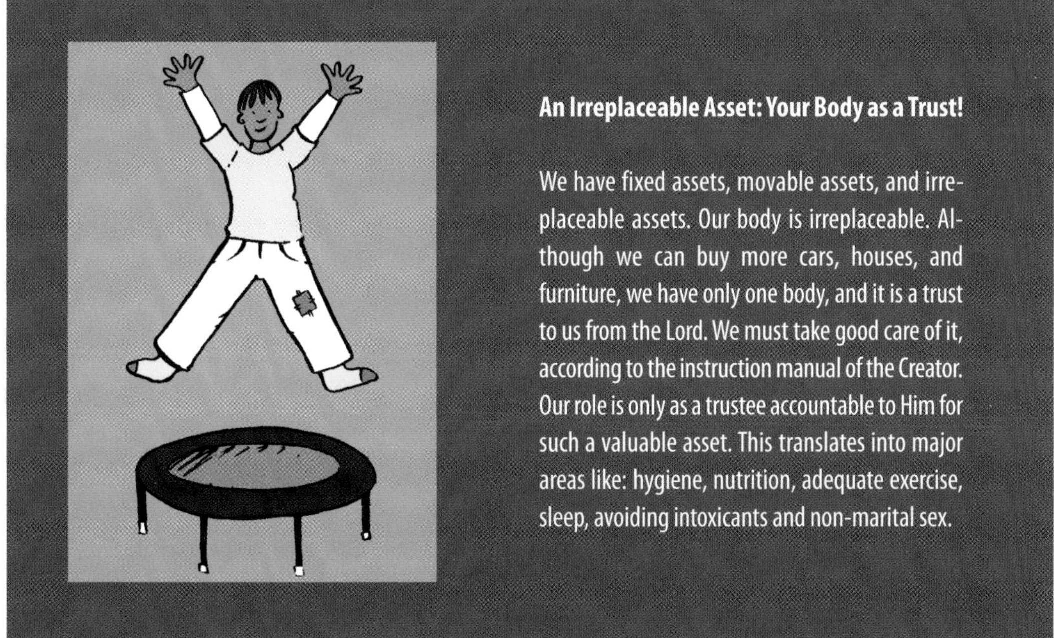

An Irreplaceable Asset: Your Body as a Trust!

We have fixed assets, movable assets, and irreplaceable assets. Our body is irreplaceable. Although we can buy more cars, houses, and furniture, we have only one body, and it is a trust to us from the Lord. We must take good care of it, according to the instruction manual of the Creator. Our role is only as a trustee accountable to Him for such a valuable asset. This translates into major areas like: hygiene, nutrition, adequate exercise, sleep, avoiding intoxicants and non-marital sex.

Activities

ACTIVITY 32: MEDICAL CHECK-UP TABLE

Sit together with your family and draw a table of regular medical check-ups, including dental care. Consult with a librarian, a teacher, a nurse, a doctor or a hospital. A copy of the final table is to be given to every member of the family.

ACTIVITY 33: FAMILY PHYSICAL FITNESS PLAN

Discuss the status of physical exercises that occur in your family with your children. Then agree with the whole family on a plan of physical activities and produce a moderate exercise schedule to follow. Try to increase the amount of exercises gradually and periodically. Try travelling on your feet instead of using the car, and doing the washing by hand instead of by machine, sometimes! A budget should be in place to purchase equipment, athletic club membership and healthier food).

ACTIVITY 34: ENGAGE BETTER WITH MEANINGFUL GREETINGS

The next time parents meet some children, instead of just saying "Hi! What's Up! How are you?" they could try greeting them in a more concerned, loving, and caring way, like:

- Did you eat nutritious food today?
- Did you exercise?
- Did you have a good sleep?
- Did you smile at your parents? Friends?
- Did you read something today?
- Did you kiss, hug or shake hands with your parents?
- Did you help anyone today?
- Did you do anything charitable?
- Did you pray?

It is not necessary to go through the whole list; just a few items will be appropriate.
Add any relevant issue depending on the children's personal occasion.

ACTIVITY 35: SLEEPING HABITS

Explain to your children healthy sleeping and eating habits:

Ibn Majah reported: The Prophet ﷺ passed by someone sleeping in the mosque, lying on his stomach. He prodded him with his foot and said, "do not lie in this manner, for it is a way that Allah and His messenger hate." Similarly the Prophet ﷺ prevented people from eating while lying on their stomachs.

Sleeping on the stomach is unhealthy for the back and the internal organs. Sleeping on the right side is the most beneficial. Sleeping on the left side causes the lungs, stomach, and liver to press against the heart, causing stress.

It is a good habit to follow daylight: go to bed (early) after the *`ishā'* prayer and rise early for the *fajr* prayer before sunrise.

The Prophet's ﷺ habit was to take a short nap after the *ẓuhr* prayer. Doctors have found that a short midday nap helps to optimize mental and physical activity, refreshing the body at a point of the day when a natural low takes place, increasing productivity and alertness, improving mood and temper, and reducing accidents.

ACTIVITY 36: CREATION OF A PROPER HOME ENVIRONMENT

Parents should sit down with their children to discuss and agree on a simple plan of action for ALL the following items in the home:

> Love, joy, laughter, free communication, mutual trust, encouragement, and recognition of achievements. Also, taking an interest in their children, eating, praying, and playing together, respecting and honoring them, kissing, hugging, and smiling at them.

Even if parents are not accustomed to these practices, it is never too late to start doing all or most of them sincerely.

ACTIVITY 37: A PROACTIVE DISCUSSION ON DRUG ABUSE SIGNS

Parents should sit together and discuss what they should do as soon as they discover signs that their child is using drugs. Steps they should take include: consulting with professionals, educating themselves, and talking to wise friends and relatives. Panic, extreme grief or beating and coercion are not helpful. (These are emotionally debilitating and only make things worse).

ACTIVITY 38: ROLE PLAY AS A POLICE OFFICER!

Parents could suggest to their teenagers to imagine themselves as police officers, magistrates or social workers, having to do their jobs. What are they responsible for? What sorts of things happen during their day? Is their work nice or unpleasant? Could they imagine themselves taking care of the community, keeping an eye out for criminals, and so forth?

> This role-play helps children to realize that probation officers, teachers, firefighters, policemen, and policewomen are normal human beings with feelings, homes, and problems just like everybody else. If teenagers are having problems in this area, then parents could introduce them to a real police officer or social worker, and let them find out more information about the job.

A visit to the court is a memorable experience. Seeing what the place is like, and learning what to do and how to behave can be a real education. It is a good idea to organize this little eye-opener visit for children.

CHAPTER 10

Breastfeeding

Introduction

AN ESSENTIAL STEP in raising strong, healthy children, physically and emotionally, is breastfeeding. The Qur'an and Islam emphasize breastfeeding and the ensuing kin relationship resulting from being breastfed by the same person (this is called milk kinship, and the children are milk siblings). For example, why cannot Salah, a 20 year old from Turkey, marry Fatimah, a young woman from Indonesia? The answer is that when Salah was one year old, he was breastfed for a couple of days by Fatimah's mother. This action makes Salah the milk brother of Fatimah, and therefore unmarriageable to her. In addition, all Fatimah's sisters and aunts also automatically become Salah's sisters and aunts, hence unmarriageable (*maḥram*) relatives. Thus, there would be no veiling (*hijāb*) between him and them. Although it is easy to understand blood relations as well as brotherhood and sisterhood in faith, how can we comprehend that a few ounces of milk can transform a stranger into a brother or a sister? It illustrates some of the importance of breast milk.

Consider blood transfusion. Even if all one's blood is replaced by the blood of another person, this does not establish a kin relationship between the two of them, even if the blood transfusion is done many times. Blood transfusions serve an essential need, and organ transplants help improve our lives, yet they do not constitute any kinship relations, no matter how major and extensive they may be. The consensus of jurists is that milk banks are forbidden in Islam. Indeed, milk kinship is put on an equal footing with biological family relationships (see verse 4:23). Laws of inheritance, however, do not apply in the case of milk siblings.

> *Forbidden to you are your mothers, and your daughters, and your sisters, and your aunts paternal and maternal, and a brother's daughters, and a sister's daughters; and your milk-mothers, and your milk-sisters; and the mothers of your wives; and your step-daughters – who are your foster children – born of your wives with whom you have consummated your marriage; but if you have not consummated your marriage, you will incur no sin [by marrying their daughters]; and [forbidden to you are] the spouses of the sons who have sprung from your loins; and [you are forbidden] to have two sisters [as your wives] at one and the same time - but what is past is past: for, behold, God is indeed Much-Forgiving, a Dispenser of grace.* (Qur'an 4:23)

The following has been presented by way of explanation:

- The baby's bones and flesh are made from the mother's milk during infancy; hence similarities exist between all those who suckle it. In other words, parts of the mother become parts of the baby from breastfeeding when s/he is less than two years old.

Jurists explain that the mother's milk causes the baby to resemble her in some ways, according to 'Umar ibn al-Khaṭṭāb and 'Umar ibn 'Abd al-'Azīz. In line with this, guidelines for nursing also prevail:

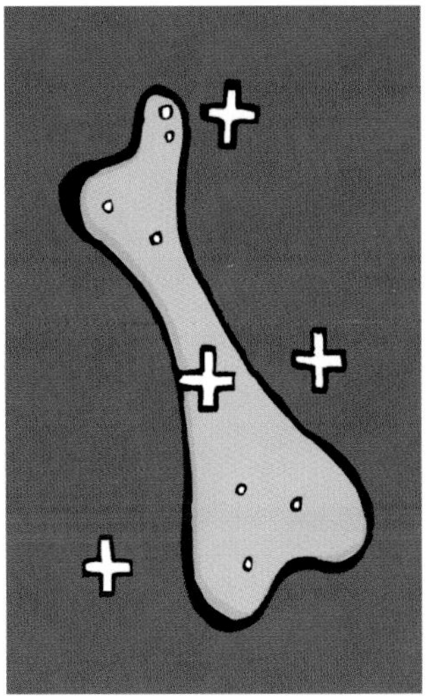

- Nursing changes the characteristics of the baby. Some jurists, for instance, have prevented a mentally imbalanced nurse from breastfeeding a baby lest s/he acquires this characteristic from her.
- Wet-nurses who smoke, eat pork, drink alcohol, or use drugs are not recommended for nursing the baby.
- Sinful foster mothers, like adulterous women, are not to breastfeed the infants.

The above are not to negate other factors. The personality of the infant is affected by many things, including the parents' genes, the environment, and the nursing milk s/he is given.

A pre-Islamic Arabian saying is that the mother's milk is from the man, so that when the baby suckles the milk of the wet-nurse, her husband's sperm and influence somehow affect her milk; therefore, the baby is somehow indirectly affected by the foster father. Thus the lineage relationship with the foster father is established. (Some Arabs used to believe that breast milk is transformed male semen). (Parkes, 2005). However, it is still unclear why we become close relatives from the milk of the wet nurse.

Dr. Fathiyyah Sulayman in Al-Ibrashi (1979) explains that some psychological studies have proven that 50 percent of the acquired intellect available at age 17 is actually achieved in the first *four* years of the child's life, 30 percent appears between the ages of 4 and 8, and the remaining 20 percent between 8 and 17. Furthermore, most of the behavior patterns observed in young and middle-aged people are attributed to events taking place in the first five years of their childhood. The Qur'an concentrates on breastfeeding and the full-time care of the loving mother in the first two years. A lack of love for and kindness to the baby may result in mental retardation. At a White House Conference held by President Clinton, experts emphasized beyond doubt that "the minds of infants are active from the time they are born and are shaped by their early experience" (Begley and Wingert, 1997). The first two years during breastfeeding contributes greatly to this shaping of the baby's brain.

The courts in Egypt have five necessary conditions that must be satisfied in order for milk kinship to be valid:

- Five feeding times at least.
- Each feeding must fully satisfy the baby.
- Each feeding must be at a separate mealtime, not rapidly consecutive sessions.
- The five feedings must be confirmed as authentic by credible witnesses.
- All five feedings must be completed before the baby is two years old.

Breastfeeding in the Qur'an

The Qur'an has dealt with breastfeeding in four different chapters, encouraging mothers to nurse their babies for two years. The nursing mother is freed from the responsibility of providing for her own sustenance, even if divorced, so that she can care for her baby full-time. If the father dies, his heir assumes the responsibility of sustenance for the nursing

mother. Religious rituals are eased for all Muslim women (including mothers); they are excused from attending daily congregational prayers and the weekly Friday sermons (to provide them with a flexible timetable to care primarily for the babies). This enables mothers to take care of babies personally rather than delegating this sensitive responsibility to babysitters. In the first two years, the baby relies completely on the mother, physically, psychologically, and emotionally.

The plastic feeding bottle cannot substitute for the soft breast and mother's love. Physical or psychological damage to the baby that is not breastfed may be difficult to cure later on; the harm may be serious and permanent. The Qur'an refers to breastfeeding in the following verses:

1. *The mothers shall nurse their offspring for two whole years, if the father desires to complete the term. But he shall bear the cost of their food and clothing on equitable terms. No soul shall have a burden laid on it greater than it can bear. No mother shall be treated unfairly on account of her child, or a father on account of his child, and his heir shall be chargeable in the same way. If they both decide on weaning, by mutual consent, and after due consultation, there is no blame on them. If you decide on a wet-nurse for your offspring there is no blame on you, provided you pay what you offered, on equitable terms. But fear Allah and know that Allah sees well what you do.* (Qur'an 2:233)

2. *And We have enjoined on man [to be good] to his parents: in travail upon travail did his mother bear him, and in two years was his weaning: [hear the command], "Show gratitude to Me and to your parents: to Me is [your final] Goal."* (Qur'an 31:14)

3. *We have enjoined on Man kindness to his parents: in pain did his mother bear him, and in pain did she give him birth. The carrying of the [child] to his weaning is thirty months. At length, when he reaches the age of full strength and attains forty years, he says: "O my Lord! Grant me that I may be grateful for Your favor that You have bestowed upon me, and upon both my parents, and that I may work righteousness such as You might approve; and be gracious to me in my issue. Truly have I turned to You and truly do I bow [to You] in Islam."*
(Qur'an 46:15)

4. *Let the women live [in 'iddah,] in the same style as you live, according to your means: do not annoy them, so as to restrict them. And if they carry [life in their wombs], then spend [your substance] on them until they deliver their burden: and if they nurse your [offspring],*

give them their recompense: and take mutual counsel together, according to what is just and reasonable. And if you find yourselves in difficulties, let another woman nurse [the child] on the [father's] behalf. (Qur'an 65:6)

Let the man of means spend according to his means: and the man whose resources are restricted, let him spend according to what Allah has given him. Allah puts no burden on any person beyond what He has given him. After a difficulty, Allah will soon grant relief.
(Qur'an 65:7)

If the mother cannot nurse the baby – if she lacks breast milk – then a wet-nurse may be assigned. The wet-nurse becomes a foster mother; she is considered the child's mother, for all intents and purposes, except for inheritance. Her children become the baby's brothers and sisters (milk siblings) and her husband becomes a milk father for the baby. No marriage is allowed between the baby and the milk mother's children, brothers, sisters and husband. The biological father is responsible for paying the milk mother's remuneration. If the father dies, the heirs should support both the nursing foster mother and the baby for the two-year period of breastfeeding.

Breastfeeding was taken seriously by the early Muslim state. At the time of the second Caliph, 'Umar ibn al-Khaṭṭāb (seventh century CE), every needy newborn baby was given an allowance as a social security benefit to ensure healthy nursing (Haq 1967).

Medical and Psychological Advantages of Breastfeeding

Al-Bar and Kandil (1986), state the following advantages:

- The mother's milk contains the nutrition a child needs, in the right proportion and in a suitable state for digestion and absorption. The nutritional elements of breast milk change daily according to the infant's needs. A premature baby has a suitable formula prepared in the mother's breast to make it a suitable diet. The mammary glands are created with the means of adjusting its secretions according to the changing needs of the growing infant.
- Human breast milk is stored naturally at the right temperature, making it free from germs and available on demand.
- No bottles need to be cleaned and no formula needs to be prepared.
- Close psychological attachment is developed between the breastfeeding mother and her baby.
- Breastfeeding helps the mother to return to her pre-pregnant size and weight. Breastfeeding makes the uterus smaller under the effect of oxytocin secreted by the pituitary gland and released by reflexes through suckling.
- Breastfeeding protects the baby from several diseases (such as diarrhea and chest infections). Breastfed infants are less likely to suffer from respiratory and gastrointestinal diseases, and have a lower mortality rate than those who

are bottle-fed. Human milk contains IgA (immunoglobulin A), an antibody in the mammary glands manufactured by lymphocytes that have migrated from the gut of the mother. (Antibodies are the tools of the immune system to fight disease). Colostrum (the pre-milk breast secretion) contains a huge amount of antibodies. The IgA forms 97 percent of the cholesterol protein on the first day, which falls to 25 percent on the fourth day of lactation. Breast milk supplies the infant with viable immunological cells and immunity against a variety of germs (especially E coli, Staph aureus, Coxsakie B5 virus, Herpes Simplex virus, poliovirus, and Pneumococcus). Tuberculin-sensitive mothers pass a long-lasting immunity to their infants.

- The colostrum has a laxative effect, which helps discharge the stool of the newborn baby.
- Cow's milk, or other non-human milk, is more likely to cause allergies in humans. The infant is at higher risk of developing eczema, bronchial asthma, and gastrointestinal upsets caused by sensitivity to the non-human proteins.
- Breastfed infants thrive better and are less liable to infections and immunological diseases. The mother's milk strengthens the developing immune system in the first few months of the baby. The mother absorbs the germs from the baby's breath. Then, through her intestines she produces the immune cells in her lymphatic nodes, which in turn excretes the required defensive antibodies that the baby suckles in the milk.
- Breastfeeding acts as a contraceptive. The lactating mother is less likely to conceive during breastfeeding, thus providing a natural and comfortable birth control for mothers.
- Humans only need breastmilk during the first 9 to 12 months.
- Human milk contains a zinc ligand, whereas cow's milk contains none. Zinc deficiency is more liable to occur in bottle-fed infants, or after premature weaning of breastfed infants.
- Breastfeeding plays a critical role in optimizing a baby's brainpower. Mother's milk contains important building blocks not found in any domestic infant formula. Babies breastfed just one month have an "8-point

Animal milk is suitable for animal babies, and the ingredients are different for each animal. The following table explains the percentages of basic contents of human, cow, buffalo and goat milk. Water content is about 88% and the rest are as follows:

Milk	% Protein	% Fat	% Sugar	% Minerals
Human	1.5	3.5	6	0.2
Cow	3	4	4	0.8
Buffalo	3	6	4	0.8
Goat	3	4	4	0.8

United States Department of Agriculture, 2010

It is recommended for mothers to breastfeed for at least 12 months. There is overwhelming evidence that breast is best. Breastfeeding may decrease the incidence of breast cancer, ovarian cancers, osteoporosis, and other female disorders. Breastfeeding stimulates the uterus to return to its original state. (CNN, December 7, 1997)

IQ advantage as kindergarteners, and that figure rises with extended breastfeeding" (BBC 2002). A study tracking over 1,000 children in New Zealand supports the link between breastfeeding and higher intelligence.

- Mother's milk includes protection against bacterial infections (such as meningitis, urinary tract infections, and earaches). Formula-fed babies suffer more from insulin-dependent diabetes, lymphoma, allergies, and digestive problems.

American Business and Breastfeeding

Despite the clear advantages of human milk for babies, fewer than 60 percent of American women breastfeed, which is lower than many industrialized nations. Only 22 percent of mothers in the U.S. are still nursing by the time their babies are 6 months old. Part of the reason is the demands of breastfeeding. Newborns breastfeed up to a dozen times during a 24-hour period, usually 10–15 minutes on each breast. Fitting that schedule into working hours is daunting.

The workplace may soon become friendlier for nursing mothers in America. Governments and companies are granting women up to an hour of paid leave per day to express milk at work, and encouraging workplace lactation programs. (Cassidy 1998)

In 1993, a UNICEF award was given to John Hancock Mutual Life Insurance Company for its introduction of workplace lactation rooms (which include an electric breast pump, comfortable chairs, and a refrigerator). With an annual average of 300 pregnant employees, the company discovered that the new program saved it money ($60,000 since its inception) because breastfed infants are healthier, so mothers are less apt to miss work. Also, the transition back to work is easier, so more new mothers are willing to take a shorter maternity leave. Because breastfed babies in the U.S. have 35 percent fewer illnesses than babies fed formula, and nursing mothers consequently miss work up to 27 percent less than new mothers who do not breastfeed. (Rona Cohen, School of Nursing, University of California at Los Angeles).

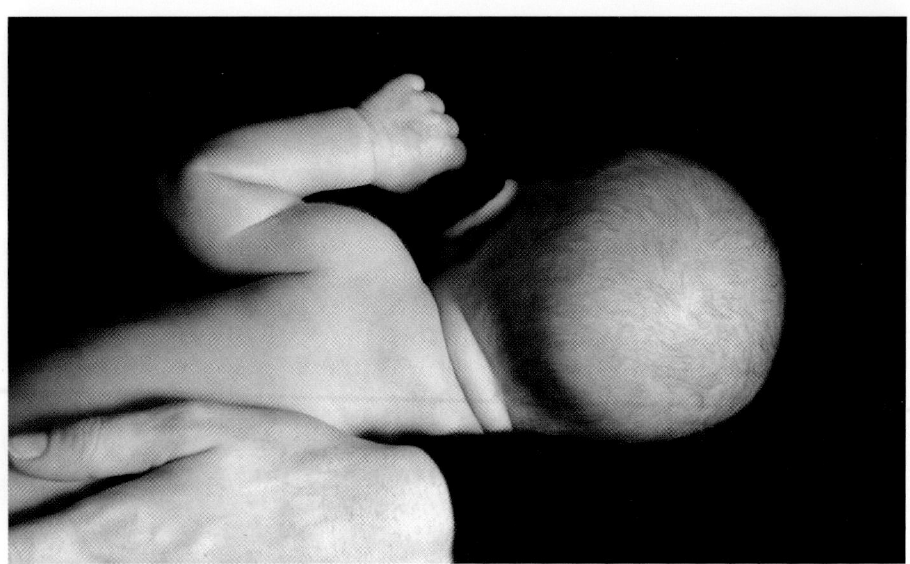

The Muslim World and Breastfeeding

Historically, Muslim communities paid great attention to breastfeeding and wet-nurses. Even when the mother nursed her baby, it was common for a neighbor, relative or friend to breastfeed the newcomer as well. Such practices had some social advantages. Many girls who marry at age 15 or less, and boys under 18, need help and guidance from older generations. Extended families help by relieving mothers of some of their burden.

Modernization is changing the pattern of social and cultural attitudes in Muslim countries. This is more pronounced in the urban areas, where breastfeeding is rapidly declining more than in rural areas. Baby food companies are behind the decline of breastfeeding in developing countries. Their sales and profits increase when mothers stop breastfeeding and buy their products.

UNICEF and the WHO consider these companies the number one killer of babies in the developing world, and have strongly advised their governments to ban the advertising of manufactured baby foods. These bottle-fed infants often receive diluted and contaminated feeds containing few nutrients and massive doses of microorganisms, owing to unclean water from unsanitary sources being used in the formula. UNICEF and WHO findings estimate that 9.4 million cases of severe malnutrition occur in the developing world annually, of which at least half are due to bottle-feeding. Similarly, there are annually about 10 million infant deaths due to digestive system diseases in the developing world. At least half of them are due to bottle-feeding, whereas breastfeeding could have saved them. Breastfeeding is also less expensive (a 6-month supply of formula in Malaysia costs $300 or more). (Allain, 1993)

Infant formula is a pale imitation of mother's milk, although researchers are learning to make it more nutritious. Fortifying formula with a class of fatty acids known as LCPUFAs (pronounced "Elsie Pufas") can help promote brain development. The University of Dundee, Scotland (Willats et al. 1998) gave half of a group of 44 babies, a formula containing the high LCPUFA concentrations found in breast milk. The other babies received the regular formula. At the age of 10 months, the LCPUFA babies scored significantly higher on a test that entailed finding a hidden toy, possibly indicating stronger nerve cell connections in their brains. Some Europeans now fortify formula with LCPU-FAs.

Imam ʿAlī's and Ibn Ḥazm's Opinions of Breastfeeding

Breastfeeding is considered a natural right of babies over their mothers. Mothers are encouraged to nurse their children. Ibn Ḥazm said,

> **"A mother should nurse her baby even if she is the daughter of the king. She is not exempted from that duty, unless she is incapable of nursing."** (Ibn Ḥazm, Vol 10)

If Islamic teachings are adhered to, many problems that befall children and their mother could be avoided. ʿAlī ibn Abī Ṭālib said:

> **"No milk suckled by the baby is more graciously blessed than the mother's milk."**

THE INTERNATIONAL BREASTFEEDING SYMBOL

Duration of Breastfeeding

Jurists differ, but the general consensus is that breastfeeding should not exceed two years. If the mother is healthy and her milk is available, it is better to wean at two years. Yūsuf ʿAlī comments on verse 46:15:

> The maximum period of breastfeeding (2 years) is again in accordance with the time that the first dentition is ordinarily completed in the child. The lower milk incisors in the center come out between the 6th and 9th months, and then the milk teeth come out at intervals, until the canines appear. The second molars come out at about 24 months, and with them the child has a complete apparatus of milk teeth. Nature now expects him to chew and masticate and be independent of his mother's milk completely. On the other hand, it hurts the mother to feed from the breast after the child has a complete set of milk teeth. The permanent teeth begin at the 6th year, and the 2nd molars come at 12 years. The third molars are the wisdom teeth, which may appear at 18–20 years, or not at all.

Some have commented that breastfeeding beyond two years might harm the baby physically, mentally, and psychologically. In 1997 the American Academy for Pediatricians (AAP) recommended mothers to nurse their babies between the months of 6 and 12 at least. In reality only 20% of American mothers actually breastfeed their babies after 6 months. The AAP later extended this by recommending mothers to breastfeed for at least a year. It listed the benefits of breastfeeding (such as reducing the chances of having uterus cancer, breast cancer and osteoporosis).

The Prophet ﷺ spoke about breastfeeding by a wet-nurse. Whenever possible, the biological mother should breastfeed, unless there is a medical reason to excuse the mother, in which case a wet-nurse may be hired. He explains:

> "Be careful who is going to be your foster brother from suckling! Use a wet-nurse only upon the necessity of hunger of the baby." (AL-BUKHĀRĪ)

One advantage of publicizing marriage is to ensure that a woman does not marry her own milk-brother or father by mistake. This gives a chance for the public to come forward and testify of the existence of such milk relations if they exist.

Helpful Hints for Nursing Mothers

(Adapted from: El-Amin 1998)

Although breastfeeding is the natural way, it is a skill that can be improved. Below are some useful tips for mothers:

- Prepare yourself before your baby is born. Read some books about breastfeeding. Take a class from your hospital, healthcare provider, or lactation consultant. Attend a meeting of a breastfeeding support organization.
- Proper positioning is essential. Make sure the nipple is 1" to 1½" into the baby's mouth. Do not bend toward the baby; bring the baby to you. A pillow is often helpful.
- Let the baby nurse at one breast until it completely softens and the baby's sucking motion changes from vigorous to slow. Then offer the other breast. It is better to soften one breast per feeding than to partially nurse at both breasts. The first portion is like *skimmed milk*, the middle like *whole milk*, and the last like *cream*. This cream balances the consistency of the feeding and helps prevent excessive crying.
- Some breast engorgement enlargement is natural in the first few days. If babies cannot nurse from engorged nipples, release a small amount of milk before feeding.
- Correct sore nipples with proper conditioning. Relieve the pain by air-drying nipples then apply natural products like organic olive oil or pure lanolin.
- Drink plenty of water. *Fenugreek tea* and *garlic* are both said to increase milk supply.
- It is important to begin in the *first one or two hours* after delivery, when the baby is alert.
- How often is enough? For the first 2–3 weeks, you might need to wake your baby for feedings. The baby nurses at least every three hours during the day, and every four hours at night. Frequent feedings are important for the baby and for building up the milk supply. The more the baby nurses, the more milk the mother makes. Once your baby is gaining weight well, follow the baby's desire for the number of feedings.
- Bottle-feeding from expressed milk: Do not give a breastfed baby a bottle with your own breast milk until breastfeeding is well established – usually between 3 and 5 weeks. It sometimes helps if someone other than the mother gives the baby the first bottle, which should contain the mother's breast milk. With a little practice, most babies can go back and forth between bottle and breast.
- Some babies are good at nursing right

from the start, others take longer to learn. It is okay if it does not work well in the beginning.
- Do not give up on breastfeeding. One mother said it took six weeks to fall into a comfortable rhythm, followed by a long, beautiful nursing relationship.
- The mother's nipples during the first week may suffer from being sore to painful. Release a bit of milk before and after feedings, and rub the milk into your nipples. Allow nipples to air dry.

Mothers enjoy breastfeeding. No food preparation is needed, a special sense of closeness develops with babies, and babies have fewer illnesses and ear infections. Before birth, mothers should make a list of support services, so if they have any difficulty during the first couple of days, they will know whom to call.

Mother's Daily Diet: A Sample

The following is a sample diet for nursing mothers:

- three servings of protein, such as chicken and fish
- two servings of food high in vitamin C, such as oranges
- five servings of calcium, such as milk or cheese
- six servings of fruits and vegetables, such as coconuts and asparagus
- six servings of complex carbohydrates, such as whole wheat bread
- one serving of iron-rich foods, such as beef or beans
- small amounts of high-fat foods, such as cheese or whole milk
- eight glasses of water
- vitamins for pregnant or lactating women

Good nutrition helps the mother maintain an adequate milk supply, gives her energy, and helps her lose excess pounds from the pregnancy. It is also important to drink plenty of milk or the mother will be robbed of calcium in the future.

The Strong Nation: Physically

The Qur'an and traditions of the Prophet ﷺ, speak of strength in all its forms:

> *...You are indeed the best community that has ever been brought forth for [the good of] mankind: you enjoin the doing of what is right and forbid the doing of what is wrong, and you believe in God...* (Qur'an 3:110)

> *... And prepare for them all you can of strength [power] and of horse power to scare the enemies of Allah and your enemies...* (Qur'an 8:60)

One mother said, "Breastfeeding is wonderful. Even in the middle of the night, when I look down at that little face and know that all that my son wants is me, how could I not want to nurse him? The emotional benefits of nursing are as much for me as for my baby."

The Prophet ﷺ said: The strong believer is better and more loved by Allah than the weak believer; there is goodness in both (Muslim). Note, the word '*qawy*' in the Hadith refers to strength of faith and body. These aforementioned descriptions, "best community," "prepare all the strength and power you can," and "the strong believer," include the physical (biological) aspects as well as the faith and moral aspects. In the light of previous chapters, the following conclusion can be drawn:

> A community can surpass in physical strength all other nations by following these guidelines:

- Choosing healthy spouses.
- Abstaining from all forms of non-marital sexual practices; this ensures that parents and their offspring will be free from sexually transmitted diseases, including, but not limited to, AIDS.
- Eating properly. Parents, pregnant mothers, and children eat *azkā ṭaʿāman* (also described as *al-ṭayyibāt*), that is: good, wholesome, nutritious, and pure food. No pork, blood, carrion, and strangled animals, are allowed for consumption. The Qur'an promotes water, milk, and honey; fruits (dates, grapes, olives, figs), meat (poultry, seafood, beef, and lamb), and vegetables (onions, garlic, cucumber, cereals, beans).
- Following a clean hygienic lifestyle. Germs are eliminated by simply washing hands before and after every meal. Use the left hand for washing in the bathroom and the right hand for eating. Perform ablution five times a day.
- Avoiding intoxicants (alcohol, drugs and smoking). The fetus, in particular, will develop and emerge healthy if its parents avoid chemicals and substance abuse.
- Breastfeeding babies. Children grow up and develop a strong character, and physical and psychological strength, making them ready to become righteous people and leaders of the pious.

Maternity leave should be longer than eight weeks. An extended leave of one year will help mothers dedicate themselves full-time to the care of their babies (to nurture future leaders, as did the mother of Moses).

In conclusion, the first five years are crucial for building a strong healthy person of good character. They constitute a window of opportunity that must not be lost. The above guidelines will lead the community to become the best of people amongst humankind.

Having raised strong, healthy children, we can teach them faith, wisdom, knowledge, and skills. These come later in life, as explained in the case of Prophets Joseph, Moses, and others.

> *When he [Moses] attained his full manhood and maturity, We gave him wisdom and knowledge: thus do We reward those who do right.* (Qur'an 28:14)

Breastfeeding has a firm basis for producing the best of nations because:

a) It gives babies physical strength, psychological power and emotional energy.
b) It is a highly customized and individualized form of nourishment as opposed to the mass produced formula used for bottle-feeding.
c) It is the most natural way of feeding babies.

While human knowledge keeps expanding and changing, the divine scriptures stress certain instructions (Do's or Don'ts) for human beings to benefit from.

> *Verily this Qur'an guides to that which is most right (or stable), and gives the glad tidings to the Believers who work deeds of righteousness, that they shall have a magnificent reward.*
>
> (Qur'an 17:9)

Muslims today are violating the basics of the Prophet's directives on living a healthy life. Not a single Muslim country is listed among the 12 countries with the highest life expectancy in the world. Afghanistan is listed as having the lowest life expectancy (43 years for men and 44 for women)! (United Nations, 2010)

Activity

ACTIVITY 39: IT BOTHERS ME ...

Parents and children should discuss these items and agree on how to avoid committing them.

IT BOTHERS ME WHEN:

- The pizza, the *baqlāva* and the cake is not cut very well.
- Children do not pick up their own litter, and the parent picks it up for them.
- The trash is thrown around the trash can, not inside it.
- People come late to their appointments.
- The husband comes home late without informing his wife.
- People forget to tie their shoelaces and nobody reminds them.
- People come out of the restrooms without washing their hands.
- People do not lock the bathroom when they are inside.
- People leave cups of tea, coffee, or water on their desk over night without emptying them completely.
- People do not comb their hair (including long eyebrows and beards).
- People leave clips, pins, and staples scattered around desks and floors.
- Parents smile at their child while s/he is misbehaving in a friend's home.
- People spread rumors and indulge in backbiting (the Qur'an describes it as if you are eating human flesh).
- The child is asked a question and the parent answers instead of the child.
- People interrupt children often while they are talking.
- The host forces the guest to eat too much.
- People make racist comments or jokes.
- People leave lots of food on their plate and throw it away.
- Visitors come unexpectedly without notice.
- Guests interfere and punish the host's children without permission.
- Parents break their promises to their children without a sincere apology.
- People ask you for advice without telling you all the sides of their story.
- Young people use the elevators instead of the stairs.
- A messenger does not convey the message to you completely and accurately.
- Visitors stay too long with the patient in the hospital.
- Someone is upset with you without telling you why.
- People waste money, food, paper, medicine, time, napkins, and soap.

- Drivers send and read text messages while driving. (In some places it is illegal to use a cell phone while driving a vehicle).
- People cough or sneeze in your face, without covering their mouths and noses.
- People do not silence their cell phones in meetings, prayers and libraries.
- People's clothes and socks smell bad.
- People wet the floors and sinks in bathrooms without wiping them dry.
- More than one person talks at the same time.
- Drivers honk their horns uselessly and aimlessly.
- Speakers repeat a word or phrase too many times inappropriately.
- A person speaks too loud, annoying others, while the other person speaks too low for listeners to hear.
- People leave lights on unnecessarily.
- Someone jumps the queue without people's permission.
- Guests do not follow the instructions of their host in his/her own home (castle).
- The host delays offering the food waiting for a guest who is very late.
- People waste tap water as they wash their hands.
- Faucets are not fully turned off.
- People do not use a napkin when needing to spit (they spit on the floor).
- People do not pick up trash from their path.
- People block corridors as they converse.
- Two persons talk or whisper to each other during meetings.
- A person commits a mistake and s/he does not admit it and apologize sincerely for it.
- People invite you and do not tell you clearly if there will be a meal or not.
- In taking a paper napkin from a box you pull out many napkins.
- Speakers take too long or too short of their allotted time.
- People frown rather than smile.
- You greet someone and s/he does not answer.
- People make the room too dark or too bright.
- People bother people by being noisy, nosy, or needy.

Each member of the family can add his/her own dislikes to this list.

CHAPTER 11

The Child's Brain: Use it or Lose it!

Introduction

It is He Who brought you forth from the wombs of your mothers when you knew nothing; and He gave you hearing and sight and intelligence and affections: that you may give thanks [to Allah]. (Qur'an 16:78)

THE QUR'AN ASSERTS that babies are born with zero knowledge. God has endowed them with the tools of acquiring knowledge: first by hearing, then seeing, and finally the *fū'ād*, the seat of feelings and emotions. Biology explains that the center of hearing is located at the front of the brain, while the center of sight is at the back. In between the two lie other centers of the brain. These constitute the cognition for which individuals are responsible for the rationality of their decisions. It is interesting that the Qur'an always mentions these three words in the same order together, as if they are inseparable: hearing, sight, and affection.

We need to understand how a child's brain is formed and developed. It brings into focus the importance of the child's early experiences and how they help form the brain's circuits for logic, mathematics, music, language, and emotions. Once we understand this, we can then appreciate the emphasis on breastfeeding in the first two years.

The Window of Opportunity

"To deal with babies properly, we have to understand their biology. Circuits in different regions of the brain mature at different times, though mostly during infancy. As a result, different circuits are most sensitive to life experiences at different ages. Give your children the stimulation they need when they need it, and anything is possible; stumble and the result is likely to be failure." (Begley 1996).

Although the human brain weighs only about three pounds (≅1360 gm), it contains trillions of brain interconnections, and immense processing power. If we imagined every two cities of the world were connected by a main highway, and more highways connected these cities to every other major city in the world, and also went on to connect villages all over the world, this would still not do the brain any justice. And if we imagined that a secondary road connecting every village to every other village in the world were built, the vast network of primary and secondary roads required would still not match the brain's complexity, not to mention the fact that the available land on our planet would not be sufficient to house them all.

The problem, in terms of brain development, is that if these roads are not built during the first years of infancy, they cannot be built later on. Alas! This is exactly what is happening, and a golden opportunity is continually being lost forever – what a tragedy! Hence, it is important to learn how to develop the brain interconnections and then make every effort to develop them in our children.

Brain Power Absorption

How many inputs can a 3-year-old child's brain absorb?
If we conceive of the brain as the most powerful and sophisticated computer imaginable, the child's surroundings act like a keyboard, inputting experience. The computer comes with so much memory capacity that for the first three years it can store more information than an army of humans could possibly input. By the end of three or four years, however, the pace of learning slows. The computer will continue to accept information, but at a decreasing rate. The process continues to slow as we mature, and as we age our brain cells and synapses begin to wither away. We have to capture this opportunity before it escapes after the age of three. (Kotulak 1993)

WINDOWS OF OPPORTUNITY

PRENATAL	BIRTH	1 YEAR OLD	2 YEARS	3 YEARS	4 YEARS	5 YEARS	6 YEARS	7 YEARS	8 YEARS	9 YEARS

MOTOR DEVELOPMENT
EMOTIONAL CONTROL
VISION
SOCIAL ATTACHMENT
VOCABULARY
SECOND LANGUAGE
MATH / LOGIC
MUSIC

Rycus and Huges 1998

To reiterate, the Qur'an asserts that at birth knowledge is zero: *It is He Who brought you forth from the wombs of your mothers when you knew nothing; and He gave you hearing and sight and intelligence and affections: that you may give thanks [to Allah].* (Qur'an 16:78)

Development of Neurons and Brain Networks

"The brain is crisscrossed by billions of nerve cells (neurons). Some of the neurons control breathing, manage heartbeat, regulate body temperature or produce reflexes. Yet upon birth trillions upon trillions of neurons are still not yet used; they are like Pentium chips in a computer before the factory pre-loads the software. If the neurons are used, they become integrated into the circuitry of the brain by connecting to other neurons; if they are not used, they may die. It is the experiences of infancy that determine which neurons are used, wiring the circuits of the brain as surely as a programmer at a keyboard reconfigures the circuits in a computer. Which keys are typed – which experiences a child has – determines whether the child grows up to be intelligent or dull, fearful or self-assured, articulate or tongue-tied. Early experiences are so powerful that they can completely change the way a person turns out." (Nash 1997)

By adulthood the brain is crisscrossed with more than 100 billion neurons, reaching out to thousands of others so that the brain has more than 100 trillion connections. It is those connections – more than the number of known galaxies in the known universe – that give the brain its unrivaled powers. The traditional view was that the wiring diagram is predetermined, like one for a new house, by the genes in the fertilized egg in the womb. Even though half the genes play a role in the central nervous system, there are not enough of them to specify the brain's incomparably complex wiring. That leaves another possibility; genes might determine only the brain's main circuits, with something else shaping the trillions of finer connections. That something else is the environment, the myriad messages that the brain receives from the outside world. "There are two broad stages of brain wiring: an early period when experience is not required, and a later one, when it is" (Carla Shatz, 1996, University of California in Nash 1997). Yet, once wired, there are time limits to the brain's ability to create itself. Called "critical periods," "they are the windows of opportunity that nature flings open, starting before birth, and then slams shut, one by one, with every additional year."

The implications of this are at once promising and disturbing. With the right input at the right time, almost anything is possible. Nevertheless, if that window is missed, then one is playing with a handicap. The gains a toddler makes in intensive school programs such as Head Start are so often temporary: this intensive instruction begins too late to rewire the brain fundamentally. Postponing instruction in a second language is also a big mistake. As Chugani asks, "What idiot decreed that foreign language instruction was not to begin until high school? It is too late then." (Dr. Harry Chugani, Children's Hospital of Michigan).

The vision, sound, emotions and movement centers of the brain can be described as follows:

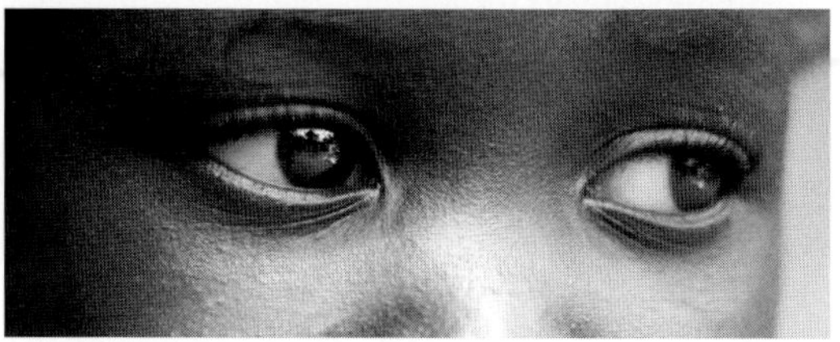

Vision

The circuit for vision has a neuron growth spurt at the age of 2 to 4 months, which corresponds to when babies really begin to notice the world, and peaks at 8 months, when each neuron is connected to an astonishing 15,000 other neurons. A baby whose eyes are clouded by cataracts from birth will, despite surgery to remove the cataracts at the age of 2, be forever blind. Vision experiments on cats confirm these findings.

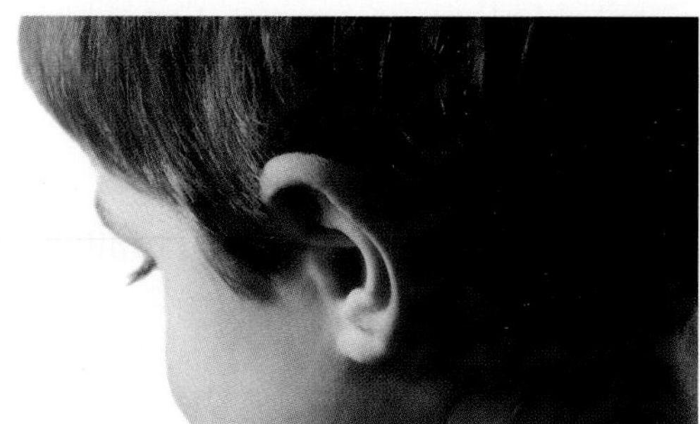

Sound

"By 12 months, infants have lost the ability to discriminate sounds that are not significant in their language, and their babbling has acquired the sound of their language," says Patricia Kuhl (The University of Washington). This explains why the Japanese are unable to differentiate between the sounds of L and R: "elects" sounds like "erects." Also, many non-Arabs equate ḍ with z sounds, where *ḍāllīn* sounds like *zāllīn*.

Learning a second language after (rather than with) the first language is so difficult. "The perceptual map of the first language constrains the learning of a second" she says. For example, if the circuits are already wired for Spanish as the first language, the remaining undedicated neurons have lost their ability to form basic new connections for Greek as a second language. A child taught a second language after the age of 10 is unlikely to speak it like a native. This is why it is crucial that babies listen to Qur'anic recitations during infancy to master the sounds of all the Arabic letters.

With this basic circuitry established, babies are primed to turn sounds into words. The more words children hear, the faster they learn language. Infants whose mothers spoke to them frequently knew 131 more words at 20 months than did babies of less dedicated mothers; at 24 months, the gap had widened to 295 words. It did not matter which words the mother used – monosyllables seemed to work. The sounds of words build up neuro-circuitry that can then absorb more words. There is a huge vocabulary to be acquired and it can be acquired only by repeated exposure to words. It is important to note here the same positive effects on babies' language development if they have several siblings who talk to them frequently.

Music

(Elbert et al. 1995) Early exposure to music rewires neural circuits. The brains of musicians who play string instruments were examined with magnetic resonance imaging. The amount of brain area dedicated to the thumb and the fingers of the left hand was significantly larger than in non-players.

Plato said that music is the most potent instrument for education. Now scientists know why. Music, they believe, trains the brain for higher forms of thinking. Researchers studied the power of music by observing two groups of preschoolers. One group of children took piano lessons and sang daily. The other did not. After 8 months the musical 3 year olds were excellent puzzle masters, scoring 80 percent higher than their playmates did in spatial intelligence (the ability to visualize the world accurately).

It is striking that this skill later translates into complex mathematical and engineering skills. According to physicist Gordon Shaw of Irvine, California, "early music training can enhance a child's ability to reason." (Begley 2000).

There seems to be a close relationship in the brain between music, mathematics and logic. Higher order thinking is characterized by similar brain patterns. Teachers working with little children do not teach them higher mathematics or chess. Nevertheless, little children are interested in and can process music. Frances Rauscher (University of Wisconsin) gave some children piano lessons and some children singing lessons. After 8 months, those children who were given music lessons "dramatically improved in spatial reasoning," compared with children given no music lessons. This improvement showed in their ability to work mazes, draw geometric figures, and copy patterns of two-color blocks. When children exercise cortical neurons by listening to classical music, they are strengthening circuits used for mathematics. Music excites the inherent brain patterns and enhances their use in complex reasoning tasks. (Nash 1997)

Children should be encouraged to learn to play a musical instrument.

Birth and Musical Therapy

What makes a baby calm when it is in its mother's arms? To answer the question, researchers performed the following experiment: Some babies who were crying for food were taken to a room where pre-recorded mothers' heartbeats and lullabies were playing. The crying babies became silent and fell asleep in a short while (Hicks, 1995). During pregnancy, babies in the womb become accustomed to the heartbeats of the mother. After the baby is born, this familiar sound becomes a sort of music that relieves the baby. Most mothers unintentionally lean their babies on their left arms during breastfeeding and over their hearts when trying to lull them. This instinctive behavior reinforces the soothing impact of the mother's heartbeat on the baby. (Sears, 1991)

Music therapy is effective during the delivery of a baby. In a study conducted at Bakirkoy Maternity Hospital in Turkey, the researcher selected a sample of women who were about to deliver their baby. She divided the pregnant women into two rooms: In one room she played the sound of water and the sound of the 'ney' (a traditional Turkish flute), and in the other room there were no sounds. She found that those who listened to the musical sounds had less pain during labor, experienced less stress, and were in a better mood. (Komurcu 1999)

Music therapy helps patients feel better and increases their self-confidence. It also improves blood circulation, improves respiration, and improves muscle functions (Davis, et al. 2008). Along the same lines, Muslims have been experiencing many positive effects from listening to the Qur'an and the recitation of poetry that praises the Prophet Muhammad (*qawāli*).

Emotions

The trunk lines for the circuits controlling emotion are laid down before birth. Then parents take over. Perhaps the strongest influence is attunement (where caregivers play back a child's inner feelings). If a baby's squeal of delight at a cat or puppy is met with a smile and hug, or if his/her excitement at seeing a plane overhead is mirrored, circuits for these emotions are reinforced. Apparently, the brain uses the same pathways to generate an emotion as to respond to one. So if an emotion is reciprocated, the electrical and chemical signals that produced it are reinforced. However, if emotions are repeatedly met with indifference or a clashing response (for example, baby is proud of building a skyscraper out of Mom's best pots, and Mom is terminally annoyed), those circuits become confused and fail to strengthen. The key here is "repeatedly": one negative word will not harm a child for life. It is the pattern that counts, and it can be very powerful. In one study, a baby whose mother never matched the baby's level of excitement grew up extremely passive, unable to feel excitement or joy.

Stress Can Rewire Emotion Circuits

Stress and constant threats also rewire emotion circuits. These circuits are centered in the amygdala, a little almond-shaped structure deep in the brain whose job is to scan incoming sights and sounds for emotional content. Impulses from the eye and ear reach the amygdala before they reach the rational, thoughtful neocortex. If a sight, sound or experience has proved painful before – Dad's drunken arrival home was followed by a beating – then the amygdala floods the circuits with neurochemicals before the higher brain knows what is happening. The more often this pathway is used, the easier it is to trigger: the mere memory of Dad induces fear. Since the circuits can stay excited for days, the brain remains on high alert. In this state, more circuits attend to nonverbal cues – facial expressions, angry noises – that warn of impending danger. As a result, the cortex falls behind in development and has trouble assimilating complex information (such as language). This may explain the guidance of the Prophet ﷺ to keep silent when angry, lest unintended and inappropriate words gush out during intense anger.

Movement

Fetal movements begin at seven weeks of pregnancy and peak between the 15th and 17th weeks. This is when regions of the brain controlling movement start to wire up. The critical period lasts a while: it takes up to two years for cells in the cerebellum, which control posture and movement, to form functional circuits. A lot of organization takes place, using information gleaned from when the child moves about in the world. If you restrict the infant's activity, you inhibit the formation of synaptic connections in the cerebellum. The child's initially spastic movements send a signal to the brain's motor cortex; the more the arm moves, the stronger the circuit, and the better the brain will become at moving the arm intentionally and fluidly. This window of opportunity only lasts a few years: a child immobilized in a body cast until the age of four will learn to walk eventually, but never smoothly. (Carmichael 2007)

Exercise is good not only for the heart, but also for the brain, by feeding it nutrients in the form of glucose, and increasing nerve connections – all of which make it easier for children of all ages to learn. Children who exercise do better in school. Children also need to be given physical activities in the classroom, not just sitting quietly in their seats memorizing multiplication tables and poetry. Knowledge is retained longer if children connect not only orally but also emotionally and physically to the material.

Vocabulary and Memorization in Childhood

These biological discoveries may explain why many non-Arabic speaking children memorize the Qur'an at a young age. Some children memorize it entirely before the age of 10. This confirms the recent findings that the window of opportunity of language learning starts to close after 10. The practice of early memorization is missing in modern nations. While the physical body needs food to grow, memorization provides the brain with the foundation to develop a language. The "windows of opportunity for learning" last until the age of 12. The more glucose the brain uses, the more active it is. Children's brains gobble up glucose at twice the adult rate from the age of four to puberty. Hence, young brains are the most capable to process new information. Complex subjects (such as trigonometry or foreign languages) should be taught at a young age. It is far easier for an elementary school child to hear and process a second language – and even speak it without an accent. Unfortunately, most U.S. schools wait until seventh grade to introduce Spanish or French, after the "windows" are closed.

How the Brain Changes

Exercise spurs growth in the brain area associated with memory, possibly leading to improved function. Researchers found that exercise increased blood volume in the dentate gyrus (a region of the hippocampus, which is used in memory), implying new brain cells were forming in the area. (Carmichael 2007)

Parents Should Speak to Their Baby Positively

The biggest difference among various households is in the amount of talking that occurs. The more money and education parents have, the more they talk to their children, and the more effective the child's vocabulary development. By age three, the children of affluent parents would have heard more than 30 million words, three times as many as the children in the least privileged families.

There were also significant differences in the ways parents talked to their children. The parents with the most income and education tended to speak more affirmatively, conveying frequent and explicit approval (with encouraging statements like "That's good," "That's right," "I love you," "Good job"). Working class parents generally praised their children, but less frequently, and they more often voiced statements of disapproval (such as "That's bad," "You're wrong," "Stop," "Quit," "Shut up"). Poor parents praised their children less often and criticized them more frequently.

The size of toddlers' vocabulary increases the more their mothers had talked to them.

Children of professional parents heard 75 percent more words per hour than did the children of working class parents, and more than three times as many words as did the children of low-income parents. The richer children were given positive feedback two to five times as often as the poorer children. Tested at the age of three, children who heard many words and had more positive experiences scored higher on standardized tests than children who heard less words and had less positive experiences. Note that low-income and working class parents love their babies as much as other parents. (Begley and Wingert 1997).

The Head Start Preschool Program in the United States

Head Start, a federal program that has provided comprehensive early childhood development services to low-income children since 1965, has not succeeded. The children's intelligence gains disappear after about three years. The reason is timing: Head Start enrolls two, three, and four year olds. In 1992, the Abecedarian Project was started. Children from 120 poor families were assigned to one of four groups for intensive early education in a day care center: Group 1, from about four months to age eight, Group 2, from four months to five years, Group 3, from five months to eight years, and Group 4, no intensive early education. What does it mean to "educate" a four month old? Giving them blocks and beads, talking to him or her and playing games (such as peek-a-boo). Each of the 200-odd "learning games" was designed to enhance cognitive, language, social or motor development. The children enrolled in the Abecedarian project as preschoolers scored higher in mathematics and reading at the ages of 15 than other children. The children in the Abecedarian Project had a higher gain in intelligence than other children. The earlier the children were enrolled, the more enduring the gain. Intervention after age five conferred no noticeable IQ or academic benefit.

The troubling question is: If the windows of the mind close before we are out of elementary school, is all hope lost for children who missed their educational opportunities? What about poor children whose parents did not have them count beads to stimulate their mathematical abilities, or talk to them to build their language ability? At one level there is still hope: the brain retains the ability to learn throughout life. Look at people who did not learn French in college only to master it later in life or during retirement. On a deeper level, however, there is a problem. Children whose brains are not stimulated before kindergarten are going to be less capable.

The bottom line is that although we are born with great potential, that potential will be realized to its maximum only if it is developed. Hence, parents must be aware of how the brain develops and how the brain retains knowledge. Three basic skills must be enhanced in the child's brain in a timely fashion:

- the logic brain (mathematics and logic),
- the language brain, and
- the music brain.

On September 30, 1997, British Prime Minister Tony Blair announced in his address at the Labor Party National Conference (Brighton, England), that pre-schooling should start at the age of three instead of four, thus capitalizing on the importance of early timing in brain development.

What Can Parents Do?

THE LOGICAL BRAIN

Skill: Mathematics and Logic

Learning window: Birth to 4 years

What we know: Circuits for mathematics reside in the brain's cortex, near those for music. Toddlers who are taught simple concepts, like one and many, do better in mathematics.

Action: Counting games can be played with toddlers. For example, have children set the table to learn one-to-one relationships – one plate, one fork per person. Meanwhile, soft music can be played.

THE MUSICAL BRAIN

Skill: Music

Learning window: 3 to 10 years

What we know: String players have a larger area of their sensory cortex dedicated to the fingering digits on their left hand. Few concert level performers begin playing later than the age of 10. It is much harder to learn an instrument as an adult. Music lessons help develop spatial skills.

Action: Parents can play Qur'anic recitation (*tajwīd*), *adhān*, and soft recordings of natural sounds and birds. They can also sing songs and *nashīd* (religious songs) with children and play soft music. Give children musical instruments to see if they show any musical aptitude or interest.

THE LANGUAGE BRAIN

Skill: Language

Learning window: Birth to 10 years

What we know: Circuits in the auditory cortex, representing the sounds that form words, are wired by the age of one. The more words children hear by age two, the larger their vocabulary will grow. Hearing problems can impair the ability to match sounds to letters.

Action: It is important that parents talk to their children – frequently. If they want their children to master a second language, they should introduce it before the age of 10. Hearing needs to be protected by the prompt treatment of ear infections.

Islam, Singing, and Music

Islam allows singing and music, provided they do not promote evil, sexual arousal, or interfere with performing religious obligations. The Companions of the Prophet ﷺ and their Successors listened to songs and music. In particular, happy occasions (like weddings, 'Īds, parties, and celebrations for the newborn) were conducted with songs and musical instruments (such as drums and tambourines). Al-Bukhārī and Muslim report that some Abyssinians were playing and dancing for the Prophet ﷺ, and the Prophet ﷺ was watching them with his wife 'Ā'ishah for a long period, trying to entertain her.

Narrated 'Ā'ishah

Allah's Messenger came to my house while two girls were singing beside me the songs of Bu'ath [a story about the war between the two tribes of the Anṣār, i.e. Khazraj and Aws, before Islam]. The Prophet reclined on the bed and turned his face to the other side. Abū Bakr came and scolded me and said protestingly, "Instrument of Satan in the presence of Allah's Messenger?" Allah's Messenger turned his face toward him and said, "Leave them." When Abū Bakr became inattentive, I waved the two girls to go away and they left. It was the day of 'Īd, when Ethiopians used to play with leather shields and spears. Either I requested Allah's Messenger or he himself asked me whether I would like to see the display. I replied in the affirmative. Then he let me stand behind him and my cheek was touching his cheek and he was saying, "Carry on, O Banu Arfidah [i.e. Ethiopians]!" When I grew tired, he asked me if that was enough. I replied in the affirmative and he told me to leave. (MUSLIM)

This is a lesson for parents to let girls and boys enjoy themselves, rather than deprive them of entertainment. Nowadays, music and art in general have been used to promote vice (such as sexual lust, drugs, and alcoholism). However, we can use music for education and clean entertainment.

There exists no authentic tradition (hadith) that prohibits music and singing. Al-Qaradawi (2007) rejects the anti-music and anti-singing hadith because they lack accuracy in meaning or narrations or both. There are no references to any prohibition at any time. Moreover, there are several pieces of evidence during the time of the Prophet ﷺ that proves the lawfulness of music and singing. For example:

1. Abū Bakr entered the house of the Prophet ﷺ and found 'Ā'ishah listening to two female singers. He tries to stop them, saying: "Instrument of Satan in the presence of Allah's Messenger?" However, the Prophet tells him: "Leave them; these are days of festivities ['Īd]."
2. When 'Ā'ishah escorted a bride to her bridegroom from the Anṣār, the Prophet ﷺ asked the bride, "Did you have some entertainment?" (the Anṣār people loved celebrating).
3. During the migration of the Prophet ﷺ from Makkah to Madinah, there were memorable celebrations: the girls came out welcoming him and singing; the ladies of Banū al-Najjār came out beating the drums and singing. Abū Bakr tried to stop them but the Prophet ﷺ said: "Leave them, our religion is joyous."
4. 'Umar ibn al-Khaṭṭāb entered the *masjid* and found the Ethiopians dancing with their spears in front of the Prophet ﷺ and his wife 'Ā'ishah during the festival of 'Īd. He tried to stop them but the Prophet ﷺ told him: "Leave them."

The general rule is that actions are judged by intention and any action that leads to falsehood and away from righteousness, is to be avoided. Sexually arousing music and obscene songs are definitely unlawful, as well as pornography. All other music and singing (that is not promoting vice) is lawful.

AVICENNA ON BREASTFEEDING AND MUSIC

Avicenna said: There are certain kinds of fever caused by psychological factors.

Breastfeeding: Avicenna stressed the strong relationship between psychology and body health. One example is breastfeeding. Hence, he emphasized the good choice of a wet-nurse.

Music: Avicenna emphasized the effect of positive music on the sick, both physically and psychologically.

Pictures and Sculptures in Islam

Pictures and sculptures are lawful in Islam (unless they depict nudity, vice and other forms of immorality). The main uses of pictures and sculptures during the Prophet's ﷺ time were for worshipping idols, so he prohibited them. The same words are used today but have a different meaning. For example, the word *sayyārah* in the Qur'an (*surah Yūsuf*) meant a caravan of travelers, whereas today, the same word means a motorcar (a completely different usage).

The same principle applies to pictures and sculptures, whether we are talking about drawings and paintings, photographs and films, electronic screens, and two-dimensional or three-dimensional sculptures. For a long time, pictures and sculptures (idols) were used by pagans for worship and religious rituals. This explains why when the Prophet ﷺ saw pictures in a non-religious setting, he did not object to them. Similarly, when he noticed children playing with three-dimensional dolls, he did not prevent it.

By the same token, any picture or sculpture used today as an idol or for worship is prohibited categorically. However, these pictures or sculptures today are not used for worship but for purposes like science, technology, media, education, entertainment, passports, identity cards, and credit cards. All these usages were not prohibited by the Traditions of the Prophet ﷺ. Our dealings with these tools should be for useful purposes and not harmful ones. A knife, for example, can serve many good purposes but it must never be used for violence and killing people (except in ritual slaughtering, self-defense, or war).

Toddlers' Brain Development

Toddlers are interested in learning languages, patterns, and relationships of all types. They do not just observe life as they did as infants; they want to become part of it. The following are a few ideas for parents to develop their toddlers' interests and to make a positive difference in their brain development.

CALLING ATTENTION TO IMPORTANT PATTERNS IN THE ENVIRONMENT

Sequences and situations are important for toddlers. *Sequences* are quite interesting to toddlers. The brains of young children naturally link events in time in a cause–effect relationship. Parents can show the correct sequence of physical occurrences (effects of light, temperature, water, gravity, and wind) and social conventions (knocking on doors before entering, taking turns, saying "thank you"). Children at this age are also intrigued by the sequences used in common tasks, such as cleaning, cooking, or dressing. A second important pattern is *situations*. Toddlers do not show an interest in situations as they do in sequences. Nevertheless, in the months from 13–19, they begin noticing grouping patterns. For instance, what are the objects, who are the people, and what are the events related to an experience at a restaurant? By pre-school age, children use this information to understand and adapt to the environment at large. Parents should point out "what," "who," and even "why" and "how" information when they are in different situations with their children.

ENCOURAGING CHILDREN'S PHYSICAL PARTICIPATION IN ACTIVITIES

The learning of spatial concepts is made much easier with physical participation. For instance, the word "under" will have more significance if the toddler goes "under" a table when the word is used. Placing toddlers in a restricted area with a restricted range of objects diminishes their development. Be present as much as possible as a guide to your child, looking out for safety issues and interacting as much as possible.

TALKING TO CHILDREN AND ELABORATING ON WHAT IS SAID TO THEM

When parents speak with their toddlers, they are helping to develop vocabulary. During the 12–24 month range, children want to know the names of objects. As parents point out these names, they should be as clear as possible about what they are referring to. Touching the objects aids language learning. Parents can also use "context" clues, such as "I am going to pick up the book" while demonstrating the action. When mothers ask questions and then repeat their children's answers with rephrased expansions, the children become more advanced in their grammar. For example, if the child answers "cage" to the question "Where is the bird?" the parent responds, "Yes, the bird is in the cage," providing the complete sentence structure.

MAINTAINING A POSITIVE, PREDICTABLE, AND REWARDING ATMOSPHERE

The feelings that parents project to their children affect the brain. Interchanges between depressed mothers and their infants actually produced brain activity in the infants that resembled the depression of the mothers (Field et al. 1988). A cheerful, optimistic atmosphere produces a more buoyant and emotionally resilient child. Young children are influenced by the emotional energy of their parents and the degree to which their caretakers are positive and supportive. Consistency in routine makes learning easier and provides greater emotional security.

ENCOURAGING PRACTICE AND WELCOMING REPETITION

Practice and repetition is important. What a child extracts from a given situation is only a part of the total knowledge possible from that object, event, or circumstance. In fact, infants and toddlers may attend to only a particular element of what is heard, seen, or felt on many occasions before noticing any other property. The brain takes time to reflect the realities of the environment. Parents need not hurry the process; there is much to be learned!

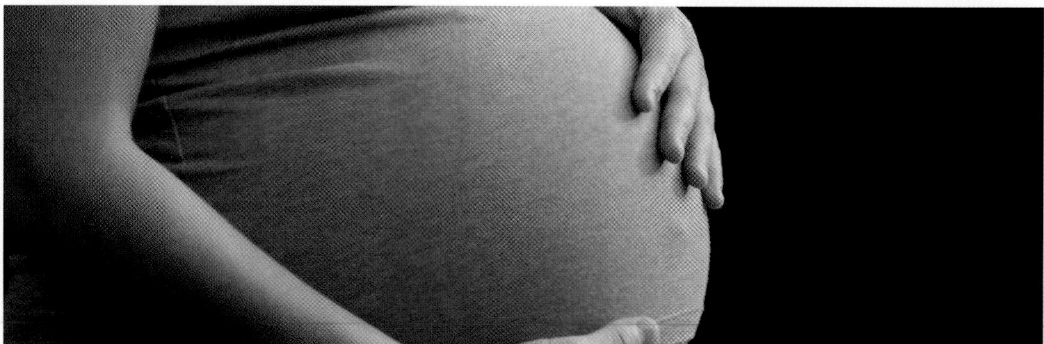

Does the Fetus Know Your Voice?

Studies show that some in-utero learning takes place in the latter weeks of pregnancy. Fathers can talk to the fetus through a rolled-up newspaper, so that the baby gets used to the dad's sound. (HENRY BILLER 1993)

How Emotions Override Reason

Truly humans are created very impatient [fearful, scared]. Whenever misfortune touches them, they become intensely horrified.

(Qur'an 70:19–20)

Although most of us do not habitually react with violence, we all get angry, give in to irrational fears, or otherwise feel overwhelmed by our own emotions from time to time. Why do we, as thoughtful human beings, allow emotional impulse to override rational thinking?

The amygdala, an almond-size part of the brain, is the physical seat of our emotions. It acts like a "home security system." The amygdala scans the senses for anything that is frightening or hurtful.

Whenever the amygdala picks up danger, it reacts instantaneously, sending out an emergency alarm to every major part of the brain. The body begins to get ready for fight or flight. Heart rate and blood pressure go up and breathing slows. Even the memory system switches into a faster gear as it scans its archives for any knowledge relevant to the emergency at hand.

The amygdala acts as a storehouse of emotional memories. The memories it stores are especially vivid because they arrive in the amygdala with the neurochemical and hormonal imprint that accompanies stress, anxiety, or other intense excitement. The brain has two memory systems, one for ordinary facts and one for those which are emotionally charged.

Problems arise because the amygdala often sends a false alarm, when the sense of panic it triggers is related to memories of experiences that are no longer relevant to our circumstances. For example, traumatic episodes from infancy, when reason and language were barely developed, can continue to trigger extreme emotional responses well into adulthood. The neocortex – the thoughtful, analytical part of the brain – acts as a "damper switch for the amygdala's surges." Most of the time, the neocortex is in control of our responses. However, it takes the neocortex longer to process information. This gives the instantaneous, extreme responses triggered by the amygdala a chance to take over before the neocortex is aware of what has happened. When this occurs, emotions override reason.

Most people learn how to avoid emotional over-reaction when they are infants. If they have supportive and caring adults around them, they pick up the social cues that enable them to develop self-discipline and empathy.

According to Dr. Geraldine Dawson (1984) of the University of Washington, the prime period for emotional development appears to be between eight and eighteen months, when babies are forming their first strong attachments. As with cognitive development, emotional development extends to adolescence and beyond, although it narrows over time. Children who have had many painful experiences (through abuse, neglect, or exposure to violence) may display destructive and antisocial reactions later in life.

Mother's Care is Indispensable

The Qur'an tells mothers to nurse babies for up to 2 years whenever possible. This motherly investment in babies during the critical stages of cognitive and emotional development will bring great rewards.

The mother is a central and essential figure in an infant's development. Working mothers need to ask themselves whether they really need to work in the first years of their babies' lives. A happy, well-balanced child is certainly worth a few material sacrifices. Mothers whose work is a matter of survival should be given more opportunities to work part-time and from home whenever possible. Their husbands, relatives, friends, and neighbors are to provide them with as much support as possible.

Having said this we do not deny that children from all families are capable of healthy psychological adjustment. A parent may be at work full-time, and raising a child single-handed but can still do a good job in raising a healthy child. This book asserts that the activities related to successful child rearing require quality time. Working mothers have less time to spend with their children than full-time mothers. Thus full-time mothers, if they are properly trained, have a greater chance of producing healthy and psychologically adjusted children, than working mothers (all other things being equal). Of course, if a working mother has extended family members helping out and a very family-friendly workplace, she may do a better job of parenting than an

uncaring or uninformed parent who may be at home full time but does not know how to spend quality time with the children.

What Makes Us Who We Are: Nature, Nurture, or Destiny?

Scientists no longer ask whether the issue is one of nature or nurture, they are now focusing on how genes and environment interact. So instead of a competition between nature and nurture we should consider them as more of a dance of two elements. **Nurture works through nature and nature works through nurture**.

The kind of traits a person will have begin with the sperm and the egg. Sperms and eggs have tiny "computer control centers" inside them called chromosomes, which carry information from the parent cells to the baby cell. Each human egg cell and sperm cell has 23 chromosomes, and when they unite, they add up to 46. These 46 chromosomes have tinier information units called genes, which are

Some mothers think they can manage full-time child rearing and a full-time career. This is impossible. Once they are mothers, the choice is made: their children come before their career. Society should reject all images that belittle housewives, mothers, and the family. Actively engaging in a celebration of childhood and motherhood is needed.

comprised of DNA. There are about 30,000 genes determining all kinds of traits, from the color of the eyes to the size and shape of the feet, and all kinds of mental and physical abilities. Some of these genes are naturally stronger, and are called "**dominant**" **genes**, whereas others are weaker, and they are called "**recessive**" **genes**.

For instance, brown eyes are dominant and blue eyes are recessive. If a man with brown eyes marries a woman with blue eyes, it is likely that most of their children will have brown eyes rather than blue, because the brown genes are stronger. Nevertheless, it is also possible, for example, for one daughter in a family of brunettes to have reddish hair just like her great-aunt (a recessive trait). Each child creates a detailed map of the dominant and recessive genes of the mother's and the father's families collected from many generations.

Genes are not the only factors that decide the kind of person we become; health care, upbringing, and education are also significant. All of these non-genetic factors that influence growth are called a child's environment, which is just as important as their genes. For instance, children from a poor, uneducated family may grow up to be more intelligent than their parents if they are well fed and receive a good education from birth. Most of our manners and behavior are learned from our environment: a Chinese baby boy raised in a European home will think and behave much like a European child when he grows up, even though he has Chinese genes. A child may be born with a stubborn and independent personality. Depending on whether the child has had a good or bad upbringing, the child can become a spoiled, inflexible adult or a person with a strong will and character who is able to achieve great things. Good manners, discipline, love, and compassion are crucial in a child's environment. Children in orphanages who receive good food and physical care but are not given enough love and attention will often suffer socially and psychologically later in life.

Beyond genes and the environment, the other factor that makes us what we are is our personal will and the destiny that God has written for us (the Will of God). The belief that certain things in our lives have already been decided by God is called determinism. The things that a soul cannot control are part of its destiny: physical and mental abilities, family, gender, and color, as well as many events during a person's life. Heredity, environment, and destiny combine to form a test for each soul. Each of us has a challenge to make the best of our life with the free will we have been given. We will return to the Almighty on the Last Day, and He will ask us what we have done with all of the things He has given us.

A simple trait like the acidity in tomatoes is controlled not by a single gene, but by as many as 30 that operate together. In the same way, many genes are required in setting up temperamental traits and psychological vulnerabilities; each gene contributes a little bit to the overall effect. DNA is constructed out of four chemicals (adenine, guanine, cytosine, and thiamine). It can take as many as a million combinations to spell out a single human gene. Genes alone do not control the chemistry of the brain, and ultimately it is the environment that determines how these genes will express themselves.

We attribute physical traits to genes (like eye color, height, the size of feet, the shape of nose and ears, the length and shape of fingers). However, it is quite difficult to decide how much of our personality characters and traits are influenced by heredity and how much are environmental. All of the following are influenced by both genes and the environment: leadership abilities, imagination, stress, courage, stubbornness, artistic talents, aggression, sociability, love, anxiety, tendency to take risks, honesty, impulsiveness, openness, conservatism, liberalism, hostility, intelligence, mood, temperament, curiosity, confidence, problem-solving ability and decision making abilities.

What a great creation of God we are!!

> *We have indeed created man in the best of molds. Then do We abase him [to be] the lowest of the low. Except those who believe and do righteous deeds: for they shall have a reward unfailing.* (Qur'an 95:4–6)

Brain Growth: Emotional Influence on Boys and Girls

BRAIN GROWTH: THE BRAIN DOUBLES IN THE FIRST YEAR OF LIFE, AND THEN DOUBLES AGAIN. Our brains make us remarkably helpless at birth, yet also flexible beyond any other species. We are born with less knowledge than other animals, and therefore we are more open to experience. It also means that what happens to us – right from the moment when our parents hold us tight or, in a dark reverse, slap us down – is enormously influential.

EMOTIONAL INFLUENCE ON BOYS AND GIRLS: Emotional connections are enormously important when we are at a very young age. Lack of affection produces bad physical results. Metabolism levels were found to drop severely in the brains of babies with depressed mothers as compared with those whose mothers were warm and cheerful (Field, et al. 1988). Children with depressed mothers do not have normal brain development. Most of the children who are deprived of love began showing signs of anger and aggressive behavior by the age of three. *Unhappy infancy produces less adult happiness and more likelihood of negative actions.*

Boys need more touch, more song, and more emotional support than we tend to give them. Maybe parents disconnect from boys early in a way that they do not with girls, pushing the boys faster toward independence. Although as grown men they may not remember this, the emotional damage still affects them.

Boys need more touch, more song, and more emotional support than we tend to give them

Is the Success of Humanity Determined Before the Age of Five?!

Is the success of society going to be in the development of the brain? The basic structure (skeleton) of the human is decided by genes, and the genes are fixed and not much can be done about them. The real utility and productivity of humanity will largely depend on the human brain. The vast trillions upon trillions of interconnections are constructed in the child's brain before the age of 10 and most of them may be formed by the age of three. Hence, nations who concentrate on caring for their babies will have a tremendous chance of success. If they do not do what is required during infancy, it may be too late to catch up. Investments made in children during this period of three years yield the maximum rate of return for any community. Optimum brain interconnections occur between birth and four years. That is one reason why the Qur'an strongly recommends breastfeeding for up to two years.

The process starts at birth, when the father recites aloud the *adhān* (call to prayer) in the right and left ears of the newborn. It continues with breastfeeding by the mother, who feeds her baby love, warmth, and a sense of belonging. Then a sense of autonomy starts developing in the baby, and parents can enhance the baby's cognitive development using the advice in this book.

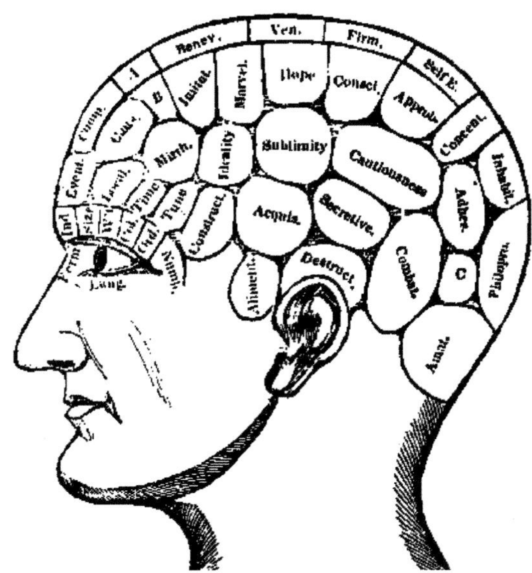

Avicenna memorized the Qur'an before the age of 10. This helped him to expand his useable brain capacity and build his memory, enabling him to maximize his brain potentials. Some believe that we normally use only five to fifteen percent of our brain's capacity.

(Morgan 2007)

Activity

ACTIVITY 40: ESTABLISH A BOOK OF THE MONTH SYSTEM

Parents and children can create a book club. Selected books can be read whether weekly, monthly or every few months according to a fixed but flexible schedule. Each member will read a book and present it, followed by an open discussion. Preferably, this can take place after a nice meal with each member telling a joke. For a schedule to work and become a habit, make it regular. For example, designate the first Friday night (or Saturday) at 7:00 pm of every month for the book club. This way there will be no need to send reminders and members are less likely to have a scheduling conflict.

CHAPTER 12

Raising Boys and Girls: Are They Different?

Introduction

DISCUSSING DIFFERENCES BETWEEN men and women is important, and it helps our understanding of their different roles and needs. As well as directly affecting the relationship between husbands and wives, it also impacts the relationship between parents and their sons and daughters. Healthy relationships are built on a mutual understanding of the similarities and differences between the sexes. A parent's idea of what constitute differences between boys and girls affects the children's relationships later in life. Concepts and thoughts become words, words become actions, actions become habits, and habits formulate personalities.

This is not a discussion about which gender is better or more important, for the Qur'an and the Prophet ﷺ settled this issue clearly by stating:

> *Women shall have rights similar to the rights against them according to what is equitable.* (Qur'an 2:228)

The Prophet ﷺ said:

> **Women are the peers "true equals" of men.** (AHMAD)

Thus, he put men and women on an equal footing, playing different but complementary roles, and not as opposites or competitors.

Specific Differences: Logic vs. Emotions

Smalley (1995), points out that some of the differences between males and females are:

- Females (XX chromosome) have a stronger immune system than men (XY chromosome).
- Males have more red blood cells than women, thus possessing more energy flowing through the body.
- Males have more muscles, thicker skulls, and thicker skin than females.

About 80 percent of men and women follow this pattern: Females use both sides of the brain, whereas males use mainly the left side. Females are more alert than men, for they hear and feel more than males. In one study, a message was flashed across a computer screen. Women were able to write down what they saw, whereas men asked one another, "Did you see that? I didn't catch that."

In general, males favor the use of the left

side of the brain, which is believed to be the location of logic, spatial ability, conquest, lecturing, accounting, and engineering. Females favor the use of the right side of the brain, which is thought to be the location of feelings, emotions, art, poetry, love, music, and verbal ability, although they can also use the left side. Females are less aggressive, whereas males are more argumentative, boastful, and more difficult to teach as children. Males have less difficulty reading maps because they are usually trained in spatial ability. Mental faculties are localized more in the male brain compared with the female brain, although both use the whole brain. Furthermore, which side of the brain is favored may vary among males (artistic types of males favor the right side of the brain and scientific types of males favor the left side of the brain). (Baron-Cohen 2002; Gilmartin et al. 1984)

Males and females can use both sides of the brain if they train themselves and learn how.

Gray (2003) states that men like to make decisions, conquer, provide solutions, and thrive on achievements. Women like to express their feelings, discuss their problems, and appreciate those who listen to them, so they need to be loved and protected.

Males tend to discover and express facts, while females tend to express feelings and emotions. In one study, young American girls and boys were told to say any words they wanted to say. All the girls said something to do with conversational words, whereas 60 percent of the boys were just making noises instead of words. An average American male speaks 12,000 words per day, while an average American female speaks 25,000+ words per day. Lip muscles move more at birth for girls than for boys. (Eliot 2009)

Males tend to give solutions when there is a problem. When a wife complains to her husband, he tries to give solutions. Females, on the other hand, like to give sympathy and love.

Males are trained to be more objective and rational, whereas women are trained to be more personal. If a man is watching a basketball game, he is not keen to know about the lives of the players. However, a woman will be more interested in watching the game if she knows the players' names and their families. Women are trained to focus on relationships more closely than men.

Males, to a certain extent, learn to separate themselves from their surroundings. Females acquire their identity from whom they know and from their surroundings. A woman does not separate herself from her house, her children, and her job. If she forgets to wash the dishes, she thinks of going back and washing them. Her house is an important part of her. A male feels differently about his house, since for him a house is mainly a resting-place, and washing dishes on time is not his priority.

Males tend to remember general things in their relationships, while females learn to focus more on the details, i.e. what they wore and ate on their first wedding anniversary.

Women have a stronger desire for good relationships and have the ability to recognize a bad relationship more quickly than men. Some researchers asked couples to ask themselves the following questions: What is our relationship on a scale of 0–10? What should we do to improve our relationship closer to 10?

Males tend to answer the first question two points higher than females, whereas females tend to be more accurate about the quality of their relationship.

The husband has a need to feel adequate, which occurs when his wife praises him and avoids criticizing him (unless he asks for it).

Women need more emotional energy, which is necessary for the proper care of babies. Men have less tolerance than women where their children are concerned. One father babysat his 4-year-old boy for one full day. He concluded that if he disciplined his son all day long, it would not be enough punishment for the nonstop mischief the boy was creating! Mothers are less likely to say such a horrible thing.

Emotionally, a man has a difficult time connecting to his wife, whereas a woman has an easier time. This may be due partly to biology and partly to upbringing and training. Women are more adept at building close friendships than men.

> Dr. Warren says that when a new client comes to him he asks: "Who are your three closest friends?" If the client is a woman, the answer is usually quick and she may describe more than three friends and may have difficulty narrowing the list to three. If the client is a man, there is often a pause followed by the question "What exactly do you mean by best friend?"
>
> Most men aren't adept at building close friendships. They enjoy being together watching games, hunting, or fishing. But are they "close" friends? (WOLGEMUTH 1996)

According to the way many men are raised, beauty is not a priority in their lives, yet financial strength is. Women are frequently brought up to concentrate on beauty rather than on financial strength. A woman is told that she needs to be attractive to catch a man and commit him to his responsibility of supporting the family.

Gur et al. (1999) have shown that women's brains seem to run at a slightly higher temperature, circulating more blood, and maintaining a little more overall charge. Girls mature faster than boys, (they talk and move gracefully at an earlier age). The brains of females and males appear to develop along different tracks although no one is sure why. These differences are not constant, for the gaps may widen and close according to age. A young girl may use words more easily than a young boy, although in later years he is likely to catch up.

Neuron-imaging studies tend to show that a biological difference will predict a particular type of behavior. Men are more likely to strike out physically and women to strike out verbally and this is usually how people tend to behave. In such cases, it is tempting to conclude that it is biology, not culture that governs behavior. However, finding a functional difference may tell us as much about culture as it does about biology. Our brains are basically alike, even if we use them differently. If we set two brains side by side, they look the same and we have to search very carefully to find the differences. The contrasts are far too tiny, and still far too mysterious, to suggest that these are profoundly different organs. Although people may do some things in different ways, the basic behavior patterns are the same between men and women.

Emotional Connection

Emotional connection has become the stuff of stereotypes and greeting cards: women seek commitment and men flee; women talk about their feelings, men change the subject to football scores; women share their emotions with friends, men regard this as an act of indecent exposure. Is it merely perception? And if it is, where does this perception originate?

The emotional responses of day-old infants are not due to training or socialization. In a test where babies simply listened to sounds – of other babies crying, of animal calls, of the weird droning voice of computer-generated language – they responded most strongly to the sound of another human in distress (Cassidy 1999). However, it was the tiny females who reacted most intensely to the sound of another's trouble – a reaction that would continue throughout their entire lives. Although both sexes respond to another's distress, even on the first day, girls are more tuned to an empathetic response. Females may be more apt to imagine how it would feel if the stimuli impinging on the other were impinging on the self. Females, for so long the first line of care giving – the first defense that an infant has against the world – are oriented to the needs of others.

The Senses

No wonder, then, that females possess such exquisitely tuned senses. The female sense of smell is more acute than the male's (especially during ovulation), and women are more sensitive to touch than men. Ability to communicate with touch is critical for the healthy survival of a child. When premature infants are held, even just gently stroked, they grow and mature faster. They gain weight 47 percent faster than those left alone, even if both receive the same amount of food. (Dodd 2005)

The vocalizations of mothers are well matched to the sensitivities and needs of infants. By playing tape-recorded voices to infants, they turn more readily toward a woman's high-note sounds than toward the tones the same woman might use to an adult. In addition, the heart of the infant slows, calms, and steadies, beating more gently as it hears that particular music of a mother's voice. The comfort that the mother gives the child appears basic, biological, and continuous with the development that takes place in the womb. It is in this intertwining of mother and child – a tale of two hearts – that the emotional differences between men and women begin.

Status

The idea of status seems to occur very early in boys. It does not seem to occur so much in girls. Overall, girls seem less determined to be number one –with some exceptions. A typical study of children's play illustrates the point by exploring the way groups of same-sex children played the game of "doctor." The boys all wanted to be the doctor – the one in charge who told others what to do. They would argue about this for an extended period. Girls would ask who wanted to be doctor. Then they would negotiate, sharing roles as doctor, nurse, and patient.

Boys, more than girls, want games with real winners. They also seem more comfortable with confrontation over the outcome of the games. Girls' games turn out to be shorter than boys'. Boys argue over their games – who did what, who had what, and their games do not end owing to an argument. However, the girls themselves complained that quarrels regularly ended their games. Boys let go of disagreements more easily than girls; girls have a stronger emotional response to conflict. Some argue that this may be the result of culture, that we encourage girls to be more emotional, whereas we discourage emotionalism in boys.

Nevertheless, much as we try to separate them, biology and culture are not mutually exclusive. They cannot be. Our questions about the role of nature versus nurture form a circle, in which one influence feeds the other. In this loop, biology is more important as a starting point. Yet how do you figure out where a circle begins?

Facial Expressions

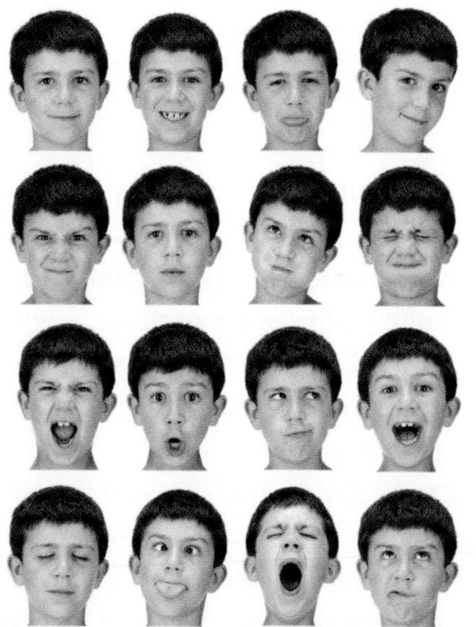

Women are far more adept than men at interpreting facial expression. Women tend to smile more often than men, and men often encourage women to smile. Some argue that this could be due to a past based on a dominant–submissive relationship between the two sexes. Women are also more adept than men at reading non-verbal expressions (such as body language and facial movements).

Studying photographs of faces, both sexes were equally adept at noticing when someone else was happy. Women also easily read sadness in a person's face, whether male or female, at about 90 percent accuracy. Men, on the other hand, accurately read unhappiness in another man's face about 90 percent of the time, but were right about 70 percent of the time when looking at women's faces. The woman's face had to look really sad for men to notice it. The subtle expressions went unnoticed by them.

Cultural Stereotyping of Boys and Girls

Some people misread the realities of our biology. The old nursery rhyme says that girls are made of "sugar, spice, and everything nice," whereas boys are "snips (slugs) and snails and puppy dogs' tails". A 5-year-old boy was outraged: Why did girls get to be the good stuff? Why did boys get stuck being garden pests and amputated dog body parts?

Some studies suggest that boys need more one-on-one attention, since affection may change the sex hormone level in the brain, which then affects brain development. Many studies of men and women show that they best survive even severe illnesses, such as heart disease and cancer, if there is a loving and supportive marriage. Even a minor marital spat sends shivers through the immune system, to the effect that after a fight couples are much more likely to come down with a cold or the flu. When a partner dies, the immune system of the survivor stays depressed between four and fourteen months.

Did you ever wonder why the chapters of the Qur'an start with "In the Name of God, The Most Compassionate, The Most Merciful"? Do you see any hint to the parents to be affectionate toward their children?

Grief

No one has ever found loneliness or grief to be good for health, whether mental or physical. Women handle grief differently than men. This may explain why husbands and wives handle the loss of a child differently (the husband usually withdraws and the wife usually sobs on everyone's shoulder). However, we cannot argue that every woman is a good emotional communicator, or that every man has a "stiff upper lip." There is a point at which science cannot define all aspects of who we are.

Sexual Differences

When some wives were asked: "If you could not have sex with your husband any more, how would you feel?" most responded that this would be fine; they just needed hugs and kisses. Men however, said that they would feel bad if they could not have sex with their wives. (Fisher, et al. 2012)

Sexually, women are stronger than men. They can avoid sex for long periods, and they usually need to be touched to be aroused. Men have a hard time avoiding sex for long periods. One word can make a man sexually excited and have an erection. Woman can indulge in sex without being excited, unlike men who need to be excited.

An average man in the United States may think of sex every few minutes. Men need to lower their gaze, because they are weaker at controlling their sexual urges. Sex is an important activity and children are its consequences. Regulating sexual relationships is paramount for a healthy society, morally, psychologically, and socially.

The Wisdom of Gender Differences: Roles, Not Preferences

A woman is created and generally taught to be sensitive and emotional, so that she can readily protect her children from any threat. This is also apparent in the animal kingdom. The mother cat protects her kittens and hides them from all male and other cats, including the father, lest they eat them like mice. Special hormones are secreted during pregnancy, which aid in the delivery, feeding, and protection of her babies.

During the monthly menstruation period, pregnancy, delivery, and breastfeeding, women are in a more dependent state. Hence, more care should be exercised during these times. Millions of women complain of discomfort during menstruation. Problems can last for days and range from mild to severe. Symptoms include bloating, cramps, breast tenderness, headaches, heavy or prolonged bleeding, mood swings, and fatigue.

A man is attracted toward a woman sexually so that he will carry the responsibility of serving her and their children. He is supposed to be generous to provide her and their offspring with their needs, while the mother has to be more concerned about herself and her babies' livelihood. He does not have the burden of monthly periods, pregnancy, delivery, and breastfeeding. Thus, he is freed to strive better for the necessary income and family needs.

The complementary differences in the human nature of men and women explain the Islamic family laws and injunctions. The distinct sexual natures of men and women is reflected in the concept of *'awrah* – the private parts of men and women. The man's private parts are defined as being between the navel and the knees so that he can engage in hard physical work unimpeded and unrestricted. At the same time, the exposed parts of his body do not unduly seduce or allure women to lose control and rationality and fall for him. The opposite is true of women. Almost the whole of a woman's body is an attraction and temptation for men. Men are easily tempted by the appearance of the woman's body; hence, all her body is defined as private parts, except the face, hands, and feet. Usually, there is no real need for women to expose their bodies to men. The face is quite different, since it has other effects and functions such as expressing the woman's personality and identity. This well-defined and detailed concept of *'awrah* is a strong protection for the family and an effective insurance policy against promiscuity, which destroys the family and society. However, within a husband-and-wife relationship, there is no restriction on each other's bodies, as the Qur'an explains.

> *...They are your garments and you are their garments...* (Qur'an 2:187)

As equitable members of society, men and women have similar rights but different and complementary roles, depending on their physiological and psychological uniqueness. The family is a special human institution that functions effectively and delivers benefits to men, women, and children.

Women aged between 20 and 40 are the foundation of the family. They are tender and caring so that they can provide peace and comfort for their families. The husband needs tranquility, especially after he returns from a long and exhausting day at work earning a

livelihood. This is a natural priority in their lives at this stage. However, this does not mean that wives cannot do many other things, nor does it excuse fathers from their duty of nurturing peace inside the home. These traits are not to be interpreted as weakness of women and harshness of men. They are fit for the specific role of each member. Islamic Law puts the legal responsibility of providing an income on the husband, not the wife, regardless of her economic status, because the issue is that of roles and the preparations to qualify for these roles. The decision of whether the wife is to go out to work is in her hands. She is not to be forced to work, because the provision of her sustenance and that of her children rests entirely with her husband. If the woman chooses to go out to work, there is nothing wrong with this. Since she can handle both roles of work and motherhood, then she has the right to be both an income-earner and a mother.

The differences in physiology and psychology between the sexes during the various stages of development does not reduce their rights and responsibilities. A certain trait or quality may be positive in a woman (such as a soft voice) and negative in a man, and vice versa.

When a man looks at a woman with lust, it is unacceptable. When a woman is attracted to a man, the consequences for the woman, if she sins, are extremely serious, especially as she may be become pregnant. It is required of the man to be committed to her and stay with her. He is obligated to support her and the baby. If he fails in his duties, he will deprive them of their God-given rights of sustenance and livelihood.

The Priority of American Men and Women: A Survey

A survey of four thousand men and women conducted by the *Washington Post* newspaper and Harvard University concluded that the priority for men and women in the United States is:

- Confronting the psychological and economic pressures of modern living.
- Strengthening family bonds.
- Communicating with children effectively.

Nowadays, unfortunately, women have been victimized in the West as well as in the Muslim world. Beyond financial pressures, women are culturally expected to go out to work in the West and they are looked upon as sex objects, cheap entertainment, and a commercial entity. In some Muslim countries, women are uneducated and unprepared for the great task of motherhood. Many of them have no assurances, are at the mercy of their husbands, and in many countries are neglected and marginalized.

The late Shaykh Muhammad al-Ghazaly states in his memoirs that during his childhood in the village, women could be seen everywhere except in the mosque. It is sad to witness that in some countries there is no place for women in the mosque. Most theology students in Turkey now are women. However, the mosque architects had "given little thought to the accommodation of worshipping women." Therefore, in Istanbul, part of the main prayer-hall and even a separate mosque have been allocated to women for the congregational prayers. (MURAD 2009). How can we expect a mother to raise children without the religious guidance and education provided week after week in the Friday sermon, potentially the most influential institutional education that exists?! This deprivation has existed for centuries, in spite of the Prophet's ﷺ tradition.

The Prophet ﷺ said:

Do not prevent the female servants of Allah from going to the Mosques of Allah. (MUSLIM)

Women, owing to their extra family duties, are free to attend prayers at the mosque or at home according to their roles and responsibilities. Indeed, it is the duty of the husbands to facilitate their wives' visits to the mosque by helping them rather than burdening them.

While men approve of women working outside the home, many men and women prefer mothers who spend all their time on the children and in the home. The majority believe that the main reason American women have jobs is to earn more income to satisfy the necessities of life (*al-Usra*, Issue 61, 1419 AH).

Sixteen Years too Late

An Arab poet said:

Do you cry for your daughter Lubna,
after you have vanquished her?
Lubna is gone, so what shall you do?!

Some parents frequently spoil, mistreat, and abuse their children, and then feel sorry for their actions.
Their sorrow may be 16 years too late!

When Does the Gender Divide Start?

Most children begin to process gender differences around their first birthday (Beal 1993). By the time they are between the ages of two and three, they have figured out their own gender. So three year olds who make loud observations about anatomy may merely be verbalizing something that they have pondered for almost two years. Gender-wise, toddlers see the world as divided into two camps. Once they know their gender, their sense of self quickly becomes identified as boy or girl and they begin to learn how to fit in. Around the age of three, a child's behavior is likely to become noticeably gender-specific. Girls may become less aggressive and choose "girl" games, such as playing house. Boys may turn rough-and-tumble and become interested in "boy" toys, like trucks and action figures.

Gender identity comes in part from glandular influences, especially from puberty onward, and partly from the recognition of anatomical differences in early childhood and the psychological reactions to that recognition. Most of all, gender identity comes from positive identification with the parent of the same sex. In cases of effeminate men and masculine women, the problem is partly traceable to problematic relationships with parents, despite normal glands.

What makes a boy feel securely masculine is loving, being loved by, and patterning himself after a father who enjoys being a man. A father needs to feel adequate in his competitive and cooperative relationships with the other men of his society. A good gender identity in a growing body does not depend on whether his father or the men of the community hunt lions or work on the assembly line or cook the meals and change the diapers at home. As long as the father feels comfortable as a man and has a good relationship with his son, the gender identity is more likely to be fine and secure.

A father who has always felt insecure about his masculinity will keep inadvertently revealing his uneasiness to his son in a variety of subtle ways. This will interfere with the boy acquiring a comfortable male identity. The father's rejection of any domestic chore as feminine or even unmanly is one of the ways in which he indicates his uneasiness to his son. The boy senses this and unconsciously takes on some of the same uneasiness.

A girl grows up wanting to be a woman, and prepares to be a successful one by being loved and approved of by a mother who enjoys a woman's role, whatever that may be in her culture, whether the mother is a peasant farmer or a busy senator.

There is no requirement to raise girls and boys identically. In the home there should be no superiority of one gender over the other. In spite of their differing roles, childcare and home care are as dignified as working in an office, factory, or public life.

Boys and girls are to be treated fairly, but not exactly the same. Boys and girls should be taught to face life, yet be able to play their own roles successfully, without boys being taught aggression and insensitivity and girls being taught to be helpless and fully dependent on males. Girls should be discouraged from being too emotional and resorting to crying whenever they do not get their own way. Boys should be discouraged from being too aggressive and resorting to violence whenever they do not get their own way.

Wherever possible, and until a person finishes college, education is equally important for boys and girls. Boys and girls need to be given gender-neutral toys rather than just representational dolls and action figures. A Lego building block set has to be placed side by side with a female doll or a male action figure.

Grooming and clothing for girls are not to be overemphasized, and grooming and clothing for boys not to be under-emphasized. Both mother and father have to give the same importance to their daughter's hair as well as their son's hair. The same concept has to be applied to clothing. Clothing is not supposed to inhibit the young girl from playing. When parents make their daughter wear a skirt, then shout at her when her underwear shows, this is not being fair to her. Parents must allow their daughter to wear comfortable trousers, not too tight, and allow her to play as actively as her brother does. The daughter has to learn to be playful and to value her physical abilities, just like her brother. The son has to be taught never to hit a girl, even when playing. The daughter has to be taught never to allow a boy to hit her and if he does that she should defend herself instead of only crying or running away.

Masculine Women and Effeminate Men

The Prophet ﷺ expressed his utmost displeasure at effeminate men and masculine women. (AL-BUKHĀRĪ)

A man is a man, a woman is a woman, and both have to be grateful for who they are! They are not to imitate each other. Within the culture they are living in, it is supposed to be easy to distinguish between boys and girls, although nowadays it has become sometimes ambiguous. God created boys and girls distinct from each other, because their roles are different but complementary. It is a blessing that we are different so that we can be attracted to each other and life becomes more enjoyable. We should not trivialize such distinctive and attractive dissimilarities.

Neither gender can win the "battle" of the sexes. There is too much fraternizing with the "enemy!" Radical feminists have had a damaging influence on Western culture. Some feminists claim that women are as tough and invulnerable as men, and they can do anything men can do. Other radical claims are: Women do not need men. A woman needs a man like a fish needs a bicycle. Whatever society needs, women can do it without men.

The predominant Christian view contradicts these claims. Jesus Christ told men not only to be gentle and kind, but also to be bold and to assume leadership. Any fool can be a "tough guy," yet it takes a real gentleman to treat a woman with honor and respect. Men can make family decisions, though only after serious consultation with women. Husbands are to treat their wives with respect, which implies that they should act respectfully. God created men to be masculine and women to be feminine, so girls should not be treated like boys.

The Qur'an addresses gender issues as follows:

> *And do not covet those things of which Allah has bestowed His gifts more freely on some of you than on others: to men is allotted what they earn, and to women what they earn: but ask Allah of His bounty. For Allah has full knowledge of all things.*
>
> (Qur'an 4:32)

Both Women and Men are Unique

- A hundred men may make an encampment, but it takes a woman to make a home. (Chinese Proverb)
- "Who is the strongest person in the world?" asked Emperor Themistocles. "The Athenians govern the Greeks; I govern the Athenians; you, my wife, govern me; my baby governs my wife; the baby governs you."
- Can a man fully understand a woman? Can a woman fully understand a man?
- Can a man comprehend the agony of pregnancy and delivery? It is impossible, but a severe colic kidney ache can be close enough.
- If you had a choice between teaching a man or a woman, whom would you choose? If you teach a man you are educating a citizen, but when you teach a woman, you are educating a nation!

Status of Parenting: Gender Wise

Nowadays, parenting in many families is Mom's responsibility and Dad helps out . The imbalance in childcare between men and women in America (in 2001) is shown as follows:

- 75 percent of fathers do not participate in daily hands-on care.
- 50 percent of fathers say that they help when their schedules permit.
- Mothers spend more time on child care (an average of 32 hours per week) than fathers (an average of 10 hours per week).

(Taffel 1994; Taffel 2001; Davidson, 1992)

The jobs and responsibilities of child rearing in the twenty-first century are no longer delineated by gender but by availability and proximity, and it has come to resemble an equal opportunity task. Diaper changes are decided by the "Who smelled it first" dictum, not by the "My father never did this, so why should I?" defense of the past.

The term "babysitter," applied to a teenage girl, is no longer used to refer to a father caring for children while the mother is away, because he is now the co-carer of his children. This being said, fathers are not equal partners in all aspects of care-giving. The prominence of women in the workplace has caused men and women to re-evaluate traditional family roles. When they both return home from work, who sits down and reads the newspaper, and who must start dinner and feed, bathe, and put the children to bed? These issues are usually resolved today with a sharing of duties: one parent attends to the meal while the other handles baths and bedtime. Even disciplining children has changed to a more evenhanded approach. Mothers rarely threaten children nowadays with the old "Wait until your father gets home." Discipline is meted out by the "Who saw it first?" rule, taking a tremendous load off the modern father's shoulders.

Why the Imbalance?

ON THE WOMEN'S SIDE, THE FOLLOWING REASONS ARE GIVEN FOR WHY WOMEN ARE MORE INVOLVED IN CHILDCARE:

- Women do not want to rock the boat or create conflict.
- Women are more inclined toward caretaking because of the way they are socialized and because of innate responses based on their biology.
- Since society still holds women primarily responsible when problems arise with the children, many women are unwilling to give up this responsibility.
- Many women are ambivalent about sharing these duties because they would lose control, they view it as having to share the attachment and affection of their children, or they do not like the way their partner does the work.

ON THE MEN'S SIDE, THE FOLLOWING REASONS ARE GIVEN FOR WHY MEN ARE LESS INVOLVED IN CHILDCARE:

- I worry that something terrible will happen when I am in charge.

- I will not be able to deal with the child's demands and will lose my temper.
- Their mother is better at caretaking and I will never be able to master it.
- If I do too much with the children, I will lose the chance of promotion at work because of too much pressure and lack of time.
- Men have fewer chances to attend babysitting or child development classes in school.
- Men do have good parenting role models.
- Men do not have a support system for their parenting role.
- Some mothers discourage the increased participation of fathers.

However, today's generation of fathers are spending more time on childcare than their fathers did, so it seems that there is now a change in behavior.

Myths and Realities About Fathers as Caregivers

A LIST OF SOME COMMON MYTHS ABOUT FATHERS AS CAREGIVERS AND THE REALITY

MYTHS	REALITIES
• Women are always better at childcare.	• Children can become just as attached to their fathers as their mothers.
• During the first few years, fathers are not that important to their children, and they need to do more with them only when their children are older.	• Fathers are as sensitive to their infants as mothers.
• The most important role of a father is to be a disciplinarian.	• American fathers play differently with children than mothers: Fathers use more physical play activities, are more tactile, and spend a larger proportion of their time together playing (40 percent fathers compared with 25 percent mothers). Parke 1996; Yogman 1981.
• Because the father is the bread winner, he need not spend much time with the children.	• Fathers are nurturant: infants who received full-time care from fathers scored above the norm on standardized tests.
• Children need to be more attached to their mothers to grow up healthy.	• A father's parenting style has a big influence on how children become socialized. Fathers who use a loving, reasonable, firm style in guiding their children's behavior produce children who have a high rate of competence. Fathers who are unloving, punitive, and authoritarian tend to produce children who are dependent, withdrawn, and anxious.
• As a son I did not have a close relationship with my father, and I turned out all right, so I do not need a close relationship with my child. • I cannot be blamed for my shortcomings as a father, because this is how my father raised me.	• We are always responsible for our own actions. If our own parents were not good role models, we should seek good role models.
• Doing well in my career is the most important thing I can do to help my family.	• The well-being of the family has a higher priority than a career.

Impact of Absent Fathers on Children

Studies show a correlation between the absence of a nurturing father and the following misbehaviors of children:

1. Drug and alcohol use.
2. Increased rates of male violence.
3. "Hyper-masculinity" in boys raised without male role models.
4. Delinquent behavior.
5. Difficulty in adjusting to their parent's divorce and remarriage.
6. Do not care about the feelings and needs of others.
7. Decline in academic achievement and a higher school drop-out rate.

Different Needs of Boys and Girls

No one knows exactly whether it is nature or nurture that causes boys and girls to have different needs. Nevertheless, parents can play a critical role in helping their children satisfy their needs. In some societies, gender roles and the behavior associated with them are strictly defined, especially in the poorer sections of society. Anyone flouting these rules is liable to punishment.

THE FOLLOWING ARE SOME HINTS TO ENCOURAGE LITTLE BOYS AND GIRLS TO FULFIL THEIR ROLES (ADAPTED FROM FRIEDMAN 1998):

WHAT A LITTLE GIRL NEEDS

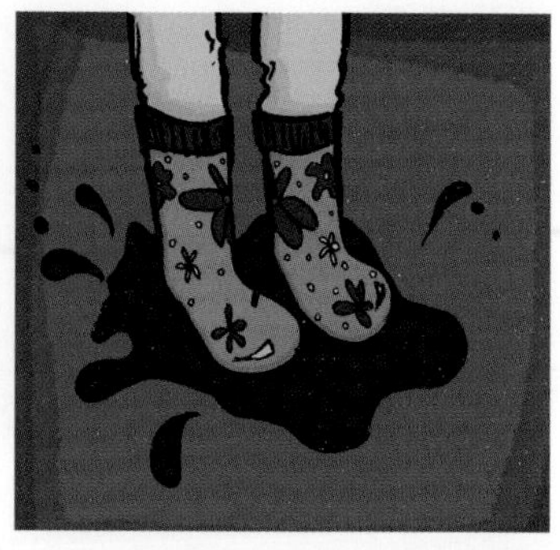

Self-Confidence**:** Girls need frequent encouragement with words that describe the characteristics that their parents want them to develop: "That was so brave of you to climb the steps all by yourself." It is important that girls know that their parents have confidence in them, and that they are bright and capable. Girls should be given more opportunities to be leaders, for example, by letting them choose an activity, make the rules, and settle disputes. A girl who has learned to lead is better prepared to take charge of her own education and career.

Self-Sufficiency**:** It is important that little girls feel competent by being allowed to accomplish whatever they can on their own – carry a cup of juice, brush their hair, or build a block tower without help. Girls should be reminded that many women may work for pay for most of their lives, and therefore, every girl needs to be prepared to support herself. Parents can cite positive role models of dynamic women who combine paid work, voluntary activities, and family life.

Spatial Relationships and Coordination**:** Girls should be given a variety of toys to play with, including trucks and cars, building blocks, water-play gear, a variety of balls, and playthings on which they can ride or climb.

Physical Fitness**:** Parents can play active games with their daughter (such as crawling, tag, and wrestling). Even girls who are still too young for organized sports can benefit from scaling the playground slide, running races, and making somersaults. The parents should avoid rescuing her; instead, they can encourage her to get dirty, disheveled, and sweaty climbing trees or playing in the grass, and thus help her rise above the "yuck" feeling. She needs also to be encouraged to play with clay or engage in outdoor sports.

Decision-Making Skills**:** Parents have to let their daughter make choices and take responsibility for her decisions. As a toddler, she could be allowed to choose which cup or plate she wants to use at mealtimes and which friend she would like to invite over to play.

Curiosity**:** Girls need to be provided with every opportunity to explore their environment. When they are infants or toddlers, the home must be thoroughly baby proofed so that they can safely roam indoors. Parents can also take their daughter on trips out into the world – to the library, the park, the zoo, the supermarket, the street market, and the places of worship. Parents could ask their children's school if it organizes visits to farms, factories, craft workshops, gardens, the law courts, and other centers of educational interest.

Body Image**:** Parents should focus on achievement more than physical appearance. It is better to talk to their daughter more about what she can accomplish than how cute she is in her dress. For example, they can say, "You did a terrific job," instead of "You look pretty today."

Critical Analysis Skills**:** If children watch television and movies, then parents can teach them to do so with a critical eye. They can discuss what they have seen together and look for "traditional" roles. For instance, start a discussion about body image. Consider how girls are portrayed on television: Are heavier girls shown as unpopular? Are they used as comic relief? Are girls with voluptuous figures shown only as sex symbols? Do they seem to be smart?

***Mathematics and Science Aptitude*:** Girls need to be given every opportunity to experience science, mathematics, and technology. Although girls are ready, willing, and eager to explore the world, they often have not had enough exposure or encouragement.

***Be an Example*:** By respecting themselves and other women, mothers, aunts and other female relatives set a standard that girls can follow. Thus, they can overcome traditional stereotypes that encourage girls to be nothing more than "sugar and spice and everything nice."

WHAT A LITTLE BOY NEEDS

A Male Role Model: Men have been redefining gender in their personal and professional lives, and wrestling with issues of identity, equality, and sexuality. In an era with more absent fathers, if boys do not learn from a male role model, then they will learn from popular culture (such as sports and television) that masculinity is defined by four things: *sex*, *violence*, *sports*, and *material possessions*. As caregivers, parents can rethink the relationship between women, men, and boys. Men should experiment with things that traditionally fall in the culture of women: share feelings, provide emotional support, and work on the art of conversation. If a boy comes to his father and says that another child is hitting him, then the father can imagine how that conversation might look between a mother and a daughter, and incorporate some of that into their discussion.

***Physical Affection*:** Little boys need as much cuddling as little girls, so parents need to comfort their infant son when he cries. They should also spend time playing gentle games with him, and keep the snuggling as their little boy grows older.

***Verbal Skills*:** Parents have to talk to their son often, even in his infancy. Their voices will provide comfort and help encourage his language development.

***Consideration for Others*:** It is important that parents explain to their son how his actions can affect other people. When a girl misbehaves, she is told that it may have disturbed someone else, but boys are simply disciplined. When they are punished, children tend to focus on how angry they are rather than learning the effect that their misbehavior has had on their parents or playmates.

***Skills for Peaceful Resolutions*:** Boys need to be provided with constructive ways to work out conflicts. If they engage in hitting or biting, as many do at the toddler stage, parents have to explain that hurting is not tolerated and suggest other ways to express their anger.

***Responsibility for His Actions*:** It is important to avoid applying double standards. If parents find certain behaviors unacceptable for their daughter, then the same standard need to be applied to their son too. They cannot use the excuse "boys will be boys" to pardon unkindness.

***Expression of Emotions*:** Boys have to be encouraged to express their feelings, including crying. If boys are led to believe that feelings of sadness are not tolerated, they will learn to repress these emotions as adults.

Rational Reactions to Gender Differences

Parents can help by making children feel good about boy–girl differences.

- They can react with proper guidance to their daughter's observations and discoveries about sex differences.
- The parents can model the behavior that they want their children to learn. For example, they can ensure that their son sees Mom mowing the lawn and driving the car and Dad dusting, cooking, or washing dishes. In some countries women do most of the heavy work (such as carrying water).
- Parents can offer gender-neutral toys. Toddlers are learning as much from their peers' behavior as from their parents', so parents should work with other parents.

Confusing Gender with Temperament

Most parents agree with psychologists that being rigidly masculine or rigidly feminine is not the best way. Both boys and girls need to be assertive AND gentle, intuitive AND analytic. Nevertheless, many parents are concerned when their child engages in "cross-gender" behavior. A father worries about his son wanting a Barbie doll and a mother is troubled when her daughter refuses to wear dresses (Kessler and McKenna 1978). How serious is any of this? What does it mean?

Each of us is born with a certain temperament. A temperament is a characteristic way of reacting to what goes on around us. Temperaments determine, to some extent, which things we are attracted to and which things we dislike. Some babies seem to be innately sensitive to and interested in people (making eye contact easily and responding to a smile with a smile). Other babies are more drawn to visual objects or sounds (their eyes are glued to the overhanging musical toy).

A problem arises if parents believe that certain temperamental styles are inherently masculine or feminine. This can aggravate the situation. For example, if a parent says to a boy who paints his nails pink, "What do you think you are – a girl?" the child might mistakenly conclude that if he wants to do "girl things" then he has to be a girl. He might then begin to talk about wishing he were a girl or "really" being a girl. This is an idea inadvertently implanted by his parents. Many girls enjoy the noise and chaos of "rough and tumble" play. If a girl likes to be physically active and enjoys rough games, parents may see her as "unfeminine," when the issue is really that she has a temperament that responds to high levels of stimulation in the environment.

The confusion of temperament and gender role expectations is particularly problematic for boys. Boys are given more negative feedback when they engage in "girl" play than girls who engage in "boy" play. "Sissy" is a much more feared label than "tomboy." Because the label "masculine" has greater prestige in society than "feminine," a man's rejection of masculinity in favor of the "lower" status of femininity is extremely stigmatized.

Parents should love their sons and daughters. Children thrive when they have strong and nurturing relationships with parents, and when parents want their children to become caring, productive, healthy, and happy human beings.

Parents have to be aware of the following:

- Be concerned if your child's play behavior is compulsive and inflexible. It is one thing for a child (boy or girl) to want to play with Barbie dolls or dress up in women's clothing. It is another if that is all the child wants to do or if the child plays in a highly repetitive way.

- In rare cases, children who are very unhappy will talk about wishing that their bodies, especially their genitals, were different. Parents should be concerned if their child tries to, or even just talks about, mutilating his/her body. In that case, it is essential to seek professional guidance.

- Parents need not turn their child's temperamental style into a sickness. If their son or daughter is unhappy, depressed, or anxious, then s/he should be taken to a child psychologist who specializes in childhood depression or anxiety.

- Drug therapy is dangerous. Providing medication to children is therefore not advisable whereas talking therapies are.

- It is not necessary to blame anyone. It is likely that the child's unusual preferences are unrelated to anything specific that the parents have done.

Girls and Boys Learn Differently

"From the time they are pre-schoolers, boys and girls absorb information at different rates, for different reasons, with different measures of success" (Gurian 2001). Young boys may be more interested in objects and things, whereas young girls may focus on people and relationships. In primary school, while boys may have an easier time finding France on the map, girls may have an easier time learning French. He will be better at circling the right answer, whereas she will excel at listening to a question and writing down her response. Unfortunately, boys and girls are still treated as if they learn the same way, which results in misbehavior and failure.

Many poor learners can be turned around if we just acknowledge the differences between boys and girls and re-educate ourselves on how to help them thrive. Michael Gurian's successful strategies have been used to transform failing students into the best students. His strategies could benefit every classroom because he capitalizes on the strengths of boys and girls and complements their weaknesses.

For girls: Parents need to strengthen their leadership roles, play movement-related games, utilize their writing skills; facilitate using computers and mastering them; and encourage them to enter mathematics and science competitions.

For boys: Parents need to encourage them to use their energy in cleaning, helping, and moving things around; help them to appreciate feelings like anger, sadness, and happiness; offer storytelling and myth making to develop their brain's imaginative and verbal skills; allow physical movement (from hugs to tumbling); teach media literacy; and make them participate in conflict resolution and community training.

The issue of separate gender education is controversial. However, since boys and girls learn differently, thus necessitating using different teaching strategies in the classrooms, why not use separate classrooms for a more efficient and effective education? How are we going to use two different strategies in one classroom simultaneously? Can it be done? And if so, at what cost in time, money, and effectiveness of results?

Michael Gilbert (2007) recommends single-sex schools. His online article is summarized and paraphrased below:

> Boys are falling behind girls and dropping out of school in greater numbers. Young men who manage to get to college find themselves in the minority, outnumbered almost three to two by women. In the 1960s, fearing that separate meant unequal, and seeking to break down sexual stereotypes, planners decided to mix the sexes at the earliest possible age. In 1965, a majority of America's public school classrooms were single sex; by 2000 barely a handful survived.

> Co-ed schooling imposes the need for sex-blind instruction material and uniform testing and standards of behavior. As a result, on the way to a perfectly balanced sexual universe in our schools, "equal to" was turned into "the same as." But there's a problem: boys and girls are not the same. They do not develop in the same way or at the same time. Most parents who have them know boys develop more slowly in everything from vocabulary to penmanship, even the simple ability to sit still.

When young boys in the U.S. arrive at school today, they enter a world dominated by female teachers and administrators. The percentage of male teachers in the nation's public schools is at its lowest level in 40 years. The girls around them read faster, control their emotions better, and are more comfortable with today's educational emphasis on cooperative study and expressing feelings. Boys favor visual processing and do not have the hand–motor control that girls readily achieve in early grades. There's hardly any of the physical action, competition, or structure boys so often crave. Boys would rather do just about anything than express their feelings.

Boys have trouble paying attention in class. They often ignore instructions and generate sloppy work. They are three to four times more likely to suffer from developmental disorders, and twice as likely as girls to be classified as learning-disabled. Many are punished for physical outbursts. Boys are controlled and medicated simply for behaving like boys (1 in 5 Caucasian boys spends time on Ritalin, a powerful drug). They may not even be allowed to run during recess. This means that boys often get off to a bad start, fail to catch up, and frequently develop an aversion to school.

Elementary school boys are 50 percent more likely than girls to repeat a grade and boys drop out of high school a third more often than girls. Boys from minority and lower-income families suffer the most. In the end, America's educational system turns out legions of young men ill-prepared or disinterested in advancing their education, even though its dramatic impact on future earnings is well documented. This is bad for men, women, and the country's economic future.

Margaret Mead, among other anthropologists, informed us that nearly all thriving cultures have trained and prepared boys and girls separately.

Out of the 90,000 co-ed schools in America less than 250 public schools opted for single-sex schools in 33 states. The single-sex option has long been popular in religious and private schools.

Single-sex private schools have long thrived. Fourth graders in a Florida elementary school were moved to a single-sex classroom. Girls as well as boys achieved amazing increases in writing tests. Other promising experiments have taken place in the U.S., Canada and Ireland. Boys and girls thrive when spared the competition and social pressures in co-ed classrooms, and discipline problems are diminished.

There are positive outcomes from single-sex education for both boys and girls, including higher reading and foreign language achievement, more time spent on homework, and higher educational aspirations. The National Association of State Boards of Education's (NASBE) 2002 report points out that in single-sex schools "positive effects are greatest among girls and among minority students of both sexes."

Segregation of Boys and Girls in Schools and Classrooms

Greene County, Georgia, USA was planning to become the first school district in America to go entirely single-sex, with boys and girls in separate classrooms. This occurred after years of poor test scores, soaring dropout rates and high numbers of teenage pregnancies. Many parents and teachers opposed the change due to not being consulted and the plan was eventually withdrawn.

School Superintendent McCollough had said that boys and girls learnt differently and that separating them would allow teachers to tailor their lessons. Also, boys would not misbehave as much because they would not be trying to impress the girls, and the girls would be more likely to speak up in class because they would not be afraid to look smart in front of the boys. (*India Times* 2008)

Separate classes tailor lessons to the sexes' strengths and needs. Girls and boys learn differently and they will be more successful if classes are designed for their particular needs. Sax (2006), contends that we as a nation do not understand gender differences and regard it as politically incorrect to discuss it. As a result, schools are not helping students to reach their potential. We are unintentionally pushing girls out of computer sciences, and pushing boys out of art and languages. Gurian (2001) shows that boys do not hear as well as girls and that girls are more sensitive to light. Boys often need to fidget and move to stay alert, whereas girls are more likely to behave and pay attention. Different teaching techniques are used to address such differences (Chandler and Glod 2008).

We recommend the following system introduced successfully by the International Islamic University, Malaysia (IIU), in its own elementary, middle, and high school:

1. From nursery school up to third grade: no separation exists between boys and girls, and teachers are women.

2. From fourth to sixth grade: boys and girls are in separate classrooms but

within the same school. Mixing is allowed in activities and during breaks. However, boys and girls can be together in the same classroom but sitting on separate sides as follows:

Suggested Classroom Configuration (4th–6th grade)

3. Seventh and eighth grades: separate schools for boys and girls, and the teachers preferably of the same gender as that of the students. This age group of around 13 to 14 is the puberty-sensitive phase and children are experimenting and learning to mature gradually. It is dangerous to mix them before they comprehend the seriousness of sexual abuse.

4. Ninth to twelfth grade: separate schools with teachers of the same sex only.

5. University education: boys and girls are in the same classroom but sitting in two columns. At this age, teenagers behave more responsibly. They may successfully choose their future spouses, particularly when the faculty and parents provide support and guidance. This is taking place satisfactorily at the IIU, where a course on Parenting is offered to all students.

Parenting and Genders: Islamically Speaking

When Islam came in 610 CE, the culture of Arab society was male dominated and chauvinist; giving birth to a girl was a disgrace and dishonor.

> *When news is brought to one of them, of [the birth of] a female [child], his face darkens, and he is filled with inward grief!* (Qur'an 16:58)

The Qur'anic response was that it is God who gives the gift of progeny, whether all girls, all boys, or a mixture of both.

The Prophet ﷺ gave good tidings to the parents of daughters who raised their daughters correctly:

> Whoever has three daughters or sisters, or two daughters or two sisters, and lives along with them in a good manner, and fears Allah with regard to them, will enter Paradise. (AL-BUKHĀRĪ AND MUSLIM)

> *O mankind! We created you from a single male and female, and made you into nations and tribes, that you may understand one another [not that you may despise one another]. Verily, the most honored of you in the sight of Allah is [he who is] the most righteous of you. And Allah has full Knowledge and is well-acquainted [with all things].* (Qur'an 49:13)

All human beings are descendants of one male (Adam) and one female (Eve).

When it comes to specific gender roles, the Prophet ﷺ established the following timeless concepts and practices in the midst of the overwhelming male-dominated Arab society:

> The best of you is the best to his family and I am the best among you to my family.
> (AL-TIRMIDHĪ AND IBN MĀJAH)

The Prophet ﷺ engaged in domestic tasks:

> ʿĀ'ishah and Umm Salamah said about the Prophet ﷺ that he used to repair his shoes, sew or mend his clothes and do what ordinary men do in their homes.
> (AḤMAD)

The Prophet ﷺ did not divide various roles into two distinctive groups as "woman's job" and "man's job." When it came to the biological roles of motherhood, pregnancy, and breast-feeding, the Qur'an established the duty on the father to provide full support, both material and emotional, for the mother and the child. Furthermore, the Prophet ﷺ gave mothers the highest honor, not the father:

Paradise lies under the feet of mothers. (Aḥmad, al-Nasā'ī, and Ibn Mājah)

The Prophet ﷺ promoted gender equality and set an example of playing a domestic role in his own life which can be classified as transformational, occurring as it did in the midst of strongly male chauvinist Arab and pagan cultures.

In the crucial issue of sex, Islam is clear and firm about preventing sexual intercourse of any kind outside of marriage between a man and a woman. This rule is to protect the family and society from disease and disintegration. Islam does not compromise on these matters, and shuts all avenues leading to unlawful sexual intercourse (such as alcohol, drugs, flirting, and seduction). When siblings attain the age of ten, they are to sleep in separate beds to prevent any sexual issues.

> The Prophet ﷺ said:
> When your children reach the age of seven years, teach them the prayers, and when they are ten years old, seriously admonish them for it [in order that they establish prayers]; and separate their sleeping beds from each other.
> (AḤMAD AND ABŪ DĀWŪD)

Islam prepares girls for the roles of motherhood and baby care, as well as work outside the home and public roles (including active participation in the military). Women in the Prophet's ﷺ time, fought side by side with him. After their children reach a certain age, mothers should be active participants in society (formally or informally, in full-time or part-time jobs, paid or

voluntary work, and political or non-political activities. Anything that fits their situation, profession, training, experience, and economic needs is encouraged. This is not a duty on women, but their own prerogative. In contrast, men's duty is to support the whole family.

Some of the gender role details are left to contemporary culture. For example, at the time of the Prophet ﷺ, men had long hair. In the West, during the mid-1900s, long hair could prevent a man from finding a good job. Now, in the twenty-first century, long hair has become acceptable. In the past, tough jobs were assigned to strong hard-working men. Nowadays, however, many of those tough jobs do not require muscles or strength owing to information technology, electronics, and computers. Professions like construction, engineering, and transportation, can easily be performed by women. By the same token, men and women can work in the areas of teaching, catering, nursing, secretarial work, information technology, and hotel management. Also, when it comes to clothing, both men and women can wear jeans and pants provided that they exhibit modesty, dignity, and respect (not too tight, not transparent, covering the body, and not vulgar). In some Muslim countries, such as Pakistan, trousers are part of women's traditional dress.

Men and women have much to learn from each other. It can be said that there is some femininity in every man and some masculinity in every woman. Both have male and female hormones in different proportions. This is not surprising at all if we analyze the following verses:

> ...*They are your garments and you are their garments...* (Qur'an 2:187)

> *And their Lord answered them: "Never will I deny the work of any of you, male or female: you are part of each other..."* (Qur'an 3:195)

> *He created you [all] from a single [soul] person.* (Qur'an 39:6)

The final position between genders is:

> *And do not covet those things of which Allah has bestowed His gifts more freely on some of you than on others: to men is allotted what they earn, and to women what they earn: but ask Allah of His bounty. For Allah has full knowledge of all things.* (Qur'an 4:32)

The Qur'an addresses all human beings. In some cases the verses address males or females when there exists a specific role to be performed. Under all circumstances, however, the Qur'an addresses women and men with respect and honor.

God's Way is the Best Way: The Examples of China, Germany, and India

The Creator of the universe has put everything in the right measure and gifted us with a balanced environment. When we tamper with divine natural laws, we cause havoc. China is a case in point. In an effort to control population growth, it instituted a controversial one-child policy. Couples had to limit children to only one child per family or else they lost benefits. This led to a society dominated by males, since people preferred their single child to be a boy rather than a girl to help provide better for the family. For several decades, parents kept boys and disposed of girls. The result was a serious shortage of women in the population, causing crimes, kidnapping, and prostitution, not to mention the damaging effects of numerous secret abortions. This disastrous imbalance forced the government eventually to abolish its "unnatural" social experiment and allow families to return to their natural state. The Qur'an explains the divine law of creation as follows:

> *To Allah belongs the dominion of the heavens and the earth. He creates what He wills [and plans]. He bestows [children] female or male according to His Will [and Plan], Or He bestows both males and females, and He leaves barren whom He wills: for He is full of Knowledge and Power.* (Qur'an 42:49–50)

Since Adam and Eve, gender balance exists naturally according to the Master Creator's design.

The Nazis tried experimenting with the qualities of individuals. Their eugenics program aimed at producing a "super human being," with several procedures of identification, isolation, and training. Again, the result was a miserable failure.

Agnivesh et al. (2005) indicate how in India, female feticide – the sex-selective abortion of girls – has led to an alarming "gender gap" of 50 million more males than females. Ironically, technology has made this easier. In the past many baby girls used to be killed after birth. Now it is easier for parents, and highly profitable for doctors, to practice female feticide by ultrasound detection without risking punitive legal actions. In an effort to curb this practice, the government has made it illegal to detect the sex of a fetus by ultrasound examination.

The practice was presumed prevalent among the poor and illiterate classes, largely owing to the high dowry demands made on brides by the grooms' families, as well as other traditional prejudices. However, today female feticide is also frequent among the rich and highly educated, apparently rising with levels of education – lowest among women with a fifth-grade education and highest among women with university degrees.

Girls are being trafficked from impoverished Bangladesh and Nepal or from disadvantaged and tribal areas in India and sold into marriage for about US$200 – while a bull costs US$1,000 (Hughes, et al. 1999). Unfortunately, across many cultures in India, the birth of a son is celebrated whereas the birth of a daughter is mourned.

Activities

ACTIVITY 41: PARENTS' CHAT

Gather several fathers and mothers to discuss "How to raise a good child," and exchange their personal experiences, both positive and negative.

> After a dinner party in our home, all the parents sat down and began discussing how to raise a good child. Many valuable experiences were offered. At the end, one wise parent said, "All that has been said is necessary, but insufficient because even if you follow all the rules, unless the Mercy of God showers on your family, your child will be a disappointment." The parents came to a consensus as follows:
>
> No matter how much effort you expend, you must always couple your knowledge and skills with seeking God's Mercy to help you with this noble and challenging task of parenthood.

It takes a family, it takes a village, it takes an Ummah, and it takes the mercy of God to raise a child. Cooperation of all, not insulation, is the answer.

ACTIVITY 42: THANK GOD FOR WHAT I AM!

All Praise Be to God "Al-Ḥamdu Lillāh"
Teach your child to say the following repeatedly:
I thank God for all the good things He bestowed on me.
I thank God for creating me as a human being.
I thank God for creating me as a girl, or
I thank God for creating me as a boy.
I thank God for creating me as black, white, brown, or yellow.
I thank God for creating me as I am!!

ACTIVITY 43: BARACK OBAMA: AN EXAMPLE OF SINGLE PARENTING!

Parents are advised to sit with their children and discuss the ascension of an African-American to the highest political office on the planet. No matter how his Presidency eventually plays out, the legacy of Barack Obama's achievement will always stand as testimony to human beings' ability to overcome the most difficult odds. Ask your children to read from Obama's two books: *Dreams from My Father: A Story of Race and Inheritance*, and *The Audacity of Hope*. Parents can explain the existence and wisdom of God's Divine plan, how it can extend over generations, travel a long way, and, despite obstacles in its path, always reach its final destination. Obama was raised by a single mother, which parents can discuss with children. They should also discuss the mothers who raised the prophets Moses and Jesus (peace be on them), and the uncle who raised Prophet Muhammad ﷺ.

Concerning Obama and the Divine plan, it is interesting to note how drastically different the outcome would have been if there were any deviation from the following steps charting his life. Consider the following "what ifs:"

- What if Obama's father (Barack Hussein Obama, Senior) was not a Kenyan Muslim and had not won a scholarship to America?
- What if he had not married a white woman (Ann Dunham) from Kansas?
- What if he had not abandoned his wife Ann when Barack was two years old, never to come back?
- What if his mother Ann had not remarried an Indonesian Muslim (Soetoro) and lived for four years in Jakarta, where Obama attended school with Muslim children?
- What if his mother had not been divorced from his stepfather (Soetoro) and returned to the United States?
- What if his mother had not died of cancer and his white grandparents (Madelyn and Stanley Dunham) had not raised him in Hawaii, where he went to school? Think of the impact of the EXTENDED family and its blessings!!
- What if he had not attended Harvard University and become the first African American to be the Editor of the prestigious journal *Harvard Review*?
- What if he had not lived in Chicago as a Christian and attended the Christian Trinity Church for decades?
- What if he had not married Michelle, a descendant of African slaves, who was also a Harvard graduate?

Man proposes but God disposes.

It is quite an achievement for humanity to transcend racism and bigotry and embrace equality, diversity, and tolerance. The White House was built by African slaves between 1792 and 1800, and for it to be now occupied by one of their own, a family unit of a father, a mother, and two daughters, is an incredible transition. Whatever Obama eventually does, he has certainly made history!

On the same theme, parents can narrate their own personal experiences in terms of the Divine plan, and share the fateful decisions taken at the various crossroads of their lives, and how it led them to marry, have children, and be where they are today!

It is all the Master Plan of the Creator:
Your "will" shall not come to pass, unless God Wills it to be!

CHAPTER 13

Sex and Sex Education: What Do We Tell Our Children?

Introduction

Sex and sex education are topics of immense importance and profound significance. Most parents feel extremely uncomfortable when discussing sex, preferring to leave the sex education of their children to schools and other people. For people to be physically fit and healthy, in mind, body, heart, and soul, they have to deal properly with sex. The unlawful practice of sex leads to tragedy, and long-term damage. The best known of these are social and physical diseases. It is not just the individuals participating in unlawful sex who can be infected with diseases, but their spouses and offspring may be harmed as well. The damage can be so severe that it becomes incurable.

Our Maker, the Creator, prohibited fornication and adultery (*zinā*). Sexual promiscuity brings disaster, so one of the foremost rules is that sex must be confined to marriage. Sexually transmitted diseases (STDs) arise from engaging in unlawful sex. When the human race behaves in an unnatural way, new kinds of diseases may strike. Parents need to take an active part in sex education for themselves and for their children.

What is Sex Education?

PEOPLE HAVE DIFFERENT perceptions of sex education. Is it about the anatomy and physiology of the human body, or sexual intercourse, or reproduction and family life, or the prevention of disease and unwanted pregnancies? Is educating children about sex equivalent to giving them permission to engage in sex? A teacher once said: "I am not planning to tell your children whether or not they should engage in sex, or how to do it. But in case they do decide to do it, they should know how to prevent disease and pregnancy." Most sex education programs are incomplete and avoid issues of morality, sexual dysfunction, deviation, and marriage.

There are two basic issues. One consists of biological facts. These deal with teenage fears that arise when youngsters have not been prepared by their parents about menstruation or nocturnal emissions. Another basic issue is giving sexually active young people enough information to avoid unwanted pregnancies and any consequent abortions. Information helps to safeguard them from danger.

Some schools teach the simple mechanics of physical reproduction as well as moral responsibility. Other schools provide bits and pieces of information. In many schools, sex education is a large part of the *Moral and Social Education* curriculum. It does little good to remove your child from these classes, for the subjects discussed may also arise in English or History, or Physical Education, or Art, or the weekly Religious Education program, or virtually anywhere else. Sex has become an integral part of our life.

Most sex education does not encourage a happy and fulfilled married life. Thus, many spouses have very frustrating married lives, frequently owing to the lack of knowledge and skills. The common misconception is that "the man's ability to arouse or satisfy his wife will just come naturally." Knowledge of how to create a happy marriage is a crucial part of education. What a pity that this education is not provided somewhere in the youngster's life.

If your teenager has become sexually active, you will probably be the last person to know about it. The teenager would obviously try to keep it secret. Moreover, teenagers have a secretive network among themselves, where they know a lot about their peers, and vice versa, but all is concealed from the parents.

The real satisfactory answer is the model of the Prophet ﷺ. The way sex education is defined and taught in schools has many positives and negatives. Hence, parents have to shoulder the responsibility of guiding their children. The sex information we are given by society, including schools, TV, the Internet, and peers, has mixed advantages and disadvantages.

The American Scene

Athar (1990) relates how children are being given value-free sex education in school as well as the wrong message from the media. (See *Sex Education: An Islamic Perspective,* edited by Shahid Athar, M.D. http://www.teachislam.com/dmdocuments/33/BOOK/SexEducation). In most schools, sex education is taught from grades 2 to 12, at a cost of billions of dollars. Teachers describe the technical aspects of sex without telling children about moral values or how to make the right decisions. After describing the anatomy and physiology of reproduction, the main emphasis is on the prevention of venereal diseases and teenage pregnancy. With the rise of AIDS, the focus is on "safe sex," which normally means using condoms. Tax dollars are paid to some schools for dispensing free condoms and other contraceptives to those who go to school health clinics. Condom vending machines are available in some school hallways and in universities.

The role of parents is minimized and sometimes ridiculed. Whenever young boys ask a question about sex, their fathers usually shun them and change the subject. Therefore, the boys learn about sex from strangers. Some vices promoted by educators are unacceptable according to religious principles. According to Dr. Shahid Athar, the beliefs of some misguided educators are as follows:

(a) Nudity in homes (in the shower or bedroom) is good and a healthy way to introduce sexuality to smaller (under 5) children, giving them an opportunity to ask questions. Yet according to a 1997 study 75% of all child molestations and incests (500,000 per year) occur by a close relative (parent, step parent or another family member) in a familiar surrounding. (Abel et al. 2001)

(b) A child's playing with the genitals of another child is a "naive exploration", is permissible and is not a reason for either scolding or punishment. This particular educator is also aware that boys as young as 12 have raped girls as young as 8. He does not inform us when this "naive exploration" becomes a sex act.

(c) Children caught reading 'dirty' magazines should not be made to feel guilty, but parents should use this as a chance to get some useful points across to him or her about sexual attitudes, values and sex exploitation. This is astonishing ignorance. Many of these magazines convey the message that sex is a commodity and that women are toys for men to play with. In fact, guilt is not a harmful emotion as long as it gets people to regret an action and to correct it. Feeling remorse through guilt (in order to evaluate and reverse a wrong act) is a learning mechanism for teaching children to measure their behavior and feel responsibility.

(d) If one's child is already sexually active, instead of telling them to stop it, the parents' moral duty is to protect their health and career by providing them information and means for contraception and avoiding venereal disease. Educators such as these do not believe that giving sexual information means giving the go ahead signal for sex. Yet, if someone is told the shape, color, smell and taste of a new fruit, and the pleasure derived from eating it, doesn't common sense dictate that they would like to try it? Parents need to initiate appropriate discussion concerning improper sexual relations. The discussion can be about a community member's unwanted pregnancy, a vulgar advertisement, lewd music or a TV show that promotes promiscuity.

True or False?

The More They Know it, the More They do it!!

Sex education in American public schools has not decreased the incidence of teenage venereal disease or teenage pregnancy nor has it changed the sexual habits of teenagers. Unfortunately, going to church is not helping much either. (Athar 1990)

Unless your children go to a school that actually tries to prevent biological knowledge, they are going to experience some sex education, and parents should be more involved. Schools usually give simple biological knowledge and contraception information needed by youngsters

who are becoming adults. Many Muslim parents, like those of other faiths, are concerned that the sexual morals imparted in government schools are not up to the standards of their faith, and that to give children advice on contraception may encourage them to have sex. This is a false fear, for the information given is factual and necessary to the young person.

Many men, Muslim and non-Muslims, are surprised to discover the sexual hunger of their wives. This is because many men have been told that it is easy for a woman to satisfy a man's sexual needs, for all she has to do is to keep still and give him access for a few seconds. However, men have not been told that it is a matter of skill and a religious duty for a man to learn to satisfy a woman's sexual needs. They have to overcome their natural shyness about a woman's private parts, to learn foreplay techniques, and grasp the understanding that if they satisfy themselves and leave the woman "hungry," they are causing severe deprivation to their wives and this is a form of cruelty.

Most parents do not want their children to start indiscriminately "sleeping around". Nevertheless, once their teenager begins to have a private life away from their watchful eye, the parents will have very little control. Although innocence is one way of protecting youngsters, the kind of innocence desired by parents has usually disappeared in the playground before the child is 10 years old. Children these days take in knowledge from the Internet, television and movies, and if your children have access to DVDs (or friends with DVDs), the sexual "knowledge" gained from what they watch is likely to be far "in advance" of your own, realistically speaking.

AIDS One of Leading Causes of Death in Thailand

AIDS in 2001 became the leading cause of death in Thailand, overtaking accidents, heart disease and cancer, according to Deputy Public Health Minister Surapong Suebwong-lee. The minister did not disclose exact figures but said the extent of HIV-AIDS had been under-reported because the relatives of victims in rural areas were reluctant to report the real cause of death.

"Village headmen reported most non-accidental deaths as being a result of 'the heart stopped beating'. This led to a misconception that most Thais die of heart disease". "But we have done a new random survey and found out that the biggest cause of deaths in the rural areas is AIDS," he said after returning from a World Health Organisation meeting in the Maldives. The UN Programme on HIV-AIDS (UNAIDS) office in Bangkok stated that AIDS deaths would continue to rise as Thais who were infected at the start of the epidemic 10 years ago have begun to sicken and die in large numbers. An estimated one million of Thailand's 60 million people have been infected with HIV and around one third of those have already died. (AIDS EDUCATION GLOBAL INFORMATION SYSTEM 2001)

Why Did an Otherwise Content Professor Choose to Leave the USA?

A professor at the International Islamic University, Malaysia (IIUM) once related the following story. His third-grade son in a government elementary school in Michigan had come home one day and explained in great detail a classmate's performance of the full sexual act in the classroom with a schoolgirl! This caused the professor to pack up and leave America with his family of five children! The result of value-neutral sex education has produced a generation indulging in sex in a casual, irresponsible way. The prevalent culture has made sex attractive, available, enjoyable, and accessible. Avoidance seems abnormal to many, because sexual images and promiscuity have become common.

Perceptions of Mothers and Daughters in the USA

Teenagers are growing more confused about sexual behavior, and they are lacking the appropriate guidance from parents and teachers. Below are some examples of what teenagers are saying:

- Says 16-year-old Selma: "I can't ask my mother anything about sex. If I do, she starts wondering why I asked the question. 'What do you want to know for?' she insists, 'unless…'"
- Says 14-year-old Juliet: "My mother believes that ignorance assures innocence. She gets mad when I ask her anything about sex. She says, 'Your husband will teach you all you need to know about sex.'"
- Says 18-year-old Louis: "I get a mixed message from my parents. One says, 'Don't do it, you'll get into trouble!' The other says, 'Sow your wild oats while you are young.' I wish parents would make up their minds. If sex is good for us, let them say so. If it is bad for us, then don't tempt, don't provoke, and don't confuse."
- Says 15-year-old Joshua: "My father always wants us to be truthful. But his honesty stops where sex begins. This is one area where my candor is not welcomed."
- 22-year-old Jonathan says: "For college boys, sex is a symbol of maturity and masculinity. For girls, it's a safeguard against unpopularity and loneliness."
- The dilemma of sex is expressed by a teenager: "If I see a comedy, I can laugh; a tragedy, I can cry; something that makes me angry, I can scream; but if I see a play that has me sexually aroused, what can I do then?"

These discussions indicate that appropriate sex education is now needed to serve as an antidote to ignorance. Society can no longer passively permit the street and the screen to set its sex standards and values.

Values and Sex: Today and Yesterday

There is a considerable conflict of values among people today. Some parents feel that the time has come to accept the new reality. They are worried about STDs, unwanted pregnancies, and ruined reputations. They hope to avoid these dangers with candid sex education. Some would supply their teenagers with information and contraception.

Other parents indignantly reject these measures. They know that contraceptives might encourage pre-marital sex. They know that society cannot support teenage sex because early erotic awakening would endanger responsible human relationships and civilization. The main task of youth is to acquire knowledge and prepare themselves for a righteous adult and family life. To accomplish this task it is best to keep the "lid on the id." Some find even discussion of sex repugnant and in bad taste. Some parents feel that open sex talk will stimulate sex acts, even when the goal is self-control. One parent talks of being role models to children: "Only when we adults set a decent example and demand decent behavior will children become the kind of people we like."

Both in life and literature, there is less sexual morality. In the United States and many other countries sex is no longer a forbidden subject; it is taught in school and discussed at home.

In these societies it is taken for granted that if exposed to temptation, youth will give in.

Therefore, boys are suspected and girls are chaperoned. Boys nowadays have cars and many girls have freedom. When maximum temptation exists with minimum supervision, how can we realistically expect youth to follow the moral rules?

In the past, nice girls insisted on chastity and when confronted with an insistent boyfriend, allowed necking or petting only. This was her compromise with conscience and society. Now, many teenagers are pushed to question this solution. Boys resent it because TV, movies and magazines leave them over-stimulated, and girls resent it because it turns them into teasers.

College girls in these countries who want to stay virgins find it hard. Many boys refuse to date them and some girls treat them as old fashioned. Those who are serious about "saving themselves for marriage" may find themselves socially isolated. Under these pressures, a virgin may start doubting her normality. In the face of temptation and ridicule, only the morally determined can maintain their high standards. Sadly, many girls have sex in this environment, not out of need but out of pressure. In the past, a girl could use the fear of pregnancy as an excuse for chastity. Now this excuse is gone. Prophylactics are sold at supermarkets, pills and diaphragms are easily obtained, and some schools and even churches distribute free condoms.

During a visit from college, Jason, aged 18, said to his father about life and love: "I have discovered the real difference between boys and girls. Girls play with sex as a way of getting love. Boys play with love as a means of getting sex. My philosophy is love them and leave them." His father asked, "What happens to the girl after you and other guys love her and leave her?" "It is not my business, I try not to think about it," said Jason.

"Well, think about it. In the Orient, they say if you save a man from death, you are responsible for his life. If you devised a strategy to lure a girl into love, her feelings become your business," answered his father.

Jason's father affirmed a basic principle: Honesty and responsibility pertain to all human relations. All situations, simple or complex, social or sexual, require individual integrity and accountability.

Why Sex Education? Should We Teach it?

Teenagers are eager to learn all they can about sex. They are troubled and perplexed and demand realistic and personal answers. When offered an opportunity to discuss sex seriously, teenagers talk freely and sensibly. They look for standards and meaning, wanting to come to terms with their sexuality.

The question is: should sex education be offered to teenagers? Often, this comes too late. Sex is already being poorly taught on the internet, in the schoolyard, and in the streets. In words and pictures, children are being exposed to sex that is often sordid and vulgar. The screens and the streets are a ceaseless source of misinformation. Smut-sellers never hesitate to share sex "facts" and feelings. Precocious peers willingly tell of experiences, real and imagined. It is the parents and teachers who often fear to share the proper information in a timely manner.

Sex education has two parts: information and values. Values are best learned at home. Experts can best give information. Not all questions on sex spring from a thirst for knowledge. Some children aim to embarrass their parents, who need not answer provocative questions. Parents cannot be expected to be candid, comfortable, and knowledgeable about every aspect of human sexuality. Information sought genuinely should be provided, whereas other questions are best referred to experts. Parents need to encourage their teenagers to take part in discussions on sex sponsored not only by the school, but more importantly by the church, mosque, and the community center. Information imparted objectively and honestly can decrease hostility and increase trust between the generations. Adults may regain their faith in youth, and young people may find that despite the age gap, adults really are concerned with their well-being and share with them a common humanity.

On the other hand, one may argue: Do children need sex education? Do you teach a baby duck how to swim or just put it in water and let it swim? For thousands of years men and women have had sex without formal education. In many traditional civilizations, sex education starts by trial and error after marriage. However, having a dozen children is not a proof of love. An appropriate and healthy sex education is crucial to the fulfillment of a happy marriage.

Who should teach sex education? Everyone has a role to play. The parents need to know the facts and the issues of concern and have to assume a more responsible role. The father has a duty to be able to answer his son's questions, and the mother, her daughter's questions. We cannot rely on sex education at school or from the media. It is our duty to supplement it with an ethical and moral dimension. Sunday school teachers, the family physician, the pediatrician, well-informed imams, and the clergy can also play a role. Within a family, the older sister has a duty toward the younger one and the elder brother toward the younger one.

Parents should not be silent about sex education. Silence sends the wrong message to children. Children are confused by the conflicting "facts" they hear from strangers and peers. They will develop undesirable attitudes about sexuality which could affect them negatively during their adult years.

Avoiding sex education is not an option any more. We must be realistic. Parents who try to prevent their children from having sex education are really banging their heads against a brick wall. It is surely better for their children to learn from a learned and ethically responsible adult, who will be able to undo any possible confusion and undesirable influences of the environment.

The Qur'an and the Prophet ﷺ discuss sex issues clearly and wisely. Sex is not a dirty word, for it is an important aspect of human lives. The Qur'an discusses in a dignified language: reproduction, creation, family life, menstruation, and ejaculation. The Prophet ﷺ discussed respectfully with his Companions many aspects of their sexual lives in this regard. One reason why Muslim parents do not discuss sex is due to the way in which they have been brought up. Parents may be ignorant about sex, or uncomfortable with their own sexuality or its expression.

What to Teach Children?

Many parents prepare their daughters for the onset of monthly periods, and their sons for their first nocturnal emission. Some parents do not prepare their kids, which causes fear and distress to the teenager. Any unexpected discharge or blood is automatically connected in the young person's mind with a disease or damage, and if it has followed any self-exploration or masturbation, the young person can feel worried and guilty. A heavy flow of blood or semen often makes them believe that

something inside them has broken or is diseased, and they are too ashamed and frightened to talk about it. One young girl was desperately trying to cope with her bleeding with handkerchiefs for months, thinking she was seriously ill, and too frightened to tell anybody. At last, a kind teacher discovered her bloodstained clothes and helped her. She had been desperately washing them out in case her mother saw them.

Some mothers need to think about their own wrong attitudes toward menstruation before they talk to their daughters about it. It is useful if boys know something about it too. It helps later, when a young man has to cope with a wife who is suffering from pain, premenstrual tension, or a bad temper. It is quite pointless to regard the whole business as unclean and embarrassing, and treat the girl during this time as a person to be shunned.

The Prophet ﷺ advised that we should not hurt menstruating women by rejecting them or making them feel unclean. Only full sexual intercourse should be avoided. However, so long as the woman's private parts were covered and the man protected from blood, the couple could find satisfaction how they liked.

With few exceptions, sex education in the American public secondary schools has mostly become a series of lessons on how to use condoms, avoid diseases, and obtain abortions. The prevailing attitude in the United States seems to be that young people are going to have sex anyway, so we should just help them to do it safely. A moral or ethical perspective is rarely given, and if it is, there are no references to religion, spirituality, and pleasing God. Mixed-sex classes remove a young person's natural sense of shyness. Even in single-sex classes children are encouraged to experiment with sex, and given tips on kissing techniques or masturbation as part of a "natural exploration of sexuality." Muslim children who have not had any previous exposure to these topics will not know how to respond, and may be too embarrassed to ask their parents about it.

Sex Abuse! How Serious is it?

According to Islam, any sexual intercourse outside marriage (*zinā*) is a form of moral and religious abuse. Some argue that when sex abuse results in illegitimate children, it may be more devastating – in some cases – to a society than murder. Adultery can have a very long-term effect on families and society for generations to come. The outcome of adultery may be manifested in one or more of the following ways: diseases, abortion, handicapped or retarded babies (if an STD – sexually transmitted disease – is passed to a pregnant wife), illegitimate children, single-parent families, broken families, confused lineage (*nasab*), betrayal of trust, and prostitution.

Adultery cheapens human dignity and interaction. A society that allows for the violation of sexual taboos (such as adultery) may end up with more serious sexual taboos (such as prostitution) regardless of whether it is illegal. Once taboos are violated on a small scale, they become easier to violate on a larger scale. Fornication and adultery are major sins punishable by the Almighty in this life and in the Hereafter.

Islam does not regard fornication and adultery as personal sins only, but rather as aggressions against society. If they become acceptable, they destroy the fabric of society, starting from its very foundation, the family. Indeed, the legal punishment for fornication and adultery in the Qur'an is a public lashing of one hundred stripes. So severe is the danger of adultery to society that in the ancient past, stoning was required (i.e. The Bible,

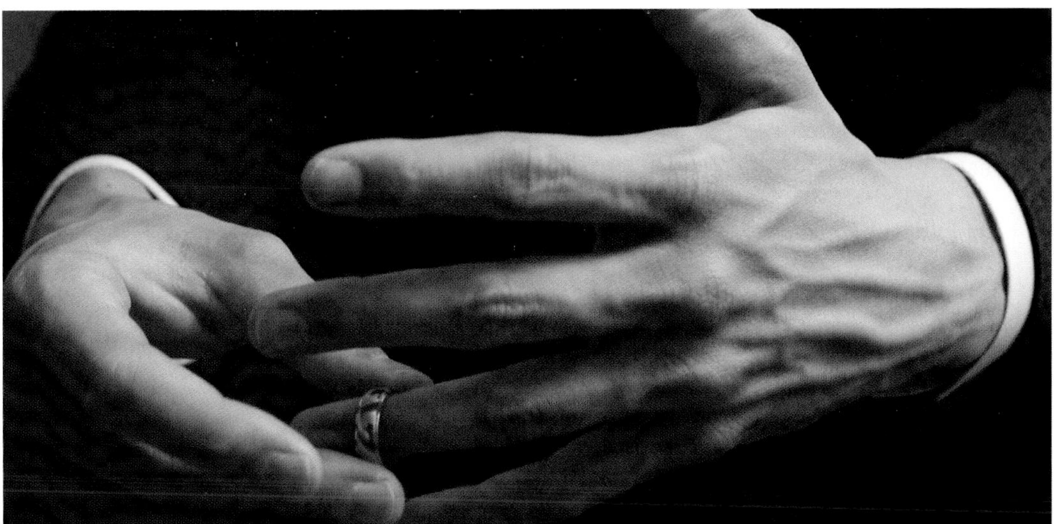

Deut. 22:23–24). Stoning however is not prescribed in the Qur'an and many Muslim scholars reject the validity of stoning outright. Owing to the seriousness and dishonor associated with the charge of adultery, four sane, reliable, adult Muslim witnesses must testify to the court the details of the act of adultery. The requirement of the four witnesses is both to protect the privacy and honor of the suspects and also to convey the message that fornication and adultery are social concerns as well. All people are innocent unless four credible witnesses testify to the contrary. Fewer than four reliable witnesses is not valid evidence and jurists may agree that DNA tests can be accepted as evidence. Adultery committed in front of four or more witnesses is a public propagation of evil in the society rather than just a personal lust satisfaction through secret means.

Adultery is, in addition, a violation of the marital contract. About half of all first-time marriages in the United States result in divorce within two years and the main reason is an extramarital affair by either spouse. Many people are not heeding either the Bible or the Qur'an. The Bible states, "Thou shalt not commit adultery," and the Qur'an resonates: "Do not approach adultery," which means that not only is it illegal, but also that we should avoid anything that leads to it. All approaches to adultery (such as dating, provocative clothing, nudity, obscenity, and pornography) are included in the condemnation. The dress codes for men and women are ordained to protect both from temptation and lust by onlookers. Some men lose self-control and fall into a major sin and possibly rape!

In matters of sex, attitudes speak louder than words. What is the society's true attitude toward sex? What is our concept of morality? As a society, we lack role models of moral excellence. Thoughtful teenagers are puzzled by a prevalent public paradox: on the one hand, society is sex-obsessed and money-motivated. For fun and profit, sex is portrayed in movies, blown up on billboards, and used for commercial enticement. On the other hand, society declares that it believes in *premarital abstinence*. This situation creates conflict and tension. If society permits continual public sources of stimulation, it cannot prevent private sources of abuse and relief. Many young people have "liberated" ideas that "being in love" consists in having sex with anyone, regardless of their lack of commitment. This leads to sexual encounters, and also divorce.

Natalie, a 19 year-old college sophomore, explains her dilemma
(Faber and Mazlish 1982):

> **My parents and I live by the grace of unspoken code: No deep questions, no real answers. They really don't want to know what goes on. And I can't tell them. I am a good girl with conventional morals. To start with, it is hard for me to find a fellow who would love me in a friendly way. I like to date. The first few meetings are pleasant. Then comes the pressure: you are invited to parties with liquor and marijuana. It is taken for granted that you will go to bed with him. And they say, "If you do, the world will smile with you. If you don't, you'll cry alone." So I'm full of integrity and tears.**

The disastrous result is that some children cannot tell right from wrong. The United States has an AIDS problem, a drug problem, and a violence problem. None of these problems will go away until schools once again make it their job to teach good character. The school curriculum must create a moral environment that complements parental guidance. Schools that are courageous enough to reinforce and practice virtue are better at building a healthy society than an army of doctors, counselors, police, and social workers.

Abrahamic Traditions Forbid Fornication and Adultery

The following sequence, totally or partially, is common in today's young generation:

Boyfriend–Girlfriend → Temptation and Seduction → Premarital intercourse → Loss of virginity and honor → unwanted pregnancy →(abortion or forced early marriage or illegitimate children followed by adoption) → poverty and misery → breaking of family ties → diseases → death!

A person who is sexually promiscuous may contract gonorrhea, syphilis, herpes, or AIDS, and then pass these disease(s) on to an innocent spouse. If the wife happens to be pregnant, the disease may harm their child permanently. The baby could be born blind or handicapped. If AIDS is contracted, the man is responsible for the slow, painful death of his wife and child, as well as himself!

Adultery causes havoc when children are involved. A man may father children from other women and refuse to take responsibility for those children since he is not legally married to their mother(s). By his deceitful actions, he denies his children the right to be brought up in a secure, dignified, and stable home. Likewise, a woman who has sex with someone other than her husband may become pregnant with another man's child. If she hides this fact from everyone, she cannot hide it from her own conscience. Also the child may never know his/her real father and other relatives. The real father will not be able to act as a father to his child, and the woman's husband is cheated and will unwittingly be responsible for a child who is not his own. By her deceitful actions, she takes away the basic right of everyone to know his/her real family. The cheated father and/or the child may discover the truth by blood-matching or a DNA test. She may also catch and spread diseases such as AIDS, threatening the lives of her husband and children. Normally, a married person who has an extra-marital affair is discovered sooner or later, and this often leads to disaster and divorce, which has serious effects on the children, the family, and society.

In Islam, the punishments for adultery can be applied only in a court that officially applies Islamic law. Individuals cannot and must not take the law into their own hands, but should go to the authority with the required evidence. Unfortunately, some fathers have lost their tempers and murdered their daughters – along with their boyfriends – who have become pregnant before marriage out of their "sense of honor." Some of these "murders" (honor killings) are based on mere suspicion of misconduct, and the boyfriends, having greater freedom of movement, usually escape.

There is so much social pressure for teenagers to fit in and listen to their peers and the media. If they would instead listen to their conscience, these problems could be avoided. Unmarried people who try out sex before marriage discover (although too late) that it was just not worth it. In exchange for a few minutes of fun, they find themselves facing a lifetime of trouble and sadness. This might have been the worst decision they have ever taken in their lives. And on the Day of Judgment, they will have to answer to the Almighty for their actions.

The Rationale Behind the Legal Punishment of Adultery and Fornication

Although it seems strange to modern ears to consider fornication and adultery a crime, yet within Islam it is just this, illustrating the great extent to which these actions inflict harm on human lives and society. The subject requires a deep understanding of the nature of human beings. We will look at four elements: the Divine Revelation, reason, nature, and the action itself.

The main aim of the law of punishment is to establish peace and security in the society. When the crime is related to material wealth or homicide, Islamic law requires only two witnesses to establish the facts. However, if the crime is related to adultery (lust and desire), four witnesses are needed. Why? Because the issue here is not just the committing of the sin individually, but also the effect of its public commission on society, that is, in the presence of at least four people. Public commission of this sin is an avenue to spreading evil and vice.

There is also the need to balance the suppression of vice and the protection of privacy and honor. There is a considerable difference between sinning in secret to satisfy a human desire and sinning publicly to spread vice among people and threaten their honor and security. A good example is that of the second caliph, 'Umar ibn al-Khaṭṭāb, who – when passing by a house – heard people singing and drinking and climbed the wall of the house to investigate. Although he wanted to prosecute them, they countered that the Caliph had no right to climb the wall and spy on them. He realized his mistake and did not take any action against them. In the case of adultery, if there are fewer than four witnesses, then they should never utter a word about what they have witnessed, otherwise they will be punished for libel and scandal in society. Islam discourages promoting sins and vices because it makes them more familiar, allowing for their gradual acceptance and toleration by society.

Sexually Transmitted Diseases (STDs)

Teenagers can contract a disease called "mono" (mononucleosis) just from kissing each other; it attacks the liver and requires several weeks of bed-rest. Other contagious diseases that are spread through sexual contact are:

- gonorrhea, which can make men and women sterile (unable to have children)
- genital herpes, which causes very painful blisters on one's genitalia and recurs repeatedly throughout a person's life
- syphilis, which can damage almost every part of the human body
- AIDS (Auto Immune Deficiency Syndrome) which leads to a slow and painful death. Treatment with antiretroviral drugs can delay the onset of AIDS for several decades.

Faithful married couples that do not have sexual intercourse with anyone except each other do not contract venereal diseases. STDs are spread either by unmarried people who have several partners, or by married people who are unfaithful to their spouses and secretly have sex with others. In the 1940's, the well known sexually transmitted diseases were syphilis and gonorrhea. Now new ones are identified every few years and are becoming increasingly harder to treat. For AIDS and herpes, there is no known cure.

In a way, these diseases are a deterrent to prevent deviation from a pure nature as a result of publicly sinful societies.

The Prophet ﷺ said:

"Whenever sexual deviation becomes spread in a society and publicly acceptable, then plague and other diseases which were not previously known to their predecessors will appear and spread among them."

(IBN MĀJAH)

The health hazards of pre-marital sex also include sexual trauma, cervical cancer, and unwanted teenage pregnancy.

A variety of injuries are possible when the sexual organs are not sufficiently mature for sex. Some of these injuries have a long-lasting effect. Cervical cancer is thought to be related to sex occurring at an early age with multiple partners.

The sexual revolution in the 1960's in the United States increased the costs of health care. In 1985 alone, ten million cases of chlamydia, two million cases of gonorrhea, one million cases of venereal warts, half a million cases of genital herpes and 90,000 cases of syphilis were diagnosed. The plague of AIDS is adding to our fears.

Risk factors for cervical cancer include: Multiple sex partners and smoking. Women at an increased risk ought to be getting regular Pap tests. (Cancer Research UK)

The US has the highest rate of curable STDs of any developed country. More than 12 million people, including three million teens, become infected annually. (Institute of Medicine 1997)

Boyfriend–Girlfriend Relations

Very young children do not mind with whom they play, although from about the age of eight, most boys prefer to play with boys and most girls prefer to play with girls. Children often form "best friend" relationships between the ages of 10 and 12, and keep these close friendships throughout their teens (D'Oyen 1996). When a man grows up, his friendships with other men continue to be important. If all is well in the family, he has a close relationship with his father, brothers, uncles, and cousins, and later on, his grown-up sons. A married woman continues to find great comfort in her friendship with other women like her mother and sisters, relatives, neighbors, or other women.

Innocent friendships are fine as long as they are kept within certain limits. A boy and a girl who are not closely related or *maḥram* (persons who are not allowed to marry each other) must not spend time alone together in a private place; they should both be modest and shy in their dress and behavior, and restrict their conversation to polite topics. Dating and intimate boy–girl friendships, which are prevalent in many societies, are not permitted in Islam. Family get-togethers, activities at the mosque, and friendly visits can provide plenty of opportunities for exchanging ideas and having a good time between boys and girls within the limits of modesty.

In many societies, it is common for boys and girls to go out together on dates and have several boyfriends and girlfriends before they finally marry. They mistakenly believe they will have a better chance of having a good marriage if they practice sex before marriage. Or they think they must try out different partners before they find the right one. Or they just want to "have fun." Sometimes they live together as husband and wife without getting married; this is called "living together." They might even have a child before they decide to get married, or they might decide never to get married.

This behavior is forbidden by many religions because of the terrible problems it causes. Sadly, the pressure on young people to behave in this way is becoming stronger. Television commercials, films, the Internet, and books at school are constantly trying to convince people that if they do not have a boyfriend or girlfriend, there is something wrong with them! Some schoolchildren as young as nine try to act much older by boasting about the things they have done with the other sex, as though they lead very exciting lives. They try to make other children feel that they are old-fashioned or stupid if they do not join them. But what really happens to these children as they get older?

Young people who are actively involved with the opposite sex at a very early age often come from problem families. Their parents may be divorced, or they may lack love or attention at home. They look for friendships with people of the opposite sex, who will kiss and touch them and keep them company. This is dangerous, because their feelings can easily get out of hand and lead to sexual intercourse before they are ready for it, and this will multiply their problems.

When teenagers have boyfriends or girlfriends before marriage, in the eyes of a Muslim, they become "used" like second-hand clothing. If they go so far as to have sexual intercourse before marriage, they lose their virginity. Many traditional cultures around the world emphasize virginity (for girls in particular) at marriage, and those girls who behave in a careless way lose their honor and have difficulty finding respectable husbands. However, Islam places a high and equal value on the self-control and chastity of both men and women. Most parents in these cultures will refuse to marry their daughter to a young man who is

known to be promiscuous and has had girlfriends. Such a man may grow tired of his wife before long and leave her for another woman, or he may not respect and treat her well.

Sexual intercourse can result in pregnancy because birth control is not always effective. If a girl becomes pregnant from fornication, it is a disaster for her and her baby and a disgrace for her family. Motherhood is an awesome responsibility even for a mature woman within a functioning family. It becomes unmanageable for a girl who becomes an unwed mother at the age of 11 to a child whose 14-year-old father is not prepared for fatherhood, and who are both thrust into these positions without the support of their families. It is less likely that they have matured educationally, emotionally, and economically. Therefore, they cannot provide a good life for themselves and their child. This is unfair to the innocent baby. More often, the boy becomes terrified and refuses to admit that he is the father of the child, and will not have anything to do with the girl after that. Then she is completely alone with a baby who will miss the love and support of a father. Such people have a very difficult time. They may not be able to finish their studies, and both parents may have to take on unpleasant work to pay the bills.

In liberal societies, what can parents do about their daughter and the obsession of girls with boys? As their daughter grows, the parents may notice that she is noticing boys. They will hear her talking about that "hot" boy over there. The first time the parents hear her talking about an illicit relationship, they might feel a little nervous. Thoughts of such a boy (who they consider a monster) taking a liking to their daughter, then attempting to form a physical relationship with her will make the parents feel nauseated.

It is important that the daughter's heart is filled with a father's love and she is taught self-respect, responsibility, and values, so that when she encounters a man with less nobility and virtue (and more active hormones), she will not be vulnerable to his pressure. Since her parents have taught her how to talk to them, she will tell them about boys. When the secrecy is gone, the parents' fear will subside.

Teaching her the art of conversation will also protect her physically from boys, for she will have the confidence and skill to say, "that's unacceptable," rather than quietly acquiesce to his requests.

Parents should explain to their daughter the myths of falling in love with boys. Many times boys try to trick girls, and some girls try to trick boys! A "good" girl can justify her passion for sex by falling in love. This is one reason why a teenage girl is so vulnerable to romance and to "sweet" words by boys. Words of love may justify to her the act of love. She assumes that what is true for her is also true for boys. A boy is physically and psychologically different, and is brought up differently. A boy can make love without loving, and often finds himself sexually excited, even in the absence of girls. He may then look for relief, and "She" can be almost anyone. The double standard permits him to make love without involvement. "Have a good time, but don't bring her home," is the misleading advice for boys.

It is a girl's task not to allow herself to be used as a tool, and it is a boy's obligation not to use a girl as a tool. Both boys and girls need to know that there are strict rules for love and sex. It is unfair of a girl to tease and provoke a boy. It is unfair for a boy to pressure a girl. A boy may follow his misguided lust blindly and may go as far as the girl will let him, without questioning her readiness or his responsibility.

Children Having Children: Abortion and Adoption in Islam

Premarital intercourse is a form of sex abuse that could result in pregnancy. In spite of all the contraception used by teenagers, a considerable number of unwanted pregnancies occur among unwed mothers. It is devastating for the unwed pregnant teenager. On top of the psychological trauma, she must decide between two evils: abortion or becoming an unwed mother with an illegitimate baby forever. Such cases are not rare: one million unwed teenage girls become pregnant in the United States every year.

FINALLY, HE ADMITTED ...

WHILST STUDYING AT LIVERPOOL UNIVERSITY IN THE UK BACK IN 1962, I HAPPENED TO HAVE A MUSLIM FRIEND WHO WOULD REGULARLY DATE THE LOCAL NON-MUSLIM GIRLS. I WOULD ARGUE ABOUT THE ILLS OF DATING, BUT IN VAIN. AFTER THREE YEARS OF CONTINUAL DATING HOWEVER, HE ONCE TOLD ME "YOU KNOW, YOU WILL BE HAPPY WHEN YOU MARRY BECAUSE BOTH YOU AND YOUR WIFE WILL BE VIRGINS ON YOUR WEDDING DAY SO IT WILL BE THE FIRST INTIMATE RELATIONSHIP THAT YOU EXPERIENCE, AND THE GIFT OF THIS WILL BE PRECIOUS AND FULFILLING. AS FOR ME, WHEN I MARRY MY WIFE WILL BE JUST ANOTHER OF THE MANY GIRLS I SLEPT WITH. SO FOR ME THE INTIMACY WILL NEITHER BE A SPECIAL NOR A DIGNIFIED ONE!"

What is life like for American teenagers who experience a pregnancy? Only 50 percent complete high school. More than 50 percent of them are dependent on welfare. They are more likely to become child abusers and their grown-up children have an 82 percent incidence of teenage pregnancy. Billions of dollars are spent every year on the financial and healthcare support of these teenage mothers in the United States.

There are No Illegitimate Children Only Illegitimate Parents with Innocent Babies!!

(WEISS 2007)

ABORTION

It is too late: parents have discovered that their daughter is pregnant. What can they do – as parents – to resolve the situation? Wisdom dictates that a DNA test be taken to identify the father of the baby. He should then be required to marry the "bachelorette" and make an honest woman of her!

A pregnant bachelorette, who realizes she cannot take care of a baby alone, may resort to an abortion. She will look for a doctor who will remove the baby from her uterus before it grows big, killing the embryo. Some believe that abortion is an acceptable practice and that an unborn baby is not really a person in the first few months of pregnancy.

However, the fetus is alive from the moment the sperm joins the egg, and if the fertilized egg is left in peace, it will grow into a complete human being. It is stated implicitly in the Qur'an and explicitly in the Hadith that the fetus is not ensouled until the fourth month. If a woman's unborn baby – from the age of four months – dies for some reason in later pregnancy and she has a miscarriage, the baby must be given a name, buried with respect, and prayed for.

Islam teaches mercy and respect for all human life. Every human being has the right to live (unless s/he has committed certain major crimes like murder, which deserve capital punishment). This is called the right to life and it is the most basic right that the Creator grants everyone. Hence, an abortion in the absence of a good reason is regarded in the same light as murder by most Muslim scholars because it kills a helpless innocent human being.

The only time a woman is permitted to have an abortion is if her own life is in danger if she continues the pregnancy, and, according to some jurists, in cases of rape and incest. Other jurists put such strict limitations only after ensoulment and consider other reasons acceptable during the first four months. Nevertheless, Islam discourages abortion at any time and prohibits abortion beginning in the fourth month. Abortion is allowed for exceptional cases: to avoid a danger to the mother's life, or to avoid grave consequences for the family honor, and to avoid a horrible psychological and social impact on the mother, the baby, and the entire family.

Although abortion is permitted in very few circumstances by some schools of thought, it is not allowed as a means of birth control or avoiding the economic cost of an unplanned pregnancy. If the pregnant girl decides to keep the baby, she will become a single parent of an illegitimate child – a situation that carries tremendous hardship for the unwed mother and the fatherless child.

ADOPTION IN ISLAM

Having done all in their power to prevent extramarital sex, if parents still find themselves with a grandchild in their home, what can they do? Many parents of unmarried pregnant girls often feel deeply ashamed of their daughter's disgraceful behavior and do not want to help take care of a baby born outside of marriage. Islam allows the mother to give up the baby for adoption. Islam encourages adoption as a way to take care of orphans. However, the orphan's wealth must be preserved, as well as knowledge of the orphan's family origins. Unmarried mothers often have to give up their babies for adoption and they may never see their children again. They will always wonder about them, and when the children themselves grow up and realize that they have been adopted, they will be curious about their biological parents and relatives.

Not all children put up for adoption end up in good homes. Some children are never adopted. They are either raised in orphanages or sent from one foster home to another, where they may be mistreated. In some societies, if it is known that a child is illegitimate, he or she is teased and not accepted by others. These children – resentful of the treatment they receive – can often grow up to be troubled children.

Can the adopted child be called by the name of the adopting father? The Qur'an considers lineage a serious issue, and it prohibits any person's true identity to be faked.

> *...nor has He made your adopted sons your sons. Such is [only] your [manner of] speech by your mouths.*
>
> (Qur'an 33:4)

Every human being must be called by the name of his true biological father:

> *Call them by [the names of] their fathers: that is more just in the sight of Allah. But if you do not know their fathers' [names, call them] your Brothers in Faith, or your mawlās [close friends].*
>
> (Qur'an 33:5)

If the biological father is unknown, the Qur'an states that they are your brothers and sisters in religion and close friends, and can receive your family name. The major issue here is not a literal naming only but to confer acceptance and dignity on the children. To confirm the principle of brotherhood, the Prophet ﷺ showed us a practical and dignified example by marrying Zaynab (his cousin) after she was divorced by his previously adopted son, Zayd ibn Hārithah.

> *Then when Zayd had dissolved [his marriage] with her, with the necessary [formality], We joined her in marriage to you: in order that [in the future] there may be no difficulty to the Believers in [the matter of] marriage with the wives of their adopted (claimed) sons, when the latter have dissolved with the necessary [formality] [their marriage] with them.*
>
> (Qur'an 33:37)

One may reflect on the similarity between the malpractice of hiding lineage during the pre-Islamic "Age of Ignorance" and that of the twenty-first century, in which calling adopted children by the adopted father's name is common. These practices need to be stopped and, if known, the true biological name revealed. The most important factor is doing what is best for the orphan and preserving the orphan's rights. The detailed mechanics depend on the prevailing culture and practices at the time.

Homosexuality and Parents

A homosexual is a person who is sexually attracted to members of his own sex, and chooses to have sexual relations with them rather than with the opposite sex. A heterosexual is a person who limits sexual relations to members of the opposite sex. Women who have sex with other women are called lesbians. Gay is a slang word for a homosexual male. We maintain from the outset that our intention is to discuss an issue which has great moral and precious significance for humanity. While we are unequivocally against the act of homosexuality and its promotion, we are not against homosexuals as people because human beings are to be treated with dignity and respect, not hatred. The idea is to help parents whose children feel they are homosexual in a world which scripturally condemns it but which under secular legal systems has given it legitimacy.

The Qur'an and the Holy Books condemn homosexual activity:

> *Of all the people in the world, will you approach males, And leave those whom Allah has created for you to be your mates? Nay, you are a people transgressing [all limits]!*
>
> (Qur'an 26:165–166)

This is an extremely uncomfortable and awkward issue for parents to face. Having performed all their duties correctly as parents, what can mothers and fathers do if suddenly confronted with the discovery that their son is a homosexual? If the teenage son seems to be adopting homosexual tendencies, it is important that his parents tread carefully and seek proper help for him.

Homosexuality is a difficult subject for parents. Some believe the less they know about it, the better. Parents take pride in seeing their sons to be masculine in every respect and their daughters, likewise, feminine. Nevertheless, facts must be faced. There are over

10 million homosexuals in the United States (Smith et al. 2001) and they were all children once; their numbers are on the rise.

Homosexuals have become more and more active in fighting for more rights. They hold parades and protest marches and try to change the laws that limit their freedom. It is possible to see men kissing each other on the lips in public or dressed up as women. The latter are called transvestites or cross-dressers (although most transvestites are heterosexual, the "gay rights" movement has embraced "transgender issues"). In some countries and states, men may even marry men and women may marry women. These homosexual couples want to be treated like normal married couples. Although they cannot have children together, sometimes they adopt children. Anyone daring to condemn their behavior is labeled "homophobic," that is, afraid of homosexuals!

Development of the birth control pill in the U.S. in the 1960s, the legalization of abortion, and the teachings of popular psychology led to what is known as the sexual revolution. People in more liberal societies began to claim that they should be free to have sex with whomever they wished, whether they were married or not, and whether they were the same or the opposite sex, and that they should be respected for their sexual orientation. Many people began to accept these ideas, with the result that today it is against the law in many countries to discriminate against homosexuals.

How does a person become a homosexual? Numerous theories have been proposed. Is it something that one can choose, or is it something one is "born" with and discovers as one grows up? Until the 1970s, homosexuality was viewed by most experts to be a type of mental illness or disorder. The medical profession maintained that certain boys with weak, cruel, and cold mothers could grow up to hate all women, and that certain girls abused by their fathers could grow up to hate all men, explaining why they would then seek to love people of the same sex. In the 1990s some medical and behavioral professionals began developing a theory which claimed that homosexuality was in fact a normal variation of human sexual orientation. They claimed that homosexuality originated in one's genes and is a trait which could be inherited (pointing to some families having more homosexuals than others, although it could equally be argued that this could be due to the way the families were raising their children). In addition, discovering rare cases of certain animals engaged in homosexual behavior, the conclusion was drawn by some that this could also be normal for people; a strange inversion of reasoning, for one should ask the question: are the activities of wild animals to be used as a barometer to define the norm of human action, or a reason to give certain behavior social acceptance? Do people consider animals to be their model of conduct?

Human values are not to be derived from animal behavior. People are different from animals; and God has honored human beings above all other creation.

Some possible reasons for homosexuality are discussed below. Genetics is suggested as one explanation. However, experience, environmental factors, and issues in the formation of relationships have major influence and importance:

- Confusion about friendship: Young people who have strong feelings for a friend of the same sex are sometimes confused by all this talk of homosexuality. They begin to wonder if they, too, are homosexual or lesbian. A girl may be so happy with her best friend that she has an urge to give her a big hug and a kiss. She may feel guilty about those urges, confusing them with sexual feelings. If she becomes convinced that she is a lesbian, she may try to persuade her girlfriend to have sex with her. The solution to this may be that parents should provide an adequate sex education for their children.
- Lack of love for children: A person may not have anyone else to turn to for love and affection. Teenagers who have poor relationships with their parents and relatives need to be touched and loved by someone. If the only friend they have is someone of the same sex, the overwhelming need to touch and hold someone may overcome their sense of decency and lead to sexual acts. The solution is a preventive one, to smother the children with love and affection, starting with breastfeeding in infancy. Loving relations should continue among all members of the same family, forever. This way, the person finds natural love within the home and does not look for it outside.
- Child molestation: Some young people are taken advantage of by child molesters and pushed into these acts against their will, until they become used to it. In a systematic study of 2881 men who had had sexual relations with other men, Paul et al. (2001) found that one fifth had experienced child sexual molestation. The solution is for parents to keep a continuous watch and check on their youngsters, ensuring that they are always in good company. Be aware that child molesters are often family members and vigilance is paramount.
- Abnormality: Some people are born with or develop rare diseases as a result of which they do not have enough male or female hormones to make them look and behave like normal men and women. Hormones are chemicals produced in various organs of the body that are responsible for physical sex characteristics (such as the growth of female breasts). Hormones also affect characteristics that are masculine (like growing a moustache and beard, developing muscles, the desire to fight and show off) or feminine (like the desire to cuddle babies). A young man without enough male hormones might not be able to grow a beard, his voice might not deepen as it should, and he might not feel masculine inside. The solution may lie with medical treatment.
- Long delays in marriages: Men and women who are deprived of marriage at the proper age may still feel a strong urge to satisfy their sexual desires. If not done

appropriately, alternative ways will creep into their minds. Early marriage is to be encouraged at the legal age, for it is the right of children. It is also the duty of parents to facilitate marriage.

Parents confronted with the discovery that their son has homosexual tendencies need to be patient and understanding, and need to seek professional help immediately. They should not withhold love from their children. Although it may be illegal for individuals to discriminate against homosexuals, they do not have to accept homosexual activity, even if they become unpopular by criticizing it, for we all have the freedom to disagree. Just as the law protects the rights of homosexuals, it also protects the freedom of religious beliefs.

Parents must be aware of the legal issues related to homosexuality: U.S. law prohibits discrimination on the basis of sex, sexual orientation, race, language or national origin. Many societies are sending the message to children that to be a homosexual is acceptable. These societies are blurring the line between what is normal and what is not.

Children are also being told to ignore their natural inhibitions and to follow their passions.

We encourage parents to make it very clear to children that homosexual behavior is wrong. Parents must also intervene if a teacher encourages homosexual behavior.

Men should be masculine
(respectful toward women, defenders of the weak, not reveal their bodies).
Women should be feminine
(wear modest clothing, lower their gaze, defend their honor against misbehaving men).

Islamic Sex Education

Islam recognizes that the Almighty created sexual need. Sex is discussed with dignity in the Qur'an and by the Prophet ﷺ within the context of marriage and family life. Islam does not treat women (or men) as merely objects of sexual pleasure but considers them with respect in a framework of a complementary relationship that fulfills the human need and the Will of God. Whereas sex outside marriage is wrong and a major punishable sin (scripturally), sex with one's spouse is a virtue rewarded as an act of worship. Islamic laws regarding sex are clear and natural; they do not change with peer pressure or the changing values of society. Virginity at the time of marriage is a virtue, unlike in some societies where it may be a disadvantage.

Sexual relationships between men and women are depicted in the verses below:

> *Did We not create you out of a devalued fluid, which We then let remain in [the womb's] firm secure place for a term pre-ordained? Thus have We determined [the nature of man's creation]: and excellent indeed is Our power to determine [what is to be]!*
>
> (Qur'an 77: 20–23)

> *And do not even approach adultery (and fornication) for, behold, it is an abomination and an evil way.*
>
> (Qur'an 17:32)

The following are some references from the Sunnah concerning husband and wife relationships:

The Prophet ﷺ considers marital intimacy as a rewardable act of virtue. He says:

> "When one of you sleeps with his wife, it is a rewardable act of virtue." The Companions were surprised and said, "How is it that we satisfy our desires and we get rewarded for it?" The Prophet replied, "If one has done it in a forbidden way, it would have been counted as a sin, but if you do it legitimately, it is rewarded." (MUSLIM)

The Prophet ﷺ teaches that intimate acts between spouses are secrets not to be told to others:

> "Worst among you on the Day of Judgment is a man who exposes himself to his wife and she exposes herself to him, then he divulges her secrets to others."
>
> (MUSLIM)

'Ā'ishah narrates:

> While I was lying with the Messenger of Allah ﷺ under a bed cover, I menstruated, so I slipped away and I took up the clothes [which I wore] in menses. Upon this he asked: "Have you menstruated?" I said: "Yes." He called me and I lay down with him under the bed cover.
>
> (AL-BUKHĀRĪ AND MUSLIM)

'Ā'ishah reveals how she had slipped graciously from the bed to leave the side of the Prophet ﷺ one night. However, when he found out that it was because she had started her period, he simply told her to cover herself and then lie down with him again. The Prophet ﷺ and his wife `Ā'ishah used to sleep "together under one cover," as several hadiths confirm. Husbands and wives are described in the Qur'an as garments for each other. A garment is very personal and is close to one's body, so similarly spouses should be very close to each other. A garment protects and shields our modesty, so spouses should also do the same for each other. Garments are put on whenever one wishes, so they should be available to each other for enjoyment at any time. A garment adds to a person's beauty, so they should beautify each other.

Sex is an expression of love, for one without the other is incomplete. The husband's responsibility is to educate his wife in matters of sexuality, especially in his likes and dislikes, and he should not compare her with other women. Wives should do the same to achieve maximum enjoyment. Wives need to realize that men's sexual needs are different from theirs. Instead of being a passive recipient, a wife should try to be an active and loving participant. Both are exposed to serious temptations outside the home, which puts the husband and wife in an unfair situation of continual competition with outside influences. Hence, in the interests of both, she has to be available to please her husband so as not to pressure him or give him an excuse to make a choice between his wife and other women, who lead him to destroy the family and earn the displeasure of God. Similarly, the husband has to be readily available to please and satisfy all the needs of his wife.

The Prophet ﷺ explains in further detail the intimate practices between spouses so that the maximum pleasure is attained. Islam discourages anal sex strongly and there is nothing in the Qur'an or the Sunnah to prohibit oral sex. Sexual organs should be kept clean and a shower (*ghusl*) should be taken after any fluid discharge or sexual intercourse.

> The Prophet ﷺ said: "No one of you should fall on his wife like the beast. There should be a [messenger] between spouses. He was asked: "What messenger do you mean?" He said: "The messenger is kissing and talking [foreplay]."
>
> (NARRATED BY AL-ZUBAYDĪ AND AL-ʿIRĀQĪ)

> The Prophet ﷺ also said: "When you sleep with your wife, you must be compassionate [considerate] to her. If you satisfy yourself before she does, you should not rush her until she is fully satisfied."
>
> (ABŪ YAʿLĀ)

Every man has the duty to look after his life partner properly. If he expects her to be faithful to him, then it is his duty to give her sufficient time to achieve full sexual pleasure. It usually takes around 15–20 minutes to satisfy a woman. A man is not supposed to fling himself on his wife like an animal – that is intercourse without sport and foreplay. This is disapproved of in Islam, and men have to be considerate. They need to understand the biological facts of female sexuality, learn techniques to pleasure their wife, and go ahead and enjoy a fulfilled and happy life. Any man who cannot spare his wife this time is causing her distress, as well as placing powerful temptations in her path.

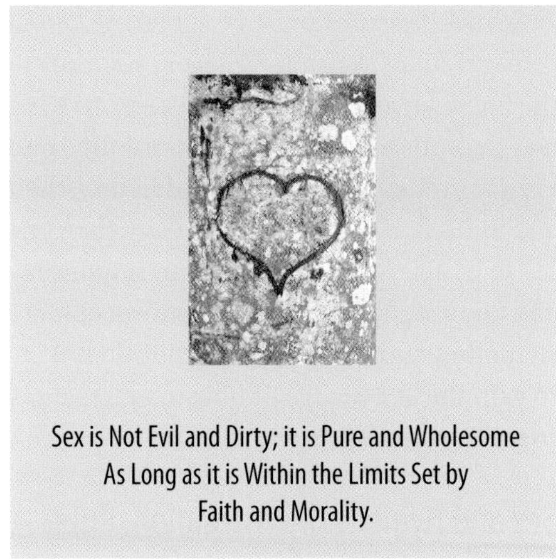

Sex is Not Evil and Dirty; it is Pure and Wholesome As Long as it is Within the Limits Set by Faith and Morality.

Parents' Duty Towards Children

It is important that parents teach their children a positive attitude toward sex: It is not the creation of the Devil, nor is it evil or dirty (if it is dealt with rightly). It is the gift and mercy of the Compassionate, and an insight into some of the joys of Paradise to come.

Although sex is an activity that is so pleasurable and wonderful (as it should be), it is also an opportunity that can be misused by Satan to corrupt, twist, deprive, and cause huge suffering. More suffering is probably caused on earth by sex than by anything else, including famine and war. The risk is so high that by committing one wrong sexual act, one may be obliged to live out one's lifetime in a minefield of endless disasters. Sex is a need that has to be satisfied according to the commands of the Creator in a pure and wholesome manner, without excess, deprivation, and suffering.

The Prophet ﷺ was open, kind, and honest in understanding the needs of men and women. He was not prudish or bigoted, and he himself obviously enjoyed his marriages. This was certainly the view of ʿĀʾishah, who undeniably knew the Prophet ﷺ more intimately than anyone else.

Sexual pleasures must be subject to moral considerations. Permissiveness in sex leads to the breakdown of family and society, to lying and deception, to lack of responsibility, and even to crimes like rape, drug addiction, theft and murder. If one really loves God, then one has to be able to resist temptations responsibly and know right from wrong. Many people are so modest and repressed that they do not try to gain the knowledge of how to practice sex in the most fulfilling way.

Sex and Hygiene: Menstruation, Pubic Hair, Circumcision, Seminal Fluid

SEX DURING MENSTRUATION: Medieval Jewish practice during the monthly period was to avoid contact with women completely. The Prophet ﷺ instructed the Companions to associate fully with their wives during menstruation, though they should avoid penetration and touching the private parts.

Girls need to be given practical advice about how to use sanitary towels and how to dispose of them without clogging the toilet. The alternative is disposable pads/rags, which can be washed, dried and reused. Monthly periods are natural and do not have to be secretive and embarrassing, especially if the daughter needs help because she suffers discomfort or pain.

PUBIC HAIR: The Prophet ﷺ recommended that pubic hair for men and women needs to be removed periodically – once a month – so that the body is kept clean and neat, ready for one's spouse to enjoy. Pubic hair is natural and healthy, and the practice of removing it brings peace of mind and cleanliness.

A boy does not mind developing a hairy chest or legs, or growing a mustache. Many girls however, do not like it. Girls can be horrified to discover long dark hair growing around their nipples, and hate it when their legs and arms become covered in thick dark hair. Mothers can be very useful in showing girls how to use depilatory creams or other means of keeping themselves smooth and attractive. Girls need not worry that they are turning into men if they grow a mustache, or have a few whiskers on their chins. These can either be removed or carefully bleached, if they become a problem. Girls should be comfortable with their body, and should not be obsessed with pleasing men in public.

CIRCUMCISION: The Prophet ﷺ strongly recommended circumcision for boys at an early age. This promotes better hygiene and more sexual enjoyment at marriage. Circumcision for males reduces cancer, decreases infections, and lessens pain during urination. Girls should not be circumcised. Islam prohibits the cutting of any part of the female genitals.

SEMINAL FLUID AND NOCTURNAL EMISSIONS IN BOYS: Some teenagers become highly embarrassed if there is any soiling or discharge on their underwear, and are terrified of their parents seeing it. It is helpful to reassure them that a certain amount of discharge is normal. If it is colored or bloodstained, or smelling, or their underwear needs changing more than once a day, then medical

advice should be sought. Semen is not to be confused with urine. Urine is filthy (*najis*) and must be washed clean. Semen is clean and need not be washed like urine, just cleaning it with a few drops of water and rubbing it should be sufficient.

Teenagers and Abstention

American and Canadian children today are reaching puberty earlier than ever. Girls may enter puberty between the ages of 8 and 13, while boys enter puberty between the ages of 9 and 14. In Britain, over the past 150 years, the average age of puberty has fallen from 16.5 years to 12.8 years. This may be due to the increased consumption of animal products, most of which come from animals intensively reared with regular doses of antibiotics and hormones as growth promoters.

On the other hand the average age for first marriage is rising. In the United States, it is about 29 for men and 26 for women. In Jordan, where the economic situation is different, the average age for marriage is 35 for men and 30 for women. People who believe in abstinence before marriage are asking their children to curb their sexual desires from the time they reach puberty till they get married, which is a wait of about 16 years, a time during which sexual desire and energy are at their peak. This is a tremendous challenge for young adults.

Up until 100 years ago most people got married soon after puberty. Societies were struggling to survive. Because of high infant mortality and frequent wars, it was important that both men and women married early when their sexual strength and vitality were at their peak.

Some societies have adapted to late marriage by unleashing sexual restraints. Religious people cannot do that, yet their insistence on abstinence is very difficult for teenagers. It does not seem likely that human beings can suppress their sexuality from puberty till marriage (possibly 20 years later). A teenager with screaming hormones is going to suffer in today's environment of continuous temptations all around.

Muslim societies must adopt early marriage to cope with the situation. The ramifications of this alternative could also be problematic. Nevertheless, parents have to find a way to tell their teenagers why sex outside of marriage is forbidden to them, even though they need it urgently. The extended family can help young couples with child-rearing, especially if family

planning is practiced wisely.

Some Muslim scholars have ruled that masturbation should be avoided, except when it becomes a relief from immense sexual desire for bachelors, and it must not become a habit. When the sex urge becomes uncontrollable, masturbation can be a much lesser evil. In his book *Rudūdun 'alā Abātīl,* the late Shaykh Muhammad al-Hamid explains that the jurists prohibit masturbation if it is used to arouse passive sexual desire. However, when the desire is so overwhelming that it occupies the mind and disturbs the stability of the person (to the extent of pushing him/her toward adultery) and if masturbation helps to pacify the compelling urge, then it is permissible. Masturbation can be neutral, earning neither reward nor punishment, neither blame nor praise; it is neither a sin nor a good deed.

Masturbation is self-centered. In isolation, instead of intense intimacy, a teenager can satisfy his fantasy. Although it may be helpful as a temporary escape from tension, for teenagers, however, it can become an easy substitute for marriage. When a teenager's main satisfaction comes from a personal relationship, self-gratification is a problem for him.

Parents should be understanding if their teenagers use masturbation as for sexual tension. Usually, it is gone by the time they mature and get married. The important thing is that parents keep their children busy in playing sports or developing a habit of fasting two days every week, and include them in group activities. They need to inform them that the misuse of masturbation could be a serious health problem and that situations of temptation and sexual pressure have to be avoided. In this way, the teenagers are discouraged from allowing masturbation to become an obsession.

Parents need to be frank with children about how to deal with their bodies. Sex occupies a considerable amount of the young adults' thinking, yet it is the subject that is least likely to be discussed between parents and their children, and when they do address the matter they are not very realistic. Muslim jurists will tell teenagers that masturbation is forbidden, although a few scholars have permitted it with some constraints. Most teenagers will practice it anyway, and live with the perception of shame or guilt. A balance has to be sought and this practice has to be used only as a last resort and even then at a minimum level, without harming the body, physically or emotionally.

The Islamic Solution to the Sexual Dilemma: A Road Map for a Preventive Approach

The basic approach is avoidance: *Lā taqrabū al-zinā*, avoid approaching adultery and fornication. Distance yourselves; do not approach any situation that leads to such a sin.

Nor come near to adultery: for it is a shameful [deed] and an evil, opening the road [to other evils]. (Qur'an 17:32)

The important phrase here is "do not approach" (*Lā taqrabū*): do not come near it; avoid it, shield yourself from it, thus implying that one should block all avenues leading to it, to the extent that it will become practically inaccessible as much as possible. The strategy of society should be preventive, to make it difficult to commit the sin by taking measures to make unlawful sex virtually unavailable and inaccessible. By cutting off all kinds of sex trade, restricting supply, and minimizing demand, society can direct behavior correctly and keep marriages clean and safe. This type of morality is not new or unique to Islam, it was originally taught by other faiths (including Christianity, Judaism, and Hinduism). No sane person thinks that it is a good idea for young or old people to practice a chaotic sexual life and become enslaved to their physical desires. People who believe in God regard the ideal place for sex as within marriage. The problem is that in many societies, this conservative attitude toward sexual practice has been rejected by the younger generations.

Nowadays, the roads leading to sexually transmitted diseases (STDs) are wide open and inviting. Avoiding them demands some sacrifice. The fruits of abstinence are rich, whereas the agony that results from indulgence in unlawful sexual intercourse is terrible. When the totality of the Islamic system is examined, it is apparent that it is clearly centered on the protection and sanctity of the family. A great emphasis is placed on things such as modesty in the dress code, no sex outside marriage, abstention from alcohol and drugs, no dating, no provocative communication between genders, no unsupervised mixing, no pornog- raphy, no vulgar sexual scenes on television, and no sexually arousing advertisements and music. All these are serious efforts to block the roads leading to adultery and fornication. In addition, parents are responsible for explaining to their teenagers the dangers of irresponsible sex.

This preventive approach to avoid *zinā* (illegitimate sexual relationships) should start early in infancy. Both individual and collective efforts are needed to moderate the sexual urge in teenagers.

The Qur'an recognizes the overwhelming sexual desire that can exist in people. Even Prophet Joseph, under the pressure of seduction, would have fallen, had it not been for the Mercy of his Lord Who saved him at the critical moment:

> *And [it so happened that] she in whose house he was living [conceived a passion for him and] sought to make him yield himself unto her; and she bolted the doors and said, "Come thou unto me!" [But Joseph] answered: "May God preserve me! Behold, goodly has my master made my stay [in this house]! Verily, to no good end come they that do [such] wrong!"*
>
> *And [with passion] did she desire him, and he would have desired her, but that he saw the evidence of his Lord: thus [did We order] that We might turn away from him [all] evil and shameful deeds: for he was one of Our servants, sincere and purified.* (Qur'an 12:23–24)

The God-given sexual urge in men and women is usually dormant, and should not be gratuitously instigated and aroused. Our sexual urges should be satisfied in marriage. If temptation is abundant, lust is awakened early and it becomes difficult to control. However, sexual arousal in men is more obvious and less controllable than in women and the passage into puberty for boys awakens sexual feelings. Women have greater control over their sexual desires and behavior than men.

The permissive sexual environment that is widely evident in many societies in the twenty-first century is not surprising. Society is doing very little to help the youth; it is in effect throwing teenagers into a lake with their hands tied and telling them: "beware of getting wet!" Temptation inflames the sexual urge in teenagers, whereas society expects them to refrain and impose self-restraint. It is like putting a tasty fish before a hungry cat and telling it "don't eat!" Abstention becomes much easier and achievable in the absence of temptation.

> He tied his hands, then threw him in the water, and told him: Beware! Beware! Don't get wet!

Man can be sexually aroused easily by touching, seeing, hearing, smelling, or even by pure imagination. It is essential that all the means of temptation, seduction, and arousal are removed as much as possible. It is much wiser to adopt the safe defensive approach by avoiding trouble rather than falling into it and then struggling to get out. Once people are aroused, their defenses are dramatically weakened and the likelihood of giving way to temptation increases.

The Qur'anic approach is preventive and holistic. The question is: How can teenagers maintain desirable ethical standards in a society that is sexually permissive? Is it humanly possible? According to Islamic law, anything that leads to wrongdoing is wrong. Hence, anything which breaks down sexual inhibition and loss of self-control over the body should be avoided.

The following is a list of many steps to block the roads leading to unlawful sex. Reducing temptation is a lifelong process that requires the cooperation of parents, the extended family, the school, the media, and the community.

MODESTY (*ḤAYĀʾ*)

It is important to establish the concept of modesty (*Ḥayā'*) from birth by respecting the private parts of the baby. Parents need not touch the baby's genitals except when bathing with hands in a cloth, and for only a short time. Also, the genitals of children aged three years and above have to be covered with a cloth, even during washing. Avoiding the exposure of the genitals augments the personal privacy of the child.

What is modesty? Modesty (*Ḥayā'*) is defined as: "bashfulness," embarrassment, and shyness from any action that degrades the person. In Arabic it means:

> A trait or an attitude that causes a person embarrassment or fear of a scandalous act.

Jurists define modesty as a character trait that discourages a person from committing vices or shameful, filthy acts.

Modesty is a quality that has to be consistently nourished by parents so that it becomes the norm in both family and society. Even in funerals, when washing the dead body, the person(s) doing the cleaning should not stare at the genitalia nor touch them directly by hand, but use a cloth to clean the private parts of the deceased. To realize the extent and dimensions of modesty, the Prophet ﷺ said the following:

> Faith has over seventy branches. The best of them is the saying "there is no God but Allah." The least is the removal of a harmful object from the footpath. And modesty is a branch of faith. (MUSLIM)

> What people have inherited from early prophethood is: If you have no shame (*Ḥayā'*), you may do whatever you please. (ABŪ DĀWŪD)

> The Prophet ﷺ said:
> Obscenity can produce only ugliness. Modesty can produce only goodness and beauty. (IBN MĀJAH)

Al-Jurjānī divides modesty into the following two categories:

a) The psychological part, which is found in all humans, such as not exposing the private parts or not having sexual intercourse in the presence of others. This type of *Ḥayā'* exists in humans, and may be a part of their innate nature; and
b) Modesty acquired from faith, which preserves the individual from committing evils owing to the love of God and fear of His punishment.

Children need to be taught the following acts of modesty:

1. to lower their gaze when looking at the other sex or at an obscene scene;
2. to walk modestly without sexual provocation or imitating the other sex;
3. to talk gently and respectfully without sexy overtones;
4. to dress modestly, covering the body nicely and with dignity.

The following three situations are where modesty is not required:

1. In scholarship: Seek knowledge (the more the better) particularly in religious instructions relating to marital sex, menstruation, pregnancy, and nocturnal emissions. Jurists, within the context of education, have coined the phrase: "There is no embarrassment (shyness) in religious learning." We may extrapolate the same phrase to state: "no embarrassment (shyness) in seeking knowledge."
2. In reform: Promote righteousness and forbid evil, for it is a duty to be discharged firmly and wisely.
3. In marriage: There is no shyness between spouses in their home. The Prophet ﷺ said:

> Conceal your private parts except from your spouse. (ABŪ DĀWŪD, IBN MĀJAH, AND AL-ḤĀKIM)

Whereas sex is completely forbidden between non-spouses, it is virtually limitless between spouses in the privacy of their bedroom.

If parents neglect implanting modesty in their children, society will suffer. Modesty is the strong foundation of immunity against temptation and seduction. The following are some observations on the results of a lack of modesty among nations:

- Under the guise of art and free expression, museums and public squares in many countries have become littered with depictions of naked men and women on posters and in naked sculptures, exposing their private parts. This is also found in some temples in India.

Arabic Poetry on Modesty

If you do not fear the consequences of how you behave and you fail to act modestly, you can do whatever you want.

But, by God, there is no goodness in an immodest life! One lives comfortably, as long as one acts modestly; just as a tree trunk stays protected as long as it is covered by bark.

For many there is a clear line between what is considered art and what is considered pornographic or obscene. Nudity in Western artistic traditions is an interesting development primarily because it often purports to be symbolic of virtue, honor, and the glory of man. A good example is Michael Angelo's statue David, a prophet, representing all that is good, sculpted entirely naked. Certain temples across the world (e.g. India) also depict full frontal nudes in a religious setting. Of course the statue of David is really a symbol of Renaissance man and not the prophet as such. The whole subject of the social acceptance and interpretation of nudity is something parents have to think more deeply about, particularly as regards their children.

- In a museum in Santiago, Chile, sculptures of a man and a woman performing sexual intercourse are on display.
- A young woman in the United States had video cameras in her bedroom and bathroom, transmitting live pictures 24 hours a day to viewers over the Internet.
- In the United States, fifty thousand people logged on to watch the first live birth delivery of a child on the Internet in full graphic detail.

(*Time*, June 29, 1998)

Some etiquettes of modesty are listed here:

- As children grow up, they have to knock before entering the bedrooms of parents and other relatives (to avoid the possibility of seeing them undressed or exposed).
- Parents and siblings should cover their bodies and dress respectfully, both inside and outside the home. The use of make-up and sexually attractive cosmetics and perfumes should be avoided. Parents need to watch their language when in the presence of children, avoiding sexual talk. Nor should there be any explicit sexual contact between parents in front of children, including deep kissing, and touching of the private parts.
- When children are 10 years old, they are to sleep in separate beds.
- Boys and girls should be taught to avert their gaze when looking at the opposite sex.

> *Say to the believing men that they should lower their gaze and guard their modesty: that will make for greater purity for them: and Allah is well acquainted with all that they do. And say to the believing women that they should lower their gaze and guard their modesty; that they should not display their beauty and ornaments except what [must ordinarily] appear thereof; that they should draw their veils over their bosoms and not display their beauty except to their husbands, their fathers, their husbands' fathers, their sons, their husbands' sons, their brothers or their brothers' sons, or their sisters' sons, or their women, or the slaves whom their right hands possess, or male servants free of physical needs, or small children who have no sense of the shame of sex; and that they should not strike their feet in order to draw attention to their hidden ornaments. And O you Believers! Turn all together towards Allah, that you may attain Bliss.*
>
> (Qur'an 24:30–31)

Lowering the gaze is essential. The Prophet ﷺ said:

> Whoever lowers his gaze away from that which is unlawful for him, Allah will grant joy in his heart. (IBN MAS'ŪD)

- Girls should be taught to walk respectfully to avoid sexual attraction. They are not to lift their dress and show off their legs. They are to avoid talking in a sexually inviting way:

> *... be not too complaisant of speech, lest one in whose heart is a disease should be moved with desire: but speak a speech [that is] just.* (Qur'an 33:32)

- Boys and girls should not be allowed to stay late at night outside the home. A reasonable curfew system can be agreed upon between parents and children.
- Certain types of music are damaging, (those that arouse sexual feelings and whose lyrics are shameful). Music may affect mood by activating melatonin, the hormone from the pineal gland in the brain that is turned on by darkness and turned off by flashing light. It is the same gland that has been thought to trigger puberty, and it affects the reproductive cycle and sexual mood. Sexually explicit rock music raises sexual desire. Some hard-rock music contains pornographic words, and children are to be prevented from listening to "pornographic rock." Once children are exposed to this music, they become desensitized to vice.
- Pornography is a menace to children, for it inflames sexual desires to an unbearable level. It has a long-term effect on the thinking of children, making them visualize these vulgar scenes for a long time, and causing them to daydream of sexual acts.
- Pornography debases women into sex objects which exist to satisfy men's lust. If a husband is aroused by anything of this nature, he should satisfy his urge with his own wife. Bachelors cannot do this, so perhaps it is yet another reason to marry early.

A man cannot be blamed for having urges; but he can be blamed if he gives way to them and hurts other people in the process. So many men hurt their wives (without realizing it) by looking admiringly at other women. The images of models and film stars on billboards, magazine covers, and posters can be a big problem. In your mind they stay forever young and lovely, in comparison with real spouses who grow old, fat, and tired. Spouses have to be considerate and kind to each other; one can be old and still remain attractive (with good planning, a healthy diet, and appropriate exercise).

Nowadays, parents have to be aware of the dangers of Internet pornography, dating, and cheap, obscene sex talk. They must supervise their children better and place computers in a public area of the house, not in the isolation of a child's bedroom.

DRESS CODE

Girls and boys need to behave and dress modestly. They must avoid provocative or seductive clothing and they must avoid drawing attention to their physical charms. They should not wear tight clothing to show the outlines of their figures to those outside the immediate family, or wear sexually oriented jewelry. "See-through" clothing for boys and girls is not allowed, and girls are to cover their heads in public. Boys and girls should not engage in cross-dressing. The following hadith clarifies this point:

> Abu Hurayrah said: The Prophet cursed the man who dresses himself to look like a woman, and the woman who dresses herself to look like a man. (ABŪ DĀWŪD)

What children wear is important. The adage "You act as you dress" implies that children are to dress modestly and respectably. People dress differently according to the occasion: for weekly worship, interviews, anniversaries, parties, or sports. They are attempting to blend in, impress, or increase their chances of being accepted within a particular group. Clothes, hairstyles, and jewelry should appear modest. Generally, parents do not like extreme attire exemplifying rebellion. If modest clothes are used for almost every situation, then the wearer will make a good impression. Clothes, behavior, and styles that do not exceed the limits are considered modest.

As far as possible, parents need to give their daughter approved "choices." There will come an age – it may be as young as two or three years old – when their daughter will have strong opinions about what she wears. She will resist her parents' choices about how she should dress. A peaceful and practical solution is to lay out two or three outfits for her to choose from, so that she feels she is being given a choice.

In schools where all students wear the same outfit (uniform), they may not like it at first, but will soon "forget" about their clothing, so that it no longer becomes an issue. This avoids frustrating discussions and decisions on "what to wear" every morning. Girls should be made aware that although the "provocative" look may appear "cute," it can convey the wrong signal to boys with unwanted consequences.

NO FREE MIXING AND NO *KHALWAH*

Khalwah is a private meeting between a man and a woman in a secluded place behind a closed door, where no one can see them (such as a hotel room or a lonely place in the country). A satanic sexual trap it is essential to prevent *khalwah* at all costs! The Prophet ﷺ gave us ample warning when he said:

> Whenever a man and a woman are alone in a secluded place, the Devil is their third party. (AL-TIRMIDHĪ)

Free mixing of boys and girls is to be avoided, but mixing supervised by parents and closely watched within the limits of decency and in a controlled atmosphere is allowed. A boy may become attracted to a girl while seeing her regularly at a mosque, a school, a library, or in the market. He might approach her and start an innocent conversation to see if she is interested in him. After talking with each other, they might make a date to meet at a more private place, such as in the park or in a home. With no one watching them, he might dare to touch or kiss her. If she allows him to do that, before long, he will become bold enough to go further. It could end in their having sex without really planning to do so, which could lead to disaster.

The Trap !

Eye Contact → Smile of Approval → Greetings → Chatting → Meeting → Touching → Arousal → Path of No Return → Sin of Sex → Problems!! The results may include STD, pregnancy, abortion, or an illegitimate child.

The above rule should never be relaxed because it is a sure prescription for disaster to happen. Even for highly religious people, it is a strong invitation to evil. All human beings are made of flesh and emotions: even Prophet Joseph had to face this challenge.

- Dating: The dating system is a 'sex gate' for teenagers. It normally brings pain and suffering for the individuals concerned, their families, and their societies. In a 1999 study conducted in the United States, 25 percent of a sample of male college freshmen said that, if on a date they have paid for the dinner and the girl does not 'go all the way,' the boy has the right to force sex on her. Many of these 'date rapes' are not reported (Norris et al. 1999; Bohmer 1993). Anything that breaks down sexual inhibition and leads to loss of self-control, such as alcohol, drugs, sexually exciting music, petting, or *khalwah*, is not to be allowed. Kissing and petting prepare the body for sex, where the body can be brought to a "point of no return." Dating and sexual freedom harms marriage. The assumption that the couple that has "tried each other out" and so will "know" each other much better is unfounded. Any society that allows these freedoms suffers from unstable families and high rates of divorce.

PEER PRESSURE AND OTHER FACTORS

- There are many reasons why children become involved in sex, the most common of which is peer pressure. Their rationale is that everybody is doing it. Other reasons for pre-marital sex are their desire for being considered competent by adults and as a way to social advancement. For some, it stems from a lack of self-esteem, which they hope to improve by becoming a father or mother. Sometimes, it is due to a lack of other options to divert their sexual energies. Lack of love and lack of appreciation at home can be a factor, whereby detachment from home can lead to attachment elsewhere. The sexual temptation is prevalent everywhere, primarily from magazines, from peers, and from television. In the U.S. about 20,000 sexual scenes are broadcast annually in advertisements, soap operas, prime time shows, and MTV. Parents must therefore flood their children with love, occupy their children's time with useful activities, and practice open communication with their children.
- Intoxicants: Alcohol and drugs are harmful because they reduce self-control and

remove inhibitions from indulging in sex.

- Dancing (which is mixed and involves inappropriate touching between boys and girls) and physical touching between the genders must be avoided, including kissing, petting, necking, massaging, rubbing, and hugging. All these actions arouse sexual urges in the body, bringing it a step nearer to sexual intercourse.

One definition of Dancing with the Opposite Sex is:

Dancing is Our Vertical Expression of Our Horizontal Desire!

WHAT TO DO

Parents have to give their children good advice. Parents are not to confine their role to providing shelter, food, clothing, and material needs for their children, but must simultaneously provide spiritual and moral guidance.

- Parents need to fill children's brains with "good thinking" and occupy them with moral and intellectual "food for thought." Higher causes and values have to be all over the menu. One model of advice is how the Prophet ﷺ spoke to a young man who asked him permission for fornication because he could not control his sexual urges. The Prophet ﷺ reasoned with him by asking if he would approve of someone having sex with his mother, sister, daughter, aunt, or wife. Each time the man answered "no." Therefore, the Prophet ﷺ replied that the woman with whom the young man wanted to have sex was surely somebody's mother, sister, daughter, aunt or wife. The man understood and repented, and the Prophet ﷺ prayed for his forgiveness.
- It is important to strengthen one's sense of identity and avoid being pushed into following the crowd! Parents can achieve this in their children by teaching them a distinct value system, a world view, and a certain code of life. In this way children will remind themselves not to drink alcohol, eat pork, take drugs, or engage in pre-marital sex. Parents themselves should not seek extramarital affairs, for they have to be good examples to their children.

EARLY MARRIAGE

No fixed age is set for marriage. It is becoming fashionable for young men to marry after obtaining a university degree, finding a job, or reaching the age of 26 or more. Similarly, young girls say that they want to marry after the age of 24, declaring, "I am not ready for it." Although they do have normal sexual organs and desires, young people have to realize that they only have two legitimate choices: marry or abstain from sexual intimacy until marriage.

The Qur'an says:

> *Let those who do not find the means to marry keep chaste until Allah makes them free from want out of His Grace.*
>
> (Qur'an 24:33)

The Prophet ﷺ said:

By God, I am the most pious among you, but I fast and break the fast, I pray and sleep at night, and I marry women. He who rejects my tradition is not of me. (AL-BUKHĀRĪ)

Marriage is half of the religion; the other half is fearing Allah. (AL-ṬABARĀNĪ AND AL-ḤĀKIM)

The Prophet ﷺ said:

> Those of you young people who have the means should marry, otherwise you should keep fasting, for it curbs desires. (AL-BUKHĀRĪ)

When a boy or a girl feels the strong urge to get married and s/he cannot wait, parents have to try their best to get them married. If they do not, they are pushing their child toward evil in one way or another. One of the duties of parents is outlined by the Prophet ﷺ:

> The one to whom a child is given by Allah, should give him/her three rights: a beautiful name, an education, and when s/he attains puberty, he should see to it that s/he is married. (Tibrizi 1985)

If the parents do not heed the child's request and fail to arrange the marriage, the responsibility of sin will also lie with the parents. However, it is equally important not to force young people into marriage. Some parents engage in wrongdoing by forcing marriage partners upon their children. They simply decide that their offspring should marry available family members without giving their children freedom of choice. They deprive them of their rights to see and know their future spouses beforehand. On the other hand, a sensibly arranged marriage with the active participation as well as the approval of the boy and girl is a duty of the parents, because this will result in a happy lasting relationship between the couple and the two families. These "arrangements" need to have as their objective the happiness and well-being of the couple rather than the selfish motives of the family agents making the arrangements.

The community has several roles to play to facilitate marriage:

- To provide a healthy environment for boys and girls to meet and know each other, while discouraging free unsupervised mixing of the sexes.
- To offer premarital education courses and counseling to boys and girls, and to prepare them for their roles as fathers and husbands and mothers and wives.

The Dilemma of the Educational System vs. Early Marriage

Our current school system has given birth to a complex sexual problem. Obtaining a college or advanced degree dictates that marriage has to be delayed till the mid-twenties. Yet the peak of sexual urge for men is during the late teens; and young women in their late teens have a strong sense of emotional dependency that makes them vulnerable to seduction. Premarital sex during early adulthood results in abortion, unwed mothers, sexually transmitted diseases, and children having illegitimate children.

The solution may seem to be either early marriage during school years or abstinence until graduation from college. Early marriage can be a satisfactory solution if the society prepares teenagers to manage a spouse, and maybe children, responsibly enough.

In modern societies, to demand from teenagers to be patient and remain virgin till the mid-twenties is very difficult nowadays in the midst of temptation and continual sexual provocation. History provides a good lesson. In the past, this problem did not arise because early marriage was the norm and the social network was designed to support that. At the time of the Prophet ﷺ and many centuries later, the following integrated system was implemented:

a) Early marriage was encouraged.

b) The extended family was a great help in taking care of children and grandchildren. It was common to have three generations living closely together and the nuclear family was the exception. Families were much less mobile than today.

c) Islam allowed birth control and population planning to help very young mothers delay pregnancies until they became ready. That depended on the cooperation of the husband and the knowledge of both husband and wife.

Nowadays, mothers who have a profession or hold a university degree can raise children full-time and may have a part time job until their mid-thirties, and then they can work full-time or part-time after their children attain puberty, whether they work as volunteers or for pay. There will be no harm to young children and the society will not be deprived of competent professional mothers with a wealth of experience and wisdom.

It is not right to regard children between the ages of 13 and 19 as incompetent and treat them merely as consumers, devoid of responsibility and productivity. The contemporary trend seems to extend the childhood phase to the early 20's. The youth depend entirely on others instead of being responsible, autonomous, and productive human beings.

The Qur'an speaks of young prophets such as Abraham, Joseph, Moses, and Jesus (peace be upon them all) and others who are meant to be our role models and who accomplished great tasks during their teenage years. There is also the story of the People of the Cave (*Aṣḥāb al-Kahf*) being young (*fityah*), rightly guided, and blessed with achievements.

The current model of delaying marriage until the mid-twenties is not satisfactory. Other successful systems of early marriages have been practiced all over the world in the past. Medically speaking, pregnancies and deliveries are easier at a young age and are not at their best during the late twenties or early thirties (and first pregnancies become more difficult with advancing age).

The issue is serious, relevant, and urgent. We must deal effectively with the dilemma of the hardship of sexual restraint, the necessity of early marriage, and the need for establishing a family during the teenage years (to be planned with or without children).

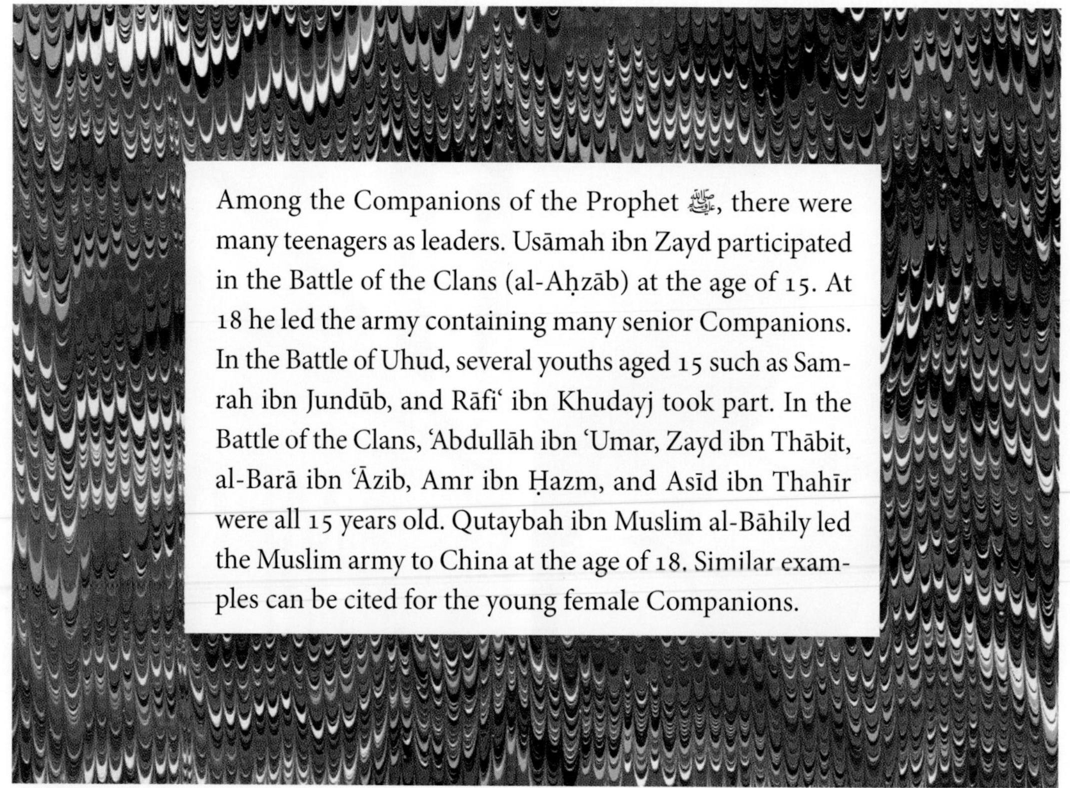

Among the Companions of the Prophet ﷺ, there were many teenagers as leaders. Usāmah ibn Zayd participated in the Battle of the Clans (al-Aḥzāb) at the age of 15. At 18 he led the army containing many senior Companions. In the Battle of Uhud, several youths aged 15 such as Samrah ibn Jundūb, and Rāfi' ibn Khudayj took part. In the Battle of the Clans, 'Abdullāh ibn 'Umar, Zayd ibn Thābit, al-Barā ibn 'Āzib, Amr ibn Ḥazm, and Asīd ibn Thahīr were all 15 years old. Qutaybah ibn Muslim al-Bāhily led the Muslim army to China at the age of 18. Similar examples can be cited for the young female Companions.

The Immoral Way	Consequences		The Moral Way	Consequences
Adultery is Easy, Attractive and Available	STD		Do Not Approach Adultery (Zinā)	Healthy parents
	Teenage pregnancy			Healthy children
	Abortion			Two-parent homes
	Unwed Children Having Children			Leaders of the righteous
	Poverty		Adultery is Made Difficult, Unattractive and Unavailable	Low crime rate
Sex is Cheap, Resulting in Irresponsible sex	Divorce	VS.		Happy family
	Broken homes			Happy children
	Single-parent families		Clean sex is dignified	Less rape in society
	Sexual chaos			
	High crime rate		Sex is organized through marriage	
	Higher incidence of rape		Responsible sex is encouraged	

Protecting Children from Sexual Abuse by Adults

It is natural for children to trust adults, and Muslim children, in particular, are trained to obey their elders. Children will be scared if they do not do what an older person asks. Rough adults can be especially scary and intimidating, although if children know what to do, they can protect themselves against abuse. Here are some tips to convey to children against evil adults:

- If a stranger is acting strangely, coming too close, staring, blocking your way, or following you, run away and look for help. If you are sure that he is after you, you can shout "Fire! Fire!" because people usually come right away and it confuses the attacker.
- Never get into a car or go anywhere with a stranger. Even if he seems friendly and knows a lot about you and your parents' name, your school or your address, do not be afraid to say "No!" loudly.
- Avoid deserted places and unsafe neighborhoods, and do not walk alone if you can help it, especially in big cities. It is best for girls to walk to school in groups, or accompanied by an adult.
- Memorize the emergency number for the police, and know how to dial it, even in the dark. Carry coins, tokens, cell phone, or a telephone card at all times to call your parents or the police.
- If you must wait inside a car or at home alone, keep the doors and windows locked. If strangers call at the door or by telephone, do not let them know that you are alone. Never give a stranger your address or any other information over the telephone! Say that your parents cannot come to the door or the phone because they are busy, or that they do not want to be disturbed. Pretend to speak with someone else in the room.
- If you feel uncomfortable about how someone has been looking at or talking to you, tell an older person whom you trust.

- Learn some form of martial arts or self-defense techniques. You do not have to be strong to protect yourself, but simply think smart and act quickly. There are self-defense classes where the emphasis is not on fighting, but on self-defense.
- Be aware of child pornography. Children should never be seen naked before others. The law in many countries restricts pornography, and child pornography is forbidden almost everywhere.
- If you are afraid of someone, recite the Qur'anic chapters of protection (*al-Fātiḥah*, the *kursī* verses, *al-Falaq*, and *al-Nās*). Keep repeating them if necessary, and make a supplication asking God for help. Allah is your best friend, Guide, and Protector.

AGE APPROPRIATE CHILDREN BE MADE AWARE ABOUT PROSTITUTION

Prostitution is a sex education topic that parents should explain to children if the context arises, taking of course account of their age. Children are not fully aware of the reality of prostitutes' lives and may have questions about them. This should also hinder those who for whatever circumstances may think of leaving home as a way out in the future. Parents are to use their professional and moral judgement. It is important that parents explain to their children the terrible details of a prostitute's life to prevent a casual attitude to sexual relations developing whilst taking account of a child's natural sense of modesty. She may be forced to have painful sex with up to twenty men every day, often contracting serious diseases (such as AIDS), dying at an early age. Very few unlucky girls choose to be prostitutes. Usually they are forced into it by evil men and miserable circumstances. Often they have had to leave their homes because of repeated beatings or sexual abuse, or are drug addicts who need the money to support their expensive habit. Some have been kidnapped when traveling alone, and are kept locked up in rooms in foreign countries where they do not speak the language and do not know how to seek help. They may never see their families again. Others have been drugged during an interview for an apparently respectable job such as a maid or a nanny. They are then stripped of all their belongings, smuggled into another country and kept in a locked room. "At least 4,000 prostitutes in Britain have been trafficked. Anti-trafficking groups say the true figure is much higher" (Morris 2008). In some cases, young girls run away from home owing to an unbearably depressing atmosphere there which feels like hell, seeking comfort outside their home. This is where pimps (men who control prostitutes and sell their services) pick them up and force them into prostitution. Only some of the money paid by customers goes to the girls with the rest going into the pockets of pimps. When parents make life miserable for their children, they are practically pushing them to escape the tortuous conditions of home and take to the streets.

Any child who has serious problems at home and does not know what to do about the situation should seek help from a trustworthy adult (such as a relative, an imam, teacher, counselor or police officer). Running away or turning to drugs to try to escape one's problems will only make things worse.

If children do not know anything about prostitution, they will concoct mental images and start fantasizing. They may think it to be nice, cool, and full of sexual pleasures. Or that it is a profitable profession, having all the cosmetics/perfume they dream of, wearing attractive clothing, causing many men to run after them, or living in 5-star hotels. All these illusions can capture their minds unless parents responsibly explain the facts to them early enough. Unfortunately, the media promote the "exciting" lives of courtesans in history who extracted a luxurious lifestyle out of wealthy men. Emma Hamilton, the mistress of Horatio Nelson, is an example.

WHEN ONE'S CHILD IS A VICTIM OF INCEST OR RAPE

It is very difficult for a parent to accept that another family member has taken advantage of a younger person by committing incest. Sometimes, it is hard to prove and s/he may not believe it or may not want to believe it. In that case, it is best to go to the imam, a teacher, a counselor, or the police. If a crime has been committed, the police must be informed. Everyone has the right to be safe and protected, and not to be forced into sinful sexual contact.

Rape has become more common today; one out of every four women in the United States is raped at least once in her lifetime. It should also be mentioned that rape victims include children of both sexes, some of them very young. Elderly ladies are also raped by male intruders breaking into their homes.

The following are two examples: "A Saudi court has ruled that a man convicted of raping 5 children will be beheaded." The youngest victim was a boy of 3, left stranded in the desert to die. (BBC News 2009)

London police arrested a man for more than 100 attacks on elderly people (aged from 68 to 93). Known as the "Night Stalker" most of his victims were women and many of the attacks included sexual assault and rape. (BBC News 2009)

If a girl has been raped, she can feel hurt, powerless, angry, and confused. She might feel guilty, thinking that she did something wrong which made the man want to rape her (which is usually not true). Or she might feel deeply ashamed and scared to tell anyone. Any girl who is raped should immediately contact the police, and seek medical help and counselling. This is important because if she

becomes pregnant or contracts a disease from the rapist, a doctor will be able to prove that she was a victim of rape and did not simply have sex with a boyfriend. This is the practical way in which she can clear her name from the accusation of adultery. If a girl is attacked, she should try to run away, or try to dig her fingernails into her attacker. Later, the police might be able to trace the DNA in the tiny bits of skin left under her fingernails to identify the rapist. Screaming may *not* be advisable during the act, for it causes the attacker to panic and he then strangles or suffocates his victim to shut her up; many women and children found murdered have been strangled or suffocated. Although screaming might attract spectators, it is unlikely to attract helpers. It is better to carry a personal alarm, switch it on and, if possible, throw it (or some other object) through the nearest window. Vandalism is guaranteed to make the occupants of the building call the police. Then, if possible before escaping, one should grab something, however small – even a button or a few hairs – of the attacker to help the police identify him. It helps to wear clothes and shoes in which one can run if necessary, such as trousers and walking-shoes. Teenagers have to be made fully aware of date rape and drug rape. These drugs can be administered in non-alcoholic as well as alcoholic drinks.

Counseling must be provided for abuse victims. The counselor can help the victim come to terms with the shock, anger, despair, fear, and disturbing emotions and feelings which the victim will experience.

A Curriculum for Islamic Sex Education

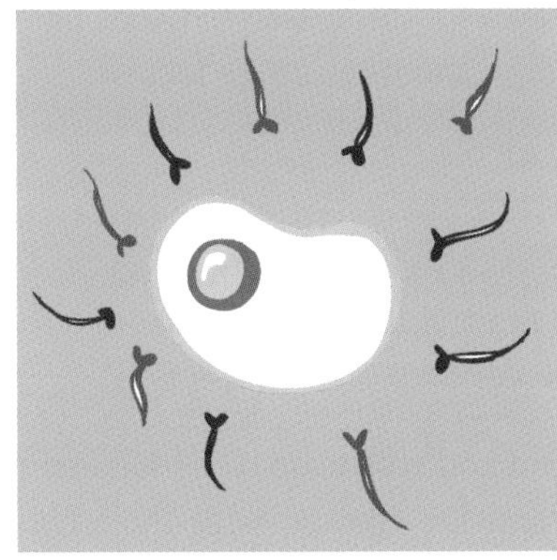

Islamic sex education has to be taught at home, starting at an early age. Before educating about anatomy and physiology, the belief in the Creator needs to be well established. Without a God-fearing belief, certain types of behavior will be thought to be permissible to satisfy lust and desire. The father should teach his son and the mother should teach her daughter. In the absence of a willing parent, the next best choice is a male teacher for boys and a female teacher for girls (preferably a physician or a nurse) at the Sunday Islamic school. The curriculum is to be tailored according to the age of the child, and boys and girls should be taught separately. Only pertinent answers to a question should be given. For example, if a six year old asks, "How did I get into Mom's tummy?" there is no need to describe the whole act. Similarly, it is not necessary to tell a six year old how to put on condoms. This might be taught in a premarital class before marriage.

The curriculum for sex education (Athar 1990) includes:

Qur'anic verses and Prophetic Hadith

Sexual growth and development
- Timetable for puberty
- Physical changes during puberty
- Mental, emotional, and social aspects of puberty

Physiology of the reproductive system
- For girls: organs, menstruation, premenstrual syndrome
- For boys: organs, the sex drive

Conception, development of the fetus, and birth
Sexually transmitted diseases
Social, moral, and religious ethics
How to resist peer pressure

It is crucial to give sex education to children; otherwise, they will learn wrong information from peers and the media. However, this has to be done in an indirect way. The explicit sexual explanations and removal of all screens between parents and children may be counter-productive. Teach children the physical differences between genders, the right conduct, and the sexual practices that are essential for a healthy Islamic life.

The different roles and objectives of men and women have to be explained in a clear way, according to the phases of development of the child. It is particularly important that parents emphasize the dangers of deviant peers. They should show distaste for improper behavior, and watch carefully for any such inclination in their children. They have to show children how to detect and avoid wrong behavior, and guide children in a practical way toward sexual health.

It is the parents' duty to ensure and facilitate contacts with good peers. Parents of teenagers should not leave them ignorant about proper sexual conduct. Parents have to prevent children from staying out late at night, and prohibit sleepovers when teenagers of the opposite sex are present except when there are trusted adults present and capable of close supervision.

Suggested ages for discussion between parents and children about sex are as follows:

- 5 years old: discuss physical differences between boys and girls
- 10 years old: discuss puberty, seminal fluid, and menstruation
- 15 years old: discuss contraception

[*Note*: Husband and wife team, Dr. Mohamed Rida Beshir and Dr. Ekram, with their two daughters Sumayah and Huda, have authored around 15 books on parenting and family matters both in English and other languages. They also have an extensive website readers may benefit from: www.familydawn.com].

Activities

ACTIVITY 44: ENRICH THE BRAINS OF YOUR CHILDREN!

Benjamin Franklin used to invite a guest for dinner with his family and engage in an intellectual conversation so that his children would hear the conversation and benefit from it without the children being aware that they were the real audience (Franklin 1909). Parents can invite such guests from within or outside the community and ask them in advance to slip certain topics into the conversation to benefit the children.

ACTIVITY 45: A GOOD DEED CHART SYSTEM FOR CHILDREN

> *And be constant in praying at the beginning and the end of the day, as well as during the early watches of the night: for, verily, good deeds drive away evil deeds: this is a reminder to all who bear [God] in mind.* (Qur'an 11:114)

> The Prophet ﷺ said: "Be God-conscious wherever you are, and follow up a bad deed with a good one to wipe it out, and behave well towards people."
>
> (AL-TIRMIDHĪ)

Parents could hang on the refrigerator a chart with each child's name, having three columns: "Extra Credit," "Good," and "Bad." When the children do as they are told, a check mark √ is inserted under the "Good" column, and if a mistake is made, an X is inserted under the "Bad" column. If they do good without being told, they are awarded 2 √ under "Extra Credit." The credit is awarded even if the children do good without the parents' presence (such as at school, or at relatives' or friends' homes); the children report the good deed to the parents, who have to trust them. The points are counted each week and each child is rewarded accordingly. If the checks outnumber the X's, then the child is given a prize (an inexpensive item). If the X's outnumber the checks, then there is no reward. If the child does not earn any prize, s/he will be encouraged to do better next time. It might take more than a week to earn a reward. It is important to check the "Good" column, even if the good deed is small, to motivate and teach children that even the tiniest good deed will make a difference. Although children should not be taught to do good just for the reward, this method helps to instill the right attitude when they are young and they appreciate tangible things (such as small gifts and words of recognition) more than abstract concepts. Parents should also explain to their children that their behavior is what is 'good' or 'bad'. The children themselves are not labelled good or bad; only their behavior is being labelled as such.

EXAMPLE OF A GOOD DEEDS/BAD DEEDS CHART

Hiba

	EXTRA CREDIT	GOOD	BAD
Monday	√√ (helped sister carry backpack)	√ (took out the garbage)	
Tuesday		√ (did her prayers)	X (loud voice)
Wednesday			X (threw trash on the floor)
Thursday		√ (helped teacher carry supplies)	
Friday	√√ (excellent report card)		
Saturday			
Sunday		√ (memorised Qur'an)	
Total	8 √		2 X
Balance	6 √ (gets prize)		

Hala

	EXTRA CREDIT	GOOD	BAD
Monday		√ (made her bed)	
Tuesday			X (hit her sister)
Wednesday	√√ (helped grandma put on socks)		
Thursday		√ (organized her clothes)	
Friday			
Saturday		√ (finished her food)	
Sunday			
Total	5 √		1 X
Balance	4 √ (gets prize)		

PART THREE

Character Building and Personality

CHAPTER 14

Character and Personality

Introduction

The Prophet ﷺ said:

People are like [minerals or metals, having their own characters]; the best of them in the pre-Islamic age of ignorance (*jāhiliyyah*) are also the best of them in the Islamic age, if they understand and comprehend. (AL-BUKHĀRĪ AND MUSLIM)

Oh Allah! Strengthen Islam with the lovable one of the two men to you, Abū Jahl or ʻUmar ibn al-Khaṭṭāb. And ʻUmar was the more lovable. (AL-TIRMIDHĪ)

THESE TWO MEN were of strong character from their childhood and earned their place as leaders of their pagan clans. They possessed excellent qualities before they acquired faith and education. The essence of child upbringing is to build strong characters, teach right concepts, and instill values that will make righteousness become habitual to children. Children imitate their parents' behavior, and therefore, parents have to be sensitive to their children's psychological and emotional development. For example, if the parents miss an appointment with adults, an apology can rectify their mistake. The same mistake made to children has a deeper impact because they may feel unimportant and insignificant. Their emotional attachment to the appointment could be tremendous and they may feel betrayed or let down. At their tender age, their parents' action may encourage mistrust or dishonesty.

In this book, the first wish of the servants of the Merciful to "produce" exemplars of the pious has already been discussed. These leaders have to be intelligent, physically fit and strong, as well as having the "right elements, minerals or character." These are the personal characteristics of leadership. Such characteristics are the building blocks that constitute the pillars of personality. If the character components are faulty or weak, then the whole human system will malfunction.

The elements of character include other aspects beside faith and education. Guidance comes from knowledge, faith, and wisdom. Misguided individuals, with strong character, can be correctly guided by rational persuasion, because their structure is robust. On the other hand, those with a weak character and personality cannot be pioneering leaders in society, even if they are strong in spiritual values. Hence, good parenting needs to concentrate on building these elements of character in children early in life because it will be quite difficult to establish them later on.

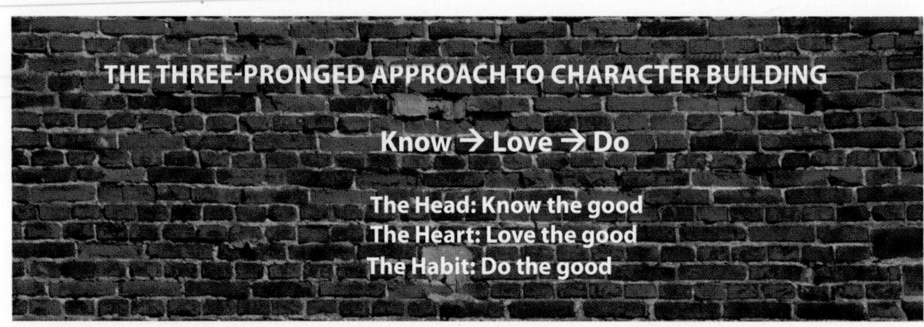

What is Meant by Character?

The relevant dictionary definitions of character are: a distinctive quality; one of the attributes or features that make up and distinguish the individual; the complex of mental and ethical traits making a person, group or nation; a person marked by notable or conspicuous traits; personage; reputation; and moral excellence and firmness.

The goal of raising children is to produce autonomous, righteous, and responsible human beings.

The Arabic meaning of character refers to personality – strong manners – morals – reputation – trait – excellence – characteristic – description – good behavior.

Parenting is concerned with building leadership traits from childhood. Several psychologists and thinkers have emphasized the traits of courage, freedom, creativity, love, responsibility, generosity, honesty, self-confidence, independence, perseverance, honor, justice, truth, sincerity, and teamwork. Some traits may be derived from a more primary trait, or come from a combination of more than one trait. Some traits may be taught later in life, while others are to be nurtured during infancy.

In this book, the focus is on the following traits:

Courage, Creativity, Honesty, Trustworthiness, Love, Responsibility, Independence, and Freedom.

Influential world leaders, whether good or bad, possess elements of the above in their personalities. Consider the great role models, starting with Adam, Eve, then Noah, Abraham, Sara, Hagar, Moses, Mary, Jesus, and Muhammad (peace be upon them all). Think also of other leaders like Napoleon, George Washington, Mao Tse-Tung, as well as the Companions of the Prophet ﷺ: Sumayyah, Khadījah, 'Ā'ishah, Abū Bakr, 'Umar ibn al-Khaṭṭāb, 'Alī ibn Abī Ṭālib, Fāṭimah, Khālid ibn al-Walīd, and the Ottoman hero, Muḥammad al-Fātih. They were all brave, creative, and responsible, otherwise they could not have earned and maintained their leadership.

The following lesson from Prophet Moses and the Children of Israel is particularly valuable. After Moses saved the Israelites from the slavery of Pharaoh in Egypt, he did not rely on this enslaved generation to achieve anything substantial, because they lacked the required characteristics of courage, freedom, and creativity. They had lived for generations as slaves suffering from fear and intimidation. He could not change their basic character with faith and education because it was too late to train them as adults. Their "metal" was faulty. He waited for a new generation to be born free in the Sinai desert, whom he could raise and build into strong men of courage, freedom, honesty, and a sense of responsibility. This process of character building took 40 years. Moses and Aaron used the open and free desert of Sinai to create strong and faithful Jews born after the exodus from Egypt.

Parents need to start character building early during infancy, because lecturing and preaching does little to change character during adulthood, when most of the personality traits have already been established. There are many guidelines for parents to follow, yet it is crucial to implement them within a friendly and happy environment in the home. Although character building is a continuous process, it is more effective during early childhood.

It is character which makes a person, not accidents nor circumstances.

Character Formation

Although character building begins in infancy and continues thereafter, the first few years are the most effective. Character formation occurs day by day, thought by thought, and action by action.

When is character formed? Can anything be done about it later? We do not know the exact answers. Dr. Spock suggests that between the ages of 5 months and 1½ years is perhaps the most significant in setting people's fundamental attitudes toward life. That is when children begin to feel like separate individuals and insist on some independence (like wanting to hold their own bottles and not be cuddled too long). They form their first real attachment to the parents. If the parent is a warm person, they expect other people to be the same. Lovingness of the parent will foster love in them. If, on the other hand, their parent is cold and suspicious, they will develop in this direction themselves. They will expect the rest of the world to be cold, and therefore will find mainly its cold aspects. Regarding their concept of themselves, babies are led at this stage to an assumption that they are basically appealing or unattractive, good or unworthy. This is when they tend to become optimists or pessimists. If babies have had little relationship with their parents, they will not relate well to things and ideas. Between the ages of one and a half and three years, children acquire a definite sense of themselves as separate people. However, they become more conscious of their dependence on their parent. The baby feels a number of conflicting pulls: independence versus dependence, cleanliness versus soiling, cooperation versus stubbornness and affection versus antagonism. How children emerge at the end of their third year depends on how warm a relationship has developed between them and their parents. Character formation also depends on how both parents and children resolve conflict during this somewhat strained period.

By the age of 18 the character building of the person has been essentially completed and stabilized. Character building occurs during the stages of nursery, kindergarten, elementary, intermediate, and high school. Further education at the age of 20 and beyond is the stage of knowledge and educational development.

To raise children well, each of the following aspects of personality has to be cared for: spiritual, moral, physical, mental, psychological, and social.

In each area, parents need to establish a strong bond with their children. For example, if parents are intensely dominating and the children are compliant, they may be made too submissive. If the parents are hostile and tactless, yet leave their children loopholes for fighting back, the children may grow up too hostile. If parents are grim, and make a serious matter of cleanliness, their children, if naturally docile, may end up overly clean and scrupulous. If anxious parents hover over their children and constantly watch them, and if the children are impressionable, they may become overly dependent.

Although various psychologists assert that a child's character is formed by three years of age, certain personality tendencies can be greatly modified later if the environment or the pressure changes. Some characteristics will not be formed until the later stages of childhood (like attitudes toward people of their own sex and the opposite sex).

The strong want peace while the weak want justice
President Theodore Roosevelt warned Americans not to become soft and complacent: "The things that will destroy America are prosperity-at-any-price, peace-at-any-price, safety-first instead of duty first, the love of soft living, and the get-rich-quick theory of life." No man he warned was above the law, and expediency did not justify wrongdoing. The virtues on which America was built are: Courage, honor, justice, truth, and sincerity.

Character is Not Skin Deep, It Has Deep Roots

Character is not something easily handed over to children by others with schooling or experience. Character building must occur in the early making of personality. It takes time for parents to build character (just like the roots of a huge tree takes time to grow into the ground). Good character preserves the child's integrity, unshaken by the events of daily life. Well-established character does not stir like the leaves of a tree or follow the herd wherever it goes. Character has a strength that grows like deep roots within children. If parents implant it at birth, the seeds of that good character germinate early.

"The best gift that a parent can pass to a child is good character." (Tawfiq 1967)

Demolishing a Child's Character

You're Stupid

What is Personality?

This is an interesting question. Broadly, there are three major theories about personality:

1. The traditional theory is that personality consists of three elements: the mind, the body, and the spirit.

2. The modern theory is that personality consists of only the mind. Shaykh al-Nabhany (a Palestinian jurist) believes this and argues that the body has no connection with what is the personality.

3. The post-modern theory holds that personality consists of, and encompasses, many elements. A majority of educators and psychologists believe that a wide range of variables form personalities: physical, mental, social, emotional, and spiritual.

The focus here is on the foundations of personality: courage, love, creativity, responsibility, honesty, trustworthiness, independence, and freedom.

According to ethics educator Michael Josephson (in Ferguson et al. 1999), the six pillars of character are: **trustworthiness, respect, responsibility, fairness, caring,** and **citizenship**.

Other qualities enumerated by various scholars are: wisdom, patience, humility, self-restraint, modesty, moderation, simplicity, self-confidence, sacrifice, and generosity. Character is internal and is related to the basics of personality, whereas behavior is its outward manifestation. A habit is a persistent, repeated behavior that becomes unconscious after a time.

Upcoming chapters will cover specific elements of character: Courage (ch.15), Love (ch.16), Honesty and Trustworthiness (ch.17), Responsibility (ch.18), Independence (ch.19), Creativity (ch.20) and Self-esteem (ch.21).

The Rose, the Baby, and the Parents

We may liken the baby to a rose. It blooms, diffuses a pleasant perfume, and inspires beauty. Nevertheless, its stalk has many thorns. The compassionate parent holds the rose gently by the stalk, carefully leaving the rose to flourish, although he may be pricked occasionally. The impatient parent, trying to avoid the thorns, holds the rose by its soft bud, thus killing it. He may save himself the pain but destroys the rose. Parents need to treat children with utmost care and patience like dealing with the rose.

Activity

ACTIVITY 46: MEMORIZATION OF A SUPPLICATION

Memorize this supplication with the family either in Arabic or English:

اللهم إني أعوذ بك من الهم والحزن وأعوذ بك من العجز والكسل وأعوذ بك
من الجبن والبخل وأعوذ بك من غلبة الدين وقهر الرجال» أبو داؤود

The Prophet ﷺ said: O Allah! I seek refuge with You from worry and grief, I seek refuge with You from weakness and laziness, I seek refuge with You from cowardice and miserliness, and I seek refuge with You from being heavily in debt and from being overpowered by [other] men. (ABŪ DAWŪD)

Discuss and identify the traits mentioned in this hadith. Why should these negative traits be eliminated in the making of personality? Can parents delay teaching their children the good traits that tackle these negative qualities until adulthood? What practical personal experiences can you relate and narrate to your children? Notice the issues portrayed in this hadith:

- Stress and Depression
- Helplessness and Laziness
- Cowardice and Miserliness
- Excessive Debts and being Disempowered by Others

CHAPTER 15

Nurturing Courage

Introduction

Courage is directly facing and dealing with anything dangerous, difficult, or painful (instead of withdrawing from it). The quality of being fearless or brave has various elements: valor, fortitude, firmness, daring, and heroism.

Courage must be encouraged in young children. We can nurture qualities like courage by enhancing hope, anticipating success, and encouraging the dreams that children have of what they can become. We can teach children to be in control of situations by remaining calm and supportive and not panicking. Parents can nurture heroism (defined as courage elevated by nobility) by caring for, rescuing, and respecting other people.

The following are behavioral definitions of courage:

1. Stand up for what is right, even if alone.
2. Reject negative peer pressure.
3. Try something even if you fear you will fail or make a mistake.
4. Express yourself even if some people might disapprove.

Some of the most common situations that require courage in children are:

1. Telling the truth when it lands you in trouble.
2. Handling bullies.
3. Handling peer pressure.
4. Beginning school.
5. Being visibly different (for Muslim girls, wearing a headscarf, or for Muslim boys, wearing a kufi).
6. Reaching higher than your previous accomplishments.
7. Expressing unpopular opinions.

However, there are situations in which courage becomes insolence, like disobeying parents, teachers, rules, and laws. Impetuous and irrational rebelling against culture and religion is also discouraged. It is crucial not to confuse religion with the many cultures of different countries, because some cultural practices completely contravene Islamic law. For example, forced marriage, giving automatic custody of the children to the father regardless of his behavior, denying children (especially daughters) an education, and denying women their rightful inheritance are violations of Islamic law. Seclusion of women and girls, whereas men and boys have the licence to go wherever, whenever, and with whomever they please unchaperoned, and the punishment of women and girls on the slightest suspicion is also prohibited in Islam. Most of these practices are erroneously passed off as "religion". It is also wrong for parents to force their children to tell lies and behave dishonestly.

Statements on Courage

The Prophet ﷺ said:

"The master of martyrs is Ḥamzah ibn 'Abd al-Muṭṭalib (the Prophet's uncle), and a man who stood up to [a] tyrant ruler, spoke the truth, and the ruler killed him." (al-Nisābūrī 1990)

When Ḥamzah embraced Islam he challenged the idol worshippers to hurt the Prophet. He earned the title of "Master of the Martyrs" when he was killed in battle by a cowardly attack from behind. He was a very brave man.

- "Courage is the first of all virtues because if you haven't courage you may not have the opportunity to use any of the others." Samuel Jackson.
- Thomas Jefferson said, "One person with courage is a majority."
- You cannot discover new continents without losing sight of the land.
- Evil will continue to triumph as long as good people do nothing courageous.

Basic Principles of Courage and Fear

The opposite of courage is fear, one of the most fundamental of human drives. Fear may be a learned reaction or an instinctive protective response. Parents need to watch out for both fluid and fixed fears. A fluid fear comes and goes (it can remain for a limited period, and then it begins to fade away). This is considered normal. A fixed fear, on the other hand, remains or may even intensify. It is not normal for children to have a fixed fear of flying, heights, dogs, spiders, and crowded places. Fixed fears may require endless patience to overcome, and may even require professional treatment. Healthy fears are a part of everyday life, for they help adults and children respond quickly to danger. Some healthy fears are fear of poisonous snakes, open flames, and mishandling hydrochloric acid. A fear is unhealthy when it prevents people from performing everyday activities.

The following are some suggestions to help children deal with fears:

- Parents should praise their children's attempts. When children make an attempt, they deserve praise for their effort, regardless of success. It is especially important to praise moral courage – not going along with others who were doing something wrong, or telling the truth when a lie would have been easier.
- The best promoter of courage is the parental model. When parents exhibit courage, children will follow. Children are enthusiastic imitators, for they want to behave as adults do, particularly their own parents. Often children's fears are the same as those of their parents.
- Parents need to clarify the difference between courage (a praiseworthy quality) and "loudness" or "showiness". Parents should not get confused between the lack of courage, shyness and deference. Children have to be taught to stand up for their own rights as well as those of others. Parents can explain to them about "quiet courage:" the courage to say "No" to what is wrong.
- Parents must create an atmosphere of acceptance and respect in the home. Children need a safe place to express their fears openly. Any fear is real to children, no matter how unreasonable it appears to adults. Parents have to avoid ridiculing or ignoring their children's fears. A fearful child should not be shamed, punished or overprotected.
- A consistent predictable daily routine provides children with a sense of power and control. Children's fears often stem from a lack of information about what is happening in their lives. When changes in the routine are necessary, then a discussion in advance will help prepare children for the event. Field trips, visitors, or fire drills can be frightening to children because they do not know what to expect. They can be asked to describe what they think will happen and then, after the event, they can be included in a discussion of the event and their experiences. Words like "afraid," "fear," and "scared" can be used to talk about how children feel.
- Do not force children into facing something which they are afraid of before they are ready. When they seem able to handle it, they can be gently encouraged to confront a fear by gradual exposure to what they find frightening. For example, if the children are afraid of the noise of the vacuum cleaner, then they can touch it when it is switched off, or someone else could

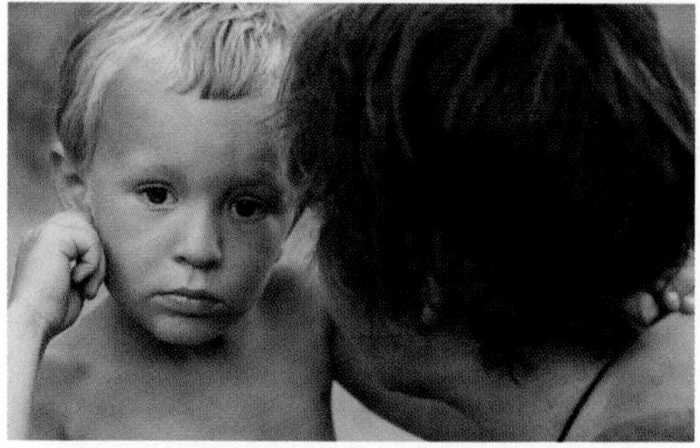

switch on the vacuum cleaner while the parents hold and comfort the children. Allowing children to decide when to put their faces under water when swimming gives them a sense of control and less fear.
- Do not show excessive concern when your children are upset. You might unintentionally reinforce their fears, giving the impression that there are grounds for feeling afraid. The children can be given information suitable for their age in a calm and reassuring tone. For example, a parent might say, "That's a very loud noise, isn't it? It's an ambulance; it must be on its way to help someone."

- Children need to be reminded with kindness and compassion of the things that no longer frighten them. This will empower them to overcome other fears too.
- Help children understand the fear. For example, "Loud noises, like fireworks and thunder, can be scary." "Dogs bark because that is how they 'talk' and sometimes they bark a lot when they are happy to see someone." Do not expect the child's fears to go away overnight; be patient.

Children take what they hear literally, such as, "The policeman will get you if you don't get in your car seat", or when a stranger says, "You're so cute I'm going to take you home with me." Death should not be described as sleep, because children may be afraid of going to sleep. Nor should children be told that they will be a big boy or a big girl when they overcome their fear. This puts too much pressure on the child.

Understanding the Development of Fear in Children

AGE	MOST COMMON EARLY CHILDHOOD FEARS
6 months	Strangers
8 months	Separation from parent, falling down
1 year	Separation from parent, noises, animals, doctors, taking a bath
2 years	Separation from parent, toilet training, bedtime, doctors, taking a bath
3 years	Loss of parent, toilet training, bedtime, monsters and ghosts, anyone who looks different than family (such as someone with a disability, beard, different skin color or different attire)
4 years	Noises, animals, bedtime, monsters and ghosts, people who look different than family, loss of parent, death of parent, divorce of parent
5 years	Noises, animals, monsters and ghosts, getting lost, going to daycare, getting hurt, loss or death or divorce of a parent

It is normal for all youngsters to be afraid of something at one point or another, whether it is thunder, dogs, bees, darkness, or imaginary things such as ugly monsters under the bed. Fear seems to be especially common between three and six years of age, when a child's ability to think about and remember scary things increases. Some children's temperaments make them naturally more fearful than others. When parents comfort their frightened children, they are helping them feel safe. This sense of security gives them the courage they need eventually to face and conquer their fears.

Infants fear loud noises, strangers, and separation from parents. Toddlers fear strangers, separation from parents, and the unknown. As their imaginations grow, preschoolers and school-age children fear the dark, being injured, animals, being left alone, and death. In addition to these fears, older school-age children worry about not living up to the expectations of parents and teachers. During adolescence, teenagers often worry about nuclear war, natural disasters, and terrorism.

Children may fear the most unimaginable things. For example, when children begin to walk and understand that they can leave their mother, they realize that their mother can leave them as well. Or the water goes down the drain (or the toilet), so they might disappear down the drain too. A child's surroundings, such as unfamiliar places, crowds, and shadows from night lights can increase fears.

When children's fears are clearly excessive and become disruptive to their lives, then parents should consider seeking professional help. When making this decision, parents need to ask themselves the following questions. How long have the fears persisted? Are the fears harmful to the children? Are the fears interfering with normal behavior or relationships? Are the fears preventing the children from playing and sleeping?

Children Need to Learn Emotional as Well as Physical Courage

Emotional courage is when you are not afraid to say something, write something, or do something emotional (such as crying). Emotional courage is a real courage, and that kind of courage is a source of strength in life. Popular movies aimed at boys seem to prize only one kind of courage: standing up to a physically larger opponent. The willingness to fight an enemy, to outwit a large animal, to defeat an alien monster, and to confront a villain with a gun, are the ways in which the media depict male courage. Boys need models of emotional courage. They need to see courage in their families and in the lives of people around them. Society needs to provide models of heroism that go beyond the muscular. Although many adults display emotional courage in their work or personal lives, rarely do they allow their children to witness their private moments of conscience or bravery. People need to speak about it. Parents should praise the emotional courage of those people who exhibit the courage to make a speech, to be active despite handicaps, to learn a new language, and to help when it would be easier to look the other way. When emotional courage is given a face and form, then a positive impression is made on the children.

> Another dimension of moral courage is the courage to control emotions and speech while becoming angry. This is in contrast to physical strength, as explained by the Prophet ﷺ:
>
> The strong man is not the good wrestler, but it is he who controls himself at the time of anger.
>
> (AL-BUKHĀRĪ)

Between Courage and Conformity

Many adults have described how their fear response was developed in childhood by parents and teachers who used threatening and shaming tactics. Children were taught that they had better conform "or else!" and they were publically embarrassed, threatened, and shamed into conforming to what others wanted them to do. Children had to blindly follow the wills of the adults. They were told: "Children are to be seen and not heard!" or "Shut up or I'll give you something to cry about!" These statements create fear and destroy courage.

Fearful and insecure children seek "security" by staying in unsuitable jobs and/or partnerships. Because of their fears of not being able to succeed they could not find more suitable work. They have fears of rejection. They exhibit guilt, shame, and inferiority. They do not have confidence, they do not feel worthy of better conditions, and they do not struggle for freedom. It takes courage to become free. These people had been taught since they were children that they were not safe on their own and needed the help of others. They were not taught how to create, but were constantly stripped of their creativity and, instead, taught to conform.

Peer Pressure

When children are young, their parents or guardians make the important decisions for them. As they grow older, however, children must learn to make their own decisions. Teenagers run into some difficult social situations where they have to make their own decisions. Friends and acquaintances may pressure them to experiment with alcohol, drugs, or sex. It is hard to say "No" and go against the group.

Imitation → Socialization → Autonomy

Three stages of growing up may be identified: the stage of imitation of parents – from birth to 7 years; the stage of socialization – from 7 to 14 years; the stage of autonomy – from 14 to 21 years.

Children want to fit in and to be part of a group, and they like to appear to be more sophisticated than they really are. They do not want to be seen as "the baby." It is not easy for them to stand up for themselves and do what they think is right (especially when friends are encouraging them to just try a beer, or a cigarette). The group may pick on one child, or leave one child out of a game. Children sometimes become involved in power struggles within a small circle of friends. "I won't be your best friend anymore" is a common weapon that young children use against each other.

Even young children want to be part of a group, and parents must explain the issue of peer pressure. Parents can talk to their children about what happens in a group. If a group of children are playing a game like hide and seek, it is important that everyone plays by the rules, otherwise, one person will spoil the game for everyone else. However, if the group wants to do something that is risky or harmful, then refusing to be part of the group is a good thing. One child's refusal to go along with the group may give others the courage to say "No" to the group as well.

Parents can discuss individual differences with their children. Does everyone have to be the same as the others in a group? If children can respect individual differences, they will have richer lives in their teenage and adult years. Parents can talk about being a leader or a follower. They have to listen to their children and let them know that they understand the difficulties of coping with peer pressures. If parents can listen to their children and discuss the issues without being judgmental, it is likely that the children will continue to talk to their parents as they grow older.

Peers can be good, yet "peer pressure" can be bad. However, some children will influence others in healthy, positive and supportive ways. When parents treat their children's friends with respect and warmth, their own children will watch and learn valuable lessons on how to behave toward others.

When parents tolerate differences in others and value individuals who may be seen as eccentric or unusual, then their children will also learn to be tolerant of others. When parents do not judge people on the basis of their income, clothes, religion or racial origins, their children will realize that there is really nothing to be embarrassed about when people are different. Although peers may have a strong influence over a growing child, parents can be even more influential.

Friends are essential throughout one's life, and learning to socialize with others is a part of children's normal development. All children have to learn how to fit in with the group while still holding onto their own values and identity. When parents help their children develop confidence and courage, then the children will be better equipped to deal with the pressures of the group. They will have the strength to say "No" to things that make them feel uncomfortable or that they believe are not right.

Parents, Bravery, and Cultural Practices

Courage has much to do with the making of a leader. Enhancing courage in children starts early. It may be easier than is generally thought, because research shows that babies are born brave, having no fear of their surroundings, and it is usually the parents who put fear in their minds. They make children fear animals, darkness, heights, ghosts, monsters, snakes, dogs, and water. The way in which children are raised has a strong influence on how brave they become. It is usual in some cultures to use threats and intimidation to make children docile and obedient. This approach has affected the way children are taught faith, religion, memorization of the Qur'an, and the beautiful names of Allah. The correct way is to start with verses containing Love and Mercy, and the welcoming names and attributes of God. In the beginning, emphasis should be on love and Heaven, not on punishment and Hell.

Tell stories about the bravery of the prophets. Prophet Abraham entered the temple, broke the idols with his axe, then hung the axe on the neck of the biggest idol; Moses and his brother Aaron fearlessly defied the powerful dictator Pharaoh; and Muhammad ﷺ prayed at the Ka'bah in Makkah, even though the pagans threatened him and threw stones and garbage at him. Use true stories of courageous people in your lifetime. It is important that children are taught to feel as if they are living with the presence of God. Teach children to be brave, secure, and righteous individuals, fearing no one but their true Lord, who loves them deeply.

Unfortunately some parents do not let their children mix and play with others, and they isolate them. They tell them how swimming could drown them, how horse-riding could hurt them, and how sports could break their legs and arms. Parents teach cowardice when they give children no choices and deprive them of decision making. This teaches children that parents are the only ones who know and that parents should decide and think for them.

They spoil children by providing everything for them and making all the effort for them. They prevent children from taking any risks in their lives, and teach them not to make any effort. Parents also make the error of being overprotective and sensitive; they do not take the children outside the home, fearing that they will fall sick or catch a cold. They teach them that children cannot be trusted and should not be allowed to take any risk. The solution is to teach children to be courageous by putting them in situations that require courage and taking reasonable risks. Teach children how to be safe in an unsafe environment. Explain to children, in a forest and a factory and a boat, what is safe, what is unsafe, and how to tell the difference. Bravery has to be part of our culture. Remember: Allah supports those who are brave!

- The uncle of the Prophet ﷺ was named Ḥamzah, meaning "Lion."

  Owing to his courage and strength, he was nicknamed "Asadu Allāhi wa Rasūluh," meaning *the Lion of God and His Messenger*!

  We can tell children stories of bravery from the animal kingdom:

  In the lion's den there is an odor, which foxes are scared to approach even when the lion is far away. There is an innate timidity in certain birds [i.e. finches] even when they are flying high. Whereas there is courage and pride within falcons even when they are dying.

- "We must build dikes of courage to hold back the flood of fear." Martin Luther King, Jr.

SHYNESS OR BASHFULNESS?

What we are advocating is bashfulness, but not shyness. Shyness is being introverted and afraid of meeting other people. Bashfulness is being initially considerate, polite, and respectful. It also implies that one does not show off.

Activities

ACTIVITY 47: SHARING EXPERIENCES OF FEAR

Talk to your children about some of the fears you experienced during your life and what you did when you were frightened. Children can share their own comments and experiences.

ACTIVITY 48: NINE WAYS TO RAISE A COWARD

Discuss the bad parenting practices below with your whole family and narrate examples and stories from your experience. If these mistakes do happen how do you rectify the damage?

- Disgrace your child and insult him, especially in front of his friends.
- Call your child bad names. Tell him that he is good for nothing.
- Never trust your child and always disbelieve in what he says. Tell him he cannot be right and that others know better than he does.
- Ignore anything good about him; focus on his faults.
- Treat his brothers, sisters and cousins better. Always compare him with them – how ugly and lazy he is, and how beautiful and hard working they are.
- Always keep your child next to you to make him feel safe.
- Spoil your child with excessive gifts.
- Do not allow your child to talk in front of anybody. He should always keep silent before others.
- Do not give your child any responsibility, no matter how small. Teach him to rely on others and to avoid all risks.

ACTIVITY 49: COURAGE AND FAITH

Discuss with your children the story of how the Quraysh tried to stop the Prophet ﷺ. The Prophet ﷺ said:

> Dear uncle, by the name of Allah, if they [the Quraysh] put the sun in my right hand and the moon in my left hand, to leave Allah's Message of light and guidance, I will not drop it until Allah reveals it, or I shall die defending it.

1. What elements of courage can you identify from the incident of the Prophet ﷺ telling his uncle Abū Ṭālib that he would not renounce his message?
2. Narrate other incidents of courage from the lives of the prophets.
3. Narrate stories of courage from the Companions of the Prophet ﷺ.
4. Narrate contemporary situations of courage by heroes from various faiths around the world.

Describe a situation in which you showed courage. What was hard about it? What did it accomplish? How did people respond to you?
Ask the children to tell their own stories.

ACTIVITY 50: COURAGE: A TEST FOR TEENAGERS

Are You a Person of Courage? Give some examples.

TRUE	FALSE	
☐	☐	I stand up for what is right, even if I stand alone.
☐	☐	I do not follow negative peer pressure.
☐	☐	Fear of failure does not prevent me from trying things.
☐	☐	I am not afraid to express myself when others disapprove.
☐	☐	I am willing to take risks and make decisions.

I think I am/am not a courageous person because: ______________________________

ACTIVITY 51: REDUCE CHILDREN'S FEAR DURING WARS AND DISASTERS

Discuss the items below with your children and execute some of them together.

More children are exposed to wars and disasters nowadays. Parents can do the following to reduce their fear about disasters:

a) Turn off the television news. Do, however, give them a summary of events.
b) Maintain their daily routine (like bedtime, soccer practice, mealtimes, and prayer times).
c) Focus on nurturing your children. Hold and cuddle them, spend time with them, and give them more attention and warmth. Encourage communication by listening and validating their feelings.
d) Give a calm response to scary events: do not become frightened or depressed, and avoid being obsessed with the news.
e) Allow your children to gain a better understanding of war by using play (like setting up a hospital for wounded soldiers and civilians; making a place for prisoners of war; deciding where, how, and what to shelter and feed refugees; setting up relief agencies for victims; and setting up a special prayer service for the people who are suffering).
f) Correspond by email or letter with the children of other countries who have been through a disaster, and exchange messages and gifts with them.
g) Write a letter to someone (that includes a supplication to God): the president of a war torn country, the enemy, or a disaster survivor. Draw a picture of peace for a soldier, bake cookies for someone who is injured, or collect money to send to a recognized survivor fund.

ACTIVITY 52: HOW TO SAY "NO" AND STILL BE FRIENDS

Practice this four-step strategy with your children so that they feel comfortable saying "No." You can act out any number of situations, making them appropriate for your children's ages.

Example: Your child's friend wants him/her to try smoking or drinking beer, or using drugs or trying sex.

- Saying "No Thanks: I Don't Want To."
  The first strategy for resisting pressure from friends and acquaintances is a simple "No thanks, I don't want to." Often, that will be the end of the incident. You have made a choice and others should respect your choice.
- Keep repeating "No Thanks".
  Sometimes, another child will keep up the pressure, urging you again and again to try it just once. Simply repeat your first answer over and over again. Say "No thanks, I don't want to" as many times as necessary. For cases in which it is appropriate, say "It is against my religion." Do not get upset if you have to keep repeating yourself and do not try to justify your decision. Eventually, the child who is putting on the pressure will tire of hearing your answer and will give up. If this still does not work then state your reason in a clear and confident voice.
- Reverse the Pressure: "Why are you pressuring me!?"
  If someone is repeatedly nagging at you, turn the pressure around. Say to the person, "Why are you picking on me?" This reverses the pressure, forcing the other person to explain the behavior. It shows that it is the other person, and not you, who has the problem. You can suggest an alternative to keep a good relationship.
- Excuse Yourself and Leave: "Sorry, I have to leave."
  In a friendly tone, just say, "Sorry, I have to leave," and then walk away without argument. You do not have to justify your actions to anyone, nor do you have to tolerate pressures that make you feel uncomfortable.
- Encourage your children to think about ways of saying "no" whenever friends or classmates want to do something unacceptable. When children learn that they can say "no" and still stay friends, it relieves them of a lot of pressure.

(Adapted from advice on www.ehow.com)

ACTIVITY 53: COURAGE IS...

Cite examples and narrate stories to your children on the following lines:

Courage is:

Following your conscience instead of "following the crowd."
Refusing to take part in hurtful or disrespectful behavior.
Sacrificing personal gain for the benefit of others.
Speaking your mind even though others do not agree.
Taking complete responsibility for your actions and your mistakes.
Following the rules – and insisting that others do the same.
Doing what you know is right – regardless of the risks and potential consequences.
Confronting evil-doers and supporting good-doers.

CHAPTER 16

Teaching Love

Introduction

BABIES ARE BORN with a capacity to love, which parents have to develop. As young as six weeks, they respond when parents coo to them. A parent's capacity to love is a very influential factor in the development of the children's capacity to love. It begins to function by the time babies are six months old.

It is good for parents to show affection, not only implicitly, but explicitly and physically as well. There has been a tradition in the Anglo-Saxon segment of American society to subdue the physical aspect of affection, especially between father and son. This may partly explain why American children are attracted to the opposite sex early, owing to lack of physical affection by their parents during childhood. Parenting expert Dr. Spock criticized the lack of affection between fathers and sons. He himself was brought up this way and mistakenly practiced it with his own children. In the Muslim and other traditions, shaking hands, kissing each other, and hugging are encouraged.

Children gain their first impression of what people are like from their parents. If parents are full of affection, this will develop the children's ability to love. Children will assume that all people are friendly, and will not be fearful of others. Parents have to avoid unnecessary conflicts with children, even at one year of age. To prevent children from touching dangerous things and breakable items (such as medicine, glasses, and knives) parents need to remove them from the baby's reach. This will reduce the number of times you tell them "No! No!" The home has to be made a friendly and safe environment for babies, physically as well as emotionally.

Building love starts from breastfeeding. Cuddling, smiling, touching, kissing, and rubbing gently is essential for the baby. Children should be given verbal expressions of love, acceptance, and approval. As children grow, they will notice how their parents behave toward others. Are they loving and affectionate, or cruel and hateful? This will affect the child's concept of the world and his behavior and attitude toward others. Children also notice how parents deal with pets, animals, plants, and the environment. Parents should show appreciation for the rain, the snow, the sun, the moon, and the stars (rather than cursing them when they bother you). When we deal with nature, we are to show a loving and caring attitude.

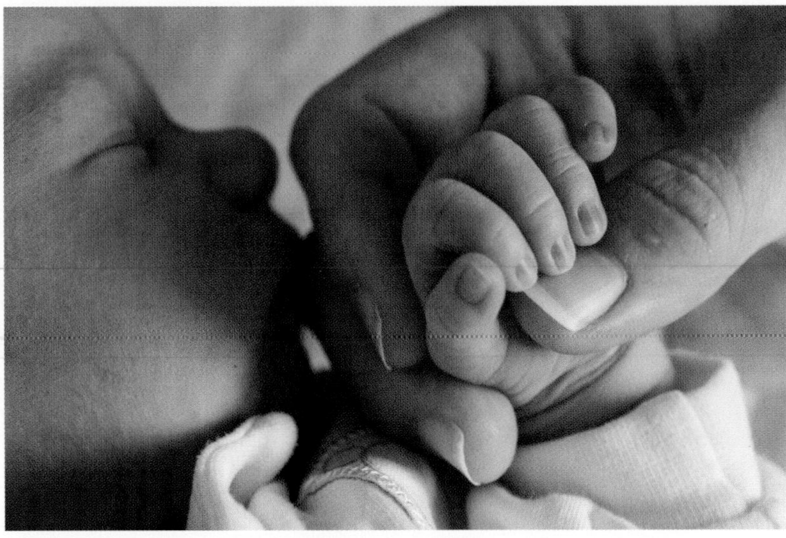

One of the greatest gifts a parent can give a child during all the ups and downs of life is LOVE. The power of a loving parent is one of the most potent forces.

Warmth and approval from caregivers are the essential ingredients for healthy emotional development. In the first two to three years children's personalities are modeled by parents and caregivers. Babies who have lived in understaffed orphanages, or who lie neglected in their cribs in day nurseries, can be harmed for life. This has been shown in the former Soviet Union. When a baby's intellect, and emotions are neglected they do not recover fully, whereas babies who are cared for by loving parents surge ahead.

Foundation of Emotional Empowerment

Parents foster emotional strength and keen intelligence when they give their children visible love. Provide your baby with pride and joy in their tiny accomplishments, thoughtful playthings, and answers to their questions. Let them play freely but safely, read to them and show them pictures. Children know that they are weak, inexperienced, and dependent; hence they rely on their parents for leadership, love, and security.

Kids are continually watching their parents and instinctively patterning themselves on them. This is how they acquire their own personalities, their strength of character, and their ability to cope. They are learning in childhood how to be adult citizens, workers, spouses, and parents by identifying with their parents.

Parents express love in countless ways: happy facial expressions, spontaneous demonstrations of physical affection, pleasure in their children's accomplishments, comfort when they are hurt or frightened, and safety when they are threatened. It is the parents' love that creates love in children. It is from this lovingness toward parents that children go on to form their positive relations in life – with friends, teachers, spouses, offspring, neighbors, and colleagues.

Children gain trust in themselves from being loved and respected by their parents. This self-assurance helps them to be comfortable with themselves and with all kinds of people for the rest of their lives. Respect and love from parents are what teach children to give respect and love to their parents and others in turn.

In a violent society, children need to be taught love in a stronger way, to compensate for the violence that is everywhere else. If parents do not teach children love, how can they learn it anywhere else?

The Prophet ﷺ said:
Surely, in the body is a piece of flesh: if it is sound, the whole body is sound; and if it is damaged, the body is diseased. Surely, it is the heart. (AL-BUKHĀRĪ AND MUSLIM)

Love: The Concept of Creative Intelligence and the Qur'an

The Qur'an describes the soul (*fū'ād*) as the seat of intuition, comprehension, affection, and empathy. The Institute of Heart Math (in Boulder Creek, California, USA) shows that the heart is a powerful agent for transforming perceptions, resolving challenges, and manifesting values. Harmonizing the heart and brain with love is what can establish a complete intelligence, a complete self. The soul (*fū'ād*) and heart (*qalb*) are spiritual and emotional centers of the body.

When 'in the heart,' people want to explore, learn, and be creative. Children are more responsive and listen better when "in the heart." When "out of the heart," frustration, anger, boredom, self-pity, or anxiety can take over, and problems appear insoluble. Children who learn to love remain wholesome and balanced, develop a more complete perspective of life, are able to make wiser decisions, care better for themselves and others, and pass the understanding of how to love on to their own children. (Bradley et al. 2009)

In his book, *Emotional Intelligence*, Goleman shows that the emotional lessons a child learns shape the brain's circuitry. People who excel in life are usually not those with the highest logical intelligence, but those with the highest emotional intelligence. Emotional intelligence includes impulse control, character and self-discipline, altruism, and compassion. (Goleman 2005)

The myth that children's intellectual abilities are independent of their ability to give and receive love is not true. Perceptions, mental and emotional attitudes, reaction times, and decision-making abilities are all directly related to the health of our heart. The higher perceptual faculties in the brain perform better when electrical rhythms produced by the heart are balanced and harmonious. Love, care, appreciation, and compassion create balanced and

THE HEART IN THE QUR'AN

The Qur'an describes the human heart in so many forms; all of these forms are indications that the heart is much more than a mechanical pump. The most important descriptions of the heart in the Qur'an are that it is the seat of:

A) POSITIVE ASPECTS	*Imān:* faith	*Takhsha'*: God consciousness	*Yuṭahhir*: purity
	Taqwā: piety, devotion	*Khayr*: goodness	*Munīb*: repentance
	Yahdī: guidance	*Yarbiṭ*: strength	*Yafqahūn*: understanding
	Ya'qilūn: reason	*Muṭma'in*: satisfaction	*Sakīnah*: peace
	Līn: softness	*Ra'fah*: compassion	*Raḥmah*: mercy
B) NEGATIVE ASPECTS	*Maraḍ*: disease	*Munkirah*: refusal	*Ghamrah*: ignorance
	Āthlmūn: sinfulness	*Ta'mā*: blindness	*Kal Ḥijārah*: coldness
	Nifāq: hypocrisy	*Ghill*: rancor, hate	*Lāhiyah*: preoccupation
	Ru'b: terror, fear	*Tartāb*: doubt	
	Qāsiyah: harshness		
	Yazīgh: deviance		

There are 145 places in the Qur'an which mention the heart. Further research is needed to expand our knowledge about the heart.

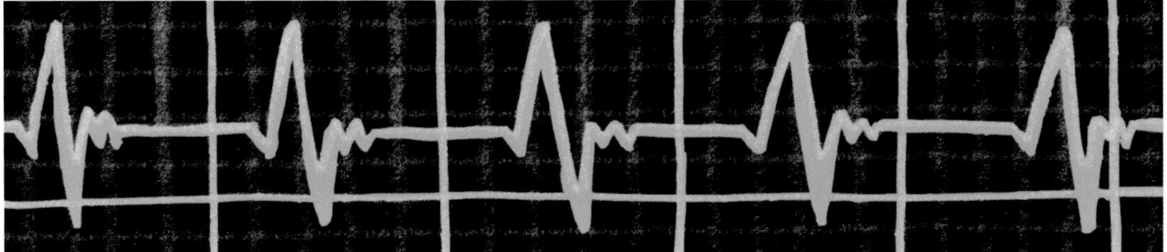

harmonious heart rhythms. By balancing head and heart, people develop wisdom, power, and integrity in making choices and communicating. With love, sensitivity increases, communication grows clearer, and understanding develops. Love, compassion and appreciation amplifies creativity, improves problem solving, and enhances our ability to make accurate choices.

When children lack love, and are continually fearful or worried, they become stressed and their ability to adapt diminishes. As they become conditioned to stress, the brain's neuronal patterns are set in stress response patterns; hence, children who lack love have a harder time learning. In a nurturing and caring environment, children love learning.

The physical heart responds to love and this can be measured in the ECG (electrocardiogram) and in the HRV (heart rate variability) rhythms. Feelings of anger, worry, frustration, or stress cause heart rhythms to become imbalanced and disordered. To hold positive and hopeful feelings about the future, children need love.

Dr. Ilham Altalib (ADAMS Center seminar, 2008) explains that the sayings "I love you with all my heart" or "I love you from the bottom of my heart" are actually correct, for the heart is also the center of human emotions, love, and feelings.

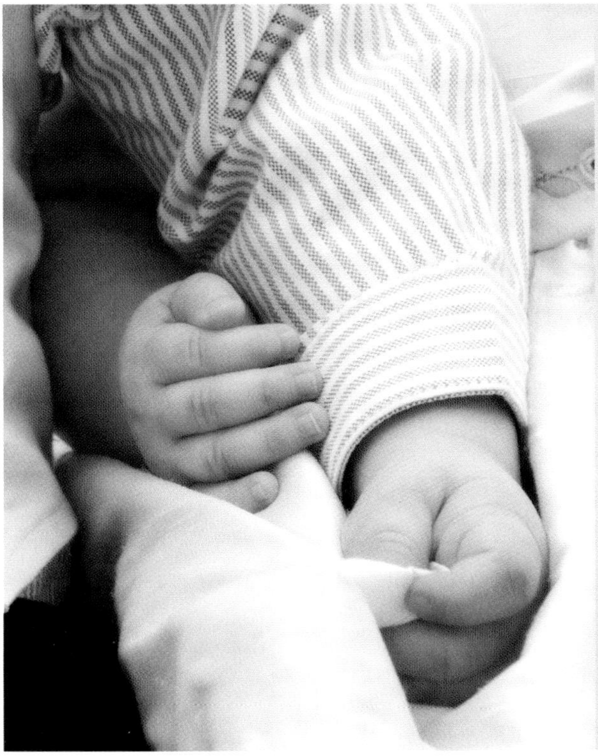

CHILDREN ARE MORE RESPONSIVE AND LISTEN BETTER WHEN "IN THE HEART."

Helpful Hints for Parents

Children are born to love. It is up to the parents to nurture that quality and to perfect it. If the parents display love to their children, it will encourage them to love in return. The following are a few practical steps to help children achieve a loving personality.

- START WHEN THEY ARE VERY YOUNG
  Instill love into your baby. Holding infants during feeding teaches them love. Holding, hugging, kissing, and talking to infants teaches them security and love.

- TEACHING CHILDREN "DO UNTO OTHERS AS YOU WOULD HAVE THEM DO UNTO YOU"
  Teach your children how to treat others without being selfish and self-centered. Considering how they would like someone to treat them makes children stop and think before acting. They realize that how they treat people is how they are going to be treated. The rule is to respond in a "better way," which will ensure friendliness instead of hostilities.

  But when you are greeted with a greeting [of peace], answer with an even better greeting, or [at least] with the like thereof. Verily, God keeps count indeed of all things.
  (Qur'an 4:86)

- LOVE IS SET BY EXAMPLE
  What really matters to children is how parents show their love toward them, toward each other, and toward other family members. Display love adequately. Your children will show love in the same way.

- APPRECIATE EACH INDIVIDUAL'S UNIQUE PERSONALITY
  Each child has a unique personality. It is not the parents' job to change their children's personalities, but to help them show love in the right way. Parents need to teach patient loving to kids who are impatient, courageous love to kids who are shy, and generous love to kids who are self-centered.

What if Your Child Says "I Hate You!"

After all of the love that you have given your children, as well as the hugs and kisses, presents and gifts, trips to the doctor, and endless comforting you have provided, those precious loving children might say: "I hate you!" Do they really hate their parents? Of course not! They hate the fact that their parents will not let them eat gum for breakfast or go to a party. They are speaking only out of anger and frustration, not hatred. Children learn early that they provoke a lot of attention when they say "I hate you," because their parents' reaction, although negative, is instant attention. Also, the parents are so riled, angry, and hurt that they will give in to their children's demands in the end, if only they will say that they did not mean it. The children are trying to push the boundaries and attract attention. It is essential that the parents keep their temper. Although they may be hated for a moment or two, the children are only looking for a reaction from them. They will soon learn that saying "I hate you" will not produce that reaction, and they will not be able to manipulate their parents in the future. The parents should, in their turn, acknowledge the feelings behind the statement. They could tell their children, "You sound pretty mad," while refraining from saying anything hurtful. It is most helpful if the parents can remove themselves from the situation, walk into the living room, sit on the couch, and take a few deep breaths. Call your spouse for some encouragement and reassurance. Prepare for further discussions with the children at a later and calmer time: "We'll talk about this later when we're not so angry."

The First Child

Parents with high aspirations want their children to have high aspirations. All that parents

accomplished in their life, they want their first child to accomplish as well. In all that they strove for and did not achieve, parents hope that their first child will be more successful. Any mistakes they have made cause them to worry that their first child may make the same ones. By contrast, these conscientious parents are more likely to take it easy with their second child. Hence, the second child is relatively more independent in his/her actions and feelings than the first one.

It is easy to tell new parents, "Relax with your first born. Let her be herself." That is like telling learners to relax the first time they ride a horse or drive a car. It helps to take the first child to places where other children play. Play is a great opportunity to learn how to be with others, and to give and take. Visiting others and welcoming other children to visit is useful. Having a good time together is the essence of being able to love.

Some sociologists advise parents to have all their children born after each other, without a long gap. This makes it easier for children to have a social life with each other, rather than being raised alone and growing up to be lonely. It is easier for many parents to raise one whole generation at once, and then move to a new phase in their life. If they leave long gaps between their children, they may end up with babies, teenagers, and young adults, thus taking care of three generations simultaneously, which is a heavy burden on parents, who will spend most of their life "babying". They will have very little time for themselves during their retirement.

Envy goes counter to love, because it is to wish that other people's good things leave them and come to you. It is a serious problem, which parents need to remove from children early in life. The Prophet ﷺ considered it a social evil. The Prophet ﷺ said:

> People continue to be well as long as they do not envy each other.
>
> (AL-TABARĀNĪ)

A new baby in the family often attracts all the parents' attention. People come to visit and often bring presents, and everyone remarks how cute the baby is. The mother may be too tired, and the father too busy doing errands, to pay much attention to the other children. Older brothers and sisters can feel left out, especially the youngest one, who may feel angry or confused, because s/he is not the youngest any more. It is natural to feel envy when a younger child is given most of the attention.

To prevent or minimize envy, parents can do the following:

- Make all the children feel that they are loved and wanted.
- When another baby arrives, ensure that the other children do not feel less love and care. It is important to continue giving them enough attention and making them feel important.
- Avoid comparison and competition among brothers and sisters.
- Tolerance, rewards, and discipline must be equitable.
- All the children need to be kissed and hugged as often as possible.
- Parents can give older children a feeling of shared responsibility for the care of the new baby, and include them in the decision making.

Why Do Parents Love Their Children?

According to Euripides, "Here all mankind is equal: rich and poor alike. They all love their children." Rabindranath Tagore said: "I don't love him because he is good, but because he is my little child."

It is a sad fact that many children are not loved, because

1. they are the result of an "accident", social pressure or rape;
2. they are seen as the cause of the wife's death in childbirth;
3. they are the offspring of a parent who turns out to be a criminal;
4. the baby is a female in a society where preference is given to males. (In some countries, parents receive congratulations only if the baby is a boy)

Why should children be mistreated for no fault of their own?

Do not link love to conduct. Without any context, it can sound as if the parents are placing conditions on their love. Parents should never say: "I will love you more when your behavior is acceptable."

Children need love, especially when they seemingly do not deserve it. Parents need to convince their children that their love for them is not based on performance and it is independent of it. They love them as they are. The success of parents is judged by the degree that children feel safe, wanted, and above all, loved. Although praise and compliments are desired by children they want love the most. Mark Twain said: "Praise is well, compliment is well, but affection – that is the last and final and most precious reward that any man can win."

Love the Actors, But Hate the Evil Actions!

The love relationship between parents and children is to be unconditional. They have to accept each other without conditions. Children have to be accepted as they are, with their fears, anxieties, and idiosyncrasies (habits, modes of expression, and mannerisms). Without conditions means without prejudice or judgment. Your children may or may not be the most attractive, well-educated, or popular children. However (with God's help) they have been brought into this world, and this qualifies them for unconditional acceptance and love.

IT IS NOT ENOUGH TO LOVE YOUNG CHILDREN SILENTLY: VOCALIZE YOUR LOVE TO THEM

The Prophet ﷺ taught the Companions to vocalize their love to each other.

> One day while the Prophet ﷺ, was sitting with his Companions, a man passed by them. One of the seated men said, "I love this man." The Prophet ﷺ asked him, "Did you tell him?" The man replied, "No." The Prophet ﷺ said, "Go and tell him." The man got up and hurried to catch the other man and said to him, "I love you for the sake of Allah." The other man replied, "May Allah love you, as you loved me for His sake." (ABŪ DĀWŪD)

Love and Parents' Self-Confidence

Parents' self-confidence is the key to a loving parent–children relationship. If the parents fail to convince their children that they know where they stand, and where they want their children to stand, then their children will test them and continue to test them. This perpetual testing to pin down the parents will elevate the level of stress in the relationship. Stress hurts affection. Reducing stress will release the flow of affection in the relationship. In the absence of love, authority is tyrannical. Self-confident parents convey both authority and love. Lovingly authoritative as well as authoritatively loving, they maintain their sense of balance. In so doing, they communicate great security to their children and secure children are relaxed and happy. Free of the need to pin their parents down, children present few discipline problems. When children misbehave, a simple reminder of who is in charge will generally suffice.

Practical Ways to Develop Compassion

Parents love their children, so that the children feel that they are being loved. But love has to be expressed in many different ways. Parents who do not speak of their love frequently are shocked when they discover that their children do not perceive that they love them.

Compassion can be developed with practice. It entails intention and action. Intention is having the desire to open one's heart to others, and show them that they matter. Action is doing something about one's intentions. For example: parents could regularly donate a little money or time (or both) to a group that they like, or offer a smile and a genuine "hello" to the people they meet on the street. It does not matter how much parents do, just that they do something. Mother Teresa explained: "We cannot do great things on this earth. We can only do small things with great love."

The following are some ways in which parents can develop love with children:

- Focus on the "big stuff" and ignore the "little stuff."
  Compassion develops gratitude. When you reflect on the great gifts of life – such as the gift that you can read this book you can develop love.
- Share with your children, since to love is to share and care. Share food, money, pens, papers, computers, cars, chairs, books, trips, and thoughts with children.
- Tell family members that you love them (especially before you go away for a few days).
- Compose a special song with your children that says, "I love you".

LOVE IS SHARING

A child has to have love and care in his heart for others; he is to love for others what he loves for himself. The Prophet ﷺ said:

> **You are not a believer until and unless you love for your brother what you love for yourself.**
> (AL-BUKHĀRĪ)

Love is...

Sharing ...our brightest hopes, our darkest fears, our loudest laughs, our softest tears, our sweetest dreams, our bitterest woes, our highest highs, our lowest lows, a growing love, always aware, the more we share the more we care.

The best way to forget our own problems is to help others solve theirs.
You may forget with whom you laughed, but you will not forget with whom you wept.

A Story from John Gray's Book: *Truly Mars and Venus*

An acquaintance whose health was deteriorating told me that she had not spoken to her son for three years because she had had a disagreement with him about his wife, and that she would not speak to him unless he called first. I suggested that she be the one to reach out, but she insisted "I can't do that, he should apologize." She was willing to die before talking to her only son. After gentle encouragement, she decided to call first. To her amazement, her son was grateful for her call, and offered an apology of his own. When someone takes the chance and reaches out, everyone wins.

Hate is like acid. It can damage the vessel in which it is stored as well as destroy the object on which it is poured.

It is important to practice affection. Although giving material things is good, it is not the same as genuine affection.

How much love is enough? Parents can make plenty of deposits in the bank of love by their demonstrations of affection to their children. No one is ever concerned about receiving too many deposits.

The more love the parents give, the more they will receive. Being a loving person is a trait that one can control, yet receiving love is beyond one's control. Parents cannot expect a return from their children, for love is its own reward. Children cannot comprehend fully how much parents love them until they become parents themselves.

Parents have to reach out first when they have a disagreement with their child. So many people hold on to little resentments from an argument or a misunderstanding, and they stubbornly wait for someone else to reach out to them, believing this is the only way in which a mistake can be forgiven or a friendship or family relationship rekindled.

Whenever people hold on to their anger, they turn "small stuff" into really "big stuff" in their minds. They consider that their positions are more important than their happiness. Peaceful people understand that being right is not more important than being happy. People must let go of their anger and reach out to others. Allowing others to be right does not mean that one is wrong. People feel much better when they experience the peace of letting go of their anger, as well as the joy of letting others be right. In return the others will become less defensive and more loving toward the former opponents.

Goodness and Evil cannot be equal. Repel [Evil] with what is better: the one with whom there was enmity will become your friend and intimate! (Qur'an 41:34)

- It is worth sacrificing time, effort, and money for the children. Love is cumulative like a positive feedback closed loop. The more the parents love their children, the more they sacrifice; and the more they sacrifice, the more they love.

- Every morning, parents can ask themselves: To whom shall I send special love to in my family today? They can expand this to include someone outside the family. Love every day keeps resentment away.

A Survey: Many Ways to Make Your Children Feel Loved

Samon (1999) asked 55 mothers and fathers of children between ages 1 and 16 how they stayed connected with their children. In every case, the answer was to spend time with their children doing something. This includes watching something, reading something, cooking something, talking about something, sharing something, and being together. Spend time together in a joint activity with your children. Below is a list of activities parents can do with their children that will increase love:

- Walking together
- Spotting shapes in the clouds/studying the night sky
- Watching home videos/listening to a radio programme/reading poetry or a play together
- Letting them brush your hair
- Wrestling together
- Filling a notebook with photos and stickers
- Taking them to the grocery store, and letting them share in the decision of what to buy for dinner
- Playing games together (like Scrabble, Twenty Questions and I Spy). They are cheap, environmentally friendly (do not need electricity or batteries), mentally more stimulating, can be played in any language, and are kinder to the eyes than looking at a video screen.
- Doing homework with them, but not for them
- Reciting Qur'an, nashīd, music, and songs together
- Washing and folding clothes together
- Painting together
- Hugging, kissing (not on the mouth), and holding hands
- Going to museums together
- Saying prayers together
- Dressing up in old clothes together
- Bringing them to the workplace
- Banging on pots and pans (without disturbing neighbors)
- Taking the children to shows, sports, movies, matches, rides, rallies, parks, and picnics (in the forest/desert/on the beach)
- Being at home listening to them fully, without answering telephone calls or opening the mail
- Visiting grandparents and other relatives together
- Cleaning and vacuuming the house together
- Baking cookies, biscuits and cupcakes together
- Looking at family photo albums together
- Picking apples, oranges, pears, and strawberries together
- Gardening together

Should Parents Teach Hate? Sometimes!

Although the focus is on love, hate must not be forgotten, for both are essential. If people love God, the prophets, parents, relatives, fellow human beings, animals, plants, the environment and the universe, then they must also hate the Devil, evil, corruption, lying, cheating, stealing, sexual abuse, drugs, drinking alcohol, smoking, jealousy, racism, bigotry, discrimination, and anger. However, although the evil actions are to be hated, the actors should not be hated. Hate the evil, not the evildoer.

Verily Satan is an enemy to you: so treat him as an enemy...
(Qur'an 35:6)

Activity

ACTIVITY 54: DAILY LOVING RITUALS

A 17 year old says: "I still like it when my mom checks in my room before she goes to bed."

Parents: discuss your daily loving rituals with your child. Do not forget *du'ā'* (supplication) every day!

CHAPTER 17

Teaching Honesty and Trustworthiness

Introduction

MOST PARENTS WORRY when their child lies for the first time. But, for most children, lying is a passing phase that is rooted in normal child development, part instinctive reaction (i.e. fear of punishment) and part learned behavior. While lying is generally nothing to worry about for most children, parents can and should strive to teach honesty. Lying is a child's response to many factors including self-defense.

Children confuse reality with their fantasies, dreams and imagination. It is important for parents not to devalue their children's fantasies. Daydreaming and imagination are key elements in terms of who people are, even as adults. Being able to pretend that one is someone else or is somewhere else is often liberating and stress releasing. Do not be overly critical. If children feel that they always have to justify themselves in the presence of parents, this may increase their level of dishonesty to avoid being reprimanded.

The pagans of Quraysh named the Prophet ﷺ from his childhood as "The Honest and Trustworthy" (*al-ṣādiq al-amīn*). Trust in

Arabic means many things: Trust, confidence, responsibility, care, and guardianship.

Honesty and trustworthiness are essential parts of the character of a righteous leader. Parents need to preach, practice, and live "honesty and trustworthiness" until this becomes ingrained into the children. Children become trustworthy when they see that others trust their parents and feel that their money, property, and secrets are safe with them. Trustworthy parents are most likely to be chosen as leaders by their communities. In fact, one of the qualities of a Muslim taught by the Prophet ﷺ is trustworthiness:

The Muslim is the one whom people feel safe and secure from his tongue [talk] and hands [actions] and the blessed believer (migrant) is the one who runs away from what God has prohibited. (AL-BUKHĀRĪ)

Trust between parents and children is essential. Establish it, maintain it, and develop it. Even if some children are difficult to trust, parents should act as if they trust them. If the children are not telling the truth, the parents should be careful and not make accusations. In cases of confrontation, the child may ask them: "Don't you trust me?"

Parents can pretend that trust is there until they find a convenient and effective way of dealing with dishonesty. Children are to be taught that with authority comes responsibility and with responsibility comes trust. For children to establish trust with parents, they need to learn how others have gained the trust of their parents and what behaviors cause distrust.

Gaining trust is an ongoing process. Although children might experience a successful relationship with their parents, sometimes it might go awry. This will cause the parents to hesitate in trusting their children again. However, it is important that they remain confident! They have to be patient.

Parents Should Trust Their Children but Verify Their Whereabouts!

Parents may trust their children when they go out, yet at the same time, they have to verify their whereabouts. Parents have to know where their children are and who they are with. This can be done without a feeling of mistrust or censorship. Parents should not assume that when they leave their children at school in the morning, they will stay there all day. Some children run away from school without their teachers' or parents' knowledge. Parents have to check on them from time to time (through school records, their friends, and neighbors, directly or indirectly). Several children have landed in trouble by running away during the day and committing crimes. It is important to check their rooms and clothes from time to time to make sure that they are not dealing in drugs, or stealing money or valuables. Explain to your children what you are doing and why you are doing it.

> Treat people as if they were what they ought to be and you will help them become what they are capable of becoming. (Johann Wolfgang Von Goethe)
>
> Trust people, and they will be true to you; treat them greatly, and they will show themselves great. (Ralph Waldo Emerson). (Exley 1997)

General Principles

The following are some significant points to consider when dealing with children:

FAMILY VALUES

Children must understand that lying is unethical and immoral. Show them that lying will have negative consequences. Teach them honesty and trustworthiness by word and deed. Parents need to discuss with their children their beliefs regarding dishonesty. Share examples of dishonesty appropriate for their age. Include a "truth" policy in your list of family values. Give children a definition of truth and trust that they can comprehend and by which they can abide.

ROLE MODELLING

Preach honesty to your children. Do not lie about your whereabouts, do not steal from stores or employers, and do not cheat on your taxes or spouses.

Parents need to ask themselves, "What message am I sending?" It is important to avoid dishonesty, especially in front of the children. Parents should never lie about their children's ages: "A child's ticket, please, he is only 11." Parents should never ask their children to lie on their behalf: "Tell Grandma I'm in the shower." Parents have to make every effort to keep their commitments, be on time, do what they say they will do, and make only promises that they know they can keep, especially when it concerns their children. If circumstances change beyond the parents' control, then offer an explanation, and refrain from making excuses and blaming others. Do not deceive with word playing, like the politician who said: "I promised, but I did not promise to keep my promises".

TEACH THE DIFFERENCE BETWEEN WHITE LIES, MALICIOUS LIES AND OTHER FICTITIOUS LIES

It is important to explain to children the difference between the malicious hurtful lie and one that is told out of politeness. Although people deny that they tell lies, everyone does so. What is the point of telling the neighbors that they are ugly? Or telling the postman, who asks how one is doing, that one is doing awful and needs psychological help? Sometimes we lie out of respect. Teach children to distinguish between lying, exaggeration, storytelling, metaphor, and deception.

TEACH THE DIFFERENCE BETWEEN FANTASY AND REALITY

Identify the difference between what is real and what is not. Discuss dreams after sleep time with children. Discuss what is in movies and what is real. Discuss what is in stories and what actually happens.

REWARD HONESTY

If the children are having a difficult time telling the truth, it is important to praise them each time they are truthful. Children like attention. Therefore, honesty has to be encouraged, even when it may cause the children to get into trouble. Parents need to praise efforts to be honest and point out good examples whenever possible, while expressing disappointment for dishonesty.

ASK BEFORE YOU TAKE

Parents can make it a rule in their home that everyone asks before taking something that belongs to another member of the family. This teaches children to mind the possessions of others and to respect each person's belongings. It will also teach that stealing from anyone is wrong.

SOLVE PROBLEMS BEFORE HAVING PROBLEMS

Immediate gratification has become a serious problem, so much so that many people have little savings, are overweight, and have serious trouble saying no to unnecessary purchases. It is especially difficult for children to postpone their desires and to own up to their wrongdoings. Teach children to admit mistakes and to postpone gratification.

Children do not have to steal before learning the bad consequences of stealing. Discuss unacceptable behavior with children before they commit it.

OLDER CHILDREN

If parents have older children who continually tell lies and are dishonest, professional help is needed. Many adults have lied as teenagers, often out of a need for privacy. Teenagers are not always willing to share their secrets with parents, and this is understandable. It is a time when they are changing quickly and are grappling with the notion of adulthood, while they are still considered children by most. It is a time when keeping secrets is common. Privacy has to be respected. However, the parents' expectations must also be respected by the teenager. The consequences of lying must be clearly defined and agreed upon. Teenagers must understand the consequences of dishonesty. If your teenagers are in the company of other teenagers who tell lies, separate them and discourage these friendships.

It is essential that children are taught the importance of trust in relationships, including the trust they should have in themselves. Therefore, they should not be put in situations where deceit or exaggeration can occur (for example, gambling, con games, multi-level marketing, and high-pressure sales), nor should they be blamed for lying unless it is clear that they are responsible for the situation. Discussions about dishonesty should be held in private so that the children are not afraid of telling the truth.

Integrating Character with the Overall World View

> *O you who believe! Why do you say that which you do not do? Grievously odious is it in the sight of Allah that you say that which you do not do.* (Qur'an 61:2–3)

Display definitions of honesty, trustworthiness, and promise-keeping in your home

Include virtues like honesty and trustworthiness into discussions on various topics (like politics, religion, history, science, literature, language, and mathematics). For example, does the mathematical ability of a bank teller to hide theft have anything to do with ethics? Do scientists have an ethical obligation to use their findings for the benefit of humankind? Were all the people mentioned in history ethical? Are all the characters in dramatic literature people of integrity?

Lying is a serious problem, which cannot be ignored and has to be dealt with promptly but wisely. Lying is so harmful that the Prophet ﷺ expressed it as follows:

> The Prophet ﷺ was asked, "Is it possible for the believer to lie?" He answered, "A believer can never lie."
>
> (KANZ AL-UMMĀL)

Pretty much all the honest truth telling there is in the world today is done by children.
(Oliver Wendell Holmes in Brown 1994)

**A nine year old said:
It is hard to lie when you are looking into your mom's eyes.**

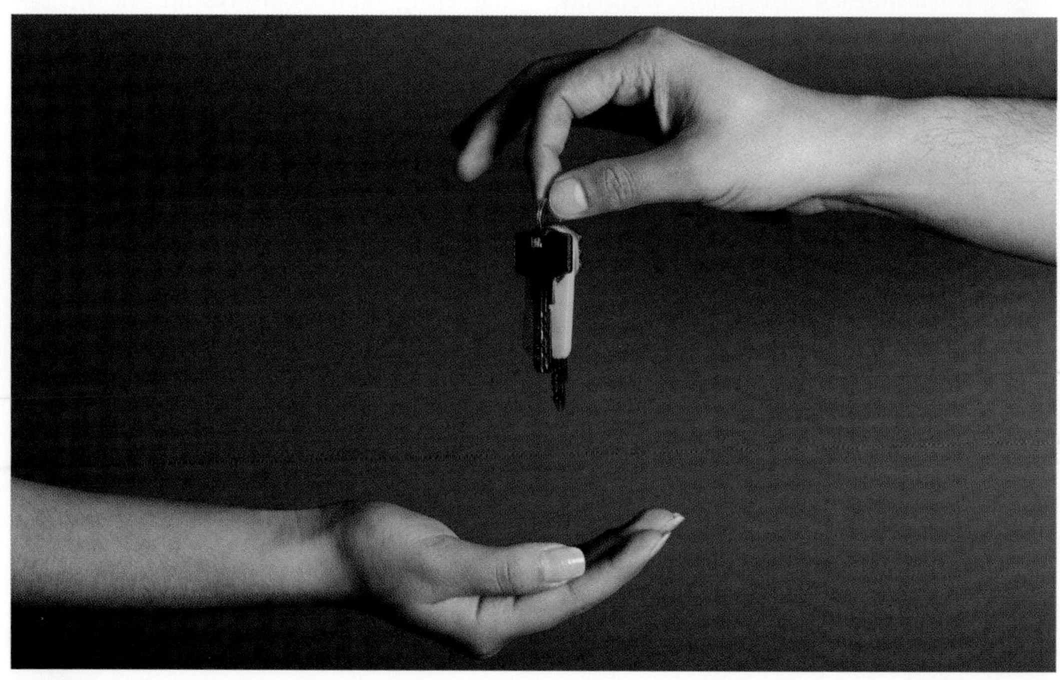

Although babies are born honest, they usually learn lying, consciously and unconsciously, from the behavior of parents and siblings. Lying is an acquired behavior, not a hereditary characteristic. Over time, children learn to lie and it becomes part of their character. Teenagers often resort to lying to justify their mistakes, conceal their secrets, and avoid embarrassing situations. The more children lie, the more lying becomes entrenched in their character. Lying breeds lying, just as honesty breeds honesty, as explained in the Prophet's ﷺ saying:

> Truth breeds goodness and goodness breeds Paradise. The man tells the truth until he is recorded as truthful. Lying breeds immorality and immorality breeds Hell fire. A man tells lies until he is recorded as a liar. (AL-BUKHĀRĪ AND MUSLIM)

Why Children Lie: How to Treat Lying

Here are some possible reasons for children lying:

- They want to avoid punishment.
- They claim ownership of items belonging to others.
- They are feeling ignored, deserted, and abandoned.
- They want to brag about themselves to their peers, asserting what they are not.
- They want to claim recognition for things they have not done.
- They may think it is allowed to lie because their parents lie.

The major reason children lie is to escape punishment. They are primarily motivated by either pleasure or pain. Whenever possible, parents should teach their children to confess their wrong doing and ask for forgiveness. If their children take something from a store without paying, then the parents should ensure that their children return it and confront the store manager directly with an apology.

If children are falling into a pattern of lying, then the parents need to examine the causes. Children are often put into a variety of activities, where they cannot keep up and the pressures to perform are too high. They may be lying because they cannot handle the pressure. Other children may lie because they are bored or do not feel that they are receiving adequate attention. Children who have gained attention from telling elaborate stories and untruths may continue to do so to get attention.

Keeping track of the children's behavior, including the times and places when they are most likely to lie, may be helpful in discovering whether a serious problem exists. Perhaps the children tell lies only during their playtime, or perhaps it is when they are doing some mischief, or perhaps it is when they are with friends and trying to be the center of attention. Each of these circumstances would require a different response.

Lying needs to be stopped from the first lie. A person who grows up lying will live a painful life. Children have to be taught that dishonesty is absolutely unacceptable. Do not punish the child for a misdeed if the child tells the truth. However, there have to be consequences for what children have done. For instance, if they hurt another child, they have to be taken to the parents and made to say sorry and ask for forgiveness; if they are caught cheating on a test at school, they must be failed instantly. However, if they tell the truth, then no direct punishment should be given. One reward for telling the truth is for parents not to respond with emotional outrage and in a frantic way. They need to react rationally and deal with the problem wisely.

This accomplishes two important aims.

- The "rope of lying is short."
- Lying will make people trust you less, and will make them feel betrayed and manipulated.
- When you tell the truth, you will not get mixed up; you do not have to remember what you have said; and you do not forget what you have said.
- Honesty will generate a force that will drive you toward greater success. When you lie, there are strong forces pushing you toward failure.

First, it ensures that the lines of communication between the parents and their children will be wide open. They will be rewarded for being truthful, since lying is usually committed because of fear of punishment.

Second, because of the good relationship established between the parents and their children (with conversation, trust, and affection) the children will want to avoid disappointing their parents. The relationship of love for each other will naturally have an "arresting" and "straightening out" effect on their behavior. Parents are not to be afraid that the "no-punishment-for-the-truth" rule will turn into reckless behavior. The mutual love will provide plenty of control.

The following treatment for lying is given in the book, *al-Khuluq al-Kāmil* [The Complete Character] by Muhammad Jad Almawla (2004 in Arabic):

- If the child lies owing to talking too much, direct him to keep silent.
- If the child lies because he is scared of a cruel punishment, be kind and compassionate to him.
- If he lies out of greed or to acquire something, then do not stand in his way to acquire what he wants.
- If he lies to trick others and fool them, then punish him.
- If he lies owing to [the influence of] some bad friends, then find him better friends.
- Confront him with the opposite of what he wants to achieve from his lies.

Teenagers have to be taught that lying is a disgrace and that it goes against goodness, honesty, justice, and respect. Ibn Khaldun advises us:

> Educating the liar about the unethical aspects of lying, and how it contradicts correct human behavior. Humans have a love of righteousness, truth, justice, and honesty.
>
> Using coercion in education is harmful to the learners, especially for children. When the child is raised in a harsh atmosphere of subjection and oppression, s/he will undergo stress and depression (which leads to laziness and the urge to lie and commit mischief).
>
> (*al-Muqaddimah*, section 32, 1992)

Fill the children's lives with compassion and care. As soon as others discover dishonesty, they will lose their trust in you and like you no more.

When parents tell their children to speak the truth, regardless of the circumstances, then the parents themselves must speak the truth, so that they are perceived as honest, and regarded as people of integrity. Truthful and honest citizens gain the respect, cooperation, and trust of other people.

Tell Children Purposeful Stories

Shaykh 'Abd al-Qādir al-Jaylāny of Baghdad narrates: "I pledged to my mother to tell the truth, always. I left Makkah and went to Baghdad to seek knowledge. My mother gave me 40 dinars for the trip. A gang of thieves attacked our caravan near Hamdan. One thief asked me: 'How much money do you have?' I said: '40 dinars.' He left me alone, thinking that I was joking. Then a second thief asked me, and I told him 40 dinars. He took me to their chief, who asked me: 'Why are you telling the truth?' I replied, 'I pledged to my mother to tell the truth always, and I don't want to break my promise.' The chief became frightened. He panicked and shouted, 'You are scared to break your pledge to your mother, and I am not scared to break my pledge to God?!' He ordered the gang to give back all our belongings and said, 'I am going to repent to Allah at your hands.' His followers told him, 'You were our leader in stealing, and today you have become our leader in repentance.' They all repented as a result of the blessing of telling the truth."

Parents: This is a purposeful story, regardless of its authenticity. The moral of the story for the children is that honesty can save you and it can save others as well.

A Prophetic Way to Treat Lying

1. A young man came to the Prophet ﷺ and said: "O Prophet of Allah, I don't pray, I commit fornication, and I lie. What should I repent from?" The Prophet said, "From lying." So the man promised not to lie. Later, when he left, he attempted to commit fornication, then he said to himself, "The Prophet might ask me if I have sinned. If I say no, I would be lying, and if I say yes, I would face the punishment of my sin." (Tibrisi 1991)

When you avoid lying – which is a major sin – you also avoid other sins and vices.

2. Telling the truth a serious issue, even in seemingly trivial situations. The Prophet ﷺ gives the following directive:

   Whoever tells a child to come and take this [candy] from his closed hand, and does not give him anything, it is considered a lie. (AḤMAD)

The Prophet ﷺ also said:

> The worst of people is the one with the double face: he puts on one face to some people and puts on another face to other people. (AL-BUKHĀRĪ)

Honesty and trustworthiness, in addition to love and courage, are character traits that are found in children who bring contentment to their parents. Let us now turn to responsibility, independence and creativity in the coming chapters.

Activities

ACTIVITY 55: SHARING EXPERIENCES

Share with your children situations when you told the truth (when you could have lied). What are the consequences, the remedies, and the lessons to learn from lying? Children may also share their own real stories.

ACTIVITY 56: ONE OF THE MOST HARMFUL VICES YOU WANT CHILDREN TO AVOID

What is one of the single most harmful vices you want your children to avoid? Answer: Lying.

- Tell children true stories of people who have ruined their lives by lying. Had they been honest, they would have had successful and happy lives.
- Remind your children and discuss with them the fact that the pagans of Makkah called Prophet Muhammad ﷺ the "Honest and Trustworthy" before his Prophethood.

CHAPTER 18

Teaching Responsibility

Introduction

BEING RESPONSIBLE MEANS acting wisely without being told, pressured or threatened into action. It is the ability to make decisions and be accountable for them. The Prophet ﷺ states:

> He who does not care about the affairs of Muslims, is not one of them. (AḤMAD)
>
> He is not a believer who sleeps on a full stomach and his neighbor is hungry, while he knows it. (AL-ṬABARĀNĪ)

Teaching responsibility to children is crucial. Children have to be trained to shoulder their responsibilities without being told or reminded. Responsible children volunteer to serve and help, without being asked or assigned the task. Responsible children also have the urge to accomplish and excel. One way of instilling responsibility in children is to teach self-monitoring. Responsible children understand the importance of their actions and the repercussions of their actions. A good habit for children to acquire is that before falling asleep at night, they hold themselves accountable for the actions they did during the day. Build an internal "policing and auditing" system. Parents have to instill the love and fear of God in their children's hearts and minds to keep them alert and on the straight path all the time. Telling children that God is with everyone wherever they are strengthens their sense of responsibility.

Responsibility is much more than just remembering to do chores or being obedient. It entails caring about right and wrong, how one's actions affect other people, and understanding why rules are important. To teach responsibility, parents themselves must be responsible.

The Good Example: Father and son are rushing to reach a store before it closes. They stop to help a woman carry the baby stroller up the stairs. The child learns that it is good to go out of one's way to help people, even if you will miss some financial gain for yourself.

When their child takes on a responsibility, parents should notice it and express appreciation. Rewarding desirable behavior encourages more desirable behavior. People often overlook occasions when the child behaved responsibly or take them for granted. Worse, many parents comment only when their children are irresponsible. As a result, the children will say to themselves: "When I am right, nobody remembers, and when I am wrong, nobody forgets." Parents need to say, "Thanks, that was a big help." They need to be especially careful to acknowledge behavior that is important to them, but that may not be important to their child, like: "I noticed that you put your books in your room instead of leaving them on the dining table. That's great – now I can set the table for dinner." Or, "I appreciate you hung up your jacket when you came in."

Making good decisions is a prerequisite to responsible behavior. Children who are simply told what to do all the time rarely learn to make informed choices. They will not be trained to be responsible. It is essential that children are given choices, for adulthood consists of making one choice after another. Instead of simply assigning chores to family members, make a list of all that needs to be done in the house, and discuss in a family meeting who will do what. Together they divide the duties, so that each person is assigned tasks s/he does not mind doing, and then work out a rotation system so that no one is stuck with the most tedious chores. Including the children in this process shows them that their parents trust them and value their opinions, and this helps them become responsible partners. It also makes them part of a team, with each member dependent on the others to run the household smoothly. This is a practical way of teaching them decision making, *shūrā* (consultation), and also responsibility.

Laying the Foundation: Attitudes and World View

If we are responsible parents, half the task is done. The other half is helping children follow in our footsteps.

Children need both adequate knowledge, as well as good character to prepare them for adult life. Responsibility is one of the most important elements of good character. Responsibility begins with a mentality, or set of presuppositions, which parents pass on to their children. If the parents' world view is that children should only play and please themselves, the children will fulfill that expectation and complain about their chores. If the parents believe that children will always be selfish, that expectation becomes clear to the child. One of the surest ways to raise selfish, contentious, unhelpful children is to have low expectations. However, if the parents' world view is that everyone, regardless of age and ability, should contribute to the well-being of all, then their actions, attitudes, and expectations will reflect that, and their children will learn the value of responsibility.

We want to raise children who succeed in life. Children who learn responsibility tend to be less dependent, and more likely to take responsibility for their own actions in adulthood. Responsibility is a learned skill, and children need to be provided with the tools to learn this critical skill.

A child should start learning responsibility at a young age. Children who are raised in a consequences-free environment miss the opportunity to learn responsibility. Some parents go too far when trying to create a safe haven for their children. These parents do not allow their children to experience the consequences of negative actions. Such parents are 'enablers' (they enable their children to be overly dependent and irresponsible). These

children grow up with a sense of entitlement. They adopt the problematic attitude of: 'the world owes me' rather than the healthy attitude of: 'the world will treat me as a responsible person if I act responsibly toward the world.'

Children cannot be responsible if they do not know how, and they can learn only if they are taught. Teaching and training are critical parts of a parent–child relationship. Being responsible is an attitude as well as a skill. Children will not put their toys away unless they are taught. Adults will not know how to return items that they borrowed or to arrive at work on time unless they have been trained. The best way parents can teach children responsibility is little by little, day by day.

Do not encourage slothful tendencies. This can be done by giving teenagers responsibilities. However, give teenagers more responsibilities than just washing dishes two nights a week and taking out the trash. When irresponsible children have to cope with a 40-hour work week (or full-time college plus a part-time job) they will be unprepared. Hard work and responsibility are necessary for a productive and successful adult life.

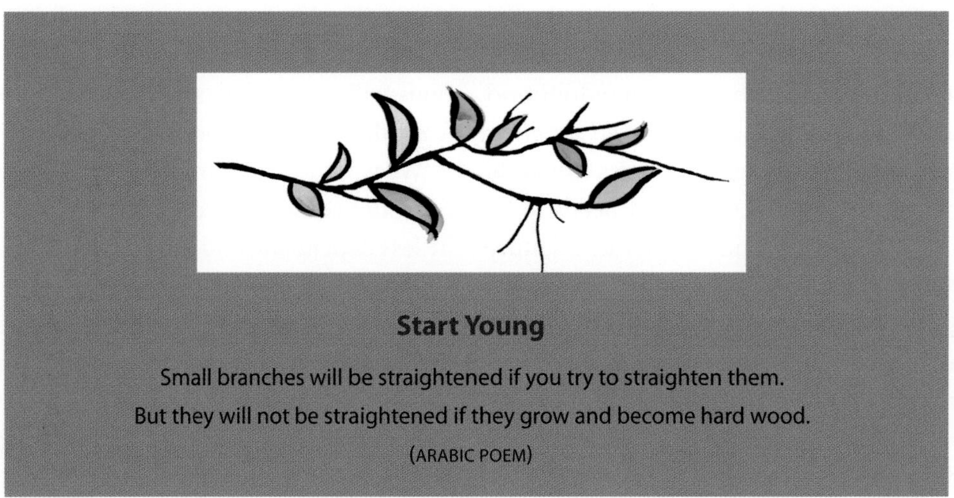

Start Young

Small branches will be straightened if you try to straighten them.
But they will not be straightened if they grow and become hard wood.
(ARABIC POEM)

Start at the preschool age. The children have to be told (when a new baby is expected): "We will have fun taking care of the baby together." They will become excited about the idea of being a responsible partner in this special project. The child can then help care for his younger brother by bringing clean diapers, putting the baby's dirty clothes in the hamper, and picking up toys that the baby drops. Teach him (by inclusion, partnership, and communication) that it is a privilege to work together and serve. The trick is "Active Engagement in Activities". Rather than just watching their parents, children should be helping.

Opportunities at Various Developmental Stages

INFANT AND TODDLER

At this stage, children begin testing their parents' boundaries. For example, the two year old child learns to repeatedly throw a toy to attract attention, then learns to throw the toy in anger, and then learns to provoke a reaction from an adult. At this point, the parents should set the boundary for their child rather than letting the child set the boundary. If he throws the toy once, then the parents can pick it up and give it back. However, if the child intentionally throws the toy again and again, then it is time to put the toy away. Thus, the child will know that negative behavior is not going to be rewarded. This age is called "the terrible twos".

As infants grow into toddlers, they will learn which actions will most test their parents' patience. At this stage, children need to learn that there can be consequences for poor behavior. If parents tell their child, "if you don't stop that…, we will go home," then they should carry out their threat. If the parents teach their child that they are making serious threats, their words will carry more weight. It is important that both parents do this.

EARLY CHILDHOOD

In the early childhood years, children need to be learning to take care of themselves. They should comb their hair, brush their teeth, tidy up after themselves. Giving young children some small chores around the house will help foster their self-esteem and increase their feelings of contribution to the household. Children who refuse to do their chores need to know that there will be consequences. If chores are not completed, then the children cannot go play with their friend, or watch television, or do something that they consider "fun." Once the chores have been completed, then the children can do what they want to do.

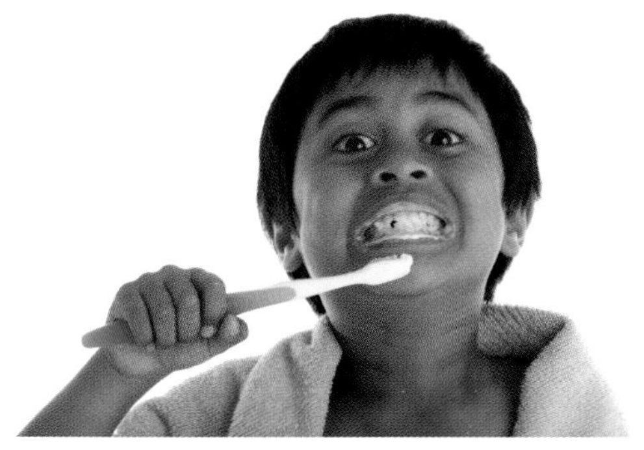

SCHOOL AGE TO PRETEEN

As children grow older, their responsibilities increase. Offering the children a regular allowance will help increase their sense of self-worth. Reward children for being responsible: More allowance for taking good care of a pet, a special treat for a good report card, or notes to say how wonderful the parents think their children are for being responsible.

If children are not performing well in school, or are not helpful around the house, then it is important to find the root of the problem. Children perform better when confronted with defined boundaries. Those children who are not held to a performance standard (either at home or in school) will cease to meet any expectations. Providing children with a sense of accountability for their actions requires a nurturing environment. Children have to be allowed to fail as well as to succeed.

Preteen children are most aggressively confronted with peer pressure. Children who have been raised in a household that teaches responsibility will more likely avoid problem behavior and negative influences from peers. Keeping the lines of communication open will give the children an outlet to discuss their fears with their parents and provide insight into their feelings.

TEENAGER

Teenagers are confronted with a multitude of opportunities for making bad choices. A teenager who knows right from wrong and understands that bad actions have bad consequences, will make the right choices.

Continue to instill a sense of responsibility in your teenagers. If the foundation for responsibility has already been laid, the parents will have a better opportunity to discuss their children's future with them. Children need to know that being responsible is necessary for their success. Help children develop targets that can be attained.

YOUNG ADULTHOOD

If you have taught your children a sense of responsibility, they are now self-sufficient and on their way to a life separate from the family. Parents who have taught dependency will find that their children are not separating (such adults remain dependent upon the family to help them survive). Adults who have never learned the consequences of their negative actions will find themselves in difficult situations, yet will be looking elsewhere to place the blame for their plight. Relationships will always be a challenge for irresponsible adults.

Principles to Develop

MAKE WORK SEEM FUN

Toddlers and preschoolers believe whatever their parents say, so they can be taught that work can be fun. Parents can make a game of putting away toys and groceries. As teenagers, these children will be hard working and helpful around the house. Parents must be careful about what they say in front of their children. If the children hear, "Mommy would like to have fun with you, but she has to work now," then the parents are sending the message that work is negative and undesirable. Instead, one could say, "You can have fun with me while I sweep the floor. You could hold the dustpan for me. Wouldn't that be fun?"

Teach children that no domestic or garden work is beneath them, since all these chores are respectable. It is important to convey the message that work is a privilege (not a right). Parents have to share with their children the blessings of physical work. What if they could no longer engage in their usual activities because they were handicapped or unemployed or had an injured back? Everyone has to be aware of the blessings of a healthy body. Parents should miss no opportunity to pass on to their children an enthusiasm for physical work and responsibility.

Parents should try to make chore time fun (with cheerful songs, tasteful joking, or interesting conversation). An atmosphere of cheerfulness helps improve children's attitude toward work and responsibility. If the whole family's work and play can be scheduled at the same times of day, it will avoid a feeling of resentment which can result from one child working at chores while the rest of the family has fun. If yard work needs to be done, it is more enjoyable if the whole family does it together.

"THE TEN RULE" TO KEEP UP ON YARD WORK

Whenever the children go outside, they are required to do ten small tasks before they can play. This could be picking ten stones or weeds, picking off ten dead flowers, putting ten large dead leaves into the trash, or picking ten diseased leaves. Or the child may do one larger task like raking or watering instead. This teaches them to help take care of property.

Parents should encourage their children to grow their own food whenever possible.

A Libyan described to me how he divided his garden into 6 strips and gave a strip to each of his 6 children, who could grow whatever they wanted. If his wife needed vegetables for the family meals, she would ask the children whether she could have some tomatoes or peppers or whatever was available. The garden was well tended and this system put an end to all the arguments about the allocation of gardening tasks!

SYLVIA HUNT

DO WORK TOGETHER

Parents might find it helpful to use the word "we" in training children. For example, they could say to them, "We always put our dirty clothes in the hamper, like this, instead of on the floor." Children like to be included, and using the word "we" encourages in them the right behavior without lecturing. Instead of telling a child "Clean up your room!" The parent could say, "Let's clean up your room together."

Children learn best and develop responsible habits when they work with their parents. They feel loved and come to associate work and responsibility with their parents' love. This gives them a more positive attitude toward work later.

Preschoolers should be allowed to make some choices. There are also times when a child needs to hear, "This is what you are going to do." Do not to make the mistake of training the children to be lazy also by failing to make them do what they do not feel like doing. An essential part of responsibility is learning to do what needs to be done no matter how one feels. Be both loving and firm at the same time.

BUILD RESPONSIBILITY GRADUALLY

One mistake parents make is to let their children play (without any work) until they reach a "responsible" age. Then suddenly there is a lot of work to do and too many responsibilities to fulfill. Help children gradually take on more work and responsibility every year. In some developing countries, children (especially girls), are expected to look after the baby and carry fuel and water as well as help with the domestic responsibilities. Children as young as 8 may be sent out to work as maids and houseboys.

A baby begins with no work whatsoever, while 19 year olds work 40 hours a week. The parents' job is to build responsibility gradually. Children who are used to increasing levels of responsibility will better adjust to full-time work when they are adults.

The schedule can be started in the preschool years (with tasks such as putting clothes in the hamper and picking up the toys). Other tasks suitable for the children's age and abilities can be slowly added. Children of six can set the table every day, make their beds, help dry dishes, feed a pet, clear the table after a meal, and put away laundry with a little help or guidance. Gradually, new responsibilities can be introduced every year. Teenagers can do the laundry and dishes (taking turns with siblings), mow the lawn, trim the bushes, and babysit younger siblings. Teenagers can also do some part-time work and voluntary work in the community.

DISCOURAGE A 'THAT'S NOT MY JOB ATTITUDE'

Children need to be taught that responsibilities should be borne by a family together. Children who are allowed to bicker over fairness miss the point of being helpful to others. If the focus is always on who picked more weeds or whether two children dried the same number of dishes, children develop contentious attitudes that are not conducive to family harmony. Build a teamwork mentality. Parents can tell the children, "When the table is cleared and wiped, we can all watch a video or go to the park," or, "If we get the yard work all done today, we can have ice cream or popcorn tonight." "After we get the cleaning done,

let's all have a special trip together to celebrate." Group rewards encourage harmony, teamwork, and responsibility. The children can be asked to fill in for one another when one child is sick. It is important to encourage them to help one another with the work and to bear one another's burdens. The older children have to help the younger children with their schoolwork and the younger children should help the older ones with their chores.

Practical Suggestions

- Do not overwhelm children with too many tasks. Parents need to take into account children's abilities and temperaments and give them tasks that they can achieve successfully. Success and praise will motivate them to do more whereas overload can result in failure and destroy motivation.
- "Expect" children to be responsible. Parent expectations motivate children. When they give children a task, they can discuss the acceptable time in which to do it. Then they should let the children do it and assume it will be done. Allow children to complete the task in their own way without watching over them or constantly reminding them about it. If they do not manage to finish the task, then the parents can help them.
- Do not call a child "irresponsible". Even if the children do something totally irresponsible, such as going to the movies when they promised to help their friends study for a test, the parents should refrain from labeling them. Instead, it is better to encourage them to make it up to their friends as soon as possible. If a child tends to be forgetful, parents should avoid making remarks such as "if your head wasn't attached, you'd probably forget that, too." Such comments are hurtful and discouraging. Label the behavior, not the person.
- Children need help in organizing their schedule. Show them how to estimate how much time homework will take and to budget accordingly. Help children make an after-school schedule. Show them how there is enough time to do all their work, and to bathe, and still have time to relax and play outside.

- Divide tasks into smaller tasks. When children are given reports to write, parents can discuss in advance how much time will be needed to go to the library or search the Internet and write the various sections of the report. Children need help to break the project into manageable parts and to make a plan to achieve each part.
- Parents should not do their children's homework for them. It is surprising how many parents are caught in the trap of doing their children's homework, either with them, or for them. Children are to be told that their homework is their responsibility, not that of their parents, since it should be a task that the children are capable of doing on their own. However, children need some help now and then, and they do need to be tested for spelling or vocabulary.
- Children have to learn to take responsibility for their own mistakes. Parents should not rush in to save them.
- Children need to be taught to manage money. Children should not spend more than they have – whether it is an allowance, gift money from grandparents, or money earned from a job. It is not acceptable to borrow when they want

something and repay it when they have more money. This is poor training. Instead, they have to wait until they have enough of their own funds and not to go into debt. Children who have jobs need to learn to set aside some money for charity and for savings. As children grow older, parents can discuss with them how adults manage their money and the types of savings and investment plans people use. This is an ideal opportunity to explain to children that usury is banned in all the Holy Books and to teach them about Islamic banking.

- Encourage children to get a job. This can be voluntary work, or an after-school or summer job. Children whose parents run a business (for example, a shop, hotel, restaurant, farm or market) should help in the workplace from an early age. Children will learn to be on time, to be pleasant despite how they feel, and to make sure their duties are done.

General Advice

- Children should not be taught when they are tired or hungry.
- Criticism is poison when it is combined with teaching.
- Responsibility requires Patience.

Just like in the real work force... but parents cannot dismiss their child!!

Irresponsible behavior is totally unacceptable in the work force. All employees know their duties and they are required to perform them at certain times or risk dismissal. Although parents cannot dismiss their children, yet they can give them guidance and train them to be responsible.

There are some days when children cannot do their jobs (because they may be spending the night at a friend's home or going on a trip). However, just like a real job, they can ask for a morning or day off, though they have to ask in advance. They cannot come up to their parents at the beginning of the day and say: "I need today off because I was at a party last night."

Connect Privilege with Responsibility: Examples

Many children believe that they are entitled to whatever advantages they have, as though their parents were created to serve them. These children have a difficult time accepting the responsibilities of adulthood. One family has an annual ritual. Each year, each child is given a new privilege and a new responsibility: One is contingent upon the other. The children discuss their choices with their parents, who then take their concerns seriously.

Example 1: Your daughter has wanted a cat for several years. She agrees to babysit her brother once a week. For this, she will earn the privilege of having a cat, although she has to take care of the cat herself. And she should be reminded that if she neglects the animal, it will be given away!

Parents should impose appropriate consequences, which means that it is unhelpful to their children to "rescue" them too quickly when they make mistakes. Parents often nag, and then bail out their children anyway. One of the best ways children learn responsibility is from the impact of reasonable punishments. If the consequences are appropriate, the children will be less likely to forget and be irresponsible next time. For example, paying a teenager's parking violation tickets is wrong, and parents are not to do it!

Example 2: Your son was asked to pick up a carton of milk on his way home from school and forgot. Instead of rushing to the store herself, Mother serves dinner with no milk, and the next morning there is none to put on her son's cereal.

Example 3: Daughter leaves the house late several times and misses the school bus, despite her mother's attempts to make her get up on time. Each time, the mother has had to drive her daughter to school, lecturing her on punctuality during the trip.

However, the daughter will be more likely to change her behavior if her mother stops talking and lets her walk to school. If this is unsafe, the mother needs to tell her daughter that she will drive her later, when she has finished some chores. Daughter will be embarrassed to arrive late at school after classes have already started, and this situation will give her a chance to correct her mistakes, for errors can be learning opportunities. There is no point in parents losing their temper at their children's failures, for yelling rarely accomplishes anything and makes everyone feel worse. Instead, they have to find ways to improve the situation, for the children will learn more than they would from scolding, and the parents will feel better too.

Example 4: It is the son's turn to make dinner. He forgets, stays late at school to play football, and arrives home late. Instead of yelling at him or starting dinner herself, Mother could try saying, "We have a problem now. What do you think we can do about it?" He may decide to boil eggs, make a quick cheese sandwich, or trade shifts with the person whose turn is the following night. Even more important than putting dinner on the table, he will be motivated to take his commitments seriously.

Some children fall into the habit of blaming other people or circumstances for their mistakes. However, this can only deny them the opportunity to become the best they can be. Parents can think of situations where they, as children, may have refused to accept total responsibility. Usually, these situations made their parents disappointed with their children because of their irresponsibility.

Children may feel that their parents are always telling them what to do. Perhaps it is because the children have not taken the initiative to accept total responsibility. The children have to take the initiative, and to change the negatives into positives, and then the parents will stop telling them what to do.

The Consequences of Sexual Irresponsibility

Between 2002 and 2007 the UK had 268 pregnant girls aged 12; 2,527 aged 13; 14,777 aged 14 and 45,861 aged 15, however these figures could be just the tip of the iceberg, many young girls could have had miscarriages or illegal abortions which would not appear in official statistics.

According to Norman Wells, of the Family Education Trust, a spiraling number of sexually transmitted infections coupled with a growing number of young people carrying emotional baggage into adulthood are just some of the bitter consequences of our highly sexualised society today where children are encouraged to dress and act in a sexually precocious way. He blames this on 'grossly irresponsible' sex educators who by 'encouraging young people to use contraception rather than in discouraging them from engaging in sexual activity in the first place exacerbate the situation. (Martin 2010)

The Qur'an addresses actions and consequences:

> *And anyone who does an atom's weight of good, shall see it; and anyone who does an atom's weight of evil, shall see it.* (Qur'an 99: 7–8)

Responsibility and accountability are basic principles that we must teach our children. In the next chapter we deal with the concept of independence, which is necessary in order to learn responsibility.

Require your children to do their share of the household chores and hold them accountable. They may be disappointed if they do not succeed, but they are doomed if they do not try.

Activities

ACTIVITY 57: GOD IS WATCHING *ALL* GROUPS

Let a child read these stories and then have everyone comment.

a) At a children's summer camp at the dinner line there was a sign saying: "Take only one apple, God is watching." At the end of the line, there were cookies with no sign. One child wrote a sign and put it on the cookies: "Take as much as you like because God is busy watching the apples." *(*PASTOR PETE MARTIN AT IIIT RAMADAN RECEPTION, OCTOBER 2007*)*

b) When 'Umar ibn al-Khattāb was Caliph and he saw a merchant cheating, he told his "announcer" to declare loudly: "Whoever cheats is not one of us. It is unlawful to add water to milk before selling it."

Afterwards, the following conversation took place in a house in al-Madinah:

Mother: My daughter, get up and add water to the milk to get more money.

Daughter (politely): Did you not know that 'Umar's announcer today declared that no water is to be added to the milk?

Mother: Do what I tell you, neither 'Umar nor his announcer will see us!

Daughter: How can I obey the ruler in public and disobey him in private? If 'Umar does not see us, the Lord of 'Umar sees us! Always!

ACTIVITY 58: A LESSON ON ACCIDENTS AND RESPONSIBILITY!

Answer the following question, and then think about the comments below.

Your 12-year-old son is playing baseball in your back yard when he hits the ball and breaks the neighbor's window. You:

a) Telephone the neighbors to tell them that you will pay for the window, then punish your son.

b) Tell your son to go to the neighbor and explain that he accidentally broke the window and that he will pay for it. You pay for the window and deduct it from your son's allowance.

c) Tell your son to go to the neighbor and admit that he accidentally broke the window and that he will pay for the repair from his savings (if any) or earn extra money to pay promptly for the repair.

COMMENTS: This is an ideal situation to teach your son to accept responsibility for his actions, without becoming angry or having to punish him. If you answered:

a) When you call the neighbor, your son does not learn anything except that someone will bail him out in a time of crisis. Why punish him? It was an accident.

b) Good first step (sending the son to tell the neighbor about the broken window).

c) Excellent! Now your son takes FULL responsibility for his action. This method works better than answer (b).

CHAPTER 19

Teaching Independence

Growing Up "Dependently" in America

Parents in America complain that many children continue to expect too much from them for too long. As a society, America is failing to prepare its children for leaving home and becoming independent.

THERE IS A TERRIBLE irony at work here. Although parents today want their children to be happy, the formula by which they raise them is a prescription for unhappiness. The children have not learned to be autonomous, because they have not been expected to be. Parents are spending more and more, financially and emotionally, on their children's well-being. They are sincere in their dedication, trying to do a good job to realize their deepest ambitions for their children.

Super-parents are identifiable in two principal ways: by what they do for their children, and by what they give to their children. Typically, they do everything they can to make sure their children have every advantage. They decorate their children's rooms in stimulating colors, they buy a wide variety of educational toys and they give the baby a series of expensive massages. They space their children according to the advice of child-development experts. They register their children for gymnastics classes, send them to the most progressive preschools and enroll them for soccer at age four. They sacrifice time, friendships, and their own interests – sometimes even their sex lives. They let their children interrupt them and drop everything to take advantage of every teaching moment. Most important of all, they take every opportunity to build up their children's self-esteem (by complimenting them on how smart, athletic, artistic, talented, and good-looking they are). They schedule elaborate birthday parties as if their children were princes and princesses. Even when the kids become spoiled, the parents keep giving them gifts and fulfilling every request. These parents do not want to deprive their kids in any way. Unfortunately, this leads to disaster.The true deprivation for their children lies in not being expected to leave the house and not being permitted to experience independence.

Many of the parents of today's young adults in the United States were raised quite differently. At that time, children only mixed with other children, and parents with other parents. Some mothers would tell their kids: "Don't bother me unless you're bleeding." Sports were after-school rather than weekend activities and parents did not always come to the games. Parents usually left their children's schooling to the teachers. Parents did not worry so much whether children were happy; they worried whether they themselves were happy.

DO WE MEAN DEPENDENCE OR INTERDEPENDENCE?

Teaching independence to children does not mean to sever relationships with parents completely. There has to be both autonomy as well as interdependence among all family members.

When today's parents were children in the United States, families were bigger, houses were smaller and services were limited. Many children worked part-time during high school and college to help pay their own expenses. They acquired cars only when they could pay for them. Both parents and children assumed that once young people graduated from high school or college and found employment, they would become financially self-sufficient. That assumption led to children's independence.

Today's parents seem to care a great deal about their children feeling good, and often forget to teach them about being good. There is not enough emphasis on becoming decent human beings who think about others and not just themselves. Children who have been given too much have less empathy for other people and too much concern for themselves. Spoiled children make bad roommates and even worse spouses. When these children grow up, the parents' job is not over. There are more requests or demands and the parents do not say no – or they say it but do not stick to it. They want their children to be happy, no matter what. These parents also believe that giving them more will make them happier. What results is an irresponsible and dependent set of adult children and an increasingly resentful group of parents. They are sick and tired and have no idea what to do about it.

This phenomenon is by no means limited to affluent families. There are American children at every income level who see their parents only as sources of money. Many parents save money and live simply, yet donate much of what is left over to their sons and daughters. The children learn to be wasteful and overly dependent.

When children's achievements matter so much that they make parents constantly intervene, an important boundary between "self" and "other" is blurred, and the children's ability to learn is stunted. Appropriate parental help is necessary and important. Yet even in cases of physical or mental illness it is wrong to give too much help and to treat adult children like infants. Sometimes, children have been so over-directed that they go on to have a terrible time making decisions, from "What should I wear?" to "Should I take this job?" or "Should I marry this person?" Those who have been given too much become young adults who resent their parents' role in their lives even as they seek it.

Developing self-reliance and confidence
Not total dependence and fear to take decisions

A Myth

THE CASE OF CRYING INFANTS

According to psychologist Jeffry Simpson: "If you are insecure at age one, you are more likely to experience negative emotions in your relationship with your current partner when you are 21."

Simpson and his colleagues have closely tracked 78 people over a quarter-century, starting when they were babies. Mothers dropped infants into a laboratory, and were asked to leave briefly. The infants became upset. When the mothers returned, some infants clung tightly to their mothers, sought comfort and in a little while, they calmed down. Others refused to calm down even after lengthy soothing. A third set of babies refused to turn to their mothers for comfort at all.

The secure child learns, "I can count on my parents to calm me down," and learns to turn to others. The insecure child learns, "my parent is rejecting" or "my parent is neglectful," or "I have to protest to get attention." If children are insecure at age one they may grow up to be weak and dependent. Infants who are cared for properly become secure, and are then able to become independent. Infants who are abandoned or neglected become insecure, and are then less able to become independent.

Crying infants who turn to their mothers for support must receive it. Once comforted, they resume their explorations of the world. Romantic partners similarly become more interdependent once their emotional needs are met. It is much easier for people to take risks and accept challenges when they know someone is available to help them and comfort them if something goes wrong. The more secure individuals are able to turn to other people for support.

People who are confident enough to reach out to others for help – and to whom help is given – become truly capable of interdependence.

Age-Specific Accomplishments

Young children think of themselves as capable and independent if their parents teach them to be capable and independent. Children learn autonomy when their parents give love and support, encourage exploration and curiosity, teach skills, and allow the children to make appropriate choices. Their enthusiasm for children's exploration sends a message that they value these activities.

"I Can do it Myself!"

Self-care tasks lead to independence. The efforts of infants to lift their heads, roll over, or sit up is a significant step toward independence. Love, affection, and nurturing will help them reach that goal.

A safe environment is paramount once children are mobile. Curious toddlers have little judgment of their safety. Independence can be encouraged by giving them small choices. Give toddlers a measure of control over their lives, like choosing which story to read, which song to sing, or which shirt to wear. Preschoolers are capable of expressing many thoughts, feelings and needs, and they are ready to take bigger steps toward independence. Encourage toddlers to put away clothes and toys, set the table, fold towels, or help with meal preparation. This builds a sense of competence and independence.

Once children reach school age, there are many opportunities to facilitate independence. Decisions about friends, school projects, and play are all a part of their daily life choices. Financial decision-making skills can be taught by giving older children responsibility with money (for example, providing a weekly allowance or designating a child as a family treasurer). It is important to honor children's choices whenever possible. By showing their genuine enthusiasm and recognizing the many small tasks young children accomplish, parents are helping them gain control over their world, and preparing them for a healthy, independent life.

Let Toddlers Find Their Own Way

Children want to try things for themselves. You may find it hard to keep up when your children switch from a demanding "let me do it" attitude one minute, to being clingy and afraid to let go of you the next. The following points help in dealing with toddlers:

> **"...do all you can to build feelings of security in children by giving lots of loving attention..."**

- Defiance and disobedience (refusing to comply with adults' requests) are an essential part of a toddler's desire of independence.
- Following the toddlers' lead will eliminate much heartache. If they want to cling to their parents, then they should be allowed to do so. If they want to do things their own way, then the parents have to go along with it (as long as it is reasonable).
- Distraction is a particularly useful tactic when toddlers do not want to follow orders. Alternatively, the children can be allowed to make choices and offered some control.
- Orders and ultimatums should be avoided. They provoke power struggles and endless battles with most toddlers. Teaching by leading is more productive. Toddlers seem to resent any form of control by adults, preferring to get dressed and feed themselves without parental help. This contrary behavior is quite normal, even if parents find it irritating.

Separation Anxiety: Handling Clingy Behavior

The parents are the most important people to their children, which is why a young child's fear of strangers and separation from the family is natural. Having spent the previous year or two attached to the parents, it seems reasonable not to let parents get out of their sight! Separation is difficult for parents and children. Here are a few guiding points in dealing with separation.

- Parents should make every effort to build security by giving as much love and attention as possible and cuddling up or playing with their child. Building a sense of security requires patience and should be continued until the child feels ready to be independent.
- Separations have to be kept short when it is necessary to leave the toddler, especially

for the first few times, and enough time needs to be allowed for the child to know his/her new caregiver beforehand.

- It is important to reassure the child. Even short partings, such as going to the nursery for the morning, may be difficult for a sensitive toddler. Parents need to take time to talk to their child in advance about the changes in his/her care and give every reassurance that they will be coming back. The handover must never be rushed.
- Parents should not just slip away behind the child's back. Although goodbyes can be upsetting, it is less worrying for the child in the end if the parents do not just disappear. It is important to be happy and avoid extending the departure, because showing stress only causes the child to feel anxious.
- "The clinging toddler" – if the child clings to the parent even during the daily routine at home or at the market, the parent should try to stay calm and continue as usual. Although it may not be easy to make lunch or continue talking to someone while the child is clamped to the parent in this way, eventually, the toddler will feel more secure and will let go.

It is natural for parents to feel rather sad when their baby moves on to the next developmental stage.

Teenagers – The Reality

Small children need to be cared for in a manner that is protective and authoritarian, for they have very little experience and knowledge. Due to their smaller size, young children have to be constantly protected and supported. Sometimes, parents cannot explain properly why they have to behave in a particular way; they just have to tell their youngsters to do as they are told.

With teenagers, it is different. Instead of being a "commander" parents have to be a skilled negotiator who makes compromises.

Teenagers have to learn how to survive on their own; they will leave home soon, and will have to survive without the help of Mom and Dad. It is the parents' duty not to cling to the children whom they have loved, and possibly spoiled, but to help them to be self-reliant. The parents have to change from a tight rein to a slack rein, and then be prepared to hand over the reins altogether. Teenagers have to learn how to be less dependent on parents. This is difficult when there is conflict with the parents.

Teens become lazy when the mother has chosen to become a household servant for her family. They do not become self-reliant at all, but grow up expecting to have someone to wait on them.

The hard thing to realize for the mother who is always a servant is that despite her good intentions, it is likely that the teenagers will feel only resentful and frustrated toward her, instead of being full of love and gratitude, as she had hoped. Their resentment builds up, because the children grow up feeling that they can do more or less whatever they want, and get away with it. If boundaries are not clear to teenagers, they may be unsure of what they are or are not permitted to do, and it is human nature to push to the limit.

Some parents are aggressive and demand to be in control of every situation. This attitude leads to conflict with the young adults, who are trying to learn independence. It is the parents' duty to help teenagers take control of their own lives. The parents themselves are going to lose some control. When parents discuss issues with an adult friend, there are many times when they have to differ because their minds are not carbon copies. Parents have to learn to allow children the same

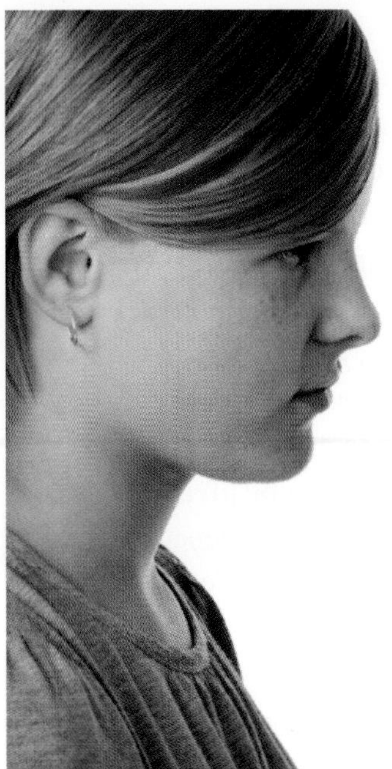

freedom to be different. They cannot control the minds of their teenagers; they can only encourage them to see a different point of view. Parents should not force them. If the parents suffer from shock, they will have to overcome it. If they suffer from disappointment, they will have to learn to live with it. These reactions are normally the parents' problem, not that of the children.

However, there is a growing problem of AIDS, drugs, and violence. The dangers to children are more insidious than ever, and "learning from one's own mistakes" can carry a very heavy price. "What happened to my baby?" and "Why don't you just grow up!" are common expressions of some parents. Adolescence is a time when parents and children redefine their relationship for the better, and when adults must offer teenagers guidance and comfort that they will appreciate and remember.

Most parents realize that they have less say over what their children do just as consequences of their children's actions become

For some fathers, turning their daughters loose to "hop down the branch" is tough. They overprotect, so their daughters develop long-term dependence on them. Then the girls do not learn to make their own decisions. They cannot renew a driver's license or fill out a car insurance form or open a bank account, or drive a two-hour trip on their own. Parents should not let this happen. They can give their daughter autonomy when she is small. A sleep-over at a friend's house or a week of summer camp under trusted parents' supervision will help.

One definition of independence!

Independence is the number of choices, options or alternatives that parents give to their child.

greater. Parents have to accept that their children will want to fire them as "manager," and hence, they have to try to be rehired as a "consultant," who offers guidance and continues to exert influence, yet learns to relinquish control. If the parents cling to control, they will have endless fights.

While teenagers are well known for telling their parents to leave them alone, former teenagers agree that most adolescents secretly do need to know that their parents are concerned about them.

Teenagers who have enough real responsibility and autonomy in their lives are less likely to look for it in risky ways.

For example, although Jimenez grew up in an area where gangs were active, his parents warned him against becoming involved with a gang. He says, "I knew my parents cared about me, so I didn't need that family structure that gangs provide, and my parents taught me to think independently and not follow other people."

Trust in Children + Parental Guidance → Autonomy, Responsibility

Parenting Styles Impact: Authority-Based vs. Power-Based

Authority-based parenting means parenting that fosters and encourages self–reliance, whereas power-based parenting means parenting that fosters and encourages dependence. Although many adults have a difficult time making decisions from time to time, for some, it is a chronic problem that wreaks daily havoc in their lives. Deciding where to go for dinner, what to purchase, or what class to take can sometimes be a painful event. For some, it seems always better to defer to the judgment of others than to make their own judgment.

Two common fears develop in children who are raised by power-based parents. The first fear is a fear of failure. For "decision-phobic" adults, their difficulty often grows out of a childhood in which someone constantly made decisions for them. Too often, there was someone willing to protect them from any possibility of failure; or it was simply easier to make a quick decision for them. The children of power-based parenting say, "why risk failing if someone else will do it for me?" These children grow up less able to think and avoid decision making. In addition, by being protected from failure, they are likewise deprived of the good feelings that accompany successful decision making.

A second fear is the fear of rejection. Children who are raised with the dependency that often accompanies power- based parenting, tend to grow up needing the approval of Mom and Dad. Although in their early years this can be healthy and desired, eventually, their self-assessment and self-approval declines. When self-approval is weak, they will transfer that need for approval from Mom and Dad to others in their life. Their attitude may be: "Since making the wrong decision could lead to disapproval and rejection, I'd better remain passive and dependent."

On the other hand, authority-based parents teach their children to bravely deal with failure and rejection. At the same time, they help children take educated risks, which is essential to good decision making. By encouraging self-reliance, parents provide children with the opportunity to learn and succeed by giving them the chance to actually fail. The saying: "show me a success and I'll show you a failure" implies that many successes come as

a result of having failed. Children will learn from those failures by evaluating what went wrong, deciding what to avoid next time, and then trying again.

Establish guidelines, but do not confuse flexibility with inconsistency. Since consistency fosters safety, predictability and an understanding of cause and effect, it is an important characteristic of parenting. The key is to be willing and able to be flexible and, at the same time, consistent. Flexibility that is an earmark of authority-based parenting refers to fairness and the willingness to reevaluate decisions, based on new information that comes to light. Guidelines established by authority-based parents sometimes change, but only when there is a good reason.

Rigidity, on the other hand, is refusal to change even when new circumstances require you to change. The message children receive from their power-based parents is "because I said so", or, "because I'm your parent", or "do as I say" (without any logic or sense). Children may eventually reach such a level of frustration that they violate their parents' rigid guidelines. They begin doing things "my way and for myself" without thinking through the "cause and effect". Since they have not learned how to survive failure and rejection their rebellion leads to more mistakes that they are not equipped to handle. The inevitable outcome is frustration, self-defeat, and poor self-esteem. We see signs of this throughout society today in the form of delinquent and destructive teens.

The other unfortunate outcome of power-based parenting is that some children react in the opposite ways to those described above. They become spineless adults who allow someone else to control them. This results in marriages where one person, needing to control and dominate, seeks another who needs to be controlled and dominated. Such a match makes for a miserable relationship that often ends in pain and sadness.

The child of power-based parents may have difficulties with his/her spouse during marriage: overly anxious or overly argumentative!

Skills to Build Autonomy in Children

Issues like gangs, drugs, or sex involve real dangers and lasting consequences. These dangers can sometimes provoke parents to become dictators instead of consultants. Young people say that during these difficult issues is exactly when trusting one's children is crucial (Faber and Mazlish 1982).

Liz, 20, who grew up in California, says she appreciated the fact that her parents dealt openly with any questions she had about sex or drugs. They recognized that children tried new things, yet they also gave her a strong message about keeping away from sex and drugs. Those of her classmates whose parents forbade discussion of drugs or drinking, were the ones who always drank behind their parents' backs. Encouraging children to exercise their own "decision-making" is wiser than making all decisions for them, no matter how much father or mother knows best. Teenagers who have enough real responsibility and autonomy are less likely to do risky things.

When people are placed in dependent positions, they experience feelings of helplessness, worthlessness, resentment, and anger. This presents a dilemma for parents. On the one hand, children are clearly dependent upon us because of inexperience. There is so much we have to do for them, and tell them, and show them. On the other hand, their dependency can lead to hostility. Fortunately, the opportunities to encourage children's autonomy present themselves every day. Here are some skills that can help children rely on themselves: (Faber and Mazlish 1982)

• Whenever parents listen to children's feelings, or share their feelings with them, or invite them to problem-solve with them, they encourage their self-reliance. One mother said: "I can still hear my grandmother saying admiringly of a neighbor, 'She is the most wonderful mother. She does everything for her child!'" Many people grew up believing that good mothers did almost everything for their children. Worse still, they thought for them as well. Over-control results in arguments over trivial issues, a contest of wills, and a lot of frustration.

• Parents have to gradually turn over to children responsibilities that rightfully belong to them. Whenever parents feel themselves starting to be involved, they need to ask themselves, "Do I have any choice here? Must I take over? Can I put the children in charge?"

• A good habit for parents is to ask themselves often: What do I say or do that keeps the child dependent upon me? And avoid it. What could I say or do to encourage my child's autonomy? And do it.

Trying to protect children from disappointment also prevents them from hoping, striving, dreaming and achieving.

AN UNBELIEVABLE TRUE STORY!

One mother related this story: I remember the satisfaction from being totally needed by my three children. And so it was with mixed feelings that I discovered that a mechanical alarm clock could wake them more efficiently than I; and it was also with mixed feelings that I gave up my job as reader of bedtime stories, when the children learned to read by themselves.

It was my own conflicting emotions about their growing independence that helped me understand a story by a nursery school teacher, who described her efforts to convince a young mother that her son would be fine if she wasn't sitting in the classroom with him. Five minutes after the mother left, the child needed to go to the bathroom. When the teacher urged him to go, he mumbled unhappily, "Can't cause my Mommy isn't here. She claps for me when I finish." The teacher said: "You can go to the bathroom and then clap for yourself." The child looked confused, but the teacher led him to the bathroom and waited outside. After a few minutes, she heard the sound of applause.

Later that day the mother called the teacher to say that her child came home saying, "Mommy, I can clap for myself. I don't need you in the bathroom anymore!"

"Would you believe it," the teacher exclaimed, "the mother said she was actually depressed about this."

LET CHILDREN MAKE CHOICES

Ask a child whether he wants a half glass of milk or a whole glass of milk, or whether he wants his toast light or dark. To him each small choice represents one more opportunity to exert control over his life. He may become resentful and stubborn if he is never given a choice.

He is always hearing commands:

"You must take your medicine".

"Stop drumming on the table".

"Go to bed now".

If we can offer him a choice, often that choice is enough to reduce his resentment.

"I can see how much you dislike this medicine. Would it be easier to take it with apple juice or orange juice?"

"The drumming really bothers me. You can stop drumming and stay or you can drum in your own room. You decide."

"It's Mommy and Daddy's time to talk and your time to be in bed. Do you want to sleep now, or do you want to play a while in bed and call us when you're ready to sleep?"

> The persons hardest to convince they're at the retirement age are children at bedtime.
> (BROWN 1994)

A forced choice is not much of a choice at all and becomes just another way to control a child. One alternative is to invite the child to suggest choices that would be acceptable to everyone. One father said: "My wife and I were about to cross the street with Hany, who is three, and the baby. He hates it when we hold his hand and struggles to get loose – sometimes in the middle of the street. Before we crossed, I said, 'Hany, you can take hold of Mommy's hand or my hand. Or maybe you have another safe idea.' He thought and said, 'I'll hold the carriage.' His choice was fine with us."

SHOW RESPECT FOR A CHILD'S STRUGGLE

When children are told that something is "easy," it may not help them. If they succeed in doing something easy, they feel that they have not accomplished much. If they fail, then they have failed to do something simple.

However, if they are told instead, "You can do it, and it is easy" or "That can be hard," they get another message. If they succeed, they can be proud of doing something difficult. If they fail, they are satisfied that this task was a tough one.

Some think that parents are being insincere when they say "That can be hard." However, if they look at the task from the point of view of an inexperienced child, they would realize that the first time one does anything new, it really is hard. (Avoid saying, "That must be hard for you". A child might think "Why for me? Why not for anyone else?").

For some parents, it is unbearable to just stand and watch a child struggle (offering just empathy). Nevertheless, rather than doing the job for the child, it is better to give useful information instead: "Sometimes it helps if you push the end of the zipper all the way down into the little case before you pull it up." Or "Sometimes it helps if you turn the knob of a lock a few times before you try the combination again." The phrase "sometimes it helps" is particularly useful here because if it does not help, the child is spared feelings of inadequacy.

DON'T ASK TOO MANY QUESTIONS

"Where did you go?"... "Out." "What did you do?"... "Nothing." Children use defensive tactics to ignore questions they are neither ready nor willing to answer. "I do not know" or "Leave me alone." This does not mean that parents may never ask the children questions. The important thing is to be sensitive to the possible effect of the questions.

One common parental inquiry that seems to be bothersome is: "Did you have fun today?" This is an unreasonable demand to make upon children. Not only did they have to go to the party (school, play, camp…) but also the expectation is that they should have enjoyed themselves. If they did not, they have their own disappointment to cope with plus that of their parents. The children feel that they have disappointed their parents by not having a good time.

DON'T RUSH TO ANSWER QUESTIONS

In growing up, children ask a bewildering variety of questions: "What is a rainbow?" "Why can't the baby go back to where he came from?" "Do you have to go to college?" Parents often feel put on the spot, and search their minds for immediate, appropriate answers. Usually, the children have already done some thinking about the answer. What they want is to explore their thoughts further. Normally, there is always time for the adult to supply the "correct" answer later, if it still seems important. Giving immediate answers is not helpful to children. It is as if the parents are doing their mental exercise or wider thinking for them. It is more helpful to children to have their question returned to them for further examination:

"You wonder about that. What do you think?"

Parents might even repeat the question.

"Why can't people just do whatever they want?"

They can credit the questioner:

"You're asking an important question, one that philosophers have asked for centuries." There need not be any hurry; the process of searching for the answer is valuable in itself.

ENCOURAGE CHILDREN TO USE SOURCES OUTSIDE THE HOME

One way to lessen children's feelings of dependency upon their family is to show them that there is a larger community out there with valuable resources waiting to be tapped. The world is not an alien place; there is help to be had when it is needed.

Aside from the obvious benefit to children, it also relieves the parents of having to be the controller all the time. The school nurse can discuss sensible eating habits with the overweight child; the shoe salesman can explain what continual use of sneakers does to feet; the librarian can help a youngster wrestle with a research paper; and the dentist can explain what happens to teeth that are not brushed or the effects of eating too much candy. All of these outside sources can replace volumes of lectures from Mom or Dad.

DON'T TAKE AWAY HOPE

Much of the pleasure of life lies in dreaming, fantasizing, anticipating, and planning. By preventing children from having any disappointment, parents can deprive them of important pleasant experiences.

Hints for Parents

Here are some additional ways of building independence in children:

LET THEM OWN THEIR OWN BODY

Parents have to refrain from constantly brushing the hair out of their children's eyes, straightening their shoulders, tucking in their shirts, and rearranging their collar. Children feel this excessive behavior as an invasion of their physical privacy.

DON'T TALK ABOUT THE CHILDREN IN THEIR PRESENCE NO MATTER HOW YOUNG THEY ARE

Parents should picture themselves standing next to their mother as she tells a friend the following:

"In the first grade he was unhappy because of his reading, now he's doing better." Or, "Don't mind him. He's a little shy."

When children hear themselves discussed this way, they are embarrassed. They are being treated like objects and possessions.

LET CHILDREN ANSWER FOR THEMSELVES

Again and again the parent, in the presence of the child, is asked questions like:

"Does he like the new baby?" "Why isn't he playing with his new toy?" The real mark of respect of the child's autonomy is to say to the inquiring adult, "Amir can tell you. He's the one who knows."

SHOW RESPECT FOR YOUR CHILD'S EVENTUAL "READINESS"

Sometimes a child wants to do something very much, but is not emotionally or physically ready for it. For example: she wants to use the bathroom like a "big girl", but she cannot yet. He wants to go swimming like his brother, yet he is afraid of the water. She wants to stop sucking her thumb, yet when she is tired, it feels so good.

Instead of forcing, urging, or embarrassing youngsters, parents can express their confidence in their children in a positive way:

"One of these days, you'll use the bathroom just like Mommy or Daddy."

"I'm not worried. When you're ready, you'll get into the water."

"When you decide to, you'll stop sucking your thumb."

WATCH OUT FOR TOO MANY "NO'S."

There will be many times when parents have to deny their children's desires. Yet some children receive a blunt "No" as a direct attack upon their autonomy. They scream, have tantrums, call names, or turn sullen. They barrage the parent with, "Why not...? You're mean...I hate you!" It is exhausting even for the most patient of parents. Should parents give in and say "Yes" to everything? Obviously not. Fortunately, there are some helpful alternatives that allow the parents to be firm without inviting a confrontation. Examples are making the home safe for children to move around in, or distracting their attention to something else without saying "No".

CONSULT YOUR CHILD

Many parents do not discuss with their children matters concerning them. If they want to reward them with dinner for passing their exams, it is only appropriate that the children choose their favorite restaurant. It is their party, not yours. Also, if parents want to buy them a toy or a game, they have to be consulted; otherwise parents will buy toys according to their own taste, not the children's. Parents end up playing with the toy and the child is bored watching or crying. It is important that children are included in the parents' affairs instead of the parents forcing their likes and dislikes on them. When children are treated as partners, it will help to improve attitudes both ways.

'Umar ibn al-Khaṭṭāb said:

Play with your child for the first seven years, teach and discipline him for the second seven years, and then make him your companion for the third seven years. Then let him be free.

To call [certain traits of character] virtues in their isolation is like taking the skeleton for the living body... Morals concern nothing less than the whole character, and the whole character is identical with the man in all his concrete make-up and manifestations. To possess virtue does not signify to have cultivated a few nameable and exclusive traits; it means to be fully and adequately what one is capable of becoming through association with others in all the offices of life.

John Dewey

TEACH YOUR CHILDREN RESPONSIBLE INDEPENDENCE

The independence advocated here is that which is responsible, value-laden, and rightly guided. It is not intended to be chaotic and lacking any sense of direction, which is the result of liberating oneself from principles, ethics, and morality. Parents are encouraged to build righteousness with autonomy so that their children make the correct decisions on their own. Equip children with autonomy and righteousness so that they are able to face any challenges.

Advice vs. Autonomy: The Daughter and Her Mother

When parents are told that giving advice to children may interfere with their autonomy, many of them are immediately upset. They feel, "Now that's going too far!" They cannot understand why they should be deprived of the right to share their parental wisdom and experience.

EXAMPLE #1

Consider the case of a persistent mother and her daughter:

"Why shouldn't my child have the benefit of my advice when she has a problem? My daughter wasn't sure she should go to her friend's graduation party because she didn't like some of the girls. They 'always whisper and call names.' What's wrong with telling her that she has to go anyway, because otherwise she'll be letting down her friend?"

When parents give immediate advice, the children may feel stupid ("Why didn't I think of that myself?"), resentful ("Don't tell me how to run my life!"), or irritated ("What makes you think I didn't think of that already?"). When children decide for themselves what they want to do, they grow in confidence and are willing to assume responsibility for their decisions.

"Should I do nothing when my child has a problem? The few times I have told her, 'It's your problem; you deal with it,' she seemed very upset." Children feel hurt and deserted if parents ignore their problems. However, between the extremes of ignoring or advising instantly, there is much that a parent can do, for example:

- Parents can help sort out the child's tangled thoughts and feelings. "From what you said, you seem to have two feelings: You want to attend, but you don't want to contend with the girls you don't like."
- They can simplify the problem as a question. "So the question seems to be, 'How do you find a way to be at the party and put up with the name-calling of some girls?'" Parents should then keep quiet after they have asked a question like this. Their silence allows the child to find solutions.
- Point out the resources available to children outside the home. "I notice that the 'Young Adult' section of the library has some books for teenagers on coping with different kinds of social problems. You may want to see what they say."

"Suppose I do all that and then think of a solution that I am sure she has not thought of. Can I mention it to her?" Yes, but after she has had time to think. She will be able to listen to her parents' idea, particularly if it is introduced in a way that shows respect for her autonomy: "How would you feel about bringing your record to the party, the one by that new comedian? Maybe the girls will be too busy laughing rather than bothering you."

Begin suggestions with "How would you feel about ..." or "Would you consider..." Advice which seems so "sensible" to us can be "not so sensible" to the child.

"Suppose I believe she should go to the party. Must I remain silent?" After a child has explored her problem, it can be helpful to hear her parent's thoughts:

"It would bother me to miss the fun of a party because of the way some girls act. I think it's important to attend and not to disappoint a friend on her graduation, even if it entails some sacrifice."

Young people are entitled to know their parents' values. Even if they choose not to act upon them at the moment, the parents have given them something to think about and a lesson to be learned.

EXAMPLE #2

One mother said: "I used to have clothing fights all the time with my daughter. Now I let her wear whatever she wants when there is no school. On school days I lay out two outfits on her bed and she decides." The advantage of a school uniform is that there is no choice – and therefore, no argument – about what to wear!

EXAMPLE #3

Samy's mother: "I finally put an end to the daily hassles with my son over whether he should wear a sweater or a jacket. I said, 'Samy, I've been thinking. Instead of telling you what to wear every day, I think you can tell yourself. Let's work out a chart and decide what clothing goes with what degree of temperature outside.' We then drew up a chart together:

OUTSIDE TEMPERATURE	APPROPRIATE DRESS
69 degrees Fahrenheit (20 Celsius) and over:	No sweater
Between 50 and 68 degrees Fahrenheit (10 -20 Celsius):	Sweater
49 degrees Fahrenheit (9 Celsius) and below:	Heavy jacket

We bought a large thermometer and he hung it outside on a tree. Now he looks at it every morning and there are no more arguments. I feel like a genius."

EXAMPLE #4

Muna asked her mother, "Why don't we ever go anyplace good on vacation, like Bermuda or Florida?" "I almost started to answer her, but remembered not to. I said: 'Why don't we?' Muna stomped around the kitchen and said 'I know, I know... Because it's too expensive... Well, at least can we go to the zoo?'"

Do You Force Veiling on Your Daughter? by Noha Beshir

My parents did not force me to do things. I can't remember a time when my parents didn't let me choose. When I came to wear the headscarf, my mom didn't say, "You must wear it because it's your religion". She explained why we wear it and that sometimes it may not be comfortable, and that wearing it in summer doesn't mean wearing a sweater and jeans. "No, you can wear light flare pants that let the wind go through them and a light button up shirt. This way, when your friends ask you why you wear it, you can actually give them a reason that YOU believe in it, not its part of my religion and my parents make me wear it." I've actually had a couple of people tell me "I should wear one of those" after I've told them why I wear it. I've been really comfortable with my parents. That doesn't mean I can't live without them. For some reason I always end up respecting them more. I really love my family and I'm glad that I can tell them almost everything. My sister and I have a great bond together. But the best thing about my family is that even though Amirah is the oldest and even though I'm the youngest, in our family we're all equal.

(Beshir and Rida 1998)

If Parents Do Not Like Their Children's Friends

Parents want their children to have friends who are polite, honest, and bright, and who do not drink or smoke or use drugs. Parents want to protect their children and, at the same time, encourage autonomy. Many of the friendships parents worry about are short-lived. Often children discover that a friend whom they admired at first is really not so terrific. Allowing an objectionable friendship to run its course may work better than actively trying to stop it. Here, it is important to address the need that the friendship satisfies, by asking the children what it is that they like about that particular friend. The answer may give parents some clues about the real reason they are attracted to that friend.

Children have to learn to deal with several kinds of people. Sometimes friendships are threatening and potentially dangerous, such as when the children align themselves with belligerent friends who engage in antisocial or delinquent acts. Parents have a responsibility to discourage friendships with those whose behavior is unacceptable.

Parental support, trust, and patience, will help children improve their social interactions. Children need guides to help them get along with people, feel good about themselves, and be responsible for their actions.

Helping Children to Make Decisions Enhances Autonomy

Parents can teach independence by doing the following:

- Give children opportunities to make decisions (such as choosing the site of a family outing or dividing the chores fairly).
- Show children how to weigh their options, gather necessary information, and consider the potential outcomes of their decisions (e.g. deciding what clothes to wear).
- Teach children that decisions have consequences for themselves and others. Use the example of smoking: A teenager may smoke because it looks "mature" without considering the consequences: yellow teeth, bad breath, and increased risk of cancer and heart disease. Tobacco cultivation is destructive. It strips the land of its nutrients. In addition, the land used for tobacco cultivation could be used instead for producing food and clothing for needy people.

- Children have to be shown that not making a decision when a decision is needed can be as bad as making the "wrong" decision.
- Parents should accept children's decisions wherever possible. No decision is perfect, so parents should support their children's ability to make decisions and improve on them.
- Children's decisions are based on their tastes and needs and may not match the parents' decisions.
- Rules or limits for decision making should be laid down. Clearly harmful decisions are unacceptable, so parents must explain why they cannot be allowed.

Decision-Making Steps

The ability to make decisions helps improve self-esteem. Children who can exercise some control over their lives are being prepared to be self-reliant, responsible, and happier adults. Independent children are able to go through the following steps:

- Recognizing that a decision needs to be made
- Gathering information to help make the decision
- Identifying alternative decisions
- Examining the potential outcomes of the decision
- Considering how the options fit with personal values and goals
- Recognizing poor reasons (such as peer pressure, a desire to prove maturity or a feeling of rebellion) for choosing certain decisions
- Implementing the decision

Activities

ACTIVITY 59: TESTING THE COEFFICIENT OF DOMINANCE OF PARENTS

Try to ask a child in the presence of his parent ten simple questions about any topic. Notice if the child gives the answers or if the parent jumps in and answers on behalf of the child. The number of questions answered by the parent is a clear indication of the "Coefficient of Dominance" of the parent. Also watch how restless and intense the parent becomes when the child struggles to answer a difficult question!

Parents have to transform themselves from being domineering managers to being guiding consultants (to facilitate proper autonomy for their children).

ACTIVITY 60: EXPLAIN YOUR FAMILY VALUE SYSTEM TO YOUR CHILDREN

It is a mistake to force our children to follow a certain career or become a copy of ourselves. Instill in them the pure creed (*'aqīdah*), the value system, and the world view that they need. Also share with them your values regarding the love of human beings, animals, plants, and the environment.

Today's children surprise their parents by their many creative ways of achieving goals and objectives. Discuss your family and ask your children how they would embody these values.

ACTIVITY 61: ARE YOU A SUPPORTIVE OR INTERFERING PARENT?

We start as singles, get married, and have children. Two decades later, children leave the nest and go to college.

General MacArthur and President Roosevelt had mothers who moved to be near them when they went to college. They did not have cell phones and e-mail available 24/7 to check on them.

Most parents point out that they respect their children's boundaries and that they do not interfere in their children's lives. Below are a few questions parents can answer to discover their true behavior:

- How often do you communicate with your child during college? Daily, weekly, monthly?
- Do you contact your child's professors?
- Do you take part in your child's papers if s/he has trouble writing them?
- When you visit your child, do you do their chores (clean his/her room, do the laundry, take out the trash)?
- If your child has trouble with a roommate, do you interfere?

Discuss your answers with your family. Here are some suggestions for dealing with students who live away from home:

- Have your child initiate the calls. It helps teach self-reliance.
- Papers and assignments should be done by the student.
- Your college student is an adult who is able to take care of his/her needs, so they should do their own chores.

(Kantrowitz and Tyre 2006)

CHAPTER 20

Fostering Creativity

Introduction

CREATIVITY IS A form of self-expression. There is a great feeling satisfaction when children express themselves openly and without judgment. The ability to create something original is an important part of good character. Experiences with all types of art can significantly enhance the development of children's creativity. Creative children can express and cope with their feelings while developing thier talents. Trying out new ways of thinking and problem solving are qualities of a creative child.

We may characterize the creative person as someone who is curious, enjoys challenge, is optimistic, is able to suspend judgment, and possesses imagination. Creative people see problems as opportunities, challenge assumptions, work hard, do not give up easily, and persevere. Many people fail because they spend only nine minutes on a problem that requires ten minutes to solve.

Children need extended, unhurried time to explore and do their best work. They are not to be stopped and asked to move to an activity when they are still productively engaged and motivated by a piece of creative work. They need a place to leave unfinished work to continue it later, and they need a space that inspires them to do their best work. A barren home environment is not conducive to creative work. Children need a space that has natural light, harmonious colors, comfortable seats and child-sized areas. The room should display examples of their own and others' work. Parents should accept mistakes, encourage risk-taking, and promote uniqueness. Creativity requires a certain amount of mess, noise, and freedom, without chaos or tight control.

As a parent, you have enormous influence on your children's creativity. Insights and problem-solving skills can be developed with originality and enjoyment. For a young child the "doing" of an activity is the important thing, the finished product is of less interest. Avoid comments like: "That looked like fun" or "You worked hard on this" rather than comments that relate to the child's own perception of the activity, and comment on the uniqueness of their product. Many sensitive children are frightened away from creative activities when they are expected to produce "something." A child who begins to draw, or build, or make up songs in order to please an adult has already lost some of the enthusiasm for creativity. Allow and appreciate creative use of ordinary household items such as pans, pots, cans, and couch cushions. Give pre-schoolers art materials as soon as possible. A 2½ year old who has a low art drawer in the kitchen can be more creative than the same-age child who has to wait until someone brings the crayons down from a high shelf. Do not make the rules so difficult to the point that art activities become more trouble than they are worth. Simplicity is the key to success in toddler art. As children grow older, you can expect more neatness.

The energy spent in conforming to rules of neatness will take away from the energy of exploration and originality. Every child needs to learn the rights of others and the safety rules. Without a framework of reasonable expectations, exploration and originality tend toward chaos.

The overly controlled child, however, sacrifices originality and exploration for the sake of approval. If a child feels his or her self-worth is totally based on being clean and orderly, then there will be little energy or courage available for creativity. Creativity is crushed if "be careful – clean that up!" is the usual response.

General Creativity Concepts

Here is some advice for fostering creativity:

- Adapt to the children's ideas rather than trying to make the children's ideas adapt to you. Accept unusual ideas from children and discuss them.
- Use creative problem solving for the problems that occur in everyday life. Give children the freedom to make mistakes. Allow children to experiment without fearing failure.
- Allow time for children to explore all possibilities.
- Encourage children to experiment with objects that are unusual. Listen to the children's questions and comments. Clarify what the children have observed by repeating what you have heard and ask further questions about the experience.
- Provide a stimulating environment that appeals to the children. Give the children a variety of materials, books, and games, and plenty of opportunities to experiment with these materials.
- Expose your children to a diversity of cultures, experiences, people, religions, and ways of thinking. Let them see that there are different ways to think about a problem. Encourage children to try new experiences within their abilities. Visit children's museums.
- Appreciate new ways of thinking. Share your own artistic, scientific, and creative projects with your child. Participation in a project about which you feel passionate will encourage passion in your children.
- Model perseverance. Encourage children to complete a project by encouraging each step of the process and helping them to understand their own strengths and weaknesses.

The Creative Student: Complexity vs. Simplicity

A student was interviewed for admission to a prestigious Management Institute. The interviewer said: "I shall either ask you ten easy questions or one really difficult question. Think well."

The boy said, "One really difficult question."

Now tell me this, "What comes first, Day or Night?"

"It's the DAY sir!"

"How?" the interviewer said.

"Sorry sir, you promised me that you would not ask me a SECOND difficult question!"

He was selected!

Technical Skill is to master complexity, while creativity is the mastery of simplicity!

- Tolerate the "offbeat." Let children know that it is not always necessary to have the "correct" answer to the problem. Innovative and unique approaches are valued as well.
- Support your child's imagination. Creative people are comfortable with weird, wild, or strange thoughts. Brainstorming will encourage a variety of unique thoughts and interesting ideas.

- Foster a belief that mistakes are welcome. Failure is not a disaster, it is an educational opportunity and can lead to success. One chief executive warns his new managers, "Make sure you make a reasonable number of mistakes."
- See the good in the bad. Creative thinkers, when faced with poor solutions, ask, "What's good about it?" There may be something useful even in the worst ideas.

See the Good in the Bad

How can we persuade students to learn better? Solution: Spank their bottoms with a stick! This is not a good solution, partly because it is illegal. However, should we just toss it out? Why not ask: "What's good about it?" It gives individual attention to the poor performers; it motivates other students as well as the student being spanked; it is easy and costs nothing. The next question is, "Can we adapt or incorporate some of these good things into a more acceptable solution, whether derivative of the original or not?"

We easily fall into either/or thinking and believe that a bad solution is bad, in every aspect. In fact, it may have some good parts we can borrow, or it may do inappropriately something that is worth doing appropriately. And often, the bad solution has just one really glaring bad part, which, when remedied, leaves quite a good solution.

Stark Historical Inventions

1. Creative people look for improvements. For example, the first margarine was made from beef fat, milk, water, and chopped cow udder. It was not tasty or healthy. Then at the beginning of the twentieth century a shortage of beef fat created a problem. What to use? The margarine makers turned to vegetable fats. The soybean, corn, and sunflower oils that they chose are still in use today. The margarine became healthier and tasted better.
2. You do not have to be a genius to be creative. Highly skilled and trained scientists working in the space industry were initially unable to develop a zero gravity pen that could be used in space. The solution: use a pencil. Ultimately, however a company developed the pen independent of the space program and then asked NASA to try it. It worked and has been adopted by both US and Soviet space agencies.
3. A problem can also be a solution. Something that one person may describe as an "obstacle" can sometimes be an "opportunity" for someone else.

   For example, soon after the advent of cyanoacrylate adhesives (super glue), it was noted that if you were not careful, you could glue your fingers together with it. This problem – a permanent skin bond – was soon seen as a solution also. Surgeons in Vietnam began to use super glue to close wounds.

   Another glue example: A chemist working at the 3M corporation in the USA was experimenting with adhesives and produced one that was so weak you could peel it off. Glue that will not hold?

Quite a problem. Nevertheless, this problem was turned into a solution. In 1980 the product was launched as Post-It Notes and is used throughout the world today.

Stifling Children's Creativity

It is perhaps ironic that we place such value on creativity but then destroy it in children. Amabile and Hennessey (1992) identify these common "creativity killers":

- Too Much Surveillance – Hovering over children and making them feel that they are constantly under observation causes risk-taking and creativity to disappear.
- Harsh Evaluation – When we constantly make children worry about how they are doing, their creativity diminishes.
- Too Many Rewards – The excessive use of prizes deprives a child of the intrinsic pleasure of creative activity. When people do not expect a reward, they are more creative and enjoy the process more. An unexpected reward that comes after a project is completed is valuable but not necessary to the creativity. Too much extrinsic motivation (such as money or special privileges) undermines creativity.
- Extreme Competition – Putting children in unfair competitions with others destroys their motivation and creativity.
- Restricting Choices – Telling children which activities they have to engage in instead of letting them follow their curiosity and passion destroys creativity.
- Pressure – Establishing grandiose expectations for children's performance leads to a decline in creativity.

Negative Attitudes that Block Creativity

There are many other ways to hinder creativity. The following are common phrases used to block creativity in children.

- *Oh no, a problem*! Sometimes, the reaction to a problem can be a bigger problem than the problem itself. A problem should not be blown out of proportion. Happy people welcome problems, looking at them as opportunities to improve. A problem is the difference between what you have and what you want. There is something better than the current situation, and creativity can help you.
- *It cannot be done*. This is like surrendering before the battle. By assuming that something cannot be done, a person gives the problem a power it did not have before. Giving up before starting is the worst disease. Imagine if we all gave up trying: humans would never fly, diseases would never be conquered, and rockets would never leave the atmosphere. The appropriate attitude should be: "The difficult we do immediately; the impossible takes a little longer."
- *You cannot do it*. Or: *There's nothing you can do*. Some people think, "Well, maybe the problem can be solved by some expert because I am not smart enough." "I can't solve it because I'm not an expert."
  In fact, most innovations in industry come from individuals (not research groups) outside of the area of the invention. A positive attitude and good skills will solve any problem. Commitment to the problem is the key. Even if you cannot totally eradicate the problem from the face of the earth, you can always improve the situation.
- *That's childish*. In our efforts to appear always mature and sophisticated, we often ridicule creativity and playfulness. However, if you solve a problem that saves your marriage or brings about your promotion or keeps your friend from committing suicide, do you care whether people describe your route to the solution as "childish?" Besides, is not play a lot of fun?
- *What will people think?* There is strong social pressure to conform, to be ordinary and to be normal. Here are some examples:
  Creative Person: "I like to put water in my orange juice so it's less sweet."
  Ordinary Person: "You're weird, you know?"
  Creative Person: "We're cooking at midnight."
  Ordinary Person: "You're crazy."
  Creative Person: "Why don't we add a little garlic or mustard?"
  Ordinary Person: "Because the recipe doesn't call for them."

Progress is made by those who are strong enough to endure being laughed at. Mistakes are not fun, but they sure are educational.

Thomas Edison, in his search for the perfect filament for the incandescent lamp, tried whiskers from a friend's beard, and 1800 other things. After about 1000 attempts, someone asked him if he was frustrated. He said, "I've gained a lot of knowledge – I now know a thousand things that won't work."

Genius of the Non-Specialists!

- The Wright brothers who invented the airplane were not aviation engineers, they were bicycle mechanics.
- The ballpoint pen was invented by a printer's proofreader, Ladislao Biro, not a mechanical engineer.
- Major advances in submarine design were made by English clergyman G.W. Garrett and by Irish schoolmaster John Holland.
- The cotton gin was invented by the attorney and tutor, Eli Whitney.
- The fire extinguisher was invented by a military officer, George Manby.
- Kodachrome (colour film) was invented by two musicians.
- The continuous steel casting process was invented by a watchmaker (fooling around with brass casting).
- Soap-making chemists turned down synthetic detergents: those detergents were invented by dye-making chemists.

- *You might fail.* Suppose you let your fears of failure guide your risk taking and your attempts. You try only 3 things in a year because you are sure of succeeding. At the end of the year the score is: Successes 3, Failures 0. Now suppose the next year you do not worry about failing, so you try 12 things. You fail at 6 of them. The score is Successes 6, Failures 6. Which would you rather have – 3 successes or 6? And imagine what twelve failures will have taught you.

Ways to Develop Creativity

There are several techniques to develop creativity, below are a few:

CREATIVE QUESTIONING

Ask your child high level questions. These questions engage the whole brain because they combine emotional intelligence with logical intelligence and spatial intelligence:

- Which would be more creative – the most wonderful, smooth and effective car imaginable, or a dome, minaret or cathedral that captured the essence of art and faith in a totally unique way?
- Does anyone create new ideas, or do people just rediscover old ones?
- Which is harder – starting a creative project, or finishing it? Why?
- Is the kind of creativity that lets people solve problems fundamentally different than the creativity to make art?

PRACTICAL ACTIVITIES

- Have a backwards day, beginning by having dinner for breakfast.
- Use a copier or computer to enlarge small objects and shrink big ones. Make a collage.
- Make up a card game. You can start by changing a game you know, and then change it again: dominos, backgammon, and two combined sets of dominos.
- Try cooking with new and unusual spices that you have never used. Use the smells to

guide your culinary exploration.

- Access the Internet and play a game where you follow links not based on what information is presented, but on the first letter of the link. See what random and amusing sites you find.
- Create a model of an environment in which you would like to live. Use only household objects and natural materials.
- Make your own poetry using random words.

VARIETIES OF EXPERIENCE

- Combine multi-ethnic, multi-cultural, and multi-religious holidays in creative ways.
- Imagine that you are from another planet. Pretend that you are visiting other planets. Imagination and pretending promote creativity.

BRAINSTORMING ACTIVITIES

- Hand a child a piece of modeling clay and ask the child to imagine that s/he is the modeling clay.
- Place a child in a different time and place. For instance, ask a child to describe how s/he would cook a meal without electricity, silverware or dishes.
- Make a list of questions that can't be answered.

CREATIVE PLAY

Have your children use familiar materials in a new or unusual way. Engage in role-playing and spontaneous, self-directed play throughout the day.

As early as infancy, play fosters physical development by promoting the development of sensory exploration and motor skills. With play and the repetition of basic physical skills, children become competent at increasingly difficult physical tasks. Children who play with blocks are confronted with challenges linked to measurement, equality, balance, shape, and spatial relationships.

Dramatic play means imitating people in society; it helps children experiment with social roles. In dramatic play, children gradually learn to take one another's needs into account, and appreciate different values.

With play, children are able to express and cope with their feelings. Play also helps relieve stress and pressure. Children can be free of adult restrictions. There's no need to live up to adult standards during play.

As caregivers, we have to be careful to avoid dominating the play ourselves. Play is supposed to be the result of the children's ideas and not directed by the adult. We need to foster their own inspirations, not ours.

To facilitate a number of skills, including reading and understanding of people, you may wish to enact a written play with your children. Each person has a character which he should explore, whose feelings he has to understand, and then learn his "part" by reading the sections relevant to him. Ask children to put on an entire performance for you, all organized by themselves with simple costumes.

CHILDREN'S WRITING

Pre-readers can dictate a story for you to write, and then they can illustrate it. As soon as your child is able to articulate some words, s/he can begin to write. Do not worry about spelling at this time. That will come later. As soon as your child is enthusiastic about writing, you can begin to teach the method of writing used by the authors of books. Typically, a writer begins with a rough draft and gradually polishes it until it is ready to be published. A good way to teach this is to ask your child to pick a favorite story, and then help him/her see how to write the story more clearly. This story can then be made into a little handmade book. Older children can do a wonderful job of creating books by using the computer. Do not forget the value of reading. Good writers are good readers and reading will give your child many imaginative ideas for writing.

CHILDREN'S ART

- *Provide open-ended art activities to children.* Instead of displaying a model of the art project for children to replicate, encourage children to use their imagination. Instead of passing around coloring book pages, all with the same line drawings, turn on some soft music and ask the children to draw what they hear!
- *Create an environment that invigorates the five senses.* Let them feel the texture of the paper, smell the crayons, listen to the sound of a crayon being sharpened, and watch the colors change as paints are mixed!
- *Encourage spontaneous exploration.* Provide a constant, easily accessible supply of basic materials such as crayons, markers, paste, construction paper, brushes, and paints. Allow children to discover the properties of these items and how to use them. Can the children use their fingers as a paintbrush? Can children draw a picture in the dirt using a stick? Make their bodies the same shape as a tree? Describe what the color purple feels like? March around the room in a happy, sad, or funny way?
- *Refrain from criticizing what you consider bad work.* We have to protect children from the criticism and judgments of peers, adults, and even themselves. There is no bad or good; each creation is unique.

This is important even in preschool. In art, everyone is the boss of her/his own work and can do it any way s/he wants. Children become tense and doubtful if their work is constantly being described as ugly or incomplete.

Misconceptions: 'Strange' or 'Unproductive' Ideas

Some personality traits that creative children develop can be viewed by others as strange or unproductive. The following gives a few examples of these:

- Free thinking: When creative children talk about ideas, they may appear undisciplined and chaotic;
- Gullibility: Creative children get excited about strange ideas and may not see the drawbacks or flaws that an adult would easily see;
- Humor: Creative children find humor in ideas that adults consider to be serious. This ability to question and see other perspectives may be interpreted as mocking and obnoxious;
- Daydreaming: Creative children learn from fantasy and solve many of their problems using daydreams. Letting one's mind wander can help the imagination form new connections, although it may be seen as being inattentive or distracted;
- Solitude: Creativity develops from simple, unformed ideas. Children might need to be alone while their ideas emerge;
- Activity: Ideas may come at times of "doing nothing." Once the idea comes, the creative child will become absorbed in the activity. A good practice is to have pencils and papers placed in strategic places in the home for children to record their thoughts.

> The gift of fantasy has meant more to me than my talent for absorbing positive knowledge.
>
> ALBERT EINSTEIN

What Parents Can Do?

- Set an Example: Honor your own child-like curiosity, enthusiasm and "crazy" ideas. Keep yourself open to new experiences, share your own creative interests, and take delight in the interests of your child.
- Trust Your Child: Children who feel loved and trusted gain the confidence to be different and the courage to create. Over-concern for societal convention or sex-role stereotypes can inhibit creativity.
- Encourage Your Child: Encourage experimentation and exploration. Practice listening to your child without being judgmental. Support your children when they fail. Avoid "empty praise."
- Enrich the Environment: Provide materials that encourage imagination and enable children to create their own artwork. Old magazines, books, newspapers, games, clothes, and jewelry can be used for a variety of projects. Fabric scaps can be used to design quilts and covers.
- Watch TV Together: The idea is controversial because of the negative influence of TV on children. Focus on documentaries and engage their imagination in discussion.
- Help Your Child to Record Ideas: Children love to paint and draw from a very early age. Before they begin to write, they can dictate their ideas to adults or other children. Later, you can encourage your child to keep a diary or journal.

A Note on Toys

Think about the toys you are buying your children. Toys have to encourage creativity and be educational. Building blocks (like Lego) stimulate thinking. Some dolls (like Bratz) bring confusing gender roles. Playing with dolls and teddy bears is a healthy thing for children; it gives children a companion, they can role play with dolls being mothers, or friends, and they can take their frustrations out on dolls. Buy toys that teach weaving, knitting, sewing, and woodwork. Little tape measures and little hammers (used under supervision) are also good. The toy that is promoted the most on TV or is the most expensive is not necessarily the best toy. If you have more than one child, try to buy toys (like board games) that allow children to play together.

Think about the toys you are buying your children. Toys have to encourage creativity and be educational. Building blocks (like Lego) stimulate thinking.

There are also toys available specifically for different abled children and children with autism designed by specialists to meet the challenges these children face.

Activities

ACTIVITY 62: FAMILY EXERCISES TO FOSTER CREATIVITY

Try the following creative tools with the children:

1. **Use creative play:** Activities such as "follow the leader" encourage a child to think of creative movement and experience the reward of others following his/her example. Construction activities can use simple materials (blocks, mud, sand, clay, water) that allow the child to build and design various structures.
2. **Use a continuing story concept:** Someone starts the story and then each person adds a part. Read a story and act it out. Use puppets to act out a story.
3. **Use objects to create new ideas:** Try the animal cracker game – the child chooses one cracker; looks at it; then eats it. Then the child becomes the animal for 1–2 minutes. Use creative movement to act out how the animal behaves and moves.
4. **Use role-playing:** Simulation games help children see the viewpoints of others and explore their feelings.
5. **Ask open-ended questions:** Show the child a picture and then ask questions. For example: "What are the people in the picture doing?" "What are the people saying?" "What was interesting in your day?" Instead of: "Did you have a good day?"
6. **Ask children to use their senses:**

- Have children close their eyes and then guess what you have placed in their hands (such as a piece of foam rubber, a small rock).
- Have children close their eyes and guess at what they hear (use such sounds as shuffling cards, jingling coins, rubbing sandpaper, ripping paper).

7. **Ask children about changes:** Ask them to change things to make them the way they would like them to be. For example:

- What would taste better if it were sweeter?
- What would be nicer if it were smaller?
- What would be more fun if it were faster?
- What would be better if it were quieter?
- What would be happier if it were bigger?
- What could be more exciting if it went backwards?
- How would English spelling be if we wrote words the way we pronounce them? Try writing a paragraph using this phonetic method. There are languages like that, can you name some?

8. **Ask questions with lots of answers:** Here are some examples using the concept of water (other concepts include: fire, wind, sand, cars, smoke, ice.):

- What are some of the uses of water?
- What floats in water?
- How does water help us?
- Why is cold water cold?
- What always stays underwater?
- What are the different colors that water can be?

9. **Ask "What would happen if…" questions:**

- What would happen if all the trees in the world were blue?
- What would happen if all the cars were gone?
- What would happen if everybody wore the same clothes? Had the same name?
- What would happen if you could fly?
- What would happen if no one cleaned the house?
- What would happen if everyone were righteous or evil?
- What would happen if everyone were sick or healthy?

10. **Ask "In how many different ways…" questions:**

- In how many different ways could a spoon be used?
- In how many different ways could a button be used?
- In how many different ways could a string be used?
- In how many different ways could a paper clip be used?

ACTIVITY 63: CHARACTERS THAT COUNT!

When the first revelation came down to Prophet Muhammad ﷺ, he was afraid and returned home to his wife, Khadījah. She comforted him and listed some of his good behaviors:

- Reaching out to next of kin
- Helping the weak
- Giving to the destitute
- Providing hospitality to guests, and
- Supporting the sick

Discuss with your children the significance of each of these behaviors. Write a story together that includes these behaviors.

ACTIVITY 64: EXPLAINING TRICKY QUESTIONS

Gather a few parents to discuss how to answer these questions, which children ask frequently (ask others if you need help).

- "Who created God?", "Why would God punish people for not believing in Him?", "Why are there so many people who never received the Divine Message?", "How can we live forever in Heaven without getting bored?"
- How do we explain the concepts of "free will" and "determinism" in a way that encourages proactive thinking on one hand and acceptance of God's Will on the other? Where do we come from? Where do we end? What is the Hereafter like? Can we see God? Why not? God can make everyone believe in Him, why doesn't He do that?

These are tricky questions for children. We need to explain to them according to their age and maturity.

In visualizing Paradise, the Prophet ﷺ explained that Heaven is so good and unique that no eye has seen it, no ear has heard it, and no heart or mind has imagined it! It is a completely new system of eternal existence that our human senses cannot comprehend.

ACTIVITY 65: IT IS THE PERCEPTION OF THE THIEF THAT MATTERS! A CREATIVE SOLUTION

Let children read the following true story. Then think together of some problems facing the family and how to solve them.

> When the Chief Executive of American Airlines saw a guard standing at an airport, he asked the Manager, "Can we cut costs?" The Manager responded by asking, "How?" The Executive said that if they had the guard for three random nights only, the thieves would not know which nights the guard was on duty. Next year, the same question arose about cutting costs, and the same response was given: "How?" The Executive suggested replacing the guard with a vicious dog. The third year, again, the same question was asked. The solution was to have the dog only part-time. The fourth year, the Executive told the Manager: "Since it is the perception of thieves that counts, why don't you make the dog very hungry and record his loud wild barking and play it randomly at night?" It worked! They saved by not having a night guard. (MSNBC, NOVEMBER 3, 2007)

CHAPTER 21

Self-Esteem vs. Spoiled Children

Self-Esteem

CHILDREN NEED ENCOURAGEMENT when they make mistakes just as much as when they find the solution. In fact, since mistakes are a part of life, it is important that children are taught to view them as learning experiences rather than failures. Do not let failures discourage children; use failures as an opportunity to encourage them instead. There is a big difference between saying "How could you be so stupid?" and saying "I know you are smart and capable!" Encouragement helps the child to learn and do better in the future. Children told they are losers by the people they admire the most will become losers.

Thoughts that are of a discouraging nature like, "I failed, therefore I am good for nothing", will diminish the children's enjoyment of life, drain their emotional energy, and increase the likelihood they will take the easy way out when stressed. Children without self-esteem will not spend their effort on goals they perceive to be unattainable. Success in the long run (through studying and resisting peer pressure) requires self-esteem. Children with less self-esteem are more impulsive and have less concern for their consequences. They have little confidence to pursue their goals. Low self-esteem kids are prone to immediate gratification through alcohol, drugs, sex, and violence.

Children should be taught that there is nothing that they lack, and to view mistakes as opportunities to learn. These children have the energy necessary to choose what is better (to study for the examination instead of going out with friends). They have hope, and are optimistic that they will succeed (by their hard work and efforts). They observe the benefits of their efforts and define themselves as winners. The happiness that follows success makes it even more likely that they will find success in the future.

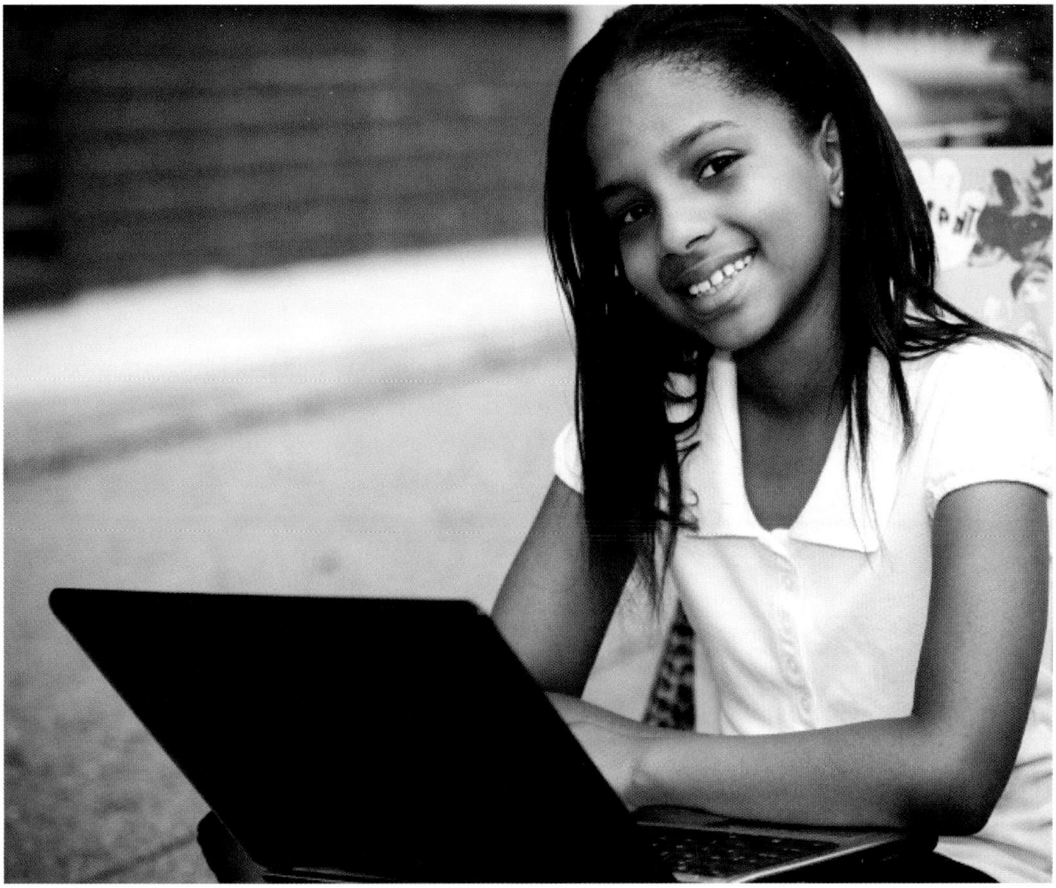

Love, courage, creativity, honesty and a sense of responsibility – directly or indirectly – builds strong self-confidence and self-esteem. All these characteristics interact and strengthen one another. They all increase the emotional energy and psychological capital in the child.

We decide whether the glass is half full or half empty. Enhance courage and self-confidence in children at every opportunity. If weeds are planted, that is what will grow. So plant flowers.

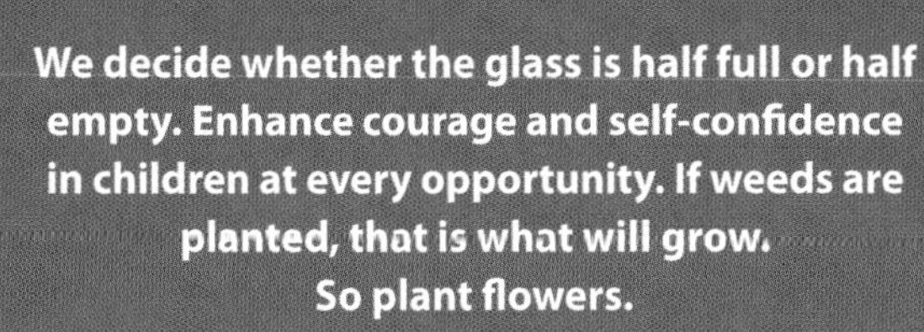

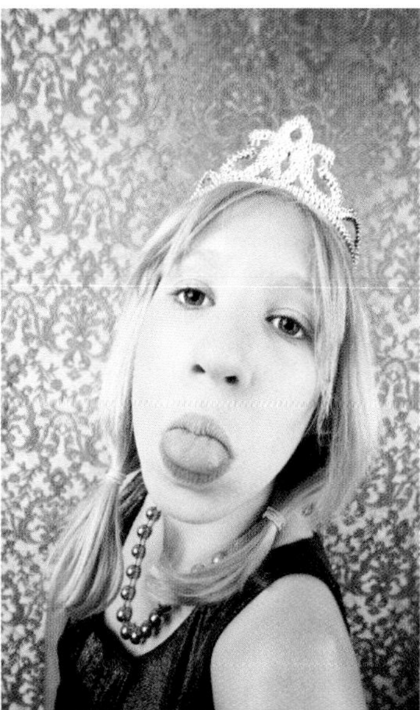

How to Avoid Raising a 'Spoiled' Child

Children have to learn how to handle competition and stress. Children need to be taught to deal with a "no" from parents and from friends, teachers, neighbors, and strangers. Train your children to deal with disappointments, denials, and refusals. The following are ways to avoid spoiling a child:

DO NOT UNDERMINE DISCIPLINE

Some parents tend to pamper children. Abundance of anything, whether toys, games, money, or chocolate, spoils children at a very young age. Children brought up in affluent families may become spoiled if they have too much of everything. Parents should not give their children more than what is necessary. Children have to be prepared for the rough times and the smooth times in life.

NEVER SATISFY ALL DEMANDS

Parents derive satisfaction from fulfilling their children's wishes. However, parent should deliberately leave some wishes unfulfilled. If every wish and desire of the child is fulfilled, the child grows up to be a narcissistic person. These children become illogical, violent and frustrated. They will be unable to accept rejection in a job interview later in life. They are prone to depression and they cannot handle disappointments.

DISCOURAGE COMPARISONS

Parents need to discourage their child's tendency to compare his or her possessions with other children. If the children demand a toy merely because a neighbor has a new one, their demand should be discouraged. These children end up constantly comparing themselves with people who have more than they have.

AVOID APPEASEMENT

To avoid conflict some parents tend to constantly please children. Appeasement has short-term gains but long-term losses. Children lose respect for such parents. Parents need to be honest and say no to unreasonable demands by their children. You cannot base your whole life on your children's demands.

DO NOT GIVE IN OUT OF GUILT

Some parents tend to please children out of guilt. For instance, many working mothers come home late and do not have time to help with the child's homework. The child asks for ice cream before dinner. The mother agrees. The child is smart enough to know the reason behind the bribe. Parents need to have the courage to say no despite the child's tantrums.

Children need to be taught to deal with a "no" from parents and from friends, teachers and neighbors.

Tantrums: Do Not Let Crying be Used as a Tool

There is crying that comes from a real need (for example, hunger, fever, pain, and fear). This requires the parents' attention. There is another type of crying that is a tantrum crying. The child wants to have something unnecessary so s/he cries and screams loudly. This type of crying should be ignored. Otherwise it will start a pattern: the screams will get louder until the frustrated parent gives in. The child will learn that s/he has control over the parent through unnecessary crying. When crying is part of a tantrum, ignore it. Do not shout at the child. Stay calm and in control, and accept the child's feelings. Do not give in. When the tantrum is over the child will learn that unnecessary crying is not acceptable behavior.

Activities

ACTIVITY 66: RELIABILITY TEST

The various characteristics of a good personality overlap with each other. In a family setting, all the members should discuss the importance of reliability and answer these questions:

- Do I keep my promises?
- Do I honor my elders?
- Do I respect my commitments?
- Do I pay my debts on time?
- Do I return what I borrow promptly?
- Do I meet deadlines?
- Do I pray on time?
- Am I punctual?

ACTIVITY 67: CONTENTMENT

Read this story and reflect on the practices of your family, your relatives and your friends.

The Messenger ﷺ said:
"Be content with what God has provided for you and you will be the richest of people."

One of the companions used to pray behind the Prophet ﷺ wearing the same torn robe. The Prophet noticed him leaving quickly after every prayer. He asked about this man: "Where is he?" They told him: "He returned home." The Prophet asked for him, so he came and the Prophet asked him: "Why do you leave quickly and do not finalize your prayers?" The companion answered: "Because my wife and I own one robe only, so I return quickly to my wife to give her the robe so that she can do the prayer before its time is up." So the Prophet gave the companion his own shirt. He took it happily to his wife, who asked: "Whose shirt is this?" He answered: "The Prophet's shirt; he gave it to us." She replied: "Did you complain about God to the Prophet of God?" He answered: "By God, I did not complain! By God I only accepted so that the shirt of the Messenger will be my shroud in the grave!"

IMAM AL-GHAZĀLĪ, *IḤYĀʾ ʿULŪM AL-DĪN*

ACTIVITY 68: ACTIVE ENGAGEMENT

Read the following with your children, then relate the specific items to their own experiences.

The most effective learning occurs when children are actively engaged in exploring the world around them: trying to figure things out, falling and then trying to get back up, and expressing their thoughts, ideas and emotions in response to what they see. Parents should pass on their ideas and lessons during the child's exploration. Give children the opportunity to test and apply their knowledge during these "teaching moments," a phrase that President Obama has often used to illustrate an encounter.

Allow a child the time to go silent, look around, take a deep breath, express frustration and think. This is not a sign of weakness, they are actually thinking and trying to determine what to do with what they have. Unfortunately, many parents will answer questions on their children's behalf, shelter them from challenging situations, and take it upon themselves to take over the situation when their child is struggling to figure something out. This has negative impact on the child's self confidence, problem solving ability, patience and negotiation skills. They have learned to only rely on others to solve their problems.

Parents should take on the roles of an expert, a coach and a mentor. Allow children the opportunity to use their own knowledge, skills and abilities. The parents should be guiding and helping their children think through difficult situations, using the child's own abilities.

Parents must allow their children to make mistakes. Help the child understand and explore what went right, what went wrong, why did they do that, how can they do it better next time, what they have learned from this experience, and what would they do different next time. It is not just the actual task that is important. The mental effort to get the task done and to avoid the same mistakes over and over again is also very important.

Through active engagement the parent-child, and child-parent bond is strengthened and a deeper relationship is created. Once this bond is established, the child will be more willing to consult with his/her parents as challenges arise in later years of life and as challenges become more complex.

CHAPTER 22

Choosing the Right Friends for Your Child

Your Child's Friends

IN PHYSICS, SIMILAR charges (polarity) repel each other, opposite ones attract each other. With animals "Birds of a feather flock together." We try to establish friendly relations with people we meet – neighbors, children at school, sellers at the market, and so forth. We must treat everyone with kindness and respect. At the same time, it is best not to form too close a friendship with people who lead valueless lives. Choose practicing believers as friends. Such friends will not mind stopping a few minutes in the middle of a game to pray with you. They will understand why you do not drink alcohol or use drugs.

Sometimes, it is not possible to make friends with those who share your values because you live far away from them. Their children do not go to the same school as your children. However, it may still be possible to find a friend nearby from a good family of any faith who share similar values and respect your customs. Community organizations, such as sports clubs, scouts and nature groups, can be good places to make friends with young people who share the same interests and want to have healthy, clean fun.

A good friend is someone who shares the values of loyalty, generosity, sympathy and understanding. As an adult, you have certain standards, but your teenagers may not agree with your standards. Friends hold the most influence on teens. They will experiment with ways of dressing, behaving, and relating to other people.

Girls tend to have a special friendship with one person or just a small group of girls. Boys tend to move in large groups, or identify their friends in connection with a particular sport or hobby. These friendships are important and can be very deep. They can also be broken up suddenly if the other person "breaks the rules" of loyalty.

Do not be irritated if your children seem to care more about their friends than they do about their families. You do not have to work hard at keeping your relatives – you were born with them. All you have to work at is how to be happy with them, because they already love

Make a thousand friends and not a single foe!!

Q: What is common between American football and a righteous leader?

A: They both value strength, courage, team spirit, and hope.

Q: What is common between soldiers and Mafia members?

A: Both show tremendous loyalty and courage to their organizations – the soldiers to their country and the Mafia to their gangs. Soldiers work for a good cause, whereas the Mafia works for an evil one.

you and care for you. As for friends, however, you have to find them for yourself. They have to be persuaded to regard you as a likeable person; you have to earn their friendship.

Note that friends are the source of tomorrow's families. The old Italian saying "Buy a cow from your own field" means it is better to go with something that you are familiar with.

There are many types of friends:

- Colleagues – people whom the teenager has to work with or co-operate in an activity. They may not like them but have to be "friendly" with them in order to get work done.
- Acquaintances – people whom they know slightly. They do not feel strongly about them.
- Ordinary friends – these are people whom they know and like; they are part of the school and neighborhood.
- Close friends – those whom they know well and about whom they care. They confide in them and can depend on them.
- Best friends – Their feelings for them are more like love than liking. They share everything, and however much they argue, they remain best friends.

Friendship is a rope with two ends – it is difficult to be connected to a person who is not connected to you. You have to give as much as you receive in a friendship: tolerance, affection, humor, concern, and sacrifice. You need to stay in touch.

Most people change. Explain to your teenagers that they should not blame themselves if their friends go through a bad time, or seem less enthusiastic than usual. Friendship requires you to share. Parents are upset if their teenagers turn up with "undesirable" friends (youngsters whose values are in conflict with what you have been trying to teach your own children). "Undesirable friends" are not God fearing, smoke or take drugs, use unpleasant language, have been in trouble with the police, or encourage dangerous behavior. Keep in mind that some "undesirable" friends may be attracted to the virtues of your children and family.

Some Problems with Bad Friends

- They damage your possessions or property.
- They are rude and unpleasant.
- They take over your house.
- They frighten you and ignore you.
- You are sad that they are taking your son or daughter away from you and leading them into evil ways.

Day-to-Day Peer Pressure at School

The school system exerts pressure on the child to be accepted by classmates. A Muslim child in a non-Muslim environment may be at a disadvantage because of language, dress code (especially for girls), and dietary habits. Different religious beliefs usually translate into a different set of actions. These differences may be perceived as threatening by other classmates. There is also the difference in skin color that may lead to difficulties for a child in a racist environment.

Choosing the Right Friends

You need to know who your children's friends are. Invite them to your home to get a good idea of who they are and what kind of influence they might have on your child. Inviting others may be the only chance they will have to see what a believer's home looks like. Imagine the tremendous impact your family could have on some youngster!

Talk to your children about their choice of friends, especially if some of those choices are giving you concern. Handle it with care. Your children must begin making their own friendship decisions. If you are making decisions for them, you are teaching them dependence. That is not helpful when they are on their own, for you will not always be around.

When discussing friends with your children, do two important things:

- *Make "I" statements.* Talk to your child about how you felt when you were around his/her friend. For example, "When you were playing with Yasmin, it seemed to me that she was always taking things from others. Seeing a child who acts selfishly makes me sad." Or, "When I talked to Sara, I noticed she said bad things about her mother. That made me feel bad."
  Here, you are giving your son/daughter a chance to make the same observations you have made without feeling defensive. You should not say, "You certainly do pick selfish, thoughtless friends to play with, don't you?"
- *Ask questions.* Ask your child if s/he noticed the same problems and ask how that made her/him feel. Listen carefully to their answers. What you are looking for is your children's honest appraisal. If they share your concerns, you may say, "Do you think it might be a good idea for you to spend more time with your other friends and less time with Yasmin or Sara?"

Start this process as early as you can. Give your children permission to openly discuss their friends with you. This will be a valuable "bridge" you can use when they are much older and the stakes are considerably higher.

What if Your Child Chooses Undesirable Friends?

Iman El-Kadi (a social worker) said:

> "A child may choose a friend who is impolite and disrespectful. Don't be alarmed, because children naturally are attracted to the unknown out of curiosity, and once this curiosity is satisfied, they usually lose interest. If we try to end this friendship abruptly on the basis of parental authorities, it may cause more attachment to this friend, if only out of sheer stubbornness." When such a friend is in your house you can say, " you are welcome but please abide by our house rules."

Perhaps the most dangerous influence on a child is that of a friend with a similar faith who does not observe the faith and commits vices. I remember the shock my two boys experienced (ages 7 and 9) when they visited Istanbul for the first time. Having been raised in a religious home environment in America, they never imagined that in Istanbul some people could drink alcohol, display pornography in the streets and openly not fast during Ramadan. I helped them realize that people may be born Muslims, but they may not act in appropriate Islamic ways.

Children are influenced by their parents' views and principles. It is crucial for parents to find out when children do not follow those principles. What are the factors that brought the child to this harmful friend? Why do we see one child who smokes and another one who does not? What is the friend providing that is not being provided at home?

Encouraging children to join useful activities is crucial to the choice of peers for them.

Here are a few more tips:

- If the child you dislike is coming over suggest inviting other friends who you do like to come also, thereby bringing a better influence.
- Keep the child busy with other things (i.e. visit a relative).
- Create a series of rules applicable to all (such as no shouting, swearing or hitting).

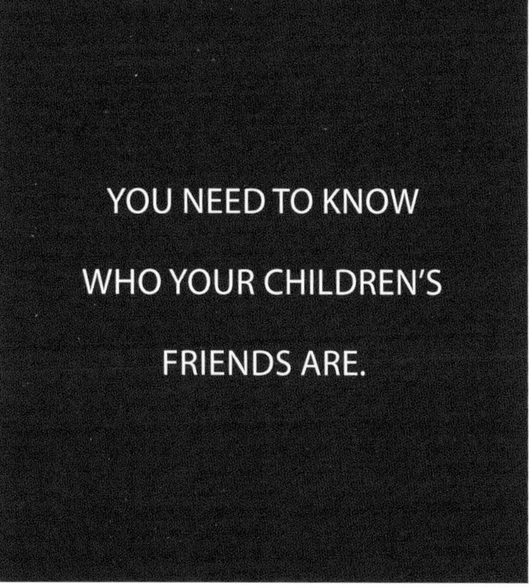

Why the Strong Attractions Among Teenagers?

Teenagers are influenced by their peers for two major reasons:

- They *choose their own friends*, unlike their family and relatives, where the relations are already chosen for them.
- Their *affinity* with peers is due to similarities in age, experience, feelings, hobbies, challenges, problems, circumstances, and school environment.

Teenagers form their own social groups with a special culture, symbols, language, values, and norms.

Teenagers tend to consult less with parents and more with friends as they grow older. The less the interaction with parents, teachers, and older people, the more the teenagers tend to interact with their peers. In financial matters, teens are influenced more by parents; in hobbies, clothes, clubs, leisure time, trips, tours, and type of cars, they follow their friends.

Varieties of Social Interaction

- Young children with their counterparts
- Wrongdoers with wrongdoers
- Youth with youth
- Smokers with smokers
- Old people with old people
- Drug users with drug users
- Righteous persons with the righteous
- Professionals with those of the same profession

Friends affect their friends. The Prophet ﷺ explained:

> A person is affected by the ways of his friend, so let every one of you look to whom he keeps as a friend. (AL-TIRMIDHĪ AND ABŪ DĀWŪD)

> A man will be with whomever he loves. (AL-BUKHĀRĪ AND MUSLIM)

> The example of a good companion and a bad companion is like that of the perfume seller, and the blacksmith. As for the seller of perfume, he will either grant you some, or you buy some from him, or at least you enjoy a pleasant smell from him. As for the blacksmith either he will burn your clothes or you will get an offensive smell from him. (AL-BUKHĀRĪ AND MUSLIM)

The following verse explains the effect of bad influences:

> *The Day that the wrong-doer will bite at his hands, he will say, "Oh! Would that I had taken a [straight] path with the Messenger. Oh, woe is me! Would that I had not taken so-and-so for a friend!*
> *Indeed, he led me astray from the remembrance [of God] after it had come unto me!" For [thus it is:] Satan is ever a betrayer of man.*
> (Qur'an 25:27–29)

Families in Undesirable Locations

Wicked friends create problems that are serious, real, and cannot be brushed aside. Misbehaving school friends, and neighborhood children can wreck a family. If the family is living in a place where they cannot find proper friends for their children, they should move to a place where there are good friends. Many parents change their child's school, or even migrate to another city, if they cannot secure good friends for their children. This is a minor sacrifice by parents compared with the great benefits they will reap later on.

The prophets migrated from one community to another, as mentioned in the scriptures.

Parents: Let your child invite his/her friend home and watch them. Study their behavior fairly and justly. Try to befriend your child's friend!

Dr. James S. Coleman, former President of the American Sociological Association, and one of the world's most famous sociologists, promoted inter-generational closure. This means that the parents know the parents of their children's friends. This promotes closure in society, meaning the ability to promote good behavior and discourage bad behavior.

Activities

ACTIVITY 69: YOUR CHILD'S ROLE MODELS

Ask your child to name three persons s/he would most like to meet and why. This can reveal much about their perception of their "role models."

Have a discussion with your kids about good and bad role models.

ACTIVITY 70: THE BAD INFLUENCE CHILD

Discuss the following situation and then discuss the options given below.

Your neighbor's nine-year-old daughter is a bad influence on your seven-year-old daughter. The children are together almost every day and you want to minimize the contact between the two. Do You:

1. Have your daughter tell the girl that she cannot play with her and that she cannot see her any more.
2. Tell the neighbor's child that she can no longer play with your daughter and she cannot come over to your home nor can your daughter visit her home.
3. Let the two friends be together only when you can completely monitor their behavior.
4. Talk to your neighbor and explain your concerns about the children being together.

The child who is a bad influence causes concern for many parents. The following are comments on each of the answers above.

1. Do not make your child try to explain the problem to the other child. They are probably too young to understand your concerns and you are certain to be everyone's "villain" with this approach.
2. Trying to explain your concerns or setting rules for a child other than your own is inappropriate.
3. This requires a lot of work. You become the full-time supervisor and your duties are required every time the children are together. This could be extremely wearisome over time.
4. It is never an easy task to confront the neighbor with what you perceive as inappropriate behavior on the part of their child. Nevertheless, this is the best way to help solve the problem.

ACTIVITY 71: IF I KNEW BETTER, I WOULD HAVE ACTED DIFFERENTLY!

In a family session, parents should answer the question: "If I were to start my life again, what would I do differently?" Admit your mistakes to your children. Encourage your children to share their mistakes as well.

CHAPTER 23

The Destructive Impact of Television, Video and Computer Games

Introduction

THERE IS SOMETHING in our home that plays an enormous part in our life yet sits quietly in the corner, that spends more time with our children than we do, although we are oblivious to it, and that can destroy entire families yet is never seen as the cause. That thing is television. Do not underestimate TV or its huge impact on our lives!

A Questionnaire for Parents

- Do children watch TV during breakfast and before going to school?
- Do the children watch TV right after coming home from school? While doing homework?
- Does the family watch TV during meals?
- How much of your child's conversation and play is TV-related?
- Is the TV on while children play with friends and toys?
- Do they ask for junk food and toys they see advertised on television?
- Is family life scheduled around what is on TV?
- Can your child turn off the TV at the end of a program or does s/he keep watching?
- Is the child often tired from staying up late watching TV?
- Does the child have fears or nightmares because of what they see on TV?
- Does the child prefer TV to play?
- Does the child ignore the arrival of a guest when s/he is watching TV?
- Does the child delay prayers because of TV?

Too much television watching is a form of addiction and has many similarities to drug use. Many children go into a trance-like state when watching TV, totally absorbed and oblivious to anything else. If you speak to them they do not hear you, and if the phone rings next to them they do not respond. Even their facial expressions undergo a transformation when watching TV, the jaw is relaxed and hanging open slightly, the tongue is resting on the front teeth, and the eyes are in a trance. Rather than being active and mentally alert, children fall into a state of stupor (numbness, dullness, and intellectual shutdown), hypnotized by the flickering screen in front of them.

The content of TV programming can be debated endlessly, with some programs being useful and some harmful. However, the issue of content is less important than whether the experience itself and the time spent are helpful or harmful.

Some children watch television endlessly, such that it becomes a substitute friend, and a killer of time. A child with a TV addiction, is likely to have more problems than other children: s/he may be too shy, aggressive, vulnerable and cannot get along with others.

One television addict in the family is sufficient to create a serious problem. It is harder to organize and enjoy family activities when one member would rather watch TV. It is much easier to go from non-TV related activities (like reading, playing, and drawing) to television viewing, than from going from TV viewing to other activities; the TV-addicted child will find the pull of TV to be too strong.

According to Marie Winn (2002) TV has a hypnotic effect on many people. They become like zombies (dull, stupid, and easily controllable). The smaller problem is what happens when a person watches TV; the bigger problem is what does not happen when a person watches TV. Children who spend hundreds of hours watching TV hurt their intellectual and social development. There will be hundreds of thousands of words not spoken and responded to by another human being, and thousands of questions not asked and answered by another human being.

Negative Effects of TV

When it comes to evaluating television, parents tend to focus on the content rather than the amount of time spent watching TV. They focus on their own needs rather than those of their children. Parents need a source of amusement for their children. They need peace and quiet in the house. Parents need an electronic babysitter who is free, does not complain, is reliable, and is always there. This is in contrast to their children's needs. TV does not meet the children's need to be independent, to discover their strengths and weaknesses and to learn how to communicate (to speak and write well). Children need to engage in make-believe fantasies that they create, rather than having them created for them by adults. Children also need the intellectual stimulation that comes from manipulating, touching, and doing, rather than just passive watching of a TV screen.

Many parents use television to sedate an overactive child because it induces a highly relaxed condition rather than intense mental concentration. The slight defocusing of the eyes while viewing television is similar to what happens to the eyes during a daydreaming state. The material on TV comes to have an unreal, dreamlike quality. Heavy TV viewers are as unbalanced in their lives by their TV "habit" as drug addicts or alcoholics are. They pass up activities that lead to growth or development or a sense of accomplishment. TV is an unproductive experience; almost any other activity is more worthwhile. Even though TV does not satisfy children, they still watch it instead of reading, planting a garden, sewing, playing games, or having conversations. These "meaningful" activities become no longer as desirable as TV viewing. Television "captures" children because it is so pleasurable. Although it is not as pleasurable as eating or being hugged, nevertheless, TV can be very attractive. It is "fake" in the sense that it does not "give" you anything the way food and loving family members give you something, yet it is so fascinating because it concentrates a vast amount of pleasure into one source: bright images, various sounds and music, and recognizable scenes as well as fantasy scenes. Over half of all American parents use television deprivation as a form of punishment and it has become the most widely used form of punishment in America.

Television overwhelms children, who can respond to it only by shutting down and becoming more passive, quiet and inactive. The constant shifting of images, the constant changes of camera angle and focus, the constant change in the viewer's reference point every few seconds, can lead to the creation of a short attention span. Hyperactive schoolchildren may be trying to recapture the dynamic quality of TV images by rapidly changing their perceptual orientation. Even TV shows for children are over-stimulating. They are "sensory overkill" for some preschoolers, who are not developmentally equipped to handle fast-paced electronic stimulation. This may be related to the frantic behavior observed with greater frequency among children today. It may also be related to the epidemic of ADHD among children (Attention Deficit Hyperactivity Disorder). Switch on a children's TV show and count how fast each scene change and camera-angle change takes place. Listen also to the volume and pace of talk by presenters: it will be loud and fast. Then understand that this type of programming stops mental development, unlike a book, which has the effect of developing the child's mind.

Many parents notice that when they turn the TV off, children become frantic and frenzied (widely excited and distracted, jumping around, running wildly, and out of control). This is called the re-entry syndrome. It is similar to the grumpiness that people experience when they go from being totally asleep to being totally awake. They are irritable, and unable to focus or use their senses properly. This also applies to those who are overcoming an alcohol binge or drug use. Children are in an almost unconscious drug-like state while watching TV for a long time. Among children who are addicted to TV, turning off the TV frequently results in rude behavior, swearing, yelling, and acting in a nasty way.

THE SESAME STREET EXPERIENCE

Sesame Street is an international children's TV show that teaches kids the alphabet and many words. The producers of Sesame Street claim that their program is an important educational experience for young children. However, there are other things that are also true of Sesame Street. It plays a very important role in causing children to be addicted to TV. Teachers note that some children enter kindergarten and nursery school recognizing letters from Sesame Street. However, TV addicts have a decrease in imaginative play, an increase in aimless running around, do not use toys and play materials, have low frustration tolerance, lack persistence, and confuse reality with fantasy.

Successful learning requires active, hands-on experience. Sesame Street and programs of this "educational" type are a poor substitute for real, face-to-face teaching experiences. Indeed, any good book is better than Sesame Street!

Elementary school teachers have become frustrated with many students, because the children do not want to read and pay attention. While television may improve non-verbal thinking skills, it does not help with other skills, which are absolutely necessary for success in school. Watching 100 hours of Sesame Street provides less educational value than spending 10 hours on a good book. A parent and a book can do a better job in much less time than Sesame Street, with more advantages for the intellectual development of the child and none of the disadvantages of TV (such as passivity, stupor, over-stimulation, and loss of vocabulary development).

The more television children view, the worse they do in school. Success in school requires a love of reading, an ability to get along with others, and the habit of concentration on boring, repetitive tasks (such as learning the multiplication tables). All of these skills are reduced or destroyed by excessive television watching.

BEFORE TELEVISION

Before television, parents were firmer with their children, not because they believed this was a better way to raise children (which it is), but because firmness was necessary for the parents' survival. Before television, parents observed their children. They trained children to play alone for periods of time, constantly monitoring their children's development. They helped children learn to entertain themselves successfully and reliably. They trained their children to take a nap because quiet rest is good for the child. Parents made sure the kids slept or remained quiet in their room, playing or listening to music or moving around quietly.

After the advent of television, many of these practices disappeared. Nowadays, children do not know how to amuse themselves. Instead of pursuing hobbies and adventures, once the TV is turned off, they do nothing. They reject fun, creative activities, reading, and experience boredom.

Before television, children were able to develop independence and change from being parent-centered (during infancy), to being environment-centered and active. To survive in society you have to be able to adapt. By the time children are three years old, they begin their interdependence and interaction with the world around them.

TV, however, is frequently used as a

babysitter during this stage of a child's life. While watching TV, young children are safe, secure, and receptive, as they were in their mother's arms. They do not have to offer anything, as they must do when they play with another child. For children, watching TV has none of the risks that normal play has: they will not hurt themselves or land in trouble, and they will not make parents angry. Just as they are beginning to emerge from their infant helplessness, television returns them to a state of attachment and dependence.

Before television, children enlarged their interests and tried new things; they overcame boredom by inventing games, playing make-believe, reading, re-reading, writing letters, and pursuing hobbies. After television, children complain that they have "nothing to do," and everything else seems less interesting. Never have they been so entertained and never have they been so bored! TV watching has become the safe, effortless, amusing way of experiencing time and life, while finding something fun to do has become like work! TV films of books take the imagination away from children and give them an unthinking experience instead of an intellectual one. They do not grow with the characters in the story, or understand their insights and struggles and values. Instead of days spent reading a story and then coming to its end, the whole story ends in 90 minutes. Children walk away from TV entertained but unfulfilled. At least while reading the book, they will have partly lived the experience, befriended the characters, and exercised their imagination. The touch, smell and feel aspect of a book allows children to connect to the story, and to be able to read passages again and again. TV involves a withdrawal feeling, a kind of depression when a film is abruptly over and they have to walk away. There is a deep bond between us and books that cannot be studied, quantified or explained. That important emotional attachment is denied by TV.

TV reinforces helplessness and dependence

on adults. In the past, free time provided children with the necessary opportunities for reducing their reliance on adults. Today, for many children, free time is a curse. The only thing they find fun doing with their free time is to watch TV. Some children even eat, spend time with friends, and do their homework in front of the TV.

Family life has been seriously affected by television viewing. Daily routines frequently revolve around the TV, and family rituals have died out. Participation in religious and community activities has decreased, and television is a primary cause. Many parents complain that their home has become like a hotel and a restaurant: just a place to eat and sleep. They are frequently unaware that when TV dominates family life this is an inevitable result. For a family to be healthy, there must be a huge amount of shared experiences. A large quantity of everyday activities that occur and recur and change and develop over many years is the ingredient that creates strong family relationships. Otherwise, parents simply become caretakers, engaging in feeding, clothing, and sheltering, and not much else; parents diminish into people in the background of children's lives.

Television undermines the family by stealing time away from dealing with real live people. The majority of American families watch television during meals, and not always at the same TV set! Even if they were all watching excellent TV programs about nature and morality and current events, they would still have deprived themselves of something more important. Did they share with each other what they did that day? Did they make plans, exchange views, share jokes, and talk about their triumphs and disasters? In what sense are they being a real family? While television by itself does not destroy family life, it certainly does not strengthen family life. However, it takes time away from creating relationships of trust and emotional security between family members, and it stands in the way of parents educating and enjoying their children.

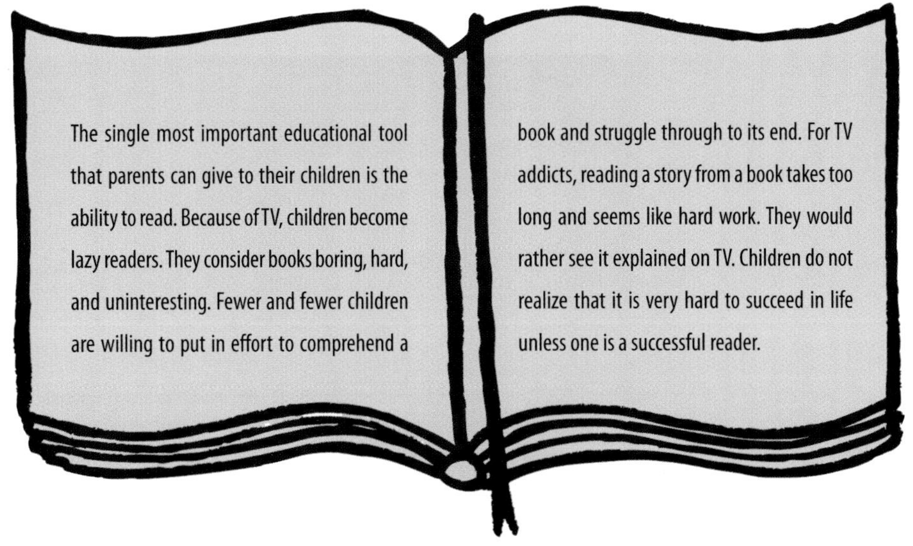

No TV Home!?

Solving the problems created by television is one of the hardest things a family will do. It is similar to the problem faced by cigarette smokers, drug addicts, and alcoholics. They know that they must stop, and they know they are doing something harmful. Nevertheless, they continue with the habit because it is difficult to stop.

Most parents know that the way to overcome the problems caused by television is simply to get rid of it permanently. Most, however, cannot find the conviction and the courage to do this. They find excuses for keeping a television in their home. Their reasons are usually related to selfishness, laziness, addiction, or immorality. Some parents need to know what is going on in the world for business reasons. Most often, however, they underestimate its harmful impact and feel its "educational" benefits outweigh its harms. Others fool themselves into thinking that they are in control of what their children watch and how much their children watch.

Delusions Formed by Television

Once I was called by a couple who had two children, to counsel them on their family problems. Both parents were practicing physicians. To my surprise, the mother said, "Before marriage, I thought that marriage would be full of fun without responsibilities, just like it is depicted on TV by Hollywood actresses." If professionals are deceived by the television portrayal of life, then what chance do our children stand?

When we were in the second grade, the teacher read to us an ancient story of a nice old couple who had a cat and a dog. The cat betrayed the couple, while the dog was faithful to them. The dog ran after the cat, which fled and climbed a tree for safety. The story ended with the statement: "From that day on, whenever a dog saw a cat, he ran after her to bite her." For many years, I really believed that the reason for dogs fighting cats was the original sin of the cat's betrayal of the nice old couple. The teacher should have explained clearly that these stories were fiction because children believe what they hear and see. Similarly, parents have to tell their children that what they see on TV is not real.

Ideas to Help You Break Free of TV

Parents can do the following to reduce TV watching:

- Move the television set(s) to a less prominent location in the home. TV is less tempting when it is not readily accessible.
- Hide the remote control.
- Remove the TV set from your child's bedroom. A television in the bedroom draws children away from family activities and distracts them from homework, thinking, reading, and sleeping. Parents will also find it difficult to monitor harmful programs.
- Keep the TV switched off during meals and have conversations.
- Place clear limits on television viewing. Try to restrict viewing to half-hour a day or one hour every other evening. Explain your rules. Try replacing "You can't watch TV" with "Let's turn off the TV so we can… "
- Designate certain days of the week as TV-free days (for example, school nights).
- Do not use TV as a reward. This can increase its power.
- Listen to your favorite recitations, songs, music, or the radio. Do not use TV as background noise.
- Do not fret if the children complain, "I'm bored!" Free time should lead children to play and do projects together.
- Do not let the TV displace what is important: Family conversations, exercise, and play.

Notable Quotes About Television

Television has changed a child from an irresistible force to an immovable object.
Author Unknown

If you came and you found a strange man... teaching your kids to punch each other, or trying to sell them all kinds of products, you'd kick him right out of the house; but here you are, you come in and the TV is on, and you don't think twice about it.
Jerome Singer

Don't you wish there were a knob on the TV to turn up the intelligence? There's one marked 'brightness' but it doesn't work.
Gallagher

Television has done much for psychiatry by spreading information about it, as well as contributing to the need for it.
Alfred Hitchcock

TV. If kids are entertained by two letters, imagine the fun they'll have with twenty-six. Open your child's imagination. Open a book.
Author Unknown

(SOURCE: WWW.QUOTEGARDEN.COM)

Fast TV Facts

- Americans watch an average of more than four hours of TV a day, or two full months of TV a year.
- 86% percent of American 12th graders who watch TV six hours a day perform badly on reading tests.
- By age 18, American children will have seen an average of more than 200,000 acts of violence, including 16,000 murders on TV.
- The proportion of overweight American children has doubled since 1980, owing, in part, to watching TV and bad diet.

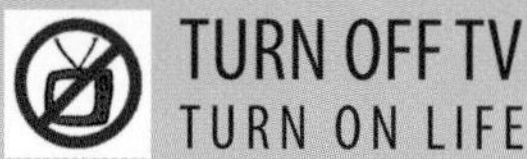

The Plug-In Drug: Television, Computers, and Family Life

Are your children watching (TV) instead of living?

"Families with rules about less TV viewing, [find] their children are happier and better adjusted than families without rules." (Winn 2002)

Surgeon General's Warning: Television Promotes Illiteracy

A GOOD RULE! NO TV ON SCHOOL NIGHTS

Firmness is important. Families that limit TV watching find that children get used to no TV.

Our TV Culture

Kilpatrick (1993) asserts that the reason for the cultural vacuum in many homes is that television has become the organizing principle of family life. Television is no longer a part of the culture; rather, "it is our culture." Television is not just the dominant medium of American entertainment; it is the single most significant shared reality in our entire society. Television shows determine how we live and move and eat and play.

Television defines our priorities, it tells us what is important and what is not important. It shapes our view of reality. It confers significance on events by paying attention to them, or by withholding attention it denies them significance. It does not, for example, confer much significance on religion. Although religious faith still plays a significant part in the lives of most American families, it is close to nonexistent in the lives of television families. Rarely does a TV character go to church, mosque, or temple, seek religious counsel, or pray for moral guidance. Another impression left by television is that sex underlies almost everything: that it is constantly on everyone's mind, or should be. At the same time, television sex rarely takes place within the context of marriage but almost exclusively outside of marriage. Schools are sometimes against parental values. Television programs are almost always against traditional values. It opens up the home to become the receptacle for whatever somebody in Hollywood wants to dump onto your living room floor and into your children's minds. Those who think that their children will not be corrupted by TV are mistaken. TV teaches children to be aware of what they lack rather than what they have. TV focuses on beautiful people and leads children to be dissatisfied with themselves. TV gives children a confused sense of morality by undermining values based on faith and belief in God. "Good guys" are seen drinking, smoking, having girlfriends, and shooting and killing people! TV gives children early exposure to sexuality, whether it is the bikini wearing Little Mermaid of Disney or the very revealing outfits of movies stars.

Parents may not want children to watch violence, vulgarity, sexual material or enticing advertisements for junk food and useless toys on TV. However, many parents ask: Is it worthwhile to watch educational programs? Parents will be surprised to learn that more and more parents, teachers, and child development researchers say NO. They know that television viewing:

- Requires less mental work than reading,
- Inhibits the learning of reading skills,
- Reduces a child's perseverance in finding answers to problems.

These disadvantages of TV outweigh any advantages.

The Stranger

"A few months before I was born, my dad met a stranger who was new to our small town. From the beginning, Dad was fascinated with this enchanting newcomer, and soon invited him to live with our family. The stranger was quickly accepted and welcomed me into the world a few months later. As I grew up I never questioned his place in our family. Mom taught me to love the Word of God. Dad taught me to obey God. But the stranger was our storyteller. He could weave the most fascinating tales. Adventures, mysteries and comedies were plentiful. He could occupy our whole family for hours each evening. He was like a friend to the whole family. He took Dad and me to our first baseball game. He was always encouraging us to see the movies and he even made arrangements to introduce us to several movie stars. The stranger was an incessant talker. Dad didn't seem to mind, but sometimes Mom would quietly get up – while the rest of us were listening to one of his stories of faraway places – and go to her room, read her Bible and pray. I wonder now if she ever prayed that the stranger would leave. You see, my dad filled our household with morals. But this stranger never felt an obligation to honor them. Profanity, for example, was not allowed in our house – not from us, or our friends, or adults. Our longtime visitor, however, used bad words that burned my ears and made Dad squirm. The stranger was never confronted. My dad did not permit alcohol in his home – not even for cooking. But the stranger offered us beer and other alcoholic beverages often. He made cigarettes look tasty, cigars look attractive, and pipes distinguished.

He talked freely about sex. His comments were sometimes rude, sometimes suggestive, and sometimes embarrassing. I know now that my early concepts of the man/woman relationship were influenced by the stranger. As I look back, I believe it was the grace of God that prevented the stranger from influencing us more. Time after time he opposed the values of my parents. Yet he was seldom rebuked and never asked to leave. More than thirty years have passed since the stranger moved in with us. But if I were to walk into my parents' house today, you would still see him sitting over in a corner, waiting for someone to listen to him talk and watch him draw his pictures. His name? We always called him TV." (AUTHOR UNKNOWN)

How to Change the TV Habit: Experiences of Some Families

Suzanne, mother of a five year old and a two year-old, found that it was her own TV addiction that she had to break first. The children watched TV occasionally, maybe two or three shows a week, but they never developed a daily TV habit. After reading Marie Winn's book *The Plug-in Drug*, and Dr. Jane Healy's book, *Endangered Minds*, she became convinced that the family should watch less television. "We discontinued cable TV service and we have no antenna," said Suzanne, "so now we have very poor reception. That keeps the television from being such a temptation."

SET LIMITS ON THE AMOUNT AND CONTENT OF THE TELEVISION YOUR CHILDREN WATCH

Pam decided to participate in National TV-turnoff Week. Her children, who were then 13, 11, and 4 grumbled at first, and then they stopped complaining as they found other things to do that week. The older boys read more and played together, even teaching their little sister to play soccer. The children organized family activities and were kinder to one another. Not having a TV made a big difference. Family time was now available.

NEVER WATCH A MOVIE IN FRONT OF YOUR CHILDREN THAT SHOWS ACTIVITIES YOU DO NOT WANT THEM DOING

Several parents have permanently turned off the TV and agreed that the effort was worth it. Kane's family made the transition on vacation: There was no TV available when we were on vacation, so it was a natural time to make a change. At first, our daughter asked about it, but we just distracted her whenever she asked.

Parents think children must be constantly entertained. Parents feel compelled to help their children: "Oh, I'll find something for you to do." After a while, however, they are comfortable letting their children find their own activities.

Young children particularly benefit from helping their parents with chores. Invite children to help with the cooking. Should parents be role models for their children? If children see parents relaxing or being busy without television, then children will learn to do this too.

A Word of Caution About TV

Television has become one of the most common objects in our society. If children feel that they are being prevented from TV by force, they may view this as a deprivation of their rights. This may force them to go to places to watch TV, where it is unsafe for them to do so or where they are vulnerable. The following approaches help to alleviate the problem:

- Occupy children with other activities that they like (scientific, cultural, spiritual or physical activities).
- Whenever possible, do not let children watch TV by themselves; parents should be with them commenting appropriately on certain scenes and programs. Hopefully, this will guide children to certain virtues and principles. It will also develop an immunity in the children against evil and violent scenes. Develop a shield of faith, which in the future, prevents sin. Strong faith is needed because parents cannot be with their children all the time.
- Blocking harmful TV shows, may be possible through the V-Chip device, which was introduced in 1999.

Experts and Research on Television for Children

Spock (1998) and the American Academy Of Pediatrics (1999) say that toddlers and children **should not** watch TV at all as "infant TV viewing is associated with delayed language, shortened attention spans and delayed cognitive development." "The scientific evidence of benefit is just not there and the best available evidence suggests harm."
Spock recognizes that this strategy is "far too extreme" for most parents.

Rosemond (1993) suggests **prohibiting** TV until a child can read and enjoy books. Even then, limit it to five hours a week.

Rankin (2006) states major studies that suggest watching three hours or more of TV a day hurts school performance, but well-chosen educational shows can help. Educational shows have also been linked to increased creativity.

Share with your child the inspiring and instructive stories and poems

(BENNETT 1996)

A List of Family Alternatives to Watching TV

Most parents allow their children to watch TV, owing to the lack of options for filling the children's time. Parents are so tired that TV gives them time to relax, keeping children out of their way. The solution is to start engaging in useful activities. We have mentioned the many evils of watching television for both children and parents. Perhaps the greatest harm that TV does to family life is to trivialize it, and this is a danger not realized by many. Families do not have interaction among themselves; TV prevents them from being together. Consider some of the alternatives to watching TV.

How would you treat a thief who steals your money? What about a thief who steals your time, and your family's life? TV is inflicting much more harm on you than stealing your money. It is taking your happiness away. Although you may restore your money somehow, you cannot restore your time and happiness.

Alternatives to Watching TV

Depending on the child's age, appropriate activities can be selected. There are books that list 1000s of activities for families to choose from:

1. Build a fort
2. Organize a community clean-up
3. Visit the library, borrow a book, attend library activities
4. Listen to the radio
5. Visit the zoo, or the museum
6. Paint a picture
7. Go to your community center or park
8. Go swimming
9. Read a book aloud to your younger sister/brother
10. Plan a picnic
11. Walk, run, or ride a bike
12. Sing a song, or memorize a poem
13. Go bird watching
14. Jump rope
15. Volunteer for a community organization or a charity
16. Go camping (even if it is just in the backyard)
17. Write a letter to a friend, a relative or a grandparent
18. Plant a flower, vegetable or herb garden
19. Read magazines or newspapers
20. Play chess
21. Make friendship bracelets; put one on one person's wrist, and one on another person's wrist
22. Donate surplus items to refugees or charities
23. Start a diary
24. Visit a local bookstore
25. Research your family history
26. Learn woodwork and make a bookshelf
27. Make crafts to give as gifts
28. Make up a story and write it down
29. Take a nature hike. Collect seeds and leaves. Make a collage with the materials you collected and post it on the refrigerator
30. Watch the night sky through binoculars: identify the different constellations. Observe the moon. Read something about astronomy
31. Bake cookies for your neighbors
32. Ask an older family member to tell you a story about his or her childhood. Write about it
33. Make jam
34. Make yogurt
35. Exercise
36. Walk to work or school
37. Go bowling
38. Play football
39. Attend religious services of various faiths
40. Run a potato sack race
41. Play soccer, volleyball and basketball
42. Learn typing
43. Learn how to use a computer
44. Learn to drive
45. Play table tennis
46. Organize a neighborhood hunt to find something hidden
47. Wash clothes by hand
48. Vacuum the house
49. Clean the windows
50. Cook dinner with friends or family
51. Reconcile bank statements
52. Write a book review
53. Discuss the family monthly budget
54. Prepare a party
55. Swap magazines with your friends
56. Clean up your room
57. Play frisbee or hockey
58. Write a letter to your favorite author, living or dead
59. Play with your pet or the neighbor's pets
60. Do yard work
61. Fly a kite
62. Go on a family trip
63. Hang a thermometer and barometer on the porch or a tree
64. Make up a play
65. Go sledding and make a snowman
66. Make a collage out of pictures from old magazines
67. Visit a nursing home
68. Babysit for new parents
69. Go hiking
70. Solve puzzles
71. Make a new friend
72. Start a book reading group
73. Play board games with your family or friends
74. Make an ant farm
75. Have a garden tea party
76. Make a miniature boat and float it in the water
77. Draw pictures of members of your family
78. Learn how to use a compass and a map
79. Learn the metric system
80. Have a conversation with an elderly person
81. Play checkers
82. Learn to sew
83. Visit the countryside
84. Milk a cow
85. Climb a tree
86. Collect jokes, record them in a book, and tell them to friends and family
87. Learn some riddles
88. Watch the sunset and the sunrise
89. Prepare a grocery list
90. Learn to say simple phrases in a few different languages. (Thank you, good morning/evening, yes, no, count 1 to 10, the days of the week….)

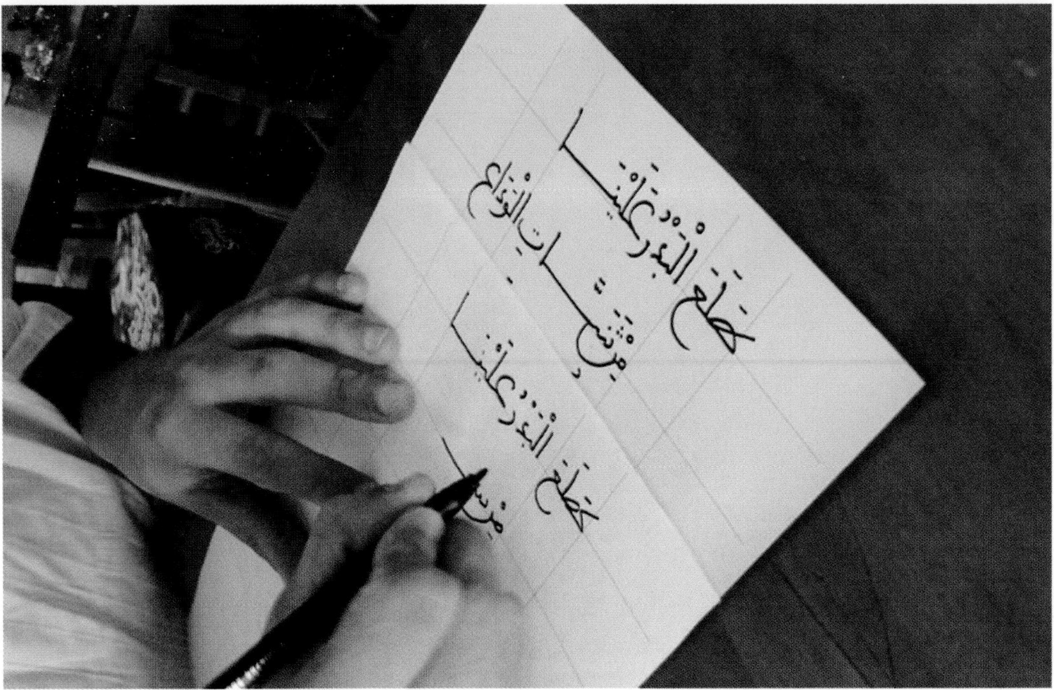

More Serious Options

The following are more serious activities for children to perform (adapted from Beshir et al. 1998).

Community Activities

- Learn another language in addition to the two crucial ones: the indigenous language of your country and Qur'anic Arabic.
- Attend youth camps: Make sure that enough useful activities are organized for the children, especially during long vacations. In addition to the intellectual and spiritual content, the camp programs should include plays, sports, skits, games, and contests.
- Join a boys' and girls' clubs.
- Join *nashīd* (song) groups. Choose songs that are decent and easy for the children to learn, and allow them to perform in community celebrations.
- Attend overnight parties: sleep-over parties organized by the children and supervised by parents provide much fun for children and help create strong bonds among them.
- Play in the rain, snow or in the sun (use proper protection).

'Umar ibn al-Khaṭṭāb said:

"Teach your children swimming, archery, and horseback riding."

- Learn self-defense.
- Join *tajwīd* (Qur'an recitation with proper intonation) and poetry lessons.
- Learn safety rules in case of fire.
- Learn public-speaking.
- Learn debating.
- Learn English and Arabic calligraphy.
- Go fishing.
- Learn CPR (cardiopulmonary resuscitation)
- Learn the Heimlich maneuver.

NATURE ACTIVITIES

- **Explore Nature at Your Own Speed.** Hiking trails should be found where the family can take a leisurely stroll or a more energetic hike to see the wonders of nature: birds, insects, snakes, flowers, and trees. Children can spend hours hunting for rocks in the river. They can also go biking.
- **Gaze at the Stars.** Stargazing is a great activity. Use a map of the constellations. Grab a blanket and some fruit and go somewhere where there is very little light. It could be your backyard or the top of a hill. When it is completely dark, try pointing out different constellations to one another. Point out the Little Dipper, and then look for Leo, the Lion. Eventually, children will start finding their own shapes in the stars, just like they do in the clouds.

GAMES

- Play the toes-and-fingers game, comparing the relative length of your fingers. Each person holds up his or her hand with the fingers right next to each other. You will discover that your index finger is shorter than your ring finger, and your middle finger is the longest, but that the pattern is different with each person. Then check your toes: take off your socks, lie on your backs next to each other, and look at your feet. Toes are different, too.
- Counting the ribs of your children can be fun, especially if done by the grandparents.
- On car trips divide the car into two teams, the left side and the right side. Silently count cows, sheep, and horses. Count dogs, cats, and birds. You can count only the animals on your side. However, if you spot a graveyard on your opponents' side, all their counted animals will be "dead," and they would have to start over.
- Play the alphabet game. Each person in the car collects each of the letters of the alphabet from road signs. They must be gathered in order. No one is allowed to turn around to see signs on the other side of the road. The first person to see "z" wins.
- On trips, "collect" license plates from as many states and countries as possible.
- Play "B.B. Bumblebee, I see something you don't see." You can keep a two-year-old busy for several minutes. You go first and say, "B.B. Bumblebee, I see something you don't see, and it's red." Then you give your daughter a chance to look around the room and guess what red thing you might be looking at. When she gives the right answer, it is her turn. Or "I spy with my little eye something beginning with A" and the child has to guess what object you have seen beginning with the letter, in this case A.
- Play chess. One of the effective ways of training your children to think and be creative is to play a game of chess. It teaches patience and it disciplines the mind. You can also learn something about the personality of your opponents by analyzing their strategy in the game. Are they aggressive or defensive? Do they take risks or not?

Sounds of Nature.

Have children sit down, close their eyes, and be as quiet as they can, counting all the different sounds they can hear. Hear the sound of birds and insects and frog.

Expose them to nature

Our children are going away from the world of woods, rivers and mountains, into the world of TV, computers, and videogames. Take them back to nature.

EATING WITH YOUR CHILDREN

According to a survey by the National Center on Addiction and Substance Abuse at Columbia University:

- Children who eat dinner with their family communicate better with their family. Family dinners are more than just sharing food. The conversations help parents learn about their children's lives, the challenges they face, and the activities that children like to do.
- Teenagers in the U.S. who never eat dinner with their families are 72 percent more likely to use drugs, alcohol, and cigarettes.
- Children who have frequent family dinners get better grades in school, have less stress at home, and trust their parents more.

The Harm of Excessive Internet Use

Much of the discussion on the negative effects of TV can also be applied to the Internet and computer games. Parents often encourage excessive use of computers. Some parents assume computers are a tool that can bring only benefit to our lives. Not so! Parents expect their children to use computers moderately and responsibly. The reality, however, is that some kids use computers to waste hours in chat rooms, to access useless websites, and to look at pornography.

Like television, excessive Internet use can foster apathy, interfere with legitimate work, increase obesity, and hinder normal socialization between children. Children are also exposed to bad ideas and plenty of advertising.

Computers are a powerful tool which can bring benefits and much-needed information. However, parents have to supervise their use, introduce passwords, block certain sites, use safety measures, and become more familiar with the medium. Do not allow children to spend excessive time on the Internet and keep computers in the living room in full view of the family.

Computer Games

Computer games also take up much of children's – especially boys' – time. What may appear to be a harmless and innocent game, can actually harm children.

Computer games contain violence and are also highly addictive. Extreme cases of addiction have also led to loss of life (several deaths occurred in South Korea from game addiction) (BBC News 2005).

These games de-sensitize reality, so that much of the real world is reduced to a game and an arena for "fun." Games that encourage combat fighting and commando-style killing lower the value of human life. Militaries train their soldiers to kill using computer games like the ones children play. Other themes include witchcraft, demons and the occult world. Magic and spells have become common in computer games.

Unfortunately, as technology advances, these games become more real and "life-like." This is highly dangerous, blending the real world into fantasy. Children should not to be encouraged to flee reality but to face life with all its challenges.

Parents need to limit the amount of time children spend on computer games and control the games they choose to play.

Videogames and Children

Videogames were introduced in the 1970's. Since then they have become very popular with children. Violence, substance abuse, and sex are becoming more common in videogames.

Paducah (Kentucky), Jonesboro (Arkansas), Littleton (Colorado), and Blacksburg (Virginia) are four American towns that experienced school shootings carried out by students who often played violent videogames. In the 1999 Columbine High School massacre (Gibbs 1999), teenagers Eric Harris and Dylan Klebold shot 13 people and injured 23 before committing suicide. These two teenagers enjoyed playing the videogame Doom, a bloody shooting game intended to train soldiers to kill. Harris had created a customized version of the game with two shooters, extra weapons, unlimited ammunition, and victims who could not fight back – similar features to the actual shootings he was about to do. (Anderson and Dill 2000). The more children practice violent acts, the more likely they are to perform violent acts. (Clark 1993)

There is a relationship between aggressive behavior by children and their exposure to aggression in videogames. The more a child engages in violence as part of a video game, the more likely the child will engage in violent behavior towards other people.

Males play video games more frequently than females.

Videogames are promoting antisocial and anti-religious behaviors (such as murder, verbal abuse, and theft).

The social content of videogames have negative portrayals of women. In the Nintendo games, women are usually cast as persons who are acted upon rather than as initiators of action; in extreme cases, they are depicted as victims. Many games were based on a scenario in which a woman is kidnapped or has to be rescued. (Funk 1993)

Extensive television viewing is associated with aggressive behavior, poor academic performance, precocious sexuality, obesity, and the use of drugs or alcohol. Violent games are associated with hostility and physical fights.

Playing violent games leads to:
1) Increased physiological arousal,
2) Increased aggressive thoughts,
3) Increased aggressive feelings,
4) Increased aggressive behaviors, and
5) Decreased pro-social helping behaviors

DEPICTION OF GENDER DIFFERENCES ON TELEVISION:

1. In TV male–female interaction, men are usually more dominant.
2. Men on TV are usually rational, ambitious, smart, competitive, powerful, stable, and tolerant, whereas women are romantic, submissive, and timid unless they are portrayed as manipulative villainesses.
3. For men, the emphasis is on strength, performance, and skill; for women, it is on attractiveness and desirability.
4. Marriage and family are not important to men in many TV shows. For nearly half the men, it was not possible to tell if they were married, a fact that was true for only 11 percent of the women.

Most females on night-time television are young, attractive, thin, and ornamental. Females are consistently placed in situations where looks count more than brains, and helpless and incompetent behaviors are expected. Men are twice as likely as women to be shown as competent and able to solve problems. Women are depicted as sex objects more frequently than men, and men are portrayed as inept when handling children's needs. (Seidman, 1999; Davis, 1990; Beal 1994)

On American music television, females are often shown as sex objects, trying to gain the attention of a male. In rap music videos women are portrayed as objects of lust. Women are four times more likely than men to wear very little clothing, whereas men are almost always fully clothed.

FAMILY DISTRACTION: Video games stress solo action rather than cooperation. A common game scenario is that of an anonymous character performing an aggressive act against an anonymous enemy. The world of video

games has little sense of community and few team players. Most video games do not allow play by more than one player at a time. The National Institute on Media and the Family has been studying and reporting on the influence of video games for many years. We have found that many videogames glorify gang culture, celebrate brutality, promote crudeness, and support violence and brutality toward women!

In Summary

- Children who play less videogames do better in school and also get into fewer fights.
- Encourage educational games and discourage violent games.
- TV and videogames have less influence on children who have good character.
- Parents must set limits on the amount of time children spend on videogames.

Turn off TV and Turn on Life

Enjoy Children More and be with them. Parenting is the most challenging and most rewarding job; it requires science, art, and faith. Enjoy your children every day (rather than the TV).

Activities

ALTERNATIVES TO TELEVISION AND VIDEO GAMES

ACTIVITY 72: EDUCATIONAL VISITS

Expose children to many different institutions. "Tell me and I will forget. Show me and I will remember. Include me and I will understand."

- Take your children to a court, to see judges and lawyers.
- Take your children to police stations and prisons.
- Visit places of worship of other faiths with your children.
- Visit museums, parks, libraries, and farms.

ACTIVITY 73: MAKE THEM FOOD CONSCIOUS

Ask children about the ingredients of food and how meals are prepared: soups, pizza, bread, yogurt, cheese, hamburgers, pancakes, waffles, curry, biryani, cakes, honey, popcorn, mayonnaise, ketchup, tea and coffee.

Show children the ingredients and preparation of: soap, shampoo, paper, ink, clothes, plastic, asphalt, shoes, furniture, and carpets.

Let each child choose one type of food and recipe and try to cook it with your help.

ACTIVITY 74: WHAT DO YOU VALUE THE MOST?

In a family meeting, ask each member: "If you have only one day to live, what will you do? Why?" Then let each one discuss the answer.

ACTIVITY 75: GEMS OF WISDOM TO CHILDREN!

Get the family together and ask a child to read aloud the following passages. Explain the meaning and share examples from your experiences. Encourage children to share their opinions.

My Child: Be cautious of…
The noble man if you insult him,
The wise man if you embarrass him,
The ignoble man if you are gracious to him,
The foolish man if you joke with him, and
The dissolute man if you associate with him.

O My Beloved Child;
I savored all kinds of delights and found nothing as sweet as health.
I suffered all kinds of bitterness and found nothing more bitter than the need for others.
I carried heavy loads of iron and rocks and found nothing as heavy as debt.
Be aware that your lifetime is only two kinds of days…one for you and one against you,
When it is your day, do not be arrogant and ungrateful,
When it is against you, just be patient.

(ʿALĪ IBN ABŪ ṬĀLIB)

ACTIVITY 76: ARE YOU MANAGING YOUR FAMILY WISELY?

A Checklist: How Am I Doing As a Parent?

Parenting is both challenging task and rewarding. Parents are involved in nurturing, disciplining, managing, leading, and counseling. Parents engage in teaching, training, coaching, and mentoring. They are like a compassionate doctor whose aim is always to help improve and do no harm. Parents empower, encourage, enhance, and extend a helping hand to children.

Review your parenting practices item by item. (It may take several sessions to cover all the points).

As a parent:

- Did I choose my spouse wisely?
  The time and effort I spend finding the right spouse is nothing compared with the time I will have to spend dealing with the wrong spouse. Search thoroughly, so that you can get along well.
- Did I explain the family mission to my children clearly?
- Did I teach the correct values? What makes a home wonderful is not walls and ceilings but values and morals.
- Did I promote the best abilities in each of my children? Each child has distinct interests and hobbies; we need to strengthen their talents.
- Did I make the best use of our family resources: time, money, and materials?
- Did I pay attention to my children's feelings and perceptions? Their perceptions matter. I need to "walk a while in their shoes."
- Did I coach my children? Children do not like to be ignored, even if they are doing wrong. They need to be worked with, included, recognized, and rewarded.
- Did I provide to my children proper guidelines? Parents need to provide discipline, feedback, and rules.
- Did I set a good example? The way you talk to one another and about one another, the types of jokes you share, the promises you keep, the friends that you have, and the credit you appropriately share…are all important.
- Did I do all my parenting duties for the sake of our Creator, Our Lord, Who gifted and entrusted me with this family?
- Did I make plans to accomplish our family goals? Your family plan should answer these questions:

- What needs to be accomplished?
- Why does it need to be done? How does it contribute to our overall mission?
- When does it need to be accomplished?
- Where are we now in relation to this goal?
- Who will be required to accomplish the plan?
- How will it be accomplished? What specific activities are entailed, and what resources are required?

Your children and spouse depend on you, just as you depend on them. Do not let them down.

Conclusion

Conclusion

WE BELIEVE THAT the family has the capacity to and is meant to produce righteous, effective citizens. This task is best be done within a happy and supportive home. Parents are the first and best teachers for their children. Parents need to act as models, shepherds, pastors, educators, trainers, disciplinarians, mentors, and coaches.

Today, neither the Western world nor the Muslim world offers a satisfactory model for parenting. We need to learn from each other. The West has adopted a lifestyle that is focused on self-gratification. Morality and values have weakened. This value-neutral system has suffered from drug abuse, alcoholism, sexual promiscuity, and the weakening of the family.

On the other hand, the Muslim world is rife with oppression, coercion, fear, corruption, and intimidation. Many Muslims possess a slave mentality, that stifles courage, creativity, and freethinking. The Muslim world has produced an irrational, superstitious, and dependent generation of children, who grow up without concern for the public interest.

Non-Muslims need to put God back in their lives and complement their great achievements in science and technology with religiosity that recognizes Allāhu Akbar (God is Greater) and Allāhu A'lam (God knows best). Muslims need to rediscover God and promote peaceful, free societies, practicing tolerance and democracy (*shūrā*).

On a micro-level, good parenting is the seed from which all this can spring. Parenting is a 24/7 task, 365 days a year. It is an effort with no vacation, no delegation, done under countless interferences and much stress. It demands a father and mother team with rationality and knowledge complemented by emotions and feelings. Psychology, sociology, medical sciences, communication, and faith are all necessary requirements for parenting. We cannot win a war with our children; we have to win them over with love, patience, and two-way communication. Never forget that every child is shouting: "Please make me feel important."

Many parents think that they know their children well and vice versa, but this is rarely the case. Children may perceive help as interference, advice as bossing, and affection as babying. There exists an erroneous perception among many children that their parents do not love them!

Reduce the negative aspects and enhance the positive traits in your child's personality. Parents need to identify what style of parenting they exhibit: autocratic, permissive, democratic or authoritative. Parents have to ask themselves: "Are we really doing the right thing?" The answer can be sought from as many sources as possible.

Learn the child's physical and emotional phases of development. Achieve the maximum potential of each child at the right time. For example, children can memorize well, and learn languages and music quite easily, before the age of ten.

Peers have tremendous influence on children. Parents have to provide a welcoming

> If I had my child to raise all over again, I'd build self-esteem first, and the house later. I'd finger-paint more, and point the finger less. I would do less correcting and more connecting. I'd take my eyes off my watch, and watch with my eyes. I'd take more hikes and fly more kites. I'd stop playing serious, and seriously play. I would run through more fields and gaze at more stars. I'd do more hugging and less tugging. (Loomans 2000)

atmosphere in their homes to their children's friends. Parents need to befriend the friends and parents of their children's friends to attract the right kind of friends.

Parents need to acquire the skills, education, and tools needed to raise their children properly.

Character building has a time limit. Breastfeeding prevents many diseases and provides the infant with psychological and emotional "capital." Teach children love, courage, creativity, honesty, freedom, self-confidence, generosity, and trust.

Parents need to teach each child time management, money management, the etiquette of disagreement, decision making, the art of supplication, problem solving, good manners (politeness, respect, patience, humbleness), the art of listening, and modesty.

Children whose fathers and mothers are too busy for them are like orphans. Most parents do not spend enough time with their children and they resort to other means to compensate (like television, babysitters, and gifts). Watching too much television is harmful. The solution is spending quality and quantity time with the family. The extended family (grandparents, aunts, uncles, and cousins) are the best babysitters, mentors and role models.

Build the character traits of love, courage, honesty, creativity, responsibility, and independence. All this has to be done within a happy home environment, which acts as an incubator to produce righteous adults. A happy home is based on continual two-way communication between parents and children. Sincere praise is a basic ingredient when complimenting your children in things they do right. Organizing monthly family meetings is an excellent practice and conducive to establishing family harmony. Touching, kissing, hugging, and smiling builds affection between parents and children. Parents need to master the art of listening to their children.

Children are good observers, but poor interpreters. They see and observe how their father and mother treat each other, and how they treat their grandparents, relatives, siblings, guests, the rich and the poor, the live-in help (maids and servants) and the neighbors. They watch how they treat pets, animals, plants, flowers, and the environment. They compare their parents' words with their deeds and uncover the truth as well as hypocrisy. "Do as I say, not as I do" is not acceptable. Parents should practice what they preach. However, when parents make a mistake, the least they can do is to confess their shortcomings sincerely to their children.

Children need role models. If parents do not provide them with good role models, children will choose the wrong ones. The best of all role models are the Prophets of God, followed by those leaders across the globe who promote morality and family values.

Mothers play the most vital role in child rearing. It is not a coincidence that Prophets Ishmael, Moses, Jesus, and Muhammad (peace be upon them all) were all raised by their mothers. To honor women in our life, men have to demonstrate their respect for them in words and actions.

One parent paused and remarked: "I am

too insignificant to make a difference!" This is not true. Parenting is a task too important to do in isolation. Forming support groups is very useful. You cannot change your ancestors but you can certainly improve your descendants. As a parent, you can make a great difference in this world, so do not lose hope. It is never too late!

Children's personalities are influenced by nature, nurture, and, above all, the Will of the Creator! Parenting is a science and an art.

This book is the first in a series and, God willing, other books will follow. We invite scholars and experts to enrich the field of parenting with their much needed contribution.

At the end of your life ask yourself the following question: "Have I been a good parent who tried to improve the world?"

Do Your Best. Have Faith in God and Rest!
What will matter at the end is not what kind of cars, houses, or bank account you had, but how good a parent you were!

Don't wait until it is too late!

Appendix 1

Selected Qur'anic Verses and Traditions of the Prophet Muhammad ﷺ on Parenting

Selected Qur'anic Verses

And those who pray "Our Lord! Grant unto us spouses and offspring who will be the comfort of our eyes and give us (the grace) to lead the righteous." (Qur'an 25:74)

And those who believe and whose families follow them in Faith to them shall We join their families: nor shall We deprive them [of any of the fruit] of their works: each individual is hostage to his own deeds. (Qur'an 52:21)

It is not your wealth nor your sons that will bring you nearer to Us in degree: but only those who believe and work Righteousness; these are the ones for whom there is a multiplied Reward for their deeds while secure they [reside] in the dwellings on high! (Qur'an 34:37)

It is Allah Who created you in a state of [helpless] weakness, then gave [you] strength after weakness then after strength gave [you] weakness and a head of white hair: He creates as He wills and it is He Who has all knowledge and power. (Qur'an 30:54)

It is He Who brought you forth from the wombs of your mothers when you knew nothing; and He gave you hearing and sight and intelligence and affections: that you may give thanks [to Allah]. (Qur'an 16:78)

O you who believe! Truly among your spouses and your children are [some that are] enemies to yourselves: so beware of them! But if you forgive and overlook and cover up [their faults], verily Allah is Oft-Forgiving Most Merciful. (Qur'an 64:14)

O you who believe! Let not your riches or your children divert you from the remembrance of Allah. If any act thus, the loss is their own. (Qur'an 63:9)

Say: "The true losers are those who lose their own souls and their families on the Day of Judgment: Ah! that is indeed the [real and] evident Loss!" (Qur'an 39:15)

Behold, Luqman said to his son by way of instruction: "O my son! Join not in worship [others] with Allah: for false worship is indeed the highest wrong-doing." And We have enjoined on man [to be good] to his parents: in travail upon travail did his mother bear him, and in years twain was his weaning: [hear the command], "Show gratitude to Me and to thy parents: to Me is [thy final] Goal. But if they strive to make you join in worship with Me things of which you hast no knowledge, obey them not; yet bear them company in this life with justice [and consideration], and follow the way of those who turn to Me [in love]: in the end the return of you all is to Me, and I will tell you the truth [and meaning] of all that you did."

"O my son!" [said Luqman], "If there be [but] the weight of a mustard-seed and it were [hidden] in a rock or [anywhere] in the heavens or on earth, Allah will bring it forth: for Allah understands the finest mysteries, [and] is well-acquainted [with them]. O my son! Establish regular prayer, enjoin what is just, and forbid what is wrong: and bear with patient constancy whatever betide you; for this is firmness [of purpose] in [the conduct of] affairs. And swell not your cheek [for pride] at people, nor walk in insolence through the earth; for Allah does not love any arrogant boaster. And be moderate in your pace, and lower your voice; for the harshest of sounds without doubt is the braying of the ass."

(Qur'an 31:13–19)

Wealth and sons are allurements of the life of this world: but the things that endure Good Deeds are best in the sight of your Lord as rewards and best as [the foundation for] hopes. (Qur'an 18:46)

"O my Lord! Make me one who establishes regular Prayer and also [raise such] among my offspring, O our Lord! and accept my supplication." (Qur'an 14:40)

"O our Lord! Forgive me, my parents, and [all] Believers, on the Day that the Reckoning will be established!" (Qur'an 14:41)

And as for that wall, it belonged to two orphan boys [living] in the town, and beneath it was [buried] a treasure belonging to them [by right]. Now their father had been a righteous man, and so your Sustainer willed it that when they come of age, they should bring forth their treasure by your Sustainer's grace.

(Qur'an 18:82)

Traditions of the Prophet Muhammad ﷺ

People are like minerals [or metals, having their own character]; the best of people in the [pre-Islamic] age of ignorance (*jāhiliyyah*) are the best of them in [the age of] Islam, if they understand [and comprehend].

(AL-BUKHĀRĪ AND MUSLIM)

The most desirable of activities after the rituals is making a Muslim happy.
(AL-BUKHĀRĪ)

It is better for a man to discipline his son than to give charity every day.
(AL-TIRMIDHĪ)

When a person dies, his acts come to an end, except for three: recurring charity, or knowledge [by which people] benefit, or a pious child who prays for the deceased. (MUSLIM)

Your Lord has a right on you; and your own body has a right on you; and your family has a right on you; so you should fulfill the rights of all those who have a right on you. (AL-BUKHĀRĪ)

It is a big sin for a man to neglect his responsibilities and withhold the subsistence from his dependents. (ABŪ DĀWŪD)

"All of you are guardians and responsible for your wards and the things under your care. The Imam is the guardian of his subjects and is responsible for them. A man is the guardian of his family and is responsible for them. A wife is the guardian of her husband's house and is responsible for it. A servant is the guardian of his boss's belongings and is responsible for them. All of you are guardians and responsible for your wards and the things under your care."
(AL-BUKHĀRĪ)

Prophet Muhammad's ﷺ Advice to a Child

Ibn 'Abbās, while he was a child, was told by Prophet Muhammad ﷺ:

"O young man: I am teaching you a few words. Feel close to Allah, Remember Allah; Allah will protect you.

Remember Allah; Allah will take care of you. If you have a need, turn to Allah to provide you. If you need help ask Allah for help.

Know that if the whole world is united against you, it will be unable to harm you unless Allah has willed so. If the whole world is united to benefit you, it will be unable to benefit you unless Allah has willed so."

(AL-TIRMIDHĪ AND AḤMAD IBN ḤANBAL)

Appendix 2

Activities List

Activities List

Bibliography

Bibliography

ENGLISH

Abd al-Ati, Hammudah. *The Family Structure in Islam*. Indianapolis, IN: American Trust Publications, 1997.

—— *Islam in Focus*, 3rd rev. edn. Beltsville, MD: Amana Publications, 1998.

Abdul Hye, Hamid. "Islam on the Rearing of Children." *The Muslim World Journal*, vol. 18 (issues 11 & 12) India, May/June 1991.

Abdullah, Nina. "Qur'an Memorization and Memory." Unpublished paper. Reston, Virginia, 1994.

Abel, Gene and Nora Harlow. *The Stop Child Molestation Book*. La Vergne, Tennessee: Ingram Content Group, 2001.

AbuSulayman, AbdulHamid. "Islam and the Family." Unpublished paper presented at the Conference on 'Youth'. Brunei, April 4, 1984.

—— "Islamic Educational Reform: Top Priority in Intellectual Islamic Work." Editorial. *The American Journal of Islamic Social Sciences (AJISS)*, vol. 15, issue 1, USA, Spring 1998.

—— *Islamization of Knowledge: General Principles and Work Plan*. Herndon, VA: IIIT, 1995.

Abu-Talib, Ali. *Nahjul Balagha* (Peak of Eloquence). Elmhurst, New York: Tahrike Tarsile Qur'an, 1996.

Adler, Jerry. "Building a Better Dad." *Newsweek*, June 17, 1996.

Agnivesh, Swami et al. "Missing: 50 Million Indian Girls". *International Herald Tribune*, November 25, 2005.

Ahmad, Imad-ad-Dean. *Islam and the Discovery of Freedom*. Beltsville, MD: Amana Publications; 1st edn., 1997.

Aids Education Global Information System (AEGIS), (website article dated August 31, 2001): http://www.aegis.com/news/afp/2001/af010886.html

Akhtar, et al. "Views on Breastfeeding in Medical Science and Islam." *Journal of Islamic Medical Association (JIMA)*, vol. 30, 1998.

Alcohol Concern. Factsheet: Young People and Alcohol. September 2009. http://www.alcoholconcern.org.uk/publications/factsheets-and-booklets/factsheet-young-people

'Ali, 'Abdullah Yusuf. *Translation of The Meaning of the Holy Qur'an*. Beltsville, MD: Amana Publications, 2004.

Allain, Annelies. *Protecting Infant Health*. Penang, Malaysia: International Baby Food Action Network, 1993.

Altalib, Ilham. The Muslim Family in North America. Ten Unpublished Articles. Reston, Virginia: 1984.

—— The Human Heart in the Qur'an, Seminar at ADAMS Center, Herndon, Virginia, September 2008.

Amabile, T.M. & B.A. Hennessey. "The Motivation For Creativity in Children" in T. Pittman & A. Boggiano (Eds.) *Achievement And Motivation: A Social Developmental Perspective*. New York: Cambridge University Press, 1992.

Athar, Shahid. "Sex Education for Muslim Youth and Their Parents." *Journal of Islamic Medical Association (JIMA)*, vol. 22, USA, 1990.

—— *Reflections of an American Muslim*. Chicago, IL: Kazi Publications, 1994.

—— (ed.) *Sex Education: An Islamic Perspective*. http://www.teachislam.com/dmdocuments/33/BOOK/

Atkins, Andrea. "The Gender Divide." *Parenting Magazine*, August 1998.

Badaraco, Joseph. *Leading Quietly*. Harvard Business Review Press, 2002.

Badi, Jamal and Mustapha Tajudin. *Creative Thinking: An Islamic Perspective*. 2nd edn. International Islamic University Malaysia: Kuala Lumpur, Malaysia, 2005.

Bailey, Joseph. *The Serenity Principle*. San Francisco, CA: Harper & Row, 1990.

al-Bar, Mohammad Ali, and Osama Kandil. "Breastfeeding and Islamic Teaching." *Islamic World Medical Journal,* July/August 1986.

Barazangi, Nimat Hafez. "The Education of North American Muslim Parents and Children: Conceptual Change as a Contribution to the Islamization of Education." *AJISS.* 7(3), 1990.

Baron-Cohen, Simon. "The Extreme Male Brain Theory of Autism." *Trends in Cognitive Sciences*, vol. 6, issue 6, June 2002.

Barzinji, Jamal. "The Prophet as a Father." Lecture at ADAMS Center, Herndon, VA, April, 11, 1993.

Bashir, Askia H. *How to Manage Your Parents (Without Manipulation).* Atlanta, GA: KYD Publishers, 1995.

Baumrind, Diana et al. Parenting for Character: Five Experts, Five Cases. Portland, Oregon: Center for Spiritual and Ethical Education, 2008.

BBC News. "Breast Milk 'Boosts Babies' Brainpower." 8 May 2002. http://news.bbc.co.uk/1/hi/health/1974976.stm

BBC News. "South Korean Dies after Games Session." 10 August 2005. http://news.bbc.co.uk/1/hi/technology/4137782.stm

Beal, C. *Boys And Girls: The Development of Gender Roles.* New York: McGraw-Hill, Inc., 1994.

Begley, Sharon. "Child's Brain: Use It or Lose It." *Newsweek,* June 17, 1996.

——"The Parent Trap." *Newsweek,* September 7, 1997.

——"A Mother's Cocaine Use: They Call Them Snowbabies." *Newsweek*, September 29, 1998.

——"Tuning Up the Brain." *Newsweek,* Fall/Winter 2000.

——and Pat Wingert. "Teach Your Parents Well." *Newsweek*, April 28, 1997.

——"Your Child's Brain", *Newsweek*, vol. 127, no. 8, p.54, February 19, 1996.

Bennett, William. *The Book of Virtues.* New York: Simon & Schuster, 1996.

Beshir, Ekram and Mohamed Rida. *Meeting the Challenge of Parenting in the West: An Islamic Perspective.* Beltsville, MD: Amana Publications, 1998.

Biller, Henry. "The Father Factor in Building a Better Dad." *Newsweek*, June 17, 1996.

—— *Fathers and Families: Paternal Factors in Child Development.* Westport, Connecticut: Auburn House, 1993.

Blum, Deborah. *Sex on the Brain: The Biological Differences Between Men and Women.* New York: Penguin Books, 1998.

Bohmer, Carol and Andrea Parrot. *Sexual Assault on Campus: The Problem and the Solution.* New York: Lexington Books, 1993.

Boorstein, Sylvia. *It's Easier Than You Think.* San Francisco, CA: HarperCollins, 1996.

Booth, Caroline and Mindy Henderson. *I Love My Grandmother Because....* Nashville, TN: Rutledge Hill Press, 1998.

Boydston, Jo Ann (editor). *The Collected Works of John Dewey.* Carbondale and Edwardsville: Southern Illinois University Press, 1969-1991.

Bradley, Raymond et al. *Facilitating Emotional Self-Regulation in Preschool Children.* Boulder Creek, California: Institute of HeartMath, 2009.

Branden, Nathaniel, *The Psychology of Self-Esteem: A Revolutionary Approach to Self-Understanding that Launched a New Era in Modern Psychology.* San Francisco, CA: Jossey-Bass, 2001

Brawer, Barney. "Raising Sons in a World of Changing Gender Roles." *Women in Higher Education,* November 1998.

Brazelton, Leach; Lemonick, Michael. "War of the Diapers." *Time*, January 25, 1999, vol. 153, no. 3.

Brizendine, Louann. *The Female Brain.* New York: Morgan Road Books, 2006.

Brooks, Arthur. *Gross National Happiness.* New York: Basic Books, 2008.

Brown, H. Jackson, Jr. *Life's Little Treasure Book On Success.* Nashville, TN: Rutledge Hill Press, 1994.

—— *Life's Little Treasure Book On Marriage and the Family.* Nashville, TN: Rutledge Hill Press, 1995.

—— *Life's Little Treasure Book On Friendship.* Nashville, TN: Rutledge Hill Press, 1996.

—— *Life's Little Treasure Book On Parenting.* Nashville, TN: Rutledge Hill Press, 1995.

Burgess. *Fathers and Parenting Interventions.* London: Fatherhood Institute, 2009.

Burt, Sandra and Linda Perlis. *Parents as Mentors: A New Perspective on Parenting that Can Change Your Child's Life.* Rocklin, CA: Prima Publishing, 1999.

Campo, Juan. *Encyclopedia of Islam.* New York: Infobase Publishing, 2009.

Canadian Child Care Federation. "Children and Creativity." Resource Sheet no. 15, http://www.cccffcsge.ca/docs/cccf/rs015_en.htm

Cancer Research UK. http://info.cancerresearchuk.org/cancerstats/types/cervix/riskfactors/

Canfield, Jack and Mark Victor Hansen. *Another Sip of Chicken Soup for the Soul.* Kansas City, MO: Andrews McMeel Publishing, 1997.

—— *Chicken Soup for the Father's Soul.* Deerfield Beach, Florida: Health Communications, 2001

Carlson, Richard. *Don't Sweat the Small Stuff – and It's All Small Stuff: Simple Ways to Keep the Little Things from Taking over Your Life.* New York: Hyperion, 1997.

Carmichael, Mary. "A Shot of Hope." *Newsweek.* October 1, 2007.

—— "Stronger, Faster, Smarter." *Newsweek,* March 26, 2007.

Cassidy, Anne. "Take Charge of Your Time." *Working Mother,* May 1998.

Cassidy, Jude and Phillip Shaver. *Handbook of Attachment: Theory, Research and Clinical Applications.* New York: Guilford Press, 1999.

Cesarone, Bernard. "Video Games and Children." Urbana, Illinois: ERIC Clearinghouse on Elementary and Early Childhood Education, University of Illinois, 1994.

Chandler, Michael Alison and Maria Glod. "More Schools Trying Separation of the Sexes." *Washington Post,* June, 15, 2008.

Clark, C.S. "TV Violence." *CQ Researcher,* (3), March 26, 1993.

Clark, Reginald. *Family Life and School Achievement.* Chicago, IL: University of Chicago Press. 1983.

Clinton, Hillary R. *It Takes a Village To Raise a Child.* New York: Simon & Schuster, 1996.

Coleman, James Samuel. *Adolescent Society: The Social Life of the Teenager and Its Impact on Education.* New York: The Free Press, 1961; Macmillan, 1963.

Coloroso, Barbara. *Kids are Worth it! Giving Your Child the Gift of Inner Discipline.* New York: Harper Collins, 2002.

Covey, Stephen R. "Secrets of Much, Much Better Family Relationships." *Bottom Line,* July 30, 1992.

Davidson, Maurice et al. *Working with Fathers: Methods and Perspectives.* Stillwater, Minnesota: Nu Ink, 1992.

Davis, D. "Portrayals of Women in Prime Time Network Television: Some Demographic Characteristics." *Sex Roles,* vol. 23, pp.325–332, 1990.

Davis, William et al. *An Introduction to Music Therapy.* Silver Spring, Maryland: American Music Therapy Association, 2008.

Dawson, Geraldine. "Imitation and Social Responsiveness in Autustic Children." *Journal of Abnormal Child Psychology,* vol. 12, 1984, pp.209–225.

Dodd, Virginia. "Implications of Kangaroo Care for Growth and Development in Preterm Infants." *Journal of Obstetric, Gynecologic, and Neonatal Nursing,* vol. 34, no. 2, March 2005, pp.218–232.

D'Oyen, Fatima M. *The Miracle of Life.* Leicester, UK: Islamic Foundation, 1996.

The Economist. "Arab Learning: Know Thyself." October 25, 2003.

eHow Website. How to Teach Kids to Say No to Peer Pressure. http://www.ehow.com/how_6108016_teach-kids-say-peer-pressure.html

Elbert, Thomas et al. "Increased Cortical Representation of the Fingers of the Left Hand in String Players." *Science Journal,* vol. 270, no. 5234, pp.305–307, 13 October 1995

Elias, Maurice, Steven Tobias and Brian Friedlander. *Emotionally Intelligent Parenting, How to Raise A Self-Disciplined,*

Responsible, Socially Skilled Child. London: Hodder and Stoughton, 2000.

Eliot, Lise. *Pink Brain, Blue Brain*. New York: Houghton Mifflin Harcourt, 2009.

Elkadi, Iman. "Construction of Muslim Communities: Raising Children." *Al-Ittihad*. Gary, Indiana: The MSA of the US and Canada, spring 1972.

Elkind, David. "The Family in the Postmodern World." *Phi Kappa Phi Journal*. 1995.

Elmore, Tim. *Nurturing the Leader within Your Child: What Every Parent Needs to Know*. Nashville, TN: Thomas Nelson Publishers, 2001.

Epinions. "Teaching our Children to Love." January 2001. http://www.epinions.com/kifm-review-3E0B-2F84CB47-3A52CFB3-prod2

Exley, Helen. *Words of Wisdom*. New York: Exley, 1997.

—— *Words of Calm*. New York: Exley, 1998.

Eyre, Linda and Richard. *3 Steps to a Strong Family*. New York: Simon & Schuster. 1994.

—— *Teaching Your Children Values*. Sound recording: 2 cassettes. New York: Simon & Schuster Audio, 1994.

Faber, Adele and Elaine Mazlish. *How to Talk so Kids Will Listen and Listen so Kids Will Talk*. New York: Avon Books. 1982.

—— *Siblings Without Rivalry*. New York: Avon Books. 1998.

Fannoun, Kathy. *Our Loving Grandparents*. Chicago, Illinois: Iqra, 1994.

Ferguson, Andrew et al. *Time*, May, 24, 1999, vol. 153, no. 20, p.68.

Field, et al. "Infants of Depressed Mothers Show Depressed Behavior Even with Non-depressed Adults." *Child Development* journal, vol. 59, issue 6, December 1988, pp.1569–1579.

Fisher, et al. "Sex on the Brain." *Journal of Sex Research*, vol. 49, issue 1, 2012, pp.69–77.

Fowler, Lynda. "Encouraging Creativity in Children." Department of Family & Consumer Sciences, Ohio State University. http://www.ohioline.osu.edu/flm97/nr04.html

Franklin, Benjamin, *The Autobiography of Benjamin Franklin*. New York: P. F. Collier and Son, 1909.

Freedman, Joshua. Creativity for Emotional Intelligence: Ideas and Activities. http://www.kidsource.com/kidsource/content4/creativity.eq.html

Friedman, Jenny. "Avoiding Gender Stereotypes: Learn How to Overcome the Typical Stereotypes in Raising Your Son or Daughter." 1998. http://www.americanbaby.com/ab/story.jhtml?storyid=/templatedata/hk/story/data/1172.xml

Funk, J.B. "Reevaluating the Impact of Video Games." *Clinical Pediatrics*, vol. 32 (Feb. 2, 1993), pp.86–90.

Geoparent, http://geoparent.com/family/growth/independence.htm

Gibbs, Nancy. "In Sorrow and Disbelief – Special Report: The Littleton Massacre." *Time*, May 3, 1999.

Gilbert, Michael. "Single-sex Schools Help Children Thrive: Bleaching Out Gender Differences Hampers the Education of Both Girls and Boys." September 20, 2007. http://www.csmonitor.com/ 2007/0920/p09s01-coop.html.

Gilmartin, Patricia and Jeffrey Patton. "Comparing the Sexes on Spatial Abilities." *Annals of the Association of American Geographers*, vol. 74, issue 4, 1984.

Ginott, G. Haim. *Between Parent and Teenager*. New York: Avon Books, 1971.

Glod, Marie. "Schools Try Elementary Approach to Teaching Foreign Languages." *Washington Post*, August 8, 2006.

Godfrey, Neale and Carolina Edwards. *Money Doesn't Grow on Trees: A Parent's Guide to Raising Financially Responsible Children*. A Fireside Book. New York: Simon & Schuster, 1994.

Goldscheider, Frances K. and Linda J. Waite. *New Families, No Families? The Transformation of the American Home*. Berkeley, CA: University of California Press, 1991.

Goleman, Daniel. *Emotional Intelligence*. New York: Bantam Doubleday Dell Publishing Group, 1996.

Gookin, Dan and Sandy. *Parenting for Dummies*, 2nd edn. New York: HarperCollins, 2002.

Gordon, Thomas. *Parent Effectiveness Training: The No-Lose Program for Raising Responsible Children*. New York: Three Rivers Press, 2000.

Gray, John. *Truly Mars and Venus: Men are from Mars, Women are from Venus: A Practical Guide for Improving Communication and Getting What You Want in Your Relationships*. New York: HarperCollins, 2003.

Gur, Ruben and Raquel Gur et al. "Sex Differences in Brain Gray and White Matter in Healthy Young Adults." *The Journal of Neuroscience*, vol. 19, no. 10, pp.4065–4072, 15 May 1999.

Gurian, Anita and Alice Pope. "Do Kids Need Friends?" March 21, 2001. http://www.aboutourkids.org/articles/do_kids_need_friends

Gurian, Michael. *Boys and Girls Learn Differently: A Guide for Teachers and Parents*. San Fransisco, CA: Jossey-Bass, 2001.

Haq, S. Moinul. Trans., Ibn Saad's *Kitab al-Tabaqat* [The Book of Classes]. India: Islamic Book Service, 1967.

Harper, Cynthia C. and Sara S. McLanahan. "Father Absence and Youth Incarceration." *Journal of Research on Adolescence*, vol. 14, no. 3, pp. 369–397, September 2004.

Harris, Judith. *The Nurture Assumption*. New York: Free Press, 1998.

Harris, Robert. "Introduction to Creative Thinking." *Virtual Salt,* July 1, 1998 http://www.virtualsalt.com/crebook1.htm

Harrison, Harry H., Jr. *Father to Son: Life Lessons on Raising a Boy*. New York: Workman Publishing, 2000.

Hart, Michael H. *The 100: A Ranking of the Most Influential Persons in History*. New York: Hart Publishing, 1978.

Harvey, Eric et al. *The Leadership Secrets of Santa Claus*. Dallas, Texas: The Walk the Talk Company, 2003.

Al-Hashmi, Muhammad. *The Ideal Muslim*. [Arabic] Riyadh, Saudi Arabia: International Islamic Publishing House, 1999.

Al-Hassani, Salim. *1001 Inventions: Muslim Heritage in Our World*. Manchester, UK: Foundation for Science, Technology and Civilisation, 2011.

Head, Christina. *An Educated Decision: One Approach to the Vaccination Problem Using Homeopathy*. London: Lavender Hill Homeopathic Centre, 1999.

Al-Hewar, vol. 13, no. 4, Spring 2002.

Hicks, Felicity. "The Role of Music Therapy in the Care of the Newborn," *Nursing Times* journal, vol. 91, issue 38, pp. 31–33.

Holy Bible: New King James Version. Austin, TX: National Publishing Company, 1982.

Hughes, et al. *The Factbook on Global Sexual Exploitation*. New York: Coalition Against Trafficking in Women, 1999.

Hwedy, Fahmy. "Islam is Greater than Waging a Battle against an Instrument or Art." (In Arabic). *Al-Mujtama*, vol. 933, January 1, 1998.

Hyde, Barbara and Brian Sansoni. "Women Better at Hand Habits, Hands Down." *American Society for Microbiology*, Washington DC. 2005. http://www.eurekalert.org/pub_releases/2005-09/asfm-wba091905.php.

Ibn Khaldun, *al-Muqaddimah*, Beirut: Dār al-Qalam, 1992.

Institute of Medicine. *The Hidden Epidemic. Confronting Sexually Transmitted Diseases*. Washington, DC: National Academy Press, 1997.

Islamic Schools Department. "Homework: Your Child and You." (Pamphlet). Plainfield, IN: Islamic Society of North America, 1994.

Islamic Society of North America. "Greatest Obstacles Confronting Muslim Children Raised in America." *Islamic Horizons*, vol. 11, no. 11, November 1986.

Ja'fari, Suzanne Fatimah. *Muslim Names*. Beltsville, MD: Amana Publications, 1998.

Jaffe, Charles A. "Your Money." *Chicago Tribune,* April 2, 1998.

Jameelah, Maryam. *The Generation Gap: Its Causes and Consequences*. Lahore, Pakistan: Muhammed Yusuf Khan, 1981.

Johnson, Anne. "Exploring Women's Creativity: The No-Push Method for Developing

Creativity." 1999. http://www.womenfolk.com/creativity/kids.htm.

Josephson, Michael S.; Val J. Peter and Tom Dowd. *Parenting to Build Character in Your Teen*. Boys Town, NB: Boys Town Press, 2001.

Kalb, Claudia. "Farewell to Aunt Flo." *Newsweek*, February 3, 2003.

Kane, Frank L. and Bathke, Leigh Anne Nicholson. "Parenting and Child Care." *Newsweek*, September 29, 1997.

Kantrowitz, Barbara and Wingert, Pat. "How Well do You Know Your Kid?" *Newsweek*, May 10, 1999.

Kantrowitz, Barbara and Peg Tyre. "The Fine Art of Letting Go." *Newsweek*, May 22, 2006.

Karp, Miriam. "Make Room for Your Child's Creativity." *Natural Jewish Parenting*, issue 3, http://www.jewishholiday.com/creativity.html.

Kasule, Omar. "Character-Building." Unpublished paper presented at the Third International Seminar on "Medical Curriculum: The Holistic Approach," Kuala Lumpur, Malaysia, February 1999.

Keller, Nuh. *Becoming Muslim*. Jordan: Wakeel Books. 2001.

Kendall, Francis. *Super Parents, Super Kids*. Johannesburg: Delta Books. 1983.

Kessler, Suzanne J. and Wendy McKenna. "Some Children are Gender Nonconformists." http://www.webehave.com/hottopic.htm

Kilpatrick, William. *Why Johnny Can't Tell Right from Wrong and What We Can Do About It*. New York: Simon & Schuster, 1993.

Kindlon, Daniel J. and Michael Thompson. *Raising Cain: Protecting the Emotional Life of Boys*. New York: Ballantine Books, 1999.

Knox, David and Caroline Schacht. *Parenting Choices in Relationships: An Introduction to Marriage and the Family*, 5th edn. Belmont, CA: Wadsworth Publishing, 1997.

Komurcu, Nuran. "Effect of music therapy on anxiety in pregnant women during labor" (in Turkish). *Hemsirelik Forumu*, 1999, vol. 2, pp.89–96.

Kotulak, Ron. cited in: "Unlocking the Mind." *Chicago Tribune*, 1993.

Kuczmarski, Robert J.; Flegal, Katherine M.; Campbell, Stephen M.; and Johnson, Clifford L. "Increasing Prevalence of Overweight Among US Adults." *American Medical Association*, vol. 272, no. 3. 1994.

Kulkarni, Chaya and Lynn Oldershaw. *Helping Children Overcome Their Fears. Comfort, Play and Teach: A Positive Approach to Parenting* (Get Set for Life program). Toronto, Ontario, Canada: 2005.

Lazear, Jonathon and Wendy. *Meditations for Parents Who do too Much*. New York: Simon & Schuster, 1993.

Lebelle, Linda. Focus Adolescent Services. http://www.focusas.com.

Leland, John. "Tightening the Knot." *Newsweek*, February 19, 1996.

Lemonick, Michael D. "Eat Your Heart Out." *Time*, July 19, 1999.

—— "War of the Diapers." *Time*, January 25, 1999, vol. 153, no. 3.

Leonhardt, Mary. "It is Never Too Soon to Foster a Love of Reading in Young Children or Too Late to Help an Older Child Gain a Love of Books." *Bottom Line*, May 5, 1991.

Longfield, Anne and Mike Fitzpatrick. "Should Parenting be Taught?" *The Independent*, December 4, 1999.

Maier, Thomas. "On the Life of Dr. Spock." *Biography Magazine*, April 1998.

—— "Raised by Dr. Spock." *Newsweek* March 30, 1998.

Maqsood, Ruqaiyyah Waris. *Living with Teenagers: A Guide for Muslim Parents*. London: Ta-Ha Publishers, 1995.

Martin, Daniel. "Schoolgirls Aged Just Ten Falling Pregnant As Underage Pregnancies Continue To Rise." *Daily Mail*, 8th February 2010.

Maternal and Child Health (MCH) Early Childhood Development and Parent Education Program. http://www.ok.gov/health/Child_and_Family_Health/Maternal_and_Child_Health_Service/

Matthews, Andrew. *Making Friends*. Singapore: Media Masters, 1990; Princes Risborough, UK: J. Wilson Booksales, 1998.

Mayhew, Mary M. *Your Star Child: Attracting,*

Birthing and Parenting an Evolved Soul. Fairfield, IA: Sunstar Publishing, 1995.

Mazrui, Ali. "North American Muslims: Rising to the Challenge of Dual Identity." *Islamic Horizons,* March–April 1996.

Meiji, Stewart. *Parenting: Part Joy, Part Guerrilla Warfare.* Novata, CA: Portal Publications, 1999.

Minawi, Kawther M. et al. *The Child's Rights in Islam.* Riyadh: Safir Press, 1992.

Mirza, Tanveer Ahmad. "Parenting." Weekly Parenting Workshops at ADAMS Center, Herndon, VA, 1994–1999.

Moir, Anne and David Jessel. *The Real Difference Between Men and Women.* New York: Delta Books, 1991.

Moran, James D. III. Creativity in Young Children, http://www.kidsource.com/kidsource/content2/Creativity_in_kids.html

Morgan, Michael Hamilton. *Lost History: The Enduring Legacy of Muslim Scientists, Thinkers and Artists.* Washington, DC: National Geographic Books, 2007.

Morris, Sophie. "Sex for Sale: The Truth About Prostitution in Britain." *Independent.* 26 November 2008.

Murad, Abdul Hakim. "Ramadan in Istanbul." *Meeting Point,* August 2009.

Murphy, Sam. "Why Barefoot Is Best For Children." *The Guardian* newspaper. August 9, 2010. http://www.guardian.co.uk/lifeandstyle/2010/aug/09/barefoot-best-for-children

Nash, J. Madeleine. "How a Child's Brain Develops." *Time,* February 3, 1997.

——"Fertile Minds." *Time,* February 3, 1997.

——"The Personality Genes." *Time,* April 27, 1998.

National Association for the Education of Young Children. www.naeyc.org

The National Center on Addiction and Substance Abuse, www.casacolumbia.org. Family Day – A Day to Eat Dinner with your Children. www.casafamilyday.org

National PTA Parenting Guide, http://www.lausd.k12.ca.us/Haskell_EL/parent%20information/decision.htm, 1994.

Natural Resources Defense Council. "Benefits of Breastfeeding", 2010. http://www.nrdc.org/breastmilk/benefits.asp

Norris, Jeannette; Nurius, Paula; Graham, Thomas. "When a Date Changes from Fun to Dangerous." *Violence Against Women,* vol. 5, no. 3, pp.230–250, March 1999.

Olasky, Marvin. *The Tragedy of American Compassion.* Regnery Publishing: 1994.

Osman, Fathi. *Concepts of the Qur'an.* Los Angeles, CA: Multimedia Vera International, 1997.

Parke, Ross (ed.). *Review of Child Development Research,* vol. 7. Chicago, Illinois: University of Chicago Press, 1984.

——*Fatherhood.* Cambridge, Massachusetts: Harvard University Press, 1996.

Parkes, Peter. "Milk Kinship in Islam." *Social Anthropology,* vol. 13, issue 3, 2005.

Paul, J. P., et al. "Understanding Childhood Sexual Abuse as a Predictor of Sexual Risk-taking Among Men who have Sex with Men." *Child Abuse & Neglect,* vol. 25, issue 4, April 2001, pp.557–584.

Piotrowski, Caroline. "Rules of Everyday Family Life." *International Journal of Behavioral Development,* vol. 21, no. 3, pp.571–598, October 1997.

Porter, Dalia and Gabriel Cervantes. *All About Dad: Insights, Thoughts, and Life Lessons on Fatherhood.* Cincinnati, Ohio: Adams Media Corporation, 2007

Positive Parenting. www.webehave.com

Preschool Education. *Encouraging Creativity in Children,* 1997–2006, http://www.preschooleducation.com/art60.shtml

Pryor, Fred. *How to Manage Conflict, Anger, and Emotion.* Fred Pryor Seminars, 1994, 3-volume video set (6 audio cassettes).

al-Qaradawi, Yusuf. *The Lawful and the Prohibited in Islam.* Trans. Kamal el-Helbawy et al. New Revised Edition by Zaynab Alawiye. London: Al-Birr Foundation, 2003.

Qutb, Sayyid. *In the Shade of the Qur'an.* Trans. and ed. Adil Salahi and Ashur Shamis. Leicester, UK: The Islamic Foundation and Islamonline.net, 2011.

Ramey, C.T. The Abecedarian Project. *Encyclopedia of Human Intelligence.* Ed. R.J. Sternberg. New York: Macmillan, 1994.

Rankin, Jane. *Parenting Experts: Their Advice, the Research and Getting it Right.* Westport, CT: Praeger, 2006.

Ricks, Shirley. "Father-Infant Interactions: A Review of Empirical Research." *Family Relations*, vol. 34, no. 4, October 1985, pp.505–511.

Riera, Michael. "Uncommon Sense with Parents of Teenagers." *Target The Family,* August 1996.

Robins, Joyce. *Naming Your Baby.* London, UK: Chancellor Press, 1996.

Robinson, Holly. "The Working Mother's Guide to Breastfeeding." *Working Mother*, May 1998.

Rosemond, John. "Tender Loving Discipline." *Hemisphere* (United Air Lines), June 1993, p.67.

——"Is Your Family a Healthy One? Family Counselor." *Hemisphere* (United Air Lines), December 1994.

Rycus, Judith; Hughes, Ronald. *Child Development and Child Welfare.* Washington, DC: Child Welfare League of America, 1998.

Samalin, Nancy. "Personal Responsibility: How to Teach Children Responsibility." *Bottom Line,* February 15, 1994.

Samon, Katherine Ann. "55 Ways to Make Your Kid Feel Loved." *Parents' Magazine,* January 1999.

Sample, Steven. *The Contrarian's Guide to Leadership.* San Francisco, CA: Jossey-Bass, 2001.

Sax, Leonard. *Why Gender Matters: What Parents and Teachers Need to Know about the Emerging Science of Sex Differences.* New York: Broadway, 2006.

Schachter, Robert and Carole Spearin McCauley. *When Your Child Is Afraid.* New York: Simon & Schuster, 1988.

Schirra, Walter. *Chicken Soup For the Father's Soul.* Deerfield Beach, Florida: Health Communications, 2001.

Scott, Buddy. *Relief for Hurting Parents: What to Do and How to Think.* Nashville, TN: Oliver Nelson Books, 1989.

Sears, William. *Keys to Calming the Fussy Baby.* New York: Barron's, 1991.

Seidman, S. A. "Revisiting Sex Role Stereotyping in MTV videos." *International Journal of Instructional Media*, vol. 26, pp.11–22, 1999.

Shamma, Freda. Literature for Muslim American Students in K-12 Islamic Schools and Homeschoolers. Presented at the Islamic Education Conference, Georgetown University, Washington, DC, April 2006.

Shapiro, Laura. "The Myth of Quality Time." *Newsweek,* May 12, 1997.

Shaw, Eva, *For the Love of Children.* Deerfield Beach, Florida: Health Communications, 1998.

Sherman, Paul; Billing, Jennifer. "Antimicrobial Functions of Spices," *Quarterly Review of Biology*, vol. 73, issue 3, 1998.

Siddiqui, Dilnawaz. *The Muslim Observer.* April 30, 1999.

Silverstein, Shel. *The Giving Tree.* New York: HarperCollins Publishers, 1986.

Sinclair, Ian. *Health: The Only Immunity: The Alternative to Vaccination.* The Informed Parent Publications, 2009.

Smalley, Gary. "Hidden Keys to Loving Relationships." 16 video cassettes, 1995.

Smith, Charles. *Mighty Hearts: 8 Steps to Raising Kids with Courage.* Paper presented at a Workshop held by the Parenting Education Institute, State College, Pennsylvania, June 2004

Smith, David; Gates, Gary. *Gay and Lesbian Families in the United States.* Washington, DC: Human Rights Campaign, 2001.

Spock, Benjamin. *Raising Children in a Difficult Time: A Philosophy of Parental Leadership and High Ideals.* New York: Norton, 1974.

Stanley, Gary, *What My Dog has Taught Me about Life: Meditations for Dog Lovers.* Tulsa, OK: Honor Books, 1999.

Staso, William. "Toddler Brain Development." *Washington Families,* July 1998.

Stein, Rob. "Scientists Finding Out What Losing Sleep Does to a Body." *The Washington Post,* Oct. 9, 2005.

Sutherland, John and Jane Stoever. "Important

Facts about Children and Nutrition." Special Advertising Section, *Newsweek*, September 29, 1997.

—— "Parenting: Child Care." Special Advertising Section, *Newsweek*, September 29, 1997.

Taffel, Ron. *Why Parents Disagree: How Women and Men Parent Differently and How We Can Work Together*. New York: William Morrow, 1994.

—— *Getting Through to Difficult Kids and Parents*. New York: Guilford Press, 2001.

Takim, Liyakatali. Overcoming Dualities: Muslim Youth in North America. Unpublished paper presented at the ISNA Conference, Indianapolis, IN, July 5, 1997.

Time, June 29, 1998. "Giving Birth Online." http://www.time.com/time/community/tran scripts/chattr061798.html

Tremblay, George, Allen Israel. "Children's Adjustment to Parental Death." *Clinical Psychology: Science and Practices*, vol. 5, issue 4, 1998.

Turecki, Stanley and Sarah Wernick. "How to Put Your Foot Down without Squashing Your Child." *Family Circle*, March 16, 1994.

Underwood, Anne and Kuchment, Anna. "Fussy Kids, Flustered Mom." *Newsweek*, August 18, 2008, vol. 152, no. 7, pp.60–62.

UNICEF. *The State of the World's Children 2007*. New York: United Nations International Children's Emergency Fund, 2006.

United Nations. *Arab Human Development Report*. New York: United Nations Development Program, 2009.

United Nations. *World Population Prospects*. New York: UN Department of Economic and Social Affairs, 2010.

Unus, Iqbal. "A–Z Guide for Muslim Fathers," pamphlet. Herndon, VA: IIIT, 1994.

U.S. Census Bureau, Current Population Survey, Washington DC: March 2002.

Versi, Ahmed. "Wonder Boy in UK." The *Muslim News*, February, 1998.

Villani, S. "Violence in the Media." *Journal of the American Academy of Child and Adolescent Psychiatry*, 38, 1208, 1999.

Weiss, Rick. "Study Debunks Theory On Teen Sex, Delinquency." *The Washington Post*. Nov 11, 2007. p.A.3

Willatts, P. et al. "Effect of long-chain polyunsaturated fatty acids in infant formula on problem solving at 10 months of age." *The Lancet*, vol. 352, no. 9129, pp.688–691, August 29, 1998.

Williams, Rowan. "Archbishop Damns Disney." *Daily Mail*, July 23, 2002, http://www.dailymail.co.uk/news/article-129452/Archbishop-damns-Disney.html#ixzzorfbjTvIV

Wimberly, Ed. *A Parent's Guide to Raising Great Kids*. http://www.raisinggreatkids.com/

Wingert, Pat et al. "Building a Better Dad." *Newsweek*, June 17, 1996

Winn, Marie. *The Plug-in Drug*. New York: Penguin, 2002.

Winnicott, D. W. *Babies and Their Mothers*. MA: De Capo Press, 1992.

Wolgemuth, Robert D. *She Calls Me Daddy: Seven Things Every Man Needs to Know about Building a Complete Daughter*. Colorado Springs, CO: Focus on the Family Publishing, 1996.

The Women's Committee of the Muslim Students Association of the United States and Canada, *Parents' Manual: A Guide for Muslim Parents*. Baltimore, MD: American Trust Publications, 1976.

Wood, Joyce. "Quality Time." *Family Circle*, March 16, 1994.

Woolf, Marie. "Children to Learn Pitfalls of Being a Parent." *Daily Telegraph*, December 30, 1999.

Wright, Robert. "The Power of Their Peers." *Time*, vol. 152, no. 8, August 24, 1998.

Wulf, Steve. "What Makes a Good School." *Time*, October 27, 1997.

Yogman, Michael. "Games Fathers and Mothers Play with their Infants." *Infant Mental Health Journal*, vol. 2, pp.241–248, 1981.

Zogby International. December 15, 2006

Zorn, Eric. "Only Way to Teach Values: Help Kids Discover Them." *Chicago Tribune*, April 7, 1998.

المراجع العربية

- محمد علي الصابوني. صفوة التفاسير ، بيروت: دار القرآن الكريم، 1981م.
- محمد علي الصابوني. مختصر تفسير بن كثير ، بيروت: دار القرآن الكريم، 1981م.
- محمد حسن الحمصي. تفسير وبيان مفردات القرآن مع أسباب النزول للسيوطي، دمشق: دار الرشيد ،1984م.

كتب وبحوث عربية

- الجزيري، عبد الرحمن، الفقه على المذاهب الأربعة، دار الكتب العلمية، 2003 م.
- سابق، السيد ، فقه السنة، بيروت: دار الكتاب العربي، 1971م.
- أبو الحب، ضياء ، الطفل: هذا الكائن العجيب، بغداد: دار الحرية للطباعة، منشورات وزارة الثقافة والإعلام، 1979م.
- أبو سلميان، عبد الحميد ، "تأملات في ظاهرية ابن حزم وإعجاز الرسالة المحمدية" ، مجلة التجديد (كوالالمبور) س2 : ع3 ، 1998 .
- أبو سلميان، عبد الحميد ، البعد النفسي في الخطاب الإسلامي المعاصر، بحث قدم في ندوة المعهد العالمي للفكر الإسلامي، الموسم الثقافي، القاهرة، 1999م.
- أبو سلميان، عبد الحميد ، أزمة الإرادة والوجدان المسلم: البعد الغائب في مشروع إصلاح الأمة، دمشق: دار الفكر ، 2004م.
- أبو سلميان، عبد الحميد ، دليل مكتبة الأسرة المسلمة، فيرجينيا : المعهد العالمي للفكر الإسلامي، 1988م.
- أحمد أحمد ، حمد ، نحو قانون موحد للأسرة في الأقطار الإسلامية، قطر : جامعة قطر ، مكتبة الملك فيصل الإسلامية، 1990م.
- البهي، محمد ، الفكر الإسلامي والمجتمع المعاصر : مشكلات الأسرة والتكافل، القاهرة: مكتبة وهبة، 1982م.
- أحمد التل، شادية، مراحل النمو الإنساني ومطالبها التربوية، إربد : جامعة اليرموك، قسم التربية، 1986م.
- الجراجرة، عيسى حسن، ريادة الإسلام في تفهم خصوصية عالم الأطفال وفي تقرير وتطبيق حقوقهم الخاصة في الرعاية والتربية، عمان: دار ابن رشد ، دار الكرمل، 1988م.
- الجمالي، محمد فاضل ، تربية الإنسان الجديد، دمشق: دار الحكمة، 1995م.
- محمد ، السيد محمد الزعبلاوي، تربية المراهق بين الإسلام وعلم النفس، الرياض : مكتبة التوبة ؛ بيروت : مؤسسة الكتب الثقافية، 1996م.
- السيد ، فؤاد البهي، الأسس النفسية للنمو من المهد إلى الشيخوخة، القاهرة: دار النهضة العربية، 1975م.

- الضامن، ريما كمال، الأسرة ورعاية الذات الإنسانية للأطفال من 6 إلى 12 سنة، عمان: منشورات دار البشير، 1989م.
- العبادي، نضال محمد أمين، الأحاديث النبوية الواردة في الأطفال، جمع وتصنيف وتحقيق، عمان: كلية أصول الدين، رسالة ماجستير، الجامعة الأردنية، 1990م.
- العظم، يوسف، براعم الإسلام (في الحياة، وفي العقيدة) ج2، عمان: المكتب الإسلامي، 1985م.
- العلواني، طه جابر، أدب الاختلاف في الاسلام، فيرجينيا: المعهد العالمي للفكر الإسلامي، 1997م.
- العيسوي، عبد الرحمن، مقومات الشخصية الإسلامية والعربية وأساليب تنميتها، الإسكندرية: دار الفكر الجامعي، 1986م.
- الغزالي، محمد أبو حامد، إحياء علوم الدين، القاهرة: عالم الكتب للطباعة والنشر والتوزيع، 2005م.
- الغزالي، محمد، كيف نتعامل مع القرآن، فيرجينيا: المعهد العالمي للفكر الإسلامي، 1992م.
- الندوي، أبو الحسن، نحو التربية الإسلامية الحرة في الحكومات والبلاد الإسلامية، بيروت: مؤسسة الرسالة، 1985م.
- النغيمشي، عبد العزيز محمد، المراهقون، دراسة نفسية إسلامية للآباء والمعلمين والدعاة، الرياض: جامعة الإمام محمد بن سعود الإسلامية، دار المسلم للنشر والتوزيع، الطبعة الثانية، 1993م.
- الهاشمي، محمد علي، شخصية المسلم كما يصوغها الإسلام في الكتاب والسنة، دار البشائر الإسلامية، بيروت، 1986م.
- بدرانة، سعد الدين أحمد سعد الدين، الأساليب التربوية في غرس القيم العقدية لدى الطفل المسلم، رسالة ماجستير بإشراف د. شادية التل ومروان القيسى، إربد: جامعة اليرموك، 1994م.
- جابر، جابر عبد الحميد، علم النفس التربوي، القاهرة: دار النهضة العربية، 1977م.
- الحامد، محمد، ردود على أباطيل وتمحيصات لحقائق دينية، دمشق: دار الفكر للطباعة والنشر والتوزيع، 2003م.
- حماد، سهيلة زين العابدين، بناء الأسرة المسلمة، جدة: الدار السعودية للنشر والتوزيع، 1984م.
- حمد، أحمد، الأسرة: التكوين، الحقوق، والواجبات: دراسة مقارنة في الشريعة والقانون، طنطا: دار الكتب الجامعية، 1986م.
- زهران، حامد، علم نفس الطفل، القاهرة: عالم الكتب، 1977م.

- زين العابدين، وجيه، الإسلام والتربية الجنسية، الكويت: مكتبة المنار الإسلامية، 1979م.
- زين العابدين، وجيه، الإسلام والطفل، مكتبة المنار، الكويت، 1980م.
- عفيفي، محمد الصادق، المجتمع الإسلامي وبناء الأسرة، موسوعة المجتمعات والنظم الإسلامية، الكتاب الرابع، مكتبة الأنجلو المصرية، 1981م.
- علوان، عبد الله ناصح، تربية الأولاد في الإسلام، دار السلام للطباعة والنشر والتوزيع، الطبعة الثالثة، جزءان، حلب: سوريا، 1981م.
- فاضل، خليل، الصحة النفسية للأسرة، الدار السعودية للنشر والتوزيع، 1987م.
- الرافع، رفاعة، المرشد الأمين للبنات والبنين، القاهرة: مطبعة المدارس الملكية، 1871م.
- قطب، محمد، منهج التربية الإسلامية، الجزء الأول، القاهرة: دار الشروق، 1989م.
- نافع، إبراهيم، في بيتنا مدمن: كيف نمنع الكارثة؟، القاهرة: مركز الأهرام للترجمة والنشر، 1991م.
- النجار، عبد المجيد، "عقيدة تكريم الإنسان وأثرها التربوي"، القاهرة: المسلم المعاصر، س19، ع74-73، 1995م.
- يالجن، مقداد والقاضي، يوسف، علم النفس التربوي في الإسلام، الرياض: دار المريخ، 1980م.

مجلات عربية

- عبد الله، عبد الستار، "في زواج الأقارب: متهم لم تثبت إدانته"، مجلة الأسرة، 1996م.
- فكار، رشدي، ندوة "الإسلام وتحديات القرن القادم"، القاهرة، 1996م.
الرشودي، فاطمة، "مقتطفات"، أمريكا: مجلة المرأة المسلمة.
- "عشرة أخطاء يرتكبها الآباء مع المراهقين وكيفية تجنبها"، مجلة صحتك اليوم، أكتوبر/ديسمبر 1997م.
- سافران، كلير، "6 أفكار تنجح ولدك في المدرسة"، المختار، مارس 1987م.
- " ذكاء الطفل: فطري أم مكتسب؟"، الكويت: مجلة المجتمع، 23/9/1999م.

Website Resources and Further Reading

Bullying
http://www.bullying.co.uk
http://www.kidpower.org
http://www.stopbullying.gov

Child Intelligence
http://www.raisesmartkid.com
http://www.mensaforkids.org
www.sciencemadesimple.com
www.kidzone.ws/dolch (*This site contains a huge collection of sight words*)

Drugs
http://www.drugfree.org
http://www.talktofrank.com
http://www.teensusingdrugs.org

Homeschooling
http://www.muslimhomeschool.net
http://themuslimhomeschool.tripod.com

Nutrition
http://www.kidsandnutrition.co.uk
http://www.healthychildren.org
http://www.usda.gov

Problem Teens
http://www.teenswithproblems.com
http://www.empoweringparents.com

Single Parents
http://www.lone-parents.org.uk
http://www.gingerbread.org.uk
http://www.thekidsandme.co.uk (*This site lists holidays for single parents to connect with their children*)

Teaching Children Responsibility and Work Ethic
http://www.myjobchart.com
http://www.theartofhomemaking.com/teachchildrenwork.htm
http://www.aish.com/family/mensch/Teaching_Children_Responsibility.asp

Television
http://www.insteadoftv.com
http://www.limitv.org
http://www.whitedot.org

GENERAL

American Academy of Pediatrics
www.aap.org

American Heart Association
www.americanheart.org

BBC
http://www.bbc.co.uk/health

Canadian Living
http://www.canadianliving.com/CanadianLiving/client/en/Family/Search.asp

Child Development Institute
http://childdevelopmentinfo.com

The Dr Spock Website for Parents
http://www.drspock.com

Family Dawn
http://www.familydawn.com

Fatherhood Institute
http://www.fatherhoodinstitute.org

Josephson Institute-Centre for Youth Ethics
http://www.charactercounts.com

Media-Awareness
http://www.media-awareness.ca/english/parents/marketing/marketers_target_kids.cfm

National Prevention Information Network
http://www.cdcnpin.org

National Safety Council
www.nsc.org

The Nemours Foundation
www.kidshealth.org

Pathfinder Parent Center – North Dakota
http://www.pathfinder.minot.com/index2.html

PBS
http://www.pbs.org/wholechild/providers/play.html

Progressive Parenting Solutions
http://www.progressiveparenting.com

SoundVision
soundvision.com/info/parenting

The Teaching Home
http://www.teachinghome.com/supplement/summer00/training.cfm

Wellness: The Wellspring
http://www.thewellspring.com

Glossary

Adhān: call to prayer
Adl: justice
Aql: mind
Fuad: heart
Ḥalāl: religiously permitted
Ḥarām: religiously prohibited
Khalifah: vicegerent
Ihsān: excellence; improvement
Imrān: civilization
Iqāmah: call to immediate prayer
Itqān: perfection
Mawaddah: compassion
Nafs: soul
Nashīd: religious song
Raḥmah: mercy
Tarbiyah: education; training
Ummah: worldwide Muslim community

Index